A HISTORY OF ROME TO A.D. 565

1 Pantheon at Rome. *Originally built by Augustus' minister Agrippa in 27–25 B.C., the Pantheon was completely rebuilt early in the reign of Hadrian (A.D. 117–138). Remaining virtually intact to the present day, it has seemed to many to be the quintessence of the Roman architectural experience. (Photo: Fototeca Unione.)*

750/56

A HISTORY OF
ROME
TO A.D. 565

SIXTH EDITION

WILLIAM G. SINNIGEN
PROFESSOR OF HISTORY, HUNTER COLLEGE OF
THE CITY UNIVERSITY OF NEW YORK

ARTHUR E. R. BOAK
LATE RICHARD HUDSON PROFESSOR OF ANCIENT HISTORY,
THE UNIVERSITY OF MICHIGAN

Macmillan Publishing Co., Inc.
NEW YORK

Collier Macmillan Publishers
LONDON

Macmillan Publishing Co., Inc.
866 Third Avenue, New York, New York 10022

Collier Macmillan Canada, Ltd.

Library of Congress Cataloging in Publication Data

Sinnigen, William Gurnee, (date)
   A history of Rome to A.D. 565.

   First–4th ed., by A. E. R. Boak, published under title: A history of Rome to 565 A.D.; in the 5th ed. Boak's name appeared first on t. p.
   Bibliography: p.
   Includes index.
   1. Rome—History. I. Boak, Arthur Edward Romilly, 1888–1962, joint author. II. Title.
DG209.B55 1977   937   76–10674
ISBN 0–02–410800–6

Printing: 3 4 5 6 7 8   Year: 9 0 1 2 3

PREFACE TO THE SIXTH EDITION

In preparing the sixth edition of this book I have tried to do three things: to improve, and especially tighten, the prose; to correct errors of fact; and to update the interpretive parts so that the book may remain abreast of its field. I also have made corresponding changes in the bibliography. I call special attention to my revision of the first seven chapters, for in the fifth edition these chapters represented Professor Boak's interpretation of certain points with which I disagreed. Throughout the book I have tried to improve the parts dealing with culture and society while keeping one of the book's main strengths, its treatment of Roman government. At a lower level of importance, I have sought to make the legends accompanying the illustrations fuller and more informative than those of earlier editions.

Permission to use most of the new illustrations was graciously given by Signora Karen Einaudi of the Fototeca Unione (Rome). The photograph of the Baalbek temple was very kindly provided by A. H. McLeod of Macmillan, to whom I owe many thanks for much else besides. The sources of still other photographs are acknowledged in their respective credit lines.

I thank my friend Professor Frank D. Gilliard of the California State University at Hayward for drawing to my attention errors and inconsistencies in the fifth edition; Professor Robert K. Sherk of the State University of New York at Buffalo, who read the entire manuscript of the sixth and made valuable and constructive critical comments; and Professor Richard E. Mitchell of the University of Illinois at Urbana-Champaign for suggesting many improvements in Chapters 12, 13, and 14. I also thank the editorial staff of Macmillan for their help and, again, my friend John S. Widdicombe for his encouragement.

Naturally, I hope that this edition has maintained the standards of scholarship characteristic of the first five and that its errors are few. For the latter I assume full responsibility.

William G. Sinnigen

PREFACE TO THE FIFTH EDITION

Faced with the possibility of declining health in the fall of 1961, Professor Boak asked me to aid in the preparation of the fifth edition of his textbook, in particular to be responsible for the revision of those chapters dealing with the Late Empire. A year later, the state of his health becoming increasingly precarious, he requested me to take over all revisions of the Imperial period and to be responsible for the work as a whole if he were not able to finish the earlier parts.

By the time of his death on December 16, 1962, he had revised to the bottom of page 97 of the fourth edition. Although I disagree with some of his interpretations of early Roman history and am less critical than he was of literary tradition, I have not drastically changed his revision of the first chapters, whose viewpoint remains essentially his. All revisions following page 97 of this edition are my own responsibility. Before his death, Professor Boak had also decided on an expanded set of illustrations. The selections I have made follow his wishes, with the exception of the mosaics from Piazza Armerina and the Basilica at Trèves, which are my own choices. Professor Boak's original Preface to the new edition follows.

I should like to thank members of the editorial staff of Macmillan for their kindness during the preparation of the revision and my friend Mr. John S. Widdicombe for his encouragement and criticism. The entire manuscript has benefited by criticism of Professor Henry C. Boren of The University of North Carolina, who has saved me from numerous errors. Lastly, I should like to express my indebtedness to Mrs. Boak for placing in my hands certain of Professor Boak's papers and notes and for much else besides.

Naturally, errors of fact and judgment that may remain in the following pages as a result of revisions made by me are my own responsibility.

William G. Sinnigen

PREFACE TO THE FIFTH EDITION

Few of the reading public have been oblivious of the tremendous advances in human knowledge made during the past eight years, but many of them have been blind to the fact that this expansion has been true of the social as well as of the physical sciences, and of history as well as of some more widely publicized humanistic studies. Some of the most spectacular achievements have been in the field of ancient history; and Roman history can claim its share of these. New and striking archaeological discoveries in all parts of the Roman world, including many important inscriptions, new papyrological publications, and new and sounder interpretations of previously known historical materials of all sorts have necessitated a fresh appraisal of many phases of the Roman experience, even though in its main outlines older evaluations maintain their validity. In the light of these considerations, a new edition of this text seems highly desirable.

The author wishes to express his thanks to Macmillan for its kindness in permitting him to rewrite much of the text, to enlarge greatly the number of illustrations, and to change radically the list of suggested collateral readings. He is also deeply indebted to Professor Paul J. Alexander of the University of Michigan for pointing out typographical errors in the fourth edition and to Professor William G. Sinnigen of Hunter College for his suggestions for improving many aspects of the work.

A. E. R. B.

CONTENTS

ILLUSTRATIONS

MAPS

PART

I

THE EARLY
PEOPLES OF ITALY

CHAPTER 1
GEOGRAPHY OF ITALY

Italy, ribbed by the Apennines, girdled by the Alps and sea, juts out like a long boot from Europe toward the North African coast. It includes two regions of widely differing physical characteristics: the northern, continental, and the southern, peninsular; together their area is about 91,200 square miles.

CONTINENTAL ITALY. Continental Italy consists of the southern watershed of the Alps and the northern watershed of the Apennines with the intervening lowland plain. East to west this region measures about 320 miles; its width from north to south does not exceed 70 miles. On the north, the Alps extend in an irregular crescent of over 1,200 miles from the Mediterranean near Nice to the Adriatic near Trieste. On the Italian side they rise abruptly like a high wall, but on the northern faces the slope is gradual and river valleys afford gradual ascents to passes leading over the divide to the plain below. From the west, there is an easy approach at the end of the Alps along the Riviera, and at its eastern approaches, a low pass facilitates access from the basin of the middle Danube. Thus the Alps formed no serious barrier to landward migration into Italy. The plain is occupied largely by the valley of the Po, the greatest Italian river, which rises in the western Alps and flows eastward for 360 miles to the Adriatic, receiving many tributaries along its route. Since the plain has been built up by silt from the rivers, it is richly alluvial. But much silt is carried down to the sea, where it chokes the river mouths and continuously extends the coastline. Thus it has formed the marshy delta of the Po and the lagoons at the site of modern Venice. Alpine rivers furnish abundant water throughout the year, however, and thus enhance agriculture of the north Italian plain. In its natural state this region was swampy and forested, and many centuries of effort were required before it was cleared, drained, and cultivated.

THE PENINSULA. The southern portion of Italy is a long, narrow peninsula, running northwest and southeast between the Mediterranean and Adriatic seas and terminating in two promontories, which form the toe and heel of the Italian boot. The length of the peninsula is 650 miles; its breadth is nowhere more than 125. In striking contrast to the plains of the Po, peninsular Italy is traversed by parallel ridges of the Apennines, which give it diversity of hill and valley. The average height of these mountains, which form a sort of vertebrate system along the peninsula, is about 4,000 feet, and even their highest peaks (9,500 feet) are below the snow line. Throughout central Italy the loftiest ranges of the Apennines lie close to the Adriatic, leaving only a narrow coastland, intersected by numerous short mountain torrents. In the west the mountains are lower and recede farther from the sea, leaving the wide lowlands of Etruria, Latium, and Campania. On this side, too, are rivers of some length, navigable for small craft—the Volturnus, the Liris, the Tiber, and the Arno—whose valleys link the coast with the interior highlands. In the south, however, the mountain chain swings over to the western coast where it ends in the rugged promontory of Calabria, the "toe" of Italy. To the north and east lie the lowlands of Apulia, which include its "heel."

The west coast of Italy with adjacent islands has always been the scene of volcanic activity. Both north and south of the Tiber River there are extinct volcanoes. Farther south are three peaks active since antiquity: Vesuvius, near the Bay of Naples; Stromboli, on one of the Lipari islands; and Etna, in Sicily, the largest European volcano. Although volcanic eruptions have caused considerable temporary damage, their effects have been ultimately beneficial. Volcanic ash and weathered volcanic rock form excellent soils particularly adapted to viticulture.

THE ISLANDS: SICILY, SARDINIA, CORSICA. The location of three large islands, Sicily, Sardinia, and Corsica, makes them a third region of Italy, with which their history has been closely linked. Sicily forms a large triangle (9,930 square miles) separated from the "toe" of Italy by the narrow Strait of Messina and from the African coast by a shallow stretch of sea about 80 miles wide. It is really a prolongation of the Apennine chain and in early geologic times formed part of a land bridge between Italy and Africa. The tiny islands of Malta and Pantelleria south of Sicily and the Lipari group to the north are mountain tops projecting from the submerged portion of the broken bridge. Sardinia (9,299 square miles) and Corsica (3,376 square miles), lying west of the Tyrrhenian Sea, are rugged, mountainous offshoots of the Italian mountains.

THE COASTLINE. In comparison with Greece, the Italian coastline is remarkably regular. Throughout a length of over 2,000 miles it has few deep bays or good harbors, almost all on the southern and western shores. On the Adriatic, the chief harbor was at Brundisium (Brindisi), far down the heel of Italy; on the southern shore was Tarentum (Taranto), at the head of the like-named gulf; on the west, the Bay of Naples; and on the Gulf of Genoa the ports of Genoa and Lunae Portus (Spezia), which, however, were important only late in Roman history. Sicily offered several good harbors for vessels of shallow draught; in particular, Syracuse on the east coast, Panormus (Palermo) on the north, and Drepanum (Trapani) on the west. Because ancient ships did not require deep harbors, they found adequate accommodation in river mouths wherever the current was not too swift or the shoals too dangerous. For this reason many cities, like Rome itself, grew up a few miles from the sea, at the head of navigation rather than directly on the coast. The character of the western coast of Italy, with its fertile lowlands, rivers, harbors, and general southerly aspect, made it more inviting and accessible to seaward approach than the Adriatic shore and determined its leadership in the cultural and material advancement of Italy.

CLIMATE. Although the climate of Italy, like that of Europe and North Africa, fluctuated greatly in prehistoric times, since the fifth millennium B.C. at least, it has been approximately the same as it is today. In general, it is "Mediterranean," characterized by a high average temperature, an absence of extremes of heat and cold, and rainy winters followed by dry summers. Nevertheless, it varies greatly in different localities, according to their northern or southern situation, their elevation, and their proximity to the sea. In the Po valley the continental climate approaches that of central Europe, with a wide difference between summer and winter temperatures and clearly marked transitional periods of spring and autumn. Here are frequent winter snows, abundant rains in spring and fall, and moderate ones in summer. Farther south through the peninsula, the winters become much, and the summers slightly, warmer. Annual rainfall decreases, summers are drier, in south Italy and Sicily almost rainless, and there is a rapid transition between wet and dry seasons. Even the rainy seasons are rather sunny, and the Italian climate is both healthful and stimulating.

MALARIA. In antiquity and modern times the disease from which Italy has suffered most has been malaria. Malaria was found in extensive marshes in river valleys and along the coast, generally formed by the blocking of channels of streams and rivers with soil washed down from the hills, and furnishing breeding grounds for malarial mosquitoes. The ravages of malaria have varied as the progress of civilization has brought about the cultivation and drainage of affected areas or as its decline has caused the undoing of such work.

FORESTS. Italy was much more wooded than most Mediterranean countries. The southern slopes of the Alps and the Po valley were forested, the former being noted for their larch and bird's-eye maple, the latter for its oaks, beeches, and chestnuts. Great forests flourished on the Apennines, particularly along the Ligurian coast, in southern Etruria, and in the valleys of the Tiber and its tributaries. Latium was also well wooded and produced much fir, pine, and beech. The forests of Corsica were famous, and even the mountains in the toe of Italy were heavily timbered. There, a single pine furnished the mast for the largest ship of ancient times, built for King Hiero of Syracuse in the second half of the third century B.C. Besides forests, there were thickets of laurel, myrtle, and similar shrubs and small trees. Italian timber was in great demand for shipbuilding among Carthaginians, Etruscans, Greeks, and Romans. It was not used extensively in household architecture owing to the preference for brick, stone, and cement, but was employed for roof and floor beams. Many articles of furniture were made from choicer woods. Coniferous forests supplied pitch and resin; oak, beech, and chestnut groves provided rich fodder for swine. At the beginning of the Christian era, Italy was still thought well wooded, although much forest had disappeared long before. Deforestation was due to the activities of woodcutters, charcoal-burners, and farmers who cleared land for tillage or pasturage. Once cut down, forests were seldom replaced. The need for reforestation was unrecognized, and the thin soil, exposed to the action of winter rains, was washed off hillsides before new growth could be established. Even where seedlings managed to take root, they were devoured by goats pastured in the clearings, which are still destructive to vegetation.

MINERALS.   The mineral wealth of Italy has never been very great. In antiquity the chief minerals mined were copper and iron, copper extensively in Etruria, Liguria, and Sardinia, iron on the island of Elba off the coast of Etruria. For a time, the gold washings in the valleys of the Graian Alps were worked. Tin was found in Etruria and some silver in Sardinia. Obsidian, much in demand before the age of metals, was quarried in Sardinia and elsewhere. Salt was mined in Sicily and was also obtained from the salt marshes at the mouth of the Tiber and along the west coast of central Italy. Various building stones, including marble of excellent quality, have always been abundant. Latium, Etruria, and many other parts of Italy had excellent clays for making bricks, tiles, and pottery.

AGRICULTURE.   In ancient times Italy was essentially agricultural and pastoral. The lowland yielded large crops of various grains—millet, maize, wheat, and barley—while peas, beans, and other vegetables were raised in abundance everywhere. Campania was especially fertile and allegedly yielded three successive crops annually. Sicily was one of the chief granaries of the ancient Mediterranean world. The vine, olive, and fig flourished and their cultivation eventually became as profitable as that of grain. Apples, pears, and other fruits, as well as nuts, were raised, but lemons and oranges, like rice, were not introduced from the East until long after the fall of the Roman Empire.

During the rainy season the coastal lowlands, and in summer the mountain slopes and meadows, afforded excellent pasturage for sheep, goats, cattle, and horses. Stock raising ranked next in importance to agriculture among the occupations of ancient Italy. The ancient Italians, unlike the Greeks and Phoenicians, therefore, never became a race of seafarers.

HISTORICAL SIGNIFICANCE OF ITALY'S CONFIGURATION AND LOCATION. The configuration of Italy, long, narrow, and traversed by mountain ridges, hindered its political unification. Yet the Apennines, running parallel to the length of the peninsula, offered no serious barrier to unification as did the network of mountains and long inlets that intersect Greece. Once Italy had been welded into a single state by Rome, its central position greatly facilitated the extension of Roman dominion over the Mediterranean basin. Because Italy was further removed than Greece from the older centers of civilization in Egypt and the Near East, it was less exposed to their cultural influences, and consequently its development lagged behind that of Greece and the Aegean area.

THE NAME ITALY. "Italy" is the ancient *Italia*, derived from the word *Witalia* which probably means "land of cattle." It was applied by the Greeks as early as the fifth century B.C. to the toe of the peninsula, adjacent to the island of Sicily. It rapidly acquired a much wider significance until, before the end of the first century B.C., *Italia* in a geographical and political sense denoted the whole country as far north as the Alps.

CHAPTER 2
PREHISTORIC
CULTURES IN ITALY

ACCESSIBILITY OF ITALY TO EXTERNAL INFLUENCES. The long coast of Italy rendered it accessible to influences from overseas, for the sea united rather than divided ancient peoples. Thus Italy was subjected to immigration and cultural stimuli from lands whose shores bordered the Mediterranean. Nor did the Alps and forests and swamps of the Po valley bar migrations and cultural influences from central Europe. Italy was the meeting place of peoples coming by sea from east and south and overland from the north, each bringing a new ethnic, linguistic, and cultural element to enrich its life. These movements had been going on since remote antiquity, until, at the beginning of history, Italy was occupied by peoples speaking different languages and living under very different political and cultural conditions.

Knowledge of this prehistoric age is derived almost wholly from archaeology, supplemented by linguistic studies of the peoples inhabiting Italy at the beginning of history. On this basis we can do little more than trace early cultural developments and indicate the course and approximate date of migrations. Uncertainty is caused by the frequently ambiguous nature of the evidence, that makes its interpretation tentative and even controversial, especially when new remains are discovered.

[8]

I. OLD STONE AGE

ITALY IN THE GLACIAL AGE. The geologic and climatic development of Italy was like that of neighboring Europe and North Africa. During the Pleistocene or Glacial Age—the Age of Man in Europe—there were four periods of glaciation in the Northern Hemisphere. These were characterized by a cold, moist climate during which ice fields formed in the mountains of Scandinavia and Switzerland and spread widely over the lowlands of northern and central Europe. Under these conditions, plants and animals of warmer zones were replaced by those of a northern or arctic character. As each glacial wave receded under the influence of moderating conditions, arctic flora and fauna retreated to be replaced by those of more temperate climes. In Italy, as in North Africa, there was no glaciation, but each glaciation brought a colder climate and increased rainfall, which affected plant and animal life.

OLD STONE AGE PEOPLES OF ITALY. The presence of man in Italy can be traced certainly to the third interglacial period, when the climate was warm and the hippopotamus, elephant, rhinoceros, and other types of tropical life roamed its forests and meadows along with the stag, bison, and horse of the northerly zone. Evidence of human occupation in Italy at this time comes chiefly from the discovery of flint tools and weapons, shaped by flaking or chipping in a fashion characteristic of the Old Stone or Palaeolithic Age. These artifacts are mostly hand axes, awls, gravers, and scrapers found in river gravels and caves in association with animal bones. Partial human skeletons have also been found in the same geologic strata and have been identified as belonging to the so-called Neanderthal race. This primitive type of man, once widespread in Palaeolithic times over Europe and the Mediterranean, was more apelike and probably less intelligent than modern man. It was predominant in Europe between 170,000 and 35,000 B.C.

The last glacial period set in about 70,000 B.C. and lasted, with temporary recessions and advances, until about 9000 B.C. During this period new types of men entered Europe from Asia and Africa, some of whom arrived in Italy.

The presence of late Palaeolithic men in Italy is attested to by discovery of their caves and rock-shelter abodes. The oldest, dating from about 10,000 B.C., are a cave on the island of Livanzo off the western tip of Sicily, rock shelters of Mt. Pellegrino on the northern coast of that island and of del Ramito in Calabria, and the grotto Polesini near Tivoli. Not much later are the Romanelli cave near Otranto in the extreme southeast of Italy and the Grimaldi caves at Balzi Rossi on the Italian Riviera.

The del Ramito grotto, the Romanelli cave, and that of Polesini reveal the naturalistic animal art of hunting peoples who decorated caves of southern France and Spain in the late Palaeolithic Age. This cultural affinity is confirmed by later burials in the Grimaldi caves that contained skeletons of the Cro-Magnon type of modern men, who were then one of the dominant peoples in southwestern Europe. Burial accessories, stone tools, and ornaments of seashells are related to the Magdalenian culture of southern France.

Like their predecessors, late Palaeolithic inhabitants of Italy were food gatherers. Living by hunting, fishing, and gathering wild fruits and edible plants, they had no domestic animals and raised no crops. They used fire, but their only durable habitations were rock shelters and caves. Under these conditions, Italy had only a small and scattered population which contributed little to ethnic elements in the historic population.

II. MIDDLE AND NEW STONE AGES

MESOLITHIC AGE.   In the centuries that followed the retreat of the last glaciers in Europe, the climate of Italy with its vegetation and animal life gradually assumed its present characteristics. Since about 5000 B.C. climatic conditions in Italy have remained relatively stable. In the transition new peoples entered the peninsula bringing with them so-called Middle Stone, or Mesolithic, cultures, characterized by the use of finely made small flint implements and by manufacture of bone tools and weapons. Their greatest contribution to human development, however, was the introduction of the bow and arrow as major implements of hunting and warfare. This weapon gave to people who had entered a Mesolithic stage of development greater mastery over wild animals and over those tribes that had remained Palaeolithic, which latter they exterminated or absorbed. Mesolithic peoples also were food gatherers, however, and consequently could not have been very numerous.

NEW STONE (NEOLITHIC) AGE.   Beginning about 3500 B.C. the inhabitants of Italy entered a new and revolutionary period of their cultural development, the New Stone Age. This was a transitional epoch from a food-gathering to a food-producing economy and so laid the foundation for a new era in history—ancient civilization. This was the result of the introduction of agriculture—the cultivation of food-producing plants and the taming and raising of various animals as a source of food. It appears that these developments took place first in the Near East, Anatolia, and the Balkans, where the earliest village communities of farmers and herdsmen appeared before 7000 B.C. From these areas the food-producing economy spread westward slowly along the Mediterranean and northwestward across Europe. It underwent modifications as it was carried by groups of immigrants filtering into Italy from North Africa by way of Sicily, from southern France into the northwest, and into the northeast from around the Adriatic. It is probable that it reached Sicily and south Italy by 3500 B.C. and had spread over the peninsula, the Po valley, Sardinia, and Corsica, by 2500 B.C. Adoption of agriculture had three very important consequences. It led to the rise of villages surrounded by fields and pastures; it made possible a greatly enlarged population by providing a regular and more abundant supply of food; and it led to conditions producing a more complicated division of labor.

NEOLITHIC TECHNIQUES AND INDUSTRIES. As the name "Neolithic" implies, the age was characterized by the use of a new technique in the manufacture of implements, that of polishing or grinding suitable stones into the required forms, although the older processes of chipping and flaking flints continued in use and became highly perfected. Characteristic products of polished stone were hammer, axe, and club heads usually with holes bored to receive wooden handles, adzes, chisels and, later, stone hoes that could be fitted into similar handles. Tools made by the new grinding and polishing technique were commonly of much denser stone than previously used and were therefore much more useful in developing agriculture. The forms of these implements set the pattern for commoner metal tools of later times. Knives, spearheads, and arrowheads were usually made of flint or obsidian.

Apart from the manufacture of polished stone tools and weapons, New Stone Age peoples introduced pottery making and cloth weaving. Pottery was hand formed and baked in open fires. Its shapes and sizes were many, to satisfy domestic needs and burial requirements. Such ware was decorated with incised and painted patterns, largely of geometric designs.

AGRICULTURE AND STOCK RAISING. Several varieties of grain—chiefly wheat and barley—and flax were the chief products of Neolithic agriculture. Neolithic man's superior tools made it relatively easy for him to make clearings for villages and cultivated fields. He domesticated goats, sheep, and dogs—the latter possibly having attached themselves to Mesolithic settlements—and perhaps pigs. Cattle were introduced later. Wild fruits and nuts were still eaten, but they were as yet not domesticated. Hunting was still an important source of food. The chief game animals were deer, wild pigs, and hares; bears and wolves were killed to defend the domestic animals.

NEOLITHIC CULTURE GROUPS. Archaeological discoveries from the Neolithic period reveal the presence of several different cultures by 2000 B.C. The people of Liguria in the northwest were still living in caves, where they also buried their dead. In the southeastern Po valley, however, many villages are evidenced by remains of hut foundations. These contain ashes from open hearths in which are embedded the charred remains of food, discarded utensils, and pottery, all of which reveal their culture. The foundations suggest the appearance of the huts. They were round or elliptical, with walls framed by wooden poles interlaced with small branches, reeds, or straw, and plastered with mud. The wall poles curved inwards until they met, forming the framework of the roof. The floors of the huts usually were excavated to about a yard below ground level. In southern Italy and Sicily the inhabitants, who lived both in caves and villages, widely used painted and incised pottery evidently influenced by ware indigenous to the Balkans across the Adriatic.

BURIAL CUSTOMS. Numerous cemeteries constitute one source of information for the Neolithic period. Despite local variations, there is general uniformity of burial customs throughout Italy. Nearly always the dead were buried in a contracted position with arms folded across the chest and knees drawn up to the body. Inhumation took place either in cave floors or in trenches or pits excavated in the open. It was also customary to strip the bones of flesh, or rebury them after the flesh had decayed, and to paint them with red ochre. Besides the corpses, which were usually interred with clothing and ornaments, the graves contained weapons and jars filled with food and drink. Graves were lined and covered with stone slabs or were filled with heaps of stone to protect the bones.

NAVIGATION. Apparently Neolithic Italians used seagoing vessels propelled by oars and sails. This explains migration from Africa to Sicily and Italy, and the occupation of Sardinia and Corsica, which seem to have been uninhabited in the Old Stone Age. Ability to use the sea enabled them to establish contacts abroad, although at the same time seafarers from other Mediterranean lands were beginning to make voyages to Italy. Thereby trade developed and with it an exchange of ideas and practices leading to continued cultural progress.

NEOLITHIC PEOPLES OF ITALY. Very little is known about the peoples of Italy in the Neolithic period, apart from their culture revealed in remains of habitations and graves. They surely did not have a common name and almost certainly were divided into many small political units. Their language, although certainly different from later Indo-European languages of Italy, has not survived. Physically, they probably belonged to the so-called Mediterranean type of the white race which from Neolithic times has been established in the Mediterranean basin and which is characterized by a dark complexion, dark hair, narrow head, and medium to short stature. This type still remains dominant in Italy and other Mediterranean countries, having assimilated both the so-called round-headed Alpine and the blond, long-headed Nordic types later introduced.

At the close of the Neolithic period, certainly after 2000 B.C., a new people entered Italy from the north by way of the central Alpine passes and settled near the lakes. Their intrusion is marked by the introduction of a new burial rite, cremation of the dead and burial of their ashes and bones in pottery. They also brought the practice of building villages on marshy shores of lakes with the houses elevated on piles or stakes for safety's sake in times of high water. Centuries later a rise in the water levels submerged the villages, and they remained unknown until a lowering of the lakes in the nineteenth century revealed them. The term *palafitte* (sing. *palafitta*), Italian for piles, is usually applied to these communities, their builders, and their culture.

The earliest *palafitte* settlement was found in the vicinity of Lake Maggiore. Its remains are purely Neolithic, but later sites belong to the Age of Metals, and a description of the *palafitte* culture in general will be reserved until later. These northern intruders possibly introduced the first Indo-European dialect into Italy.

III. COPPER-STONE AGE

From contacts abroad Neolithic peoples of Italy acquired knowledge of copper, the first metal used as a substitute for and an improvement on stone. Copper was probably first brought to Italy by sea from Cyprus along a trade route leading through Crete and the Aegean to southern Italy, Sicily, Sardinia, Corsica, and Liguria. Northern Italy was in touch with the central Danubian valley, and there was communication between the islands and Spain, so that these regions, rich in copper, were supplementary sources of supply. Local copper ores were unworked. Stone implements were not discarded upon the introduction of copper, as its supply was limited and for some purposes it was not as satisfactory as stone. Hence the new period has been called the Chalcolithic, Aeneolithic, or Copper-Stone Age. Chief metal objects were daggers and chisels of pure copper. Not only did stone implements remain in use, but the technique of stoneworking then reached its height. Its finest products were axe and hammer heads, pierced for the insertion of wooden handles.

There is no evidence of any extensive immigration into the peninsula during the Copper-Stone Age. Cultural conditions developed gradually from the preceding period, so that at times it is almost impossible to distinguish between Neolithic and Chalcolithic remains. In central and southern Italy and on the islands, the use of natural caves as tombs induced the inhabitants to excavate artificial ones in cliffs and hillsides. Stone-lined trench graves developed into great stone tombs built above ground in south Italy, Sicily, and Sardinia. Some of these are dolmens or chambers, each side and the roof being formed by a single huge stone block. Associated with dolmens are monuments called menhirs—single great stones set upright in the ground. Most of the megalithic tombs, like the larger rock ones, were collective burial places used for many generations. This is true of the "giants' graves" of Sardinia, long chambers built rather like dolmens with stone sides and roofs of flat stone slabs.

THE PALAFITTE CULTURE. In northern Italy *palafitte* peoples were reinforced from beyond the Alps, and they gradually spread southward and eastward in the Po valley. *Palafitte* villagers were hunters, fishermen, and farmers. They made wooden dugout canoes for use on the lakes and cleared the shores for fields and pastures. Wheat and millet were main crops, and among their domestic animals were oxen, sheep, dogs, and, later, horses. Their handmade pottery was gray in color, ornamented with incised horizontal bands of circles and zigzags. Spindle whorls and traces of cloth attest that they wove. They used stone axes with perforated heads, but also tools and weapons of copper, later of bronze. There is some evidence for the use of wheeled carts.

IV. BRONZE AGE

BRONZE AGE IN NORTHERN ITALY. In northern and southern Italy alike, the transition from the Copper-Stone to the Bronze Age, begun about 1800 B.C., was accomplished by about 1300 B.C. The technique of mixing melted copper with tin to form bronze alloy was discovered in the Near East before 3000 B.C., but many centuries elapsed before the use of bronze made its way to Italy, where it was introduced by trade and by the arrival of new immigrants who were familiar with it in their homelands. Tools and weapons of bronze were superior to those of copper because they were harder and sharper. In the Bronze Age the use of stone implements virtually disappeared. In the Po valley, the Bronze Age was marked by the appearance of new groups of immigrants from beyond the Alps who brought with them a fully developed Bronze Age culture from central Europe. They did not arrive in large tribes to cause a violent displacement of the natives, but in a succession of small units which formed several culture groups. The best known of these is that of the so-called *terramaricoli*, who settled in the central part of the valley and spread southwest. Their arrival was contemporary with the later *palafitte* settlements.

VILLAGES OF THE TERRAMARICOLI. Remains of these villages have been recently discovered in deposits of rich black earth which had accumulated on their sites as the result of human occupation. This earth was known in the local Italian dialect as *terramara* (plu. *terremare*), a name used to designate both these villages and their culture. Since the identity of the builders of the *terremare* villages is unknown, they have been called, for convenience, *terramaricoli*. The *terremare* villages had no uniform plan. The houses were huts, at first round and later oblong, with walls of wickerwork and clay strengthened by wooden posts whose lower portions are in many cases still standing. Only rarely is there any proof of pile foundations, and these are late and due, apparently, to protracted flooding of sites. The villages were sometimes surrounded by crude earth walls, ditches, and palisades.

TERREMARE CULTURE. *Terramaricoli* were much more advanced than *palafitte* peoples and had close affinities with the contemporary Bronze Age culture of Hungary. These northern invaders were primarily farmers and cattle raisers. They were also hunters, practised weaving, and were skillful workers in wood and bronze. Seeds of flax, beans, and two varieties of wheat found in remains of their villages indicate their crops. Their domesticated animals were horses, oxen, sheep, swine, and dogs. Their coarse pottery, their bronze tools and weapons, and their ornaments had distinctive Central European forms. Besides axes, spearheads, and daggers, they used two-edged cutting swords, or rather long knives of bronze. They seem also to have used wheeled carts, and for musical instruments had bronze horns or trumpets.

Terramaricoli cremated their dead and buried the ashes in jars known as ossuaries or cinerary urns. At first these were deposited, closely packed in rows, in cemeteries adjacent to the villages. Later, urns were separated by stone slabs, and finally individual graves were constructed. For a time, the dead were burned clothed, but no equipment of any sort was buried with the ashes. With the use of separate pits for the urns, however, it became customary to deposit weapons, ornaments, and pottery, along with the cinerary urn. Greater wealth, consciousness of individuality, and influence of the older inhabitants, with whom peaceful relations began to develop as subjects or neighbors, modified the original simplicity and uniformity of their rites.

BRONZE AGE IN THE PENINSULA. The picture of the origins of the Bronze Age cultures of peninsular Italy is as yet unclear. This is the period when there must have been an infiltration of new peoples in sufficient numbers to spread over the area Italic dialects which almost everywhere had displaced the older language by the beginning of history. Italic dialects were Indo-European and show a close relationship with both Greek and Celtic. Accordingly their appearance in peninsular Italy must be explained by the general movement of Indo-European speakers whose pressure can be traced from Iran across upper Mesopotamia and Asia Minor to the Balkan peninsula in the period 2000 to 1000 B.C. Although the *palafitte* villagers, the *terramaricoli*, and certain others may be regarded as belonging to this speech group, they were rather isolated from the main stream of peoples who apparently originated in the Balkans, crossed the Adriatic, and gradually spread westward across the peninsula. It seems very probable that the occupation of most of the peninsula and of Sicily by these Indo-Europeans took place in the late Italian Bronze Age and was completed by about 800 B.C., when they had reached a line running, roughly, from the future sites of Rimini to Rome.

BRONZE AGE IN SICILY AND SARDINIA. In Sicily and South Italy Bronze Age culture developed under influences from Crete and the Greek mainland and perhaps antedated its appearance in the north. From before 2000 B.C., trade relations were maintained with Minoan and Mycenaean centers as is shown by the contents of the Sicilian Bronze Age tombs. Among these may be mentioned long, narrow, Cretan swords, hatchets of bronze, leaf-shaped daggers, Mycenaean pottery, and various ornaments. In this period Sicily enjoyed greater prosperity and a higher cultural development than South Italy and exercised a strong cultural influence upon the mainland. It was also in the Bronze Age that the prehistoric culture of Sardinia reached its height. Great stone tombs were still built, but more unique and impressive were the massive stone towers called *nuraghi*, probably fortresses.

V. EARLY IRON AGE

TRANSITION FROM BRONZE AGE TO IRON AGE IN ITALY. The transition from the Bronze to the Iron Age was a slow development brought about by contacts with the Aegean and Danubian areas, which had anticipated Italy in the development of Iron Age cultures. Local mineral deposits of the peninsula and the islands still remained unworked for some time. The transition was completed by about 900 B.C. in Sicily but not until a century later in some parts of the peninsula. There was no large-scale immigration into Italy early in the Iron Age, but instead a steady infiltration of small groups from across the Adriatic which reinforced the already present speakers of Indo-European dialects. The early or prehistoric phase of the Italian Iron Age lasted until about 600 B.C.

EARLY IRON AGE.   The Early Iron Age in Italy was marked, like the Bronze Age, by the formation of many regional cultures. There was also a considerable distinction between the northwestern and southeastern zones that met along the Rome–Rimini meridian. In the former, the dominant non-Indo-European population cremated their dead; in the latter, where Indo-Europeans were in the majority, inhumation was the normal practice.

In the Po valley the chief cultures were the Comanine-Golaseccan in the central and the Atestine in the eastern sector. In the north of the peninsula

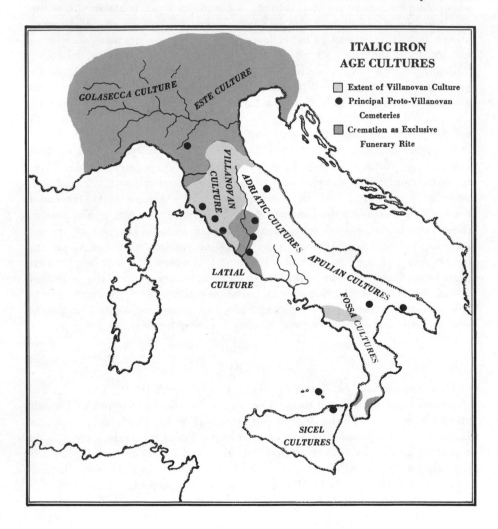

there are distinguished the Villanovan ranging from modern Bologna across the Arno into Tuscany and the upper reaches of the Tiber, the Latian in the lower Tiber valley and Latin plain, and the Picene in the highlands of Picenum on the Adriatic. In the south, there were the Campanian, Apulian, Bruttian, and Sicilian cultures, each named for the region where it developed. Sardinia and Corsica lagged behind Italy and Sicily in passing from the Bronze to the Iron Age and, in fact, the Iron Age in Sardinia was marked by cultural decline.

VILLANOVAN CULTURE AND THE ORIGIN OF THE ETRUSCANS. The Villanovan culture of the Bologna district may be regarded as the most important one in the northwestern part of the peninsula in the Early Iron Age. Here, settlements were irregular villages of round huts. Earthenware and, later, bronze jars, peculiarly biconical, were used to hold the ashes and bones of the dead. These jars were buried in pits covered with stone slabs or in rectangular stone-lined trenches. Swords, spears, and axes of iron served as weapons; rings and armlets of gold, pins with colored glass heads, amber beads, and disks were the chief ornaments. Garments were of wool fastened with elaborate bronze safety pins. A great improvement gradually took place in bronze work, owing to the introduction of the process for making hammered bronze plates, which made possible the manufacture of bronze helmets, shields, and body armor, as well as vases, boxes, and other articles for domestic use.

Villanovan culture is especially significant because of its relationship to the "origins" of the Etruscan people, whose vital civilization played so important a role in Italy at the very beginning of the historical period ca. 600 B.C. This subject will be discussed in some detail in the next chapter. It is enough to note at this point that Villanovan culture should probably be viewed as a primitive stage in the development of Etruscan civilization. It seems likely that the Villanovan peoples were, in fact, early Etruscans.

GREEK MIGRATION. Migrations into Italy from across the Adriatic which fell in the Late Bronze and Early Iron Ages ceased by 800 B.C. In the period that followed, a new people came by sea from the east and settled on the shores of the peninsula and Sicily. These were the Greeks, who planted their settlements on the southern coast from the heel of the Italian boot to the Bay of Naples, and in eastern and southern Sicily, between the middle of the eighth and the middle of the sixth century B.C. The settlement of the Greeks was of great significance, for it brought Italy into much closer contact with the older cultures of the eastern Mediterranean. Under the influence of these contacts, the various peoples of Italy emerged from barbarism into conditions of civilized life and into the light of history, for it is to the Greeks that we owe the earliest surviving written records concerning Italy and its inhabitants.

VI. THE PEOPLES OF ITALY IN THE SIXTH CENTURY B.C.

The Early Iron Age in Italy witnessed the formation of the various peoples who were to play important historical roles. Beginning with the sixth century

B.C., a connected historical outline of their political, cultural, and economic development may be presented. At the dawn of the historic period of the Italian Iron Age, as a result of the series of migrations described above, the distribution of peoples and languages in Italy was as follows.

THE LIGURES. The northwest corner of Italy, including the Po valley as far east as the Ticinus river and the coast as far south as the Arno, was occupied by the Ligures (Ligurians). They were descendants of the Neolithic population with an admixture of culturally superior northerners who settled in the central Po valley in the Chalcolithic and Bronze Ages. By the opening of historic times they spoke an Indo-European dialect. An important part of the population of Corsica was also of Ligurian stock.

PEOPLES OF THE CENTRAL AND EASTERN PO VALLEY. In eastern continental Italy from the Po northward to the Alps and from Lake Garda eastward to the peninsula of Histria (Istria) the chief people were the Veneti whose language was Indo-European and showed a remote affinity with Latin. They occupied the area in which the Atestine Iron Age culture had emerged. To the north and west of the Veneti, in the Alpine valleys and foothills, dwelt the Raeti, who apparently spoke an Indo-European dialect. By the sixth century the western Raeti, like the other peoples of the Po valley living between the Ligures and the Veneti, had come under the domination of Etruscan invaders from south of the Apennines. The Etruscans had also overrun the coastal strip to the north and east of the Apennines.

THE LATINS. South of the Tiber dwelt the Latins, destined to become the leading people in Italy and to make enduring contributions to civilization. The Latins probably had been formed by a union of invaders of Indo-European speech with the previous inhabitants. To these two elements there was added, about the beginning of the sixth century B.C., a small percentage of Etruscans. Several small tribes bordering on Latium, such as the Falisci and the Hernici, were substantially the same as the Latins in ethnic background and language.

NORTH CENTRAL PEOPLES. In the valleys of the central and southern Apennines lived a large group of tribes often called the Umbro-Sabellians. They were not confined to the mountains, for in the sixth century B.C. they extended down to the west coast south of Latium and to the middle Adriatic shore on the east. The Umbri, Sabini, Aequi, Marsi, Volsci, Vestini, Frentani, and the Samnites or Sabellians were their chief tribes. Basically, they seem to represent a survival of the older population with a strong admixture of invaders infiltrating westward from the Adriatic, who introduced an Indo-European element into their speech. Later these tribes expanded toward the southwest and south. The Umbro-Sabellians, together with the Latins and their kinsmen, formed the block of peoples usually called Italic, in contrast to Etruscan, Greek, Ligurian, and Illyrian. Their chief dialects were Umbrian in the north and several variations of Oscan in the south. All these were closely related to each other, and more distantly to Latin.

ITALY
IN THE SIXTH CENTURY B.C.

Scale of Miles
0   25   50   75   100

CAMPANIA AND SOUTH ITALY.   Until the coming of the Greeks by sea toward the close of the eighth century and the Etruscans over land early in the sixth, Campania was occupied by a people called the Oscans who, apparently, had been little affected by contacts with the north. In historic times, their dialect, Oscan, was Indo-European, but this was a late development due to Samnite migrations, for originally the Oscans spoke another tongue. In Apulia, along the lower Adriatic coast of Italy and around the Gulf of Tarentum, the population was known as Iapygians. They included several tribes of which the most important were the Daunii, Peucetii, and Messapi. They spoke a common Indo-European tongue usually called Messapian, but their origin and that of their language are obscure. Possibly the latter was the result of an Illyrian intrusion from across the Adriatic. To the southwest, in Lucania and Bruttium, the basic population seems to have been much the same as that found by the Greeks in Campania and called Oscan or Oppican and Oenotrian. Later thay were overrun by expanding Samnites who brought in their Italic dialect, but quite possibly they had earlier learned an Indo-European tongue in the same way as the Messapi. Along the southwestern and southern coasts the Greeks were dominant, but they did not penetrate far into the interior.

THE ISLANDS.   The population of Sicily prior to Greek occupation was closely affiliated with that of the adjacent regions of south Italy. The Greeks distinguished an earlier element they called Sicani, later known as Siculi (Sicels). The Sicels spoke an Indo-European dialect. How this came about is not known, although here, too, there is the possibility of an Illyrian intrusion. In western Sicily dwelt a people called the Elymi whose origins are unknown. By the sixth century B.C. the southern, eastern, and part of the northern coasts were in the hands of Greek colonists, who had pushed well into the heart of the island. A few Phoenician settlements had been established on the far western coast. Sardinia was largely occupied by the people who had established themselves there in the Neolithic and Bronze Ages, but the Carthaginians had obtained a foothold on the southern coast. Likewise on Corsica, the older population remained almost undisturbed, although the Etruscans won control of a strip along the eastern shore.

From the foregoing survey of the peoples of Italy at the close of the sixth century B.C., it can be seen that there was neither ethnic nor cultural unity among various sections. This condition added a still more serious difficulty to the topographical obstacles placed by nature in the path of political unification and the growth of an Italian nation.

CHAPTER 3
ETRUSCANS AND
GREEKS IN ITALY

I. THE ETRUSCANS

ETRURIA. In the sixth century B.C. the region between the Tiber and the Arno west and south of the Apennines was dominated by the Etruscans. These people were known to the Greeks as Tyrsenoi or Tyrrhenoi and to the Romans as Etrusci or Tusci. According to a Greek tradition, they called themselves Rasenna. The memory of the Etruscan occupation is preserved in the name *la Toscana*, derived from the Roman form *Tuscanus*, which is the modern designation of their homeland, whereas their Greek name is perpetuated in that of the Tyrrhenian Sea, which lies between the west coast of Italy and Corsica, Sardinia, and Sicily.

ORIGIN OF THE ETRUSCANS. Authorities in antiquity disagreed about the origin of the Etruscans, who differed from all the other historic peoples of Italy in language and certain other aspects of their culture. Most ancient historians followed the account of Herodotus, who believed that the Etruscans emigrated by sea to Italy from western Asia Minor and that they came in two waves after the Trojan War. Another tradition, known to Dionysius of Halicarnassus writing in the first century B.C., held that they were aboriginal Italians.

The contradictory nature of ancient literary traditions cannot be clearly resolved by the use of such modern tools as comparative philology and scientific archaeology, even though the Etruscans, a literate people, left thousands of inscriptions, and even though the cities and cemeteries of Tuscany have been extensively investigated. Their language can at least be pronounced because they wrote in a Greek alphabet adopted, it seems, from Cumae. Etruscan survived as a spoken language in Italy until as late as the second century A.D. Written records in the language existed in sufficient abundance at the middle of the first century to aid the Roman Emperor Claudius in his composition of a lengthy history of the Etruscans, a work no longer extant. Etruscan eventually became a dead language, however, and today its vocabulary and structure are scarcely understood because surviving Etruscan inscriptions are mainly funerary and tend to repeat a narrow range of short phrases. Those whose meaning can be translated bear no relationship to any other known language, and it seems certain that the Etruscan language is not Indo-European or Semitic.

Even without easily interpreted linguistic evidence, many prominent authorities, following Herodotus, continue to believe that Tuscany received Etruscan immigrants from Asia Minor early in the Iron Age. They note that a few inscriptions found on the Aegean island of Lemnos and in neighboring western Asia Minor appear to be written in a language either closely related to, or identical with, Etruscan. The erection of burial mounds (*tumuli*) over tombs, the practice of divination and reading of omens, and the use of fantastic animals like the chimera and griffin in artistic motifs, were typical in both areas, suggesting direct, initially intimate contacts. The emergence of city life in Tuscany during the eighth through seventh century B.C. occurred simultaneously with the increasingly eastern tone of Etruscan civilization, and many authorities attribute these possibly related phenomena to the influence of immigrants from Asia Minor.

Such arguments in favor of a Near Eastern provenance for the Etruscans are forceful but not convincing. The tradition recorded by Herodotus looks very much like a learned myth which cannot easily be reconciled with archaeological evidence. The historical civilization of the Etruscans emerged in the very heartland of Villanovan culture; archaeological investigation of sites occupied by Etruscans attests to evolution from characteristic Villanovan remains without revealing a clear break that might suggest the imposition of a foreign, oriental culture on earlier indigenous Iron Age settlers. Many of the great Etruscan cities of historical times—Veii, Cerveteri, Tarquinia, Vulci, Vetulonia, Populonia, and so on—had been important Villanovan centers whose subsequent development was clearly evolutionary.

One of the most striking characteristics of Etruscan civilization was its constant receptivity to Greek influences, even though the Etruscans tended always to interpret these influences on their own artistic terms. The first clearly "Etruscan" style of the seventh century B.C. was certainly orientalizing, but so was Greek civilization of the same period; it seems simpler to derive that style from evident Greek influence than to see it as part of a cultural tradition inherited by the Etruscans from any putative Near Eastern ancestry. The apparent linguistic similarities between Tuscany and Asia Minor may easily be explained by assuming (1) that there was a prehistoric linguistic substratum common to the central and eastern Mediterranean basin before the arrival of Indo-European speakers and (2) that Etruscans and the population of western Asia Minor kept their common, or related language(s), independently of one another, down to historic times. Etruscan would then resemble a language such as Basque, a linguistic island surrounded by Indo-European languages which has kept its identity for millennia.

It cannot be stated categorically, of course, that no wayfarers ever found their way from Anatolia to Tuscany during the prehistoric period. But such casual immigration, if in fact it did occur, is irrelevant to the idea that Etruscan civilization can be appreciated only in terms of its historical environment in Italy. This argument is attractive because it is comprehensible in terms of other Iron Age Italic cultures, which, except for the Greeks, were not imported by clearly defined ethnic groups but evolved under a medley of cultural influences on Italian soil.

EXPANSION IN ITALY. There is a tradition that twelve Etruscan cities were united in a league primarily for joint celebration of religious festivals; all the cities, however, were politically independent. At first they were governed by kings assisted by the heads of noble families called *lucumones*. Later the kingships disappeared, and the governments became aristocratic. Although the political and military expansion of the Etruscans outside Tuscany was a remarkable phenomenon, in the long run their position was insecure because they failed to build up a stable political organization. Both within Etruria and without, their conquests had been effected by small bands of warriors acting in loose cooperation. These bands founded separate states that were not united by any firm alliance and did not recognize any central authority, although they regularly helped each other in wartime. At the same time, they oppressed their subjects, causing them to be disloyal or indifferent to Etruscan rule. Accordingly, the more the Etruscans expanded, the more precarious their rule became. Nevertheless, for a time during the sixth century B.C. they were the most powerful political group in Italy.

Toward the close of the seventh century B.C. or early in the sixth, bands of Etruscans crossed the Tiber and conquered a large part of Latium. They occupied Rome and other important sites. Not much later they pushed on southward into the rich lowlands of Campania, where they founded Capua. Finding the coast already occupied by the Greeks, they tried in 524 to capture the Greek city of Cumae but were vigorously repulsed. A little earlier, however, they had been more successful in dealing with Greek colonists on the island of Corsica. With the help of the Carthaginians, they forced the Greeks to abandon their colony of Alalia (about 536) and retained for themselves sole access to the vast Corsican forests, although they never occupied more than a narrow strip along the eastern coast.

Late in the sixth century the Etruscans crossed the Apennines and descended into the Po valley. Here they conquered the central region between the Ligures and the Veneti from the Adriatic coast to the Alps. North of the Apennines, their chief city was Felsina near modern Bologna. Their seaport Adria, founded in the territory of the Veneti just north of the mouth of the Po, has given its name to the Adriatic Sea. Another flourishing port was Spina, south of the Po delta.

DECLINE OF ETRUSCAN POWER. The first losses were suffered in Latium. In 507 Latin cities, aided by Aristodemus, the Greek ruler of Cumae, defeated an Etruscan army at Aricia, and at about the same time the Romans shook off Etruscan rule. Later, in an effort to strengthen their position, the Etruscans launched a great attack on Cumae by sea and by land. Hieron, the ruler of Syracuse, came to the rescue and destroyed the Etruscan fleet (474). Etruscan sea power was broken, and ships of Syracuse raided Corsica, Elba, and the coast of Etruria. These attacks were repeated in the early fourth century by Dionysius I of Syracuse, who also seized the Etruscan ports on the Adriatic. In Campania the expansion of the Samnites from the central Apennines brought about the downfall of Etruscan rule, which ended with the fall of Capua in 438. About 400, Celtic tribes descended the central passes into the Po valley and soon overran the territory which the Etruscans had held in continental Italy. Henceforth the Etruscans were confined within the limits of Etruria proper, and their later history will be treated in connection with the expansion of Rome and their absorption into the Roman state. The decline of Etruscan power did not result in destruction of Etruscan culture, which continued to progress and to produce interesting work for several centuries. The economic decline of Etruria dates from the later stages of Roman conquest of the area in the third century B.C. and was gradually followed by cultural decay until the beginning of the Christian era.

ETRUSCAN CIVILIZATION. Etruscan civilization is a synthesis of their own developed Villanovan culture and that of the Italian peoples whom they conquered. It also contained a liberal admixture of Greek influences, largely the result of commercial contacts with the Greek colonies to the south. Their civilization was based on agriculture, industry, and commerce, all of which experienced a great impetus under Etruscan direction.

The Etruscans planted vineyards and olive orchards, cultivated grain for export, and bred horses. In order to provide new land for cultivation and to prevent soil erosion they dug tunnels and built dams on an extensive scale. They fully exploited the mineral resources of areas under their control, promoting ironworking in Etruria and opening up the iron mines of Elba. They also worked copper deposits of Corsica and the copper and tin ores of Etruria. Their bronzes, especially their mirrors and candelabra, enjoyed high repute even in fifth-century Athens Their goldsmiths and silversmiths, too, fashioned elaborate ornaments of great technical excellence. They developed an excellent black pottery called *bucchero nero* and expanded their ceramic industry by producing imitations of imported Greek ware.

The Etruscans were active seamen at the very dawn of the historical period and long continued to be a powerful maritime people. At an early date they established commercial relations with the Phoenicians and the Carthaginians. By the early seventh century B.C. they had developed an active trade with Greece, as is evidenced by the contents of their tombs and the influence of Greece upon their civilization. In the sixth century they traded directly with Athens, largely by means of their own ships. There was also an extensive trade with the Greek cities of South Italy, and groups of Greek traders settled in Etruscan seaports on the Tyrrhenian and Adriatic coasts. The growth of commerce ultimately led to the introduction of coinage. About the close of the sixth century the Etruscans gave up using rough lumps of copper as a medium of exchange and employed coins of the Greek cities of Ionia. After 500 B.C. Populonia and other Etruscan cities began to issue gold, silver, and copper coins, using at first a standard adopted from Lydia but later discarding this in favor of the Greek standard in vogue in Euboea and Campania. The Etruscans, as well as the Carthaginians, were jealous of Greek expansion in the western Mediterranean, and about 536 B.C. a combined effort of these two peoples drove the Greek colonists from Corsica. From this time Etruscan domination in the Tyrrhenian Sea was firmly established, and this may have been responsible for the reputation for piracy which they enjoyed among the Greeks.

CITIES AND CEMETERIES. Our knowledge of Etruscan civilization is derived mainly from the ruins of their cities and from their tombs. Frequently, Etruscan cities developed out of Villanovan settlements which, for the most part, were situated on hilltops or in other easily defensible positions. These communities grew into prosperous towns fortified with ramparts of earth sometimes partly faced with stone. The purely stone city walls of polygonal blocks or of regular ashlar masonry once regarded as Etruscan work of the sixth century B.C. must now be dated in the late fourth century B.C. or subsequent centuries, and outside of Etruria proper they are post-Etruscan. The most important public buildings were the temples. The typical Etruscan temple was an almost square structure set on a high base and having a portico or pillared entrance porch almost as large as the interior chamber (*cella*). The *cella* itself was often divided into three parts to accommodate the cult of a triad of deities. Walls were of sun-dried brick resting on stone courses; columns and the beams of the steeply pitched roof were of wood. All wooden parts were faced with colored terra cottas, and the roof was ornamented with figures of the same material. Private houses were of wood or sun-dried brick and in some cases were built around a central, open court, in the so-called Greek peristyle fashion.

II Tomb of the Leopards. *An early fifth-century B.C. example of vivacious Etruscan funerary art, this is one of the many tomb frescoes discovered at the site of ancient Tarquinii (modern Tarquinia), chief of the league of twelve Etruscan cities and alleged home of two of Rome's early kings. (Photo: Alinari.)*

The Romans credited the Etruscans with developing distinctive types of column and domestic hall (*atrium*), both later called Etruscan.

In their burial rites the Etruscans practiced both inhumation and cremation. The graves of the poor were pits or trenches in which ash urns or sarcophagi were deposited. The tombs of the nobles, the most striking memorials of Etruscan civilization, were of various types: *tumuli* or artificial mounds of earth enclosing a burial chamber, *tholoi* or circular stone vaults built into hillsides, and corridor tombs with many chambers excavated in solid rock. The larger corridor tombs were evidently family burial vaults and were elaborately decorated with reliefs carved on their walls or with painted friezes, from which decorations we derive most of our information regarding the Etruscan appearance, dress, and customs. Many gold ornaments and other costly articles found in Etruscan tombs of the seventh and sixth centuries B.C. attest the wealth of the aristocracy.

ART. Etruscan art takes many forms: painting on vases and the walls of tombs, incised designs on bronze chests and mirrors, statues and statuettes of bronze and terra cotta, reliefs on grave steles, sarcophagi, and cinerary urns, terra cotta architectural ornaments, and gold and silver jewelry. The greatest impulse to artistic productivity came to the Etruscans from the Greeks in the sixth century, and they derived continuous inspiration from Greek art. Some Greek artists seem to have settled in Etruria and founded schools there, but Etruscan artists were by no means slavish imitators of Greek originals. While they copied the form, subjects, and technique of the latter, they always preserved their own basic conceptions and thus succeeded in creating a native art of their own. Although this art lacked the idealism, rhythm, harmony, and restraint of the Greek, it excelled in naturalness, force, and vivacity—characteristics also of Villanovan art at a much more primitive level—and is a reflection of the Etruscan outlook on life in this world and in the hereafter.

RELIGION. Religion played a very prominent part in Etruscan life. The Etruscans worshipped numerous gods and believed in powerful malicious spirits which controlled the afterworld. In their desire to interpret the will of the gods and to ward off impending evils, they developed an elaborate system for forecasting the future by examining the livers of sacrificed animals and by interpreting the significance of flashes of lightning and numerous other omens. The Etruscans readily adopted both Italian and Greek gods, and with the Greek deities came a great deal of Greek mythology. Among the higher gods, they paid particular reverence to a triad composed of Tinia, Uni, and Menerva, corresponding to Jupiter, Juno, and Minerva in the Roman pantheon. In order to honor their dead and to ensure them immortality, the Etruscans believed that it was necessary to offer to the gods the lives of others. Here is the origin of gladiatorial combats at funerals and perhaps the explanation of the cruel massacres of prisoners of war which the Etruscans perpetrated.

THE ETRUSCANS AND ITALIAN CIVILIZATION. The general impression of the Etruscans is that they were a wealthy, luxury-loving people, but by no means the voluptuaries whom certain Greek writers depict. Quick to appreciate and adopt the achievements of others, the Etruscans were rather unoriginal. A strain of cruelty is revealed in their religion, particularly in the rites celebrated in honor of the dead. Bold and energetic warriors, they nevertheless lacked a spirit of discipline and cooperation and were incapable of developing a stable political organization. Yet on the whole, they were most active in the promotion of civilization in early Italy. In town planning, road building, architecture, art, warfare, political organization, and religion, they influenced the Italian peoples with whom they came into contact, particularly those of the central and northern part of the peninsula.

II. THE GREEKS

GREEK COLONIZATION. It has been pointed out that as early as the eighth century B.C. the Greeks had begun their colonizing activity in the western Mediterranean. In the next two centuries, they settled the eastern and southern shores of Sicily, stretched a chain of settlements on the Italian coast from Tarentum to the Bay of Naples, and established themselves at the mouth of the Rhone and on the Riviera. The opposition of Carthage shut them out from the western end of Sicily and from Spain; the Etruscans closed to them Italy north of the Tiber; while joint action of these two peoples excluded them from Sardinia and Corsica.

In the fifth century B.C. the Greek cities in Sicily and Italy were at the height of their power and prosperity. In Sicily the Greeks penetrated from the coast far into the interior, where they brought the Sicels under their domination. Their position was challenged by the Carthaginians; but the victory in 480 B.C. of Gelon, ruler of Syracuse, at Himera secured the Sicilian Greeks in the possession of most of the island and freed them from danger of Carthaginian invasion for over seventy years. Six years later, his brother and successor, Hieron, crushed Etruscan naval power off Cumae, and delivered the mainland Greeks from all fear of Etruscan aggression. The tip of the toe of the Italian peninsula, known to the Greeks as Italia, was completely under their control from sea to sea; but northward as far as Posidonia on the west coast and eastward to Tarentum their territory did not extend far from the seaboard. Likewise in Campania, their cities Cumae and Naples were closely confined to the coast by the Etruscans. It was in this region, apparently, that the Romans came to call the Greeks "Graeci" instead of "Hellenes," the common name they had adopted for themselves. How firmly the Greeks were established in south Italy and how deeply it was permeated by their culture may be judged from the name Great Hellas[1] which they applied to this area.

The Greeks possessed even less political cohesion than did the Etruscans. Each colony was a city-state, a sovereign independent community, owing no political allegiance even to its mother city. Thus colonial Greece reproduced all the political characteristics of the motherland. Only occasionally, in times of extreme peril, did some of the Greek cities lay aside their mutual jealousies and unite in common cause. Larger political structures, such as those that the tyrants of Syracuse built up by the subjugation of other cities, were purely ephemeral, barely outliving their founders. Individual cities also were weakened

---

[1] In Latin *Magna Graecia*.

by incessant factional strife within their walls. The result of this disunion was to restrict Greek expansion and to pave the way for eventual conquest of the Western Greeks by Italian "barbarians."

DECLINE OF GREEK POWER IN ITALY AND SICILY. Even before the close of the fifth century B.C. the decline of the Western Greeks had begun. In Italy their cities were subjected to repeated assaults from expanding Samnites of the central Apennines. In 421 Cumae fell into the hands of a Samnite band, and thenceforward the Greek cities further south were engaged in a struggle for existence with the Lucanians and the Bruttians, Samnite offshoots. In Sicily the Carthaginians renewed their assault upon the Greeks in 408. For a time (405–367) the genius and energy of Dionysius I, tyrant of Syracuse, welded the cities of the island and the mainland into an empire which enabled them to withstand their foes. His empire had only been created by breaking the power of the free cities, and after his death they were left weaker and more disunited than ever. After further warfare, by 339, Carthage permanently occupied the western half of Sicily, while in Italy only a few Greek towns, such as Tarentum, Thurii, and Rhegium, barely maintained themselves against the Italians. Even by the middle of the fourth century B.C. an observant Greek predicted the speedy disappearance of the Greek language in the West before that of the Carthaginians or Italians. Their final struggles, however, must be postponed for later consideration.

THE GREEKS IN ITALIAN HISTORY. The Greeks brought Italy into the the light of history and into contact with more advanced civilizations of the eastern Mediterranean. From Greek geographers and historians we derive our earliest information regarding Italian peoples, and they, too, shaped the legends that long passed for early Italian history. The presence of Greek towns in Italy gave a tremendous stimulus to the cultural development of the Italians, both by direct intercourse and indirectly through the Etruscans. In spreading Greek influence, Cumae, the most northerly of the Greek colonies and one of the earliest, played a very important part, as did individual Greeks who, by about 500 B.C., had settled in Latin towns at Rome's doorstep and probably in Rome itself. The more highly developed Greek political and military institutions, art, literature, and mythology found a ready reception among Italian peoples and profoundly affected their political and intellectual progress. Traces of Greek influence are nowhere more noticeable than in the case of Rome itself, and the cultural ascendency which Greece thus early established over Rome was destined to last until the breakup of the Roman Empire.

PART

II

PRIMITIVE MONARCHY AND REPUBLIC: FROM PREHISTORIC TIMES TO 27 B.C.

CHAPTER 4
EARLY ROME TO THE
FALL OF THE
MONARCHY

I. THE LATINS

LATIUM AND THE LATINS. The district south of the Tiber, extending along the coast to the promontory of Circeii and from the coast inland to the slopes of the Apennines, was called Latium. The northern part of Latium, now known as the Roman Campagna, is an undulating plain intersected by watercourses and dominated by the isolated volcanic mass which culminates in the Alban Mount rising over 3,000 feet above sea level. At the opening of history this region was occupied by an Italic people called the Latins (*Latini*), a mixed people in which the dominant element was formed by the descendants of invaders, part of the westward movement of Indo-Europeans, who arrived at the Tiber about the close of the Bronze Age. These invaders absorbed the previous occupants of the country, probably a sparsely settled pastoral folk, who had been there since Neolithic times. Later, in the Early Iron Age, there apparently was an intrusion of people, probably Sabines, who descended the Tiber valley and ultimately amalgamated with the Latins. South of the Alban Mount, however, the land was held by Sabellian peoples, in particular the Volsci.

EARLY LATIN CULTURE. Until the close of the seventh century B.C., the Latins remained agricultural and pastoral, little affected by cultural developments taking place elsewhere in Italy. They settled in villages built on defensible

[33]

eminences, with cemeteries placed outside the inhabited area. In these cemeteries they deposited the ashes of their dead in clay urns made like the huts in which they lived. They were round or elliptical structures with wattle and plaster walls supported by a wooden framework. The sloping thatched roof was held in place by exterior beams which extended from the ridgepole part way down the sides. In the roof was a hole which served as a vent for the hearth smoke. The roof terminated in overhanging eaves, and the single opening was flanked on either side by one or two wooden pillars. The opening was large and served not only as a doorway but also, since there were seldom windows, to admit light and air to the interior.

CULTURAL PROGRESS.   From the end of the seventh century B.C. Latium enjoyed a much richer cultural life. The change was mainly due to Etruscan influence, which in many places was accompanied by their political domination, but also to Carthaginian, and more particularly Greek, traders who began to frequent the coast towns. The villages developed into towns with fortified citadels and protecting earthen walls and were adorned with temples built and decorated in Etruscan style. Grave deposits show the presence of a wealthy class easily distinguishable from the majority of the people. It seems also that the population had increased considerably and that arable land was in demand and had to be intensively cultivated, if to this age may be attributed the dams and drainage works, still visible today, that were constructed at various places to win new ground or protect fields from erosion.

POLITICAL CONDITIONS.   The Latins were divided into many independent units called *populi* (peoples). Each *populus* occupied a definite district (*pagus*) and had its central point in its fortified town (*oppidum*). There was, however, a marked tendency by the stronger of these petty states to absorb the weaker, and many of the sixty-five towns whose names have been preserved had merged with their neighbors before the close of the sixth century.

LATIN LEAGUES.   The general feeling among the Latins that they were united by ties of common inheritance and interests found expression in associations of towns for the joint worship of deities widely recognized among all the Latins. Most important of these associations was the religious league which celebrated the annual festival of the Latin Jupiter (*Jupiter Latiaris*) on the Alban Mount. It is uncertain how many Latin towns participated in the Alban festival. Tradition has preserved the not improbable number of forty-seven for the end of the sixth century. Tradition also records that the town of Alba Longa on the west shore of the Alban Lake was the early head of the league, but this refers to religious and not political leadership. Each community which joined in the celebration contributed its quota of the offerings and received a share of the sacrifices. Despite the political fate of the Latin towns, this festival of prehistoric origin was maintained until well into the Christian era. The Latins also had a military league for mutual defense. In this association, leadership passed from one town to another as their respective military and political

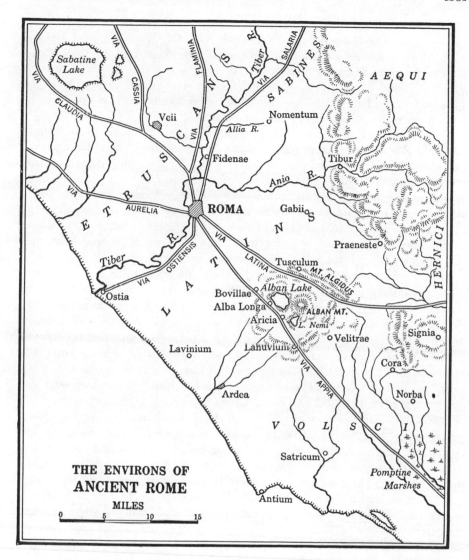

THE ENVIRONS OF
ANCIENT ROME

MILES

0   5   10   15

strength changed. This league had as its patron divinity the goddess Diana, whose cult was celebrated jointly by all of the allied cities in a sacred precinct consisting of a grove and an altar maintained by the *pro tempore* dominant city.

II. ORIGINS OF ROME

Site of Rome. Rome, the Latin *Roma*, is situated on the Tiber about fifteen miles from the sea, where the river flows through a cluster of low hills. There, on the left or eastern bank are the three buttes, the Capitoline, Palatine,

and Aventine hills. Stretching out toward them from the high ground farther
east are the spurs known as the Quirinal, Viminal, Esquiline, and Caelian
hills. All these formed part of Rome of the later Republic and the Empire, the
City of the Seven Hills, which also extended across the Tiber to the west bank
where it included both the low ground along the river and the height of the
Janiculum hill. This extent was the result of a long period of growth; the
beginnings of Rome were much more humble.

GROWTH OF THE CITY. The origins of Rome go back to prehistoric
times. As Rome grew in importance, men's curiosity on this point was aroused,
and speculation began to supply the want of historical evidence. Legends arose
which ultimately came to form the traditional version of the founding of Rome.
In this can be detected contributions from both the Romans and their Greek
neighbors in Italy and Sicily. Before the close of the fourth century B.C., the
Romans attributed the foundation of the city to a figure called *Romulus*, whose
name is derived from that of Rome itself. Romulus, son of the god Mars and
the daughter of a king of Alba Longa, was credited with the establishment of a
city on the Palatine hill. Meanwhile the Greek desire to explain the origin of
Rome by linking it with their own past had given rise to myths in which the
founder of the city appears as the descendant of a Greek hero. The most sign-
nificant of these Greek tales was the one whose roots go back to the sixth century
and which eventually established a connection between Rome and the Trojan
prince Aeneas, son of the goddess Aphrodite. In his wanderings after the
destruction of Troy, Aeneas made his way to Italy, where either his son or his
grandson founded Rome. Owing to the Greek cultural ascendency over the
Romans, the latter partially accepted Greek myth and by the end of the third
century B.C. combined it with the native tradition. The resultant composite
version was that Aeneas came to Latium and founded Lavinium, his son
Ascanius founded Alba Longa, and Romulus, his descendant after many
generations, was the founder of Rome. In this legend there is little of historical
worth, except perhaps a faint reflection of the early importance of Alba Longa
in Latium and the memory of a prehistoric settlement on the Palatine. Roman
writers of the late third and the second centuries B.C. differed widely on the
date of the founding of Rome, but in the first century the date 753 B.C. became
canonical and served as the basis for reckoning events in terms of years "from
the founding of the city." If by the "foundation" of Rome is meant the appearance of an Iron Age settlement on the Palatine, then this date may well be
approximately correct; at the very least it is not contradicted by the surviving
archaeological evidence. In default of written records we must rely mainly on
such evidence to picture the early stages in the growth of the city.

The find of some Apennine Bronze Age pottery in a fill on the low ground
near the Tiber indicates that there was a settlement on the site of Rome about
1500 B.C., but its location is unknown, and there seems to be no continuity
between this settlement and those of the early Iron Age. Excavations have

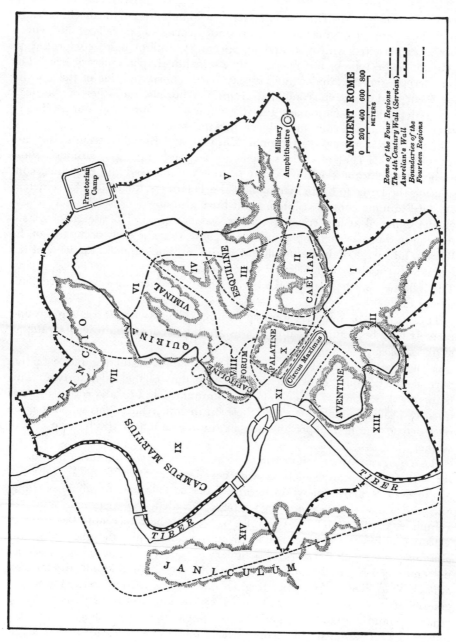

shown that in the latter period, from the ninth to the seventh century B.C., there were several communities on the hills overlooking the marshy area which later became the site of the celebrated Forum. One of these, and at first prob-

ably two, occupied the Palatine hill. Here the foundations of the dwellings show
that they were rectangular huts with rounded corners and walls of interwoven
branches plastered with mud and supported by upright posts, conforming in
general to the type of hut revealed by Latin hut-shaped cinerary urns. The
cemetery of the Palatine community lay on the northeast side of the Forum.
Here the earliest graves contained cremation burials, the ashes of the dead
being deposited in customary hut-shaped urns. Inhumation burials began
later, but cremation continued along with the new rite.

Similar cemeteries on the Quirinal, Viminal, and Esquiline seem to indicate
the presence of contemporary settlements on these hills also, although some
authorities deny the existence of any on the Viminal and the Esquiline, con-
sidering the latter to be an extension of the Palatine settlement. The cemetery
on the Esquiline contained inhumation burials almost exclusively, but in that
on the Quirinal at first cremation alone was practiced. The use of these contrasting burial rites contemporaneously suggests that the early occupants of the
Roman hills were of different cultural traditions, and supports the view of the
Romans themselves, who believed they were a people of heterogeneous origins.
The inhumers may possibly have been Sabine intruders in a region predominantly Latin.

These early communities were sprawling villages with no regular ground
plan. It may be assumed that each was an independent political unit ranking
as an *oppidum*.

About 650 B.C., the old Palatine cemetery ceased to be used and an extensive
part of the Forum area was built over with huts of the Palatine type. This
points to an expansion of the Palatine community and its absorption by conquest or peaceful amalgamation of those on the other hills. This union may be
regarded as the first important step in the formation of the historic city of
Rome.

ROME OF THE FOUR REGIONS. The next step was the urbanization of
the earliest community which can with certainty be called Rome. It is the city
of the Four Regions, known in historic times as Palatina, Esquilina, Collina,
and Sucusana (later Suburana). These included the Quirinal, Viminal,
Esquiline, Caelian, and Palatine hills, as well as the intervening low ground.
This probably was the area included from the earliest historic times within the
pomerium, the ritually consecrated boundary of the city. Within the *pomerium* but
not embraced in any of the four regions was the Capitoline hill, the fortified
citadel. Thus, Rome of the Four Regions may be regarded as an expansion and
consolidation of the town formed earlier by the union of the Palatine with its
adjacent communities. In the period 625–575 B.C. the marshy land between the
hills had been drained and people began to move down into it. Thus, the
originally isolated hill villages began to grow together and form a single
community. City life began about 575 B.C. under Etruscan influence. This
view finds support in the name *Roma* itself, which seems to be of Etruscan origin.

The new city was not surrounded by a continuous wall, although by the sixth century the individual hills were protected by earthen embankments with ditches in front. The Aventine hill, as well as part of the plateau back of the Esquiline remained outside the *pomerium* until the time of the Emperor Claudius in the first century A.D.

HISTORIC ROMANS. The archaeological evidence shows that the Roman tradition of a strong Sabine element in the population of the early city has a substantial basis. But though it is true that the population of Rome was the result of a fusion of different elements, Latin and Sabine mainly but with a slight admixture of Etruscan and probably even pre-Italic, nevertheless the Romans were essentially Latin. In language, in religion, in political institutions, they were characteristically Latin, and their history is inseparably connected with that of the Latins as a whole.

ROME'S STRATEGIC SITUATION. The location of Rome, on the Tiber at a point where navigation for seagoing vessels terminated and where an island made transit easy, made it commercially important. It was also the gateway between Latium and Etruria and the natural outlet for the trade of the Tiber valley. Furthermore, its central position in Italy gave it a strategic advantage in its wars. But the greatness of Rome was not the result of its geographic advantages; it was the outgrowth of the energy and political capacity of its people, qualities which became a national heritage because of the character of the early struggles of the Roman state.

III. THE EARLY MONARCHY

TRADITION. "In the beginning," wrote the Roman historian Tacitus, "kings ruled the city Rome."[1] The accuracy of this statement is attested by the mention of the king (*rex*) in an inscription of the sixth century B.C. and by the survival of this term in later times in the title *rex sacrorum* or "king of the sacrifices," borne by a higher priest, as well as by the strength of the Roman tradition regarding an early period of monarchy. It is quite impossible, however, to present any reliable history of Roman monarchy because, when Roman historians began to write they found scarcely any records of the regal age, and oral tradition had become confused. Consequently the Roman account of the reigns of the kings is a reconstruction by annalists and antiquarians who sought to attribute the origins of Roman political and religious institutions to these rulers.

According to the accepted Roman version, seven kings ruled Rome between the founding of the city and the establishment of the Republic about 509. The first of these, Romulus, and his alleged Sabine colleague Titus Tatius, may not have been historical personages. The six successors of Romulus—Numa Pompilius, Tullus Hostilius, Ancus Marcius, Lucius Tarquinius Priscus, Servius

---

[1] *Annales*, 1, 1.

Tullius, and Lucius Tarquinius (Superbus)—probably were historical, although we can place little reliance upon their characteristics and exploits. Apparently the first three were pre-Etruscan and may have ruled the Palatine community before and after the absorption of its neighbors; the last three date from the sixth century when Rome was under Etruscan domination. By name and tradition, the Tarquinii were Etruscan, and Servius Tullius may have been an Etruscan whose name has survived in a Latin form.

Despite the unreliability of the Roman account of the age of the kings, it is possible to draw a general picture of conditions in Rome under its monarchy, based on the survival in later times of religious, political, and social institutions originating in the early Roman state, and on the results of archaeological studies that have revealed much of the character of early Roman civilization.

POLITICAL ORGANIZATION OF THE REGAL PERIOD. The political institutions of early Rome bore a strong resemblance to those of other city kingdoms built up by Indo-European immigrants in Greece and Italy. They comprised the kingship, a council, an assembly of the people, and the smaller units into which the citizens were grouped for the better performance of their obligations and the exercise of their rights.

The Roman monarchy apparently was not purely hereditary but elective within the royal family, like that of primitive Greek states, where the king was the head of one of a group of noble families chosen by the nobles and approved by the people as a whole. The king was warlord, chief priest, and judge in matters affecting the public peace. His authority, called the *imperium*, included the right of scourging and execution. Its symbols were the *fasces*, small bundles of rods enclosing an axe, carried by attendants called lictors. The royal power was not absolute, for its exercise was tempered by custom, by the lack of any elaborate machinery of government and by the practical necessity for the king to avoid alienating the community.

The council was called the Senate (*senatus*), which, as its name indicates, was originally a council of elders but, following the pattern of similar councils in the city states of Greece, had become a council of nobles. The details of its organization are not known, but its functions were primarily advisory. From a very early date the Roman people were divided into thirty groups called *curiae*, apparently derived from an ancient Italic (but non-Latin) term, *coviria*, meaning a "fellowship of men" in the sense of a community or village, like an Attic *deme*. It seems that the number of *curiae* gradually grew under the monarchy as various villages on and near the seven hills were admitted into the state. Under the last kings of the sixth century B.C. they apparently numbered twenty-seven, attaining the ultimate and permanent figure of thirty in 495, after which the Romans used other institutions to absorb new citizens. Membership in the *curiae* was probably hereditary, and each *curia* had its special cult, which was maintained long after the *curiae* had lost their political importance. Apparently the *curiae* were grouped into three larger units called tribes, eventually ten *curiae* to each tribe. The names of these tribes, *Ramnes, Tities,* and *Luceres,* survived in later time as the names of cavalry corps in the army, which was recruited at first on a tribal basis.

When the members of all the *curiae* met, they constituted the popular assembly known as the Curiate Assembly (*comitia curiata*). It was convoked at the pleasure of the king to hear matters of interest to the whole community such as adoptions, wills, and grants of citizenship. It did not have legislative power, but such important steps as the declaration of war or the appointment of a new *rex* required its formal sanction. Even then, strictly speaking, the Curiate Assembly was not a legislative body, although its very existence presupposed the idea that government was in some sense responsible to the citizenry, one that was important for future political development.

EXPANSION UNDER THE KINGS. According to literary tradition, Rome grew to be the chief city in Latium under the kings, having absorbed several smaller Latin communities in the immediate neighborhood, extended her territory along the lower course of the Tiber to the seacoast, where later the port of Ostia was founded, and even conquered Alba Longa, the former religious center of the Latins. Atlhough occasionally doubted, the tradition that Rome was, in fact, the leading city of Latium, at least under the Etruscan monarchy of the sixth century B.C., seems well-founded. One of the greatest temples of all Italy, that dedicated to Jupiter Capitolinus on the Capitoline hill, was begun by the last Etruscan king, Tarquinius Superbus, and certainly seems to symbolize the wealth, power, and hegemony of Rome in Latium. Another credible tradition ascribes Rome's first commercial treaty with Carthage to about the same period (508), one in which the Roman government clearly defined its exclusive sphere of interest as being in Latium.

CENTRALIZATION OF POWER AND THE FALL OF THE MONARCHY. According to Roman tradition, the monarchy came to an end in 509 B.C. with the abolition of the kingship, although it survived as a shadow of its former self in a lifelong priesthood. This date may be accepted as approximately correct even if no confidence can be placed in the dramatic Roman account of the misdeeds of the second Tarquin as the cause of a revolt that swept away the Etruscan dynasty. Rather, it seems as if Tarquin's downfall was the result of a movement by aristocrats against centralizing measures undertaken by the monarchy to curb their own power.

The kings had apparently weakened the originally noble senate of 100 men by packing it with their own appointees (*conscripti* = the "enrolled"), 200 wealthy native commoners and Etruscans, to create a powerful clientage of their own within the governing establishment. Even more important were military reforms attributed to King Servius Tullius. Before his reform, the main offensive arm of the Roman army had been mounted infantry (*celeres* or *equites*) drawn almost exclusively from the nobility, who were practically the only ones wealthy enough to equip themselves with horses and armor. In battle they did not charge in solid ranks but engaged in individual, heroic duels with enemy leaders. If necessary, they dismounted and fought on foot, and if the enemy fled they remounted for pursuit. Servius probably expanded and revolutionized the army by introducing so-called "hoplite" tactics which the Etruscans had learned from the Greeks. Hoplites were heavily armed shock troops, normally infantry (*pedites*), wearing leather caps with bronze plates, bronze body armor and greaves, leather shields, iron swords, and spears. They fought in a regular line of battle or phalanx, a solid formation of foot soldiers identically armed and organized in centuries of 100 (later 60) men. The effectiveness of this "new model" army depended on teamwork and made it much more amenable to discipline than the aristocratic horsemen. Servius called out a levy (*legio*) of those few thousand citizens, both nobles and commoners, wealthy enough to outfit themselves with a suit of armor and so serve as shock troops. His reform undoubtedly made Rome the leading military power in Latium and dominant over the Latin League.

Servius seems also to have undermined the political power of noble clans by emasculating the *curiae* and tribes through which they functioned. The Curiate Assembly continued to confer the kingship on nominees presented to it by the Senate, but Servius may have given his centuriate army the right to choose its leaders, even though a centuriate assembly in a political sense is unattested during the monarchy. He almost certainly abolished the three old tribes, creating on a geographical basis in city and countryside nineteen new tribes that cut across areas inhabited by fellow clansmen, thereby dividing them. Mere domicile in a geographical tribe, not membership in a *curia*, became the basis of citizenship, which was extended to many immigrants, grateful clients of the monarchy.

The emphasis on wealth, not aristocratic blood, in senatorial and military service and the curbing of tribes and clans were centralizing measures, not unlike those of Solon and Cleisthenes in sixth-century Athens. Nobles, however, were restive under novel monarchic discipline, and their power remained considerable. The Servian reforms were only imperfectly effective, and the aristocracy revolted against Servius' successor, Tarquinius Superbus, expelling him from the city and reorganizing it as a republic (*res publica* = "commonwealth"), permitting free play to their ambitions. The fall of the Etruscan dynasty did not mean the expulsion of all Etruscans from Rome, for some of the leading families of the Roman nobility were of Etruscan origin and a district in the city continued to be called the Etruscan quarter.

ETRUSCAN INFLUENCE IN EARLY ROME. While Etruscan domination failed to alter the Latin character of the people, it left many traces in various aspects of Roman life, notably in official paraphernalia, military organization, and religious practices, such as the employment of *haruspices* or Etruscan diviners. The *Cloaca Maxima*, or great sewer, probably at first an open ditch, which drained the Forum, belonged to the Etruscan period. In early Roman art and architecture Etruscan influence is particularly noticeable. The earliest temple of Jupiter on the Capitoline was built in the sixth century in Etruscan style, and the statue of Jupiter it contained and its terra cotta roof decoration were ascribed to Etruscan artists. Indeed, the association of the three divinities— Jupiter, Juno, and Minerva—in a triad worshipped in this temple was an imitation of widespread Etruscan practice. Under the Etruscan kings there was some development of industry in Rome, particularly in pottery, bronzeworking, and ironworking. In this connection may be noted the introduction of the worship of Minerva, goddess of handicraft and patroness of trade guilds. It is possible that the organization of the eight early trade guilds of free craftsmen, the names of which reveal the scope of the industrial life of kingly Rome, fell within the period of Etruscan rule. These trade guilds were those of flute players, goldworkers, smiths, dyers, shoemakers, leatherworkers, bronze-workers, and potters. The use of music on state occasions and the celebration of public games and festivals were popular Etruscan practices that were early adopted by the Roman state.

IV. EARLY ROMAN SOCIETY

POPULUS ROMANUS. The oldest name of the Romans was *Quirites*, a name which long survived in official phraseology but which was superseded by the name *Romani*, derived from that of the city. The body of those eligible to be soldiers, to participate in the public religious rites, and to attend the meetings of the popular assembly, with their families, constituted the Roman state—the *populus Romanus*.

At the base of Roman society was the household (*familia*), a closely knit economic as well as social unit. Such households claiming descent from a common ancestor formed a clan or *gens*. These *gentes* were social rather than political groups, for they did not form political subdivisions, even though they might exercise a great deal of influence upon the public life of the community. Each clan was distinguished by its gentile name,[2] borne by all its members, and each celebrated its own religious rites (*sacra*), from which all outsiders were excluded.

SOCIAL STRUCTURE. Early Romans evolved a characteristic social structure, whose origins are obscure. They seem never to have believed that all men were created equal and preferred to organize their lives on the assumption that certain men were born to lead and that others were natural followers. This view was expressed in the institution of patronage and clientship, which, if not uniquely Roman, was fundamental to their development. Clients were obliged to follow their patron to war and to the political arena, to render him respectful attention and, on occasion, pecuniary support. Such duties were called "offices" (*officia*). The patron, in his turn, was obliged to do anything of

---

[2] For example: all members of the Cornelian *gens* were called Cornelius, those of the Julian *gens*, Julius. In addition, each had a personal name (*praenomen*) used before the clan name (*nomen*), and in later times a family name (*cognomen*) regularly followed the *nomen*. These three elements appear in such names as Lucius Cornelius Scipio, Gaius Julius Caesar.

benefit (*beneficia*) to his client, such as protecting his life and interests, especially in courts of law. Legal protection was important to clients, since patricians controlled the judicial system. The ties that bound client and patron were based on mutual faith, and at least in the historical period were accordingly extralegal and moral in nature. For either patron or client to fail in his obligations was sacrilege. This relationship, called *patronatus* on the side of the patron, *clientela* on that of the client, was hereditary on both sides. The client-patron relationship was one of the most important, characteristic, and permanent features of Roman life, and, in one form or another, it was to determine the further development of society, politics, and even foreign policy.

Assertive clan patriarchs, backed by numerous kinsmen and clients and supported by extensive landholdings, tried to monopolize their right as senators, acknowledged by the community, to nominate and advise the kings. According to one theory that right became hereditary in certain families, called patrician, that claimed noble status because they provided the "fathers" (*patres*) of the state and were thus distinguished from the rest of the citizenry. The latter were mainly peasants, although apparently there always existed some wealthy, ambitious squires backed by clients and clans of their own. The patricians were quarrelsome, their ideals warlike, and they occasionally used their power selfishly and even unscrupulously to maintain their economic and political preeminence, even if it meant injury to the weaker classes in the state. In attempting to protect, consolidate, and expand their power against the rival pretensions of kings and leading commoners, patricians insisted on their tenure of priesthoods, thereby controlling the interpretation of law, which was as yet unwritten custom often influenced by religious taboo. Since they led most clans and clients, they dominated the Curiate Assembly, and on the battlefield they competed as warlords with the king, except when temporarily checked by the Servian military reforms.

The patrician aristocracy tended to form a social caste, although it apparently had not become totally exclusive by the end of the monarchy. At least some of the *conscripti* nominated by the kings to the Senate seem to have been recognized as patrician, since later tradition acknowledged a difference between "lesser" or more recent noble clans (*patres minorum gentium*) and "greater" or established ones (*patres maiorum gentium*). Class distinctions between nobles and commoners were clearly becoming more rigid under the kings, although commoners, as citizens, could always at least claim membership in the *curiae* and a voice in the Curiate Assembly. As the social system evolved, these latter—peasants, craftsmen, laborers, tradesmen, and even some wealthy, non-noble landlords— tended to emerge as a caste of their own, ultimately given the name plebeian (*plebs* = the many). The increasingly sharp social and political distinction between nobles and commons, between patricians and plebeians, is the outstanding feature of early Roman society and affords the clue to the political development of the early republican period.

CHAPTER 5
EXPANSION OF ROME
TO UNIFICATION OF
THE ITALIAN
PENINSULA:
CA. 509–265 B.C.

The history of the two and a half centuries after the fall of the monarchy rests upon a somewhat more secure foundation than that of the age of kings. Although there was no contemporary historical writing and no important literary productivity of any kind, documents and records of various sorts like the Law Code of the Twelve Tables, individual statutes, census records, lists of magistrates and official calendars were increasingly committed to writing. No more than a skeleton narrative could be made from these written sources for the period before 300 B.C., however, and later Roman historians had to rely largely on folk tales and the oral traditions maintained by Rome's leading families. For several reasons these stories and traditions came to be padded heavily with fictitious details by the time Romans were first writing history about 200 B.C. History was written by members of the new senatorial oligarchy that developed in the course of the third century, and their reconstruction of past events had to satisfy the pride of its two elements, the old patrician families and their newer plebeian associates. Furthermore, national pride required them to present a narrative that would command respect by those masters of historical writing, the Greeks, with whom they were establishing ever closer cultural relations. Accordingly, much biased or fictitious information ultimately found its way into the extant canonical versions of early Roman history in the works of Livy and Dionysius of Halicarnassus, written towards the end of the first century B.C. In some cases archaeological data can be used as a check on literary tradition, but the interpretation of such data is often controversial. Accordingly, only the bare outline of the history of the early Republic can be reconstructed, and that outline must be based on an often unreliable source tradition.

I. THE YOUNG REPUBLIC AND ITS NEIGHBORS:
509–392 B.C.

ROME AND THE LATIN LEAGUE. The initial effects of the revolution ousting Tarquin from Rome were politically decentralizing and socially unsettling; it also appears likely that hoplite discipline, imposed on the Roman army by the last kings, may have temporarily loosened under patrician leadership. In any case her military ventures in the period were anything but brilliant. It appears that the Latin cities took advantage of Rome's momentary weakness to challenge her hegemony over the Latin League, which the patrician government aggressively intended to reassert.

The result was the battle of Lake Regillus near Tusculum in 496 (489),[1] in which Rome was only barely victorious. This victory was followed by a treaty drawn up by a Roman, Spurius Cassius, and dated in 493 (486). The terms ascribed to the treaty may have been drawn from a much later pact,[2] but one result was that Rome was formally recognized as the dominant city in the League. This primacy was marked by the dedication of a grave and altar to Diana on the Aventine hill.[3] This was a suitable site for a sanctuary common to the members of the League, since it was outside the *pomerium* and thus open to foreigners for purposes of worship. This alliance of Rome with the other Latin cities had a natural basis in their common ethnic and cultural traditions as well as in the common dangers which threatened all Latins from the Etruscans on the north and highland Italian peoples to the east and south. One great advantage Rome derived from this league was that the Latin cities formed a barrier between its territory and the aggressive Aequi and Volsci. Not long after the Romans and Latins had concluded their alliance, they extended it to include the Hernici, on the eastern border of Latium.

WARS WITH THE AEQUI AND VOLSCI. On the northeast, east, and south the Latins were confronted with Italic tribes of the Sabellian group: Sabines, Aequi, and Volsci. According to Roman tradition, the fifth century

---

[1] There is considerable uncertainty in the chronology before 300 B.C. For this reason both traditional and corrected dates have been given, the latter in parentheses.

[2] These terms were agreed to when the alliance was renewed in the early part of the fourth century. A bronze copy of the treaty drawn up at that time, which may have been the treaty actually concluded by a Spurius Cassius, survived into the first century B.C. The terms are discussed later in the present chapter.

[3] According to another view, the foundation of the Roman sanctuary to Diana dates from the regal period and is to be ascribed to the wishes of Servius Tullius to cement relations with the Latin League.

was a period of intermittent warfare with these peoples, who sought to encroach upon Latin territory. Although accounts of these wars are unreliable and some of the wars themselves may be fictitious, it is apparent that the Sabines and the Aequi, pressed by overpopulation in their mountain valleys, sought to expand into the lowlands of Latium. Sabine raids seem to have been unsuccessful border forays, but by the middle of the century the Aequi had penetrated into the heart of Latium, as far as Tusculum and Mt. Algidus. By about 500 B.C. the Volsci already occupied the southeastern part of the Latin plain as far as the coast, and there they seem to have met with a Latin attempt to win new territory for settlement. Evidence for this comes in the establishment of Signia and Norba as Latin foundations in Volscian territory during the fifth century. It was not until toward the close of the century that the Latins with Roman support definitely overcame both Aequi and Volsci and freed themselves from the danger of encroachments by these two peoples.

VEII. In addition to these frequent wars, the Romans had to sustain a serious conflict with the powerful Etruscan city of Veii, situated across the Tiber about twelve miles north of Rome. Veii was a flourishing town, controlling a larger and richer territory than Rome. Excavations have shown that it was an important place from the tenth to the beginning of the fourth century B.C. It had come under Etruscan influence in the course of the eighth century and was now the bulwark of Etruscan power in southern Etruria. The contents of its tombs reveal the wealth and extensive foreign trade of the Veientes, while imposing sculptural remains from its temple show that they were in contact with Greek cultural influences, then so powerful throughout Italy. It is probable that the cause of the war with Rome was a conflict of political interests in northern Latium. It broke out in 407 (402), shortly after the Romans had taken Fidenae, a town which controlled a crossing of the Tiber above Rome. According to tradition the Romans blockaded Veii for eleven years before it fell, but this tale looks like an invention of Roman annalists in imitation of the legendary ten years' siege of Troy. In the course of this war the Romans introduced the custom of paying their troops, a practice which enabled them to keep citizen soldiers under arms throughout the year if necessary. Veii was destroyed, its population enslaved, and its territory incorporated in the public land of Rome. This annexation was the first great expansion of Roman territory, which doubled as a result.

II. THE GALLIC INVASION

GAULS IN THE PO VALLEY. The Romans had scarcely beaten Veii when a sudden disaster overtook them from an unexpected quarter. About 400 B.C., Celtic tribes crossed the Alps, probably by way of the Brenner Pass, and moved into the Po valley. This inroad was part of the expansion of Celts from their homeland in the upper Danubian region of central Europe, from which they were slowly being ousted by pressure of Germanic peoples to the north. The invaders belonged to that branch of the Celts known as Gauls. They conquered the Etruscans, who formed the ruling class in the central part of the valley, and well before the close of the fourth century had occupied all the land from the Ticinus river and Lake Maggiore southeastward to the Adriatic between the mouth of the Po and Ancona. This district came to be known as Cisalpine Gaul, i.e., Gaul on the near side of the Alps.

The Gauls formed eight tribes, which were often at enmity with one another. Each tribe was divided into many clans, and there was continual strife between the factions of various chieftains. They were a barbarous people, living in rude villages and supporting themselves by cattle-raising and primitive agriculture. Their chief industry was metalworking, in which they displayed considerable skill and artistic ability. Drunkenness and love of strife were their characteristic vices, war and oratory their passions. Ancient writers describe them as tall, blond, and blue-eyed. Brave to the point of recklessness, they were formidable warriors, and the ferocity of their first assualt inspired terror even in the ranks of veteran armies. Their chief weapons were long, two-edged swords of soft iron, which frequently bent and were easily blunted; for defense they carried small wicker shields. Their armies were undisciplined mobs, greedy for plunder, disinclined to prolonged, strenuous effort, and utterly unskilled in siege operations. These weaknesses nullified the effects of their victories and prevented their occupation of Italy south of the Apennines. During the fourth century, however, before they settled down to exploit the rich agricultural resources of the Po valley, they were very restive. Large bands frequently invaded the peninsula in search of adventure and plunder.

SACK OF ROME. In 390 (387) a band of these marauders crossed the Apennines and besieged Clusium in central Etruria. Thence, angered, as was said, by the hostile actions of Roman ambassadors who had been sent to persuade the Gauls to withdraw, they marched directly on Rome. The Romans mobilized their forces and met the Gauls near the Allia, a small tributary of the Tiber above Fidenae. The fierce onset of the Gauls routed the Roman army. Many were slain, and most of the survivors took refuge within the ruined fortifications of Veii. Deprived of the protection of their army and having no city wall, the citizens in a body evacuated Rome and fled to neighboring towns. The Capitol, however, being adequately fortified, was left with a small garrison. The Gauls entered and sacked Rome but failed to storm the citadel. Apparently they had no intention of settling in Latium, and, after a delay of seven months, upon information that the Veneti were attacking their new settlements in the Po valley, they accepted a ransom of 1,000 pounds of gold[4] and marched home. Their decision may have been hastened by knowledge of the gathering of a Roman and allied force at Veii. The Romans at once reoccupied and rebuilt

---

[4] In view of the comparative poverty of early fourth-century Rome, it is likely that the ransom has been greatly exaggerated.

their city and soon after provided it with more adequate defenses in the wall later miscalled Servian. This wall consisted of a thick earthen embankment faced with stone and protected by a ditch.

LATER GALLIC INCURSIONS. For some time the Gauls raided the peninsula, even penetrating as far south as Apulia. But not until 360 (357) did they appear again in Latium. On that occasion they raided as far as the Alban hills, but the Romans feared to meet them and remained within their walls. When, however, a fresh band appeared in 349, the Romans were prepared. They and their allies blocked their path, and the Gauls retreated, unwilling to risk battle. Rome thus became the successful champion of the Italian peoples, their bulwark against the barbarian invaders from the north. In 331 the Gallic tribe of the Senones and the Romans concluded peace and entered upon a period of friendly relations which lasted for the rest of the fourth century.

III. CONQUEST OF THE NORTH AND CENTER OF THE PENINSULA, DISRUPTION OF THE LATIN LEAGUE, AND THE SAMNITE WARS: 390 (387)–280 B.C.

WARS WITH THE AEQUI, VOLSCI, AND ETRUSCANS. The disaster that had overtaken Rome impressed the civilized world profoundly and was noted by contemporary Greek writers. But the blow left no permanent traces, for only the city, not the state, had been destroyed. Encouraged by their enemy's defeat, the Aequi, Volsci, and the Etruscan cities previously conquered by Rome took up arms; but each met defeat. Rome retained and consolidated her conquests in southern Etruria. Part of the land was allotted to Romans, and four tribes were organized there. On the remainder, two Latin colonies, Sutrium (383) and Nepete (372), were founded. It was not until 351 that the Etruscans were so badly beaten that they abandoned their attacks on Rome and sued for peace. The Aequi and Rome's former allies, the Hernici, who had seized the opportunity to assert their independence, were speedily subdued. The Volsci, however, fought long and bitterly to preserve their independence and regain control of Southern Latium. In 358 the Romans annexed most of their territory and settled it with Roman colonists organized in two tribes. But even this did not end the struggle. Only with the fall of their chief city, Antium, in 338 did the Volsci abandon their resistance and accept a Roman alliance.

EXPANSION OF THE SABELLIANS.[5] While the Romans were consolidating their power in southern Etruria, Latium, and northern Campania, the more southern regions were being overrun by peoples of Sabellian stock from the valleys of the central Apennines. While Roman expansion was that of a settled agricultural people whose conquests were motivated fully as much by

---

[5] Sometimes called Oscans. But the term *Oscan* seems originally to have applied to part of the pre-Sabellian population in south-central Italy (see p. 20).

the necessity of protecting themselves from foreign attacks as by the desire to find new lands for colonization, that of the Sabellians was caused almost entirely by overpopulation. About once in each generation, bands of young men were forced to emigrate and descended upon the neighboring lowland areas to win homes.

From the middle of the fifth century these migrations affected all south Italy. Capua (438) and Cumae (421) fell into Sabellian hands. Farther south, Sabellian settlements gave rise to the people known as the Lucanians, before whose advance the Bruttians were driven into the toe of Italy. During the fourth century both the Apulians and the Greek cities of the south were forced to defend themselves against repeated attacks by expanding Sabellians. Unlike the Romans, who created a single powerful state supported by military alliances, the Sabellians split up into several independent groups. Those who settled in the Campanian cities amalgamated with the older population and were repeatedly at war with fresh waves of invaders from Samnite territory. The Lucanians were united in a military federation free from the control of their kinsmen in their former homeland. The Samnites, as the latter were called, also formed a loose confederacy of kindred peoples whom poverty drove to plundering raids or attempted conquests at the expense of the descendants of earlier emigrants from the same mountain hinterland.

END OF THE LATIN LEAGUE: 338 (336) B.C. An even greater menace than hostility of the Etruscans and Volsci and the potential hostility of southern mountaineers was the attempt of the Latins to break their alliance with Rome. Before Rome had recovered from the shock of the Gallic victory, several of the more important Latin cities deserted the Latin League and challenged Rome's predominance in Latium. Although they received support from the Hernici and Volsci, they were defeated and forced to join with the rest of the Latins in accepting a close alliance with Rome (358). It was probably at this time that most of the terms later ascribed to the accord between Rome and the Latins early in the fifth century were formally agreed to. It is noteworthy that in this new pact Rome does not appear as one of the cities of the Latin League, *primus inter pares*, but as an outside power confronting the cities of the League. The treaty provided for a close offensive and defensive military alliance with each party contributing equal forces for joint military enterprises and dividing the spoils of war. At the same time they exchanged private rights of citizenship. This meant that a Roman could transact business in a Latin city with the assurance that his contract would be protected by the law of

III Capestrano Warrior (*Chieti Museum*). *Statuette of a soldier in festive attire, including sun helmet, dating from ca. 550–500 B.C. and illustrative of the vigorous, if primitive, art practiced by the Samnites of east-central Italy in what is called today the Abruzzi region. (Photo: Alinari.)*

the said city, and could also acquire and hold property there (right of *commercium*), while if he married a woman from a Latin city this would be a legitimate union and his children would inherit both his property and his citizenship (right of *conubium*). Conversely, a citizen of a Latin community would enjoy the same privileges in Rome.

Perhaps more important than renewal of Rome's treaty with the Latin League was the defensive alliance she made in 354 with the Samnites of the southern Apennines. This, the first treaty Rome signed with any Italian power outside the immediate vicinity of Latium, showed how sophisticated and venturesome her foreign policy had by then become. It was a major event, leading to her eventual domination of all Italy. The treaty of 354 provided not only for mutual defense by the contracting parties against Celtic raids but also for a division of respective spheres of influence in central Italy along the Liris river.

This treaty alarmed the Latins, for, even while providing for defense against the Gauls, it unilaterally assumed Roman domination as far as the Liris. Two other actions reinforced the growing realization that the Roman government was coming to view the Latins as something less than sovereign states. In 358 Rome had not allowed them any part of the land annexed from the Volsci. Then in 348 another treaty was concluded between Rome and Carthage, in which the Romans clearly asserted their suzerainty over Latium.

What ultimately provoked revolt within the Latin League were the results of a Roman alliance with Capua (343), the second city of Italy, which requested Roman aid against the Samnites. The Romans, apparently assuming that a major war with the Samnites was only a matter of time, wished to fight before the League became too disunited. The result was the First Samnite War (343–341 B.C.), an inglorious episode in Roman military history marked by mutiny, reverses, and a peace treaty that callously abandoned to the Samnites some of Rome's recently acquired Campanian allies. It seemed to the Latins and Campanians that there was no longer any reason for acknowledging Roman hegemony and protection if their interests were to be treated so cavalierly, and they combined forces to continue the war against the Samnites and to attack their own erstwhile Roman leaders. The Latin War followed in 340 (338)–338 (336) and the Romans, materially aided by their former Samnite enemies, were completely victorious. The Latin League was dissolved, and the individual cities had to accept Rome's terms. Five of them were deprived of their independence and incorporated in the Roman state. The rest, including the Latin colonies, became Roman allies with the obligation of furnishing troops. They lost the rights of trade and intermarriage with each other but continued to enjoy them with Rome. They also lost the privilege of forming leagues or other associations.

ROME AND THE CAMPANIAN CITIES. In the first year of the Latin War the Romans succeeded in detaching the Campanians from their alliance with the Latins and induced them to make a separate peace. Three Campanian cities, including Capua and Cumae, were granted Roman citizenship and thus became part of the Roman state. The same treatment was accorded to two other strategic cities between Latium and Campania. Thus Roman territory was extended to the Bay of Naples. The members of these communities did not receive full Roman citizenship, for they lacked the right to vote and to hold office in Rome, although, like full citizens, they had the obligation of military service. Nevertheless they had advantages. They were now assured of protection against foreign attack, in particular against their new enemies the Samnites, and in their private and business relations with Romans they had the full benefit of Roman laws. These cities also remained at least locally self-governing communities and retained their constitutions and laws, except where they voluntarily accepted those of the Romans.

Following the Latin War, the Romans strengthened their communications with Campania by occupying the Volscian hill-country. This territory was secured by alliances with some peoples, the annexation of others, and the planting of strategic Roman and Latin colonies.

CLASH OF ROMANS AND SAMNITES IN CAMPANIA. Fear of the Samnites had induced the cities of northern Campania to accept incorporation in the Roman state, and it was this resumed policy of supporting the more civilized and peaceful lowlanders against their aggressive highland neighbors that led to a prolonged and desperate struggle between Rome and the Samnites. In this conflict all the peoples of the central and northern parts of the peninsula became involved; its result was the establishment of Roman supremacy throughout the whole area. Having used the Samnites to help subdue the Latins in the recent war, the Romans thereafter ignored their alliance with the mountaineers. The latter, for a time at least, do not seem to have regarded Roman annexation of northern Campania as a hostile act. It may have been that this apparent indifference was due to the preoccupation of the Samnites with a war against the Tarentines, who were supported by an able ally, Alexander, king of Molossia in Epirus (334–331).

When the war with Tarentum ended, the Samnites, who still looked upon Campania as a legitimate field for expansion, intervened in the party struggles in Naples and garrisoned the town with the support of one faction. Cumae became involved and sought Roman support. In 327 (325) the Romans besieged Naples and took it when the Samnite garrison was induced to evacuate the city by the pro-Roman party. Thereupon Naples became a Roman ally, and open warfare began again between Romans and Samnites.

SAMNITE WARS: SECOND PHASE, 326 (324)–304 B.C. The Second Samnite War was the first one fought by Rome for which the sources permit detailed description. It was tedious, challenging Roman generals with novel problems of organization and logistics involving campaigns in distant, rugged terrain against a resourceful enemy. The Samnites were brave and warlike. They were not greatly inferior to the Romans in numbers, and their military organization was better adapted to mountain fighting. On the other hand, the

Romans were superior in the open country and had the advantage of greater centralization of authority, which insured unity and continuity of policy in a long conflict. The Roman plan was to encircle the Samnites by alliances with peoples of central Italy to the north of Samnium and with the Apulians to the southeast.

Apparently the Romans won some initial successes, but these were more than counterbalanced by an overwhelming defeat in 321 (319). A Roman army attempting to march from Campania through Samnium into Apulia, was trapped in a valley called the Caudine Forks and compelled to surrender. The terms of surrender included the acceptance of a peace under which the Romans evacuated some of the border territory claimed by the Samnites and agreed not to renew the war.

During the next few years the Romans strengthened their position in Apulia and increased and reorganized their army. They adopted a formation which was more suitable for maneuvering in rough country and perhaps rearmed some of their troops by providing them with javelins in place of spears. In 316 they reopened hostilities, and initial success lay with the Samnites, who won a great battle at Lautulae near Tarracina in southern Latium (315). For a moment Campania wavered in its loyalty, but a Roman victory recovered the lost ground and placed the Samnites on the defensive. In the upper valley of the Liris river, in Campania, and in Apulia, the Romans planted colonies that served as fortresses to block the exits from Samnium and as bases for Roman attacks. The Romans also constructed a paved highway, known as the Via Appia, from Rome to Capua, which assured them of uninterrupted communications with Campania, even in the rainy season.

Seeing that the extension of Roman influence across central Italy would cut them off from the north, the Samnites persuaded the Etruscan cities, whose treaties with Rome were lapsing, to create a diversion by attacking Roman territory in southern Etruria. This attack obliged the Romans to divide their forces and momentarily relieved pressure on the Samnites. In two swift campaigns, however, Roman armies penetrated north-central Etruria and forced the revolting cities to accept a new peace (309–308).[6] The Samnites then succeeded in detaching the Hernici, Aequi, and Paeligni from their alliance with Rome and thus prolonged hostilities in the central Apennines. By 304, however, the Romans had reduced these tribes and also brought the Samnites to terms.

The Samnites retained their independence and territory, with the exception of certain frontier districts, but their position in regard to Rome had become much weaker. By virtue of alliances the Romans acquired control of Apulia and southern Campania. Other alliances assured them of the support of the

---

[6] So the later Roman version, but there are several improbabilities in the narrative, and these campaigns seem to have been invented from the later Roman invasion of Etruria of 295 B.C.

warlike Marsi, Marrucini, Frentani, Paeligni, and some Umbrian city-states. The revolt of the Hernici was punished by confiscation of territory and annexation of several of their towns as citizen communities. At the close of the war the Aequi met a similar fate, and part of the Sabine country was annexed with the grant of citizenship to its inhabitants. Colonies were planted on some of the confiscated land. The rest was divided up among individual Roman citizens and this expansion of territory was organized as tribes.

THIRD PHASE: 298–290 B.C. In 298 the Samnites resumed their war against Rome. During the Second Samnite War the Romans had an alliance with the Lucanians, which had kept them friendly to Rome although militarily inactive. Still later, in 303, Rome cooperated with them in a war against Tarentum, which was aided by Cleonymus, king of Sparta. Afterwards, for some unknown reason, some Lucanians, supported by Samnites, became hostile to Rome, but despite Samnite intervention, the Romans were able to induce the Lucanians to resume their alliance.

A more serious threat arose from joint action by the Gauls, Samnites, and Etruscans. Stirred by the arrival of new transalpine migratory bands, the Gauls of the Po valley were restive and began to raid the peninsula. As Rome would inevitably oppose these inroads, it was easy for the Samnites to secure the cooperation of the Gauls against the common enemy, and some Etruscan cities were encouraged to rise again against Rome. The Sabines also joined Rome's enemies, whereas the Picentes, who had good reason to fear Gallic expansion, made an alliance with Rome. In 295 the Samnites sent an army to meet the Gauls in Umbria, where the united forces fought the Romans at Sentinum. Here the Romans won a decisive victory, which proved to be the turning point. The Etruscans were defeated in their own country, and Samnium lay open to Roman attack. By systematically ravaging the country the Romans forced the Samnites to sue for peace. A portion of their land was confiscated, and they were obliged to accept the status of Roman allies (290). The Romans then turned their attention to the Sabines, who could offer little resistance. Their territory was annexed, and they were made Roman citizens without voting rights. Rome was now the dominant power in peninsular Italy.

WARS WITH THE GAULS AND ETRUSCANS. The Samnite Wars considerably widened Roman horizons and produced after 290 B.C. disagreement in the Senate concerning the priorities of foreign policy. One faction advocated caution, since adventurous expansion tended to involve Rome simultaneously on widely scattered fronts, and since her power was not yet consolidated. Although the Samnites had been conquered, the Gauls were still restive and for a time constituted a serious threat. In 284 the tribe of the Senones, who were settled on the Adriatic north of Picenum, attacked Arretium in Etruria. While attempting to relieve this allied city, the Romans suffered a costly defeat. Aroused by this disaster, Rome invaded the Senones' country, defeated them, and drove them out of the peninsula. Their former territory was added to the public land of Rome but continued to be known as the Ager Gallicus (The Gallic Land). Another tribe, the Boii from the Po valley, then marched into Etruria and joined forces with certain Etruscan towns that had broken their alliances with Rome after the battle of Arretium. The Romans crushed their united armies at the Vadimonian lake near Volsinii (283). When a second raid in the following year met a like fate, the Boii made peace and by 280 the warring Etruscan cities again accepted an alliance with Rome.

IV. ROMAN CONQUEST OF SOUTH ITALY: 281–270 B.C.

ITALIANS AND GREEKS IN SOUTH ITALY.   Peace in the north came none too soon for the Romans, who had become involved in the conflict between the Greeks of South Italy and their Italian neighbors. Ever since the collapse of the empire of Dionysius I of Syracuse, in the years following his death in 367, Greek cities in the far south of the peninsula had been exposed to constant attacks by Lucanians, Bruttians, and Messapians, and only a few of them had succeeded in remaining free. Of these, Tarentum was by far the largest and most powerful. A manufacturing and trading city, it had the strongest navy in Italy and gradually assumed the role of protector of Italian Greeks. The forces of the Tarentines were by no means a match for those of the Italians, however, and they were from time to time to enlist the services of military adventurers from the Greek world. The first of these was King Archidamus of Sparta, who fell fighting against the Lucanians in 338. Four years later Alexander, king of Molossia and uncle of Alexander the Great, succeeded in defeating the Lucanians and Bruttians. He made a treaty with Rome, in which the Tarentines were probably included, but when the latter realized that Alexander intended to create an empire of his own in South Italy, they deserted him, so that he was defeated and killed by the Italians (330). Still later, in 303, they called in another Spartan king, Cleonymus. More fortunate than his predecessors, Cleonymus pacified the Lucanians. Since the Romans had supported their allies, the Lucanians, in this war, they must also have agreed to the peace.[7] A few years later Agathocles, king of Syracuse, assisted the Italian Greeks against the Bruttians (after 298). He also made an alliance with the Messapians and Peucetians of Apulia, perhaps directed against the Romans. When Agathocles died in 289 his kingdom disintegrated, and the western Greeks were left without a protector. When the Lucanians attacked the Greek city of Thurii, the Thurians appealed to Rome for aid, since they regarded the Romans as more powerful than the Tarentines and more reliable than Greek mercenary kings. As the Lucanians had broken their alliance with Rome after the Gallic victory at Sentinum, the Romans accepted Thurii as an ally and came to its rescue (282.) A Roman army defeated the Lucanians, who

---

[7] Livy represents Cleonymus as having been defeated by the Lucanians and Romans, but this seems to be a falsification dictated by Roman pride.

were supported by the Bruttians, relieved Thurii, and left a Roman garrison there. Two other Greek cities, Locri and Rhegium, also became Roman allies and received Roman garrisons.

Roman intervention at Thurii confirmed the suspicions of the Tarentines which had been aroused by Rome's establishment of a Latin colony at Luceria (315) in Tarentum's Apulian sphere of interest. When a small Roman fleet appeared off the harbor of Tarentum contrary to the terms of a treaty (either that of 334 or that of 303), which excluded Roman warships from the Gulf of Tarentum, they attacked it without delay. Some Roman vessels were sunk, and the Tarentines ousted the Roman garrison from Thurii and occupied the town. A Roman demand for reparations was rejected, their ambassadors were publicly insulted, and a Roman army thereupon invaded Tarentine territory to enforce the demand.

In the meantime, the Tarentines had enlisted the support of Pyrrhus, king of Epirus. They could also count upon cooperation from Messapians, Samnites, Lucanians, and Bruttians. With this backing they were prepared to defy Rome.

WAR WITH PYRRHUS AND TARENTUM. Pyrrhus was probably the most skillful Greek general of the time, and he brought with him into Italy an army organized and equipped according to the Macedonian system of Alexander the Great, which had become the standard in the Greek world. His force comprised 20,000 heavy-armed infantry forming the phalanx, 3,000 Thessalian cavalry, and 2,000 archers. He also had twenty war elephants— animals that had first appeared on Greek battlefields twenty years before but were as yet unknown to the Romans. The first engagement was fought near Heraclea (280), and the Romans were driven from the field after a severe struggle. The superior generalship of Pyrrhus and the consternation caused by his war elephants won the day. As fighters the Romans had shown themselves the equal of the foe, and their tactical organization, perfected in the Samnite Wars, had proved its value in its first encounter with the military experts of Greece. In consequence of his victory at Heraclea, Pyrrhus advanced as far north as Latium, but he withdrew again without accomplishing anything. He also sent an embassy to Rome to propose peace, but his terms were rejected. The next year Pyrrhus won another hard-fought battle near Asculum in Apulia in which he was wounded, his own losses being so heavy as to give rise to the expression "a Pyrrhic victory." Although he was unable to exploit his victory, the Romans now opened negotiations that Pyrrhus welcomed. Before an agreement was reached, however, the Carthaginians, who feared the intervention of Pyrrhus in Sicily, offered the Romans money and ships. Their offer was accepted, the negotiations with Pyrrhus dropped, and Rome and Carthage agreed that if either of them should make a treaty with the common foe it would reserve the right to aid the other if the latter's country were invaded. In the meantime the Carthaginian fleet was to cooperate with the Romans.

IV   Via Latina and Sepulcher of the Valerii. *One of the earliest of the great arterial highways radiating from Rome, the Via Latina ran southeast from the city, joining the Appian Way at the Volturno River. It was used by both Pyrrhus and Hannibal in their invasions of central Italy. The ruin is the tomb of the Valerii, a prominent Roman family. (Photo: Fototeca Unione.)*

PYRRHUS IN SICILY: 278–275 B.C. Pyrrhus determined to answer an appeal from the Sicilian Greeks and to leave Italy for Sicily. After the death of Agathocles in 289 the Greeks in Sicily fell upon evil days. The Carthaginians renewed their attacks, and a new foe appeared in the Mamertini—Campanian mercenary soldiers of Agathocles who seized Messana and made it their headquarters for raiding the Greek cities. Caught between two enemies, the Greeks appealed to Pyrrhus, who came to their aid, possibly with the hope of uniting Sicily under his own control. His success was immediate. The Carthaginians were forced to give up all their possessions except Lilybaeum, and Pyrrhus stood ready to carry the war into Africa. At this juncture the exactions that he laid upon his Sicilian allies and their fear that his victory would make him their permanent master made them desert him and seek peace with their enemies. Deprived of their assistance and seeing that his allies in Italy were hard pressed by the Romans, he abandoned his Sicilian venture.

END OF THE WAR. Pyrrhus returned to Italy but lost part of his fleet in a naval battle with the Carthaginians. He reorganized his forces and advanced into Samnium to meet the Romans. Near Beneventum he attempted to surprise a Roman army, but he failed and suffered a repulse (275). He then abandoned the offensive and retired to Tarentum. Leaving a garrison there, he transported what remained of his forces to Greece, where conditions seemed favorable for him to conquer Macedonia. Three years later he was killed while fighting in southern Greece, and his garrison at Tarentum turned over the citadel to the Romans. Tarentum had to surrender to Rome and receive a permanent Roman garrison. Along with the other Greek cities of South Italy, it then became a Roman ally.

As a penalty for continued hostility, the Samnite confederacy was broken up. Much land in Samnium was taken by the Romans and used to found Latin colonies. The Lucanians received more generous treatment, having to surrender only the former Greek city of Paestum and its territory. The Bruttians became Roman allies but were forced to give up half of their forests on the Sila mountains.[8]

In the north, the Romans experienced further trouble with certain Etruscan towns and had to fight with their former allies, the Picentes. The latter were punished with loss of territory, but most of them, together with the Sabines, received full Roman citizenship in 268. By 265 all of peninsular Italy was united under Roman suzerainty.

V. ROMAN ORGANIZATION OF ITALY

ROMAN FOREIGN POLICY IN ITALY. Rome united Italy in a conglomerate organization. In retrospect, the successive steps in this process appear so methodical and consequential as to create the impression of deliberate and

---

[8] Some scholars believe that the confiscation of this area occurred after the Hannibalic War, i.e., after 201 B.C.

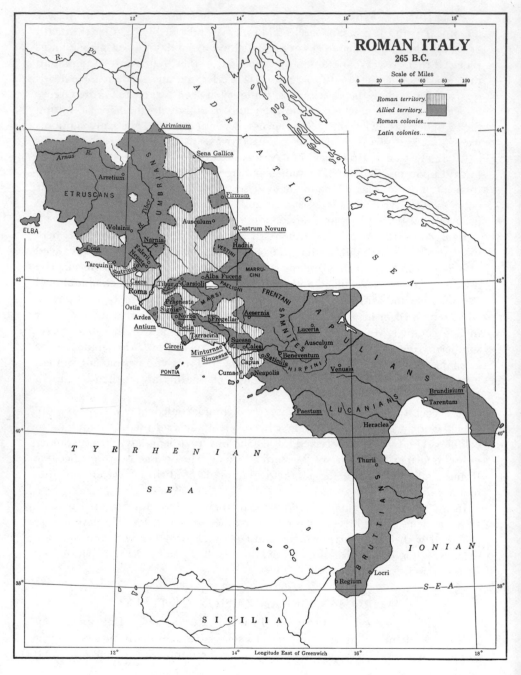

ROMAN ITALY
265 B.C.

Scale of Miles
0   20   40   60   80   100

Roman territory
Allied territory
Roman colonies
Latin colonies

relentless planning. The early Romans were no different, of course, from many
other peoples of any age in their belief that an increase in their territory could

be a desirable end in itself, but a conscious goal was probably not consistently pursued through many generations by Roman statesmen. Probably it was not until nearly the end that the Romans realized where their policy was leading them. In any case, one cannot believe in the protestations of Romans writing much later that the wars they waged were inevitably just and purely defensive. War was the normal state of affairs in primitive Italy, and the Romans as well as their fellow Italians lived in constant threat of attack by hostile neighbors. The early Romans were certainly not possessed of a political morality different from that of other Italian peoples and were guilty of their share of aggressive wars. Many early Italian peoples sought to rationalize their own warlike acts, and the Latins, Faliscans, and Umbro-Sabellians all had special ceremonies and priestly colleges to justify them. At Rome it was the business of the priestly Fetiales solemnly to proclaim that Rome resorted to war only in answer to aggression and when other means of redress had been exhausted. Such attempts to place the responsibility for a war upon the enemy are common to all ages and are not always convincing. If the Romans may not be convicted of consistent imperialism prior to 265, at any rate the methods they pursued in their foreign relations made their domination inevitable in view of their national character and their political and military organization. These methods early became established maxims of Roman foreign policy. The Romans waged even their defensive wars offensively and rarely made peace save with a beaten foe. As a rule, the enemy was forced to conclude a treaty that assured Rome of military support against other foes. Such a treaty was regarded as perpetually binding, and any attempt to break it was regarded as a hostile act. Possibly the Romans considered this as the only policy that would guarantee peace, but it inevitably led to further wars, for it resulted in the extension of the frontiers defended by Rome and therefore continually brought Rome into contact and conflict with new peoples. The voluntary allies of Rome were not allowed to leave the Roman alliance; such action was treated as equivalent to a declaration of war and punished severely. This practice gradually transformed Rome's independent allies into dependents.

From the middle of the fourth century Rome seems deliberately to have sought to prevent the development of a strong state in southern Italy and to this end gladly took under her protection weaker communities threatened by stronger neighbors, although such action inevitably led to war with the latter. Thereby she avoided the limitations of the fetial law, which sanctioned war only in response to direct aggression. Although Rome's protection of weaker powers in this period was typically expressed in formal alliances and treaties, at the same time her statesmen were coming to realize the possible advantages in regarding as clients those states seeking her help. Such client states could be bound to Rome not by formal treaty but by unwritten moral obligations that Rome could interpret to her own advantage. The realization of this idea was to have a profound effect on the development of a more sophisticated Roman foreign policy.

A conquered state frequently lost much of its territory. Portions of this land were set aside for the foundation of fortress colonies to protect the Roman conquests and overawe the conquered. The rest was incorporated in the public domain to the profit of rich proprietors and landless citizens. Usually Roman soldiers shared in the distribution of the movable spoils of war, sometimes a huge booty, as after the subjugation of the Sabines and Picentes in 290. Rome's long series of successful and profitable wars (for she was ultimately victorious in every struggle after 387) engendered in her people a self-confidence and martial spirit that soon led them to conquests beyond Italy. During this period of expansion within Italy, Roman policy was guided by dominant factions in the Senate, a determined body of statesmen, who not only made Rome mistress of the peninsula, but laid enduring foundations for her power.

It is difficult to say how far the Romans were consciously influenced in their foreign policy by overpopulation. The ability to stand the losses of so many serious wars without apparent diminution of military strength and to found many colonies, particularly in the latter part of the fourth and the first half of the third centuries, suggests a surplus population and unsatisfactory economic conditions among the rural classes. A demand for new land and the ambition of a new element in the ranks of the Roman governing circles may account for the more aggressive foreign policy pursued after the overthrow of the Latin League.

THE ROMAN STATE.[9] Roman Italy was really an empire consisting of Rome as the dominant power and a number of allied states as dependents. Broadly speaking, there were two classes of allies: (1) Latins and (2) federated states.

As a result of confiscations of territory and the extension of Roman citizenship to various cities and tribes, the area of the Roman state (the *ager Romanus*) had expanded from some 50 square miles in 509 to about 10,000 square miles in 265, and it comprised about one fifth of the peninsula. Along the west coast it extended in a broad strip from near Tarquinii in Etruria southward to the Bay of Naples, and from Rome it stretched northeastward across the Apennines to the Adriatic.

Roman citizens who constituted the free population of this territory were of two classes: (1) full citizens and (2) citizens without the right to vote or hold office in Rome.[10] Full citizens resided in the city Rome, in municipal towns, and in small rural communities. For administrative purposes, the citizenry was organized into tribes on the basis of residence in districts into which Rome and Roman territory were divided. There were also colonies of Roman citizens planted mainly in harbor towns that lay at one time beyond the Roman frontiers. These were really small garrisons of citizens, usually only three

---

[9] See map on p. 60.
[10] *Cives sine suffragio et iure honorum.*

hundred in number, who protected the ports from sea raids and insured the loyalty of their inhabitants to Rome. Twenty-seven of these citizen colonies came to be established altogether. Their military character is clearly expressed in the exemption of the colonists from active army service.

The second class of Romans, who had all the obligations but only the private rights of citizenship, comprised the inhabitants of towns in Etruria, Latium, and Campania that had received, in most cases voluntarily, this form of association with Rome. These towns were called municipalities (*municipia*), a term implying originally that their inhabitants had the full burdens but not the full rights of citizens. The *municipia* of citizens without the right of suffrage retained much local independence and their former officials. In their external relations, however, they were under the jurisdiction of higher Roman magistrates. *Municipia* of full citizens also appear to have enjoyed some local autonomy under their former constitutions, although the functions and powers of their magistrates undoubtedly suffered serious curtailment. The municipal system was a distinctly Roman contribution to solving the problem of local government in an enlarged city-state. Rome was not only the capital city; it was the *state*, for all Romans were citizens and could exercise their public rights of citizenship only in Rome itself. The municipalities were a means of incorporating other city-states into the Roman without the dissolution of their community life or a violent break with their previous traditions, customs, and culture. The status of municipalities without suffrage was a halfway stage in the complete amalgamation with Rome of previously independent communities, for they all ultimately attained full citizenship. For the new citizens it brought advantages as well as obligations, while preserving for them much local independence. For the Romans it brought an increase of manpower, which helped to meet growing military burdens and also saved older citizens from having to share their power and responsibilities with too many unassimilated foreigners.

LATIN ALLIES. Of the non-Romans in Italy, the people most closely bound to Rome by ties of blood and common interests were the Latin allies. They included: (1) the old Latin towns of Tibur, Praeneste, and one or two others not absorbed by Rome in 338, (2) the nine Latin colonies founded by the Latin League prior to its political dissolution at that date, and (3) twenty-one new Latin colonies founded by Rome after 338. Most colonists in these later colonies were poor Roman and Latin citizens, but in some cases citizens of other allied states were also enrolled. Whatever their origin, members of a Latin colony took the status of Latin allies, but if any of them left a son of military age in his place, he had the privilege of moving to Rome and becoming a citizen. Each colony had full rights of local self-government, with its own laws, magistrates, and the right to issue coins and control its own census. Its constitution was modeled upon Rome's, and its citizens enjoyed rights of *commercium* and *conubium* with Rome and with the other Latin towns, except that the last twelve colonies founded between 268 and 181 had *commercium* only. Latin colonies were large towns having citizen bodies comprising 2,500, 4,000, or 6,000 heads of households. As each colonist received enough land to support a family, large areas had to be assigned by the state from confiscated territory for these settlements. Latin colonies were primarily military. Founded at strategic points on conquered territory, they formed one of the strongest supports of Roman power. Such colonization also served to relieve overpopulation and satisfy land hunger in Latium. Contrasted with the other allies of Rome, the citizens of Latin towns formed the *nomen Latinum* (people of the *Latin name*). If they happened to be in Rome they could vote in the Plebeian Council[11] in a tribe determined by lot. Unlike the Roman citizens without suffrage, they did not serve in Roman legions but formed separate detachments of horse and foot.

ITALIAN ALLIES. The rest of the peoples of Italy—Italian, Greek, Illyrian, or Etruscan—were federate allies of Rome, *socii Italici*. These constituted some 150 separate communities, city or tribal, each bound to Rome by a special treaty (*foedus*), determining its relations to Rome. In all these treaties, however, there were two common features, namely, the obligations to lend military aid and to surrender control over foreign relations. No taxes could be imposed by Rome on an allied community. Allied troops were not incorporated in the legions but were organized as separate infantry and cavalry units (*cohortes* and *alae*), raised, equipped, and officered by the communities themselves. They were, however, commanded by Roman generals and, if several allied detachments were combined in one corps, by a Roman officer. Allied troops received subsistence from Rome and shared equally with the Romans in the spoils of war. The Greek cities of South Italy were excused from service on land but were obliged to furnish warships with their crews to the Roman fleet, and for this reason they were called naval allies (*socii navales*). All the federate allies had *commercium*, and the majority *conubium* also, with Rome. Apart from their obligations toward Rome, each of the allied communities was autonomous, having its own language, laws, and political institutions.

In many cases, as in Etruscan cities, treaties of alliance with Rome were strengthened by the strong bond of sympathy that existed between local aristocracies and the senatorial order at Rome. The foreign relations of Rome were directed by the Senate, which represented the views of the wealthier landed proprietors, and it was only natural that senators should have sought to ally themselves with the corresponding social class in other states. This class represented the more conservative and, from the Roman point of view, more dependable element, while the support of Rome assured to local aristocracies control within their own communities.

ROMAN EXPANSION IN ITALY. Although peninsular Italy was united under the Roman *imperium*, it by no means formed a single state. Rather, it was an agglomerate of many states and many peoples whose sole point of

---

[11] See page 78.

contact was that each was allied militarily with Rome. These alliances, for all practical purposes, created a Roman empire in Italy. In the organization, the Romans exhibited much statecraft. They did not seek rigid uniformity but adapted themselves readily to varied conditions in different areas. Where they found a high degree of urbanization, as in Latium, Campania, the Greek South, northern Apulia, and Umbria, they left city-states as the existing political units. In less highly civilized areas, such as Bruttium, Lucania, southern Apulia, Samnium, and other regions of central Italy, they recognized tribal states and accorded them a place in their system of alliances. Although they made extensive annexations at the expense of obstinate foes, under pressure of military necessity and need of room for colonization, this practice was not carried to an extreme. Relentless in the prosecution of war, the Romans showed themselves lenient in imposing peace. Most of their conquered opponents received moderate terms, and nowhere did the Romans interfere internally. The reward of this tolerant attitude came in the loyalty displayed by the allies during wars of the following century.

Although there was as yet no such thing as an Italian nation, still it was at this time that the name *Italia* was first applied to the whole of the peninsula and the term *Italici* (Italians) was employed, at first by foreigners but later by themselves, to designate its inhabitants.[12]

---

[12] The several elements in the Roman military confederation may be seen at a glance from the following scheme:

I. Roman citizens   (*a*) with full civic rights (*optimo iure*)
                     (*b*) with private rights only (*sine suffragio*)
II. Roman allies   (*a*) Latin allies
                     (*b*) federate peoples of Italy

CHAPTER 6
GROWTH OF THE
COMMONWEALTH:
509–287 B.C.

While the Romans were expanding and building up their organization of Italy, the Roman state experienced a profound internal evolution. This was brought about in part by the necessity of modifying the government to meet the needs of a rapidly growing community and in part by a successful struggle by the plebeians to secure political and other privileges monopolized at first by the patricians.

I. EARLY REPUBLIC

CONSTITUTION OF THE EARLY REPUBLIC: THE MAGISTRATES. The revolution ousting Tarquin and the subsequent attempt of the patricians to dominate Rome in the period ca. 500–450 B.C. were perhaps inspired by the experience of nobles in Etruria, who were just then reducing the power of their own kings and establishing aristocratic regimes. The patricians wisely refrained from repealing certain reforms introduced by the monarchy, like the new tribal organization and the reliance on essentially infantry armies. They enlarged the patriciate ca. 500 B.C. by admitting to it a few powerful foreign clans, like the Sabine Claudii, and for a time they grudgingly acquiesced in the occasional election to high office and achievement of senatorial status by the descendants of squires and *conscripti*. In the long run, however, the patricians intended to exclude all outsiders from political power, which was exercised through new offices they created. The chief executive office was filled by two annually elected magistrates, or presidents, called at first praetors, but later, consuls. Together they exercised the kingly power (*imperium*), symbolized by rods and axes (*fasces*) carried by the lictors. The *imperium* also involved *auspicium*, the right to take the auspices or omens by which the gods were believed to declare their approval or disapproval of public acts. Both consuls enjoyed these powers equally and, by his veto, one could suspend the other's action. Thus from the beginning of the Republic annuality and collegiality (the division of authority among colleagues of equal rank) characterized the Roman magistracy. As time went on, the Romans recognized the advantage of an occasional concentration of all state power in the hands of a single magistrate; and so, in times of emergency, the consuls, acting on the advice of the Senate, nominated a dictator, who was senior to the consuls themselves for a maximum period of six months. The dictator, or *magister populi*, as he was called in early times, appointed as his assistant a master of the horse (*magister equitum*). The dictatorship was Latin, not Roman, in origin. It was the title given to the commander in chief of the forces of the Latin League, and when dominant in the League, Rome must have supplied such dictators. It was thus natural that Rome should later adopt the concept of dictatorship into her own constitution as well fitted to deal with emergencies, while it was given a specific Roman character. Most of the dictators whose names have been preserved with any degree of reliability belong to the late fifth and fourth centuries B.C. Only patricians were eligible to hold the consulship, the dictatorship, and the mastership of the horse.

THE SENATE. At the side of the magistrates stood the Senate, appointments to which were made by the consuls. The senators held their seats for life unless guilty of grave public or private misconduct.

Disappearance of the monarchy greatly increased the importance of the Senate. Its primary duty was to advise the consuls, as it had the kings. Since the consuls were annual officers who became private citizens when their terms ended, the Senate, as a permanent body, had much more influence over them than it had over monarchs who had ruled for life. It can hardly be said that consuls were subordinate to the Senate at this period, but they would be reluctant to act contrary to its advice. The Senate also acquired the right to sanction or to veto resolutions passed by the Assembly, which could not become laws without the Senate's approval. The composition of the Senate and the life tenure of its members made it a very conservative body devoted to maintaining the interests of the patrician aristocracy.

THE ASSEMBLY OF THE PEOPLE. During the early years of the Republic, the only Assembly of the People was the old Curiate Assembly of the regal period. The Assembly elected the annual consuls and approved or rejected such proposals as the latter placed before it. Its powers were limited to voting, for it did not have the right to initiate legislation or to discuss or amend measures that were presented to it. Its legislative power, furthermore, was limited by the Senate's right of veto.

In the Assembly the voting was open, either by show of hands or oral declaration. The members of each *curia* voted as a unit, the majority within the *curia* determining the vote. Under these conditions it is probable that the voting in the *curiae* was often controlled by the patricians, through their personal influence and the support of their clients who would fear to oppose their wishes.

THE PRIESTHOODS. Public religion in Rome was a special branch of the administration which dealt with official relations of the community with its divine protectors. This sphere was under the direction of a college of priests, headed by the *pontifex maximus*. Special priestly brotherhoods or guilds cared for the performance of particular religious ceremonies, while divination in its political aspect was supervised by the college of augurs. With the exception of the *pontifex maximus*, elected by the people from an early date, the priests were nominated or coopted, and their tenure was lifelong. Rituals previously performed by the king were carried out by a priest who preserved the memory of the kingship in his title King of the Sacrifices (*rex sacrorum*). In the order of the priesthoods the "king" ranked first, even though appointed by the *pontifex maximus*. Priestly offices did not form a separate caste in the community, and, since they were held by men who were also magistrates and senators, the official religion was subordinated to the interests of the state and tended to become purely formal.

At the beginning of the Republic priests exercised much influence on public affairs. They were custodians of religious law, which was enforced by punishing crimes looked upon as offenses against the gods; they alone knew the exact formulas employed in important legal transactions; the *pontifex maximus* had charge of the calendar, fixed the dates of public festivals, and announced each month days open and closed to public business. The members of the college of augurs could postpone any public acts by proclaiming an unfavorable omen. For these reasons it was not merely a matter of prestige but also of practical advantage to the patricians that all priesthoods be filled by fellow nobles.

PATRICIAN DOMINATION. It is apparent that the patricians were in control of the government at the opening of the fifth century B.C. They virtually monopolized the magistracies, the Senate, and the priesthoods. Through these they controlled the Assembly and the administration of justice. At this time there were between forty and fifty patrician clans. It has been estimated that these comprised about 1,000 families, or a total of 4,500 persons, who constituted between 7 and 8 per cent of the total citizen population.[1] Although

---

[1] Beloch, *Römische Geschichte*, pp. 220–223. The chief objection to these figures is that they imply too high a total number of citizens, in view of the size of the military levy. In a rural society the larger landholding families may have formed a much larger proportion of the population than in one with a more complex economy.

little accuracy can be claimed for these figures, they are at least a fair approximation; and it is not surprising that the domination of this aristocratic minority was soon challenged by the plebeian majority.

II. TRIBES, REORGANIZATION OF THE ARMY, AND ESTABLISHMENT OF THE CENTURIATE ASSEMBLY

NEW TRIBAL SYSTEM. Many details of the development of the new tribal system are obscure. It seems likely, however, that under King Servius Tullius the original division of Roman citizens into three tribes was supplanted by the formation of four new urban tribes, named after regions of the city, and fifteen rural ones named after patrician *gentes*. These were all territorial divisions of the *ager Romanus* inhabited by Roman citizens. About 495 B.C., it seems, two new rural tribes were organized; one of them, the Claudia, was founded about fifteen miles north of Rome on the left bank of the Tiber to accommodate the newly immigrant Claudian clan and their clients. Thereafter, no new tribes were created for more than a century, until 387, when the substantial increase in Roman territory following the war with Veii necessitated the creation of four new ones. Subsequent expansion added two new rural tribes each in the years 358, 332, 318, 299, and 241, when the full component of thirty-five, 4 urban and 31 rural, was reached. All tribes created after 495 bore topographical names. After 241, colonists in new areas, or non-Romans who received grants of citizenship, were assigned to one or another of the existing rural tribes, a practice which also had been occasionally in use from the middle of the fourth century. The thirty-five tribes served as administrative units for registration of citizens and their property and so became the basic divisions for raising military levies, for collecting property taxes, and for the classification of citizens into new voting groups.

MILITARY DEVELOPMENTS. According to Roman tradition, which here seems factual, the army of the regal period was a levy of 3,000 infantry and 300 cavalry, recruited equally from each of the three early tribes. Thus each tribe supplied a regiment of 1,000 infantry commanded by a tribune of the soldiers (*tribunus militum*) and a troop of 100 cavalry. We know practically nothing, however, of the army of the early republic except that the number of centuries (i.e., units of 100 men) of cavalry at some time had been increased from three to six. Circumstantial evidence suggests that hoplite discipline and the phalanx may well have fallen into abeyance in the first years of patrician rule. The success of Roman arms was at best rather indifferent in the period ca. 500–450 B.C. On one occasion, the Battle of the Cremera River in 477 (463), tradition holds that the Fabian *gens* was almost wiped out fighting Veii, which suggests a temporary return of the disorganized melee on the battlefield to which aristocrats had been accustomed. In any case phalanx tactics were again normal during the second half of the fifth century when the infantry levy was raised from thirty to forty centuries, a total of 4,000 men. Such an increase seems to indicate a corresponding increase in the number of citizens who could furnish the full equipment of a heavy soldier. Those who possessed this equipment were called the class (*classis* or "calling"); the rest of the citizens were rated as "below the class" (*infra classem*). The latter could be called upon for military service for which inferior equipment was adequate; but they were not included in the phalanx. In 366 (362) the levy apparently was raised to 6,000 men, organized in two legions. This was accomplished by forming new "classes" from poorer property holders, who furnished fewer centuries than the original "class," which now became the first class. Evidently the struggle for existence compelled the state to draw more and more heavily upon the less privileged plebeian class for military service, with consequent pressure for increasing the political rights of the plebs.

This is clearly seen in the formal establishment of a new political assembly of the people, organized by military centuries as they existed in the second half of the fifth century B.C. (440?) but, it seems, deriving ultimately from the military reforms of Servius Tullius one hundred years earlier. In this assembly the citizens of military age voted by centuries in the order of the property classes in which they were enrolled for the performance of military duties, and the number of voting centuries assigned to each class was equal to the number furnished by that class for military service. Thus, at first, the *equites* or horsemen had six centuries or, we may say, six votes. In the first class, the juniors (*iuniores*) or men between seventeen and forty-six years of age who were liable to active service were given forty centuries, and the juniors in the second and third classes ten centuries each. These were the men who served as the heavy-armed infantry. The total number of their voting centuries was sixty, which corresponded to the infantry levy of 6,000 men. Since the assembly was a political and not a military body, provision had to be made for the senior men, those forty-six years of age and over only liable for garrison duty. This was done by assigning to the seniors of each class the same number of voting centuries as to the juniors, except in the case of the cavalry. The former *equites* apparently voted in the senior centuries of the first class. Because the assembly voted century by century it came to be called the Centuriate Assembly (*comitia centuriata*) to distinguish it from the older Assembly of the Curiae.

The foregoing account of the early organization of the Centuriate Assembly is a reconstruction based upon the description of that body at the close of the fourth century made by Romans writing much later. About 300 B.C. there were eighteen equestrian centuries and five property classes.[2] In the classes, the number of junior centuries was now eighty-four, corresponding to a levy of 8,400 men or two legions of 4,200 each. As before, the number of senior centuries in each class was equal to that of the juniors, so that the five classes

---

[2] The property ratings of each class were fixed in terms of bronze currency; the earlier method of assessment is unknown.

comprised one hundred and sixty-eight centuries of juniors and seniors. The first class had eighty; the second, third, and fourth, twenty each; and the fifth, thirty. Besides these, there were five supernumerary centuries made up of two centuries of mechanics and two of musicians (both crafts originally detailed to special military duties), and one for those who lacked the property qualification for the fifth class and were called proletarians.[3] Altogether one hundred and seventy centuries of the classes together with eighteen equestrian and five supernumerary centuries totaled one hundred and ninety-three voting units.

In its completed form, the Centuriate Assembly was a political and not a military organization. It included many who were unfit for military duties, and the term *century* had lost its original meaning—a company of one hundred—with the organization of the senior centuries, for the men of that age group were far less numerous than the juniors. By the close of the fourth century the equestrian centuries were also ceasing to function as a cavalry corps and becoming merely a special class of well-to-do patrician and plebeian property holders. The bulk of the active cavalry in the Roman armies was now supplied by the Italian allies, although many young aristocrats continued to serve in this branch throughout the Republic. The old infantry phalanx made up of centuries had been superseded by the new legionary formation, in which the units were maniples of sixty men and experience, not wealth, determined a man's position in the ranks. Nevertheless, the memory of the military origins of the assembly was perpetuated in the use of classes and centuries and in certain practices. For a long time it continued to assemble in military formation with officers and corps standards; it regularly met on the parade ground, the Campus Martius, outside the *pomerium*, for an army could not be assembled within the city; it could be convened only by a magistrate with military authority; and when it was meeting a war flag was raised on the Janiculum hill where a guard was stationed.

When the Centuriate Assembly was organized it took over the most important functions of the Curiate Assembly and became the chief popular assembly. It elected all the higher magistrates, acquired the sole right to declare war, voted on legislative proposals submitted to it by consuls or other magistrates with *imperium,* and acted as a court of appeal for citizens on whom a magistrate had pronounced a capital penalty, scourging, loss of citizen rights, or a heavy fine. The legislative power of the Centuries was limited for a long time, however, by the veto power of the patrician senators (the *patrum auctoritas*), who had to ratify measures passed by the assembly before they became law. This restriction was practically removed by the Publilian Law (339), which required the *patres* to ratify in advance proposals that were to be presented to this assembly. In like manner, the elections of the Curiate Assembly were subject to the

---

[3] That is, those who had no taxable property, only offspring (*proles*). They were called also *capite censi*, or those registered by name only.

patrum auctoritas, and in the case of officials with *imperium* this authority had to be conferred upon the successful candidates by a law of the Curiate Assembly. A Maenian Law (ca. 287) reduced to a mere formality approval by the *patres* of the Curiate law sanctioning the *imperium* of candidates elected by the Centuriate Assembly.

In the Centuriate Assembly many practices established by the Curiate were maintained. There was no right of discussion or amendment, and business was restricted to matters presented by the presiding magistrate. The system of unit voting was retained also, each century having a single vote, determined by the majority within the century. The centuries voted in a fixed order, and the vote of each was reported as soon as it had completed its polling. The eighteen equestrian centuries voted first; they were followed by the centuries of the first class; these by the centuries of the second class, and so on until a majority of centuries had voted in favor of or against a measure or in favor of the number of candidates to be chosen at any election. Once a majority was reached, the voting ceased, and on many occasions the centuries of the lower classes were never called upon to express an opinion. This was true particularly whenever equestrian centuries and those of the first class voted unanimously, for together they had 98 votes, which was a majority of the total of 193. We have no means of ascertaining, however, how often these two groups voted in unison. Establishment of the Centuriate Assembly put the higher propertied classes in control of the voting in elections and legislation. This broke down the influence of the patrician clans exercised through the *curiae* and organized the citizenry strictly on the basis of property. In place of aristocratic control it set up a timocracy or rule of wealth in which the dominant part was played by that class which then made the greatest contribution to the military. The Curiate Assembly was not abolished. In addition to conferring the *imperium* on the consuls and praetors elect, it met under the presidency of the *pontifex maximus* to witness or confirm ceremonial acts that were mainly religious. By the close of the Republic, the function of this assembly had become so purely formal that its meetings were attended only by thirty lictors who represented the *curiae*.

III. EXPANSION OF THE MAGISTRACY

CONSULAR TRIBUNATE. Increased military activity in the second half of the fifth and the first half of the fourth centuries frequently created the need for more than two officials qualified for commands over the army in any given year. Roman government in such cases replaced the consuls by boards of officials called military tribunes with consular power (*tribuni militum consulari potestate*). The title *tribune* means tribal officer, and the military tribunes were the commanders of levies from the respective tribes. Because these originally numbered 1,000 from each one, the title military tribune came to be used for the commanders of thousands even when the army was no longer organized on a tribal basis. It is in this sense that it still appears to have been employed during the late fifth and early fourth centuries. Accordingly, the military tribunes with consular power were simply magistrates who held the consular *imperium* while keeping their traditional military title.

The ancient literary tradition for these consular military tribunes held that plebeians could, and indeed were, elected to the office. It also knew of six boards of three tribunes between 444 and 427 (436–418); three boards of three and seven of four from 426 to 406 (417–402); and thirty-three boards which normally comprised six members from 405–367 (401–363). That tradition as we know it, however, derives from a much later period, the first century B.C., and it appears to be both muddled and consciously falsified. The Consular Tribunate was probably not founded in 444 (436), perhaps not until 426 (417). There were probably at first three such tribunes, later four, but never six, in an age when the military levy rose only from 3,000 to 4,000 men.[4]

CONSULSHIP RESTORED.   In 366 (362) the use of military tribunes with consular power was abandoned permanently. The dual consulship was restored and, for the future, military tribunes appear only as legionary officers under the command of consuls or other magistrates. In that same year, the levy was increased to 6,000 men and the number of legions to two; six military tribunes were then elected, three for each legion.

PRAETORSHIP.   When the consulship was restored, the numerical weakness of this office was corrected by the establishment of a new magistracy, the praetorship. Its holder, the praetor, was elected annually by the Centuriate Assembly and took charge of civil jurisdiction, relieving the consuls of this responsibility. The praetor was regarded as a junior colleague of the consuls and exercised the *imperium*. Consequently he could command an army, convene the Senate or an assembly, and exercise other consular functions.

CENSORSHIP.   An important step in the expansion of the magistracy was the creation of the censorship about 443 (435). As their name indicates, censors were originally officials who took the census; and since in Rome this happened normally every five years, censors were elected only at the beginning of each new census period. The censors were two in number, and, unlike other magistrates, they held office for eighteen months. They were chosen by the Centuriate Assembly but did not have *imperium*. Their earliest duty was to register all citizens and their properties by tribes and to assign them to appropriate classes and centuries as soldiers and as voters in the Centuriate Assembly. The development of this system of registration adequately explains the inauguration of the censorship, since neither consuls nor military tribunes could have performed the duties of censors in addition to their other obligations. At an early date, perhaps from the foundation of their office, the censors had charge of letting public contracts, and their assessments formed the basis for collection of the property

---

[4] See page 69.

tax (*tributum*) in wartime. By the end of the fourth century they had acquired the right to revise the list of senators when they took the census. Since this involved an examination of the public and private conduct of senators, there arose that power which has survived in the modern conception of a censorship, namely, the supervision of morals. The loss of the right to enroll the Senate tended to diminish the influence of the consuls over that body.

QUAESTORSHIP. In the early Republic the consuls appointed two officers called quaestors to act as their deputies in administering criminal justice. Not long after 450 B.C. the quaestors became magistrates and were elected by the people. In 421 their number was increased to four, of whom two served as public treasurers (*quaestores aerarii* or *urbani*). The other pair acted as assistants to the consuls; they accompanied the latter to war and performed the duties of quartermasters in charge of supplies and payment of troops.

AEDILESHIP. Evidence for the growth of the city Rome and the increasing burden of municipal administration this entailed is found in the establishment of the aedileship, probably when the quaestorship became a magistracy.

Like the dictatorship, this office was of Latin origin, and its original function was the care of records and public money. It appears first as attached to the temple of Diana on the Aventine hill, which once served as a shrine for the Latin League. By ca. 450 this shrine had become the center of a plebeian movement against the patricians, and the aediles appear as assistants of plebeian officials, the tribunes of the plebs. In the early fourth century they were associated with the temple of Ceres, the new center of plebeian activities. When they became state magistrates, they acted as superintendents of public works, as market commissioners, and as police magistrates. At first there were two of them and they were elected from the plebeians. In 366 (362), however, upon the restoration of the consulship, their number was increased to four by the addition of two "curule" aediles, so called because they could use the seat known as the curule chair, which had been a prerogative of the higher magistrates. For some time the curule aedileship was a patrician magistracy, but its duties were the same as those of the plebeian aediles.

PROMAGISTRACY. Roman magistrates were elected for one year only, and after 342 reelection to the same office could be sought only after ten years. This entailed some inconveniences, especially in the conduct of military operations, for when campaigns lasted longer than one year the consul in command had to yield to his successor when his own term of office expired. Thus the state was unable to use for a longer period men who had displayed special military capacity. The difficulty was overcome during the Second Samnite War by the prolongation, at the discretion of the Senate, of the command of a consul in the field for an indefinite period after the lapse of his consulship. The person whose office was thus extended was no longer a consul but acted "in the place of a consul" (*pro consule*). The proconsulship first appeared in the campaign at Naples in 327; and, although for a time rarely employed, its use eventually became very widespread and extended to other offices.

CHARACTERISTICS OF THE MAGISTRACY. By the close of the fourth century the Roman magistracy had attained its canonical republican form. It consisted of a number of committees, each of which, with the exception of the quaestorship, had an independent sphere of action. They were the executive branch of the government, entrusted with enforcing laws and carrying out routine administration in consultation with the Senate. Certain of them had military as well as civil authority. Among these committees there was a regularly established order of rank ascending as follows: quaestors, aediles, censors, praetors, consuls. Except for the censorship, which was regularly filled by ex-consuls, politicians usually advanced from one magistracy to another in this order. A distinctive feature of the committee system was the right of any magistrate to veto the action of his colleague or colleagues. This applied to the consulship as well as to lower magistracies; but in order to avoid too frequent use of veto, the consuls alternated each month in taking charge of the administration when both were in the city, and when both were with the army they held the chief command on alternate days. Magistrates of higher rank enjoyed greater authority (*maior potestas*) than all those who ranked below them and as a rule could forbid or annul their actions. In this way the consuls, or the dictator, were able to exercise a negative control over the activities of all other magistrates. The unity which was given to the administration by this theory of *maior potestas* was increased by the Senate, a council whose influence over the magistracy grew as the consulate lost in power and independence through the creation of new offices. All magistrates were said to have *potestas*, but only the dictator, consuls, and praetor had *imperium*. Consequently, these latter were the only ones who could exercise military command, summon the people on their own authority to assemble for elective or legislative purposes, and try more important civil and criminal cases. All magistrates, however, had the power to enforce their orders by the arrest of disobedient persons. The great power and the relative freedom of action enjoyed by the magistrates, who were immune to prosecution while in office, are outstanding features of the constitution. The respect for public authority which they implied is one of the characteristics of early Roman society.

IV. PLEBEIAN STRUGGLE FOR EQUALITY

CAUSES OF THE STRUGGLE. Patrician interests were narrowly self-serving and produced an increasing polarity in Roman society early in the fifth century. Aristocratic unwillingness to meet burgeoning grievances caused squires and peasants to agitate together for changes in the regime and led to their formation of a distinct social class called the plebeian, first clearly discernible early in the Republic. Thereafter, for some 200 years, a series of confrontations took place between plebeians and patricians, which were typically backed up by threats of succession. These threats never resulted in outright civil war, however, because patricians grudgingly and gradually agreed to plebeian demands.

The grievances were rather diverse. Prominent plebeians, many of them landholders of means, could at least make their will felt, along with the patricians, in the upper classes of the evolving Centuriate Assembly; but they bitterly resented patrician intentions to deny them utterly a leading role in affairs of state and officeholding, to which they aspired. The patrician commonwealth demanded their frequent service in the heavy infantry, to which their wealth qualified them, yet denied them corresponding political importance. It must be remembered, however, that they shared potentially common interests with the patricians as members of the economic upper class, even though they shared socially and politically inferior status with the rest of Rome's citizenry, who were mainly poor peasants.

The grievances of these latter, on the other hand, resembling those of Athenians in pre-Solonian times, were mainly economic. Peasants, operating in a subsistence economy and farming only a few acres of land, were vulnerable to a succession of bad harvests, aristocratic feuding, raids by Rome's neighbors, imposition of the *tributum* or property tax levied in wartime, and a general lack of capital to help them make ends meet. Those seeking protection or help from patrons tended to sink to the status of serfs, like their opposite numbers in Etruria, while peasants not yet clients were at the mercy of patricians and their clans under the prevailing informal enforcement of unwritten law. A particular problem for bankrupt plebeians was *nexum*, the customary right of creditors to the persons of defaulting debtors, who could then be sold abroad. Later Romans came to regard as fundamental to their citizenship protection under the law, guaranteed by the state, but such protection was scarcely developed early in the patrician Republic. Patrician judges and priests would "find" law in their own vested interests. There was no appeal from the judgment of consuls in capital cases; crimes against individuals, for example, homicide and assault, were investigated by consular aides to establish the fact of their commission, but punishment or compensation in such cases was still left to the kinsmen of the aggrieved party, as it was in prehistoric times.

Evidence that discontent was rife at Rome may be found in the tradition of three unsuccessful attempts to set up a tyranny, that is, to seize power by unconstitutional means, made by Spurius Cassius (478), Spurius Maelius (431), and Marcus Manlius (376), patricians who figure in later tradition as popular champions.

PLEBEIAN REVOLT. The first objectives of the plebs in their struggle to equality with the patricians were to find officers to act as their spokesmen and to defend them against exploitation by the patricians; to organize plebeian assemblies for the regular election of such officers and for passing legislation in the interest of the plebs; and to force the patricians to make public written law.

CODIFICATION OF THE LAW. In the middle of the fifth century B.C. the patricians, under plebeian pressure, and following the example set by Greek city-states some two centuries earlier, drew up and published a law code.

There can be little doubt that this was influenced by the codes which had long been in use in Greek cities of Italy with which the Romans had contact, and there is a not implausible tradition that a Roman commission was sent to Athens to study the laws of Solon.

The task of codifying the law was entrusted to ten magistrates called decemvirs who replaced the consuls for the year 450 (443). According to later accounts, this commission had not completed its task at the end of a year and was succeeded by a second board of ten. Probably this second decemvirate is fictitious, and the work of the original commission seems to have been completed by the consuls of the following year. The code which was thus compiled was set up in public on twelve wooden tablets and for that reason was known as the Law of the Twelve Tables.[5]

Only scattered quotations from the Twelve Tables have survived, but these, supplemented by references in later writers, give a general idea of their character and content. It was in no sense a constitution but simply a compilation of customary civil and criminal law, with rules for legal procedure and certain social regulations, as, for example, restrictions upon elaborate funeral rites. Though primitive in many respects, the code was simple and logically arranged, which qualified it to serve as the basis of a more highly developed legal system. It was held in great respect by Roman jurists of later centuries. The Twelve Tables sanctioned the arrest and imprisonment of insolvent debtors by their creditors and the right of the latter to sell them into slavery in default of other means of recovering the debt.[6] They also gave legal force to the patrician refusal to recognize intermarriage between the orders, the culmination of aristocratic attempts at being exclusive. In spite of illiberal provisions, publication of the code was advantageous to the plebeians, for the law was now known to all and not, as heretofore, only to patricians.

TRIBUNES OF THE PLEBS. The initial steps taken by plebeians to produce spokesmen occurred in the first half of the fifth century, but they cannot be reconstructed with any degree of reliability owing to the meagre and contradictory character of the Roman tradition.[7] A crisis surely developed about the middle of that century, which brought the state to the brink of civil war and resulted in an agreement between the two orders to improve the position of the plebeians. Important concessions were wrung from the patricians by the plebeian revolt, which, Romans believed, was a secession of the plebs to their center on the Aventine hill and a threat to form a new state. Henceforth the plebeians elected annually ten officials of plebeian birth called Tribunes of the Plebs (*tribuni plebis*) in imitation of the military tribunes. The tribunes were clearly men of some standing in the community. The patricians recognized

---

[5] This posting of the law implies some degree of literacy among the Romans.

[6] The code specified that these debtors should be sold across the Tiber, i.e., not to a Roman or a Latin but in enemy territory.

[7] One Roman source placed the organization of the plebeian tribunate in 494 B.C. with two tribunes. Boards of four and five are reported, but the names of these tribunes are suspect.

them as officials but not as magistrates in the strict sense of the term, for they were elected by the plebeians alone. They also acknowledged the right of such a tribune to intervene on behalf of any person who sought his aid against unjust or oppressive acts of a patrician magistrate or private citizen, and by uttering the word *veto* (I forbid) to stop such action. The tribune was able to make his veto effective since the plebs swore to treat as accursed and to execute without trial any person who disregarded the tribune's veto or violated his person. This proves that in origin the tribunate was an unconstitutional, revolutionary office.

PLEBEIAN COUNCIL AND TRIBAL ASSEMBLY. Legal status was accorded also to the meeting of the plebeians under the presidency of their tribunes. They met in the Roman Forum by tribes, which recorded their votes. The majority within each tribe determined its vote, and a simple majority of the tribes decided the action of the body as a whole. Since patricians were excluded from its meetings, it was called the Council of Plebs (*concilium plebis*) and not a tribal assembly. Its resolutions, called plebiscites,[8] were binding on plebeians only; but, after 287 B.C. they were recognized as full-fledged laws, i.e., valid for both classes. Beginning about 447 B.C., the consuls began to summon for electoral purposes an assembly that virtually duplicated the Council of Plebs but was called the Tribal Assembly (*comitia tributa*) because it was presided over by a magistrate with *imperium* and was open to all citizens, including patricians. Voting in the same way as the Council of Plebs, it elected quaestors and transacted certain minor matters. Thus, the early Roman Republic had *four* primary political gatherings: the Curiate, Centuriate, and Tribal Assemblies and the Plebeian Council. Despite an eventual blurring of terminology, the Romans always scrupulously kept the distinction between Council of Plebs and Tribal Assembly to the end of the Republic. The Plebeian Council and Tribal Assembly were by no means inherently radical bodies. Despite their grievances, most plebeians retained the conservative outlook of a rural society, and in many of the tribes the patricians exercised great influence through the votes of their clients.

CANULEIAN MARRIAGE LAW. The Law of the Twelve Tables affirmed the illegitimacy of marriages between patricians and plebeians. This was a mark of inferiority strongly resented by the plebs. At the same time it came to be a practical disadvantage to the patricians in view of their declining numbers, which made it desirable for them to contract marriages with wealthier plebeian families. This disability was accordingly removed by the Canuleian Marriage Law attributed to 445 (437).

PLEBS AND THE HIGHER MAGISTRACIES. The plebeians were not content with holding the quaestorship and aedileship, when the monopoly of the magistracies with *imperium* still gave patricians control of army commands,

---

[8] From the opening formula *plebi scitum* (resolved by the plebs).

administration of justice, and public policy. Here the patricians tenaciously maintained their prerogatives until after the mid-fourth century. The struggle for control of the chief magistracy is reflected in the tradition of a period of anarchy in Rome, one for which no magistrates with *imperium* were recorded in the official list, presumably because those who held office did not obtain it constitutionally. How long this condition persisted is uncertain, although it may have not exceeded one year. The writers who made it of longer duration did so to fill a gap in their chronology. At any rate, the anarchy should be placed perhaps between 375 and 370.

To the year 367 (363) tradition assigned several laws, called Licinian-Sextian from their authors, the plebeian tribunes Lucius Sextius and Gaius Licinius. One of these is said to have prescribed that at least one consul in each year should be a plebeian and to have recognized formally the right of plebeians to hold that office. The consular lists, however, show that this alleged law was not observed on seven occasions between 355 and 342 when both consuls were patricians, which make the commonly accepted tradition doubtful. More likely, another law passed in 342 decreed that one consul of any given year must be plebeian, less probably that both of them might be, because the consulship was not held by two plebeians until 172.

The plebeians simultaneously entered the other higher magistracies. They gained the dictatorship in 356, the censorship in 351, and the praetorship in 337. The curule aedileship was also opened to them and was held by patricians and plebeians in alternate years.

THE PLEBS AND THE SENATE. Because the custom was early established that ex-consuls, and later ex-praetors, should be enrolled in the Senate, the opening of these offices to the plebs began to give them an ever-increasing representation in that body. The fusion of leading plebeians with patricians in the Senate, first noticeable during the Second Samnite War, gave rise to a new ruling class in the Roman state: the senatorial oligarchy of officeholders. This consisted of a large group of influential patrician and plebeian families which, for some time at least, was continuously given new life by the accession of prominent plebeians who entered the Senate by holding magistracies. From 366 to 265 about ninety consulships were held by members of thirty-six plebeian *gentes*, which may be considered in this way to have attained the rank of nobility. Thus the Senate, by opening its ranks to the leaders of the plebs, emerged from the struggle with its prestige and influence increased.

CENSORSHIP OF APPIUS CLAUDIUS: 312 B.C. One of the censors who entered office in 312 was a patrician of the bluest blood, Appius Claudius, the first Roman politician with a discernible personality, who was responsible for the construction of the Via Appia and the Aqua Appia, Rome's first aqueduct. Appius apparently resisted the emergence of a new, hybrid senatorial oligarchy that might well escape the control of his own patrician *gens* and its faction. With the idea of strengthening his political power by enlarging his clientele, he used

V Via Appia and Tomb of Caecilia Metella. *The Via Appia, the most famous of Roman roads, was built by the Censor Appius Claudius Caecus in 312 B.C. to link Rome with Capua. It was later extended to Brundisium on the southeast Italian coast. The conspicuous monument is the tomb of Caecilia Metella, daughter-in-law of Marcus Crassus, the triumvir. (Photo: Anderson.)*

his censorial powers to patronize the sons of freedmen by enrolling them in the Senate. He also permitted city residents to register in rural tribes, where their votes would tend to have much greater weight. It is said that the consuls ignored his senatorial list and summoned the Senate according to its previous membership, and the censors of 304 apparently restricted city residents once more to the urban tribes. Despite these rebuffs Appius continued for a long time as one of the most influential public figures, attaining the consulship twice and being also praetor and dictator.

A sequel to the censorship of Appius Claudius was the aedileship of Gnaeus Flavius. Flavius was the son of a freedman and a clerk to the curule aediles. Through the patronage of Appius he was elected curule aedile, the first Roman whose father had been a slave to obtain that office (304). To Flavius was attributed the publication of a handbook explaining procedure in the courts for the benefit of plaintiffs and defendants.

THE PLEBS AND THE PRIESTHOOD. The last stronghold of patrician privilege was the priesthood. Until the close of the fourth century, the only religious office which had been opened to the plebeians was that of the board in charge of public sacred books, which also regulated religious ceremonies. In 368 (364) the membership of this board was increased from two to ten (called *decemviri sacris faciundis*), half of whom were plebeians. In 300 the plebs gained access to the higher priesthoods by virtue of the Ogulnian Law, which increased the number of pontiffs by four and that of the augurs by five and required the new places to be filled with plebeians. Henceforth it was impossible for patricians to use religious law and practice to hamper plebeian political activity.

VALERIAN LAW ON APPEALS: 300 B.C. One of the characteristic features of the early constitution was the power of magistrates with *imperium* to enforce their orders by various penalties, the most severe being scourging and execution. In 300 a Valerian Law restricted the magistrates' right of coercion by forbidding the execution or scourging of anyone who had appealed, presumably to an assembly provided in the Law of the Twelve Tables. Similar Valerian Laws were assigned by Roman writers to the years 509 and 449, but if they are historic, it is difficult to see the necessity for the law of 300. In any case the right of appeal could only be exercised within the limits of the *pomerium* or possibly one mile beyond; it was not valid against the power of the magistrate outside these limits where military authority prevailed.[9]

HORTENSIAN LAW: 287 B.C. The end of the struggle between the orders came in 287 with an economic crisis which had far-reaching political repercussions. Throughout the fourth century, the problem of debts owed by Roman peasants had become increasingly acute, and tradition knows several attempts to alleviate their burdens. It is probable that overpopulation and soil deterioration in Latium had something to do with these conditions, but perhaps the chief cause of indebtedness at this time was the demand for military service made upon poorer landholders. The pay which these received was little more than enough to purchase their food, which they had to buy for themselves; and though they might share at times in spoils of war, their frequent absence from their farms made it hard for them to raise crops to support their families or to supplement their harvests by wages earned as farm laborers. Tenant farmers were especially hard hit. Demands for relief followed the conclusion of the long Samnite Wars. The Senate, which represented the creditor class, repeatedly

---

[9] The sphere in which the *imperium* was subject to appeal was called *domi* (at home), that in which it was unrestricted was known as *militiae* (on service).

refused to approve remedial legislation proposed by the tribunes and passed in the Council of Plebs. The obstinacy of the Senate forced the plebeians to take drastic action. Plebeian soldiers under arms marched up the Janiculum hill across the Tiber and threatened to secede.[10] In the face of this threat the Senate yielded and appointed Quintus Hortensius, a plebeian, as dictator to settle the controversy. He succeeded in alleviating the distress of the debtors, although how he solved the problem is not known. He then passed the Hortensian Law which provided that all future measures voted in the Council of Plebs should become law without either previous or subsequent approval in the Senate.

THE CONSTITUTION AFTER 287 B.C. As a result of the Hortensian Law the Council of Plebs acquired greater independence than the Centuriate Assembly and tended to become the legislative assembly *par excellence*, while the Centuriate remained the senior elective assembly. For legislative purposes and for the election of the plebeian tribunes and aediles, the Plebeian Council was always summoned by a tribune. The distinction between Plebeian Council and Tribal Assembly was still maintained, the latter body being convoked by a magistrate and electing quaestors, curule aediles, and eventually, twenty-four military tribunes for the annual levy. The Centuriate Assembly, which elected the consuls, praetors, and censors, and which could also pass laws, had to be convened and presided over by a magistrate. As noted, centuries composed of the wealthy outnumbered those of the poor in the Centuriate Assembly. The Tribal Assembly and Plebeian Council were more democratic only to the extent that each tribe represented a cross section of every economic and social class. The Curiate Assembly, which formally conferred *imperium* on magistrates, had by this time become a purely ceremonial body.

INCREASED IMPORTANCE OF THE TRIBUNATE. The influence of the tribunes was greatly enhanced by the Hortensian Law, as well as by privileges which they had already acquired by 287 or shortly thereafter. The more important were the right to sit in the Senate, to address and even to convene that body, and to prosecute any magistrate before the Plebeian Council. The first was an extension of their veto power, which could thus invalidate a proposal under discussion in the Senate without waiting for a magistrate's attempt to execute it after it had become law. To permit the tribunes to veto at this stage, they had to be allowed to hear the debates in the Senate. At first they did so from their bench, which they set at the door of the meeting place, but finally they were permitted to enter the chamber itself. The power of prosecution made the tribunes guardians of the state against any magisterial misconduct. From this time on the tribunes had practically the status of magistrates.

The struggle of the orders left its mark on the Roman constitution in providing Rome with a double set of government organs. The tribunate and Council of

---

[10] Roman tradition records five such secessions. Of these, the two that seem authentic are those of ca. 450 and 287 B.C.

Plebs arose as purely plebeian institutions, but they came to be incorporated in the organization of the state along with the magistracies and the assemblies, which had always been institutions of the whole people.

After 287 all political distinctions between patricians and plebeians disappeared. Although social prestige still clung to the old patrician families, intermarriage with plebeians weakened even this distinction, and sole remnants of the former patrician prerogatives were exclusive rights to certain older priesthoods of no political significance and to the curule aedileship in alternate years. In form, at least, the constitution was a democracy with sovereign power vested in popular assemblies. In practice the coalition of leading plebeian families with patricians largely nullified the power of the assemblies and gave to the government a decidedly oligarchic character. This oligarchy was itself split up into factions based on various *gentes* that competed for the important magistracies and for the conduct of public policy. Details of the operation and significance of factional politics will be reserved for a later chapter.

V. ROMAN MILITARY SYSTEM

Upon the history of no people has the character of its military institutions exercised a more profound effect than that of Rome. The military system rested on the obligation of citizens to render military service, but the degree to which this obligation was enforced varied at different periods. For the mobilization of manpower was dependent upon equipment, methods of fighting, and organization of tactical units in vogue at various times, as well as on the ability of the state to equip its troops and the strength of their martial spirit.

RECRUITMENT. In the latter part of the fifth century the Romans apparently reinstated the regal system of recruitment on the basis of property and remodeled their tactical organization so as to make better use of their infantry. At first one and eventually three higher property classes supplied heavy armed infantry; two lower property classes furnished light troops. On the battlefield the centuries or companies of heavy infantry were united in the phalanx. From this time the strength of the Roman army rested in its infantry, and cavalry became less important. The relation of this new system of recruitment and tactical organization to the formation of the Centuriate Assembly has been discussed. The introduction of pay for troops in the field at the time of the siege of Veii both lessened the economic burden of service on poorer soldiers and enabled the Romans to undertake campaigns of longer duration, even in winter.

MANIPULAR LEGION. The phalanx did not survive the Samnite Wars. In its place appeared a legionary formation, in which the largest units were legions of about 4,200 infantry, divided into maniples of 120 men, each broken down into two centuries of 60 men.[11] This arrangement allowed increased

---

[11] For battle, the legion was drawn up in three separate lines with intervals between the maniples in each.

flexibility of movement in broken country and the adoption of the *pilum*, or javelin, as a missile weapon. Both the javelin and the *scutum*, or oblong shield, were typical Samnite weapons, and the Romans by tradition had adopted them in imitation of the Samnites. While reorganizing their infantry, the Romans developed a more efficient cavalry force, although they came to rely more and more on the mounted troops of their federate allies.

Apparently property qualifications no longer determined positions in the battle line, as men now were assigned to their places in the ranks on the basis of age and experience, and the state furnished the necessary weapons to those who did not provide their own. By the third century all able-bodied men holding property valued at 4,000 asses[12] were regularly mobilized for military duty. Others were liable to naval service, but only in emergencies were they enrolled in the legions. Ordinarily the service amounted to sixteen campaigns in the infantry and ten in the cavalry. The field army was raised from men between seventeen and forty-six years of age; those forty-six and over were liable only for garrison duty in the city. The regular annual levy consisted of four legions, besides 1,800 cavalry. This number could be increased, and the Roman forces in the field were supplemented by at least an equal number of Italian allies.

ROMAN DISCIPLINE. The Roman army was a national levy, a militia. It was commanded by the consuls, the annually elected chiefs of state. Yet it avoided the characteristic weakness of militiamen, for the frequency of wars and the length of liability for service assured the presence of many veterans in each levy and maintained a high standard of efficiency. The consuls, if not always good generals, were generally experienced soldiers, for a record of ten campaigns was required of the candidate for public office. Their subordinates, the military tribunes, were also veterans, some having seen five and others ten years of service. The factor that contributed above all else to the success of the Roman armies was their discipline. *Imperium* gave consuls absolute power over the lives of soldiers in the field, and death was the penalty for neglect of duty, disobedience, or cowardice. Roman discipline is indicated by their habit of constructing a fortified camp after every march, laid out according to fixed rules and protected by a ditch, a wall of earth, and a palisade for which they carried the stakes. They never neglected this task, in contrast to the Greek citizen armies, which could not be induced to construct such works. The fortified camp rendered the Romans safe from surprise attacks, allowed them to join battle when they chose, and gave them a secure refuge after defeat. It played a very large part in the operations of their armies, especially those conducted in hostile territory. Her military system thus proved superior to that of the other peoples of Italy and was the chief single factor in its conquest.

---

[12] At this time the *as* was probably reckoned as a pound of bronze (see p. 90).

CHAPTER 7
SOCIETY AND
RELIGION IN THE
EARLY REPUBLIC

I. SOCIAL AND ECONOMIC LIFE

THE HOUSEHOLD. The cornerstone of the Roman social structure was the household (*familia*). The state was an association of households, and it was the individual's position in a household that determined his status in the community. The Roman household was an extended family, comprising the father (*pater familias*), his wife, his sons with their wives and children, his unmarried daughters, and the household slaves.

PATRIA POTESTAS. The *pater familias* possessed authority over most, and frequently all, the household. His power over free members was called *patria potestas* (paternal authority), over slaves *dominium* (lordship). Paternal authority was in theory unrestricted and gave the father the right to put to death those under him. In practice, however, the exercise of *patria potestas* was limited by custom and by the habit of consulting older male members of the household before action. The household estate (*res familiaris*) was administered by the *pater familias*, and at his death his sons, in turn, became heads of *familiae*, dividing the estate.

The position of women in this patriarchal system was interesting. Their status varied according to whether they were patrician or plebeian, free or slave, young or old, respectable or disreputable, but especially according to their marital condition, wives married only once (*univirae*) being especially honored. Except for the Vestal Virgins tending the public hearth, all women were legal wards of either fathers or husbands or, in the case of spinsters and widows, guardians who may or may not have been male relatives. The *pater familias* decided the form his daughter's marriage would take, whether she should remain under his legal authority even as a married woman, or whether she would come under the power (*manus*) of her husband, in which case she became part of her husband's family, worshipped his ancestral gods, and had rights of inheritance to his property as if she were his daughter. In such a case her *pater familias* and his family continued to be actively interested in protecting her welfare.

If we believe Roman folklore, the demands of the patriarchal system on women, who were ideally expected to be chaste and obedient homemakers, could be severe and exacting, involving as they did high male standards of honor. Tradition knew of the plebeian Verginia, raped in 449 B.C. by a Claudian, who was killed by her father because her honorable death was preferable to her life as a dishonored woman. Yet Roman women could also be influential and respected for exercising a will of their own, if we may credit the story of Coriolanus, a traitor dissuaded by his wife and mother from attacking Rome in the early fifth century. Despite the sometimes stringent limitations imposed on women by *patria potestas*, they at least seem to have been far freer and less secluded than their Athenian counterparts, even at an early date.

EDUCATION. There was no system of public education, and Roman boys received instruction from their fathers. It consisted of training in sports, such as running, swimming, boxing, wrestling, and in the use of arms; of instruction in habits of cleanliness and good conduct; of practical training in farming; of instruction in the traditions of the state and legends of Roman heroes; and of an introduction to the conduct of public business through attendance at the Forum and the courts. Naturally, the quality and scope of such training varied according to the social and economic status of each household. Little is known about the education of young women, although it seems that, quite aside from practical training in housekeeping, they might be exposed to at least rudimentary schooling in letters, just like their brothers.

At the age of eighteen the young Roman man entered a new relation to the state. He was now liable to military service and qualified to attend public assemblies. In these respects he was emancipated from paternal authority. If he subsequently was elected to a magistracy, his father obeyed him like any other citizen, although he might make use of *patria potestas* to influence his son's political actions.

The discipline and respect for authority acquired in the family were carried by the Roman into his public relations and aroused in him a sense of obligation to the state that was perhaps the strongest quality in the Roman character. It was supplemented by the characteristic Roman seriousness (*gravitas*), developed under stress of the long struggle for existence. For the Romans the highest

HOUSEHOLD LIFE. In this period Roman household architecture shows but a slight advance from prehistoric times. The main part of each house was a large hall or room with an open hearth. This room, from its smoke-blackened appearance, was called the *atrium*. The *atrium* was the center of domestic life and served as a common work, reception, and dining room for the master and his servants. Food was simple, the main item in the daily menu being cakes or porridge of wheat or oatmeal. This was supplemented by beans and other vegetables. Bread was a later addition. Meat, not a staple, was enjoyed at festivals and sacrifices. For fruits there were pears, apples, grapes, and figs, while olive oil took the place of butter. Wine, usually mixed with water, was the regular beverage. As far as possible each household was self-sufficient. The farm and pastures provided food and drink, and clothing was largely homemade. Extras could be secured by barter in the markets, occurring every ninth day. In Rome, where there was a large landless population which could not furnish its own necessities, the cattle and vegetable markets were important. Here also flourished the craftsmen and shopkeepers who provided manufactured articles of necessity or luxury.

ECONOMIC CONDITIONS. After the overthrow of the monarchy Rome's commerce seems to have declined gradually during the fifth century, as evidenced archeologically by fewer finds of Etruscan and Greek pottery, indicative of Rome's temporarily loosening economic ties with the more advanced parts of Italy. The one large-scale commercial enterprise in which they participated from the fifth century was the salt trade. Salt was brought from the salt pans north of the lower Tiber up the right bank as far as Rome. There it was brought across to the left bank and transported by Roman merchants across Roman territory and up the Tiber valley by way of the Via Salaria, "Salt Road" (see map, p. 35), into the Sabine hill country.

Until the second half of the third century B.C. the Romans, apart from the city populated by merchants, shopkeepers, and artisans, were almost exclusively a stock-raising and agricultural people. This is reflected in the Law of the Twelve Tables, which presents a picture of a primarily agrarian society. Not only was there private ownership of land, but the rights and obligations of landholders were clearly understood and enforced. By contrast, the law of contract was in a very undeveloped state. The laws regulating the rates of interest also reflected the view of an agrarian people. By the Twelve Tables the annual rate was fixed at $8\frac{1}{3}$ per cent, and a usurer who exceeded this limit was liable to fourfold damages, whereas a thief was obliged to restore only twice the value of the stolen property. The same rate was said to have been re-established in 357, apparently owing to neglect of the older law, and ten years later it was reduced to $4\frac{1}{6}$ per cent. In 342, apparently, all loans at interest were forbidden, but this restriction did not long remain in force. Enslavement for debt and imprisonment of a debtor by his creditor, which had been permitted by the Twelve Tables, were abolished in 326. This measure was a great relief to the poorer citizens but must have been regarded as a severe blow by the creditor class.

It was the agrarian and not the commercial and industrial class that profited most from the Roman conquests in Italy. With the founding of colonies and the opening up of large sections of public land for individual settlement, the number of landholders increased greatly, and the oligarchy, which held aloof from commerce, leased large sections of public land for cultivation or stock raising. As a result, the senatorial order gradually developed into a class of agricultural capitalists. If a Licinian-Sextian law, limiting the size of holdings of public land, really was passed in 367 (363)as some Roman writers believed, it would seem that agricultural capitalism had become a menace before the middle of the fourth century.

Slavery was well established but does not yet seem to have been economically important. Most slaves were prisoners of war who had not been exchanged for Roman capitives or ransomed by their own state. As the early wars were waged chiefly with neighboring Italian peoples, these slaves were of the same general stock as the Romans. It is not surprising, then, that when a slave was set free with proper formalities, he was admitted to Roman citizenship. These *liberti*, as they were called, became clients of their former masters, although the old hereditary clientage disappeared by the third century and a much looser relationship took its place, one in which most of the client's obligations to his patron were based on some form of contract. Freedmen citizens were not eligible for public office, but this restriction did not apply to their descendants.[1]

DEVELOPMENT OF A SYSTEM OF COINAGE. The lack of interest in commerce displayed by the governing class in the early Republic was the chief reason Romans were so slow in issuing coinage of their own, although they were in direct or indirect contact with Etruscans, Greeks, and Carthaginians, all of whom had their own systems of coinage. Romans made use of more primitive standards of value in public and private business transactions. Their word for money, *pecunia*,[2] derives from a time when they reckoned values in cattle or sheep, a practice common to other pastoral and agricultural peoples on a similar cultural level. During the fifth century this practice was still in use but was giving way to the use of bronze as a common standard of value. This bronze was current in lumps or bars which could be broken into pieces of varying weight (*aes rude*). Since the bronze lacked any mark that would guarantee its weight and purity, it had to be weighed at each transaction. The standard unit of weight was the Roman pound of twelve ounces. In the latter part of the fifth century a law fixed the value of one ox or ten sheep as 100 pounds of bronze in payment of fines. This must have corresponded closely to the current market price.

Until the close of the Samnite Wars (290) the Romans got along without any coinage of their own, although their ally, the Greek city of Naples, seems to have issued bronze coins with a Greek inscription indicating affiliation with

---

[1] See p. 81. In public law *liberti* were called *libertini*.
[2] From the Latin *pecus*, a flock or herd.

Rome (ca. 327). Early in the third century, however, having acquired capital through the sale of booty and slaves in the Third Samnite War, Rome circulated bronze bars weighing about six pounds and marked with designs on two sides that indicated a Roman origin and probably served as marks of weight and purity. Possibly their appearance should be connected with the appointment of Rome's first mint masters, traditionally ascribed to 289. These bars called *aes signatum* continued in use until they yielded to the competition of true coins. The earliest Roman coins were issued in 269 in both silver and bronze. The standard silver coin was a two-drachm[3] piece worth ten pounds of bronze. The standard bronze coin was an *as* weighing one pound (*aes libralis* or *grave*). There were also smaller bronze coins worth fractions of the *as*. This system of coinage remained unchanged until ca. 235.

BACKGROUND OF ROMAN LITERATURE. Although the art of writing was introduced into Rome through Etruria as early as the sixth century B.C., it can hardly be said that the Romans had developed a literature even by the time they unified Italy under their domination. In this they resembled their closest neighbors, the Etruscans and Oscan-speaking Sabellians. Even at this early period, however, one can detect certain features of Roman writing which remained basic throughout its development and which differentiated it from its Greek counterpart. Unlike prose, the writing of poetry in early Rome never really attained the high degree of respectability it enjoyed among the Hellenes, and there was not even a word for "poet" native to the Roman vocabulary. Poetry, although recognized as decorative, was not central to public life, and the broadly based support of and interest in poetic literature, apparent in the best periods of Greek history, were almost totally absent. The Romans were always conscious of their literary inferiority to the Greeks and borrowed or adapted Hellenic forms and themes to serve their own artistic purposes, which tended to be practical and nationalistic rather than disinterestedly aesthetic.

It is characteristic that, although many things were committed to writing at Rome at an early date, they were technical or professional rather than artistic. Among them were public documents and records, such as laws, treaties, lists of magistrates, commentaries of the consuls, census lists, and the annual notices of important events compiled by the pontiffs. There were also religious works, including ritual ordinances, books of the pontiffs and augurs, and religious hymns. Of a different character were the inscriptions placed below the wax masks of family ancestors in the houses of the nobles, the funeral orations held in their honor, and songs sung to celebrate their exploits. Drama was foreshadowed by the presentation of Etruscan stage performances and Oscan farces (*fabulae Atellanae*) in Rome in the fourth century B.C. at public festivals. But the former were limited to dancing and music, and the latter consisted chiefly of coarsely humorous improvisations. There were also crude forms of popular

---

[3] Two drachms or drams = $\frac{1}{4}$ ounce.

versification, the so-called Fescennine and Saturnian verses, of a mocking and joking character, composed for weddings and triumphal processions. About the beginning of the third century Greek influences began to affect the development of literary forms. Greek meters were adopted in popular verse, and the first Roman book of a literary character, the *Sententiae (Proverbs)* of Appius Claudius the Censor, was composed in verse on a Greek model. The same writer published a speech he had delivered before the Senate in 279, opposing peace with King Pyrrhus.

LEGAL PROGRESS. For the period under consideration the Law of the Twelve Tables remained in force with only slight modifications introduced by statutes or interpretations. Primitive though it was, this code shows that the Romans had already made considerable progress in the development of private law. The separation between law and religion was almost complete, and the right of a person who had been wronged to take private vengeance upon the wrongdoer had been superseded by the state regulation of penalties to be paid by the guilty party. Self-help had not entirely disappeared, however, and in private suits the plaintiff was authorized personally to bring the defendant before the magistrate or to arrest him if he was a defaulting debtor. As might be expected in a community where many citizens were illiterate, the spoken words of a contract attested by witnesses (and not a written copy) were legally valid. One great weakness in the code was the limited means provided for defense of rights and enforcement of obligations. A remedy was found in the development of additional forms of prosecution or "actions at law" (*legis actiones*), published, as has been noted, by Gnaeus Flavius about 304. In these actions both parties had to use set phrases, and the slightest verbal error caused the one who misspoke to lose his suit.

II. RELIGIOUS BELIEFS AND PRACTICES

ROMAN CONCEPTIONS OF DEITY. By the opening of the Republic Roman religion was a composite of beliefs and ceremonies reflecting past political and cultural experience. The basic stratum was what we may call the Roman element—that is, religious ideas which the Romans held in common with the Latins and other closely related Italic peoples. As early as the sixth century this element was overlaid and permeated with Etruscan and Greek influences.

Although traces of a belief in magic and the worship of natural objects and animals or of gods conceived in animal form survived from earlier stages in Roman religious experience, the basis of specifically Roman religious ideas is found in "animism." Animism is the belief in spiritual beings more powerful than man, residing in the phenomena and processes of the natural world. These spirits were thought of as incalculable, impersonal forces, and the power exhibited by any of them was called *numen* (plural *numina*). In time, such *numina* were thought to emanate from divinities who were regarded as personalities with definite characteristics and names. These were the "gods," *dei*, who belong to the more advanced stage of religious development called "deism."

Since Roman gods developed from the spirits of an earlier age, we can understand why for a long time the Romans worshipped them without images or temples. Each god, however, was regarded usually as residing in a certain locality, and there only could his worship be carried on. These early gods lacked human attributes, their power was admitted, but they inspired no personal devotion. Until influenced by more sophisticated religious ideas, the Romans did not develop any unified and coordinated view of divine powers or their relation to man and the universe, nor did they create a body of religious myths. Roman theology consisted almost entirely of ideas about individual gods and their special powers and ceremonial acts to avert their ill will or obtain their favor.

IMPORTANCE OF RITUAL. While recognizing their dependence upon divine powers, the Romans considered their relationship contractual. If man observed the proper ritual in his worship, the god was bound to act propitiously; if the god granted man's desire, he must be rewarded with an offering. If man failed in his duty, the god punished him; if the god refused to listen, man was not bound to continue his worship. Thus Roman religion consisted essentially in the performance of ritual, wherein correctness of performance was the chief factor. This is illustrated by the use of the Latin word *religio* (religion). At first the term seems to have meant the general feeling of fear experienced by men in the presence of natural phenomena they did not understand. Then it came to mean the obligation to perform certain acts suggested by this feeling of awe, that is, religious duties.

Because the power of the gods could affect both community and individuals, it was necessary for the state to observe its obligations toward the gods with the same scrupulous care as did individual citizens. Knowledge of these obligations and their performance constituted the sacred law, a very important part of public law. This sacred law was guarded by the priesthood, the source of power of the pontiffs, who not only preserved the sacred traditions and customs, but also added to them by interpretation and the establishment of new precedents. The pontiffs performed or supervised all public acts of a purely religious nature and likewise prescribed the ritual to be observed by the magistrate in initiating public business.

The power of the augurs rested on the belief that the gods issued warnings to men through natural signs and that it was possible to discover their attitude toward any contemplated human action by observing natural phenomena. The augurs were official guardians of the science of the interpretation of such signs or auspices. The magistrate undertaking important public business had to take the auspices, and if the augurs declared any flaw therein or held that any unfavorable omen had occurred during that business, they could suspend or render invalid the magistrate's action.

Roman priests were not intermediaries between the individual Roman and his gods but rather officers in charge of one branch of administration. They were responsible for the due observance of public religious acts, just as the head of the household supervised the family cult. Thus Roman religion was essentially social and marked by an absence of individualism. Prophecy and private divination were discouraged.

CULT OF THE HOUSEHOLD. True Roman religious ideas are best seen in the cult of the household. The chief divinities of the household were Janus, the spirit of the doorway; Vesta, that of the hearth; the Penates, guardians of the pantry; the Lar Familiaris, which may be regarded as the spirit of the cultivated land transplanted within the house to guard the family fortune; and the Genius, originally conceived as the male procreative force, especially that of the head of the household, which only at a later date was regarded as his spiritual double. The corresponding female quality, the Juno, was quickly anthropomorphized and, as the like-named goddess, became part of the Capitoline triad.[4] Besides these powers there were many others which were in control of the manifold aspects of life of the household and its individual members, including birth, marriage, and death. Although the *pater familias* may be regarded as its priest, the worship of certain powers revered within the house was carried out by his wife and daughters.

Historic Romans maintained two burial rites of inhumation and cremation. Under Greek and Etruscan influences, they came to believe that the spirits of the deceased went down to the underworld, realm of the gods below (*di inferi*). Thence, at certain times of the year, they returned to visit the earth, and upon these occasions festivals of commemoration and propitiation were celebrated which served to keep alive the memory of the ancestors and to ward off any baneful influences they might otherwise exercise on their descendants.

STATE CULT. Earliest knowledge of the public or state cult is derived from the calendar of the annually recurring public festivals, which in its earliest form dates from about 500 B.C. At this stage state religion was essentially agricultural and consisted mainly in the performance of certain rites of the household and of the farm by or for the people as a whole. Such were the cults of Vesta and the Penates, as well as the festival of the Ambarvalia, the annual solemn purification of the fields. State religion also included the worship of divinities whose personalities and powers were conceived more distinctly than those venerated in the house and in the fields. Some of these had originally been gods of certain clans whose cults had been taken over by the state. Chief among the state gods originally were the triad, Mars, Jupiter, and Quirinus. By the time of the dedication of the temple of Jupiter on the Capitoline hill (509) they had given way to a new triad—Jupiter, Juno, and Minerva. Jupiter Optimus Maximus, called also Capitolinus from his place of worship, was

---

[4] See p. 43.

originally a sky god but, acquiring other attributes, was finally revered as the chief protector of the state. Juno was the female counterpart of Jupiter and was the great patron goddess of women. Minerva was the patroness of craftsmen. Mars, originally a god of agriculture as well as of war, became the patron deity of warlike activities and gave his name to the military training ground of Rome, the *Campus Martius* or Field of Mars.

FOREIGN INFLUENCES. The earliest calendar of state festivals included the worship of foreign gods whose cult had been adopted officially by the community. Some of these are obviously Etruscan; others, though partly disguised by Etruscan and Latin names, belong to the earliest circle of the gods of Greece. Such were Ceres, the Greek Demeter, and Liber, the Greek Dionysos, both earth deities closely connected with agriculture. In the latter part of the sixth century, under the influence of Etruscan kings, there was a fresh influx of Homeric Greek divinities. Among these were Apollo, Minerva (= Athena), and Diana (=Artemis). Greek religious influence was fostered by the acquisition of the Sibylline Books, a collection of oracles brought from Cumae to Rome toward the close of the regal period, placed under the care of a priestly commission, and consulted by pontiffs in times of emergency. To the Etruscans the Romans owed the introduction of temples and statues in divine worship, although here the Etruscans themselves were probably indebted to the Greeks. The great Temple of Jupiter on the Capitoline hill, begun by the last king but dedicated at the beginning of the Republic, was built in Etruscan style and decorated with the work of Etruscan artists. Greek artists, however, were called in to adorn the temple on the Aventine, erected in 493 in accordance with a Sibylline oracle, for the cult of Ceres, Liber, and Libera, that is, the Greek Demeter, Dionysos, and Kore. This marks the beginning of the predominance of Greek influences in religious art and architecture. Also built in the fifth century were temples for the worship of other Greek gods established earlier; for Mercury (=Hermes) in 495, for Castor in 484, and somewhat belatedly for Apollo in 431 B.C. Thus, from the beginning of the fifth century and at least externally, Roman religious life presented a synthesis of Greek, Etruscan, and native elements. With the adoption of Greek sculptural forms for Roman gods came the acceptance of Greek mythology, which served to enrich the growing body of Roman religious ideas. Roman deities were identified with their closest Greek equivalents and acquired corresponding myths and forms of artistic representation.

Even later Etruscan and Greek rites were introduced. After the capture of Veii the cult of Juno Regina practiced in that city was brought to Rome in 392 and worshipped with a Greek ritual. In 291 a new Greek cult was established officially at Rome with the erection of a temple to Aesculapius (Asklepios), the god of healing, whose worship was introduced directly from Epidaurus in Greece, upon recommendation of the Sibylline Books, which were said to have urged this step as the means of checking a pestilence then raging in Rome.

RELIGION AND MORALITY. From the foregoing sketch it will be seen that Roman religion did not exert profound moral or inspirational influences. The early Romans asked their gods to grant them material rather than spiritual blessings, to grant them health and wealth rather than virtue. Its hold upon the people was chiefly due to the fact that it symbolized the unity of groups whose members participated in the same worship, i.e., the unity of family and state. Nevertheless, the idea of obligation inherent in the Roman conception of the relation between gods and men and the stress laid upon the exact performance of ritual inevitably developed a strong sense of duty, a considerable moral factor, and the power of precedent and tradition in their religion helped to develop and strengthen their characteristic conservatism.

CHAPTER 8
CONQUEST OF THE
MEDITERRANEAN.
FIRST PHASE—
THE STRUGGLE WITH
CARTHAGE: 264–201 B.C.

For the period from 264 to 133 B.C. there is a sound chronology and a historical tradition which is both detailed and, in the main, dependable. Roman historical writing began about 200 B.C. and from that time steadily increased in volume along with the development of literary taste and historical interest among educated classes. Not content with presenting annalistic narratives of the more remote past from the scanty materials at their disposal, Roman writers composed contemporary histories, for which they had more abundant and reliable information. Greek historians also devoted considerable attention to Rome, particularly its relationship to the Greek world. The works of most writers of this period have been lost, but the substance of their contributions has been preserved by historians of later date. The only one of the earlier writers whose work has survived to any considerable degree in its original form is the Greek Polybius, the foremost historian of his age. Brought to Rome as a political exile from Achaea in 167, he enjoyed the close friendship of leading Romans of his day and gained a keen insight into Roman political life. He wrote an account of the establishment of Roman supremacy throughout the Mediterranean between 220 and 145, prefaced by a brief survey of the period 264 to 220. But only his first five books reaching to 216 have come down to us intact; of the rest, nothing remains but excerpts. For other substantial

[96]

accounts of the period we have to turn to writers of much later date. The most important of these is the Roman historian Livy (59 B.C.–A.D. 17), whose narrative of the years 218 to 167 B.C., contained in books 21 to 45 of his great history of Rome, has been preserved. In the biographies written by Cornelius Nepos and Plutarch and in the historical works of the Greeks, Diodorus the Sicilian and Appian, there is much valuable information derived from the missing portions of Polybius and the lost works of other early writers.

I. CARTHAGE AND HER EMPIRE

ROME A WORLD POWER. With the unification of Italy Rome entered upon a new era in her foreign relations. She was now one of the great Mediterranean powers and was inevitably drawn into world politics. No longer indifferent to events outside Italy, she assumed new responsibilities, opened up new diplomatic relations, developed a new outlook and new ambitions. At this time the other first-class powers were, in the East, three Hellenistic monarchies —Egypt, Syria, and Macedon—which had emerged from the ruins of the empire of Alexander the Great, and, in the West, the city-state of Carthage. This latter state, dominant in the western Mediterranean world from Sicily to the Strait of Gibraltar, was the determining factor in Rome's foreign policy throughout the remainder of the third century B.C.

Carthage had been founded on the northern coast of Africa near modern Tunis, opposite the western end of Sicily, as a colony of the Phoenician city of Tyre, toward the end of the eighth century B.C.[1] In the sixth century, when the cities of Phoenicia passed first under Babylonian domination and later were incorporated in the Persian Empire, their colonies, among them Carthage, severed political ties with the homeland and were left to defend themselves against surrounding natives.

The weakness of the other Phoenician settlements was the opportunity of Carthage. In the sixth and following centuries she brought them under her control and founded new colonies of her own. She also extended her sway over the native Libyan population nearby. These Libyans were henceforth tributary and obligated to render military service to the Carthaginians, as were dependent Phoenician allies. In the third century the Carthaginian empire included the northern coast of Africa from the Gulf of Syrtis westward beyond the Strait of Gibraltar; the southern and eastern coasts of Spain as far north as Cape Nao; Corsica; Sardinia; and Sicily, with the exception of Messana in the extreme northeast, the Kingdom of Syracuse in the southeast, and a few smaller Greek states that still maintained their independence. The smaller islands of the western Mediterranean were likewise under Carthaginian control.

---

[1] The ancients believed that Carthage was founded in either 825 or 814, but modern archeological research makes the period 725–700 more likely.

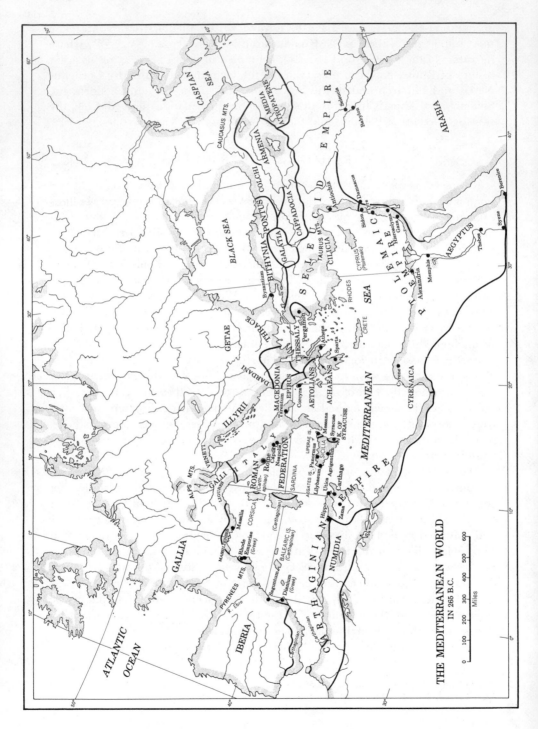

THE MEDITERRANEAN WORLD
IN 265 B.C.

The government of Carthage was republican and strongly aristocratic. There was a primary Assembly for all citizens who could satisfy certain age and property requirements. This body annually elected the two chief magistrates, called suffetes, and the generals. For the former, qualifications of wealth and merit were prescribed. There was also a Senate and a Council, whose organization and powers are uncertain. The Council, the smaller body, prepared the agenda for the Senate. The Senate was consulted by the suffetes on all matters and usually gave the final decision, although the Assembly was supposed to be consulted in case Senate and suffetes disagreed. The suffetes exercised judicial, financial, and religious functions and presided over the Council and Senate. The aristocracy was a group of families whose fortunes, made in commercial ventures and invested in estates, were handed down for generations in the same houses. From this circle came the Council and Senate, which directed state policy. The aristocracy was split into factions, struggling to control the offices and through them public policy, which they frequently subordinated to their own interests.

The prosperity of Carthage depended on her empire and the maintenance of a commercial monopoly in the western Mediterranean and the Atlantic north and south of the Strait of Gibraltar. This policy of commercial exclusiveness made Carthage oppose Greek colonialism in Spain, Sardinia, and Sicily and led to treaties which placed limits on the trading ventures of the Romans and their allies and of the Greeks from Massilia and her colonies in Gaul and northern Spain.

Such a policy could only be maintained by a strong naval power, and Carthage was mistress of the seas west of the Strait of Messana. The Carthaginians were expert shipbuilders, and their powerful fleet was manned by highly trained crews of citizen rowers and sailors. Unlike Rome, Carthage had no organized national army but relied upon mercenaries recruited from all quarters of the Mediterranean, among such warlike peoples as the Gauls, Spaniards, Libyans, Greeks, and Italians. Generally speaking, these mercenary armies served Carthage well throughout its history. They made up in experience what they occasionally lacked in discipline. When properly led and promptly paid, they were equal in fighting capacity to the armies fielded by the enemies of Carthage.[2]

This was the state Rome now faced, having conquered South Italy, and it was the first power she was to challenge in a war for dominion beyond the peninsula. Until shortly before the outbreak of hostilities, relations between the two powers had been good. The trade treaties they made with each other in 508 and 343 suggest that there were no economic reasons to disturb the peaceful relations they enjoyed. A third treaty, concluded in 279, provided for military

---

[2] The Carthaginians were known to the Romans as *Poeni*, i.e., Phoenicians, whence comes the adjective "Punic," used in such phrases as the "Punic Wars."

cooperation against Pyrrhus, but this alliance ended after the defeat of the latter; and with the removal of the common enemy a feeling of mutual suspicion seems to have arisen between the erstwhile allies.

II. THE FIRST PUNIC WAR: 264–241 B.C.

ORIGINS OF THE WAR. The first war between Rome and Carthage arose out of the political situation in Sicily. There the town of Messana was occupied by the Mamertini, a band of Campanian mercenaries, who had been in Syracusan service, deserted, and seized this town about 284. Because of their perpetual brigandage, they were a menace to their neighbors, the Syracusans. Now under an energetic ruler, King Hiero, the Syracusans blockaded Messana in 265, and its ultimate capture seemed certain. The Mamertini, without realizing the possible consequences of their action, appealed for help both to Rome and Carthage, since either power might be interested in humbling a city recently allied with Pyrrhus. A Carthaginian naval commander who happened to be near Messana with his squadron accepted their request and introduced a garrison into the town. The appeal to Rome arrived after this development and placed the Senate in a quandary. Even though the Mamertini were not exactly the kind of friends Rome might wish to have, it was traditional Roman policy to accept as allies any weaker power that appealed for her protection.

The Senate realized that to grant this request might lead to war with Carthage, but it also recognized that Carthaginian occupation of Messana would give Carthage control of the strait and constitute a threat to southern Italy. The more conservative senators may well have feared that a war would aid the careers of new men of talent from the plebeian class who would attain the higher magistracies, thus enlarging the plebeian senatorial aristocracy. But this very prospect may have appealed to those who advocated interference in Sicily regardless of the consequences. The strength of these conflicting considerations made the Senate unwilling to assume responsibility for a decision, and the matter was apparently referred to the Centuriate Assembly. Although allegedly the people were war-weary and had no enthusiasm for another conflict, they were persuaded to approve the alliance with the Mamertini by the consul, Appius Claudius Caudex, who wished to distinguish himself in a military campaign. Claudius especially emphasized the rich booty a Sicilian war might provide the people.

A consular army of two legions was levied to relieve Messana, and an advance force made its way into the harbor despite the presence of the Carthaginian fleet in the strait. Thereupon the Mamertini, apparently having reconsidered their position, decided that Roman protection was preferable to Carthaginian and compelled the Punic garrison to withdraw. At Carthage, the government decided to recover Messana. An army was sent for that purpose into Sicily, Hiero of Syracuse was won over to a Carthaginian alliance, and both parties joined in blockading the city. The main Roman force crossed over from Rhegium to Messana, and its commander, after some futile negotiations, attacked and defeated Hiero and the Carthaginians in turn. Messana was saved, but Rome was now at war with both Carthage and Syracuse.

On the basis of surviving evidence it is difficult to decide the question of "war guilt." Against the Romans it may be said that their fears of Carthaginian occupation of Messana as a threat to Italy were exaggerated. Carthage apparently regarded Roman occupation of the city as interference in her sphere of influence. On the analogy of recent developments in Italy, Carthage could expect that Roman "protection" of Messana would lead to eventual incorporation in the Roman state. This she was determined to prevent.

WAR IN SICILY: FIRST PHASE, 263–256 B.C. The next year the Romans sent a large army into Sicily to fight against Hiero. Their initial attacks were so successful that the king became alarmed. Given the opportunity of making peace upon paying an indemnity, he abandoned the Carthaginians and concluded an alliance for fifteen years with Rome.[3] Aided by Hiero, the Romans besieged the strongly fortified city of Agrigentum, a Greek town on the south coast of the island, which sided with Carthage and had received a Carthaginian garrison. When Agrigentum fell in 262, the Romans determined to drive the Carthaginians out of Sicily.

Roman operations, however, were conducted only at considerable risk, and the coasts of Italy remained exposed to continued raids as long as Carthage controlled the sea. This resulted from the Romans' traditional aversion to the sea and their consequent lack of interest in naval affairs. They had apparently felt no need for any naval organization at all until 311 B.C., when they built twenty triremes, manned by allies. Even this modest navy was maintained only intermittently and was allowed to fall into complete decay after the Pyrrhic War, when the Romans relied on a squadron of triremes supplied by Italian allies. By 261 they realized the absolute necessity of building a large fleet on modern lines that could challenge Carthaginian naval supremacy. This was a turning point in the war. According to tradition, they took as their model a stranded Carthaginian warship and constructed 120 vessels, of which 100 were quinqueremes,[4] the regular first-class battleship of the day. The complement of each quinquereme was 270 rowers and 120 fighting men. With this armament, and some vessels provided by Roman allies, the consul, Gaius Duilius, put to sea in 260 and engaged the superior Carthaginian fleet off Mylae on the north coast of Sicily. Although the Carthaginian seamen were superior to the Roman and could maneuver their ships more speedily and skillfully, the Romans offset this advantage by employing a device at one time used by the Greeks. Whenever

---

[3] This alliance was renewed on a permanent basis in 248 B.C.

[4] The trireme had a total crew of 200 men; the oars were banked in threes and each man manipulated one oar. The quinquereme was propelled by large oars each manned by five rowers with a single bank of oars on each side.

a hostile ship came close enough to ram or board a Roman, the latter dropped a crane armed with long spikes upon the opponent's deck. By thus grappling the enemy, they enabled legionaries, serving as marines, to board Carthaginian ships and capture them in hand-to-hand fighting. The Romans thus neutralized superior Carthaginian seamanship by converting sea battles into land warfare. The Roman victory was as decisive as it was unexpected. As a result they occupied Corsica and attacked Sardinia in the next year; and, since they found it impossible to force a decision in Sicily, they were in a favorable position for attacking Carthage in Africa.

ROMAN INVASION OF AFRICA: 256–255 B.C. Another naval victory, off Ecnomus on the south coast of Sicily in 256, cleared the way for the successful landing in Africa of an army under the consul Marcus Atilius Regulus. He defeated the Carthaginians so severely that they sought to make peace. A peace honorable to both sides might have been made then and there, but Regulus, overconfident and unimaginative, imposed such impossibly harsh terms that the Carthaginians decided to resume hostilities. At this juncture there arrived at Carthage, with other mercenaries, a Spartan soldier of fortune, Xanthippus, who reorganized the Carthaginian army. Early the next year he offered battle, and by skillful use of cavalry and war elephants he inflicted a crushing defeat on the Romans and took Regulus prisoner. A Roman fleet rescued the remnants of the expedition but was almost totally lost in a storm off the southern Sicilian coast.

WAR IN SICILY: SECOND PHASE, 254–241 B.C. The Romans again concentrated their efforts against Carthaginian strongholds in Sicily, which they attacked by land and sea. In 254 they took the city of Panormus, and the Carthaginians were soon confined to the western extremity of the island. There they successfully maintained themselves in Drepana and Lilybaeum. Meanwhile the Romans encountered a series of disasters on the sea. In 253 they lost 150 ships on the voyage from Lilybaeum to Rome, in 250 the consul Publius Clodius suffered a severe defeat in a naval battle at Drepana, and in the next year a third fleet was destroyed by a storm off Phintias in Sicily.

In 247 a new Carthaginian general, Hamilcar Barca, took command in Sicily and infused fresh life into the Carthaginian forces. From the citadel of Hercte first, and later from Eryx, he continually harassed the Romans in Sicily and on the coast of Italy. Finally in 242, when their public treasury was too exhausted to build another fleet, the Romans by private subscription equipped 200 vessels, which blockaded Lilybaeum and Drepana. A Carthaginian relief expedition was destoyed off the Aegates Islands, and it was impossible for their forces, now completely cut off in Sicily, to prolong the struggle. Carthage had to make peace in 241.

PEACE AND ITS CONSEQUENCES. Carthage surrendered to Rome her remaining possessions in Sicily and adjacent islands, besides agreeing to pay an indemnity of 3,200 talents (about 200,000 pounds of silver) in twenty years. For the Romans the long struggle had been very costly. At sea alone they and their allies had lost some 500 ships and 200,000 men. Rome won the war not merely because of her characteristic tenacity and her superior generalship, but largely because in Italy she could tap manpower reserves far larger than those available to Carthage. Furthermore, the Carthaginian fleets never found a satisfactory defense against Roman boarding tactics. The Romans themselves preferred to believe that their victory was due to the superior bravery and discipline of Roman and allied troops, but in reality the war had shown that Roman legionaries were not noticeably better disciplined than properly led Punic mercenaries. As a result of the conflict Carthage had been bled white, she had lost the cornerstone of her empire in Sicily, and she had been replaced by Rome as the dominant power in the western Mediterranean basin.

Weakened as she was, Carthage immediately became involved in a life-and-death struggle with her mercenary troops. Upon their return from Sicily, these troops demanded payment of rewards promised by their general, Hamilcar. When these were refused, they mutinied and, joining with the native Libyans and the inhabitants of the subject Phoenician cities (Libyphoenicians), began a war. After a struggle of more than three years, in which the most shocking barbarities were practiced on both sides and in which they were brought face to face with utter ruin, the Carthaginians, under the leadership of Hamilcar Barca, finally stamped out the revolt (238).

During the war, the Romans showed open sympathy with Carthage. They furnished the city with supplies, which they prevented their allies from selling to the rebels, and even permitted the Carthaginians to recruit troops in Italy. When the Carthaginian garrison in Sardinia revolted and asked the Romans to take over the island, they refused to do so, but after the struggle in Africa came to an end the Roman attitude changed. A Carthaginian force sent to recover Sardinia in 239 mutinied and joined the rebellious garrison. Hard-pressed by the natives, the mutineers sent another appeal for Roman intervention. The Roman Senate reversed its former attitude and made preparations to occupy the island. Carthage protested and proceeded to fit out a new expedition against the mutineers. The Romans interpreted this as a hostile act and declared war. It is difficult to account for the Roman change of policy. In the early stages of the revolt the Romans may have helped Carthage because they mistrusted anarchic or revolutionary movements wherever they occurred. Later, they perhaps did not wish the Carthaginian recovery to proceed too far and mistrusted the ambitions and influence of their old enemy Hamilcar. Perhaps also the Senate had come to feel the natural unity of Italy and adjacent islands and was determined to prevent the occupation of the latter by any foreign power. Carthage could not think of accepting the challenge and bought peace at the price of Sardinia, Corsica, and a penalty of 1,200 talents, but this unjustifiable act of the Romans caused much bitterness. As a result of the acquisition of Sicily, Sardinia, and Corsica, the Tyrrhenian Sea became a Roman lake.

III. THE ILLYRIAN AND GALLIC WARS: 229–219 B.C.

THE FIRST ILLYRIAN WAR: 229–228 B.C.   In assuming control of relations between her allies and foreign states, Rome had assumed responsibility for protecting their interests; and it was the somewhat reluctant fulfillment of this obligation that brought Roman arms to the eastern shores of the Adriatic. Rome's involvement in this area was an important step in the development of her foreign policy. It was here that she extended the principle she had already established in dealing with certain Sicilian cities during the First Punic War— that of association without formal treaty. Rome thus extended the status of patron and protector of weaker client states to areas outside of Italy and Sicily. As a patron her obligations were moral rather than legal and could therefore be interpreted flexibly. Although the client states were technically free to pursue policies of their own, in fact their capacity for independent action depended on Rome's sufferance. In the absence of any written treaties, Rome could judge their actions in the light of her own interest and reward or punish client states accordingly.

Under a king named Agron, an extensive but loosely organized state had been formed among the Illyrians, a semibarbarous people inhabiting the Adriatic coast north of Epirus. These Illyrians were allied with the kingdom of Macedonia and sided with the latter in its wars with Epirus and the Aetolian and Achaean Confederacies. In 231 Agron died and was succeeded by his queen, Teuta, who continued his policy of attacking cities on the west coast of Greece and practicing large-scale piracy in the Adriatic and Ionian Seas. Among those who suffered thereby were the South Italian cities. In 230, as the result of fresh and more serious outrages, they appealed to Rome for redress. The Romans demanded satisfaction from Teuta; and, having their demands contemptuously rejected and one of their ambassadors killed, they declared war.

In the summer of 229 the Romans attacked the Illyrians with a fleet and an army so strong that the enemy could offer little resistance and in the next year was forced to sue for peace. Queen Teuta had to give up her recent conquests in Epirus (Albania) as well as the Greek cities which she had seized on the coast of the Adriatic and Ionian Seas, to promise not to send any armed vessels south of her own territory in Illyria, and to pay an indemnity to Rome. The territory surrendered by Teuta became client states of the type described above. The island of Pharos and some adjacent territory in Illyria were given to a Greek adventurer, Demetrius of Pharos, as a reward for having aided Rome in the war. The cities of Corcyra, Epidamnus, and Apollonia also became clients, neither subject to tribute nor formally accepted by treaty as Roman allies.

The fact that Rome first crossed the Adriatic to fight against the Illyrians aroused the hostility of their ally, Macedonia, the greatest Greek state. Although Macedonia was unable to aid the Illyrians because of dynastic troubles that followed the death of King Demetrius II[5] (229), it regarded with suspicion

---

[5] Not to be confused with Demetrius of Pharos.

Rome's success and the establishment of a Roman sphere of influence east of the Adriatic. Conversely, the war established friendly relations between Rome and the enemies of Macedonia, the Aetolian and Achaean Confederacies, which approved the suppression of Illyrian piracy. The way was thus paved for the participation of Rome, as a partisan of anti-Macedonian forces in the struggles which had so long divided the Greeks.

SECOND ILLYRIAN WAR: 220–219 B.C. The revival of Macedonian influence led indirectly to Rome's second Illyrian war. The alliance of Antigonus Doson, the new king of Macedonia, with the Achaean Confederacy and his conquest of Sparta (222) united almost all Greece under Macedonian suzerainty. Thereupon Demetrius, the client prince whom Rome had established as ruler in his native Pharos but who had gone over to Macedonia, attacked other Illyrian peoples and cities under Roman protection and led a piratical squadron into Greek waters (220). Rome acted with energy to crush a client, who, by believing in his absolute freedom of action, had dared to pursue a foreign policy hostile to that of his patron state. Macedonia, under Philip V, the successor to Antigonus Doson, was involved in a war with the Aetolians and their allies. Deprived of support from this quarter, Demetrius took refuge in Macedonia. His subjects surrendered, and Rome occupied his chief fortresses, Pharos and Dimillos. Having thus taught her Illyrian clients the real meaning of patronage, Rome preferred to maintain her protectorate rather than annex the area directly opposite the heel of Italy on the eastern Adriatic shore. Thereby she retained command of the Strait of Otranto. Although the Romans made no effort to exploit their victory at the expense of Macedonia, Philip regarded their Illyrian protectorate as a menace and made preparations for ousting them from what he considered to be the natural outlet of his country to the Adriatic Sea.

WAR WITH THE GAULS IN NORTH ITALY: 225–222 B.C. In the interval between the two Illyrian wars, Rome became involved in a serious conflict with the Gallic tribes settled in the Po valley. For about half a century the Gauls had lived at peace with Rome, ceasing their raids into the peninsula and becoming a prosperous agricultural and pastoral people. The reasons for the new Gallic incursions are obscure. Probably they were caused by fresh swarms from across the Alps, which some of the Cisalpine Gauls, who had forgotten the defeats of half a century earlier, perhaps invited, and certainly joined, for the sake of plunder. As early as 236 such a band of Transalpines had been brought in by the chieftains of the Boii to aid them in an attack upon Ariminum. But owing to dissensions among the Boii themselves this project came to nothing, and no further inroad into Roman territory was attempted until 225.

In that year a coalition of four Cisalpine tribes, reinforced by large numbers of Transalpine adventurers called Gaesati (spearmen), prepared to invade the peninsula. Both the Romans and their allies were alarmed, for the memory of the Roman defeat at the Allia (387) was still alive. Rome called for a special census of the whole federation. The returns, according to Polybius, showed

over 700,000 infantry and 70,000 cavalry, of whom the Romans accounted for
250,000 foot and 23,000 horse, while the rest belonged to Latin and federate
allies. Two consular armies, each over 50,000 strong, took the field. In addition
the Cenomani, one of the Gallic tribes north of the Po, and the Veneti, joined
the Romans, supplying 20,000 more troops. Expecting the Gauls to advance
southward through Umbria, the Romans stationed one consul with his army
near Ariminum to block their path. The defense of Etruria was entrusted to a
smaller force, and the other consul was sent to Sardinia, possibly in fear of a
Carthaginian attack on that island.

Avoiding the army at Ariminum, the Gauls crossed the Apennines into
Etruria, plundered the country, and defeated the army that had been left to
guard this region. The consul from Ariminum came to the rescue, the army in
Sardinia was recalled, and the Gauls began to withdraw northward to place
their spoils in safety. The Romans followed, and as the army from Sardinia
landed north of the foe and cut off their retreat, the latter were surrounded and
confronted at Telamon. They were annihilated in a desperate struggle won by
Roman tactics and generalship. One of the Roman consuls fell on the battlefield.

Italy was saved, and the Romans decided to follow up their victory by a
conquest of the lands of the Boii and the Insubres, as a penalty for their
conduct and as a guarantee against future invasions. In three hard-fought
campaigns the Romans, although they failed to exterminate or dispossess these
peoples, subjected them, forcing them to surrender part of their territory and
to pay tribute. The Romans suffered heavy losses, and their ultimate success
was largely as a result of the cooperation of the Cenomani.

Between 221 and 219 the Romans extended their area of domination around
the head of the Adriatic as far as the peninsula of Histria by the conquest of
peoples who dwelt to the east of the Veneti. Thus, with the exception of Liguria
and the upper valley of the Po, all Italy south of the Alps was brought within
the Roman sphere. The Latin colonies Placentia and Cremona were founded
in the territory taken from the Insubres to secure this region, but Hannibal's
invasion of 218 found most of the Cisalpine Gauls ready to revolt against the
Romans.

IV. THE SECOND PUNIC WAR: 218–201 B.C.

CARTHAGINIAN EXPANSION IN SPAIN. Almost immediately after the
loss of Sardinia and Corsica a new field for Carthaginian expansion was opened
in Spain. The initiative was taken by Hamilcar Barca, victor in the mercenary
war, who saw in this quarter an opportunity for repairing Punic fortunes and
compensating Carthage for the loss of the islands. Carthaginian interest in
Spain dated from the latter part of the sixth century B.C., when Carthage
conquered Tartessus on the southern coast and closed the Strait of Gibraltar

to foreign ships. Older Phoenician settlements in this region, such as Gades, became subject to Carthage, as did some of the neighboring Iberian tribes. From her Spanish territory, Carthage obtained much silver, copper, and iron, besides foodstuffs and fish. Tin from England and gold and ivory from the west coast of Africa were brought to the Mediterranean by the sailors of Gades, who made regular Atlantic voyages. This early Carthaginian empire was overthrown by the ancient rivals of Carthage, the Greeks of Massilia, together with some of the Iberians. Gades, however, and the strait remained in Carthaginian hands.

In 237, Hamilcar, then commander of Libya, invaded Spain, where he found the Phoenician subjects of Carthage hard pressed by native Iberians. By skillful generalship and able diplomacy he extended Carthaginian dominion over many Spanish tribes and built up a strong army, devoted to him and his family. Roman tradition accused Hamilcar of nursing an undying hatred toward Rome and interpreted his Spanish conquests as part of a carefully laid plan to develop the military strength of Carthage to a point where she could avenge her defeats of the First Punic War. His actions, however, do not seem to indicate any planned resumption of the conflict with the victorious enemy. A Roman mission sent in 231 to investigate his actions returned satisfied that he was merely seeking new resources to pay off Punic indemnity to Rome.

When Hamilcar was drowned during the siege of a Spanish town in 229, he was succeeded in command by his son-in-law Hasdrubal, who carried on his program and founded New Carthage (Cartagena) to serve as the Punic center in Spain. Although Hamilcar may have begun his Spanish campaigns without authorization from the Carthaginian Senate, his policy there, like that of Hasdrubal, was supported by a substantial faction in that body. The annual revenue of from 2,000 to 3,000 talents derived from Spanish silver mines may have been a potent factor in inducing the Carthaginians to acquiesce in the regal position that the Barcidae enjoyed in Spain.

The Carthaginian advance in Spain alarmed the Greeks of Massilia, and of their Spanish colonies, Emporiae and Rhode, whose commerce and independence were endangered. Friendship with the Massiliots had been the cornerstone of Rome's western policy, since they had traditionally been her eyes and ears in Gaul and Spain. They are said to have contributed to the ransom which the Romans paid the Gauls in 387, and they surely secured the intervention of Rome at this time on their own behalf. In 226 the Romans sent an embassy to Hasdrubal and concluded a treaty which prohibited him from waging war north of the river Ebro but allowed him a free hand to the south even at the expense of the interests of Massilia. The terms of the treaty do not indicate that Rome was disquieted over the consolidation of Carthaginian power in Spain, and Hasdrubal did nothing to provoke hostilities. At this time the Romans were too alarmed by the impending Gallic invasion to be concerned very seriously with remote Spain.

ROMAN ALLIANCE WITH SAGUNTUM. A possible cause of future friction lay in Rome's relations with the port of Saguntum, a town south of the Ebro. At some uncertain date, probably after the treaty with Hasdrubal, the Saguntines requested Roman protection. The Senate granted an alliance without a formal treaty, which meant the extension of Roman influence into Spain and which probably violated the spirit, if not the letter, of the Ebro river treaty. This was but another instance of the increasingly frequent Roman practice of using client states as levers against other, larger states.

HANNIBAL AND ROME. Upon the assassination of Hasdrubal in 221, Hannibal, son of Hamilcar, then in his twenty-fifth year, was appointed to the Spanish command. Soon afterward hostilities broke out between Saguntum and Spanish allies of Carthage who aided Saguntine political exiles. The Romans had recently interfered in the internal politics of Saguntum and helped to bring an anti-Carthaginian faction into power there, and now, fearing Carthaginian attack, the Saguntines appealed to Rome. A Roman commission appeared before Hannibal in 219 and reminded him of the existence of the alliance. Hannibal avoided an immediate conflict by referring the commission to Carthage. By this time, however, it seemed to Hannibal that Saguntum was about to become another Messana, a Roman bridgehead in a properly Carthaginian sphere of interest. Relying on his army and his own military genius, he resolved to consolidate the Punic position in Spain and, calling Rome's bluff, to attack Saguntum.

Having obtained the backing of his government. Hannibal besieged Saguntum in 219 and captured it after eight months. The Romans did nothing to aid the Saguntines, and the Senate obviously was not willing to fulfill its role as patron and go to war in defense of a client state in Spain. Roman inactivity seems to have encouraged Hannibal to embark on a second and even more daring campaign: the conquest of Spain as far north as the Pyrenees, a clear violation of the Ebro river treaty. He mistakenly believed that Rome would tolerate this menacing advance to the north as she had the conquest of Saguntum. In 218 a second Roman embassy appeared at Carthage to demand the surrender of Hannibal and his staff as the price of averting war. The pro-Barcid faction prevailed, and the Carthaginian Senate accepted the responsibility for the act of their general, whatever its consequences. The Roman ambassador then declared war.

The First Punic War had destroyed the maritime supremacy of Carthage, which never subsequently contested Rome's dominion of the sea, and consequently, while extending her empire in Spain and Africa, she had not rebuilt her navy, a fact of decisive importance in the coming struggle. The dominant faction in the Roman Senate, led by the Aemilian and Scipionic clans[6] responsible for the declaration of war and the conduct of the opening campaigns

---

[6] On factional politics within the senatorial oligarchy, see pp. 137ff.

until 216, relied on Carthaginian naval weakness and planned an offensive war. One army, under the consul Publius Cornelius Scipio, was to proceed to Spain, supported by the fleet of Massilia, and pin down Hannibal there, while a second army, under the other consul, Tiberius Sempronius Longus, assembled in Sicily to embark for Africa.

The Romans, however, had not taken into account the military genius of Hannibal, who realized that the best defense of Carthage and his Spanish base was an attack on Italy. He knew that he could not transport his army to Italy by sea; and since he was already in northern Spain when Rome had declared war (May–June, 218), it seemed best to cross the Pyrenees, traverse southern Gaul, and to descend on Italy via the Alps. Among the Gauls of the Po valley he hoped to find recruits and he expected that, once in Italy, Roman allies would seize this opportunity to recover their independence. Strategic and military problems preoccupied Hannibal, and he seems to have paid little attention to ultimate war aims other than defeating Rome and/or concluding a quick peace. Eventually he seems to have planned to destroy Roman hegemony in Italy and to reduce the Roman state to the limits attained in 340. In the long run this would have been the same as destroying Rome, since it would have made her politically insignificant, a prey to the ambitions of other Italian states.

INVASION OF ITALY. Late in the spring of 218 Hannibal forced a passage of the Pyrenees, leaving the passes under guard and resuming his march with a picked army of Spaniards and Numidians. His brother Hasdrubal[7] was left in Spain to collect reinforcements and follow with them. Hannibal arrived at the Rhone and crossed it by the time Scipio reached Massilia on his way to Spain. The latter, failing to force Hannibal to fight on its banks, returned to Italy but sent his army, under the command of his brother, to Spain—a decision which had the most serious consequences for Carthage. Meanwhile Hannibal continued his march and, overcoming the intransigent opposition of Alpine peoples whose territory he traversed, as well as the obstacles of bad roads, dangerous passes, cold, and hunger, crossed the Alps and descended into the north Italian plain in the autumn of 218, after a march of five months.[8] His army, perhaps originally 40,000 strong, was reduced to 20,000 infantry and 6,000 cavalry. Two thirds of his elephants had perished.

Hannibal found support and an opportunity to rest his troops among the Insubres and the Boii, the latter having already taken up arms against the Romans. At the news of his arrival in Italy, Sempronius was recalled from Sicily; but Scipio, who had anticipated him, ventured to attack Hannibal with his own forces. He was beaten in a skirmish at the river Ticinus, and

---

[7] Not to be confused with his namesake, Hamilcar's son-in-law.

[8] Authorities differ as to the pass which Hannibal used in crossing the Alps, arguing variously for the Little St. Bernard, Mont Genèvre, or Mont Cenis. Polybius, the best authority, seems to indicate Mont Cenis.

Hannibal was able to cross the Po. On the arrival of Sempronius, both consuls attacked the Carthaginians at the Trebia, only to receive a crushing defeat (December, 218). Hannibal then began his attempt to detach Roman allies by releasing his Italian prisoners to carry word to their cities that he would free them.

Hannibal wintered in north Italy and in the spring, with an army raised to 50,000 by the addition of Celtic recruits, invaded the peninsula. The Romans divided their forces, stationing one consul at Ariminum and the other at Arretium in Etruria. Hannibal crossed the Apennines and Etruria, where he surprised and annihilated the army of the consul Flaminius at the Trasimene lake (217). Flaminius himself was slain. This victory was soon followed by another, in which the cavalry of the army of the second consul was cut to pieces. Hannibal then marched into Samnium, ravaging the country as he went.

These defeats caused a temporary eclipse in the influence of the Aemilian-Scipionic faction, and leadership of the war effort now swung over to that more cautious group of senators led by the Fabian clan. The Centuriate Assembly elected as dictator in this emergency the leader of this faction, Quintus Fabius Maximus. Fabius recognized the superiority of Hannibal's generalship and of the Carthaginian cavalry and consequently refused to do battle. He followed the enemy closely and continually threatened an attack, so that Hannibal could not divide his forces to raid and forage. Hannibal penetrated into Campania, however, and thence recrossed the mountains into Apulia, where he established winter quarters. The strategy of Fabius, who received the nickname of Cunctator (the Delayer), had not prevented the enemy from securing supplies and devastating wide areas. It grew so irksome that the Centuriate Assembly violated all precedent in appointing Marcus Minucius, the aggressive master of the horse, as a second dictator. But when Marcus risked an engagement, he was badly beaten, and only prompt assistance from Fabius saved his army.

CANNAE: 216 B.C. Next spring the Romans and Carthaginians faced each other in Apulia. The Romans were led by new consuls, Lucius Aemilius Paullus and Gaius Terentius Varro, who were authorized to risk a decisive battle to protect the territory of Rome's allies. This change of strategy brought on the battle of Cannae, one of the greatest battles of antiquity and the bloodiest of all Roman defeats. Here the Roman and allied forces lost perhaps 30,000 men killed and missing, half of them Roman. At Cannae the consummate military genius of Hannibal was displayed, and his masterly tactics on this occasion have found admirers and imitators among the great commanders of subsequent ages. Knowing that the Romans would try to crush his troops by a frontal attack, he drew up his infantry with their center of Gauls and Spaniards thrown well forward. Under pressure of the Roman assault, these troops retreated while the wings, where the Libyan infantry were posted, held firm until the line became a crescent with the Romans crowded between its encircling horns. Meanwhile, the Carthaginian cavalry routed the Roman horsemen on both flanks and, turning back from pursuit, attacked the legions from the rear. Surrounded on all sides and thrown into confusion, the Romans were cut down. The consequences of the battle were serious. For the first time Rome's allies showed signs of disloyalty. About half of Rome's allies in Italy either defected to or were conquered by Hannibal. Under the circumstances these were surprisingly few, but such behavior was sufficient to frighten the Romans and to induce them on occasion to institute a reign of terror when they recaptured disloyal cities. In Apulia and in Bruttium Hannibal found many adherents. Ambassadors from Philip of Macedon appeared at his headquarters, the prelude to an alliance in the next year. Syracuse also wavered after the death of Hiero, the friend of Rome, and finally went over to Carthage. Most serious of all, Capua, the second city of Italy, defected to Hannibal.

Still the Romans never wavered. In 214 they lowered the property qualification for military service to 4,000 *asses* and, it seems, enrolled even the landless to fill their depleted ranks. In what was perhaps the most important decision of the war, they decided to persevere in their Spanish campaign when the temptation was strong to withdraw all available forces to Italy. Hannibal, having to maintain a small army in a hostile country, was on the march continually and could not undertake siege operations, for which he also lacked engines of war. Thus the Romans, avoiding pitched battles, were able to reduce systematically the towns which yielded to Hannibal and to hamper seriously the provisioning of his forces. At the same time they still held command of the sea, kept up their offensive in Spain, and held their ground against Carthaginian attacks in Sicily and Sardinia.

ROMAN RECOVERY. In 213 the Romans invested Syracuse. The Syracusans, with the aid of engines of war designed by the physicist Archimedes, resisted desperately, but the general Marcellus pressed the siege vigorously, and treachery caused the city to fall (211). Syracuse was sacked, its art treasures looted, and it became subject and tributary to Rome. In Italy, although the consul Tiberius Sempronius Gracchus was surprised and killed and Hannibal occupied the cities of Tarentum (without its citadel), Heraclea, and Thurii, he could not prevent the Romans from besieging Capua. The next year he tried to force them to raise the blockade by a sudden incursion into Latium, where he appeared before the walls of Rome. But Rome was garrisoned, the army besieging Capua was not recalled, and Hannibal's march was in vain. Capua was starved into submission, its nobility put to the sword, its territory confiscated, and its municipal organization dissolved (211).

After allying with Hannibal, Philip of Macedon attacked the Roman possessions in Illyria, but failed to take Corcyra or Apollonia, which were saved by the Roman fleet. Rome's command of the sea prevented his lending any effective aid to his ally in Italy. Before long the Romans were able to induce the Aetolians to ally with them and attack Macedonia. Thereupon other enemies of Philip, among them Sparta and King Attalus of Pergamon, joined the war on the side of Rome. Although the Achaean Confederacy supported Philip, the coalition against him was so strong that he stopped attacking Roman territory. Rome was able to support her Greek allies with a small fleet, while she devoted her energies to other theaters of war.

THE SCIPIOS IN SPAIN: 218–209 B.C.   The fall of Capua was most opportune for the Romans, since reinforcements were immediately needed in Spain. The army sent there in 218 under Gnaeus Scipio, who obtained a foothold north of the Ebro, was joined the next year by another under his brother Publius Cornelius Scipio. The Romans then crossed the Ebro and invaded Carthaginian dominions to the south. A revolt of the Numidian prince Syphax caused the recall of Hasdrubal to Africa, and the Romans were able to capture Saguntum and induce many Spanish tribes to desert the Punic cause, but upon the return of Hasdrubal and the arrival of reinforcements from Carthage, her commanders united their forces and were able to crush the two Roman armies (211). Both Scipios fell in battle, and the Carthaginians recovered all their territory south of the Ebro. They were unable to capitalize on their Spanish success, however, because of dissension among their generals.

Despite these disasters, the Romans determined to continue their efforts to conquer Spain because it was a recruiting ground for Punic armies and because continuance of the war there prevented reinforcements being sent to Hannibal. In 210, dissatisfied with the cautious strategy of the propraetor Nero, then commanding north of the Ebro, the Senate dispatched a more aggressive commander from the Scipionic group, Publius Cornelius Scipio, son of the like-named ex-consul who had fallen in 211. Although he had won fame already as a military tribune, he was only in his twenty-fifth year and, having filled no magistracy except the aedileship, was technically disqualified from exercising the *imperium*. The Centuriate Assembly therefore had to pass a special law, which appointed him to the command in Spain with the rank of a proconsul. This is the first instance of the conferment of *imperium* upon a private citizen.

Since the armies of his opponents were divided in widely separated winter quarters, Scipio took the offensive, crossed the Ebro, and daringly seized the chief Carthaginian base, New Carthage (209). Here he found vast stores of supplies and, more important, hostages from the Spanish peoples subject to Carthage. His liberation of them and his generous treatment of the Spaniards in general so contrasted with oppressive Punic measures that he rapidly won over both their enemies and adherents. In preparation for future campaigns he drilled his troops in intricate maneuvers and rearmed them with the finely tempered Spanish sword, adapted to cutting as well as thrusting, in place of the shorter Roman sword used solely for thrusting.

HASDRUBAL'S MARCH TO ITALY: 208–207 B.C.   Meanwhile in Italy the Romans proceeded steadily with the reduction of strongholds taken by Hannibal. Tarentum was recovered in 210, and although Hannibal defeated and slew the consuls Gnaeus Fulvius (210) and Marcus Marcellus (208), his forces were so diminished that his campaign depended on the arrival of strong reinforcements. Since his arrival he had received but insignificant additions to his army from Carthage, whose energies had been directed to other theaters. Up to this time also Roman activities in Spain had prevented Punic troops leaving that country. After the fall of New Carthage and the subsequent successes of Scipio, Hasdrubal had to decide whether to face the Romans in Spain or to leave for Italy to support his brother. He courageously chose the latter course, and, although he was defeated by Scipio, he saved the bulk of his forces, eluded pursuit, and crossed the Pyrenees (208).

Next spring he arrived among the Gauls of the Po valley. Reinforced by them, he marched into the peninsula to join Hannibal. The Romans divided their forces to prevent this. The consul Gaius Claudius faced Hannibal in Apulia, while Marcus Livius went to intercept Hasdrubal. Through the capture of messengers from the latter, Claudius learned of his position. Leaving part of his army to detain Hannibal, he withdrew the rest in secret and joined his colleague Livius. Together they attacked Hasdrubal at the Metaurus; his army was cut to pieces and he himself slain. With this battle Hannibal's doom and that of Carthage were sealed. Hannibal himself recognized that all was lost and withdrew into the mountains of Bruttium. Although in 205 Hannibal's other brother Mago landed another army in Liguria, he failed to accomplish anything of importance and was recalled in 203.

END OF THE WAR IN SPAIN AND GREECE. For the first time the Romans could look forward with confidence to the issue of the war. In the two years (207–206) following the death of Hasdrubal, Scipio completed the conquest of Punic Spain. In 205 he assumed the consulship in Rome and then went to Sicily to prepare for the invasion of Africa, since the Romans were now able to carry out their plan of 218, which Hannibal had interrupted.

At the same time the Romans were free from any embarrassment from Macedonia. In Greece the war dragged on without any decided advantage for either side until 207, when the temporary withdrawal of the Roman fleet enabled Philip and the Achaean Confederacy to win such successes that their opponents listened to the intervention of the neutral states and made peace (206), as the Romans did the next year.

THE CAMPAIGN IN AFRICA: 204–202 B.C. In 204 Scipio transported his army to Africa. At first he could do nothing before the combined forces of the Carthaginians and the Numidian chief, Syphax, who had renewed his alliance with them. In the following year, however, he routed both armies decisively, captured and deposed Syphax, and set up in his place a rival chieftain, Masinissa, whose adherence to the Romans brought them welcome superiority in cavalry. The Carthaginians now asked for peace, and an armistice was granted. Hannibal and all Punic forces were recalled from Italy, and the preliminary terms of peace were drawn up (203). Hannibal left Italy with the remnant of his veterans after campaigns that established his reputation as one of the world's greatest generals. For nearly fifteen years he had maintained himself in enemy country with greatly inferior forces. Now, after inflicting many defeats and never losing a major battle, he was forced to withdraw because he lacked resources, not because of the superior generalship of his foes. Before leaving Italy he set up a record of his exploits in the temple of Hera Lacinia in Bruttium, which survived to be read by the historian Polybius.

Hannibal's arrival in Carthage meant the return to power of the more intransigent and aggressive faction in the government bent on continuing the war. Consequently, the Carthaginians broke the armistice by attacking Roman transports and refused to meet Scipio's demand for an explanation. Thereupon hostilities were resumed. At Zama (202), the final battle of the war, Scipio applied the tactics of encirclement which he had learned from Hannibal and adapted to Roman military formations. Hannibal anticipated such a maneuver and checkmated it by a proper disposition of his own forces. In spite of this, the retreat of the Carthaginian mercenaries at a critical moment and the timely return of Roman and Numidian cavalry from pursuit of the routed Carthaginian horse resulted in a complete victory for Scipio.

PEACE: 201 B.C.   Zama did not decide the outcome of the war, which Carthage had already lost, but it did determine the kind of peace terms that Rome would impose. These were the surrender of all territory except the city of Carthage and the surrounding country in Africa, an indemnity of 10,000 talents, the surrender of all warships except ten triremes, and of all war elephants, and the obligation not to make war anywhere without Rome's consent. The Numidians were united in a strong state on the Carthaginian borders, under the Roman ally Masinissa. Scipio returned to Rome in triumph and received, from the scene of his victory, the name of Africanus.

V. EFFECT OF THE SECOND PUNIC WAR UPON ITALY

The destruction of the Carthaginian empire left Rome mistress of the western Mediterranean and by far the greatest power of the time. This victory had been attained, however, only after a tremendous struggle, probably the greatest the ancient world ever witnessed, which called forth in Rome the patriotic virtues of courage, devotion, and self-sacrifice to a degree that drained her resources of men and treasure and aroused the admiration of subsequent generations.

One of the main factors in deciding the issue was Roman command of the sea, which Carthage never challenged seriously. Another was the larger citizen body of Rome and the basic friendliness between herself and her federate allies. This, with the system of universal military service, gave her a citizen soldiery superior in morale and numbers to the armies of Carthage. As long as Hannibal was in Italy, Rome kept close to 100,000 men under arms, perhaps 10 per cent of the free population. Once only, after Cannae when she had to arm the proletariat and even 8,000 slaves who were promised freedom as a reward for faithful service, was she unable to replace her losses by the regular system of recruiting. On the other hand, Carthage raised her forces from mercenaries or from subject allies. As her resources dwindled, the former became even more difficult to obtain, while the demands made upon the latter caused revolts difficult to subdue. It required the personality of a Hannibal to develop an *esprit de corps* and discipline such as characterized his army in Italy. A third factor was the absence in the Roman commanders of the rivalries and lack of cooperation which so greatly hampered the Carthaginians in Spain and Sicily. The Romans overcame the disadvantage of the annual change of commanders in chief by the use of the proconsulship and propraetorship often long prorogued, so that officers of ability year after year retained command of the same armies. This system enabled them to develop such able generals as Marcellus and the Scipios.

The cost of maintaining her fleet and her armies taxed the financial resources of Rome to the utmost, and at times the government had to use extraordinary measures to prosecute the war. In 216 a loan of money and supplies for the army in Sicily was sought and obtained from Hiero of Syracuse. The next year, to maintain the armies in Spain it was necessary to appeal to the patriotism and generosity of several companies of contractors, who agreed to furnish supplies at their own expense upon promise of repayment as soon as the treasury was again in funds. In 214, when there was pressing need to outfit a navy to meet the rebellion in Sicily, a special "liturgy" or public obligation was laid on the wealthy, who had to furnish the cost of rowers out of their private resources. Four years later senators voluntarily contributed gold and silver for a similar purpose. In 209 the government had to tap the reserve fund accumulating in the treasury for thirty years from the returns of the 5 per cent tax on the value of manumitted slaves. This fund, known as the "sacred treasury," then amounted to 4,000 pounds of gold. When Scipio was preparing to invade Africa, the state was unable to furnish him with the necessary levies and ships, and with official approval, he had to appeal for volunteers and for donations of money and material.

An additional burden was inflation and the danger of famine, caused by the disturbed conditions in Italy and Sicily and the withdrawal of so many men from farming. In 211 the situation was relieved only by an urgent appeal to Ptolemy Philopator of Egypt, from whom grain had to be purchased at three times the usual price. This crisis passed, however, with the pacification of Sicily the next year.

A heavy tribute had been levied upon the manpower of the Roman state. The wastage of blood in the struggle was undoubtedly reflected in a sharp decline in the number of men eligible for military service,[9] and the federate

---

[9] Rome's estimated manpower potential fell from about 285,000 at the beginning of the war to 235,000 in 203 B.C.

allies must have suffered at least as heavily. In 210, twelve of the Latin colonies refused to supply their quotas of troops, giving as an excuse the exhaustion of manpower. The greatest losses fell upon southern Italy, especially Campania and Bruttium. The devastation there, sometimes described as catastrophic, actually seems to have been localized and temporary, except in Bruttium, which long after remained wilderness.

CHAPTER 9
CONQUEST OF THE
MEDITERRANEAN.
SECOND PHASE—ROME
AND THE GREEK EAST:
200–167 B.C.

I. POLITICAL SITUATION IN THE NEAR EAST IN 200 B.C.

During the thirty-five years after Zama, Rome attained the same dominant position in the eastern Mediterranean that she had won in the West as a result of the Punic Wars. The explanation of Roman interference in the East and the rapid extension of her authority there lies in the political situation of the Hellenistic world at the close of the third century, one which Rome exploited by virtue of her increasingly important role as patron to states east of the Adriatic. To understand this situation it is necessary to survey briefly the character and policy of the more important Hellenistic states: Egypt, the Seleucid Empire, and Macedonia.

EGYPT. In the third century B.C. Egypt, ruled by the Macedonian dynasty of the Ptolemies, comprised the ancient kingdom of Egypt in the Nile valley, Cyrene, Palestine and the coast of southern Syria, Cyprus, and a number of cities on the shores and islands of the Aegean Sea. In Egypt the Ptolemies ruled as foreigners over a subject native population. They maintained their authority by a small mercenary army recruited chiefly from Macedonians and Greeks and by a highly centralized administration staffed by Greeks. Since the ruler owned all the land, the native Egyptians—mostly peasants tilling the rich soil of the Nile valley—were mainly tenants of the crown and the restrictions and obligations to which they were subject made them serfs. A highly developed but oppressive system of taxation and government monopolies, largely an inheritance from previous dynasties, enabled the Ptolemies to wring from their subjects revenues to support a brilliant court at their capital, Alexandria, and to finance their imperial policy.

After 276 this policy aimed to secure Egyptian domination in the Aegean, among the states of southern Greece, and in Phoenicia, whose value lay in the forests of Lebanon. Occupations of the outlying possessions brought Egypt into conflict with Macedonia and the Seleucid Empire, whose rulers made continual efforts to oust the Ptolemies from the Aegean and from Syria. Consequently, the Ptolemies were obliged to support a navy to give them command of the sea in the eastern Mediterranean.

Destruction of the Egyptian fleet by the Macedonians in 242 ended the naval supremacy of the Ptolemies but did not force them to relinquish their territory in Syria and the Aegean. In 217, theatened by a Seleucid invasion, the Egyptian government was forced to arm native soldiers. With this aid the enemy was defeated and the immediate danger averted, but realization of their military importance led to demands by native Egyptians for greater privileges and so to racial difficulties which permanently weakened the dynasty. Internal strife made the Ptolemies helpless to protect their foreign possessions or even to defend Egypt itself against future attacks.

THE SELEUCID EMPIRE. The empire of the Seleucids, known to the Romans as Syria and with its capital at Antioch on the Orontes, was by far the largest of the Hellenistic monarchies in extent and population, and in wealth it ranked after Egypt. It stretched from the Aegean to the borders of India and included southern Asia Minor, Mesopotamia, Persia, and northern Syria. Its very size was a source of weakness because of the distances which separated its various provinces and the heterogeneous ethnic elements it embraced. As in Egypt, dynastic power was upheld by a mercenary army and by the loyalty of many Greek cities founded by Alexander the Great and his successors. These islands of Greek culture did not succeed to any great extent in Hellenizing the native subjects, however, which remained indifferent or hostile to their conquerors. The strength of the empire was sapped by repeated revolts in its eastern provinces and dissensions among the members of the dynasty.

These disintegrating forces temporarily disrupted the empire about 220, but the situation was retrieved by an energetic ruler, Antiochus III. After crushing the revolting governors of Media, Persia, and Asia Minor in a series of successful campaigns (212-204), Antiochus established his authority as far as the borders of India, gaining for himself the surname of "the Great."

MACEDONIA. The kingdom of Macedonia, ruled by the Antigonid house, was the smallest of the three Hellenistic states in extent, population, and resources, but it possessed an internal strength and solidarity lacking in the others. In Macedonia the Antigonids, by preserving the traditional character of the patriarchal monarchy, kept alive the national spirit of the Macedonians, which made them loyal to the dynasty. They also retained a military system that fostered the traditions of the times of Philip II and Alexander and, since the Macedonian people had not lost their martial character, furnished a small but efficient national army. Outside of Macedonia the Antigonids controlled Thessaly and eastern Greece as far south as the Isthmus of Corinth. Their attempts to dominate southern Greece were thwarted by the opposition of the Aetolian and Achaean Confederacies, frequently supported by the Ptolemies. Rivalries among the Greek states eventually brought the Achaeans over to the Macedonian side, and in 222 Macedonia united most of central Greece and the Peloponnesus in a league under her suzerainty. This position was maintained by Philip V in spite of attacks by the Aetolians, Pergamon, and Rhodes during Rome's First Macedonian War (215–206).

In addition to these three great monarchies, there should be noted as powers of some importance the Confederacies of the Aetolians and Achaeans, located respectively north and south of the Gulf of Corinth; the kingdom of Pergamon; and the island republic of Rhodes. Pergamon on the northwestern coast of Asia Minor, lying between Macedonia and the Seleucid Empire, feared any increase in strength by its more powerful neighbors, while Rhodes, at that time the commercial center of the Aegean and a considerable naval power, was inclined to share the fears of Pergamon.

CRISIS OF 202 B.C. The death of Ptolemy IV in 203 placed upon the throne of Egypt an infant who was controlled by corrupt and incapable advisers. Antiochus III, encouraged by his recent triumphs, judged it a favorable moment to renew his attempt to take from Egypt its Syrian provinces. At the same time Philip V of Macedonia, wishing to balance the successes of Antiochus by conquests of his own, unexpectedly attacked and occupied several cities under Aetolian protection on the coast of Thrace and certain islands in the Aegean (202). Later writers claimed that Antiochus and Philip had allied to partition the Ptolemaic empire or at least the territories of the Ptolemies outside of Africa, but this is very doubtful. Philip received an Egyptian embassy requesting his aid against Antiochus and seeking his daughter in marriage for the young king of Egypt, and he seems to have abstained from attacking Ptolemaic possessions in the Aegean before 200. In 201 his activities in the Aegean brought him into conflict with Attalus I of Pergamon, and the Rhodians, who, being unable to check them and fearing a possible alliance between Macedonia and the Seleucid Empire, appealed to Rome for support. Although the action of Philip's allies in Greece had involved him in hostilities with Athens, it does not seem that the Athenians joined in the appeal to the Roman Senate. This step, taken by Pergamon and Rhodes, brought about Roman intervention in the Greek East and led to Rome's Second Macedonian War.

II. THE SECOND MACEDONIAN WAR: 200–196 B.C.

ROME'S EASTERN POLICY TO 201 B.C. Until the year 201 Rome can hardly be said to have had any definite eastern policy. Diplomatic intercourse with Egypt had followed the visit of an Egyptian embassy to Rome in 273, but this had no political consequences. Since then she had fought with the Illyrians and with Macedonia and had established a small protectorate across the Adriatic, but her actions had been spasmodic, brought about by the attacks of the Illyrians and Macedonians on her allies or herself and were not the result of any aggressive policy. The interest and outlook of Rome's agrarian oligarchy did not include Hellas as a whole or the Greek East. This may be seen in the favorable peace terms granted Philip V of Macedonia in 205, by which Rome abandoned her formal alliances with Philip's enemies, especially the Aetolians. This is the first known instance in which Rome failed to fulfill to the letter her written agreements with her friends and marks an important stage in the growing sophistication of her foreign policy. These actions made her very unpopular in Greece. Her erstwhile allies, especially the Aetolians, protested that they had been left in the lurch, while other Greek states felt antagonistic because Rome had permitted the Aetolians to treat them brutally during the recent war. Rome still found it possible to maintain friendly relations, albeit without formal and possibly entangling treaties, with Pergamon, the Illyrians, some city-states of the Peloponnesus, and possibly Athens. Rome's general attitude toward the Greek world in the period 205–201 was watchful rather than disinterested; she had no vital or definite commitments in the area except the defense of her Illyrian clients.

ROMAN INTERVENTION: 200 B.C. A combination of circumstances involving Illyria brought about the Second Macedonian War. After the peace of 205 Philip apparently misread the Roman attitude toward Greece as one of total disinterest and attempted by diplomacy to seduce the Illyrians from their connection with Rome. Just as Rome was observing the Illyrian situation with increasing disquiet in 202, the envoys of Rhodes and of Attalus I, king of Pergamon, arrived to inform the Senate of Philip's aggressions in the East and of his alleged pact with Antiochus to partition the Egyptian Empire. They exaggerated the situation and requested Roman help. The Senate, initially unconcerned with what was going on in the Aegean, but made somewhat fearful by the Rhodian and Pergamene envoys and their account of Macedonian and especially Seleucid expansion, was interested in humbling the king who had stabbed Rome in the back during the recent war with Hannibal and who was now tampering with her Illyrian clients. The Senate, for a number of reasons, but basically because of fear and hatred, decided to make war. It seized upon Philip's aggressions against Attalus as a possible *casus belli*. Roman ambassadors went to Greece in 201/200 to proclaim a basic change in Roman policy—protection of all Greeks against future Macedonian aggression—and to mobilize Greece under the Roman aegis against Philip. They also carried an ultimatum for Philip which they delivered to one of his generals, a demand that he refrain from war with any Greek state and that he submit his differences with Attalus to arbitration. Roman diplomacy leading up to the war shows that at this stage of her history Rome took states unilaterally under her protection without the formality of a treaty and tended to regard her friends not as equals but as clients. The ultimatum revealed Rome's new aims: the reduction of Philip to the status of a client prince and the consequent conversion of Greece into a Roman protectorate. Although the Senate was apparently committed to war when these demands were not met, the Roman people as a whole shrank from fighting another war so soon after the close of the desperate conflict with Carthage. At first the Centuriate Assembly voted against the proposal, and at a second meeting was induced to sanction it only when the people were told they would have to face another invasion of Italy if they did not anticipate Philip's action. When the assembly finally gave its approval, one of the Roman ambassadors whom the Senate had already sent to Greece to threaten Philip and encourage his opponents presented the formal declaration of war to the king, who was at that time besieging Abydos on the Hellespont, whereupon the conflict began. In accordance with their instructions the ambassadors then visited Antiochus in Syria, perhaps to intercede on behalf of Egypt or to assure him of Roman good will so that he might not abandon his Syrian campaign and unite his forces with those of Philip in Macedonia.

DEFEAT OF PHILIP. Late in 200 an army under the consul Sulpicius Galba invaded Illyricum and tried to enter Macedonia. Both in this and in the succeeding year, however, the Romans, although aided by the Aetolian Confederacy, Pergamon, Rhodes, and Athens, were unable to inflict any decisive defeat on Philip or to invade his kingdom.

With the arrival of one of the consuls of 198, Titus Flamininus, the situation speedily changed. The Achaean Confederacy was won over to Rome, and Flamininus forced Philip to evacuate Epirus and to withdraw into Thessaly. In the following winter negotiations for peace were opened. At the insistence of her Greek allies, Rome now demanded not merely a guarantee that Philip would refrain from attacking the Hellenes but also the evacuation of Corinth, Chalcis, and Demetrias, three fortresses known as "the fetters of Greece." Philip refused.

The next year military operations were resumed in Thessaly. Early in the summer a battle was fought on a ridge of hills called Cynoscephalae (the Dogs' Heads), where the Romans won a complete victory. Although the Aetolians rendered valuable assistance in this engagement, the Macedonian defeat was primarily the result of the superior flexibility of the Roman legionary formation ever the phalanx. Philip fled to Macedonia and sued for peace. The Aetolians and his enemies in Greece sought his destruction, but Flamininus realized the importance of Macedonia to the Greek world as a bulwark against the Celts of the lower Danube and would not support them. The terms fixed by the

Roman Senate were autonomy of the Hellenes, in Greece and Asia; evacuation of Macedonian possessions in Greece, in the Aegean, and in Illyricum; an indemnity of 1,000 talents; and the surrender of nearly all his warships. Philip was obliged to accept (196) these conditions. Soon afterwards he became a Roman ally.

PROCLAMATION OF FLAMININUS: 196 B.C. At the Isthmian games of the same year Flamininus proclaimed the autonomy of former Macedonian subjects. The announcement provoked tremendous enthusiasm among most of the Greek states. After spending some time in effecting this policy and in settling the claims of various states, Flamininus returned to Italy in 194, leaving the Greeks to make what they would of their freedom. Rome's interest in Greek freedom was not sentimental, but was rather the natural result of political and strategic considerations growing out of the recent war. Rome was now merely applying throughout Greece a policy that she had previously used in Messana, Saguntum, and Illyricum. If the Greeks were free, from the Roman point of view they enjoyed the freedom of client states, which, as a matter of course, would pursue a foreign policy compatible with Roman interests and which would form a bulwark against any hostile action by Philip or Antiochus.

III. WAR WITH ANTIOCHUS THE GREAT AND THE AETOLIANS: 192–189 B.C.

CAUSES OF FRICTION. Even before Flamininus and his army had left Greece, the activities of Antiochus had awakened the mistrust of the Roman Senate and threatened hostilities. The Syrian king had completed the conquest of Lower Syria in 198. Profiting by the difficulties in which Philip of Macedon was involved, he had then turned his attention toward Asia Minor and Thrace with the hope of recovering the possessions once held by his ancestor, Seleucus I. The Romans were at the time too occupied to oppose him. Outwardly he professed to be a friend of Rome and to be limiting his activities to the re-establishment of his empire. Eventually, in 196, he landed in Europe and took Thrace; the Romans tried unsuccessfully to induce him to withdraw. Two years later Antiochus himself negotiated with the Senate to recognize his claims to Thrace and to certain cities in Asia Minor which, relying upon Roman support, refused to acknowledge his overlordship. Rome, cynically enough, was willing to abandon its self-proclaimed status as protector of the Greeks in Asia if Antiochus would evacuate Thrace. Since Antiochus, although harboring no designs against Rome, refused to be forced out of Europe, he decided to support anti-Roman elements in Greece to make Rome yield the points at issue. Accordingly he willingly received deputations from the Aetolians, the leading opponents of Rome.

The Aetolians, Rome's allies in the war just concluded and greatly exaggerating the importance of their services, were disgruntled because Macedonia had not been dismembered, and they had been restrained from enlarging the territory of the Confederacy at the expense of their neighbors. In short, they wished to replace Macedonia as the leading Greek state. Accustomed to regard war as a legitimate source of revenue, they did not easily reconcile themselves to Rome's imposition of peace. Ever since the battle of Cynoscephalae they had striven to undermine Roman influence among the Greeks, and now they sought to draw Antiochus into war with Rome.

WAR IN GREECE AND ASIA MINOR. In 192 they brought matters to a head by unexpectedly attacking Rome's supporters in Greece and seizing the fortress of Demetrias, which they offered to the king, to whom they also made an unauthorized promise of aid from Macedonia. Trusting in the support promised by the Aetolians, Antiochus sailed to Greece with an advance force of 10,000 men. Upon his arrival the Aetolians elected him their commander. It so happened that Hannibal, forced to flee Carthage in 196 owing to machinations of his enemies and the Romans, was then at the court of Antiochus as a refugee. Although it is sometimes alleged that he advised his protector to invade Italy, it seems likely that he was rather concerned with intrigues that might result in his reinstatement at Carthage. He may even have counseled moderation and tact in Syrian dealings with the Romans. He had little influence over Antiochus after 193, and the Syrian king made no serious use of his talents in the ensuing war.

In 191 a Roman army under the consul Acilius Glabrio appeared in Greece and defeated Antiochus' army at Thermopylae, the king fleeing to Asia. Contrary to his hopes he found little support in Greece. Philip of Macedon and the Achaean Confederacy adhered to the Romans, and the Aetolians were made helpless by an invasion of their own country. The Rhodians and Eumenes, the new king of Pergamon, joined their navies to the Roman fleet.

As Antiochus would not listen to Roman peace terms, Rome invaded Asia Minor. Two naval victories, won with the aid of Rhodes and Pergamon, secured the Aegean, and in 190, a Roman force crossed the Hellespont. The Senate had wished to designate Scipio Africanus as commander, but since he had recently been consul he was now ineligible for that office. The law was circumvented by election of his brother Lucius to the consulate and his assignment to the command, and by the appointment of Africanus as his legate. This arrangement permitted Africanus to assume practical direction of the war.

One decisive victory over Antiochus at Magnesia in the autumn of 190 brought him to terms. He agreed to surrender all territory north of the Taurus mountains and west of Pamphylia, to give up his elephants, to surrender all but ten of his warships, to pay an indemnity of 15,000 talents in twelve annual installments, and to abstain from attacking the allies of Rome. Unlike Carthage, he still could defend himself if attacked. Peace upon these conditions was formally ratified in 188. This time Rome did not "free" the Greeks as she had done in 196, since such an action would have produced too many petty states and future imbroglios. Some Greek city-states did receive their freedom, but

Rhodes and Pergamon were the principal beneficiaries of the peace, which brought them an accession of territory at the expense of neighboring Greeks and non-Greeks alike.

The Romans also demanded the surrender of Hannibal, but Antiochus connived at his escape. Hannibal took refuge with Prusias, the king of Bithynia. In 186 Prusias attacked Rome's ally, Eumenes of Pergamon, and appointed Hannibal as a commander. Hannibal won a naval victory, but Rome intervened on behalf of Eumenes, and Prusias was forced to make peace. Again the Romans insisted on the surrender of Hannibal, and Prusias was not in a position to refuse. Rather than be captured, Hannibal took poison, dying in 182, about a year later than Scipio Africanus, his conqueror at Zama.

THE SUBJUGATION OF THE AETOLIANS: 189 B.C. The Roman campaign of 191 against the Aetolians caused the latter, who were also attacked by Philip of Macedon, to seek terms. The Romans demanded unconditional surrender, and the Aetolians decided to continue the struggle. No energetic measures were taken against them at once, but in 189 the consul Fulvius Nobilior pressed the war vigorously and besieged their chief stronghold, Ambracia. Because obstinate resistance defied all his efforts and because the Athenians were trying to act as mediators in ending the war, the Romans abandoned their demand for unconditional surrender. The Aetolians proved that they had not understood the meaning of clientship, and the Romans were determined that any peace treaty with them should express their dependent status. Peace was finally made on the following conditions: the Aetolian Confederacy was granted a permanent alliance with Rome, with the obligation to support Rome against all her enemies; the Confederacy gave up all territory captured by its enemies during the war; Ambracia was surrendered and sacked; and the Romans occupied the pirate nest of Cephallenia.

IV. THIRD MACEDONIAN WAR: 171–167 B.C.

ROME AND THE GREEK STATES. Although by her alliance with the Aetolians Rome established herself permanently in Greece and in the war with Antiochus claimed to exercise a protectorate over it, the Senate as yet gave no indication of reversing the policy of Flamininus, and the Greek states remained friends of Rome in the enjoyment of political "independence." It was not long, however, before these relations became seriously strained and Rome was induced to embark upon a policy of political and then military interference in Greece, which ultimately put an end to its apparent freedom. The fundamental cause of the change was that, while Rome interpreted Greek freedom to mean liberty of action provided that the wishes and arrangements of Rome were respected, the Greeks understood it to mean the perfect freedom of sovereign communities and resented any infringement of their supposed rights. Under these circumstances, it is easy to see how difficulties arose, inevitably to be settled according to Rome's wishes.

The chief causes for the change in Roman policy are found in the troubles of the Achaean Confederacy and the reviving ambitions of Macedonia. The Confederacy included many city-states which had been compelled to join it and which sought to regain their independence. One such was Sparta, and the policy of the Achaeans toward it in the restoration of Spartan exiles led the Spartans to appeal to Rome. The Roman reaction alienated the Confederacy without settling the problem, and the tendency of the Achaeans to stand on their rights irritated the Romans. Within the Confederacy there developed a pro-Roman party, ready to submit to Roman domination, and a national party determined to assert their right to freedom of action. After 180 the Romans deliberately fostered aristocratic factions throughout Greece, feeling that they were the more stable element and more in harmony with senatorial policy. The democratic factions then began to look for outside support in Macedonia.

Philip V of Macedon considered that the assistance he had furnished to Rome in the Syrian War was proof of his loyalty and warranted the annexation of territory he had overrun in that conflict. The Senate would not allow the power of Macedonia to attain dangerous proportions, and he was forced to forego his claims. Henceforth, bitter toward Rome, he developed his military resources with the ultimate view of challenging once again Rome's authority. At his death in 179 he left an army of from 30,000 to 40,000 men and a treasure of 6,000 talents. His son and successor Perseus inherited his father's anti-Roman policy and established relations with the enemies of Rome everywhere in Greece.

ROMAN ATTACK ON PERSEUS. The Senate was kept abreast of his schemes by his enemies, especially Eumenes II, king of Pergamon, the successor of Attalus I. Therefore it determined to forestall his plans and force him into war. In 172 a Roman commission visited Perseus and required of him concessions which meant loss of liberty. Upon his refusal to comply with their demands, Rome declared war. When success depended on energetic action, Perseus sought to avoid the issue and tried vainly to placate the Romans. In 171 a Roman force landed in Greece and invaded Thessaly. In the campaigns of this and the following year the Roman commanders were too incapable and their troops too undisciplined to make any headway, but Perseus showed no ability to take advantage of his opportunities. Furthermore, by his parsimony he lost the chance to win valuable aid from the Dardanians, Gesatae, and Celts on his borders. Finally, in 168, the Romans found an able general in the consul Aemilius Paullus, who restored morale and won a complete victory over Perseus in the battle of Pydna. Perseus fled but soon was obliged to give himself up. Taken to Rome, where he was treated ignominiously, he died in captivity. The Macedonian kingdom was ended. Its territory was divided into four autonomous republics, which were forbidden mutual privileges of *commercium* and *conubium*. A yearly tribute of 100 talents was imposed; royal mines and domains became Roman property, and, for a time, the gold and silver mines were shut down.

ROMAN SETTLEMENT IN THE EAST. Having disposed of Macedonia, the Romans turned their attention to other Greek states, intending to reward their friends and punish their enemies. During the recent war the Greeks had realized that Perseus' defeat would make Roman power unchallengeable, and consequently anti-Roman parties had arisen everywhere. The situation was worsened, especially in the Peloponnese, by social disorder which added to political strife. Death or exile awaited the leaders of the anti-Roman parties, many of whose names became known from the papers of Perseus. Although the Achaeans had given no positive proof of disloyalty, 1,000 of their leaders, among them the historian Polybius, were carried off to Italy, nominally to be given the chance of clearing themselves before the Senate, but really to be kept as hostages in Italy for the future conduct of the Confederacy.

The Rhodians, because they tried to make peace between Rome and Perseus, were forced to surrender their possessions in Asia Minor despite a speech to the Senate by Cato the Elder, who counseled moderation and common sense. Their commercial prosperity was crippled by the establishment of a free port at the island of Delos. Eumenes of Pergamon, whose actions had made him suspect to Rome, was subjected to humiliation, although he kept his kingdom. In Epirus, seventy towns were sacked and 150,000 of the inhabitants carried off into slavery.

Henceforth it was clear that Rome was sovereign in the eastern Mediterranean and that her friends and allies enjoyed only local autonomy, while expected to be obedient to the orders of Rome. This is well illustrated by the anecdote of the circle of Popilius. During the Third Macedonian War, Antiochus IV, Epiphanes, king of Syria and former Roman hostage, invaded Egypt. After the battle of Pydna a Roman ambassador, Gaius Popilius, was sent to request his withdrawal. Popilius met Antiochus before Alexandria and delivered the Senate's message. The king asked for time to consider, but the Roman, drawing a circle around him in the sand, bade him answer before he left the spot. Antiochus yielded and evacuated Egypt.

The spoils of this war with Macedonia brought such an enormous booty into the Roman treasury that after 167 the war tax on property—the *tributum civium Romanorum*—ceased to be levied. The income of the empire enabled the government to relieve Roman citizens of all direct taxation.

V. CAMPAIGNS IN ITALY AND SPAIN

PACIFICATION OF NORTHERN ITALY. During the Macedonian and Syrian Wars the Romans were busy strengthening and extending their hold upon northern Italy and Spain. Cisalpine Gaul, which had been largely lost to the Romans since Hannibal's invasion, was recovered by wars with the Insubres and Boii between 198 and 191. The great military highway, the *via Flaminia*, built from Rome to Ariminum in 220, was extended under the name of the *via Aemilia* to Placentia by way of Bononia in 187. Another, the *via Cassia*

(171), linked Rome and the Po valley by way of Etruria. New fortresses were established: Bononia (189) and Aquileia (181) as Latin colonies; Parma and Mutina (183) as colonies of Roman citizens. In this way Roman authority was firmly established and the way prepared for the Latinization of land between the Apennines and Alps.

In the same period falls the subjugation of the Ligurians, whose border raids had proved annoying. In successive campaigns, lasting until 172, the Romans gradually extended their sway over various Ligurian tribes until they reached Massilia in southern Gaul. In the process of pacification, 40,000 Ligurians were transplanted from their homes to vacant public lands in South Italy. A Latin colony was founded at Luca (180) and one of Roman citizens at Luna (177). Between 181 and 176 the Sardinian tribes rebelled, and this led to thorough subjugation of that island.

SPAIN. The territory acquired from Carthage in Spain was organized in 197 in two provinces, Hither and Farther Spain. The allied and subject Spanish tribes were not yet reconciled to the Roman occupation, however, and serious revolts broke out. One of these was subdued by Marcus Porcius Cato in 196, another by Lucius Aemilius Paullus between 191 and 189, and a third by Tiberius Sempronius Gracchus in 179 and 178. The settlement effected by Gracchus secured peace for many years. In Spain Rome's first colonies were founded beyond the borders of Italy. Italica, near Seville, was settled in 206, and Carteia in 171, the former as a town (*oppidum*) of Roman citizens, the latter a Latin colony.

CHAPTER 10
THE CRISIS OF ROMAN
EXPANSION: 167–133 B.C.

CLIENT STATES AND PROVINCES. In the East the battle of Pydna marked a decisive turning point in Roman foreign policy. After 168 the entire Hellenistic world was effectively reduced to the status of Roman clients. In the West, Carthage had been reduced to the same status since the Second Punic War, while Spain, where the Senate had attempted direct provincial administration, was restive. Throughout the period 167–133 control of foreign powers through the organization of client states remained the preferred policy of the Senate. This avoided annexation of territory as provinces, which would have meant too great a drain upon the resources of the state and created administrative problems. Only when the client-state system failed to produce the peace and subservience that Rome demanded were provinces formed. Such a failure was evident by mid-century in a crisis originating in wars in Rome's Spanish provinces and spreading to the dependent states when the latter revolted. The Spanish wars were to have important internal repercussions on the state, and the revolts elsewhere forced the Senate to abandon the client system in strategic areas, to annex Carthage and Macedonia, to establish direct control over Greece, and eventually to acquire territory in Asia Minor.

I. THE SPANISH WARS: 154–133 B.C.

REVOLTS OF CELTIBERIANS AND LUSITANIANS: 154–139 B.C. In 154 revolts broke out among the Celtiberians of Hither and the Lusitanians of Farther Spain. The ensuing campaigns, long and bloody, were prolonged by the incapacity and cruelty of Roman commanders. This so-called "Fiery War" was comparable in unpopularity and in its impact on army, government, and society to the modern experience of the French in Algeria and of the Americans in Vietnam. The long pursuit of illusive victory necessitated progressive lowering of property qualifications for military service in order to find levies and occasioned a revival of the initiative of some tribunes in protecting the interests of hard-pressed Roman peasants. In 151 and 138 tribunes actually imprisoned consuls enforcing the draft for the Spanish campaign. The war also exacerbated political strife within the oligarchy, which found expression in the conversion of courts and popular assemblies into the scene of what were essentially political trials. Above all, they brought out the worst features of brutality in the Roman character.

In 150 the proconsul Galba treacherously massacred thousands of Lusitanians with whom he had made a treaty. His indictment before a special court at Rome was proposed, but no trial was held. The massacre led to a renewed outbreak under Viriathus, an able guerrilla leader who defied Rome for about eight years (147–139). Forced eventually to yield, he was assassinated during an armistice by traitors suborned by the Roman commander. The complete subjugation of the Lusitanians soon followed.

WAR WITH NUMANTIA: 143–133 B.C. Meantime in 143, war broke out afresh in the nearer province, where the struggle centered about the town of Numantia. In 140 the general Pompeius made peace on easy terms with the Numantines but later repudiated it when the Senate ignored his arrangements. A surrender of the consul Mancinus and his army of 20,000 Romans to the Numantines took place in 137. By concluding a treaty the consul saved the lives of his men, but the Roman Senate rejected his agreement, made him the scapegoat, and delivered him to the Numantines, who humanely returned him.

At length, weary of defeats, the Romans re-elected to the consulship for 134 their experienced general Scipio Aemilianus, the conqueror of Carthage (146),[1] and appointed him commander in Spain. His first task was to restore military discipline. Then he began a blockade of Numantia. After a siege of fifteen months, the city was starved into submission and razed. A commission of ten senators reorganized the country, and Spain began a long era of peace.

II. DESTRUCTION OF CARTHAGE: 149–146 B.C.

THE THIRD PUNIC WAR: 149–146 B.C.— ITS CAUSES. The treaty which ended the Second Punic War forbade the Carthaginians to make war anywhere without the consent of Rome, which thus made Carthage a client.

---

[1] See p. 130.

At the same time their enemy Masinissa was established as a powerful client prince on their borders. In such a situation future Roman intervention was inevitable, but Carthage was left in peace for a generation. After the exile of Hannibal in 196 the Carthaginians realistically accepted their dependent status and devoted their energies to peaceful revival of their commerce and to payment of reparations. The Romans would have been undisturbed by a remarkable economic revival if this had not suggested a possible resurgence of Punic political power as well. The Romans continued, perhaps exaggeratedly, to fear and suspect their former enemy and were therefore prepared to seize on any sign of political independence at Carthage as an excuse for her destruction.

The opportunity came through the action of Masinissa, who, knowing the restrictions imposed on Carthage by her treaty with Rome and understanding the Roman attitude toward the city, frequently attacked Punic territory. Carthage could only appeal to Rome for protection, but Roman commissions repeatedly sent to adjust the disputes decided in favor of Masinissa. One member of a commission investigating Carthaginian complaints of frontier violations was old Marcus Porcius Cato, who was still obsessed with the fear Carthage had inspired in his youth and who returned from his mission filled with alarm at the city's wealth. Henceforth he devoted all his energies to accomplish its overthrow. In the following years he concluded all speeches in the Senate with the words, "Carthage must be destroyed."

Further friction with Masinissa occurred in 151 and resulted in a war which Carthage lost disastrously. The Romans at once prepared to fight. Conscious of having overstepped their rights as clients, and fearful of Roman vengeance, the Carthaginians offered unconditional submission, hoping for pardon. The Senate assured them of their lives, property, and constitution, but required hostages and told them to follow the commands of the consuls, who landed in Africa with an army and ordered them to surrender their arms and war machines. The Carthaginians, desirous of appeasing the Romans, complied. Then came the ultimatum. They must abandon their city and settle at least ten miles from the seacoast, practically a death sentence to the ancient mercantile city. The faction in the Carthaginian government advocating cooperation with the Romans was overturned by one demanding a last-ditch defense of the city. The Carthaginians improvised weapons and, manning their walls, defied the Romans.

THE SIEGE OF CARTHAGE: 149–146 B.C.   For two years the Romans, owing to the incapacity of their commanders, accomplished little. Then disappointment and apprehension led the electorate to demand as consul Scipio Aemilianus, talented officer and adopted grandson of Scipio Africanus. He was only a candidate for the aedileship and legally ineligible for the consulate. But the restrictions upon his candidature were suspended by a law passed in the Plebeian Council, and he was elected consul for 147. Another law entrusted him with the conduct of the war in Africa. Scipio restored discipline in the army, defeated the Carthaginians in the field, and energetically besieged the city. The Carthaginians suffered frightfully from hunger, and their forces were greatly reduced. In the spring of 146 the Romans forced their way into the city and captured it after desperate house-to-house fighting. The survivors, about 50,000, were enslaved, their city leveled to the ground, and its site declared accursed. Out of Carthaginian territory the Romans created a new province, called Africa. The last act in the dramatic struggle between the two cities was ended.

III. ANNEXATION OF MACEDONIA AND DISSOLUTION OF THE ACHAEAN CONFEDERACY: 149–146 B.C.

THE FOURTH MACEDONIAN WAR: 149–148 B.C. Rivalries among the Greek states, which frequently evoked senatorial intervention, and ill will occasioned by Roman harshness toward anti-Roman parties everywhere, caused a large faction among the Hellenes to look for the first favorable opportunity to free Greece from Roman suzerainty.

Relying on this antagonism to Rome, a certain Andriscus, pretending to be a son of Perseus, appeared in Macedonia in 149 and claimed the throne. He made himself master of the country and defeated the first Roman forces sent against him. He was crushed the following year at Pydna by the praetor Metellus, however, and Macedonia was annexed as a province (148).

WAR WITH THE ACHAEANS. The Achaean Confederacy was especially anti-Roman. There, realization of the Roman protectorate was heightened by the return of 300 survivors of the political exiles of 167. The anti-Roman party, supported by extreme democratic elements, was in control of the Confederacy when border difficulties with Sparta broke out afresh in 149. The matter was referred to the Senate for settlement, but the Achaeans did not await its decision. They attacked and defeated Sparta, confident that the Romans were preoccupied by the wars in Spain, Africa, and Macedonia.

The Senate determined to punish the Confederacy by detaching certain important cities from it. In 147 the Achaean assembly tempestuously refused to carry out the orders of Roman ambassadors, although the Macedonian revolt had been crushed. Their leaders, expecting no mercy from Rome, prepared for war and were joined by the Boeotians and other peoples of central Greece. Everywhere they were supported by the poorer city-dwellers, who saw hope for economic betterment in social revolution. The next year the Achaeans again refused to follow Roman advice, whereupon the Romans sent a fleet and an army against them under the consul Lucius Mummius. Metellus, the conqueror of Macedonia, subdued central Greece, and Mummius routed Confederate forces at Leucopetra on the Isthmus (146). Corinth was sacked and burnt, its treasures were carried off to Rome, and its inhabitants enslaved. Its land, like that of Carthage, was added to Roman public domain. Like Alexander's destruction of Thebes, this was a warning which other cities of Greece could not misinterpret. A senatorial commission dissolved the Achaean Confederacy as well as those of the Boeotians and Phocians. The cities of Greece entered into individual relations with Rome. Those which had taken Rome's side, as Athens and Sparta, remained Roman allies; the rest were made subject and tributary. Greece was not organized as a province but was put under the supervision of the governor of Macedonia.

IV. ACQUISITION OF THE KINGDOM OF PERGAMON

PROVINCE OF ASIA.   In 133 died Attalus III, king of Pergamon, the last of his line. In his will he made the Roman people heir to his kingdom, probably with the feeling that otherwise disputes over the succession would end in Roman interference and conquest. The Romans accepted the inheritance, but before they took possession a claimant appeared, an illegitimate son of Eumenes II, one Aristonicus. He occupied part of the kingdom, defeated and killed the consul Crassus in 130, but was himself beaten and captured by the latter's successor Perperna.

Out of the kingdom of Pergamon the province of Asia was then formed (129). Occupation of this country made Rome mistress of both shores of the Aegean and gave her a convenient bridgehead for an advance farther eastward. For the unfortunate subjects of Attalus, incorporation in the Roman Empire proved the reverse of the blessing he had anticipated. Struggles of rival political factions in Rome made them victims of a long period of maladministration and fiscal oppression.

CHAPTER 11
ROME, ITALY, AND THE
EMPIRE: 264–133 B.C.

Domination of the Mediterranean world entailed serious consequences for Rome. The wars described in the preceding chapters were, in fact, the ultimate cause of the crisis that led to the fall of the Republic. The present chapter will trace the changes and indicate the problems that had their origin in these wars and ensuing conquests. It will begin by consideration of the character of Roman government during the epoch.

I. RULE OF THE SENATORIAL OLIGARCHY

CONSTITUTION FROM 265 TO 133 B.C. During this period of expansion there were few important changes in the organization of the state. The dictatorship had been discarded, although not abolished, before the close of the Hannibalic War, a step in harmony with senatorial policy which sought to prevent any official from attaining too independent a position. In 242 a second praetorship, the office of *praetor peregrinus* or alien praetor, was established. This officer presided over trials of disputes between foreigners or Roman citizens and foreigners. Two additional praetorships were added in 227 and two more in 197, to provide provincial governors of praetorian rank. Further increase in the number of praetors was avoided by the use of proconsuls and propraetors as governors after 148.

GOVERNING OLIGARCHY. The victory of the commons in the patricio-plebeian struggle broke the patrician monopoly of political power and provided the state with institutions that gave it the appearance of a democracy. It never became such in fact. Despite recognition of the sovereign power of the people, the government continued after 287 to rest, as before, in the hands of an oligarchy. This oligarchy itself was far different from the old patrician aristocracy. The patrician *gentes* formed an important element of the government and for a long time supplied many political leaders, besides enjoying great social prestige, but the new oligarchy also included a large group of plebeian families, some of which had taken the lead in the struggle for political equality, while others were immigrants to Rome from municipalities that had received the franchise and where they had been local aristocrats. Community of economic interest, cemented by frequent intermarriage and adoptions, tended to promote solidarity among all elements of the ruling class. As the patrician *gentes* were gradually dying out, the oligarchy as a whole came to assume an increasingly plebeian character.

Although all families that had an ancestor in the Senate belonged to the Roman oligarchy, there were within this group distinctions based upon the rank of the offices which these ancestors had held. The highest distinction was reserved for the narrow circle of those to whom the Romans applied the term nobles or nobility (*nobiles, nobilitas*). Strictly speaking, this mark of respect was applied only to the descendants of those who had once held the consulship.

The absorption of plebeian leaders into the senatorial class helped assure that Roman democracy would be stillborn. Once wealthy plebeians realized their political ambitions, they normally failed to support continuing reforms that might have given governmental initiative to the citizenry at large, and they jealously protected senatorial prerogatives. Even plebeian tribunes abandoned espousal of revolutionary movements and used their vetoes in the Plebeian Council or the Senate itself to protect the senatorial class against hostile legislation in return for support of their future careers by patrons among the oligarchy. The essentially popular character of the tribunate, however, was merely lying dormant during most of the period. During the Spanish wars in the middle of the second century B.C., tribunes interceded to protect the peasant yeomanry and even proposed legislation to that end at variance with the wishes of the senatorial oligarchy. Such action portended the eventual reactivation of the tribunate as a revolutionary instrument challenging the status quo.

The new oligarchy was one of wealth and office. During the third century B.C. the enlarged group of senatorial families succeeded in creating for themselves a real, if not legal, monopoly of magistracies and thus of the regular gateway to the Senate and so tended to become a closed caste. They were able to maintain this monopoly and prevent a further enlargement of their circle partly because of the expense involved in holding public offices, which were unsalaried, and partly because of the increasingly high cost of conducting election campaigns. The demands made upon the time of magistrates and senators also deterred all but rich men from seeking office. The candidate who bore the name of one of the families that had guided Rome for generations had an enormous advantage over one of unknown ancestry. The great development of voluntary clientage owing to changing economic conditions, the formation of far-reaching political alliances, and the personal canvassing of influential supporters were all on the side of a son of a wealthy and prominent house.

Access to the consulship, the hallmark of nobility, was jealously guarded. The number of consuls from families that had only recently attained senatorial status declined steadily during the third century B.C. and of the 108 consuls elected from 200 to 146, only some eight belonged to families that had not held this office previously. By the second century B.C., control of Roman policies rested with less than twenty senatorial families, which, by virtue of their position, held an inordinate number of consulships. It was only individuals of exceptional force and ability, like Cato the Elder and later Marius and Cicero, who could penetrate these barriers and reach the highest office in the state. Such a one was styled a "new man" or "parvenu" (novus homo).

SENATE'S CONTROL OF LEGISLATION AND ADMINISTRATION. Even though the will of the people was theoretically sovereign after the passing of the Hortensian Law in 287, in fact from that date to the tribunate of Tiberius Gracchus in 133 the Senate exercised practically unchallenged control over the government as a result of social and economic changes among the citizenry and the further development of the popular assemblies. By the early third century B.C., abolition of debt slavery and usury and colonization throughout Italy created a numerous but dispersed yeoman class, conservative in outlook and willing to let the oligarchy guide the state. The Senate then evolved from a mere advisory council to the magistrates into an executive body with a wide range of customary powers over foreign policy, finance, and even legislation. The prestige of the Senate, in the absence of pressing internal problems, rested on its conduct of foreign policy and was probably greatest during and just after the Second Punic War. Senatorial resolutions (senatus consulta) were in fact frequently regarded as law by the magistrates, even though only popular assemblies had the constitutional right to legislate.

The Centuriate Assembly was replaced as the chief lawmaking body after 287 by the Plebeian Council, presided over by tribunes in their new role as tools of the senatorial establishment. In 241 the Council attained its final organization when the number of tribes was raised to thirty-five, four urban and thirty-one rural. Thereafter, when new Roman colonies were founded or new peoples admitted to citizenship, they were assigned to one or another of the old tribes. The organization of this primary assembly lent itself to various kinds of manipulation. Legislative assemblies could be called at any moment and were composed of those voters who happened to be in Rome; these were mainly city dwellers who had only four voting units out of thirty-five. In creating new, rural tribes the censors had made those distant from Rome as large as possible, thus minimizing the number of rural tribesmen in Rome on voting days and facilitating control by politicians of a relative handful of voters through patronage.

It was easy for the oligarchy to control the election of consuls and praetors by the Centuriate Assembly, especially since that body was reorganized at some time between 241–218 (probably in 241/240) in such a way as to create voting centuries that were amenable to manipulation. As a consequence of the reform, it seems that centuries were distributed on a tribal basis, an equal number of centuries of juniors and seniors of the classes being assigned to each tribe. Thus the first class was reduced from eighty to seventy centuries, thirty-five of juniors and thirty-five of seniors, while the total number of centuries was maintained at 193. The equestrian centuries no longer cast the first vote—a right henceforth exercised by a first-class century chosen by lot for each meeting. The equestrian centuries then voted with the rest of the first class, followed by the votes of the second class. It might seem that this reform placed control of the assembly in the hands of a less wealthy group of rural landholders than before, since the equestrian centuries and those of the first class no longer constituted a majority. In reality, however, the reform only put the ruling oligarchy more firmly in control of the assembly. Granted the increasingly proletariat nature of the capital's population and the growth of large estates in its immediate vicinity, tribes in and near Rome had few citizens with enough property to vote in the first class. Thus, centuries based on such tribes, like the tribes themselves, were easily manipulated by senatorial patrons. Furthermore, as a result of this reform the value of the individual vote was grossly unequal in the first class, since centuries based on more populous tribes in the hinterland had no more influence than those less populous ones in and near Rome. Consular and praetorian elections also came at fixed times, so that the gentry, on whose votes the candidates depended, could plan in advance to attend.

Romans conceived of liberty as meaning protection by law, not the right of ordinary citizens to free speech. Before legislative assemblies, mass meetings (contiones) were held to publicize the issues, and, although they were sometimes tumultuous, no formal provision was made in them for discussion from the floor. Only men recognized and called to the podium by presiding officials could express opinions. In formal assemblies themselves, presiding magistrates controlled the agenda. Candidates for office, easily distinguished by chalk-whitened togas, did not discuss issues with the public but personally solicited votes of the electorate on election day. Legislative assemblies were normally held in the Forum, the citizens lining up successively by tribes to vote, the ballot being recorded orally until 139 B.C., when the secret ballot was introduced. Tribes or centuries voted simultaneously in electoral assemblies, which were held usually in the Campus Martius as they required more space. Voters there approached the tellers through a corral-like enclosure called the "sheep-fold" (ovile).

Romans believed that their electoral system was superior to that of the

Athenians because the sorting of votes in units gave proper weight to the classes that mattered and because public balloting by individuals induced a feeling of responsibility they found lacking in the secret ballot or when anonymous hands were counted. They insisted that deliberation by the electorate should precede voting by several days and regarded as unseemly and even dangerous the Greek habit of discussing issues while conveniently seated in theaters immediately before a vote. The Roman establishment inhibited discussion by insisting that the electorate vote on their feet. To avoid the temptations of seated assemblies, it seems, they prevented the construction of the first permanent stone theater in Rome until 55 B.C. Some undemocratic features of Roman assemblies resembled those of the conventions of American political parties in recent times. They were susceptible to bandwagon techniques when units voted successively, and the order of balloting by tribes or centuries, an important matter, was determined by lot, often manipulated by presiding magistrates. These wielded great power, especially in the Centuriate Assembly, since they could refuse to recognize the candidacy of their enemies, could dismiss or postpone assemblies on religious grounds if they disapproved of the way voting was going, and could appoint as poll watchers their own partisans.

SENATE AND PUBLIC POLICY.   Since the Senate was a permanent body, easily assembled and regularly summoned by the consuls to discuss all matters, it was natural that foreign policy should be entirely in its hands—subject, of course, to the right of the Centuriate Assembly to sanction the making of war or peace—and hence the organization and government of Rome's foreign possessions became a senatorial prerogative. The Senate also dealt with all sudden crises that constituted a menace to the state, such as the spread of the Bacchanalian associations, which were ended by a senatorial decree of 186.

Even though the Greek historian and statesman, Polybius, an intimate of governing circles in Rome about 150 B.C., viewing the Roman constitution, could call it a nice balance among monarchy as represented by the consuls, aristocracy as represented by the Senate, and democracy as represented by the tribunate and assemblies, in practice the state was governed by the Senate. It is evident, however, that the Senate's power rested mainly on custom and precedent and on its prestige and influence as a corporation and on its individual members, not on powers guaranteed by law.

FACTIONAL POLITICS AND THE SCIPIOS. From earliest times the Senate had been divided into a number of rival groups of allied families which sought to monopolize as far as possible the highest offices and honors in the gift of the state. Such political cliques were known as *factiones* or *partes*. They were not parties in the modern sense with doctrinaire political, social, or economic programs, but were rather fluid groupings within the oligarchy aimed mainly at furthering the political careers of their members. Clans were the core of factions, whose leaders extended their influence by appropriate marriage alliances with other senatorial *gentes*. Membership in factions was very fluid, ambition and self-interest being frequently more important than previous commitments or even family ties in changing political affiliations as the great *gentes* on which they were based gained or lost prominence. Factions depended on patron-client relationships, the giving and receiving of political favors within the senatorial class and between it and the electorate at large. The nobility patronized the careers of lesser senators by getting their clients to vote for them and expected similar cooperation when lesser senators established followings of their own in the popular assemblies. Although the Roman electorate was not noted for its independence of mind, there were always, but especially after 200 B.C., many factionally uncommitted voters, the objects of blandishment by politicians.

Politicians enlarged their factions within the electorate by acquiring the reputation of service to individual voters and to the state. Between 233 and 217, for example, the popular Gaius Flaminius, with the political backing of the Aemilian and Scipionic *gentes*, as tribune, consul, and censor, sought to build up a political following among the nonsenatorial gentry by encouraging, under his own patronage, the election of new men to high senatorial office. Through a statesmanlike act strengthening the state and improving his control over the elective assemblies, he reinvigorated the class of yeoman voters and soldiers by bringing about the subdivision of the Gallic Land among poorer Roman citizens. Nevertheless, a brilliant military career was a far surer guarantee of election to high office and great influence, because generals dispensed patronage in the form of booty to soldiers who became grateful voters when demobilized.

This was especially true of Scipio Africanus. Scipio reached the height of his influence at the close of the Second Punic War (201), after which he devoted much attention to strengthening his faction. His own position and that of his friends were not a foregone conclusion, and he had to campaign against other rival factions that were determined to reduce him to size. Although he was elected to his second consulship in 194 and engineered the election of many friends to the highest offices, he also received rebuffs, as when Hannibal, toward whom he felt lenient, was driven from Carthage by a senatorial commission. Both Africanus and his brother Lucius were recalled from the East at the termination of the latter's consulship (end of 190), although normally a successful general was continued in his command until the end of his campaign.

The chief spokesman of the anti-Scipionic factions was Marcus Porcius Cato, a prosperous farmer who had entered politics as a new man under the patronage of Scipio's foes and who compensated for lack of ancestry by oratorical ability and a display of sincere puritanical virtue. His intransigent hostility to Scipio may be explained by his complete acceptance of oligarchic political ideals, and he instinctively distrusted excessively brilliant careerists like Scipio. In 190 a series of political prosecutions began through which Cato and others sought to undermine Scipionic influence by convicting some of that faction of misconduct in public affairs, and the latter tried in turn to discredit their opponents. Finally, in 187 Cato sponsored a demand that Lucius Scipio account to the Senate for a sum of 500 talents, which King Antiochus III had paid to him as the first installment of the indemnity imposed after his defeat at Magnesia. Africanus, who refused to admit that a commander was obliged to account for his disposal of booty won by his army, tore up his brother's account books in the presence of the Senate. His enemies claimed that the money in question could not be regarded as spoils of war. In 184 a tribune called on Lucius to render an account to the Plebeian Council, and only a personal appeal by Africanus to the people stifled the prosecution for the moment. At a later meeting of the Council, a heavy fine was imposed upon Lucius for peculation. When he refused to give security for payment, he was saved from imprisonment only by the intervention of a friendly tribune. Although the case was not pressed further, the influence of the Scipios was broken, and Africanus retired from public life until his death in 183.

Factional politics did not cease, of course, after Africanus' death, and the remainder of the second century B.C. witnessed a kaleidoscopic shifting of marital and other alliances attesting the rise and fall of influential families. After ca. 150 the political arena tended to be dominated by the faction led by the brilliantly successful Scipio Aemilianus, destroyer of Carthage, who was challenged by two other factions clustering around the patrician Appius Claudius Pulcher and the plebeian nobleman Caecilius Metellus Macedonicus. This three-way political alignment characterized the period until the Gracchan revolution gave a new direction to party politics.

RACE FOR OFFICE. It is frequently alleged that, following the Second Punic War, the Senate gradually abandoned virtues of self-sacrifice, steadfastness, and patriotism, which had contributed to Rome's triumph, and that it deteriorated in capacity and morale. Such a view demands serious qualification. Even before 200 the oligarchy had resisted changes that might threaten its economic and social predominance; in times of crisis, like the Second Punic War, political rivalries within the Senate were common. In much earlier times, despite later Roman attempts to idealize them, senators had not shown ethical qualms about treating weaker peoples brutally when it seemed advantageous for Rome to do so. During the second century B.C. the prizes of officeholding in an expanding empire became evermore tempting, however, and opportunities for corruption and illicit gain multiplied. Personal ambition and class interest, always characteristics of the senatorial order, were then merely operative in a larger political arena and for greater stakes than before. Officeholding, with the opportunities it offered for ruling subject peoples and of commanding in profitable wars, became a ready means for securing for oneself and one's friends the wealth needed to maintain the new standard of luxurious living affected by the senatorial class. Higher magistracies seemed especially valuable to senators, since they were excluded by custom from banking and undertaking public contracts and were prohibited by a Claudian Law of 218 from owning ships of sufficient capacity to engage in overseas commerce. As a consequence, rivalry for office became intense, and customary canvassing for votes tended to degenerate into bribery of individuals and of the masses.

ATTEMPTS TO RESTRAIN ABUSES. There are indications that the Senate realized the greater temptations of the age and that it attempted to check political abuses. This may be seen in legislation regulating the senatorial *cursus honorum*. In 197, or shortly thereafter, tenure of the praetorship became a necessary qualification for the consulship. In 180 the Villian Law (*lex Villia annalis*) established minimum ages for holding the various curule magistracies: thirty-six for the curule aedileship, thirty-nine for the praetorship, and forty-two for the consulship. It is not certain whether this law made previous tenure of the quaestorship a necessary qualification for higher office or whether it provided for a fixed minimum age at which the quaestorship could be held. An interval of two years was required between successive magistracies. Normally a man would hold the quaestorship, and then the aedileship, which, although not imperative, involved the supervision of public games and festivals and thus was a good opportunity for winning popularity. Excessive ostentation was never the less regarded as an unconventional means for politicians to impress voters and led to sumptuary laws, like that of Cato the Elder's strict censorship (184). The praetorship and the consulship completed the *cursus honorum* in that order.[1] Somewhat later, about 151, reelection to the same office was forbidden. The willingness of politicians and voters to disregard the law boded ill for the future control of brilliant careerists. This was the case in 147 when the Centuriate Assembly, confronted with the languishing Third Punic War, elected their hero of the hour, Scipio Aemilianus, consul and commander, largely on the basis of the reputation he had acquired previously in Spain. This occurred despite the fact that, under the Villian Law, Scipio was ineligible to hold the consulship because of his youth and because previously he had not held the praetorship.

In 181 and 159, laws established severe penalties for bribery of electors. Whatever the immediate reason for introducing the secret ballot in assemblies, its use surely tended to curb the same abuses. The Gabinian Law of 139 provided for the secret ballot in elections, two years later the Cassian Law extended its use to trials in the Plebeian Council, and in 131 it was finally employed in the legislative assemblies.

These laws accomplished little, as they dealt merely with symptoms, and not with the cause, of the problem. Granted its traditionally conservative outlook, the Senate was facing administrative, military, and social problems beyond its power to solve. The Senate's prestige rested largely upon its successful

---

[1] The tribunate was not considered as one of the regular magistracies, and the censorship, according to the custom previously established, followed the consulship.

foreign policy; but its initial failures in the last wars with Macedonia and Carthage and the long and bloody struggles in Spain had weakened its reputation. It was also ignoring a fundamental social change within Italy that threatened to undermine Roman military power: the decline of the yeomanry.

ROME AND HER ALLIES IN ITALY. On the whole the Roman state respected the treaty rights of the allies, both Latin and federate; and we hear of but few occasions when any infringement of their local independence occurred as the result of action by Rome. Such trespasses tended to be isolated acts of Roman magistrates who exceeded their authority in making demands on officials of allied communities, particularly in the matter of supplies and entertainment when passing through allied territory, and in punishing them for failure to obey or for showing lack of respect. There is no question that the allies made greater military contributions than the Romans themselves to the conquest of Empire, sometimes out of proportion to their population. The allies suffered like the Romans during the Second Punic War, and the devastation and depopulation of their lands are reflected in a decline of one third in the levy made upon their manpower in the second century B.C.

As for spoils of war—which, as a rule, were divided among the troops by their generals—the allies received the same share as their Roman comrades in arms except on one particular occasion. In the assignment of public lands for colonization, it appears that they received a share, but perhaps not always the share they were entitled to. It was inevitable that the growth of the Roman imperial power should react adversely on the status of the allies. For example, Roman citizens probably received better treatment in Roman law courts. In fact, the Italians tended to sink into a position of greater inferiority and to assume the status of clients at the disposal of Roman patrons. Although they had no share in the government of the Empire, at least some of them were in a position to derive the same financial advantages as the Romans, as traders and bankers, from the exploitation of subject territories outside Italy. The generally disadvantageous position of the Italians was felt the more keenly as the cultural Romanization of Italy steadily, if slowly, progressed; ultimate absorption of the whole peninsula into the Roman citizenry was inevitable.

Before 133, however, there was no demand for Roman citizenship by the allied communities. On the contrary, down to the middle of the second century, they were more anxious to maintain their independence than to be merged with Rome. In 216 the Latin town of Praeneste refused an offer of Roman citizenship. On several occasions in the period 187–168 Latins and other allies who had migrated to Rome and had been enrolled there as Roman citizens in accordance with a long-established privilege were removed from the rolls and forced to return to their former homes. In particular, a Claudian Law of 177 ejected those who had fraudulently attained citizenship. This must be interpreted as revealing not a jealous exclusiveness on the part of Roman government but rather a compliance with the desires of allied states themselves. The attractions of life as artisans and laborers in the capital, which was booming in the first half of the second century, caused many small farmers throughout Italy to leave their homes and seek their fortunes in Rome. As a result, many allied states lost population, particularly in the classes on which they relied for their military strength. They protested to the Senate against the Roman absorption of their citizens and secured their restoration to their own census lists. Conversely, the Romans were not so conscious of their own superiority as to pursue a narrow policy of exclusiveness towards their allies. The Campanians, who had been deprived of partial citizenship in 210, were restored to their former position in 189, and in the next year full citizenship was extended to three communities on the southern frontiers of Latium—Fundi, Formiae, and Arpinum—which formerly had only limited rights. The censors of 169 were extremely negligent in enforcing the law against fraudulent usurpation of citizenship by the allies, and Latins continued to receive Roman status after having held a magistracy in their respective towns. No matter how enlightened the Romans claimed to be in treating the Italians, the fact remained that the legal differences between the two groups were increasingly unrealistic and galling to people who realized that they were not masters in their own house.

II. IMPERIAL ADMINISTRATION

SUBJECTS OR ALLIES? The annexation of Sicily in 241 and of Sardinia and Corsica in 238 raised the question whether Rome should extend to her non-Italian conquests the same treatment accorded to the Italians and include them within her conglomerate military organization. The status of federate allies was accorded only to communities that had previously attained this relationship or merited it by zeal in the Roman cause and whose territory did not form a part of Roman dominions. The rest were treated as subjects, not as allies, even though they might be so called, and enjoyed only such rights as the conquerors chose to leave them. The distinguishing mark of their condition was their obligation to pay a tax or tribute to Rome. Except on special occasions, they were not called on to render military service. This practice, once established, was extended to all other regions subsequently incorporated in the Empire.

PROVINCES. At first the Romans tried to conduct the administration of Sicily, Sardinia, and Corsica through regular city magistrates. Finding this unsatisfactory, they created in 227 two separate administrative districts—Sicily forming one, and the two adjoining islands the other—called "provinces" from the word *provincia*, which usually meant the sphere of duty assigned to a magistrate. Special magistrates were in fact assigned to them, two additional praetors being annually elected for this purpose. In like manner the Romans in 197 organized the provinces of Hither and Farther Spain, in 148 the province of Macedonia, in 146 Africa, and in 129 Asia. Subsequent conquests were treated in the same way. For the Spanish provinces two more praetorships were created, "with consular authority" because of their military importance.

For those organized afterwards, no new magistrates were added, and the practice was established of appointing as governor an ex-consul or ex-praetor with the title of proconsul or propraetor. This change of policy is explained by the opposition of the nobility to creating new praetorships, which would increase the number of candidates annually available for the consulship, and to making a corresponding increase in the quaestorships, which would enlarge the opportunities for "new men" to enter the Senate. City magistrates welcomed the innovation because it increased their chances of obtaining a provincial command with all its opportunities for acquiring wealth. The new method of appointing provincial governors subsequently became the rule for all provinces under the republican regime. As a rule the Senate decided what provinces should be "consular" and what "praetorian," but the actual allocation among eligible candidates of each rank was determined by lot subject to possible rearrangement among the appointees. Occasionally, one of the regular provinces was entrusted to a consul in office. This was usually done by the Senate, although technically either the Centuriate Assembly or Plebeian Council could do so by enacting a law.

PROVINCIAL GOVERNMENT. Although each province had its own peculiar features, in general all were organized and administered in the following way. A provincial charter (*lex provinciae*), drawn up on the spot by a commission of ten senators and ratified by the Senate, fixed provincial rights and obligations. Each province was an aggregate of communities (*civitates*) enjoying city or tribal organization, but having no political bond of unity. There were three classes of these communities: free and federate, free and nontributary, and tributary (*civitates liberae et foederatae, liberae et immunes, stipendiariae*). The first were few in number and, although within the borders of a province, did not really belong to it, since they were free allies whose status was assured by a permanent treaty with Rome. The second not very numerous class derived ultimately from states over which Rome had assumed a protectorate without a formal treaty and enjoyed exemption from taxation by virtue of the provincial charter, a privilege the Senate could revoke at will. The third group was by far the most numerous and furnished the taxes laid upon the province. As a rule each of the communities enjoyed its former constitution and laws, subject to the supervision of Roman authorities.

Over this aggregate of communities stood the Roman governor and his staff. His term of office was annual but might be extended for several years by prorogation or simple failure to appoint a successor. His duties were threefold: military, administrative, and judicial. He commanded Roman troops stationed in the province for maintenance of order and protection of the frontiers; he supervised relations between the communities of his province and their internal administration, as well as collection of tribute; he presided as judge over more serious cases arising among provincials, over all cases between provincials and Romans or between Roman citizens. Upon entering his province, the governor published an edict, usually modeled upon that of his predecessors or the praetor's edict at Rome, stating what legal principles he would enforce during his term of office. The province was divided into judicial circuits (*conventus*), and cases arising in each of these were tried in designated places at fixed times.

The governor was accompanied by a quaestor, who acted as his treasurer and received the provincial revenue from tax collectors. His staff also comprised three *legati* or lieutenants, senators appointed by the Senate but usually nominated by himself, who assisted him with their counsel and acted as his deputies. He also took with him a number of companions (*comites*), usually young men from the families of his friends, who were given an opportunity to experience provincial government and who could be used in any official capacity. The governor also brought his own retinue, comprising clerks and household servants. Although he received no salary, he was allowed a very handsome sum for his expenses and his staff.

PROVINCIAL TAXATION. The taxes levied on the provinces were at first designed to pay for occupation and defense. Hence, they bore the name *stipendium*, or soldier's pay. The term *tributum* (tribute), used of the property tax imposed on Roman citizens, did not come into use for provincial revenues until later. As a rule Romans accepted the tax systems already in vogue before their occupancy and exacted either a fixed annual sum from the province, as in Spain, Africa, and Macedonia, or one tenth (*decuma*) of the annual produce of the soil, as in Sicily and Asia. The tribute imposed by the Romans was usually lower than that exacted by previous rulers. The public or royal lands, mines, and forests of conquered states were incorporated into Roman public domain, and the right to occupy or exploit them was leased to individuals or companies of contractors. Customs dues (*portoria*) were also collected in the harbors and on provincial frontiers.

The methods of tax collection varied from province to province according to different types of taxation. Normally, where the direct tax took the form of a fixed levy (the *stipendium* in a strict sense) as in Spain, the total sum was apportioned among tributary communities, which raised their respective quotas as they wished and turned them over to the provincial quaestor. Where this tax was a percentage of the annual crops, however, the Romans followed the custom employed in Italy and which was common throughout the Mediterranean world—that is, they leased the right to collect the tax within specific areas to private corporations of professional tax farmers (*publicani*) that made the highest bid for the privilege. These corporations profited from the excess they collected over the amount they had contracted to turn over to the state. The same method was employed in collecting indirect taxes such as customs dues, rentals, and pasturage taxes for the use of public lands in the provinces. In Sicily the *decuma* was farmed out to local *publicani*; only after the annexation of Asia (122) was the collection of a provincial tithe for the first time assigned to a company of Romans. Earlier in the century, however, Roman companies probably already had a monopoly over the collection of indirect taxes and rentals in all provinces. Roman corporations of *publicani* were joint-stock companies, with central offices in Rome and agencies in the provinces where they were active. A general manager (*magister*) with a board of associates directed the offices in Rome, and provincial agencies were entrusted to district managers. The company officials were all members of what, at a later date, was called the equestrian order;[2] their employees might be Romans of lower standing, Italians, provincials, freedmen, or slaves.

OPPRESSION IN THE PROVINCES. Under the systems of tax collection that obtained during most of the second century B.C. there was ample room for misgovernment by greedy governors and their staffs. The temptations of un-restricted power proved too great for many senators, especially in provinces where they supervised local tax farming and so could easily divert revenue into their own pockets through extortion. There were, it is true, Roman governors who maintained high traditions of integrity, but there were also many who abused their power to enrich themselves. While the shortness of his term prevented a good governor from thoroughly understanding the conditions of his province, it served to augment the criminal zeal with which an avaricious magistrate, often heavily indebted from the expenses of his election campaigns, sought to wring a fortune from provincials. Bribes, presents, illegal exactions, and open confiscations were the usual means of amassing wealth. The almost sovereign position of the governor, with his military command and absolute power of life and death over all persons in the province and his freedom from immediate senatorial control, guaranteed him a free hand.

Another cause of oppression was found in the activities of Roman bankers and moneylenders (*negotiatores*) who swarmed all over the provinces and even over adjacent districts where they might still have some protection by Roman authority. They were particularly numerous in the Greek East, where cities in a state of chronic bankruptcy were vulnerable to contracting loans at exorbitant interest rates. The bankers were drawn from the same class of Roman society as the *publicani*, although in many cases they were agents of senators, who were prohibited from engaging directly in such financial transactions. Consequently, when the *negotiatores* called upon the governors to help them collect outstanding debts, the latter frequently complied out of regard for their own political future. By placing soldiers at the disposal of the creditors or quartering troops on delinquent communities, they forced the debtors to meet their obligations even if it ruined them.

Commands and governorships were highly desired, and not merely because they gave senators power and wealth during their tenure of office in the provinces. Rome's subjects were quick to realize the almost absolute power of their governors, and senators were just as quick to take advantage of the situation

---

[2] See p. 151.

by assuming the familiar role of patrons toward provinces they ruled, which continued after they laid down their offices and returned to Rome. As patrons they might arbitrate differences among the provincials, and, more importantly, facilitate their diplomatic relations with the Senate. In return, provincial clients might be called on to further a patron's political career at the capital by attesting (not always sincerely or voluntarily) to his justice or clemency, or by contributing to his campaign fund. Provincial clienteles thus established very often passed to the descendants of the original commander who had conquered a province or of some outstanding or beneficent governor. Such ties accounted in large measure for the unity and even the survival of the Empire in times of gross mismanagement or crisis.

THE FIRST STANDING CRIMINAL COURT. Since control of provincial administration was vested by custom in the Senate, that body exercised a general supervision over the governor. Upon his return to Rome, it examined his accounts, his arrangements, and his claims to the honor of a triumph for any military exploits. Deputations from provincial communities approached the Senate to complain of a governor's action or, often under pressure, to commend his conduct. At first complaints were taken before special ad hoc tribunals trying damage suits or, more typically, they might be prosecuted before the Plebeian Council on the initiative of tribunes, there being as yet no standing criminal courts of any kind. Such procedures, however, circumvented senatorial control over governors, and to obviate such an eventuality the Senate successfully sponsored a Calpurnian Law in 149. This law established Rome's first in a series of standing criminal courts. This one tried suits for the recovery of damages from officials accused of extortion or other offenses (*quaestio de rebus repetundis*). It was essentially a senatorial committee, composed of fifty senatorial jurors presided over by a praetor. Provincials themselves could not plead before it but were represented by Roman patrons who could plead but not argue their case. There is no real indication that the Senate was especially moved by sympathy for provincials in founding this court. As a matter of fact, when first used in 139 and 138 the court was the instrument of intense factional in-fighting. The trials were occasioned by the disgraceful behavior of commanders in Spain, but they were essentially political in nature and only peripherally concerned with protecting Spanish provincials.

III. ECONOMIC AND SOCIAL DEVELOPMENT

Roman expansion between 264 and 133 was marked by important and almost revolutionary changes in the economic and social life of Rome and Italy. An inevitable result of the extension of her control over the Mediterranean was closer contact between Italy and lands of older culture and more advanced economic development in the Greek East. The Romans and their Italian allies thus felt the broad impact of Hellenistic civilization and appropriated for good or ill whatever of its features appealed to them. Italian agriculture, in particular, benefited by the introduction of new varieties of fruit trees and garden crops, of improved farm implements and superior agricultural techniques. To meet the needs of empire, ca. 213 the Romans abandoned coinage based on a bronze standard for one based on a silver standard, common among the Hellenistic states. Thereafter, the basic silver coin was the denarius, whose weight was ultimately stabilized at about four grams. As the system of coinage evolved in the second century B.C., the denarius in turn was divided into four brass sesterces and sixteen bronze asses. The new Roman coinage not only speedily supplanted the products of other Italian mints but gradually became dominant throughout the Mediterranean. The most important developments in Italy were the rise of large estates operated by slave labor, the decline of the free Italian peasantry, the growth of a numerous urban proletariat in Rome, the formation of a Roman business and commercial class, and the introduction of a new scale of living among the well-to-do.

THE GREAT ESTATES. Several causes contributed to the rapid growth of great estates (*latifundia*) as the dominant factor in Italian agriculture. Among them were the Roman system of administering public domain, the inability of small proprietors to maintain themselves in the face of the demands of military service, their increasing preference to find a livelihood in one of the booming cities of Italy, and the abundant supply of cheap slave labor provided by numerous prisoners of war.

For centuries it had been established practice that public land not reserved for colonization should be open to occupation by Roman citizens or allied communities for farming or pasturage. For this privilege the occupants were expected to pay rent to the treasury, which amounted to one tenth of the produce in the case of field crops, one fifth in the case of fruits; that of pasture lands was a tax based on the number of cattle or other animals. The amount of land available for occupation by private individuals increased as a result of Hannibal's campaign in Italy, especially in Bruttium where lands left depopulated and ownerless were taken over by Rome. In addition, the Romans punished the states defecting to Hannibal by confiscating a large portion of their territory, as a rule one third. The transplanting of thousands of Ligurians from their native country to Samnium in 180 indicates how much unoccupied land was at the disposal of the Roman government.

Those who profited most from disposal of public land were wealthier landholders who commanded the labor necessary to bring considerable areas under cultivation and who possessed sufficient capital to stock new farms. After several generations, the occupants of public lands regarded them as family property. In many cases all records of the original conditions of tenure and of the boundaries of the plots had disappeared, and the rents had ceased to be paid to the state.

In the second century B.C. new conditions arose which favored still further the rise of the *latifundia*. Ever since 218, members of the senatorial order had

been prohibited by law from engaging directly in commercial enterprises outside
of Italy. Banking and contracting were considered beneath the dignity of a
senator, while agriculture ranked as the most honorable gainful occupation, so
the governing class was practically compelled to invest in Italian land the new
capital it acquired from the conquest and administration of the Empire. It not
only sought to increase holdings of public land but also to buy up farms of
smaller proprietors wherever possible. At the same time, new trends in Italian
agriculture developing under the influence of Hellenistic practices favored the
capitalist farmer at the expense of his peasant neighbor.

Cereal agriculture remained important everywhere, most cultivable land
being kept under grain or fallow, but agriculture was also becoming more
diversified. In some areas grain fields gave way to vineyards, olive orchards,
market gardens, and, particularly in South Italy, to extensive grazing ranches.
Farming became much more capitalistic than heretofore. It was carried on by
improved methods, both expenses and profits were carefully calculated, and
production on large estates was definitely directed toward local markets.
Capitalistic agriculture was already highly developed in the Near East, in
Carthaginian Africa, and in Sicily, and it was from these regions that the Romans
learned about the new farm economy. About 150, Cato the Censor wrote his
book *On Agriculture*, a practical manual for large estate owners. Some four years
later the Senate had translated into Latin the much more elaborate work of
the Carthaginian Mago, much of which must have been applicable to Italy,
although dealing specifically with conditions peculiar to Africa. The typical
Italian *latifundia* were not very large when judged by American standards.
Holdings of 100 and 240 *iugera* (66 and 158 acres) fell into this class. In ancient
Italy where, owing to the absence of agricultural machinery, the normal size
of a farm tilled by a single family was from four to eight acres, they constituted
substantial domains. Many of the great proprietors owned a number of such
farms scattered in various parts of the peninsula. According to Cato, an orchard
of 100 *iugera* required the labor of 16 slaves, in addition to workers hired for
specific tasks like harvesting olives.

For the development of *latifundia*, an abundant supply of cheap labor was
essential and was furnished throughout the second century B.C. by hordes of
captives taken in the course of Rome's victorious wars who flooded the slave
markets of the Mediterranean. When these failed to meet the demand, the
deficit was made good by the piratical slave-raiders of the Greek East. In
addition to imported slaves, some were bred on estates. So long as slaves could
be procured cheaply, they were preferred to hired free labor because they were
not liable for military service and could be exploited ruthlessly without fear of
consequences. Cato's directions for handling slaves show that they were treated
like cattle, and he callously recommended that they be turned out to starve
when they were no longer fit for work. On the plantations slaves often worked
in irons and at night were housed in underground prisons. The potential

danger of the presence of large masses of slaves so brutally treated was realized in the First Sicilian Slave War, which broke out in 135. In this struggle some 70,000 slaves revolted and defied Roman arms for three years. At the same time there were minor revolts in Italy, which were suppressed with great severity.

DECLINE OF SMALL FARMERS. The spread of *latifundia* was accompanied by a corresponding decline in the numbers of peasant farmers throughout Italy. In certain areas great proprietors resorted to illegal means to oust peasants from their holdings on public land and seized every opportunity to buy up their private allotments. A still more serious cause was the burden imposed upon the peasantry by the foreign wars of Rome. Since only citizens who had a property assessment of 4,000 asses were eligible for military service and since the great majority of them were farmers, Roman armies were recruited mainly from the rural population. When wars were no longer fought in Italy but all over the Mediterranean area and when it became necessary to maintain provincial garrisons, armies could no longer be disbanded in the autumn and reassembled for summer campaigns, so that peasant soldiers could return to their farms to attend to at least part of the necessary agricultural tasks. Once in the ranks the Roman soldier could be kept away from his home for as long as six years in succession, to the inevitable detriment of his fields and his finances. Prolonged periods of military service, with the chance of temporary profits from the spoils of war, often unfitted men for the steady, laborious life of the farm. Many discharged soldiers, returning to farms which had been mortgaged for the support of their families and being unable or unwilling to gain a livelihood on their small holdings, were only too glad to sell out to their richer neighbors. There was little room for them as tenants on private land, and work as farm laborers was seasonal and uncertain. Many of them migrated to Rome and to other expanding cities where life was exciting and where, until after the middle of the second century, there were plenty of jobs. Others migrated to Cisalpine Gaul, where new lands were still available for them. Losses in war also made a heavy drain on the peasantry. As a result of these conditions, the number of men available for army service declined as the second century progressed and many yeomen lost their property, so that it became increasingly difficult to raise necessary levies. The tribunes intervened on several occasions to spare peasants from the draft, while the property qualification for service was progressively lowered in order to find the manpower to fight wars. The rural population among the Roman allies suffered just as the Romans themselves, as is indicated by their migration to Rome on such a large scale that their native cities had to ask the Senate to force them to return home. A very serious problem began to confront the Senate. Unless it was willing to adopt a passive foreign policy and give up its distant foreign possessions, it needed to raise armies to prosecute wars of conquest and to garrison and defend the provinces, and these increasing military obligations had to be met by a population declining in eligible manpower.

The Romans were not altogether blind to the consequences of the expansion of the great estates. As early as 367 (362), if we may believe the tradition recorded by Livy, they had placed a limit of 500 *iugera* (310 acres) on the size of individual holdings and also restricted the number of animals which any one person might run on the public pastures. The former restriction had soon become a dead letter, however, and public pastures had been taken up by private occupants. Much later, in the period 201–167 B.C., another law was passed which forbade anyone to hold more than 500 *iugera* of crop-producing public land or to maintain more than a cumulative total of 100 head of cattle and 500 head of smaller stock on additional tracts of public pasture. Although this was evidently an attempt to check the spread of *latifundia* and to limit the encroachment of grazing lands on areas under cultivation, its provisions actually favored the landed oligarchy and did little to preserve the small farmer. Even the restrictions of this new law were openly disregarded, and the Senate felt both unwilling and unable to bring transgressors to account. Once occupied, public land was regarded as an hereditary possession. In 173, the Senate authorized a consul to fix the boundaries of public and private lands in Campania in order to check the encroachment of the latter upon the former, but eleven years later it found the whole region in the hands of private possessors and succeeded in recovering only 50,000 *iugera* by actually buying it back from the occupants. Thus, although the virtual abolition of the regressive land tax or *tributum* in 168 B.C., one of the most important legislative acts of the century,[3] certainly helped middling and small property holders, it was ineffective in sustaining the yeomanry, and victory rested with the great proprietors. The whole of Italy was not affected equally by the growth of the *latifundia*, however. In South Italy, Campania, Latium, and Etruria they dominated the scene, less so in the highlands of Central Italy and Umbria.

GROWTH OF THE CITY MOB. Rome itself, like Italy, underwent a profound transformation during the period of conquest that began with the First Punic War. As a result it became the political and the economic center of the Mediterranean world. By 133 it had a population of perhaps a third of a million, rivalling Alexandria and Antioch, the great Hellenistic capitals. Although not a great manufacturing center, Rome had always been an important market, and now her streets were thronged with traders from all lands. There was a large proportion of slaves belonging to the mansions of the wealthy and of freedmen engaged in business for themselves or for their patrons. Hither flocked also the peasants who for various reasons had abandoned their farms to depend on the bounty of patrons to whom they might attach themselves in voluntary clientage or to pick up a hand-to-mouth living. Many of these former peasants found employment in the urban building boom financed by the influx of booty and tribute. But about 138 this boom ended, and staple

---

[3] See p. 126.

grain prices rose simultaneously because of a slave war in Sicily. These events combined to produce a serious economic crisis among the urban proletariat. The entertainments and largesses of food characteristic of the public festivals and election campaigns attracted this element and helped to support it. Owing to slow transportation by land and its uncertainties by sea, the congestion of population in Rome made the problem of supplying the city very difficult, since a rise in the price of grain or a delay in the arrival of the Sicilian wheat convoy caused famine in the city.

Thus, by the second century B.C. the social structure of the city of Rome was fast assuming characteristics that remained typical for the rest of antiquity: a small wealthy class, principally senators, with their sizeable retinues of slaves and clients; no real "middle" class in the modern sense to speak of; and the vast bulk of the population, in which freedmen were coming to predominate numerically over resident or immigrant citizens. These latter lived at a subsistence level even in good times and tended not to reproduce themselves. The urban proletariat was an increasingly unsettling element, because it was open to political manipulation and could react tumultuously and even violently to issues of the day in mass meetings and political assemblies. This situation was potentially dangerous to the stability of the state, because the constitution provided no adequate means for policing Rome. Except for the magistrates and their personal attendants, there was no police force in the city, and since consuls lacked military authority within the *pomerium*, there were no armed forces at their disposal.

EQUESTRIANS AND BUSINESSMEN. Political and commercial developments caused the gradual emergence during the third and early second centuries B.C. of a subclass within the Roman gentry called, eventually, the equestrian order, so named from the right of wealthy men to serve in the cavalry and to vote in the prestigious equestrian centuries of the Centuriate Assembly. Although of lesser rank and having a different social function, the equestrians were related to the senatorial class. Cadets of senatorial families held equestrian rank themselves before embarking on senatorial careers, and some equestrians of even nonsenatorial lineage competed for lesser senatorial offices, although more infrequently after ca. 200 B.C. The class came to consist basically, however, of those wealthy Romans who eschewed political careers when already established families tended to monopolize public life. Therefore, although many of them were wealthier than some senators, they lacked the *dignitas* that could only be obtained at Rome through senatorial offices.

Like senators, equestrians always regarded estates as the safest and most genteel investments, whose management was their chief vocation. An active and very visible minority within their class, however, used profits from the land as capital to pursue business careers compatible with their respectability. Such careers were open to them because, whereas law and custom severely restricted business activities of the senatorial order, the state also relied on private enterprise for the conduct of public business. During the Second Punic War and as publicans organized in joint stock companies they began to bid for state contracts to produce armaments. By about 150 they predominated in bidding for contracts let out for the construction of various public works; the operation of the Spanish and the reopened Macedonian mines; and the collection of rentals from public lands in Italy and of harbor dues in Italy, Sicily, and Spain, where they competed with native, provincial tax collectors. Apparently they also were active in shipping, particularly in the transportation to Rome of grain collected as taxes in Sicily, Sardinia, and Africa.

While playing an important but not predominant role in the business community, they generally disdained involvement with commerce unrelated to the needs of the state, which was largely in the hands of wealthy commoners and freedmen. There was, however, one important exception to this rule. They shared with such entrepreneurs the profession of banking, which included moneylending, another profitable activity in Italy and especially the provinces, where lending money at usurious rates to bankrupt cities was lucrative. Because bankers paid interest on deposits, they must have found ample opportunities to make successful investments. Otherwise, Roman businessmen did not as yet engage actively in strictly foreign enterprises.

THE CHANGING STATUS OF WOMEN. During the latter part of the third and early second centuries B.C. the status of upper-class Roman women began to change markedly, in part because of the impact on society of Hellenistic *mores*, which permitted wellborn women much education, independence, and self-assertiveness, in part because of the increasing affluence of the Roman oligarchy. Women learned that they had greater independence when they married without *manus*, escaped the close guardianship of their husbands, and remained under the more distant and relatively looser tutelage of their fathers. Widows and spinsters enjoyed more freedom, since guardians, who had many other things to do, exercised increasingly light control over their wards. Since the Twelve Tables, upper-class women could inherit estates rather freely; a Voconian Law of 169 B.C. restricted that right, but the law was circumvented and the number of wealthy heiresses continued to increase.

Two noblewomen of the period may be cited as examples of increasing emancipation: Aemilia, Scipio Africanus' wife, and Cornelia, their daughter, mother of the Gracchi. Aemilia (d. 162 B.C.), it seems, was one of the wealthiest Romans of her generation and maintained a standard of living worthy of a Hellenistic princess. Cornelia (d. after 122) was even more interesting, since she combined the old-fashioned ideals of a Roman matron with the new, more liberated ones of the Hellenistic East. Having produced a brood of twelve children, she was widowed, lived unpretentiously, refused remarriage, and remained *univira*, despite the blandishments of suitors, including no less a personage than a Ptolemy of Egypt. She seems to have managed her household and made her decisions independent of any help from a guardian. She was also a well-educated philhellene, having been taught, it seems, by Scipio Africanus, her father; in any case she was enough of a literary artist that her letters later achieved publication.

NEW SCALE OF LIVING. During campaigns in Sicily, Africa, Greece, and Asia Minor, Romans came into close contact with civilizations older and more sophisticated than their own, where the art of living was practiced with a refinement and elegance unknown in Latium. In this respect the conquerors showed themselves ready to learn from the conquered, and all the luxurious externals of culture were gradually transplanted to Rome. The simple Roman house with its one large *atrium*, serving at once as kitchen, living room, and bedchamber, was slowly transformed. The *atrium* became a pillared reception hall, special rooms were added for the various phases of domestic life, in the rear of the *atrium* arose a Greek peristyle courtyard, and the house was filled with sculpture and other works of art, plundered or purchased in Hellas. The standards of living of the upper classes were rising, and an increasingly wide gulf yawned between the life of rich and poor.

TAXES ON LUXURIES. The gradual change in living standards did not come about without vigorous opposition from the champions of old Roman simplicity, who saw in the new refinement and luxury a danger to Roman morality. The spokesman of the conservatives was Cato the Elder. In his censorship in 184 he assessed articles of luxury and expensive slaves at ten times their market value and made them liable to taxation at an exceptionally high rate, in case the property tax should be levied. Although the next censors disregarded these regulations, Cato's censorship was by no means the only strict one in the second century B.C., and other senators were also disturbed by growing sophistication of Roman life. Attempts to check the growth of luxury by legislation were futile, however. The Oppian Law restricting female extravagance in dress and ornaments, passed under stress of the need for conservation in 215, was repealed in 195, and subsequent sumptuary legislation in 182, 161, and 143 was largely ignored.

RECAPITULATION. In 133 the Roman state faced a series of critical problems, the result primarily of continuing and excessive military demands made on the yeomanry. The economic basis of Roman society was unhealthy. Rome was now living largely from the exploitation of the provinces. The income derived from this source passed mainly to the officeholding oligarchy and, to a lesser degree to the equestrian class. The lower classes profited little therefrom, and their condition deteriorated steadily as the Empire expanded. The same was true of the Roman allies in Italy. Far-reaching economic reforms were needed, reforms that would diminish the idle masses by providing them with profitable occupations in industrial or commercial pursuits or by rendering agriculture again attractive to the small farmer. At the same time, political reforms were urgently required. The popular assemblies and the magistrates, organs of government adapted to a city-state, were proving incompetent to grapple with the problems of imperial administration. Signs of dissatisfaction were appearing among the Latin and Italian allies. Military resources were declining, while military burdens were increasing. The threat of mob violence and famine hung over Rome. This crisis had to be met at a time when the ruling class was unwilling to change its social, economic, and political attitudes and was therefore unable to find solutions to problems confronting the state.

IV. CULTURAL PROGRESS

GREEK INFLUENCES.   In addition to creating new administrative problems and transforming economic life, the expansion of Rome gave a tremendous impulse to cultural development. The chief stimulus was close contact with Hellenistic civilization. Rome had been subject to Greek influences both indirectly through Etruria and directly from the Greek cities of South Italy, but with the conquest of the latter and the occupation of Sicily, Greece, and part of Asia Minor these influences became much more immediate and powerful. They were intensified by Greeks who flocked to Rome as ambassadors, teachers, physicians, merchants, and artists, and by multitudes of educated Greek slaves employed in Roman households. Because Hellenistic civilization was more ancient and more sophisticated than the Latin, it was inevitable that the latter should borrow largely from the former and consciously or unconsciously imitate it. The reception of Hellenism was also unsettling, however, because some parochial and puritanical Romans resisted as impractical and even immoral a style of life stressing the cult of leisure and development of mind for the purposes of enjoyment. Thus, the intellectual life of Rome never attained the freedom and richness of that of Greece, upon which it was always dependent. In this domain, as Horace later phrased it, "Captive Greece took captive her rude conqueror."

NEW TENDENCIES IN ROMAN EDUCATION.   One very important consequence of the contact with Hellenism was that Roman education developed new forms and ideals. The upper classes were no longer content with traditional training based on familiarity with ancestral customs. In the third and second centuries they demanded an acquaintance with Greek literature, rhetoric, and philosophy. Appreciation of these studies was stimulated by the visits to Rome of some of the most famous intellectual figures of the Hellenistic World, such as the Stoic philosopher Panaetius of Rhodes and Carneades, the founder of the New Academy at Athens, both of whom came to Rome on diplomatic missions. The Hellenistic point of view that training in rhetoric and philosophy should equip a man to attain success in public and private life through the practice of virtue accorded well with the practical tendencies of Roman character and helped to develop a broader Roman conception of cultured citizenship expressed in the word humanity (*humanitas*). Among the chief patrons of Hellenism were men of the type of Scipio Africanus the Elder; notably Titus Flamininus, Aemilius Paullus, and Scipio Aemilianus, at whose house gathered the leading intellectuals of the day, including the Achaean historian Polybius.

The influence of Greek philosophy on the senatorial class should not be over-estimated, however. Romans at first regarded philosophy with some suspicion, since epistemology in general seemed useless and impractical. Fears of the possibly subversive effects of Epicurean doctrines, sophistry, and skepticism on traditional religious, moral, and political beliefs actually led in 173 and 161 to the temporary banishment of Greek philosophers. Philosophies offering rules of life seemed more interesting because useful, although their study by the increasing numbers of senators who embraced them seems to have been superficial. Thus Epicureanism, which was brought back from banishment and won many converts, was often misinterpreted at Rome as advocating sensuous living. More influential senators followed Stoicism, the first famous convert being Scipio Aemilianus, who patronized Panaetius, the Stoic sage. Because Stoic notions of duty and fate appealed to traditional Roman stolidity (*gravitas*), Panaetius' doctrine was congenial to persons like the younger Scipio, but did not noticeably make their political views more humane. Furthermore, despite genuine admiration for the Greek cultural achievement, the political ineptitude of the Greeks caused contemporary Romans to regard them with some contempt.

A knowledge of Greek now became essential for every educated man, and the demand for instruction in that language and in other subjects led to the appearance of schools conducted by professional teachers, although Roman practice remained hostile to any obligatory system of public education, and each parent directed his children's training as he saw fit. Schools were private, for the most part under the patronage or even in the houses of prominent men. Teachers were mainly educated slaves or freedmen, usually Greek, and accordingly had low social status. To a certain degree those who conducted schools of rhetoric and philosophy shared in this lack of respect, for they too were Greeks, although freemen and of a higher social standing. In a certain sense Cato and other conservatives opposed these new cultural tendencies, but it would be a mistake to regard Cato as a blind opponent of Hellenism on either political or cultural grounds. He learned to speak Greek at the age of thirty, and the buildings erected during his censorship were based on Greek models. He was acquainted with Greek philosophy, literature, and educational theory, and his own written works owe much in organization, and even content, to the Greeks. He introduced Ennius to Roman society and quite probably knew Polybius. What Cato counseled was the acceptance of Hellenism after due consideration of what the Greeks had to offer that would suit the more staid and "puritanical" Roman ethic.

PERSISTENCE OF OLDER CUSTOMS AND IDEALS. In many respects the Romans remained faithful to traditional ideals. They continued to stress the value of practical experience and home environment rather than literary studies and kept up ancient practices. Among these was the custom of entrusting a young man to an older person of reputation, whom he should attend constantly and who should be his model in both public and private life. Another custom peculiar to Rome was that of a funeral procession and panegyric oration accorded to distinguished members of aristocratic families. In the funeral cortège death masks of the deceased's ancestors were worn by mourners clad in the robes of office they had filled and bearing inscriptions recording their titles and honors. At the grave or before the funeral pyre an oration was delivered glorifying the dead and the services he and his house had rendered the state. By this reminder of the greatness of their ancestors, noble Roman youths were inspired to emulate their character and achievements.

THE RISE OF ROMAN LITERATURE.   Native Roman genius produced little literature before the Punic Wars. Close contact with Hellenistic civilization thereafter created both a taste and a demand for literary works. At first these developed in close imitation of Greek models, and as usual in the history of literature, poetry preceded prose. The low social status of the early poets, almost all of them foreigners, of servile origin, or both, attests an ambivalent Roman attitude toward poetry, esteemed primarily for practical qualities like its ability to inspire patriotic feelings or entertain the masses. Its personal, aesthetic aspects only gradually won respectability. The social function of poets producing plays under the curule aediles was thus both defined and limited, although they might experiment with epics and other genres and even establish personal relationships with the gentry. Senatorial patrons, even if they at first refused to write poetry because it was ungentlemanly, saw the advantage of cultivating writers who might publicize artistically their own services to the state.

A pioneer in poetry was Livius Andronicus (ca. 284–204), a Greek freedman from Tarentum, who translated Homer's *Odyssey* into Latin Saturnian verse as a text for school use. In 240, at the request of the aediles, he translated a Greek tragedy and comedy for production at public games. These were followed by numerous other translations and adaptations, as well as a hymn to the gods which he composed on the occasion of the invasion of Hasdrubal in 207. A contemporary of Andronicus, the Italian Gnaeus Naevius (ca. 270–199), showed greater independence and versatility. He was probably not a Roman citizen, since he failed to understand the Roman attitude toward free speech. He lampooned the Metelli, a prominent aristocratic family, and suffered imprisonment and self-exile. Not only did he create new plays by combining plots taken from more than one Greek original, he also wrote plays with purely Roman subjects. Perhaps his most notable achievement was an epic poem on the First Punic War, written in the native Saturnian meter. This probably gave inspiration to another literary pioneer, Quintus Ennius (239–169), a literary giant who, perhaps even more than Livius Andronicus, deserves to be called the father of Latin literature. A native of Calabria of Greek culture, he served as a soldier in Sardinia, was brought to Rome by Cato, and became a Roman citizen and protégé of the Scipios. His great work, a landmark in Latin literature, was the *Annals*, an epic poem in which he recounted the history of Rome from her legendary beginnings to 172. The *Annals* pointed the way for future generations of Latin epic poets by having as its central theme Rome's destiny as a world power and the glorification of her patriotic ideals. Vergil's *Aeneid* eventually ranked with it in popularity, but of its eighteen books only six hundred lines have survived. For his epic Ennius replaced the old Saturnian verse with the Latin hexameter, which he developed in imitation of the Greek. Ennius was a pioneer in the development of native Italian satire (*satura*), originally a medley of prose and verse, narrative and drama, the most original and Roman of poetic genres. He was also a comic and tragic playwright; his tragedies, which were especially regarded, followed the models of Aeschylus and Euripides.

Dramas became yearly fixtures at the chariot races, and by ca. 200 B.C. six tragedies and comedies were produced annually by the curule aediles. The first poet to devote himself entirely to the comic stage was the Umbrian, T. Maccius Plautus (ca. 254–184), who learned his Latin at Rome, where he allegedly eked out a living, at first, as a laborer in a flour mill and as an actor and stagehand. Twenty-one plays survive from his pen. They follow closely the Attic New Comedy, essentially a comedy of manners, whose atmosphere and characters were as predictable as they were un-Roman: the misadventures of the lovesick swain, the braggart soldier, the woman of easy virtue, the misanthrope, and the social parasite. Plautus infused his works with a language and meter that were genuinely Italian. There can be no mistaking the earthy Latin quality of his ebullient wit, which, at least in his early plays, is characterized by a sheer love of slapstick farce and general buffoonery, later to be reflected in Shakespearean comedy. Another interesting figure among the comic playwrights of the second century was Caecilius Statius, a captive from the Gallic tribe of the Insubres in north Italy. A friend of Ennius, Statius copied Greek models closely but was noted for the ingenuity of his plots. Much better known, however, and ranking with Plautus as a playwright of distinction is Terence (P. Terentius Afer, ca. 195–159), who came as a slave from Africa to Rome, where he received his education and his freedom. All of Terence's six plays, produced in the period 166–160, have survived. Like Plautus, Terence was dependent on New Comedy, but his works are much less broadly humorous than his predecessor's. He was not so interested in the rowdy and boisterous, devoting much more attention than Plautus to subtle interplays of characterization and to a refined and elegant Latin style. For this reason he tended to appeal to a selected and cultivated audience rather than to the public at large.

Poetry was clearly becoming more respectable during the second century B.C. as changes in education produced a small but influential upper-class audience preferring to read books than to attend public dramas. This may be seen in the work of Gaius Lucilius (ca. 180–ca. 103), a native of southern Latium, an equestrian, a friend of Scipio Aemilianus, and thus the first Roman poet from the gentry. Like Ennius, he wrote satires, but his were more striking, a poetry that was almost prose (*sermones*), the freewheeling talk of a member of the upper classes. An outspoken critic of a wide range of human foibles, he was a model and inspiration to many other famous poets, especially Horace and Juvenal. The disappearance of his poetry, except for fragments, is a very serious loss to our appreciation of Latin literature. The recognition that Lucilius' verses won him guaranteed the respectability of writing poetry as a leisure activity of gentlemen.

Tragedies continued to be written after Ennius, although our knowledge of notable figures and of works in this field is meager. One may mention Ennius' nephew Pacuvius (ca. 220–ca. 130) and L. Accius (ca. 170–ca. 85), who based their works on the Athenian dramatists Sophocles and Euripides. Accius' melodramatic works were extremely popular among his contemporaries and were highly regarded by sensitive Romans of later generations like Cicero, Horace, and Quintilian. By the last generation of the second century B.C., however, the most important period in Roman dramatic literature was drawing to a close. In both comedy and tragedy Greek plots and characters were abandoned gradually for those of Roman origin. Tragedy, in particular, declined in popularity, since the Roman public was in general too uneducated to appreciate its worth and preferred pageants, comedies, mimes, and gladiatorial combats.

Latin prose developed more slowly, and the first prose literary works of the period were written in Greek. At the very beginning of the development of prose writing in either language at Rome, certain basic characteristics are evident. Unlike poetry, writing prose was always a gentlemanly occupation, especially befitting the attention of Rome's governing elite. The favorite prose genres, as might be expected, were history, in which Rome's ideals and traditions were emphasized as much as in epic poetry, and oratory, one of the chief by-products of statecraft. Roman senators deemed it worthy to write in prose on a variety of other subjects, provided they had practical value.

Earliest among prose works was a history of Rome from its origins to the end of the Second Punic War compiled about 200 by Fabius Pictor, a senator who had fought in that war. His annalistic work was based on pontifical records and such other documentary records as were available, but it depended also on oral tradition. Pictor chose to write in Greek because the only available historical models were in that language and because he wished to justify and explain the growth of Roman power to a Greek audience. Cincius Alimentus, a contemporary of Pictor, wrote a similar history in Greek beginning with 729, and other annalists used Greek during the first half of the second century B.C. But in the meantime, the first historical work in Latin prose, albeit on a Greek rather than an annalistic model, was produced by Cato the Elder. His *Origines*, an account of the beginnings of Rome and other Italian states and of the wars of Rome from 264 to 150, was a rambling, disconnected narrative interrupted by lengthy digressions. Although the *Origines* has perished, Cato's earlier work on agriculture (*De agri cultura*) has survived as the oldest work in Latin prose to be preserved intact. This type of technical handbook also had Hellenistic precedents. A set of instructions for his peers, it is interesting for the insights it gives into the economy of the second century B.C. and into the folklore of rural society. Cato also wrote on a variety of other subjects, such as medicine, rhetoric, and probably law.

After Cato, Latin became the language of Roman historians, and many annalistic works were written. A beginning was also made in historical studies involving not merely chronological narratives but analysis and interpretation as well. Such was the history of the Second Punic War by Coelius Antipater. Closely related to history was the publication of personal memoirs and collections of letters, which began in this period. There was also some specialized and scientific writing, including works on constitutional law, astronomy, and natural history.

JURISPRUDENCE. In law we find a unique achievement of the Roman genius, affected little by Greek influences. Roman legal literature was an outgrowth of the need for interpretation of law in the code of the Twelve Tables and subsequent legislation. At first, interpretation was the advice given by pontiffs to magistrates or citizens seeking aid in applying law to definite cases. Tiberius Coruncanius, who became the first plebeian *pontifex maximus* in 253, began to admit to his discussions of legal problems any persons interested in improving their legal knowledge. His example was followed by others outside the pontifical college. In this way there grew up among the senatorial class a group of specialists called *iuris prudentes* or *iuris consulti*, "men learned in the law." They did not limit themselves to discussions and giving advice but soon began to write books on various aspects of the law. One of the earliest of these writers, the founder of Roman juristic literature, was Sextus Aelius Paetus, consul in 198, whose ability won him the nickname of Catus, "the shrewd". He published a work which later generations regarded as basic. It contained three parts: one devoted to an exposition of the Law of the Twelve Tables, the second to its interpretation, and the third to legal procedure. Paetus was followed by many juristic writers, among them Cato the Censor and his son, whose fame as a lawyer excelled his father's. Jurisconsults were not professional lawyers in the modern sense. They were a small circle of leading senators who held various public offices. They did not practice law as a business and took no fees but studied law because of its importance in the conduct of their offices and because, by interpreting the law for their friends, they increased their prestige and influence and thus their clientele. Through their interpretations, which shaped the decisions of magistrates and judges, jurisconsults exercised a great influence upon the understanding and enforcement of law.

PRAETOR'S EDICT. The most important line of development in Roman law was through the edicts issued by annual magistrates, especially those whose duties were largely judicial, such as the city praetor, the praetor for the aliens in Rome, and provincial governors. Of these the most important was the edict of the city praetor who administered the law for Roman citizens in Italy. At the beginning of his term the praetor stated the principles which he would observe in enforcing laws and the conditions under which he would admit prosecutions and suits. Thus, both new principles and remedies were introduced into law by virtue of the praetor's authority without resort to legislation. As a later Roman jurist expressed it, the purpose of the edict was "to aid, supplement, and correct" civil law. A noticeable improvement was made in procedure. In addition to, and in place of, the old actions at law which were few in number and unalterable in language, the praetor issued formulas suited to individual cases. He formally laid the claim of the plaintiff before the judge and instructed the judge to render his decision according to whether the evidence supported or contradicted it. The formulary procedure proved so flexible and efficient that the Aebutian Law, passed in the latter half of the second century B.C., approved it and paved the way for disappearance of the old actions at law. In general, the praetor's edict served the interests of equity rather than a strict interpretation of the law. Each praetor's edict was valid only for his own term, but it became the custom for a new praetor to incorporate into his own edict most or all of that of his predecessor. So reforms once introduced were perpetuated, and the edict grew to be a long document and came to need interpretation itself by jurists, just as the Twelve Tables.

RELIGION. During imperial expansion, penetration of Roman religion by Greek influences was increasingly marked. This followed the already established syncretism of similar Greek and Roman divinities and the adoption of Greek mythology. By ca. 200 B.C. there was formally recognized in Rome a group of twelve greater divinities identical with the Olympian gods of Greece. Minor Latin divinities fell rapidly into neglect, while their place was taken by others of Greek origin. The transformation of the old impersonal Roman deities into anthropomorphic Hellenic gods is reflected in the acceptance of Greek types for statuary, a strong demand for which arose following acquaintance with works of art looted from Syracuse and other Greek cities.

In the addition of Greek gods to those officially worshipped in Rome and in the acceptance of Greek ritualistic practices, the Sibylline oracles played a large part. At critical moments during the First and Second Punic Wars, when the state was in danger and appeals to the older gods were ineffectual, these oracles were consulted and frequently interpreted as authorizing a new cult or ceremony. Thus, in 205 the oracles recommended institution of the cult of the Great Mother of Pessinus in Asia Minor and of her consort, Attis. This cult was formally established in the next year, with the transfer of the cult image, a black stone, from Pessinus to Rome. The Great Mother was a nature goddess whose worship was native to Asia Minor, although somewhat rationalized by Hellenistic influences. Shocked by the orgiastic character of this worship conducted by a professional priesthood of mutilated devotees, the Senate quickly withdrew its sponsorship.

The third century B.C. marked the end of the introduction of Greek deities under official auspices. After 200 the Senate tried to discourage innovations and would permit only the grafting of new cults on to traditional ones. This conservative attitude is shown in the suppression of the Bacchanalian societies in 186. Throughout South Italy the worship of Dionysos or Bacchus had flourished among the Greek population. Captives carried northward as slaves from this area following the war with Hannibal spread its rites throughout Campania and Etruria and introduced them to Rome itself. The adherents of the cult formed secret and mystical religious associations. Some of these sectaries were accused and convicted of violent crimes and immoral practices. The Senate concluded that the societies were conspiring against the state and ordered the consuls to disband them on both Roman and allied territory. Probably the charges were exaggerated and the real grounds for action were the illegality of secret associations and a genuine Roman aversion to orgiastic religious rites. Despite this suppression, the Senate permitted individuals to worship Dionysos under official supervision. This was an expression of a definite religious policy. The state did not inquire into matters of belief, but neither did it tolerate ceremonies contrary to Roman standards of propriety and morality. Mistrust of foreign cults and their ritual observances also explains the banishment of Chaldean astrologers from Italy in 139.

Although the formalities of religion in government were still scrupulously observed, there was an ever-increasing skepticism with regard to the existence and power of the gods of Graeco-Roman mythology and the efficacy of augury and divination. After about 200 there was a corresponding decline in the status of priesthoods. This was because educated classes were influenced by the rationalism of Euhemerus, whose work on the origin of the gods had been translated by Ennius, and even more by the pantheism of Stoic philosophy.

PUBLIC FESTIVALS. Of great importance in the city were the annual public festivals or games, of which six came to be celebrated regularly by the middle of the second century, each lasting several days. Five of these were celebrated by the aediles, one by the city praetor. A fixed sum was allotted by the state to defray expenses, but custom required that they be largely supplemented at the cost of the presiding magistrate. In this way the aedileship afforded an excellent opportunity to win public favor by generous outlay. To the original horse and chariot races there were added scenic productions, wild-beast hunts, and gladiatorial combats, like those exhibited by private citizens. The first private exhibition of gladiators was given at a funeral in 264, and the first wild-beast hunt in 186; they soon became the most popular of all.

ROME THE CITY. The growth of Rome in population and wealth changed the appearance of the city, and in the third and second centuries B.C. it increasingly assumed the mannered and even elegant aspect of a Hellenized Italian town. The erection of tenement houses of several stories and a rise in rentals reflected the influx into the capital. Public buildings assumed monumental character. The Circus Flaminius, which was used for horse races, wild-beasts hunts, and gladiatorial combats, dates from the end of the third century B.C. No less than fifteen temples and shrines were dedicated between 200 and 133. Two large basilicas or public halls, so-called after similar structures built by Hellenistic kings in the Greek East, were built for magistrates and businessmen. Additional facilities for trade were provided by a new fish and meat market, new blocks of shops, and a dock on the Tiber to facilitate the unloading of ships. There were also a considerable number of porticoes to provide shelter for merchants and idlers. Two new aqueducts were constructed to meet the needs of the growing population. Streets were paved with stone blocks and the sewage system repaired and extended. Arches adorned with statues were set up to commemorate Roman victories. Many other statues, the work of Greek sculptors and spoils of war, were placed as votive offerings in the new temples. Improvements were made in the quality of building materials. Public buildings were generally constructed of stone, sometimes coated with stucco; harder travertine blocks were used in place of less durable tufa. As early as the third century B.C. Romans knew of concrete; its use, perfected in the course of the second century B.C., was to have a long history in the development at Rome of Hellenistic architectural ideas on a monumental scale. It permitted the Romans to transcend the limitations of post and lintel architecture, to use the arch and barrel vault as novel means of opening space, and to give a more plastic conception to public buildings. For the temples of Jupiter and Juno dedicated in 146, marble was imported from Greece. Private buildings, however, continued to be built mainly of crude brick and wood.

ROMAN ART. In the third and second centuries B.C. the Hellenistic style of art became general throughout Italy where, however, local variations in its interpretation had already appeared among Etruscans and Italians. Greek influences therefore continued to affect artistic tastes and techniques in Rome itself. Few artists of note appeared among the Romans, who depended upon other Italians or Greeks for the execution of works they planned. The Latin genius was revealed in the creation of practical rather than ornamental works, like the paved highways, bridges, and aqueducts. In temple building the Romans blended with the Greek architectural orders traditional Italic and Etruscan elements like the emphasis on axiality and the use of high podiums and entrances. Although a Greek architect was imported for the temples of Jupiter and Juno built in 146, architecture was highly esteemed in Rome, and Roman architects were winning recognition abroad. As early as 170 the Syrian

VI Tabularium at Rome. *This, the ancient Roman state archives building, was was erected in 78 B.C. on the Capitoline hill by the consul Q. Lutatius Catulus. It is the earliest notable example of use by Roman architects of arcaded porticoes, later to become a typical feature of Roman building. (Photo: Fototeca Unione.)*

virtue was piety (*pietas*), which meant the dutiful performance of all one's obligations, to the gods, to one's kinsmen, and to the state. It was toward the state in particular that a Roman ideally showed loyalty and devotion. Friends, relatives, life itself, must all be sacrificed for the good of the state. There can be no doubt about the importance of such values to Roman life. Later generations of Romans looked back to the lives of statesmen and generals of this period to find examples of patriotism worthy of imitation. These included Brutus the Elder, traditionally one of the first consuls, who had his own sons executed for treason; the Decii, who in three successive generations were said to have deliberately sacrificed their lives to save Roman armies; Manlius Torquatus, the consul who executed his son for a breach of military discipline; Manius Curius, who preferred poverty to wealth won by betraying his country. Even if such stories preserve kernels of historic truth, they represented a highly idealized and romanticized notion of the "good old days" thought up by Romans of the third and second centuries B.C. to furnish a contrast with the alleged moral decline of their own epoch. One may justly doubt whether early Roman aristocrats very frequently lived up to such self-effacing patriotic standards, despite their respect for authority.

Although the Romans were a serious, hardheaded, practical people, Roman life did not lack opportunities for relaxation and enjoyment. The festivals, public and private, were occasions of entertainment and merrymaking. This is true in particular of the "Great Games" celebrated after the harvest and of the Saturnalia at the end of the winter sowing in December.

RESPECT FOR TRADITION. Characteristic Roman conservatism affected Roman religious beliefs and was further strengthened by the respect paid to parental authority and by the absence of intellectual training. In public affairs this conservatism was shown by the influence of ancestral custom—the *mos maiorum*, a very potent factor in Roman government, since the constitution was not a single comprehensive document but rather a number of laws supplemented by custom and precedent and so interpreted. The importance of conservatism and respect for *mos maiorum* may be seen in several important concepts loaded with a meaning only palely reflected in their obvious English cognates and basic to Roman values for centuries. These included *dignitas*, that quality uniquely distinguishing great men who had served the state well, a prestige whose attainment gave meaning to the lives of senatorial statesmen; *auctoritas*, the main corollary to *dignitas*, a quasi-legal quality which demanded that the Romans follow the advice of elder statesmen by virtue of their character, station, and acknowledged superiority in public life; and *libertas*, freedom not to challenge or change the established order, but rather to do what laws and *mos maiorum* allowed. These attitudes go a long way toward explaining why democratic development at Rome was to be abortive. The Roman public tended not to question leadership and to be content with a society which gave and demanded unequal privileges and responsibilities, so long as *libertas* guaranteed at least a minimum of personal rights.

King Antiochus IV Epiphanes hired a Roman to complete the famous temple of Olympian Zeus begun in the sixth century B.C. in Athens. The frequent use of round buildings, especially in the case of smaller temples, shows an independent Roman tradition going back to round huts of prehistoric times.

Through familiarity with masterpieces looted in war or acquired by provincial governors, a taste for fine statuary and an appreciation of Greek ideals in this field of art slowly developed. Although such acquisitions at first decorated public buildings, a demand soon arose for a similar adornment of private homes. This led to a regular business of copying works of Greek masters for the Roman market.

Roman taste asserted itself most clearly in painting and secular sculpture. In painting there appeared the naturalness and the feeling for depth and movement that characterized tomb paintings of Etruria and Campania, as well as the decorative designs on Etruscan bronzes. Romans frequently painted their tombs, but also developed the practice of exhibiting for popular edification large-scale pictures illustrating battles and victorious foreign campaigns. Although fragments of Roman tomb paintings have survived from as early as the third century B.C., the triumphal paintings, which were housed in temples and private buildings, have all completely disappeared. Characteristically Roman was the fondness for portrait busts and statues. Their antecedents may be found in the busts and figures which adorned the Etruscan ash urns and sarcophagi, as well as in Etruscan bronze and terra cotta statuary. The Roman love of portraiture found its expression in wax death masks of ancestors in aristocratic houses and the lifelike ancestral statues carried in funeral processions. In addition, from an early date, the government had bronze statues erected to commemorate the kings and heroes of the early Republic. Later it so honored famous generals of the historic period and others who had rendered distinguished service to their country. By the end of the second century it had become a well-established custom for magistrates to set up statues in their own honor in public places. The outstanding feature of Roman portrait sculpture is its intense realism, which went far beyond the naturalness of Etruscan art and insisted on the representation even of ugliness. This emphasis on realism melded easily with some current Hellenistic styles and was one to which Greek artists, flocking to Rome, adapted without difficulty.

CHAPTER 12
A PERIOD OF
FACTIONAL STRIFE:
133–78 B.C.

R OMAN REVOLUTION. The century which began with the year 133 B.C.
is frequently called the period of the Roman Revolution. It was an era of
increasingly bitter strife that eventually erupted into civil wars, which ultimately
destroyed oligarchic government and replaced it with a disguised monarchy.
This century of crisis was the final outcome of the failure of the senatorial class
to achieve a satisfactory solution to the economic, social, and political problems
confronting Rome. Although the reasons for the Roman Revolution were in
large measure social and economic, the course it took and its ultimate resolution
were mainly political. Unlike most modern revolutions, it ended not with a
dramatic change in the existing social and economic order, but rather with a
gradual reorganization of the governing elite in the service of one-man rule.

The crisis was manifested by an intensification and broadening of factional
political strife, which had been traditional for centuries in a milder form within
the ruling oligarchy. That oligarchy continued to be split up into rival
groups competing for high office but normally presented a united front against
mavericks or brilliant careerists who might not play politics according to
traditional rules. By the latter part of the second century B.C. the burgeoning
problems of Empire gave such mavericks or careerists an opportunity to create
unorthodox political clienteles by championing various groups that were
discontented with the existing order and demanding various kinds of reform.

Such groups on occasion included the urban and rural proletariat in Italy, the Italian allies, the equestrians, and to a certain extent Rome's subjects, so that completely new dimensions were given to factional politics. Unlike some modern political systems, there was never any neat dichotomy within the Senate between "reformers" and "reactionaries." Even those leaders most enthusiastically committed to the dominance in government of the Senate as a corporation were capable of a high degree of statesmanship and of advocating reform legislation on their own or of coopting that of their rivals, although they sometimes did so reluctantly, in terms of their own vested interest.

Ultimately factional strife involved the whole Roman world and even some of the peoples beyond the frontiers of the Empire; the surest path to power lay in successful generalship, and hence ambitious men sought military force adequate to carry them to victory in their struggle to dominate the government. For this reason, despite internal disorders, the century marked an imperial expansion rivaling that of the Punic and Macedonian Wars. In Gaul, Roman domination was extended to the Rhine and the Ocean; in the East practically the whole peninsula of Asia Minor, as well as Syria and Egypt, was incorporated in the Empire. With the exception of Mauretania (i.e., modern Morocco, really a Roman dependency), Roman provinces completely encircled the Mediterranean. Another important result of the struggle was the creation of an Italian nation by the admission to Roman citizenship of practically all peoples dwelling south of the Alps. For most citizens and subjects of Rome the era of the Roman Revolution meant oppression and misery on a large scale, because the military needs of rival factions and leaders caused continued, serious drains on Italian manpower and even greater exploitation of provincial wealth.

The period 133 to 78 B.C. covers the first stage in the struggle, the events of which were recorded in detail by contemporary Roman historians. Their works have not survived, however, and knowledge of the period today depends chiefly on later writers. From them a fairly clear idea of the main course of events is derived, but frequently their exact sequence and the motives and influences that resulted in courses of action or legislation are uncertain. The chief sources are Plutarch's *Lives* of Tiberius and Gaius Gracchus, Marius, and Sulla, and Appian's *Civil and Mithridatic Wars*, supplemented by the *Epitome* of Livy, and Sallust's *Jugurthine War*. To these must be added the short histories of Velleius Paterculus and the epitomists of the imperial period, as well as fragments from the more extensive histories of Diodorus and Cassius Dio. There are isolated but important references in Cicero's speeches and other writings and in some Roman antiquarians. Inscriptions are few but include considerable portions of important laws.

I. AGRARIAN REFORM OF TIBERIUS GRACCHUS: 133 B.C.

Land Law of 133 B.C. The struggle was brought into the open by the agrarian legislation proposed by Tiberius Sempronius Gracchus, a tribune for the year 133. Gracchus, then thirty years of age, was one of the most prominent young Romans of his time, the son of the like-named consul and of Cornelia, daughter of Scipio Africanus. Under his mother's supervision he had received a careful education, which included rhetoric and Greek Stoic philosophy. As quaestor in Spain in 137, he distinguished himself for courage and honesty in dealing with the natives and acquainted himself with the military needs of Rome.

The motives for the reform program he embarked on as member of the Claudian faction are complex and obscure. In part they were political. His *dignitas* had recently been wounded and his patronage with his Spanish clients undermined when the Senate rejected a treaty he had negotiated with them. His espousal of reform would restore his *dignitas* and damage that of his opponents, especially the then-dominant faction led by Scipio Aemilianus. Some have seen at work liberal influences of his Greek education. Basically his motives were probably statesmanlike. He was aware of the economic crisis in Rome recently brought about by high prices and underemployment, and he saw in the decline of the free peasantry of Italy a potential military crisis, since normally soldiers still had to be landholders. When elected tribune he drafted a law aimed at solving the problem of urban unemployment and reestablishing the free Italian peasantry.

The bill was essentially conservative. Some years before, one Laelius (consul in 140), who belonged to the party of Scipio Aemilianus and who was scarcely radical, had broached the question of land reform but had withdrawn his proposals because of the protests they aroused. Tiberius' own bill was opposed by leaders like Scipio Aemilianus but found the support of some influential politicians, notably his father-in-law and factional chief, Appius Claudius Pulcher, Dean of the Senate. It was primarily designed to enforce existing but long-disregarded legislation that restricted the amount of public land that might be occupied by a single tenant. In a conciliatory spirit Tiberius Gracchus suggested that senatorial squatters should henceforth enjoy in full security possession of 500 Roman acres of public land.[1] Occupied land under the legal limit was to be granted to the holders in perpetuity without liability to tax or rent. In addition, the state was to compensate former holders for improvements they had made on land surrendered according to this law. Land recovered for public use was to be assigned to landless Romans in small plots that they could not transfer to others and for which they were to pay a nominal rent. A commission of three men (*III viri agris iudicandis assignandis*) was to be elected to take over the land claimed by the state and reapportion it to the new colonists.

Despite the rather generous treatment accorded to great proprietors by this Sempronian Law, it was stubbornly opposed by most senators. This was not

---

[1] Tiberius' law dealt only with occupied public land and did not include *ager publicus* that had been used as pasturage.

because the Senate did not recognize that the land question was serious but because a majority of its members had already decided against alteration in the status quo. Some of the aristocracy saw that a considerable portion of their holdings was threatened. In many cases it must have become impossible to distinguish between their private property and public lands in the possession of their families for several generations, and they did not know how much they stood to lose. Furthermore, the oligarchy traditionally had looked upon a division of public land as associated with the creation of a clientele by unorthodox means, and now they began to suspect Tiberius of ulterior political ambitions.

Angered by the opposition, Tiberius withdrew from his measure the proposals for compensation for improvements and the granting of ownership rights to public landholdings of less than the maximum legal size and sought to present his amended law directly to the Plebeian Council, a step which, although not illegal, was a deliberate bypassing of the Senate. The Senate then resorted to the traditional means of holding tribunes in check and induced one of the other tribunes, Marcus Octavius, to veto the law. Tiberius persevered, and, after all attempts at compromise had failed, he reluctantly appealed to the Plebeian Council to depose Octavius because he was thwarting popular will. The Council responded by ousting Octavius, and the land law was passed without further opposition. The deposition of Octavius alarmed most senators because it was apparently unprecedented, Rome never having recognized the principle of recall from office. Tiberius himself, his younger brother Gaius, and his own father-in-law, Appius Claudius, were elected as the three commissioners to enforce the law. They received authority to enable them to judge cases where disputes arose regarding ownership of land claimed by the state.

FALL OF TIBERIUS GRACCHUS. Once the law was passed, its legality was recognized, even by the opposing factions. Nevertheless, the Senate tried to hamper the commissioners by refusing to provide adequate funds for their expenses, which included stocking of the allotments assigned to poor settlers. Tiberius proposed that money for this purpose be provided from the treasure of his father's client, King Attalus III of Pergamon, who had just died after bequeathing his kingdom to Rome,[2] a notable instance in which a provincial client affected factional politics at the capital. Tiberius' proposal was a revolutionary challenge to traditional control by the Senate of finances and foreign affairs. Senatorial animosity was further aroused by the declaration of Tiberius that he would seek reelection to the tribunate for 132. This was not unprecedented, but it was certainly very unusual and contrary to established practice of the third and second centuries B.C. Tiberius felt that only as tribune could he assure enforcement of the land law and refused to be dissuaded from his course. He was also credited with raising the question of giving citizenship to the Italian

---

[2] See p. 132.

allies to compensate for losses they might suffer from the operation of his land law. It seems unlikely, however, that he was concerned with the allies, the basis of his power resting solely on the urban plebs and the rural proletariat. Senatorial extremists determined to prevent his reelection. The consul, Scaevola, related by marriage, like the Gracchi, to the Claudian faction, refused the appeal to take action against him. Tiberius' opponents organized their clients and slaves and attacked Tiberius and his followers at a meeting in the Forum. Tiberius and 300 of his adherents were lynched and their bodies thrown into the Tiber. A judicial commission of doubtful constitutionality, although authorized by the Senate and presided over by the consuls of 132, sought out and punished with death or exile many of his faction.

FATE OF THE LAND COMMISSION. For the moment Gracchan opponents, led by the Scipionic faction, had triumphed but only by resorting to force. Almost at once a popular reaction set in against the party that had killed the Gracchans. This led to an important, if gradual, political realignment leading to the eventual dissolution of the once-powerful faction centered on Scipio Aemilianus. This faction, which had in the last analysis opposed the Gracchans primarily on political rather than economic grounds, for the moment did nothing to impede the land commission, which, staffed by advocates of reform, continued its work.

Apparently in 130–129 the commission, presided over by the Gracchan partisan Fulvius Flaccus, disturbed the Italian allies by questioning their right to plots bordering on public land and by the way in which they selected those plots to be reclaimed by the state. The allies claimed that their treaty rights were being disregarded and appealed to Scipio Aemilianus, under whom their troops had served against Carthage and Numantia, to represent them before the Senate. Scipio successfully sponsored a law permitting appeal to the consuls of judgments on land made by the commission. How far he would have gone in securing concessions for the allies is unknown, for he died unexpectedly in April or May of 129.

When the question of allied rights was raised again, it was on the initiative of Flaccus, ex-land commissioner and a consul for 125. He sponsored a law to grant citizenship to Latin and Italian allies with an alternative of the right of appeal from the judgments of Roman courts and magistrates for the citizens of communities that did not want Roman citizenship. This won the allegiance of the allies to the Gracchan party, and his proposal was energetically opposed by other factions, who saw in the temporary alliance of the bulk of the Roman electorate and Italians a threat to oligarchy. The question of citizenship for the allies was to become a matter of party politics and could not be judged on its merits. A political maneuver by Gracchan opponents succeeded in removing Flaccus to a military command in Gaul, and he had to abandon his proposal. This angered the allies, as did a law concerning the consular elections of 126 that had excluded them from Rome, preventing Latins in particular from voting by right of domicile in the capital or even from influencing other voters. Of the Latin allies, Fregellae in Latium near the Samnite border had been most active in demanding Roman citizenship, and, when this was rejected, the inhabitants revolted. The situation was serious, for the rebellion might have spread to other Latin communities and from them to the Italian allies. The Romans at once besieged the city. As a result of treachery it soon fell and was brutally razed by the praetor, Opimius, as a warning to states that might be tempted to follow its example. None did so, and the revolt ended.

The census taken in 125 B.C. showed an increase of about 75,000 Roman citizens over that of 130 B.C.: a total of 394,736 as against 318,828. No far-reaching conclusions can be drawn from all these figures, which are surely inaccurate. In any case, the gain cannot all be ascribed to the land commission, although it had continued to function since 133, for the census lists included all Roman men of eighteen years and over, and not merely those who had sufficient property to qualify them for military service. Undoubtedly many who failed to register after they lost their properties reported themselves when they received new allotments, but surely many landless who hoped to share in the division also enrolled. At the same time, in the struggle for control of the assemblies, patrons saw to it that their clients, in particular their freedmen and other dependents, were properly enrolled in the tribes and centuries.

II. GAIUS GRACCHUS AND THE SENATE: 124–121 B.C.

GAIUS GRACCHUS, TRIBUNE: 124–122 B.C.   In 124 Gaius, the younger brother of Tiberius Gracchus and a former member of the land commission of 133, returned to Rome from a term as quaestor in Sardinia and successfully ran for the tribunate, despite intense oligarchic opposition, entering office on December 10, 124. Gaius was a passionate orator, one of the most moving speakers in Roman history. He was also more energetic and more statesmanlike than his brother. Political traditions as well as ties of blood called him to support his brother's agrarian policy, but his aims were more far-reaching and ultimately brought him into conflict with other factions over questions of policy. For a time, however, he avoided any clash with his opponents while managing to retain the enthusiastic support of the poorer citizens. His popularity and influence were proved by his reelection to the tribunate in the summer of 123. In this his opponents seem to have acquiesced, although no special legislation seems to have been passed since the death of Tiberius sanctioning successive terms, for it was custom, not law, that forbade the practice. Among the colleagues of Gaius in his second tribunate were his fiery ally Fulvius Flaccus, ex-consul of 125, and Marcus Livius Drusus, an opponent of the Gracchi.

LEGISLATION OF GAIUS GRACCHUS.   Because the order in which Gaius Gracchus proposed his extensive legislative program is not clearly known, it is hazardous to assign definite proposals to either of his two terms of office. It seems, however, that the bulk of his legislation fell between his reelection in 123 and the close of his career in December 122. For convenience, his measures may be grouped under three heads: judicial, economic and social, and imperial.

(a) *Judicial.* His first judiciary law condemned retroactively sentences pronounced by courts unauthorized by the Plebeian Council, such as the senatorial court that had punished the followers of Tiberius in 132. As a result, the ex-consul Popillius, who had presided over that tribunal, went into voluntary exile. Then, at Gaius' instigation a colleague named Acilius successfully introduced a law drastically reorganizing the court for the recovery of damages from officials guilty of extortion and other crimes in the provinces. According to the mutilated text that has survived, the Acilian Law excluded magistrates in office, senators, and fathers, brothers, and sons of senators from the panel from which the fifty judges hearing each case were selected. Although the statement of specific qualifications of the new jurors has been lost, it is almost certain that it included the class of wealthy publicans and landholders who had a property assessment of at least 400,000 sesterces. This is perhaps the earliest formally legal definition of the equestrian order in its widest extent. The equestrians thus became more conscious of their power and special interests, since control of the court became a bone of contention between them and the Senate. Gaius undoubtedly had the welfare of provincials at heart when he transferred control over the tribunal from the senatorial order, but his reform did not noticeably improve their lot.

(b) *Economic and social.* One of the first steps taken by Gaius to deal with impoverished Roman citizens was the enactment of a grain law (*lex frumentaria*), which provided that the state should sell a certain quantity of grain each month to citizens residing in Rome at a fixed price not subject to speculation. There can be little doubt that this law was supposed to stabilize prices for the benefit of the poor, who lived in perpetual danger of famine. Even before this, in emergencies, the Roman government had occasionally resorted to such an expedient, but now it became a permanent charge on the treasury. In the larger cities of the Greek East it had become a generally accepted doctrine that the state was responsible for the food supply, and it is probable that Gaius was both familiar with this doctrine and inspired by it. He also undoubtedly saw that this law would greatly increase his popularity with the city plebs and might weaken—to his advantage—the ties between other senators and their clients, who would be less dependent on patronage for their daily bread. He may have justified the expense involved in offering grain at such a low price on the ground that the people were entitled to share in the income derived from the Empire. Since recipients of cheap grain had to pay for it, Gaius cannot strictly be said to have instituted a dole, although a step had been taken in that direction. In order to store supplies of wheat, Gaius directed the construction of large granaries, and this work doubtless provided temporary employment for many free laborers.

Another project Gaius pushed vigorously was the construction or improvement of roads throughout Italy. These were probably intended to facilitate the transport of grain and other agricultural produce to the nearest markets, for the city depended mainly upon supplies drawn from Sicily, Africa, and other countries by sea. Here was also a policy of providing work for the unemployed, as well as of agrarian colonization, for the lands abutting the roads were assigned to farmers who undertook to keep them in repair in place of paying rent to the state.

Gaius was also the author of a special agrarian law, but little is known about it. A chance notice records that he restricted the amount of land which anyone might hold in Italy to 200 *iugera* (132 acres), which might be interpreted to mean that, in his desire to obtain more land for settlement, he greatly reduced the maximum set by Tiberius for occupants of public lands. If this were correct, it hardly would have been ignored by all the more important writers. Perhaps this law authorized the founding of a number of colonies throughout Italy, although that may have been the subject of special legislation. At any rate Gaius resorted to colonization to relieve overpopulation. Of the several colonial foundations attributed to him, two at least—Neptunia, adjacent to Tarentum, and Scolacium—were seaports. For these the colonists seem to have been persons of some means, willing to engage in commerce rather than farming. By far the most important colonial project was his attempt to found the first overseas colony near the site of Carthage, which had been uninhabited since its destruction in 146. This colony, called Junonia, was authorized by a law sponsored by the tribune Rubrius. In the spring of 122 Gaius and Fulvius Flaccus, two of the commission appointed to supervise the enterprise, went to Africa and organized the colony. The colonists, who numbered about 6,000, were enrolled from all Italy and received unusually large allotments, 200 *iugera* each, which they held as personal property not subject to rent.

A minor piece of legislation carried by Gaius in the interests of the poorer citizens required that the state should furnish soldiers with clothing free of charge and make no deductions for this from their pay. This law, also prohibiting enlistment of recruits under seventeen years of age, suggests the pressing manpower shortage felt by the military.

(c) *Imperial.* Although the direction of imperial administration customarily rested with the Senate, Gaius did not hesitate to intervene in this sphere. One of his laws changed the system of allocating consular provinces—that is, the spheres of duty, in particular foreign commands, assigned to incoming consuls each year. The Senate had regularly designated these provinces after the elections, when they knew who the consuls-elect were. This made it possible for senators to assign provinces according to the proven capacities of nominees, but it also allowed them to use their power to reward their friends and punish their political opponents, as had been the case with Flaccus in 125. This power was lost when the law of Gaius compelled the Senate to designate the two consular provinces in advance of the election.[3]

Another law dealt with taxes in the recently organized province of Asia. It provided that the contract for collecting the tithe on the produce of all agricultural land in the province should be let by the censors in Rome to a single company of *publicani*. The result was that provincial tax collectors were practically excluded from bidding, since the sum involved was beyond their resources, and they would be at a great disadvantage in meeting the terms of the censors. Since Asia was by far the richest province, an opportunity was thus created for publicans to make huge profits. By this act, as well as by the Acilian Law, Gracchus won the temporary support of the equestrian order. Gracchus undoubtedly believed that the change in tax collection would aid the provincials of Asia (who were his family's clients), since corrupt senatorial governors, conniving with native tax farmers, had extorted more than the legal amount from the population; but the result was unfortunate for the people of Asia, who were exposed to merciless exploitation by a largely irresponsible tax-collecting agency operating from the capital of the Empire and cooperating with sometimes corrupt governors.

The agrarian reforms of Tiberius Gracchus had brought up the question of the status of Roman allies in Italy, and events had made the Gracchan leaders champions of their rights. Early in his second tribunate, Gaius proposed to grant Roman citizenship to the Latins. This was countered by Livius Drusus, who suggested that they be given complete immunity from scourging by Roman magistrates. Gaius' opponents thus succeeded in dividing non-Romans on the question of citizenship as protection against arbitrary treatment by Roman magistrates. They apparently supported Drusus' measure at the price of abandoning the cause of the federate allies. Gaius dropped his agitation for the moment but later drafted a more comprehensive measure, again proposing Roman citizenship for the Latins and, at the same time, Latin rights for the federate allies in Italy. This met with even stronger opposition in the Senate than the earlier proposal. Italians flocked to Rome to support the law and influence the plebs on its behalf, but the Senate ordered the consuls to exclude from the city and environs all nonvoters. Whether the law was vetoed by Drusus or was defeated in the Plebeian Council, it failed to obtain the approval of the electorate, which considered that its own interests would be endangered by the addition of many new voters. Thus the question of the allies was shelved for the time, and Gaius suffered a major political defeat which revealed that his influence with the Council had been seriously undermined.

FALL OF GAIUS GRACCHUS: 121 B.C. The decline of influence with the Plebeian Council, which meant the end of Gaius' political power, was

---

[3] This rule applied also to proconsular provinces, that is, those to which the consuls were to go as proconsular governors at the end of their year of office.

brought about largely through maneuvers of his opponents, many of whom had former connections with the faction of Scipio Aemilianus. Alarmed at Gaius' successful reelection as tribune and at the dominant part which he played in government, his enemies in the Senate planned his overthrow. They found an agent in his colleague, Livius Drusus, who weaned the city electorate from Gaius by outbidding his proposed laws with others that appealed even more to interests and prejudices of the voters. When Gaius proceeded slowly with the organization of his colonies in Italy, Drusus introduced a law authorizing the foundation of twelve colonies immediately. Each of these was to consist of 3,000 colonists selected from the very poorest citizens, and there was to be no rent paid to the government for individual allotments, as was the case in the Gracchan colonies. The Livian colonies were actually never founded. After the fall of Gaius Gracchus, when it was no longer necessary to appeal to the proletariat, the matter was dropped. It may be, however, that the provision affecting rents was enforced and extended to Gracchan colonists. When Gaius renewed his attempt to enfranchise the Latins, while granting Latin status to other Italian allies, his opponents openly appealed to the exclusiveness of the voters. The campaign against Gaius culminated in an attempt to discredit his colony of Junonia during the period of seventy days he spent in Africa early in 122. He was accused of having exceeded the authorized number of colonists and of illegally admitting non-Roman settlers. Rumors of unfavorable omens greeting the attempts to inaugurate the colony were circulated. Opposing factions obviously feared that Gaius might become the patron of flourishing and far-flung colonies. The effect of these efforts was seen when Gaius sought the tribunate for a third time in the summer of 122. His bid failed, and in the following December his tribunate ended.

In 121 the Senate sponsored an attempt to annul the Rubrian Law authorizing the founding of Junonia. Gaius, who seems to have feared assassination, allowed his friends to provide a bodyguard. An unimportant member of the staff of the consul Opimius was killed in a brawl between the Gracchans and their opponents. The latter used this pretext to eliminate Gaius. They would have perhaps preferred to destroy him judicially, as they had the supporters of Tiberius in 133, but they were effectively prevented from doing so by Gaius' own legislation against kangaroo courts. They therefore had recourse to something novel, passage by the Senate of a so-called "decree of last resort" (*senatus consultum ultimum*), which authorized the consuls to take all measures to safeguard the state. Opimius promptly organized an armed force of senators, equestrians, and their slaves. He then summoned Gaius and his former colleague Flaccus before the Senate. Since it was clear that they would not be treated fairly, they resisted arrest and occupied the Aventine hill with their supporters. There they were attacked by Opimius at the head of his levies and a force of Cretan archers in Roman service who happened to be in the city. The Gracchans were routed, Flaccus was killed, Gaius had himself stabbed by a faithful slave to

avoid capture, and about 3,000 of his followers were arrested and executed. The Gracchan faction was thus obliterated.

THE GRACCHI AND THE CONSTITUTION. The careers of the Gracchi marked an important watershed in political and constitutional developments. They gave a new dimension to politics by raising such novel issues as land reform, judicial corruption, and provincial organization that cut across traditional factional and class lines. Gaius in particular broadened horizons outside the senatorial oligarchy by further politicizing the equestrians and Italians, thus heightening oligarchic awareness of social and economic concerns of classes outside their traditionally limited clienteles and producing a much more flexible situation within the Senate presaging novel factional arrangements. Of more immediate moment was the awkward limitation on the ability of the Senate to deal judicially with domestic crises, which led to the use of the "decree of last resort" in 121. In 120 the strength of the Senate's position was tested by the trial of the ex-consul Opimius for his actions under that decree. His unpopular acquittal legally sanctioned slaughter of the Gracchans and justified the decree itself.

The immediate fate of Gracchan legislation shows how their opponents had learned that the question of land reform could not be championed by any particular faction and that successful politicians would in future have to take into account the interests of groups which the Gracchi had activated. With the exception of the Rubrian Law, which was repealed, statutes of the Gracchi remained in force, and even the colonists in Africa were allowed to remain on their land. Three laws finally settled the question of public lands. The first, possibly passed in 121 or 120, permitted the Gracchan colonists to sell their allotments. This measure may actually have been welcomed by peasants who had failed at farming. About 112, and without any hint of opposition, the land commission was abolished, because there was little *ager publicus* left to distribute. Interestingly enough, this very law guaranteed present possessors of public land in their tenure if they paid rent, which was to be disbursed to the poor. The third law, passed in 111, declared private property free from any form of rent all lands assigned by Gracchan commissioners and all former holdings of public land up to the limit of 500 *iugera* set by Gracchan legislation. Further encroachment on public pasture lands was forbidden and their use was strictly regulated. It is difficult to estimate the net results of this period of agrarian legislation, nor is there any way of knowing how many new settlers remained on their farms after they were allowed to sell them nor how far the potential military strength of the state was increased. It seems, however, that any expansion of the peasant class by virtue of Gracchan reforms was only temporary.

FRONTIER WARS DURING THE GRACCHAN PERIOD. Although at Rome interest centered on the struggle between the Gracchans and opposing factions, frontier armies of the Empire were engaged in continuous warfare

to defend Roman territory. On the borders of Macedonia and Illyricum there were struggles with Celtic tribes south of the Danube, in northern Italy raids of Alpine people had to be suppressed, and in the western Mediterranean depredations of pirates compelled the Romans to occupy the Balearic Islands. Seizure of these islands in 123–121 secured to Rome command of the sea route to Spain. On Majorca, the largest, two colonies of Roman citizens were founded with settlers recruited among Italians resident in Spain. More important was the Roman advance after 125 in Transalpine Gaul. Here the Romans, in answer to an appeal from their ally Massilia, fought against the Gallic Saluvii, a people whose territory lay north of that city. The subjugation of the Saluvii and of neighboring Ligurian peoples in 123 gave the Romans control of a route across the Maritime Alps from Italy to the Rhone valley, secured by permanent occupation of a fortified post at Aquae Sextiae.

Roman success alarmed more powerful Gallic tribes, particularly the Allobroges east of the Rhone and the Arverni to the west. These two peoples allied to oppose further Roman advance, while a rival nation, the Aedui, to the north of the Arverni, took the side of Rome. Hostilities began when the Romans demanded the surrender of fugitives from the Saluvii. In 121 the Allobroges and Arverni were defeated in a great battle fought near the junction of the Rhone and the Isère by the consul Fabius Maximus and the proconsul Gnaeus Domitius Ahenobarbus. This victory made the Romans masters of southern Gaul from the Alps to the Pyrenees, except for Massilia. Despite senatorial opposition, a colony of Roman citizens from Italy was founded at Narbo, the second colony of its type to be founded beyond Italy.

III. RISE OF GAIUS MARIUS

DOMESTIC POLITICS AFTER THE GRACCHI. It appears that once tensions evoked by the Gracchi subsided, the united oligarchic front mobilized against them broke up, and senators regrouped in a new political constellation, a faction led by the Metellan clan emerging as dominant, the Gracchan and Scipionic parties as such having disappeared. Very fragmentary evidence suggests that Metellan dominance was frequently challenged by other individuals and groups, many of the latter, it seems, having had connections with the defunct Scipionic faction. Oligarchic competition frequently surfaced in the courts, where charges of corruption, malfeasance, or military incapacity were frequently made. Noteworthy in this connection is the institution of a second permanent court trying cases of electoral bribery (*quaestio de ambitu*) shortly before 116.

JUGURTHINE WAR. Shortly after the occupation of southern Gaul, the Romans became involved in a much more serious conflict, which suggested incapacity of its ruling class and shattered the deceptive tranquility of the post-Gracchan period. The scene of the new struggle was North Africa, and its occasion was the death in 118 of Micipsa, successor to Masinissa as king of

Numidia and a loyal ally of Rome. He bequeathed his kingdom jointly to his two sons, Adherbal and Hiempsal, and a nephew, Jugurtha, whom he had adopted some years before. Jugurtha was able, ambitious, and unscrupulous. As commander of the Numidian contingent in the Roman army under Scipio Aemilianus at the siege of Numantia, he had gained military experience and an insight into the mentality of the Roman oligarchy. While preparations were being made to divide the kingdom among the three heirs, Jugurtha had Hiempsal assassinated and expelled Adherbal. The latter fled to Rome and appealed for aid on the basis of the alliance with Rome that he had inherited from his ancestors.

Making a difficult decision, the Senate exercised its rights of patronage over Numidia in order to pacify the quarreling princes through compromise and diplomacy. In 116 Roman commissioners partitioned Numidia between the rivals, Jugurtha receiving the western, Adherbal the eastern half of the country. Jugurtha, however, aimed at ruling all of Numidia and so provoked Adherbal to war. In 113 he defeated him and blockaded him in his capital, Cirta, which was defended with the aid of resident Roman and Italian businessmen. Roman commissioners again appeared before Jugurtha, who promised that he would abandon aggression, but he had no intention of keeping his word. He forced the surrender of Cirta in 112 and executed Adherbal and all the defenders of the city.

The slaughter of so many Romans and Italians raised a storm in Rome, where the equestrians and populace forced the Senate, which had hitherto avoided direct involvement in Africa, to declare war. In 111 an army under the consul Bestia invaded Numidia. Jugurtha's wily diplomacy secured terms of peace from the consul after a sham submission. A case could well be made that senatorial conduct of relations with Jugurtha in peace and at war were at best incompetent, and at worst downright corrupt. A tribune, wishing to challenge the oligarchy, summoned Jugurtha to Rome under safe conduct to testify concerning his relations with Roman officials in Numidia. He came, but his testimony was vetoed by a tribune friendly to the senatorial establishment, which closed ranks against an attack on them that seemed reminiscent of the Gracchi. While in Rome, Jugurtha daringly arranged for the assassination of a rival claimant to the throne. The actual assassin was spirited out of Italy, and Jugurtha was permitted to return home.

The war reopened, and the first operations ended late in 110 or early in 109 with the defeat and capitulation of a Roman army, which was forced to pass under the yoke and released only when its commander recognized Jugurtha's position and an alliance between him and Rome. Popular revulsion at Rome at this turn of events prompted the Plebeian Council to approve a proposal of the tribune Mamilius to create a special court, staffed by equestrians, to try senatorial commanders who had dealt with Jugurtha since the beginning of the war. About seven of them, including Bestia, were convicted of acts hostile to the state and exiled. Their bribery by Jugurtha was alleged and widely believed, but the degree and nature of their venality were probably exaggerated.

In the same year the consul Quintus Caecilius Metellus took command in Africa. One of his officers was Gaius Marius, born of an equestrian family of Arpinum and therefore a "new man," but having political ambition equal to that of any senatorial noble. Like other parvenus, he had to build up a faction with the help and patronage of established and influential senators. He was first a protégé of Scipio Aemilianus, whom he served in the Numantine War. He had then successfully managed state contracts and, with the patronage of the Metelli, had been elected tribune in 119, only to break with them. He returned, it seems, to their patronage to be elected praetor in 115, and pro-praetor in Spain in 114. Marius was not content merely to be a senator but had his eye on becoming a leading statesman. His further career, in which he again turned against the very oligarchs who had launched him, is explained in part by the failure of the latter to encourage his claims to preeminence.

In contrast to former commanders against Jugurtha, Metellus was both energetic and capable. He began to devastate Numidia and forced Jugurtha to resort to guerrilla warfare. He also tried to stir up disloyalty among the king's followers, but he failed to terminate the war quickly by either killing or capturing Jugurtha. When Metellus scornfully refused Marius' request to be allowed to return to Rome and stand for the consulship in 108, Marius intrigued to get the command transferred to himself, alleging that Metellus was purposely prolonging the campaign. Finally, Metellus let him go, and, with the support of anti-Metellans and his own faction, numbering many equestrians, he was elected consul for the following year (107). The Senate, wishing to keep Metellus in command, had not designated Numidia as a consular province, and so the Marians passed a law in the Plebeian Council conferring the command against Jugurtha on Marius. This intervention of the Council in the traditional right of the Senate to distribute provincial commands boded ill for the oligarchy. Despite constant senatorial attempts to block him at every step, Marius superseded Metellus in 107. His quaestor was Lucius Cornelius Sulla, scion of an impoverished patrician family, who was destined to become the rival of his chief.

In the meantime, although the position of Jugurtha had been strengthened by an alliance with his father-in-law Bocchus, king of Mauretania, Marius continued the strategy of Metellus, seizing towns and fortresses that might serve as enemy bases. Ultimately he won two hard-fought victories over the united forces of the two kings, and Bocchus, fearing an inevitable Roman victory, opened negotiations. At length, pressed by Sulla, who had risked a journey to the camp of the Mauretanian, Bocchus turned Jugurtha over to the Romans. This ended the war, and Marius returned in triumph to Rome in 105. There he found that, in defiance of precedent, he had been elected consul for the ensuing year, owing to the fear of barbarian invasion of Italy from the

north and to popular confidence in him as a result of his success in Africa.
Jugurtha, after gracing his victor's triumph, was executed at Rome.

Apart from adding a part of Numidia to the province of Africa, the Senate
did not take the opportunity presented by the defeat of Jugurtha to annex more
territory The section of Numidia that bordered on Mauretania was united
to the kingdom of Bocchus as a reward for his services; the rest was made a
client kingdom under the rule of a native prince. The restoration of peace
opened this country once more to Roman and Italian business interests. Upon
Rome itself the repercussions of the Jugurthine War were very important. The
prestige of the Senate, already weakened by the actions of the Gracchi, was
diminished still further by its own bungling and by the intervention of the
Plebeian Council and equestrians in foreign policy.

IV. INVASION OF THE CIMBRI AND THE TEUTONS

GERMANIC MIGRATION. The barbarian menace that led to the election
of Marius to his second consulship resulted from the wanderings of Germanic
and Celtic peoples, principally Cimbri and Teutons. These tribes, suffering
from overpopulation and perhaps from the pressure of warlike neighbors in
their homeland in Jutland, migrated in search of new and richer homes. After
making their way into the middle Danube valley, they turned westward and
in 113 invaded the lands of the Taurisci, allies of Rome, who lived north of the
Alps between the upper Drave and the Danube. A Roman army sent to help
the Taurisci was badly beaten. The migratory horde then turned west toward
the Rhine, being joined by the Tigurini, a branch of Celtic Helvetians, and
by the Ambrones, a tribe of uncertain origin. In 111, these peoples crossed the
Rhine into Gaul, where they came into conflict with the defending Roman
armies. Upon refusal of their demand for lands within Roman frontiers, the
Cimbri severely defeated the consul Marcus Julius Silanus in 109, although they
failed to follow up their success. The Tigurini, however, kept threatening South
Gaul and caused a revolt of Roman allies in the vicinity of Tolosa. In 107
another consular army was almost annihilated by the Tigurini, and its commander Lucius Cassius Longinus was killed. A year later the consul Quintus
Servilius Caepio, a noted Metellan adherent, recovered Tolosa without
opposition from the invaders, who had withdrawn from allied territory, and
punished it by carrying off its immense temple treasures. Three years afterward
he was tried and perhaps acquitted for defrauding the state of this booty, which
disappeared mysteriously on its way to the coast. Danger threatened again when
the Cimbri and Teutons marched down the Rhone valley. Two Roman armies,
one under Caepio as proconsul and the other under the consul Gnaeus Mallius
Maximus, moved to meet them. The jealousy and incompetence of the commanders led to the destruction of both their armies in a great battle near
Arausio (Orange), in which perhaps 20,000 Romans fell, the greatest disaster
suffered by Roman arms since Cannae. The way to Italy lay open, but once

more the Germans failed to take advantage of their opportunity. The Cimbri crossed the Pyrenees into Spain, while their allies withdrew beyond the Roman sphere in Gaul.

MILITARY REFORMS OF MARIUS. At this juncture (105) the people voted Marius his second consulship, for 104, and gave him the command against the barbarians, thereby disregarding the legal requirement of an interval of ten years between holding the office. He set to work at once to create an army for the defense of Italy. He made use of his experience in raising troops for the Jugurthine War and, as before, accepted proletarian citizens as recruits. His recruiting practices were only marginally original. Although soldiers normally had to be landholders before 107, there never had been any statutory exclusion of proletarians from the legions; in fact, in times of crisis, as after Cannae, the state had drafted them. Marius simply enlisted men who had not normally been enlisted. His proletarian conscripts in any case were scarcely poorer than propertied recruits of the preceding generation, the government having successively lowered the property qualification to tap ever poorer classes of men as those possessing adequate property declined in number. Marius simply went one step further; his recruitment of proletarians is a certain indication that the Gracchan land reforms had no lasting effect in sustaining the yeomanry. Although volunteers were recruited after Marius, the normal method of conscription remained the military draft until the end of the Republic, an indication of continued pressing manpower needs and the general unpopularity of military service, even, it appears, among *proletarii*, who only infrequently flocked to the colors.

It is sometimes contended that proletarian soldiers were no longer anxious to return to civilian occupations but were willing to serve for many years under the command of a successful general. In reality, however, they regarded military service rather as a means to an end—a plot of land or a bonus provided by their commanders—and they were by no means anxious to serve long terms under arms. Most significant was the fact that loyalty to the state might, under certain circumstances, be supplanted by devotion to a successful patron-general. The latter might look to his soldiers to support him against civil authority or to his veterans, who remained his clients, to back him in his subsequent political career.

Marius also made important changes in legionary equipment, tactics, and organization. In part he generalized developments in the miiltary establishment that preceded him, in part the reforms were his own innovations. He instituted weapons training based on those used in the gladiatorial schools and introduced an improved type of *pilum* or throwing spear, whose metal head broke away from the wooden shaft on impact and thus prevented the spear's being thrown back by the enemy. To increase mobility he had his troops carry their entrenching tools. He generalized the practice of combining maniples into larger units known as cohorts, which then became the standard tactical unit in the legion.

Thereafter the paper strength of the legion was 6,000 men,[4] grouped into ten cohorts of 600 each, consisting of six centuries of 100 troops. Legions no longer fought in three separate lines, and all the infantry received the same arms. In the Marian legion the officer cadre subordinate to the commander, normally a consul, consisted of six military tribunes and sixty centurions, six in each cohort. The centurions, superbly disciplined and experienced veterans, were the real backbone of the army. There was no noncommissioned officer cadre. Beneath the centurionate, the Roman army officially recognized only the existence of private soldiers (*milites*) who could perform tactical and administrative functions that were, however, sometimes highly specialized. The military reforms of Marius were thus important not only because of their social and political consequences, but also because they notably increased the fighting strength of the army.

DEFEAT OF THE BARBARIANS. During the years 104 and 103 Marius kept his army in Gaul, guarding the passage to Italy, while he trained his troops and dug a new channel at the mouth of the Rhone to facilitate the passage of his transports into the river. He was reelected to the consulship for 103 and again for 102, since the barbarian danger continued. In 102 the Cimbri returned from Spain and, joining the other tribes, prepared to invade Italy. The Teutons and Ambrones followed the direct route from southern Gaul, while the Cimbri and Tigurini moved north of the Alps to enter Italy by the eastern passes. Marius permitted the Teutons and Ambrones to march by him; then he overtook and annihilated them at Aquae Sextiae. In the meantime the Cimbri forced the other consul, Quintus Lutatius Catulus, to abandon the Brenner Pass and withdraw south of the Po, allowing them to winter north of that river. Marius returned to Italy to join his colleague and face the new danger. The next year, consul for the fifth time, he met and destroyed the Cimbri on the Raudine plains near Vercellae. The Tigurini then gave up their attempt to penetrate Venetia and returned to their former home in Switzerland. Italy was saved from a repetition of the Gallic invasions of the fourth century B.C. Soon afterwards Gallia (Narbonensis) was organized as a province.

Roman victories, won over greatly superior numbers, were due largely to the superior equipment and discipline of their troops but also to the total lack of strategic planning or organization by the barbarians. The defeat of the barbarians also showed that the vitality of the Roman state was by no means exhausted and that men of energy and ability were not lacking, although under the existing regime it required a crisis to bring them forward. Such a man was Marius, now the dominant figure in politics.

SECOND SICILIAN SLAVE WAR: 104–101 B.C. While the barbarians were threatening Italy, Rome suppressed disorders in other parts of her Empire, some only after considerable effort. In 104 occurred a serious rebellion of the

---

[4] Occasionally before Marius, as at Pydna (168), specially afforced legions of 6,000 had been deployed.

slaves in Sicily, headed by two leaders, Salvius and Anthenion, the former of whom took the title of King Tryphon. The rebels became masters of the open country, defeated the first forces sent against them, reduced the Sicilian cities to the verge of starvation, and were only subdued by a consular army under Manius Aquilius in 101.

ROME AND THE CILICIAN PIRATES. Before the slave war in Sicily was ended, the Romans were forced to try to suppress piracy. Piracy had spread ever since the decline of Rhodian sea power following the Second Macedonian War. Rome neglected to maintain a navy adqeuate even for policing the seas, since there was no longer any rival maritime power. The pirates were at the same time slave traders, kidnapping all over the Mediterranean, particularly in the East, to supply the slave mart of Delos. In 104 the king of Bithynia complained to the Senate that half of his able-bodied men had been enslaved. This traffic was winked at by the Romans because they needed many slaves for their plantations and their business interests profited by the trade. The depredations at length became too serious to be ignored, and in 102 the praetor Marcus Antonius was given a special command against them. They had their chief strongholds on the Cilician coast and the island of Crete; Antonius proceeded to Cilicia, destroying several of their towns and annexing some territory, which became a province. The trouble was not over, however, and probably in December of 101 a law was passed closing harbors under Roman control to pirate vessels.

V. MARIANS AND FACTIONAL POLITICS

ATTACKS UPON THE SENATE. The prestige of dominant senatorial factions, shaken in the Jugurthine War, suffered still further blows from incompetence and disregard of public interest by their members holding commands in the war with the Cimbri and Teutons. This situation encouraged certain politicians, who counted heavily on the support and popularity of Marius, to attack vulnerable senators. One of the leaders in this movement was Gaius Servilius Glaucia, who, probably as tribune in 104, sponsored a law in effect abrogating one sponsored two years before by the Metellan Caepio. That law had changed the composition of ad hoc and standing courts trying criminal cases, including extortion, from equestrian membership to one of both senators and equestrians. By the Servilian Law they were once again staffed exclusively by equestrians. In the same year a second tribune, Gnaeus Domitius Ahenobarbus, put through a law lessening the control of nobles over appointments to official priestly colleges. The Domitian Law limited cooptations to vacancies in these colleges to persons previously elected in an assembly of seventeen tribes chosen by lot, as was the practice in the election of the *pontifex maximus*. A year later another tribune, Lucius Appuleius Saturninus, engineered the condemnation of Caepio and Mallius, who were responsible for the disaster at Arausio, by the Plebeian Council for acts hostile to the state.

VI. ATTEMPTED REFORMS OF LIVIUS DRUSUS: 91 B.C.

AFTER MARIUS. The nobles did not repeal Marian legislation, but, characteristically, returned to factional wrangles expressed by prosecution in the criminal courts of rival leaders on various charges. Marius thought it prudent to leave Rome on a mission to the East (99–97), returning to attempt reconstruction of his scattered following by playing orthodox factional politics rather than by demagoguery, but with indifferent success. The Metellan clique remained dominant in the face of attacks by other factions. Underlying domestic politics was increasing tension between Rome and the Italians, expressed in a law of 95 that banished Latin and Italian allies from the city and instituted a search to find those illegally-enrolled as Roman citizens. Although this action conformed to previous senatorial policy, it was not provoked by any special danger and was a gratuitous insult to the allies, whose loyalty in the Jugurthine and Cimbric Wars had been crucial.

TRIAL OF RUTILIUS RUFUS. Although senators and equestrians had temporarily combined against terrorism in 100 B.C., their coalition was fluid and precarious. Except when their own advantage was involved, equestrians generally kept aloof from politics. They were scornful of the senatorial prosecutions brought before their courts since 98, which they regarded as blatantly political rather than substantial, and they had acquitted all the accused. A situation arising in the province of Asia, however, deeply involved their financial interests. In 98 the governor, Mucius Scaevola, and his legate, Rutilius Rufus, both Metellan adherents, reformed provincial administration and curbed unjust exactions by agents of the *publicani*. The equestrians were furious, and upon Rutilius' return to Rome in 92 he was brought to trial on the ridiculous charge of extortion and found guilty by the equestrian jurors. His fate was an intended warning against other senatorial officials who might take their provincial obligations seriously.

LEGISLATIVE PROGRAM OF MARCUS LIVIUS DRUSUS. Equestrian activity in the courts and restiveness on the part of Italians and provincials suggested an impending domestic and imperial crisis. This, the oligarchy, led by the Metellan faction, wished to avoid. Their agent of reform was one of the tribunes of 91, Marcus Livius Drusus, son of the like-named opponent of Gaius Gracchus. Change in the jury system was initially their most important objective, attainable only by preliminary wooing of an otherwise uninterested populace. Therefore, Drusus first sponsored laws authorizing the foundation of new colonies, fresh distributions of public land, and continuance of distributions of cheap grain. Only then did he propose the reform of standing courts staffed by equestrians, by admitting 300 equestrians into the Senate, doubling its size to 600, and by choosing jurors from that enlarged body. He also proposed to include equestrians under the Gracchan law punishing conspiracy to condemn innocent men and apply it retroactively to the judges of his uncle, Rutilius

Rufus. Then, impetuously, he departed from Metellan intentions by suggesting enfranchisement of Latin and Italian allies.

His program was extremely controversial. The equestrians opposed the judiciary law, and many senators, although they thought equestrians should be curbed, objected to swamping the Senate with new men and the popular assemblies with enfranchised allies. Popular sentiment agreed on the latter point. Despite the opposition Drusus' laws were passed in assembly, only to be declared unconstitutional by the Senate, since they were parts of omnibus legislation. In the midst of great political tension, Drusus was assassinated before the end of the year.

VII. ITALIC OR MARSIC WAR:[5] 90–88 B.C.

The death of Drusus triggered revolt of the Italian allies. They had been in close contact with him and had planned rebellion if his bill should fail to pass. After the Senate had refused to entertain a renewed demand for their admission to citizenship, they took up arms. Led by the Marsi and the Samnites, a group of peoples in the central highland region organized a confederacy with its capital at Corfinium in the territory of the Paeligni, which was renamed Italia. Military necessity demanded some organization to manage the war effort. The confederacy established a council of war, while the actual conduct of operations was entrusted to two generals in chief and twelve subordinate commanders chosen from the peoples participating in the struggle. A federal coinage was issued, specimens of which have survived, many bearing a figure of the goddess Italia, the guardian deity of the union, and showing the Italian bull goring the Roman wolf.

Practically all the warlike peoples of central and southern Italy either were included in the confederacy or fought with it. The rebels were a match for the Romans in numbers; through long service in Roman armies they had become thoroughly versed in Roman military organization, tactics, and discipline, and they could count on leaders of proved ability. The Latin colonies remained true to their allegiance, as did the Greek cities of South Italy, whose action virtually cut off the Italians from the coast. Umbria and Etruria, although disaffected, did not take up arms at once. Rome possessed a great advantage in her control of the sea, which enabled her to draw provincial resources in men, money, and materials, and thus was in a much better position to sustain a prolonged struggle.

ITALIC VICTORIES AND ROMAN CONCESSIONS. Hostilities opened in 90, the allied forces attempting to reach Etruria and occupy Campania, the Romans seeking to forestall them by vigorous thrusts into the heart of allied territory. In the south the Italians, despite one defeat, achieved great success.

---

[5] Later called the Social War, i.e., the War with the Allies.

They overran a large part of Campania and broke through to the coast. Further victories gave them control of Apulia and Lucania. In the north the struggle was more even, and the Romans balanced several disasters by equally significant successes. In this sphere Marius, who served as a *legatus* or deputy commander, rendered valuable service. On the whole the balance of success favored the allies, and the Romans began to doubt the future. The allied cities in Etruria were prevented from joining the rebels only by a timely promise of citizenship, and both Senate and people were ready to make further concessions. Early in the year the consul Lucius Julius Caesar sponsored the Julian Law, which granted Roman citizenship to all Latin colonies and to all allied communities that had not taken up arms. Another provision empowered commanders to grant citizenship to non-Roman soldiers in the field. By these measures the Romans won the support of Etrurians and Umbrians and rewarded loyal Latins and Greek federate allies. Shortly afterward, two tribunes of the year 89 carried the Plautian-Papirian Law, which offered Roman citizenship to all members of Italian communities who would claim it within sixty days. This offer applied to individuals, both citizens of allied communities under arms and those who had not accepted citizenship under the Julian Law. A third law, the work of Gnaeus Pompeius Strabo, consul in 89, gave Roman citizenship to all communities in Cispadane Gaul, and Latin rights to those north of the Po.

A minor legal by-product of the war was a change in the criminal court system. A *lex Varia* of 90, sponsored by enemies of Drusus and the Metelli, was so worded that advocates of allied enfranchisement before hostilities could be, and were, accused of treason. The failure of the equestrian court hearing such cases to convict accused senators again triggered a movement for reform. In 89 a law decreed that fifteen jurors were to be chosen annually by each tribe, without regard to social status of the candidates. Such a system was much more adaptable to senatorial control through the exercise of patronage.

THE COLLAPSE OF THE REVOLT. Concessions not only checked the spread of the rebellion, but, by giving allies the rights for which they were fighting, they caused serious desertions, dooming the movement to rapid failure. The effect was seen in the change in the fortunes of war in 89. Despite desperate resistance on the part of those who insisted on independence, the Romans were everywhere successful. The consul Pompeius practically ended hostilities in the north and Sulla, in his capacity as *legatus*, broke the allies in South Italy. Organized resistance among the rebels died out in the course of the year 88.

By taking up arms, the Italians had won for themselves and the Latins the rights reason had long conceded as their due but withheld from them through national and factional jealousy. This jealousy continued to show itself in proposals to limit their influence by enrolling them in a fixed, small number of tribes. Naturally they were dissatisfied with this arrangement, and the question of their distribution became a burning political issue. Virtually all Italians were now Romans, however, and in the course of the next few generations the various ethnic elements in Italy became a single nation. It was impossible for the magistrates of Rome to oversee local administration throughout the peninsula, and Italian communities were organized as municipalities with limited rights of self-government, regularly administered by boards of four magistrates (*quattuorviri*) elected by the local citizens. With the adoption of Roman public and private law came the spread of Latin. Local dialects gradually disappeared, and a uniform culture developed on the basis of common citizenship.

VIII. FIRST MITHRIDATIC WAR: 89–85 B.C.

MITHRIDATES VI, EUPATOR, KING OF PONTUS. In 89 the attention of the Senate was drawn to a threat to its suzerainty over client kingdoms in Asia Minor. This resulted from the establishment of the kingdom of Pontus under an able ruler, Mithridates Eupator, and the Senate was anxious to settle the Italic question as quickly as possible. Mithridates succeeded in 121 to the throne of northern Cappadocia, a kingdom on the south shore of the Black Sea, whose population was Hellenized and whose rulers claimed descent from the ancient royal house of Persia and, with more justice, from Seleucus, the founder of the Greek kingdom of Syria. Mithridates shared the throne with his brother for over six years, under his mother's regency, but when he became eighteen years of age in 115 he seized sole power. Subsequently he extended his control over the eastern and northern shores of the Black Sea, as far west as the Danube. Thus he built up the kingdom of Pontus (the coastland of the Black Sea), a name later applied to his native state of North Cappadocia.

Mithridates also sought to extend his sway in Asia Minor, especially in Greater Cappadocia. This brought him into conflict with Rome, whose policy was to prevent the rise of any dangerous neighbor in the East and which refused to allow its arrangements in Asia Minor to be disturbed. Mithridates attempted no less than five times between 112 and 92 to conquer this district, but each time he was forced by Rome to forego the fruits of his victories, since he was not yet prepared for a major war. In 91 he occupied the kingdom of Bithynia, which lay between Pontus and the province of Asia, but again he yielded to Rome's demands and withdrew. When Roman commissioners encouraged the king of Bithynia to raid his territory with impunity, he decided to challenge Roman arms, observing Rome's involvement in the war with her Italian allies. Hostilities began late in 89.

MITHRIDATES IN ASIA AND GREECE. Mithridates was well prepared. He had a trained army and a fleet of 300 ships. He experienced no difficulty in defeating forces raised by Roman authorities and speedily overran Bithynia and most of the province of Asia. Meanwhile his fleet swept the Aegean Sea. Roman provincials, who had been unmercifully exploited by governors, tax-gatherers, and moneylenders, greeted Mithridates as a deliverer in many cases.

At his order on a set date in 88 they massacred the Romans and Italians resident in Asia, possibly several thousand strong, a step intended to bind provincials firmly to him.

In the same year the populace of Athens, hoping to overthrow their oligarchic government set up by Rome, seized control of the state and joined Mithridates. One of the king's generals, Archelaus, en route to Athens, exterminated the Italian community at Delos, the center of Roman commercial and banking interests in the East. From this blow the island never fully recovered. Archelaus soon won over most of southern Greece to his master's cause, while Mithridates sent a large army to enter Hellas by the northerly route through Thrace and Macedonia.

SULLA AND THE MARIANS IN ROME. This situation produced a political crisis in Rome. To revive declining dominance, the Metellan faction turned to Sulla, who was elected consul with their backing for 88. He was allotted the command in the East upon the outbreak of hostilities but was unable to leave Italy because his army was besieging Nola in Campania, where a last-ditch stand was made by the Italians in the south after almost all resistance elsewhere had disintegrated. Political events in Rome then also prevented immediate action against Mithridates. Marius, in his sixty-eighth year, was as ambitious as ever and schemed to secure the command against Mithridates for himself. He was supported by a faction containing many equestrians, who remembered his past connections to their class, and by the tribune Publius Sulpicius Rufus, who brought forward a bill to enroll new citizens and freedmen equally in each of the thirty-five tribes. Sulpicius organized a bodyguard of equestrians and instituted a reign of terror, pushing his law through by force despite consular opposition. When Sulla left the city to join his army, another law was passed in the Plebeian Council transferring his command in the East to Marius.

Sulla refused to admit the legality of the act and, relying on his troops, marched on Rome. Having taken the city by surprise, he had Sulpicius, Marius, and others of their faction outlawed. Sulpicius was killed, but Marius escaped to Mauretania. Sulla's behavior was an unnerving revelation to the nobility as a whole—even to his own faction—of the dangerous lengths to which he would go to enhance his *dignitas*. He had exploited the revolutionary potential of his client army and used it to promote his *coup d'état*. The Sulpician laws were abrogated, and Sulla introduced a number of reforms to strengthen the position of the Senate. The most significant of these made senatorial consent necessary before any measures could be submitted to one of the legislative assemblies and restricted the type of legislation that could be brought by tribunes before the Plebeian Council. Upon the conclusion of his consulate, Sulla embarked with his army for Greece early in 87.

SULLA IN THE EAST. After driving Archelaus and the Athenians from the open country, Sulla besieged Athens and its port Piraeus in the autumn of 87. Athens was completely invested, but in spite of hunger resistance lasted until March 86, when Sulla's troops penetrated the walls and sacked the city. Many inhabitants were massacred, but public buildings were spared. Piraeus was stormed soon after at heavy cost to the victors, but its citadel Munychia held out until evacuated by Archelaus.

From Athens Sulla confronted the army of Mithridates, which had penetrated to Boeotia. At Chaeronea the numerically inferior but better disciplined Romans won a complete victory. At this point the consul Lucius Valerius Flaccus arrived in Greece at the head of another army, with orders to supersede Sulla. The latter refused to give up his command, and Flaccus, fearing to force the issue, set out for Asia by way of Macedonia and Thrace. This left Sulla free to meet a new Mithridatic army that had crossed the Aegean. At Orchomenus he attacked and annihilated it. Mithridates still controlled the sea, and Sulla, unable to cross into Asia, was forced to winter in Greece.

Lucius Lucullus, Sulla's quaestor, appeared in the Aegean in 85 with a fleet he had gathered among Rome's allies in the East. He defeated the fleet of Mithridates and secured Sulla's passage to Asia. The king's position was now precarious. His exactions had alienated the Greek cities, which now began to desert him. Flaccus, after recovering Macedonia and Thrace, crossed the Bosphorus into Bithynia, where he was killed in a mutiny and was succeeded by his legate Fimbria, who was popular with the troops because he let them plunder. Fimbria proved energetic. He defeated Mithridates and recovered the coast as far south as Pergamon (86). Mithridates was ready for peace, and Sulla was anxious to be free to return to Italy, where the Marians were again in power. The king opened negotiations soon after the battle of Orchomenus, but it was not until 85 that peace was concluded on the following terms: the king was to surrender Greater Cappadocia, Bithynia, the Roman province of Asia and his other conquests in Asia Minor, to pay an indemnity of 2,000 talents, and to give up part of his fleet. His kingdom of Pontus remained intact.

Sulla wintered in Asia, readjusting provincial affairs. The rebellious communities were punished by quartering troops on them, and they were forced to buy peace by contributing to Sulla the huge sum of 20,000 talents which he intended to use to finance his campaign to rewin Italy. To raise this amount they were forced to borrow from Roman bankers and incur a crushing burden of debt. In 84 Sulla crossed to Greece, there to complete his preparations to return to Italy. The Greek states suffered heavily in the recent campaigns. Sulla carried off the temple treasures of Olympia, Delphi, and Epidaurus. Attica and Boeotia were ravaged and depopulated, the coasts raided by the Mithridatic fleet.

IX. SULLA'S DICTATORSHIP

MARIANS IN ROME: 87–84 B.C. While Sulla was fighting in Greece, the Marian party gradually won the upper hand in Italy, as part of a general reaction against Sullan extremism and ruthlessness. Scarcely had Sulla left

Italy with his army when the consul Lucius Cornelius Cinna reenacted the Sulpician laws. Cinna, originally uncommitted either to Sulla or Marius, was interested in building up a faction of his own among the Italians, but this only earned him the enmity of his consular colleague, Gnaeus Octavius, and the dominant senatorial faction, which drove him from the city and deposed him. Cinna found the support of the army in Campania and of the Samnites, who were still under arms, although the Senate tried to win them over by a promise of citizenship. Meanwhile Marius returned to Italy, raised an army in Etruria, and took Cinna into alliance. Together they advanced on Rome. They forced their opponents to capitulate, had Cinna reinstated as consul, and the banishment of Marius revoked. Sulla's laws were repealed and his property confiscated. Of particular importance was the final distribution of Italian allies throughout all the tribes, a measure designed to expand the Marian clientele, which was begun by Cinna during the censorship of 86–85.

Upon his return to Rome, Marius, with Cinna's concurrence, massacred his leading opponents, including the consul Octavius. On January 1, 86, Marius entered his seventh consulship; he planned to fight Sulla while Cinna reorganized the government but died a few days later. His successor, Lucius Valerius Flaccus, was sent to supersede Sulla, a mission which cost him his life. Cinna, the leading figure at Rome thereafter until his death, attempted to forge a consensus in Italy to conciliate all important elements—Marians, anti-Marians alarmed by Sulla's violence, equestrians, and Italians. The three years of his domestic leadership were tranquil, in part because he stifled dissent.

In 85 the war with Mithridates ended, and the government had to face the prospect of Sulla's return at the head of a victorious army. Cinna, now in his third consulship, and his colleague Gnaeus Carbo, proceeded to raise an opposing force. They illegally prolonged their office for the next year (84) and prepared to cross the Adriatic and meet Sulla in Macedonia, but the army gathered for this purpose at Brundisium mutinied and murdered Cinna. Carbo prevented the election of a successor and held office as sole consul, while the Senate undertook negotiations with Sulla to prevent further civil war. He now demanded the restitution of property and honors both for himself and all those who had taken refuge with him. The Senate was inclined to yield but was prevented by Carbo.

RETURN OF SULLA. In the spring of 83 Sulla landed at Brundisium with an army of 40,000 veterans who had sworn to remain under his orders. Sulla had two problems. He had to neutralize the possibly hostile feeling toward him on the part of the Italians and somehow create a favorable public opinion at Rome. He promised to respect Italian citizenship rights, winning their allegiance except for the Samnites. He then masked what was really a civil war with the faction controlling the government as an anti-Samnite crusade. In the operations that followed the Marian leaders lacked cooperation and military skill. Sulla penetrated into Campania, where he defeated one consul,

VII Model of the Temple of Fortune at Palestrina. *This was perhaps the largest sanctuary in all Italy during the republican period. It was the site of a long-famous oracle. Its existing ruins date, it seems, from the first century B.C. The model suggests how impressively the architects adapted to the hilly slope by using a series of terraces and ramps. (Photo: Fototeca Unione.)*

Norbanus, at Mount Tifata. The other, Scipio Asiaticus, began negotiations with him and was deserted by his army, which went over to Sulla. Simultaneously, fence-sitters and previously ill-disposed nobles flocked to him as the prospective winner in a civil war.

In the following year Sulla advanced into Latium and won a hard-fought victory over the younger Marius, now consul, at Sacriportus. Rome fell into his hands, and Marius took refuge in Praeneste. Sulla then attacked the second consul, Carbo, in Etruria and, after several victories, forced him to flee to

Africa. In a final effort the Marians, united with the Samnites, tried to relieve Praeneste. Failing to accomplish this, they made a dash upon Rome. Sulla appeared in time to save the city and utterly defeat his enemies in a bloody battle at the Colline Gate. Praeneste fell soon after; Marius the Younger committed suicide, and, except at a few points, all resistance was over.

SULLA'S VENGEANCE. Sulla was absolute master of the situation and at once proceeded to punish his enemies and reward his friends. Cold-bloodedly, without any legal condemnation, his leading opponents were proscribed, their names being posted in lists in the Forum to indicate that they might be slain with impunity and that their goods were confiscated. Rewards were offered to informers who effected the death of such victims, and many were included in the lists to gratify the personal enmities of Sulla's friends. The goods of the proscribed were auctioned off publicly under Sulla's direction, and their children and grandchildren were declared ineligible for public office. From these proscriptions the equestrians suffered particularly; 2,600 of them are said to have perished, together with ninety senators. Italian municipalities also felt Sulla's vengeance. Widespread confiscations of land, especially in Samnium and Etruria, enabled him to provide for perhaps 80,000 veterans. Thousands of slaves of the proscribed were set free by Sulla and took the name of Cornelii from their patron. Apparently these arrangements were given the sanction of legality by action of the Senate and subsequent legislation. After this initial period of violence, Sulla seems to have been very careful to respect legal precedent and there were no further acts of lawlessness.

SULLA'S LEGISLATION. Sulla's aims went far beyond mere elimination of Marian rivals for, also a statesman, he was sincerely interested in assuring a stable government. His coalition consisted of loyal Sullani, but also of others who had defected to him at the last minute in 83. Like Augustus fifty years later, he strictly observed constitutional forms. As both consuls were dead, he caused the appointment of an *interrex*, who, by virtue of a special law, could appoint a dictator for an unlimited term to enact legislation and reorganize the commonwealth (*dictator legibus scribundis et rei publicae constituendae*). Sulla's appointment to that office occurred late in 82. The scope of his powers and their unlimited duration gave him unprecedented autocratic authority.

He diagnosed the threat to established authority as coming from unorthodox use of traditional magistracies, and he thought he could curb them by legislation. Tribunes lost the right to initiate legislation in the Plebeian Council, and their intercession was restricted in some way, possibly limited to interference with the exercise of the magistrate's *imperium*. To deter able and ambitious men from seeking the tribunate, the office of tribune was made a bar to further posts. The Domitian Law of 104 was abrogated, and the practice of coopting the members of priestly colleges was revived. The customary order of offices in the *cursus honorum* was enforced, as were age limits set for eligibility to each office, and an interval of ten years was required between successive tenures of the same post.[6] The number of quaestors was increased to twenty, that of praetors from six to eight. In this connection the method of appointing provincial governors was regulated. Sulla realized the danger to stability inherent in prolonged provincial commands and therefore sought to circumscribe the powers of promagistrates and to limit their tenure of office. By the organization of the province of Cisalpine Gaul, the number of provinces was raised to ten. Each year the eight praetors and probably the two consuls, on completion of their year of office in Rome, were normally to be appointed in the provinces as propraetors and proconsuls for one year only. This system also recognized the possible desirability, in times of crisis, of proroguing provincial commands beyond the annual term.

As before, the Senate designated consular provinces prior to the election of the consuls who would be their proconsular governors. Consuls were not deprived of the right of military command, and as before, they regularly assumed control of military operations in Italy. The consular *imperium* remained senior to that of provincial governors and might be exercised beyond the frontiers of Italy.

Sulla was especially interested in reorganizing the standing criminal courts, which so frequently had been embroiled in politics. Without being much of an innovator, he gave them greater order and clearer jurisdiction. He broadened and clarified the definition of treason, increased penalties for electoral bribery, consolidated procedures for treating various kinds of murder, and established a new standing court to control counterfeiting. The archaic procedure of holding trials before the Plebeian Council under tribunician presidency thus became a dead letter. The future administration of criminal justice was based on his reforms. To promote governmental stability as he conceived it, he restored the Senate to full control of all courts. To provide a sufficient number of jurors for them, he increased the membership of the Senate from 300 to 500 or 600 by enrolling senatorial cadets, friendly equestrians, and distinguished Italians, all elected to the tribunals by the tribes. He thus realized a similar measure proposed in 91 by Livius Drusus and thereby extended his clientele throughout Italy.

The larger Senate was maintained by the annual admission of the twenty ex-quaestors, whereby censors were rendered unnecessary for enrolling senators. No censorship was held during the decade following Sulla's dictatorship, because the Senate did not wish to increase the number of voters in the first classes of the Centuriate Assembly by admitting wealthy Italians and thereby decrease its own ability to manipulate that organization through patronage.

---

[6] The minimum age for the quaestorship was thirty years, for the praetorship, thirty-nine, and for the consulship, forty-two. Possibly as a result of Sullan legislation, the minimum age requirement for tenure by patricians of the senior magistrates was two years below that of plebeian senators.

While Sulla was settling affairs in Rome and Italy, Marians in Sicily and Africa were crushed by his lieutenant Gnaeus Pompeius, better known as Pompey. In 82 Sulla had the Senate confer on Pompey the command in this campaign with the *imperium* of a propraetor, although he had not yet held office. The campaign ended, Pompey demanded a triumph, an honor previously granted only to regular magistrates. Sulla, secretly resentful, nevertheless yielded with good grace and even accorded him the honor of the name Magnus, or "the Great." Pompey returned to Italy and celebrated his triumph on the 12th of March, 79.

SULLA'S RETIREMENT AND DEATH: 78 B.C.   Sulla undoubtedly did not aim at a dictatorship for life or at the introduction at Rome of a kind of Hellenistic kingship. Having "restored" republican government in the year 81, he apparently abdicated his power in stages, resigning his dictatorship at the end of that year, being consul with a colleague in 80, and becoming a private citizen without office in 79. This unusual abdication has occasioned comment from antiquity to the present day. Julius Caesar is said to have remarked that Sulla's resignation was the act of a political dunce, and some modern commentators have been as incredulous.

SIGNIFICANCE OF SULLA.   Sulla's accomplishments were both military and political. He added new dimensions to the role played by the military in affairs of state, and he was the first to realize the use of client armies as a means of guaranteeing political predominance, through civil war if need be. Like other politicians of his age, Sulla was not doctrinaire, nor was he committed as a matter of principle to any faction or program. Rather, like Marius and other statesmen, his political outlook and affiliation were determined largely by those factors that might gratify his ambition. At first a Marian, then a Metellan affiliate, his pursuit of *dignitas* led him into civil war, and he ended up by leading and consuming all other factions. Finally, he believed that only his autocratic leadership could restore stable government. All things considered, his reforms were rather unsuccessful in that they did not, in fact, promote political stability. Sulla's lasting reform, of course, was of the courts, but this was a question of reorganization rather than of bold innovation. His other reforms scarcely survived him, Pompey in particular, one of his supporters, contributing much to their demise during the next decade. Among the graver weaknesses of the Sullan system of government was that the recreated Senate, although enlarged, was unrepresentative of the classes that mattered throughout Italy, and in governing it failed to take into account new social, economic, military, and political trends that were emerging.

CHAPTER 13
RISE OF POMPEY THE
GREAT: 78–60 B.C.

A<small>FTERMATH OF SULLA</small>. Sulla's constitution did not preclude the creation of extraordinary commands to deal with emergencies. Such commands invariably involved a military *imperium* exceeding that of regular constitutional officers. Too much should not be made of these commands as a threat to orderly government. They were well within the Roman tradition, having been a fairly regular institution at least since the third century B.C., and for a generation after Sulla they at least did not lead to military revolution. Under the Sullan system of government the senatorial oligarchy freely resumed its pursuit of factional politics, uniting, as always, however, to confront perceived threats to their control of the state. Initially, Sulla's henchmen cooperated to dominate politics, but soon they were competing to establish new factional combinations. The most striking political phenomenon of the period was the meteoric rise of Pompey the Great, who aimed at attaining preeminence within the aristocracy by means and for ends that, in the long run, were incompatible with the Sullan constitution.

I. POMPEY'S COMMAND AGAINST SERTORIUS IN SPAIN: 77–71 B.C.

T<small>HE</small> R<small>EVOLT OF</small> L<small>EPIDUS</small>. The government was initially threatened by those dispossessed of their property and disqualified from office. The discontented were championed by a member of the Sullan establishment, Marcus

Lepidus, consul in 78, the very year of Sulla's death. Lepidus apparently sought a dominant political role within the oligarchy, attracting a clientele among the electorate by promising to renew distribution of cheap grain to the masses in Rome, to restore Marian exiles, and to reinstate the dispossessed. When his program failed, discontented elements in Etruria revolted, and Lepidus embraced their cause. With their backing, he marched on Rome, demanding reelection to the consulship for 77. Near Rome he was defeated by his colleague Quintus Lutatius Catulus but managed to escape and to land in Sardinia with many soldiers. There he died shortly after, but the bulk of his forces, under Marcus Perperna, withdrew to Spain to join Sertorius, who was also leading a rebellion against the government. In the meantime supporters of Lepidus in north Italy were crushed by Pompey, to whom the Senate had given an extraordinary command in view of his military experience.

SERTORIUS IN SPAIN.   Quintus Sertorius was the ablest of the remaining faction once associated with Cinna and Marius. As early as 88 his military talents had earned him the jealousy of Sulla, who then prevented his election to the tribunate. During the following years he showed his statesmanlike qualities by opposing excesses of his own party. In 83, he was appointed propraetor of Hither Spain, but two years later, after the defeat of the Marians in Italy, he was driven out of his province by Sulla's nominee and forced to flee to Africa. Thence, after various adventures, he returned to Spain in 80 to lead a revolt of the Lusitanians. His ability as a guerrilla leader, the confidence he aroused among the Spaniards, and his initial successes alarmed the government in Rome. To crush him, Sulla dispatched Quintus Caecilius Metellus, one of the consuls of 80, as governor of Farther Spain, but he failed to make any headway. In 79 the propraetor of Hither Spain was defeated and killed by the forces of Sertorius, as was the proconsul of Gallia Narbonensis, who came to the aid of Metellus (78). By the close of 77 Sertorius had won control of almost all of Hither Spain and much of the farther province. He regarded himself as leader of the legitimate government in exile and professed to have revolted not against Rome but against the Sullan faction then dominant in the Senate. He employed former Marians as his civil and military subordinates and organized a senate from among them.

POMPEY'S EXTRAORDINARY COMMAND: 77 B.C.   The Senate, unwilling to come to terms with Sertorius, was forced to send a new commander and army to Spain. As neither consul was willing to face Sertorius, Pompey, who had evaded requests by Catulus to disband his troops, sought the command. Although he was ineligible because of his youth and lack of a previous official career, he was the obvious choice, and the Senate conferred on him proconsular *imperium* and entrusted him with the war in Hither Spain. Even after the arrival of Pompey with an army of 31,000 men, Sertorius was more than able to hold his own throughout the campaign of 76. At the close of the year, through the agency of pirates, he allied himself with Mithridates, king of Pontus, who was again about to fight Rome. In 75 Pompey and Metellus were more successful—their superior numbers and resources were beginning to tell. Sertorius still kept the field, however, and Pompey had to call on the Senate for reinforcements.

Their arrival enabled him to gain the upper hand in 74 and 73 and made victory a certainty. In order to prevent desertions, Sertorius resorted to severe punishments, which alienated the Spaniards, who were already estranged by acts of his subordinates. He was further hampered by dissensions in the ranks of his Roman supporters. The center of disaffection was Perperna, who treacherously assassinated Sertorius in 72 and assumed command of his forces. Soon afterward Perperna himself was defeated by Pompey, taken captive, and executed. The revolt was broken and pacification of Spain speedily followed. Pompey returned to Italy in 71.

II. COMMAND OF LUCULLUS AGAINST MITHRIDATES: 74–66 B.C.

ASIA MINOR AFTER SULLA'S SETTLEMENT. After concluding peace with Sulla in 85, Mithridates consolidated his kingdom and reorganized his forces and expected to renew the struggle with Rome. He recognized that Sulla had made peace (85 B.C.) only for money and because of the situation in Italy, and his inability to secure written confirmation of the terms of the treaty warned him that the Romans still contemplated his complete overthrow. He was attacked in the years 83 and 82 by Lucius Murena, proconsul of Asia, but defended himself, and Sulla once more brought about a cessation of these hostilities, generally called the Second Mithridatic War. During the years 78–75, the Romans proceeded systematically with the conquest of the mountainous districts in southern Asia Minor, including Lycia and Pamphylia. Tigranes of Armenia, son-in-law of Mithridates, in the meantime enlarged his dominions by the annexation of Greater Cappadocia and Syria (83), where he terminated the rule of the house of Seleucus.

THIRD MITHRIDATIC WAR. In 75 Nicomedes III, king of Bithynia, died and bequeathed his kingdom to the Roman people. The Senate accepted the inheritance and made Bithynia a province, but Mithridates championed the claims of a son of Nicomedes and disputed the possession of Bithynia. He raised an efficient army and navy, allied with the pirates and with Sertorius, who supplied him with officers and recognized his claims to Bithynia and parts of Asia Minor. Rome was threatened with another serious war. A former Sullan partisan, the consul Lucius Lucullus, had himself assigned by senatorial decree to the provinces of Cilicia and Asia with command of the main operations against Mithridates, while his colleague Cotta received Bithynia and a fleet to guard the Hellespont. Simultaneously a praetor, Marcus Antonius, was given an extraordinary command against the pirates with an unlimited *imperium* over the Mediterranean Sea and its coast. He proved utterly incompetent, however, was defeated in an attack on Crete, and died there.

Early in 74, Mithridates invaded Bithynia, where he was confronted by Cotta, whom he defeated and blockaded in Chalcedon. Thereupon he invaded Asia and besieged Cyzicus. Lucullus cut his communications, and in the next winter he was forced to raise the siege and retire with heavy losses to Bithynia. The following year Lucullus defeated a fleet of Mithridates in the Aegean. This enabled the Romans to recover Bithynia and invade Pontus. In 72 Lucullus routed Mithridates and forced him to flee to Armenia. In the course of this and the two following years, Lucullus completed the subjugation of Pontus by reducing its fortified cities. Cotta besieged Heraclea in Bithynia and on its fall in 71 returned to Rome. Lucullus spent the winter of 71–70 in Asia reorganizing finances. The cities there were laboring under heavy indebtedness to Roman bankers and taxgatherers, a result of the exactions of Sulla. Lucullus interceded for the provincials and, by achieving a reduction of the accumulated interest, enabled them to pay off their debts in annual installments. This care for the provincials won him the enmity of Roman financiers, who sought to deprive him of his command.

As the war could not be ended so long as Mithridates was at large, Lucullus demanded his surrender from Tigranes. When the latter refused, Lucullus invaded Armenia, defeated the king, and took his capital, Tigranocerta, in 69. The following year Lucullus tried to subjugate Armenia completely but was prevented by mutiny of his troops. He was unpopular with them because he maintained discipline and protected the subject peoples from their excesses. Some of his legions had come to the East with Fimbria in 86 and demanded the discharges to which they were entitled. In 68 Mithridates reappeared in Pontus, and the next spring Lucullus had to return from Armenia to face him, whereupon Tigranes began to recover lost ground. Because of mutiny in his army Lucullus was forced to remain inactive. He had already been superseded in the command of Asia, Cilicia, and Bithynia, which came under his control with the return of Cotta, and his enemies in Rome deprived him of all authority in 66.

III. REVOLT OF THE GLADIATORS: 73–71 B.C.

SPARTACUS. While Pompey was fighting Sertorius in Spain and Lucullus was pursuing Mithridates in Bithynia, a serious slave war arose in Italy, the last and greatest of a series of servile uprisings occurring in many parts of the Mediterranean ca. 140–70 B.C. It began in 73 with the revolt of gladiators from a training school in Capua under the Thracian Spartacus and the Gauls, Crixus and Oenomaus. Taking refuge on the slopes of Vesuvius, they rapidly recruited many runaway slaves. They defeated the armies of two Roman praetors and overran Campania, Lucania, and all southern Italy. By the end of the year 73 their number had grown to perhaps 70,000.

The next year they divided their forces; the Gauls and Germans followed Crixus, the Thracians, Spartacus. The consuls took the field against them, and

Crixus and his horde were defeated in Apulia. Spartacus then marched north, intending to make his way via the Alps to Thrace. The consuls pursued him, but were defeated in turn. He likewise cleared the way north by defeating the proconsul of Cisalpine Gaul, but his followers refused to leave Italy and turned southward, plundering as they went. Not venturing to attack Rome, Spartacus retired to South Italy.

COMMAND OF CRASSUS: 72–71 B.C. In view of the defeat of the consuls of 72, the Senate appointed as extraordinary commander the praetor Marcus Licinius Crassus, one of Sulla's officers, who volunteered his services. After restoring martial discipline, Crassus succeeded in penning up Spartacus in Bruttium. Spartacus hired some Cilician pirates to transport him to Sicily, but after payment they sailed off, abandoning him to his fate. He then forced his way through Crassus' lines, but his followers split into two detachments, each of which was overtaken and defeated. Spartacus fell in battle, and 6,000 of his following were crucified. Crassus tried to suppress the revolt before Pompey arrived in Italy on his way from Spain and perhaps gladly obey a summons to crush the rebels. This Crassus could fairly claim to have accomplished, even though a body of 5,000 slaves escaped to north Italy, where they were met by Pompey and annihilated.

The Sparticist revolution derived from intolerable conditions on *latifundia* and from the desire of slaves to be free, but this and other slave revolts were not part of a class revolution. The revolutionaries never aimed at eradicating the principle of slaveholding nor did they solicit, or receive, support from other economically depressed, but free, classes like the citizen proletariat. The revolt, although possibly causing some improvement in working conditions, is important chiefly for its political repercussions, in particular for the confrontation between Pompey and Crassus that it brought about.

IV. CONSULSHIP OF POMPEY AND CRASSUS: 70 B.C.

MODIFICATION OF THE SULLAN CONSTITUTION. Both Pompey and Crassus, respectively victorious in Spain and Italy, now sought the consulship for 70. Both Sulla's protégés, they had developed into bitter rivals, each building up strong factions in the Senate and electorate by virtue of their military exploits. Crassus was eligible for election, having held his praetorship probably in 73. Pompey's candidacy was unconstitutional, however, for he was still below the required age and had not qualified by holding the quaestorship and praetorship. Under the circumstances, it was unreasonable to disqualify him as if he were a political and military neophyte, and the aristocracy acquiesced willingly enough in suspending the rules to let him be a candidate. Temporarily burying their rivalry and supporting each other, Pompey and Crassus were both elected consul.

The legislation they sponsored apparently reflected the desires of the senatorial factions supporting them. The latter apparently felt secure enough to back restoration of rights to tribunes abrogated by Sulla, which would be conciliatory to opponents of his regime without seriously damaging it. As early as 75 an Aurelian Law permitted tribunes once again to seek other offices; in 70 they regained in full their previous legislative rights and the exercise of veto. Another Aurelian Law in 70 revised the composition of the juries. For the future, each panel was to be equally drawn from senators, equestrians, and tribunes of the treasury (*tribuni aerarii*). The exact status of these tribunes is uncertain, but it seems that they were persons of considerable property, whose assessment was equal to the equestrians'. Sulla had defused equestrian hostility toward the Senate by admitting many equestrians into it; the law of 70 affecting juries was apparently motivated by the desire to increase the potential pool of jurors by extending jury duty to a class already acknowledged as an essential part of the establishment. The Senate also backed other sensible measures advocated by Pompey, notably an agrarian law to benefit the veterans of the Sertorian War; an amnesty for the followers of Lepidus, the revolutionary consul of 78; and, it seems, a law aimed at sedition and violence against individuals. Pompey's desire to strengthen the Senate is also apparent in the actions of the censors of 70, his friends, who purged it of corrupt and otherwise unworthy members.

TRIAL OF VERRES.   In the year 70, prior to the passing of the Aurelian Law reforming the juries, the trial of Gaius Verres, ex-propraetor of Sicily occurred, a case notable because the prosecution was conducted by Marcus Tullius Cicero. Cicero's accusation, contained in his published *Orations Against Gaius Verres*, is illuminating commentary on a notorious instance of provincial misgovernment. Verres had robbed from Sicily money and valuables estimated at 40,000,000 sesterces. He openly boasted that he intended the profits of one year for himself, those of the second for his friends and patrons, and those of the third for his jurors. At the beginning of 70 the Sicilian cities sued Verres for restitution of damages and chose Cicero as their advocate. Roman government had always tolerated a certain amount of graft by governors dealing with provincials, but Verres had far exceeded acceptable limits. It appeared to Cicero, however, that even so Verres might get off unpunished by his peers if the trial were unduly delayed.

Cicero (106–43), a native of Arpinum, the birthplace of Marius, was then in his thirty-sixth year, a *novus homo* and supporter of Pompey. He had chosen the bar rather than a military career to break into the senatorial circle. He, too, had Sicilian clients, because his quaestorship in western Sicily in 75 had earned their confidence and his successful conduct of the defense in several previous trials had marked him as an exceptionally able barrister. Verres entrusted his case to his friend Quintus Hortensius Hortalus, a prominent oligarch, Rome's leading orator, but a man lacking in integrity. Every conceivable device was used to prevent the case from being heard. Another prosecutor appeared, claiming a better right than Cicero's to sue Verres, which necessitated a trial to decide who should represent the Sicilians. Cicero exposed the falsity of the claims of his rival, who was acting in collusion with Verres. He then proceeded to Sicily, where he gathered his evidence in 50 of the 110 days allowed him. Before the trial, elections for the next year were held, and Hortensius was elected consul, but Cicero was returned as aedile in spite of all efforts of his opponents to defeat him.

The trial was set for the fifth of August, and, as there were fifty holidays for festivals between that date and the end of the year, the defense hoped to drag out the trial until after January first, when a praetor friendly to Verres might preside over the court. Cicero thwarted them by abstaining from a long speech, contenting himself with a brief statement of the obstacles the defense erected, a threat as aedile-elect to punish any attempts at corruption, and a short accusatory statement against Verres. He then called his witnesses. Hortensius could not refute the evidence. Before the trial ended, Verres went into exile, an indication that he, after all, expected to be found guilty by his senatorial peers. He was condemned in his absence, and Cicero became Rome's leading advocate.

PROVINCIAL MISGOVERNMENT. The evidence brought out against Verres was afterward used by Cicero to write his *Second Accusation Against Verres* (*actio secunda in Verrem*), which was never delivered, being a political pamphlet and a fictitious oration. It explains the alleged devices the governor used in amassing a fortune. By initiating false accusations, by rendering or intimidating other judges to render unjust decisions, Verres confiscated property whose sale price he then pocketed. He auctioned off justice; he saved himself expense by defrauding tax collectors of dues on the valuables he shipped out of Sicily, and he added to his profits by the sale of municipal offices and priesthoods. He entered into partnership with the *decumani*, collectors of the tithe on produce, and ordered farmers to pay whatever they demanded and, if dissatisfied, to seek redress—which was never gained—in his court. He loaned public funds at usurious interest rates, and he either did not pay in full or paid nothing for wheat purchased from Sicilian communities for the Roman government, although he charged the state the market price. At the same time he insisted on cities commuting into money payments, at rates far above current prices, the grain allotment due for upkeep of the governor's retinue. At times the demands he made on cultivators exceeded the total of their annual crop, and they abandoned their holdings. Verres also amassed a costly treasure of works of art, which he collected from individuals and cities by theft, seizure, and intimidation. Even the sacred ornaments of temples were not spared. All who resisted or denounced him, even Roman citizens, were subjected to imprisonment, torture, or execution. It is obvious that Verres was an unsavory character. It is sometimes doubted that senatorial juries under the Sullan system normally condoned such flagrant corruption in office. But Cicero's persistent legal action against Verres, suggests that he at least believed that this was in fact the case and that only extraordinary pressure would result in the conviction of such a wrongdoer.

V. COMMANDS OF POMPEY AGAINST THE PIRATES AND
IN THE EAST: 67–62 B.C.

THE PIRATE SCOURGE. Both Pompey and Crassus declined proconsular appointments to follow their consulship because there were no provinces available promising an opportunity to augment their influence or military reputation. Pompey eventually found such an opportunity in the ravages of the Cilician pirates. After the failure of Marcus Antonius (74–72), Caecilius Metellus had been sent to Crete in 69. In the next two years he reduced the island and made it a province, but his operations did little to check the pirates. So bold had they become that they freely raided the coasts of Italy and even plundered Ostia. When their depredations finally cut off importation of grain for Rome, famine threatened, and decisive measures had to be taken.

THE GABINIAN LAW: 67 B.C. It was necessary to appoint a commander to operate anywhere against the pirates, and Pompey was the obvious choice. In 67, his supporter, the tribune Aulus Gabinius, proposed a law appointing a single commander of consular rank over the entire Mediterranean and all Roman territory 50 miles inland. His appointment was to be for three years, and he was to nominate senatorial *legati*, to raise money in addition to funds received from the quaestors, and to recruit soldiers and sailors. This command was modeled on that of Antonius, the praetor in 74, but it conferred even higher authority and greater resources. The law was warmly supported by the city *plebs* and by Pompey's faction, including some powerful figures, Cicero, and a rising young aristocrat seeking political connections, Gaius Julius Caesar. Other senatorial factions opposed the measure as unduly enhancing Pompey's power and prestige, but their opposition disappeared in the wake of popular rioting on his behalf. The Gabinian command was duly passed. Although no person had been nominated in the law, the opinion of the voters had been so clearly expressed in a *contio* that the Senate appointed Pompey. He received twenty-four *legati* and a fleet of 500 vessels.

FATE OF THE PIRATES. Pompey worked energetically and systematically. In forty days he swept the pirates from the western Mediterranean. In forty-nine more he cornered them in Cilicia, forcing the surrender of their strongholds. His victory was hastened by the mildness shown to those who submitted. They were granted their lives and freedom and in many cases were used as colonists to revive depopulated Mediterranean towns. Within three months he triumphantly concluded the pirate war, but his *imperium* had three years still to run and he was anxious for further victories.

THE MANILIAN LAW: 66 B.C. Opportunity soon arrived. The conclusion of the pirate war coincided with the defeat of Roman arms in Pontus, as a result of the disaffection of Lucullus' troops and the machinations of his enemies in Rome. Pompey now sought to have Lucullus' command added to his own. Early in 66, another friendly tribune, Gaius Manilius, proposed a law transferring to Pompey the provinces of Bithynia and Cilicia and conduct of the war against Mithridates and Tigranes. Cicero, then a praetor, supported the measure in his speech, *For the Manilian Law*, as did the many, and more influential, senators in Pompey's following. Objections of rival factions were brushed aside by the Plebeian Council, and the bill was passed. Pompey took over the Lucullan command with unlimited power to make peace or war and a hitherto unexampled concentration of military power. His eastern command strongly impressed contemporaries and was a prominent landmark on Rome's road from republic to principate.

POMPEY IN THE EAST. After allying himself with the king of Parthia, who diverted the attention of Tigranes by invading Armenia, Pompey advanced into Pontus to attack Mithridates. The latter was soon forced to withdraw into Lesser Armenia, where Pompey overtook him and dispersed his army. Failing to find refuge with Tigranes, who distrusted him, Mithridates fled to Greek cities of the Crimea that were under his control. Tigranes came to terms with Pompey and retained his kingdom as a Roman ally who might check possible aggression by Parthia. The following year (65), Pompey conquered the inhabitants of the hill country south of the Caucasus between the Black and the Caspian Seas, who then became dependent allies of Rome. The district of Pontus on the north coast of Asia Minor was broken up. The western part was joined to the province of Bithynia, known henceforth as Bithynia and Pontus; the rest was assigned to allied states.

In 64 Pompey turned to Syria, where chaos had reigned since Lucullus took it from Tigranes and left it prey to rival local dynasts. Pompey treated it as conquered territory and annexed it as a province. He then intervened in a struggle between rival claimants to the kingdom of Judaea. After a brief conflict, in which the temple of Jerusalem was stormed by Roman troops, he installed his nominee as high priest at the head of government but without the title of king. Much of Judaea was annexed to Syria and that portion left under the rule of the high priest became a Roman dependency closely supervised by the provincial governor.

The career of Mithridates ended while Pompey was in Judaea. Energetically, he had recruited new forces among his subjects on the north shore of the Black Sea and proposed to join Celts of the Danube valley in an invasion of Italy, but his soldiers and subjects were hostile to the undertaking. A revolt against him was suppressed, but a mutiny of the soldiers headed by his son, Pharnaces, trapped him in his citadel at Pantacapaeum, and he had himself killed (63). Thus the Mithridatic War finally ended. As leader of the Greek East against Rome, Mithridates displayed undeniable talent and perseverance. In the long run, however, he was unable to convert his war into a crusade that might have unified various peoples he sought to lead who were bound to him only by their common dislike of Roman rule. The Mithridatic Wars were, nevertheless, very important because they forced the state to create extraordinary commands for their resolution and since they compelled the Romans to control more closely a restless East.

POMPEY'S EASTERN SETTLEMENT. Pompey used his immense power in the East to treat kings and cities as their lord and, incidentally, to enrich himself in so doing. He displayed much political and even statesmanlike acumen in his eastern territorial arrangements. He created a continuous belt of Roman provinces along the coasts of the Black and Mediterranean Seas from northern Asia Minor to Syria. Behind these provinces to the east he extended Rome's sphere of interest through a band of client states, which, although not administered by Rome, followed her lead in foreign affairs and formed a buffer against the powerful Parthian Empire. In his provincial arrangements Pompey fostered the development of cities wherever possible. He did so partly because Hellenism, the most important unifying cultural force in the Near East, had been traditionally urban. He was also interested in using cities as a basis of local government and taxation, and, through his political reorganization, he became the patron of many communities that would swell his foreign clientele. As a result of his rational system of organization, tribute to Rome increased by 70 per cent, and, in the eventual civil war with Caesar, Pompey could find support in the East where he was regarded by many as a benefactor.

After regulating the political situation in Asia Minor, Syria, and the adjacent countries, Pompey triumphantly returned to Italy with his victorious army and booty.

VI. CONSPIRACY OF CATILINE: 63 B.C.

ROME IN THE ABSENCE OF POMPEY. While Pompey was increasing his military reputation in the East, his activities were watched jealously by rivals and competitors for leadership of the state. Their attitude is revealed in the prosecution of two tribunes who had been among his active supporters in 67 and 66 on charges of disruptive conduct while in office. Gaius Cornelius, tribune in 67, responsible for a law obliging praetors to render decisions according to their own edicts and largely responsible for another prescribing both a fine and exclusion from public life for persons guilty of bribery at elections, was acquitted. Manilius, whose law had transferred the command of Lucullus to Pompey in 66, was the object of two indictments and convicted.

The departure of Pompey left Crassus as his most obvious competitor in Rome. Crassus' clientele had been built up primarily by his military reputation earned in the Spartacist war and by his immense wealth, which he used judiciously to patronize the careers of new men in the Senate, including many former equestrians, who formed the bulk of his following. He tried as a censor of 65 to extend it even further by sponsoring the enfranchisement of Transpadane Gauls, but he was rebuffed by his own rivals. There is also a doubtful tradition that he unsuccessfully induced a friendly tribune to propose a law authorizing annexation of Egypt that same year and that he hoped, thereby, to secure a military command of his own to balance Pompey's. Whatever the facts of the matter, Crassus remained a potent factor in politics.

A potential although not yet actual rival to both Pompey and Crassus was Gaius Julius Caesar, who was rapidly becoming a leading figure in public life. Caesar was born in 100 of the patrician Julii. Since his aunt was Marius' wife and he himself had married Cinna's daughter, he obviously began his career as a Marian partisan. As a young man he had gained notoriety by refusing to divorce his wife at Sulla's behest, and Sulla had been, with difficulty, induced to spare his life. For a time Caesar judged it prudent to withdraw from Rome to the East. After the death of Sulla, Caesar returned to Rome and pursued his career. Although always courting the people by stressing his Marian background, he did not deign to seek connections with the Sullan oligarchy and was an early supporter of Pompey. In 69 he was quaestor in Farther Spain, and in 65, as aedile, he won popularity by his lavish celebration of public festivals, by the restoration of public monuments to Marius, and by support of the prosecution of agents in the Sullan proscriptions.

Political activity in Rome during Pompey's absence was played out against a background of unrest throughout Italy on the part of Marians dispossessed by Sulla, senators who had squandered their resources or been excluded from the Senate by the censors of 70, and property holders, many of moderate means, whose debts were being called in by creditors eager to invest capital in the East, which Pompey was pacifying. Discontented elements were shortly to revolt under the leadership of Catiline (Lucius Sergius Catilina), a patrician with important aristocratic connections and possessed, like many of his peers, of great daring, ambition, and sense of his own *dignitas*. Like Crassus and Pompey, he launched his career under Sulla; he rose to a praetorship and served as propraetor in Africa. He was also, in 65, indicted, perhaps unjustly, for misgoverning his province and acquitted. That same year he ran for the consulship, but his candidacy was rejected, apparently on a technicality.

CICERO CONSUL. In the year 64 there were three leading candidates for the consulship: Catiline once again, Gaius Antonius, a disreputable but well-connected noble who temporarily collaborated with Catiline in the electoral canvass, and Cicero. Cicero, although a *novus homo*, ran first at the polls, winning every century in the assembly, so successfully had he established a following as a supporter of Pompey, a leading barrister, and a spokesman for equestrians and the municipal gentry of Italy. Antonius was also elected, with Catiline running a close third.

On the first day of his consulship in 63, Cicero delivered a speech scathingly critical of a land bill proposed by the tribune, Servilius Rullus, to whom he attributed sinister and self-serving motives. Actually, the bill seems to have been a statesmanlike effort to attain worthwhile social and economic goals: the settlement of some urban proletariat and, eventually, Pompey's veterans of his eastern campaigns, on the land, and the accommodation of failed Sullan colonists wishing to sell their plots and invest their capital elsewhere. The bill proposed creating a commission of ten ex-praetors, elected in a special assembly of seventeen tribes chosen by lot and for five years. They could buy private land and sell public land in Italy and the provinces, could exercise judicial authority, and found colonies. Servilius dropped the law when he found it had little support, the urban plebs being rather uninterested in becoming farmers and the oligarchy fearing that the land commissioners would usurp senatorial prerogatives in the fields of foreign policy and public finance.

CONSPIRACY OF 63 B.C. In July of 63, the consular elections for the next year were held with Catiline again as a competitor. By proposing a general cancellation of debt, he sought to rally around him both nobles of broken fortunes and all needy and desperate citizens throughout Italy. He was bitterly opposed by Cicero, who capitalized on the apprehension of the urban plebs, equestrians, and most senators that Catiline might resort to violence. Rejected for a third time as a consular candidate, Catiline conspired to attain the office through the use of armed force. While one of his associates raised an army among Sullan veterans in Etruria, Catiline prepared to seize the capital and open the gates to these troops, who were to be concentrated secretly near Rome. Cicero got news of the conspiracy and produced enough evidence to induce the Senate to pass the "decree of last resort" and empower him to take all necessary measures to save the state. For want of adequate proof of his complicity, Catiline was not arrested in Rome, which he soon left to join his supporters in Etruria. The Senate then declared him a public enemy and ordered Cicero's colleague Antonius to take the field against him. In the meantime the conspirators who remained in the city set December 17, the opening day of the festival of the Saturnalia, as the date for revolution, when the city was to be fired, the consuls and other prominent men killed, and a reign of terror instituted. This plan was betrayed to Cicero by a delegation of Allobroges from Gallia Narbonensis who happened to be there and whom the plotters had endeavored to enlist. Cicero arrested five leading Catilinarians and took precautions to prevent an outbreak. Catiline now realized the futility of a march on Rome and tried to escape with his army into Cisalpine Gaul, but he was overtaken by Antonius and forced to give battle near Pistoria, where he and most of his followers fell. Instead of resorting to the regular courts, Cicero convened the Senate to decide the fate of the prisoners. He favored their immediate execution and was supported by the more prominent senators. Caesar proposed that they be confined to certain Italian municipalities for life. When a majority seemed likely to approve this sentence, a strong speech by Cato the Younger, an uncompromising supporter of the oligarchic establishment, won them back to Cicero's viewpoint.

The Catilinarian episode is interesting for several reasons, especially because it bore witness to the desperate straits of rural plebs throughout Italy and the interest of the propertied establishment in preserving the status quo. It is also noteworthy because of Cicero's not disinterested involvement in it and because it is so extensively documented in surviving sources. The legality of the *senatus consultum ultimum*, of course, was always hotly debated whenever it was applied, because it involved the basic rights of citizens. In this regard Caesar's arguments were the most moderate and "constitutional," whereas the viewpoint of Cicero and Cato seemed to be that of a governing class willing to sacrifice custom and even law to make outlaws of its enemies and to deny them legal protection. Cicero's execution of the conspirators without trial therefore exposed him to future attack.

VII. THE COALITION OF POMPEY, CRASSUS, AND CAESAR: 60 B.C.

POMPEY'S RETURN. Toward the close of 62, Pompey arrived in Italy from the East and, contrary to the expectations of those who saw in him a second Sulla, immediately disbanded his army. Pompey wanted enhancement of his *dignitas* no less than any man of his age but, rather naively, he thought that the oligarchy would give him his due. The following September he celebrated a memorable triumph. From the spoils of his wars, he deposited 50,000,000 denarii in the treasury, gave half as much to his higher officers, and distributed 71,000,000 denarii as a bonus among lower officers and soldiers. Largess to higher officers was politically important, because it cemented the patron-client relationships between aristocrats and successful commanders like Pompey. In addition, the taxes from his annexations increased the revenues of the Empire by 35,000,000 denarii annually.[1] To bring his achievements to a fitting conclusion, Pompey now pressed the Senate to ratify the arrangements made in the East and to provide land grants for about 25,000 veterans discharged from his legions. He was opposed by factions led by Lucullus, Crassus, and Cato the Younger, who was emerging as the most vigorous opponent of any potential dynast. Their position was aided by the inept politics of consuls friendly to Pompey in 61 and 60. The Senate insisted on examining his acts in detail and refused to ratify them *en bloc* as he demanded; when in 60 one of the tribunes proposed a land bill for his veterans, the opposition was so effective that the plebiscite was abandoned. The opposition to Pompey was itself unstable, however, encouraging a possible shift of political alignments in his favor. Crassus in particular began to have second thoughts about the efficacy of his alliance with Pompey's enemies, especially when Cato successfully campaigned against a reduction in the amount of taxes promised to the state by publicans operating in Asia Minor. They may well have needed help after Sulla and Pompey had taken so much out of the East. In any case, Crassus was an investor in their companies and stood to lose money if they did not receive some relief.

---

[1] The denarius was the average daily wage of a Roman laborer.

Such was the situation when Caesar returned to Rome in 60. His promise at this point was such that he attracted, for the first time it seems, the patronage of Crassus, who stood surety for his debts amounting to 25,000,000 denarii. He had held a praetorship in 62 and for the following year had been governor of Farther Spain, where he waged successful border wars and conciliated the provincials. Upon his return, Caesar requested a triumph and permission to stand for the consulship while waiting outside the city for the right to make a triumphal entry. Owing to Cato's intervention, the Senate failed to act on his petition, and he at once decided to forego the triumph and press his candidacy. Supported by Crassus and Pompey, he was elected consul; his colleague was Calpurnius Bibulus, the nominee of the Catonian faction hostile to Pompey. Once consul, Caesar reconciled his two patrons and formed with them a coalition to attain their particular aims. In the light of subsequent events, this unofficial coalition became known as the First Triumvirate, an important alliance of factions.

CHAPTER 14
RIVALRY OF POMPEY
AND CAESAR AND
CAESAR'S
DICTATORSHIP:
59–44 B.C.

For the history of the thirty years between the First Triumvirate and the close of the civil wars in 30 B.C., our literary sources are in large measure the same as for the years following the death of Sulla: Appian, Cassius Dio, Velleius Paterculus, the *Epitome* of Livy, Plutarch, and Cicero. To the *Lives* of Plutarch already mentioned must be added those of Caesar, Mark Antony, and the younger Cato; Cicero's speeches and other works are supplemented for the years 60 to 43 by his invaluable collection of *Letters*, which at times give an almost day-by-day account of events in Rome. Of great importance also are Caesar's own *Commentaries* on the Gallic War and on the Civil War, the first of which was completed by his friend Hirtius, who also wrote an account of the Alexandrine War. These are supplemented by similar narratives of the African and Spanish Wars written by anonymous officers of Caesar's staff. A Roman account of Caesar's career is found in the biography written by Suetonius Tranquillus early in the second century A.D. Many fragmentary inscriptions of important laws also throw light on Caesar's administrative reforms.

I. TRIUMVIRATE IN ACTION

CAESAR'S CONSULSHIP: 59 B.C. Once in office, Caesar began to accommodate his partners in the Triumvirate. Exact dating of his measures is difficult, but it seems that the early spring of 59 was a crucial period for the triumvirs, because Pompey then revealed the extent of his commitment to Caesar's designs by marrying Caesar's daughter Julia. Early that year Caesar laid before the Senate a law to provide lands for Pompey's veterans and needy citizens in Rome through the distribution of arable public land outside Campania and other properties to be purchased. This legislation was similar to agrarian measures rejected in 63 and 60 without, however, features objectionable to the oligarchy. Nevertheless, when it met with strong opposition, largely instigated by his critic, Cato, he brought his bill directly before the Plebeian Council, where it was vetoed by hostile tribunes and by obstructive use of the *auspicium* by Bibulus. Caesar then called upon Pompey and Crassus for support. Aided by Pompey's veterans he chased his opponents from the Forum. The bill became law, and Bibulus shut himself up in his house in protest and refused to carry out public business. Because the land to be used in this measure proved inadequate, Caesar introduced in late April a second law, opening for colonization public land in Campania then under lease to state tenants. This law also passed over the vigorous opposition of Cato. Caesar made use of his henchman, the tribune Vatinius, to pass through a law ratifying all Pompey's dispositions in the East and a second granting to delinquent tax-farmers of Asia a remission of one third of their contract price. Although much of Caesar's legislation was determined by the personal interests of the triumvirs and was passed by means of violence and terrorism, it was basically statesmanlike. Less partisan measures included a *lex Iulia de repetundis* that remained on Rome's statute books for six hundred years as a measure to control extortion of provincial populations by their governors. Another law decreed the publication of senatorial resolutions in a kind of "Congressional Record," (*acta diurna*) which prevented the garbling of official documents by interested magistrates and, incidentally, publicized Caesar's own legislation.

CAESAR'S PROCONSULAR COMMAND.   Caesar laid the foundations for his future career by securing for himself an extraordinary military command, probably in the early spring of 59. For 58 the Senate apparently had designated the forests and cattle roads of Italy as the province for both the consuls of the preceding year, probably to control widespread banditry and brigandage caused by hard times. The last thing Caesar wished to be was a kind of Secretary of the Interior, and he seized upon the first excuse to set aside this arrangement. He seems at first to have been interested in campaigning to the northeast of Italy, along the Danube, against the Dacians who were threatening Macedonia. Vatinius proposed a law, passed by the Plebeian Council, conferring on him the combined provinces of Cisalpine Gaul and Illyricum, with a garrison of three legions, for a term of five years (ending on March 1, 54). Cisalpine Gaul was to be an important source of strength and wealth for him eventually to rival Pompey. He had won clients there in 65 by championing a proposal to extend full Roman citizenship to all those of Latin status, and the Po valley was an excellent recruiting area. Somewhat later in 59 the governor of Transalpine Gaul died, and the Senate, at Pompey's instigation, added this province to Caesar's command on a yearly basis and gave him another legion. Caesar's primary interest promptly shifted to this area. Disturbances among the Gauls, due to a Germanic invasion from across the Rhine and a threatened migration of the Celtic Helvetii from their home in Switzerland, held out hopes for winning military laurels.

For the rest of the year Caesar's proconsular command ran concurrently with the consulship, and he was able to raise and maintain troops in Italy and thus exert pressure on the political situation in Rome. The length of his proconsular command also assured him immunity for a long time from attempts to hold him responsible for unconstitutional acts perpetrated during his consulship.

COALITION CONTINUES. The strong-arm methods of the Triumvirate produced considerable opposition among the oligarchy and even the electorate, Pompey especially losing the support of many influential members of his clientele among the nobility. Although temporarily dominant, the Triumvirate was in the long run fragile, because it was an alliance of convenience depending on the ambitions of three men who were really rivals. Far from controlling the state in subsequent years, the triumvirs only infrequently worked for the election of their own supporters to the consulship, which was normally occupied by their opponents in the nobility.

The triumvirs at least cooperated to secure the election of friendly consuls for 58 and to remove temporarily their two ablest opponents, Cato and Cicero. The latter had refused all proposals to join them and had sharply criticized them in public. His banishment was secured by the tribune Clodius, whose transfer from patrician to plebeian status Caesar had facilitated. Clodius was an adroit politician, slippery and mercurial, ready to use the triumvirs when it suited him in an attempt to establish his own, independent following. To this end he sponsored legislation, such as conversion of grain distributions into an outright dole, that would make him popular. He hated Cicero, who had testified against him when he was on trial for sacrilege. Early in 58 Clodius carried a bill outlawing any person who had executed Roman citizens without regular judicial proceedings. This law was obviously aimed at Cicero because of his execution of the Catilinarian conspirators. Finding that he could not rely on the support of his friends, Cicero went into exile without waiting trial and found refuge in Thessalonica, where the governor of Macedonia protected him. Clodius then sponsored a second law, banishing Cicero by name and confiscating his property. Cato, also Clodius' enemy, was entrusted with a special mission to incorporate Cyprus into the Empire, and his Stoic conception of duty prevented him from refusing the appointment. Caesar remained with his army near Rome until after Cicero's banishment and then left for his province.

II. CAESAR'S CONQUEST OF GAUL: 58–51 B.C.

DEFEAT OF THE HELVETII AND GERMANS: 58 B.C. In 58, Caesar, relatively untried as a commander, entered Gaul, where subsequent campaigns revealed his fascinating personality. He soon demonstrated a serene quality of self-confidence that communicated itself to his staff. A soldier's general, solicitous of his troops, especially of centurions, he was a man who regarded warfare, like politics, as an analytical exercise of the mind and was a master of both men and events. Primarily a commander who appreciated the use of infantry, he did not understand so well, nor did he have much faith in, cavalry, and he was even less of an admiral.

Transalpine Gaul (Gallia Narbonensis) embraced the coast between the Alps and Spain and the land between the Alps and Rhone as far north as Lake Geneva. The country stretching from the Pyrenees to the Rhine and from the Rhone to the ocean was called *Gallia comata* or "long-haired Gaul" and was occupied by many different peoples. These fell into three groups, (1) those of Aquitania, between the Pyrenees and Loire, where there was a large Iberian element, (2) the Celts in a narrow sense of the word, stretching from the Loire to the Seine and Marne, and (3) the Belgian Gauls, dwelling between these rivers and the Rhine. Among the latter were Germanic peoples.

The culture of the Gauls showed marked contrasts. Living in a very rich area, they had developed agriculture, animal husbandry, and mining. In part as a result of their proximity to the Greek trading city of Massilia, they learned the arts of commerce and used both Greek coinage and their own. In some areas they lived in small towns. They were illiterate, except for their priestly class, the Druids. The latter were judges and controlled religious observances and beliefs. These included belief in immortality of the soul, worship of gods in sacred groves, and human sacrifice. Although conscious of a general unity of language, race, and customs, the Gauls had not developed a national state, owing to the mutual jealousy of the individual peoples. Tribal chiefs ruled the Belgian Gauls. Elsewhere, aristocrats who feuded among themselves and with the Druids were in control. The bulk of the population was semiservile.

Rome had sought to protect the Narbonese province by establishing friendly relations with some Gallic peoples and had long before (ca. 121) allied with the Aedui. Conditions in *Gallia comata* were disturbed about 70 by an invasion of Germanic Suevi from across the Rhine, under their king, Ariovistus. They had been invited by the Sequani to help them fight their rivals, the Aedui, and had been promised lands in return for their services. In 61 the Aedui suffered a crushing defeat, which forced them to come to terms with the Sequani. The Aedui appealed to Rome for aid on the basis of their alliance, but the Romans were engaged in suppressing a serious revolt in Gallia Narbonensis, occasioned by the exactions of officials and greed of Roman money-lenders, and did not respond. Two years later, Ariovistus, whose people had settled in the region now known as Alsace, sent an embassy to the Senate. The Senate recognized him as a "friend of the Roman people," which was tantamount to approving his present status in Gaul. The next threat to peace came from the Helvetii, who planned to migrate from Switzerland as early as 61 but did not set out until March of 58 on a search for new homes in western

Gaul. They planned to traverse part of Gallia Narbonensis, but Caesar's timely arrival prevented their crossing the upper Rhone into the province. In provoking war he was certainly motivated by the desire to enhance his *dignitas* as well as by the wish to safeguard the Roman province to the south. As the Helvetii turned westward into the territory of the Sequani and Aedui, Caesar followed, overtook, and defeated them in two battles, forcing them to return home and to accept an alliance with Rome. He then learned that Ariovistus had taken advantage of Roman indifference to strengthen his position in Gaul. He had conquered the Sequani and was threatening the Aedui with a fresh band of Suevi about to cross the Rhine to support him. It now became Caesar's aim to prevent the development of a strong Germanic state in Gaul. Because Ariovistus refused to limit his freedom of action, Caesar marched against him, defeated him near Strassburg, and drove him and his people across the Rhine. Caesar's victories made him the dominant power in Gaul outside the Roman province, and this caused many leading Gallic tribes to ally themselves with Rome. Of the warlike Belgae, however, only one people, the Remi, came over to Rome's side.

SUBJUGATION OF THE BELGAE, VENETI, AND AQUITANIANS: 57–56 B.C. The next year (57) Caesar marched against the united Belgae, defeated them, and subdued many tribes, especially the Nervii. Simultaneously his legates received the submission of the peoples of Normandy and Brittany. During the following winter some of them, led by the Veneti, broke their alliance and attacked Caesar's garrisons. Thereupon he built a fleet, which in the course of the next summer destroyed that of the Veneti and captured their coastal strongholds (56). Henceforth, the Romans possessed naval supremacy on the Atlantic coast of Gaul. The same year witnessed the submission of the Aquitani, which brought practically all Gaul under Roman sway.

THE CONFERENCE OF LUCA: 56 B.C. The political situation at Rome was meanwhile extremely fluid. In the course of his violent tribunate in 58, Clodius had alienated influential aristocratic factions including the triumvirs'. To undermine Clodius, Pompey supported his own adherent, the tribune Titus Annius Milo, who pressed for Cicero's recall. A law of the Centuriate Assembly withdrew his sentence of outlawry, his property was restored, and the orator returned in September 57, by his own admission to a warm reception in the towns and at the capital. The senatorial oligarchy also acquiesced in the appointment of Pompey as grain commissioner (*curator annonae*) for five years to relieve famine in the city. This gave him proconsular *imperium* in Italy and abroad and control of ports, markets, and traffic in grain within the Empire. Pompey relieved the situation but could not suppress disorders in Rome, where Clodius and Milo ran riot with their armed gangs.

Once the grain crisis eased, the oligarchy resumed sniping at Pompey, and even Crassus lent his name to attacks on his fellow triumvir. Caesar, too, was the object of bitter senatorial criticism, and there was a movement afoot in the

Senate to recall him from Gaul. The triumvirs had to reach a new agreement if their influence on the government were to be effective. Accordingly, while wintering in Cisalpine Gaul, Caesar arranged a conference at Luca in April 56, where the three settled their differences and laid future plans. They agreed that Pompey and Crassus should be consuls in 55; that the former should be given Spain and Libya for five years; Crassus, Syria for an equal period; and, very probably, that Caesar's command in Gaul should be prolonged until sometime in 50.

These arrangements were duly executed. Because it was too late for Pompey and Crassus to be candidates at the elections in 56, they forcibly prevented any elections being held. The following January, after compelling the other candidates to withdraw, they were elected. Thereupon a law of the tribune Gaius Trebonius effected the assignment of provinces agreed to at Luca. Cicero, indebted to Pompey for his recall, was forced to support the Triumvirate; the senatorial oligarchy found their boldest leader in Cato, who returned to Rome early in 56.

CAESAR'S CROSSING OF THE RHINE AND INVASIONS OF BRITAIN: 55–54 B.C. During the winter of 56–55 two Germanic tribes, the Usipetes and the Tencteri, crossed the lower Rhine into Gaul. The next summer (55) Caesar attacked and annihilated them, only a few escaping across the river. As a warning against future invasion, Caesar bridged the Rhine and made a demonstration on the right bank, destroying his bridge when he withdrew. Toward the close of the summer he crossed the Straits of Dover to Britain, nominally to punish the Britons for aiding his enemies in Gaul. However, because the season was late and his force small, he returned to Gaul after a brief reconnaissance on the Kentish coast.

The following year, after gathering a larger fleet, he again landed on the island with a large force. This time he forced his way across the Thames and received the submission of Cassivellaunus, the chief who led the British tribes against the invaders. After taking hostages and receiving promises of tribute, Caesar returned to Gaul. Although southeast Britain was not subdued, Caesar could claim to have rendered its inhabitants subject and, besides enlarging geographical knowledge, he brought back many captives. In Rome the exploit produced great excitement and enthusiasm.

REVOLTS IN GAUL: 54–53 B.C. Although the Gauls had submitted, they were not yet reconciled to Roman rule, which ended their intertribal wars and feuds among the nobility. Many tribes were restive and not inclined to surrender all hopes of freedom without another struggle. During the winter 54–53 the Nervii, Treveri, and Eburones in Belgian Gaul attacked Roman detachments stationed in their territories. One of these was cut to pieces, but the rest held out until relieved by Caesar, who stamped out the rebellion.

REBELLION OF VERCINGETORIX: 52 B.C. A more serious movement started in 52 among the peoples of central Gaul, who found a national leader in Vercingetorix, a young noble of the Arverni. The revolt surprised Caesar when he was in Cisalpine Gaul and his troops still were scattered in winter quarters. He recrossed the Alps hastily, secured the Narbonese province, and united his forces, strengthening them with German cavalry from across the Rhine. A temporary check in his attack on Vercingetorix at Gergovia caused the Aedui to desert the Romans, and the revolt spread throughout Gaul. Caesar was about to retire to the Narbonese province, but after repulsing an attack, he penned up Vercingetorix in the fortress of Alesia instead. A great Gallic effort to relieve the siege failed to break Caesar's lines, and the defenders were starved into submission. The crisis was over, although another year passed before revolting tribes were all reduced and Roman authority reestablished (51). Caesar was generally mild in his treatment of the conquered, and the Gauls were both pacified and won over. In the future they were among his most loyal supporters. The conquest of Gaul was a supremely important event for the future of the Empire and for the development of European civilization. For the time *Gallia comata* was not made a province. Its peoples became allies of Rome under the supervision of the governor of Narbonese Gaul; they were obliged to furnish auxiliary troops and for the most part were liable to a fixed annual tribute. Caesar's campaign in Gaul gave him the opportunity to develop his unusual military talents, to create a devoted veteran army, and to develop an enthusiastic clientèle in Gaul and the capital.

III. DISSOLUTION OF THE TRIUMVIRATE

PARTHIA. The Parthians were originally a seminomadic people speaking a kind of Persian, who settled to the southeast of the Caspian Sea about 250, gradually extending their control over the Mesopotamian and eastern satrapies of the declining Seleucid Empire. They remained a landholding minority ruling various subjects. Their kingdom, even though it covered an area permeated by Greek culture following the conquest of Alexander the Great, was only superficially Hellenized. They were important particularly for their contributions to warfare, as they excelled in the use of both heavily mailed cavalrymen, known as cataphracts, and swift mounted bowmen whose tactics at first baffled the Romans. Relations between Parthia and Rome dated from a mission of Sulla (92) and were friendly until 65, when Pompey refused the claim of the Parthian king to northern Mesopotamia. Ten years later Aulus Gabinius, as proconsul of Syria, had contributed to the worsening of relations by supporting a rebel claimant to the Parthian throne. It was under such circumstances, and with the design of winning military prestige in a Parthian war to balance that of the other triumvirs, that Crassus left for Syria in the autumn of 55.

DEATH OF CRASSUS: 53 B.C. Crassus had no real excuse for opening hostilities, but the Parthians were potentially dangerous neighbors and a campaign against them promised profit and glory. In 54 he briefly invaded Mesopotamia and then withdrew to Suroa. The next year he again crossed the Euphrates, intending to penetrate deeply into enemy country, but he underestimated the strength of the Parthians and the difficulties of desert warfare. Surenas, the Parthian commander, had organized a force of mounted archers, supported by a supply train of camels carrying a reserve supply of arrows, which enabled the bowmen to maintain their fire for long periods. The archers were backed by mail-clad lancers mounted on heavy war horses also partially protected by armor. In the Mesopotamian desert near Carrhae the Romans were surrounded and cut to pieces by the Parthian horsemen. While endeavoring to lead the survivors to safety, Crassus was enticed into a conference and treacherously slain, and only a portion of his force of eight legions escaped (53). The Parthians were slow to follow up their advantage, and Crassus' quaestor, Gaius Cassius Longinus, was able to hold Syria. Roman prestige in the East had received a severe blow, however, and for the next three centuries the Romans found the Parthians dangerous neighbors.

PRINCIPATE OF POMPEY: 52 B.C. At the end of his consulship Pompey remained in Italy with the concurrence of the other triumvirs on the pretext of his curatorship of the grain supply and governed his province through legates. In Rome disorder reigned. No consuls were elected in 54 or before July of the following year. The partisans of Clodius and Milo kept everything in turmoil. Because of riots between supporters of the candidates, no consuls or praetors were elected for 52. In January of that year Clodius was slain by Milo's body-guard on the Appian Way, and the ensuing outburst of mob violence in the city forced the Senate to appeal to Pompey. He was made sole consul until he should choose a colleague and was entrusted with the task of restoring order. This was another notable instance when the Romans temporarily suspended normal constitutional practice to cope with emergency. His troops pacified the city. Milo was tried on a charge of public violence, convicted, and banished. Pompey had attained the height of his official career. He was sole consul; he had provinces embracing the Spains, Libya, and the grain curatorship; he governed his provinces through *legati*; and his armies were maintained by the treasury. He was the chief power in the state, as the Senate was helpless without him, and he was justly regarded by contemporaries as First Citizen or Princeps. At least superficially, his position foreshadowed the principate of Augustus.

Relations between Pompey and Caesar remained cordial after Crassus' death, and Pompey in particular steadfastly aided and abetted his colleague's political ambitions and aimed at strengthening a clientele that could support both of them. Caesar's immediate aim was to step directly from his provincial command into a second consulship. With Pompey's active support he influenced the tribunes of the year 52 to carry a law permitting him to be a candidate for the consulship in absentia. Initially, he apparently planned to run for election in 50 and to hold office in 49, even though he would be technically ineligible for a second consulship before 48.

Two laws carried by Pompey during his consulship of 52 are sometimes cited, without good reason, as attesting to increased estrangement in that year between him and Caesar. One of these contained a clause forbidding candidates in general to seek magistracies when absent from Rome, but Pompey saw to it that Caesar was specifically exempted from the prohibition, with the understanding that he would be a consular candidate in 50. The second, more important enactment repealed the Sempronian Law of 123, which required that consular provinces be designated before the election of possible appointees and that provincial governors be the outgoing consuls and praetors of any given year. Pompey's measure decreed that governors could be nominated at any time from among all ex-magistrates whose terms had expired at least five years before their provincial appointment. The gap between the city magistracy and provincial governorship was designed to curb lavish electoral expenditures of candidates, who, under the old system, could recoup by immediately holding a lucrative post abroad. This law might have meant that Caesar would be forced out of Gaul before settling affairs of the province and compelled to campaign for the consulship as a private citizen, with much less chance of success and unacceptable loss of *dignitas*. Such was not the case, however, as Pompey's law for the first time permitted tribunician veto of senatorial disposition of consular provinces, giving Caesar adequate protection.

POMPEY'S BREAK WITH CAESAR. The question of Caesar's recall from Gaul became the focal point of politics in Rome for the next two years, and the failure to reach agreement on this issue was the cause of a new civil war. One of Caesar's enemies, the consul Marcellus, agitated for Caesar's recall as early as 51, on the grounds that the war in Gaul was over, but his proposal was defeated in the Senate. A senatorial resolution was finally passed, however, postponing discussion of the Gallic succession until after March 1, 50. Pompey's attitude toward Caesar, in the meantime, wavered and became ambiguous. Pompey's increasing jealousy of Caesar and his desire for acceptance within the aristocracy was inducing him to join senatorial conservatives who were also Caesar's bitter opponents and to abandon his partner. This he would not at first do, although he did not object to discussion of Caesar's recall right after March 1, 50. At about this time Caesar decided to postpone his candidacy for the consulship until 49, as organization of Gaul was necessary to its future peace. This violated the spirit, if not the letter, of the law of 52 permitting his candidacy in absentia and was bitterly opposed as unconstitutional by the Catonian faction and also by Pompey, who finally moved toward a complete rupture with Caesar. For the first time, late in 50, the possibility of civil war loomed even though the vast majority of the Senate, fearful of this eventuality, went on record as sanctioning Caesar's consular candidacy in absentia for the year 49.

Caesar, sensing this mood, offered to disband his army and return to Rome if Pompey would likewise disband his troops, but Pompey declined. The proconsul thus appealed to the senatorial majority and to propertied classes who wished to avoid civil war, for which he wanted Pompey himself, Cato, and his clique to seem responsible. So long as he could protect his *dignitas*, Caesar probably wanted to avoid a confrontation with Pompey. The latter, however, apparently wanted Caesar to surrender everything, while he, Pompey, would promise nothing in return. In any case, most senators wished that *both* dynasts would retire and so approved such a resolution on December 1, 50, by a vote of 370 to 22, only a hard core of four families, led by Cato, being willing to force the issue. The resolution was ignored by Caesar's enemy, the consul Marcellus, at whose request Pompey then assumed command of the government forces in the peninsula. On January 1, 49, the Senate, railroaded by Pompey and the Catonians, voted that Caesar should surrender his command by a fixed date or be outlawed. The resolution was promptly vetoed, however, by Marcus Antonius (Mark Antony) and Quintus Cassius, two of the new board of tribunes. Angry at being thwarted, the Catonian faction drove Antony and Cassius from the Senate by threats of death. Then, on January 7, the Senate passed the decree of last resort, calling on the consuls and other magistrates, including Pompey as proconsul, to protect the state and at the same time pronouncing Caesar a public enemy. Caesar's friends fled the city and hurried to meet him in Cisalpine Gaul, where he and a small part of his army were waiting, ready for this emergency. The fugitive tribunes appealed to him for protection, and he could rightly claim that he was defending both himself and the sanctity of the people's chosen representatives.

IV. CIVIL WAR BETWEEN CAESAR AND THE SENATE: 49–46 B.C.

CAESAR'S CONQUEST OF ITALY AND SPAIN: 49 B.C. Caesar was aware of the minute size of the senatorial faction dedicated to war and knew that many equestrians, Italian aristocrats, and not a few senators, had supported him from the beginning. Other landholders wished only to be left in undisturbed enjoyment of their property. He eventually won adherents among the latter by leaving them just that. He possessed the advantages, also, of a loyal army ready for immediate action and undisputed control over his troops. His land laws had given him many clients in Campania, the city populace was now well disposed toward him, and his generous treatment of the towns of Cisalpine Gaul in the matter of Roman citizenship had made them his backers. His opponents had only two veteran legions in Italy, and although Pompey acted as commander-in-chief of the senatorial forces, he was hampered by having to defer to the judgment of the consuls and senators who were in his camp. It was obviously to Caesar's advantage to take the offensive and force a decision before his enemies could concentrate provincial resources against him. Hence, he determined to act without delay to forestall his own annihilation, and, upon receiving news of the Senate's action on January 7, he crossed the Rubicon, which divided Cisalpine Gaul and Italy, with a small force, ordering the legions beyond the Alps to join him at once.

The Italian municipalities opened their gates at his approach, and the newly raised levies went over to his side. Having failed to destroy Caesar politically, the Senate sought to slow his advance by opening negotiations. Caesar, although he renewed his offer to disband his troops if Pompey did so—an offer which his opponents would not accept—maintained the tempo of his southward march. Everywhere his mildness to his opponents won him new adherents. Pompey originally planned to fight in Italy and had gone to Apulia to raise troops, but his plan was thwarted by the stubbornness of the governor designate of Transalpine Gaul, L. Domitius Ahenobarbus. Against Pompey's advice, Ahenobarbus insisted on doing battle against Caesar at Corfinium in central Italy. Ahenobarbus was defeated, his troops went over to Caesar, and Pompey's cause in Italy became hopeless. Pompey was thus forced to abandon Italy and withdraw to the East, intending later to surround the peninsula—a plan made feasible by his control of the sea. Caesar divined his intention and tried to cut off his retreat at Brundisium but could not prevent embarkation. With his army and a majority of the Senate, Pompey crossed to Epirus. Lacking a fleet, Caesar could not follow, and he returned to Rome. There some magistrates were still functioning, in conjunction with a rump Senate. Needing money, he wanted funds from the treasury. When a tribune opposed him, Caesar ignored his veto and forcibly seized the reserve treasure the Pompeians had left behind in their flight. Meantime Caesar's lieutenants had seized Sardinia and Sicily and landed in Africa to secure the grain supply of Rome. He himself determined to attack the well-organized Pompeian forces in Spain and destroy them before Pompey was ready to attack from the East. On his way to Spain Caesar began the siege of Massilia, which resisted him. Leaving the city under blockade, he hastened to Spain where, after an initial defeat, he forced the surrender of the Pompeian armies. Some of the defeated joined his forces; the rest were dismissed to their homes. Caesar returned to Massilia. The city capitulated on his arrival and was punished by requisitions, the loss of its territory, and the temporary loss of its autonomy. Caesar then pressed on to Rome, where he had been appointed dictator. After holding elections in which he and an approved colleague were returned as consuls for 48, he resigned his dictatorship and set out for Brundisium. There he had assembled his army and transports for the passage to Epirus.

BATTLE OF PHARSALUS: 48 B.C. During Caesar's Spanish campaign Pompey gathered a large force in Macedonia—nine Roman legions reinforced by contingents from the Roman allies. His fleet, recruited largely from the maritime cities in the East, commanded the Adriatic. Nevertheless, at the beginning of winter (November 49), Caesar landed on the coast of Epirus with part of his army and seized Apollonia. Pompey arrived from Macedonia in time to save Dyrrhachium. Throughout the winter the two armies remained inactive, but Pompey's fleet prevented Caesar from receiving reinforcements until the spring of 48, when Marcus Antonius landed with another detachment. As Caesar's troops began to suffer from shortage of supplies, he was forced to take the offensive and tried to blockade Pompey's larger force in Dyrrhachium.

The attempt failed, Caesar's lines of investment were broken, and he withdrew to Thessaly where he was followed by Pompey. Relying on superior numbers and, in particular, his preponderance in cavalry, Pompey yielded to the demands of the senators in his camp and risked battle. Near the town of Old Pharsalus he attacked Caesar, but was defeated and his army dispersed. Pompey himself sought refuge in Egypt. There he was killed by order of the king, whose father he had protected in the days of his power. Nobles surviving Pharsalus dispersed to Asia and Africa. Caesar's victory assured his future rule; had Pompey won, republican institutions would perhaps have fared no better, because his was more the appearance than the substance of constitutionalism. Other senators sided with him only because they thought, for the moment, to use him because he seemed to be less dangerous to them than Caesar.

CAESAR IN THE EAST: 48–47 B.C. After Pharsalus Caesar pursued Pompey but arrived in Egypt after the latter's murder. His ever-pressing need for money probably induced him to intervene as arbiter in the dynastic struggle then raging in Egypt between the twenty-year-old Cleopatra and her thirteen-year-old brother, Ptolemy XIV Dionysos, who, following the Egyptian custom, was also her husband. Caesar, having seized the young king, brought back Cleopatra, whom the people of Alexandria had driven out. Angered at this and resenting his exactions, the Alexandrians revolted and from October 48 to March 47 besieged Caesar in the palace. Having few troops with him, Caesar was in danger and able to maintain himself only through his control of the sea, which enabled him eventually to receive reinforcements. He released the king, who promptly joined the besiegers. Caesar's relief was effected by a force raised by Mithridates of Pergamon, who invaded Egypt through Syria. In cooperation with him Caesar defeated the Egyptians, Ptolemy Dionysos perished in flight, and Alexandria submitted. Cleopatra was married to a still younger brother and given the kingdom. Caesar succumbed to the charms of the Egyptian queen and spent the rest of the winter in her company. He was finally called away to face a new danger in Pharnaces, son of Mithridates Eupator, who had taken advantage of the civil war to emerge from the Crimea and overrun Pontus, Lesser Armenia, and Cappadocia. Traversing Syria, Caesar entered Pontus and defeated Pharnaces at Zela. After settling affairs in Asia Minor, Caesar hurried to the West, where his presence was urgently needed. *Veni, vidi, vici.*

CAESAR'S CAMPAIGN IN AFRICA: 46 B.C. Both the fleet and the army of Pompey had been dispersed after Pharsalus, but Caesar's delay in the East had given his opponents an opportunity to regroup. They gathered in Africa, where Caesar's lieutenant Curio, who invaded the province in 49, was defeated and killed by the Pompeians through the aid of King Juba of Numidia. From Africa they were now preparing to attack Italy. In Rome Caesar was appointed dictator for 47 with Antony as his master of the horse. Here disorder reigned as a result of financial distress caused by the war. Antony, who was in Rome, proved unable to deal with the situation. Caesar reached Italy in September

COALITION OF SATURNINUS, GLAUCIA, AND MARIUS. During his tribunate of 103 Saturninus sponsored some important legislation. One law established another standing court to try cases of treason, which was conceived of as an offense against the majesty (*maiestas*) of the Roman people. This court was also staffed by equestrians and was essentially a revival of the Mamilian tribunal of 109 that tried the generals implicated with Jugurtha. Saturninus perhaps also instituted a fourth standing court, identically staffed, on embezzlement (*peculatus*). He courted both the electorate by reducing below the Gracchan level the price of grain sold to the urban plebs and the good will of Marius by another law, which provided for what proved to be an abortive colony in Africa for his veterans.

A coalition among Saturninus, Glaucia, and Marius came about to secure a sixth consulship for Marius, for 100, and at the same time the praetorship for Glaucia and a second tribunate for Saturninus. They were successful, but they entered office without any program. Saturninus proposed laws providing lands for veterans in Gallia Narbonensis and authorizing the founding of colonies of Latin status in Sicily, Achaea, and Macedonia. Special clauses required all senators to swear they would recognize the provisions of the laws as valid once they had been passed. The factional background to this legislation was revealed when Marius' erstwhile patron, Quintus Metellus, refused to take the oath. In a *cause célèbre* demonstrating the power of Marius' coalition, Saturninus brought capital charges against Metellus, who was forced into exile. During his previous tribunate and his recent election campaign Saturninus appealed to violence, and on this occasion he made use of Marius' veterans to rout the opposition. The laws were enacted, but the proposed settlement in Gaul was never carried out, although some colonies were founded elsewhere. Marius was already alarmed at the violence of his associates, and its continuance led to a break with them. He had never been a social revolutionary, and now that he enjoyed high honors, he became estranged from his associates and gradually sought a *rapprochement* with the oligarchy.

Seeking to perpetuate their position, Saturninus and Glaucia became candidates for office for 99. Saturninus was reelected tribune for a third time, but Glaucia, illegally a candidate for the consulship while still praetor, played into the hands of his enemies by having his chief rival murdered. As during the Gracchan and Jugurthine crises, rival senatorial factions drew together in the face of threat, the Senate passing the decree of last resort and calling on Marius to restore order. Marius broke completely with his former henchmen and forced the surrender of Saturninus, Glaucia, and their followers, who had taken refuge on the Capitoline hill, and placed them for safekeeping in a public building. There they were killed by their enemies, who tore off the roof and stoned them to death with tiles. Marius' coalition evaporated; he had been unable to control his own partisans or to protect them from mob violence when he had taken them into custody.

(47) and soon restored order in the city. He then faced a serious mutiny of his troops, who demanded money, land, and demobilization. By boldness and quick thinking Caesar won back their allegiance and left for Africa in December 47. He landed with only a portion of his troops and was checked at first by senatorial forces under Scipio and Juba. He was supported by King Bogud of Mauretania and a Catilinarian soldier of fortune, Publius Sittus. After receiving reinforcements from Italy Caesar besieged the seaport Thapsus. Scipio came to the rescue but was defeated in a bloody battle near the town, and the province fell into Caesar's hands. Cato, who was in command of Utica, did not force the citizens to resist but committed suicide, thus earning martyrdom for the republican cause. Other senatorial leaders, including Juba, either followed his example or were executed by the Caesarians. Caesar returned to Rome, where he celebrated a lavish triumph over Gaul, Egypt, Pharnaces, and Juba. He was now undisputed master of the state and settled the problem of governing the Roman world autocratically.

V. DICTATORSHIP OF JULIUS CAESAR: 46–44 B.C.

CAESAR'S FACTION. Caesar has been called a "Sulla with clemency, a Gracchus without a revolutionary program." Between the end of the civil wars and his own death, he consolidated his power, but he effected no general program of reform that addressed itself to the basic problems of the state. Wielding powers based mainly on the dictatorship for life he held after July 28, 46, he relied on a motley faction whose potential had first been realized by Gaius Marius: political adventurers from the nobility, the urban plebs, veterans and their officers, and, most notably in Caesar's case, a broad equestrian following from Italy and the western colonies, whose promotion into the Senate he patronized on an unprecedented scale. Caesar also succeeded in attracting some nobles who had followed Cato and Pompey, although many resented the dictator's genuine clemency as a patronizing or, even worse, a regal gesture. A few, like Cicero, resisted his personal blandishments and refused to support his regime as a matter of principle. The goal of his policy will be understood best from a consideration of his official position during the year and a half following the battle of Thapsus.

HIS OFFICES, POWERS, AND HONORS. Caesar's autocratic position was legalized by his tenure of various offices, special powers, and unusual honors. Foremost among them was the dictatorship. He had already held this for a short time in 49 and again in 47. In 46 he was appointed dictator for ten years, in the following year for life. Simultaneously he was consul, an office which he held continuously from 48, usually with a colleague but as sole consul in 45. In addition he enjoyed the personal inviolability of the tribunes of the plebs and the right to sit with them on certain public occasions. It is unlikely that he received full tribunician authority (*tribunicia potestas*) as the historian Cassius Dio suggests. He had been *pontifex maximus*, head of the state religious organization, since 63 and in 48 was admitted to all patrician priestly corporations. In 46 he was given censorial powers under the title "prefect of morals" (*praefectus morum*), at first for three years and later for life. In addition to official positions of rather established scope, Caesar received other powers independent of any office. He was granted the right to appoint both Roman and provincial magistrates, until in 44 he had authority to nominate half the officials annually, and in reality appointed all. In 48 he received power to make war and peace without consulting the Senate, in 46 the right of expressing his opinion first in the Senate (*ius primae sententiae*), and in 45 the sole right to command troops and to control public money. The next year advance ratification was given to his future arrangements, and magistrates entering upon office were required to swear to uphold his acts. Concentration of these powers placed Caesar above the law and made public officials his servants. Honors to match his extraordinary powers were given him, partly by his own desire, partly by the servility of the Senate. He was granted a seat with the consuls in the Senate, when not consul himself; he received the title "father of his country" (*parens* or *pater patriae*); his statue was placed among those of the kings, his image in the temple of Quirinus; the month Quintilis, in which he was born, was renamed Julius (July); a new college of priests, the Julian Luperci, was created; a temple was erected to his Clemency and a priest (flamen) appointed for worship there; and he was authorized to build a house on the Palatine with a pediment like a temple. Most of these honors he received after his victory over the Pompeians in Spain in 45. The title *imperator* (Emperor), however, regularly the prerogative of a general entitled to a triumph and surrendered along with his military *imperium*, was employed by Caesar continuously from 49 until after the battle of Thapsus in 46, when he celebrated his triumph over the Gauls and other foreign enemies. He assumed it again after the Battle of Munda the following year.

CAESAR'S AIM: MONARCHY. The powers Caesar wielded and his lifelong tenure of certain offices, show that he intended to establish autocratic government at Rome. It has been alleged that he wished to transplant to Rome a Hellenistic type of kingship, in which the monarch sought justification for autocracy through deification. There is no convincing evidence that this was so, and the exalted honors he received, although unprecedented, are explicable within the Roman tradition. That ultimately he would have dared to assume the title "rex," which was anathema to the Roman upper class, is more doubtful. At the time of the Latin festival in January 44, some of the mob actually hailed Caesar as "rex," and at the feast of the Lupercalia in February, Antony publicly offered him a diadem, which he ostentatiously refused. Monarchy, of whatever form, implies succession, but Caesar had not named a successor before his sudden death.

CAESAR'S REFORMS. Upon his return to Rome after the battle of Thapsus, Caesar began a series of reforms that reveal his astonishing versatility and competence. One of the most useful of these was calendar reform that he effected as *pontifex maximus*. Hitherto the Romans used a lunar year of 355 days, with its New Year's Day originally on March 1, after 153, for civil purposes at least, on January 1.[1] It was customary to correct this lunar year approximately to the solar year by adding an intercalary month of 22 days in the second, and one of 23 days in the fourth year of each successive four-year period. For personal or political reasons the pontiffs in recent years had neglected to make necessary intercalations, so that in 46 the Roman year was over two months ahead of the solar year. By adding the requisite number of days to the year 46, Caesar brought the Roman calendar back into harmony with solar time. He then introduced a new calendar, worked out by the Greek astronomer Sosigenes of Alexandria, that went into effect on January 1, 45. It was based on the Egyptian solar year of $365\frac{1}{4}$ days and provided for cycles of four years of which the first three had 365 days each, and the fourth or "leap" year 366 days with an extra day added in February.[2]

Abuse of the grain dole was partially rectified by the reduction of the number of recipients from about 320,000 to 150,000. This decrease was made possible in part by establishing many poor persons in colonies, in part by excluding those not really dependent on the dole for their livelihood. In interests of public order, Caesar dissolved plebeian guilds, with the exception of the ancient associations of craftsmen. Many of them had become political clubs and contributed to recent disturbances in the city. For reasons that are unclear, the composition of the juries was changed by the removal of the tribunes of the treasury. Penalties for criminal offenses were increased. Caesar also laid plans for a much-needed codification of the Roman law, but these were not effected. To meet administrative needs and to have more positions to dispense patronage, he increased the number of quaestorships from twenty to forty and the praetorships from eight to sixteen. There was a corresponding increase in the number of priesthoods. Pompey's law requiring provincial governors to be selected from ex-magistrates five years out of office was disregarded, and a new law restricted proconsular governors to terms of two years and propraetorian governors to one. Some plebeian families were elevated to patrician status to replace extinct patrician clans and to fill patrician priesthoods. The number of senators was raised from 500 or 600 to 700, the new recruits coming from Caesar's partisans, including Italian equestrians, his veteran officers, and adherents from the western provinces whom he had enfranchised. Thereby he strengthened his faction in the traditional way. As early as 48, and again in 46, he relieved a financial crisis by alleviating debts, but he also protected creditors from excessive losses. Intending to obtain more farmland, he planned to drain

---

[1] The religious year which regulated festivals and the like had also come to be reckoned from January 1 at some date prior to Caesar's reform.

[2] This Julian calendar, as it came to be called, survived the Roman Empire and remained the calendar of the Christian world until it was corrected, at the orders of Pope Gregory XIII, in 1582 by the omission of ten days then and of three intercalary days in every 400-year period since, as the Julian year was about eleven minutes longer than the true solar year.

the Pomptine marshes in Latium and the Fucine lake in the Marsic country. To minimize the danger from rural slaves, he required at least one third of the shepherds and herdsmen be freemen. Other projects he did not live to carry out were the construction of a new highway across the Apennines to the Adriatic and the improvement of the harbor at Ostia, both commercially important.

Caesar's reorganization of local government in Italy was very important. This was accomplished by a series of laws, some of which did not come into effect until after his death. As the result of the creation of new municipalities in rural districts, all of Italy was divided into areas, consisting of a town and the territory dependent upon it for local administration. These communities received local autonomy of a uniform type, irrespective of their origin as colonies or *municipia*. Each was governed by a board of elected magistrates, whose functions were the same everywhere although their titles might differ, and by a council recruited primarily from ex-magistrates. The development of municipal autonomy in Italy removed a heavy burden from Roman magistrates, in particular the praetors, and laid the basis for the later extension of the municipal system throughout the provinces.

COLONIZATION. Caesar carried out a broad program of colonization that revealed a keen appreciation of economic needs and was also significant for the future relationship between Italy and the provinces. He provided for many of his veterans by settling them in Italy on properties confiscated from dead or unreconciled enemies. In so doing he did not found new colonies or upset any existing municipalities, so that there was no serious disturbance of the agricultural population as a result of land grants. Many others received lands in the provinces, particularly in Narbonese Gaul and Africa, where they either formed the nuclei of new colonies or augmented the population of older ones. Indeed, the first large-scale settlement of Romans abroad begins with Caesar's colonization program. Colonies were also founded in the provinces with colonists drawn from the urban proletariat of Rome, who were more fitted for commercial and industrial occupations than for farming. It is reported that some 80,000 of the city populace were so cared for. Many of these colonies were seaports, like Sinope and Heraclea on the Black Sea, Corinth, where Caesar proposed to dig a canal through the Isthmus, and Carthage, where he successfully revived the project of Gaius Gracchus. Many colonies arose in Spain, partly through conferment of colonial rights on communities that had supported Caesar loyally and partly through actual colonization. Among communities of the latter sort was Urso, made up of freedmen from Rome who settled on a site confiscated from Pompeian inhabitants. A large part of the charter of this colony is extant[3] and corresponds closely to the municipal government Caesar had organized in Italy. Widespread establishment of Roman colonies, generous conferment of

---

[3] The *Lex Coloniae Genetivae Iuliae.*

citizenship upon individual provincials, and the liberal granting of Latin rights in Narbonese Gaul as a preliminary step to Roman status all characterized Caesarian policy abroad.

MUNDA: 45 B.C. Caesar was a magnanimous conqueror. After Pharsalus he permitted most republican leaders (among them Cicero) to return to Rome. Even after Thapsus, at the intercession of friends he pardoned bitter foes like Marcus Marcellus, one of the consuls of 51. There remained some irreconcilables, led by his old lieutenant Labienus, Varus, and Gnaeus and Sextus Pompey, sons of Pompey the Great, who fled after Pharsalus with a small navy to the western Mediterranean. In 46 they were joined by Labienus and Varus and landed in Spain, where they rallied to their cause Pompeian veterans who had entered Caesar's service only to be alienated by his *legatus*, Quintus Cassius. The Caesarians could make no headway against them, and the dictator had to campaign in person. In December 46, he set out for Spain. Throughout the winter he tried vainly to force the enemy to battle. In March 45 the armies met at Munda, where Caesar's eight legions defeated thirteen Pompeian legions. The Caesarians gave no quarter, and the Pompeian forces were annihilated. Labienus and Varus fell on the field, Gnaeus Pompey was later taken and executed, but his brother Sextus escaped. Caesar returned to Italy in September 45 and celebrated a triumph.

ASSASSINATION OF JULIUS CAESAR: MARCH 15, 44 B.C. His victory at Munda strengthened Caesar's autocratic position and was responsible for granting of most of his exceptional honors. It was now clear at Rome that Caesar did not intend to restore the Republic which he made no bones about calling a sham. In the conduct of government he allowed no freedom to the Senate or public assemblies, and although in general mild and forgiving, he resented any attempt to slight him or question his authority. The realization that Caesar contemplated autocracy aroused bitter animosity among many of the old governing oligarchy, who chafed under the restraints of his power and resented degradation of the Senate to a mere advisory council. It could hardly be expected that the Roman aristocracy, with all their traditions of imperial government, would tamely submit to exclusion from political life except as ministers of an autocrat who had been only lately one of themselves. This attitude was shared by many who had hitherto been active in Caesar's cause, as well as by republicans who had been reconciled to him. Among these disgruntled elements a conspiracy was formed against the dictator's life. The originator of the plot was the ex-Pompeian Gaius Cassius, whom Caesar had made praetor for 44, and who won over Marcus Junius Brutus, a member of the house descended from that Brutus reputed to have delivered Rome from the Tarquins. Brutus had gone over to Caesar and was highly esteemed by him, but Brutus was persuaded that it was his duty to emulate his ancestor. Other conspirators of note were the Caesarians Gaius Trebonius and Decimus Junius Brutus. In all some sixty senators were implicated. They set the Ides of March,

44, as the date for executing the plot. Caesar was now busily preparing a campaign against the Dacians north of the lower Danube, to be followed by a war against the Parthians, who had been a menace to Syria ever since the defeat of Crassus—which Caesar aimed to avenge—and, in addition, to secure the eastern frontier. An army of sixteen legions and ten thousand cavalry was being assembled in Greece for this campaign, as Caesar prepared to leave Rome to assume command. He is said to have disregarded information that a conspiracy against his life was under way, dismissed his bodyguard of soldiers, and refused one of senators and equestrians. On the fatal day he entered the Senate meeting, where the question of granting him the title of king in the provinces was to be discussed. A group of conspirators surrounded him and, drawing concealed daggers, stabbed him to death.

ESTIMATE OF CAESAR'S CAREER. Roman writers who preserved the republican tradition honored Brutus, Cassius, and their associates as tyrannicides who tried to save the Republic in the name of liberty. Cato, who died rather than witness the triumph of Caesar, became their hero, and they regarded Caesar as an adventurer. This is an extremely narrow and partisan view. The Republic Caesar had overthrown was no popular government but one of a small group of Roman nobles who exploited for their own ends millions of subjects. Republican government had ceased to voice the opinion even of the whole Roman citizenry. Governing circles had proven incapable of improving the situation and were completely unable to keep peace. In his resort to corruption and violence in furthering his own career and in his appeal to arms to decide the issue with the Senate, Caesar must be judged by the practices of his time. What set him apart was his dedication to his goal, enhancement of his *dignitas*, and his ability to realize it. Although, strangely enough, he did not appear so to contemporaries, Caesar deserves to rank as one of the most fascinating and genial personalities in Roman history and, indeed, in the whole course of Western civilization. He was at once in the front rank among Roman writers, statesmen, and generals. In war he was remarkable as a tactician and a strategist, and in political life he displayed a similar capacity to develop a plan of action and to manage the details of party conflicts. Better than his contemporaries he appreciated the political tendencies of the age, which he intended to shape and guide. Although he was ruthless and cold-blooded and maintained an aristocratic aloofness, his personal charm enabled him to create a remarkable *esprit de corps* among his troops and evoked loyalty and solidarity among his political adherents. The autocratic ideal he strove to realize was the logical outgrowth of the power and independence he enjoyed in this proconsular command. His courage and self-confidence are revealed in his acceptance of the responsibility for guiding the Empire. To do so he was willing to provoke civil war, and he crossed the Rubicon to prevent an ignominious defeat and even his own annihilation. Caesar fell because he was too open and direct in assuming autocratic powers. In spite of his capacities

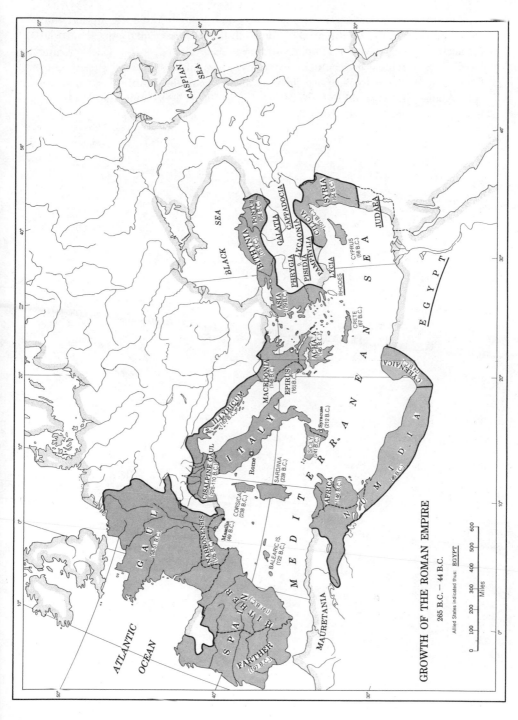

GROWTH OF THE ROMAN EMPIRE

265 B.C. – 44 B.C.

Allied States indicated thus: EGYPT

0 100 200 300 400 500 600
Miles

as statesman and politician, he had been unable to build up a faction that would embrace all the influential elements in the state, especially the senatorial oligarchy, without which Rome could not be governed. After Caesar some form of monarchical government was inevitable, but a successful successor to Caesar would have to be more devious and gradual in establishing one-man rule. Above all, he would have to reconcile the oligarchy to such rule, as Caesar had failed to do.

CHAPTER 15
PASSING OF THE
REPUBLIC: 44–27 B.C.

I. RISE OF OCTAVIAN

POLITICAL SITUATION AFTER CAESAR'S DEATH. Caesar had made no arrangements for a successor, and the conspirators evidently expected that control of affairs would revert back to the Senate. Instead of finding their act greeted with an outburst of popular approval, however, they discovered that, although Caesar was dead, the Caesarian party lived on in his officers, his veterans, and the city populace, led by the consul Mark Antony and Marcus Aemilius Lepidus, Caesar's master of the horse. The Senate met on March 17, and a majority evidently supported the assassins, but they were afraid of the legion Lepidus had under his orders and of the Caesarian veterans in the city. Antony, who possessed Caesar's papers and money, led the Caesarian party and came to terms with its opponents. His actions are revealing. For the time being at least he had no quarrel with them, provided they did not prevent his consolidating his position as head of the Caesarian faction. It was agreed that the conspirators should go unpunished but that Caesar's acts should be ratified, even those which had not yet been effected, that his will should be approved, and that he should receive a public funeral.

Caesar left his gardens on the right bank of the Tiber as a public park, bequeathed a donation of 300 sesterces (two and a half months' wages) to each Roman, and adopted his grandnephew, Gaius Octavius, as his son and heir to three fourths of his fortune. Although the oration Antony delivered on the day of Caesar's funeral seems to have been mild, it was sufficient to inflame popular sentiment against the tyrannicides. The mob seized Caesar's corpse, burned it in the Forum, and buried the ashes there. The chief conspirators did not dare to remain in the city. Decimus Brutus went to his province of Cisalpine Gaul, Marcus Brutus and Cassius lingered near Rome. Antony was master of the capital and overawed opposition by his bodyguard of 6,000 veterans, restraining Lepidus and other Caesarians who called for vengeance upon the conspirators. Lepidus was won over by his election to the position of *pontifex maximus* to succeed Caesar and was induced to leave the city for his province of Hither Spain to check Sextus Pompey, who had reappeared in Farther Spain and defeated the Caesarian governor. It was hoped that Sextus would be satisfied with permission to return to Rome and compensation for his father's property. Caesar's arrangements for the provincial governorships assigned Macedonia to Antony and Syria to Dolabella, who became Antony's consular colleague at Caesar's death. Antony altered this assignment by a law granting him Cisalpine Gaul and the Transalpine district outside Gallia Narbonensis for six years, violating a law of Caesar's, which limited proconsular commands to two years. Dolabella was to have Syria for a like period, and Decimus Brutus was given Macedonia in exchange for Cisalpine Gaul. The consuls were to occupy their provinces at once. For the next year Brutus and Cassius were assigned the provinces of Crete and Cyrene; for the present they were given a commission to collect grain in Sicily and Asia. The two left Italy for the East, however, with the intention of seizing Macedonia and Syria. Although Antony showed no signs of following Caesar's path to absolute power, for their own protection they needed force to balance his.

OCTAVIAN.   Antony found an unexpected rival in Caesar's adopted son, Gaius Octavius, a sickly but able youth of eighteen years. At the time of Caesar's death he was at Apollonia in Illyricum with an army being assembled for the Parthian war. From the beginning Octavius showed determination equal to that of his adoptive father. He aimed at one goal: leadership of the Caesarian faction, and he coolly contemplated the struggle with Antony that would result. Against his family's advice, he returned to Rome and claimed his inheritance. Antony, who was not about to help a rival, had spent Caesar's money and refused to refund it. Octavius began the creation of a Caesarian party of his own. Lacking influential family connections, he made good Caesarian legacies to citizens and veterans by selling property, by borrowing, and by dispersing the Caesarian war chest he had commandeered upon landing at Brundisium. Gradually he acquired a following, especially among equestrian financial interests. Despite delays caused by Antony, his adoption was legalized the next year, and he assumed the magic name of Caesar.[1]

---

[1] After the adoption his full name was Gaius Julius Caesar Octavianus. Although he was known as Caesar by his contemporaries, it is more convenient to refer to him henceforth as Octavian, to distinguish him from his adoptive father.

Antony clearly underestimated the cunning ambition of this youth, although he soon became aware of his mistake. He himself was anxious to occupy Cisalpine Gaul. When Decimus Brutus refused to evacuate it, Antony determined to drive him out, and he obtained permission to recall the four legions from Macedonia for that purpose. Before their arrival Octavian, on his own, raised a force among Caesar's veterans in Campania, and two of the four Macedonian legions deserted to him on the march from Brundisium to Rome. The Caesarians were now divided into two parties, and Octavian began to cooperate with the republicans in the Senate, since the backing of senior statesmen would increase his own authority. The latter were thus encouraged to oppose Antony, with whom reconciliation was impossible. Cicero, who was not among the conspirators but who had subsequently approved Caesar's murder, was on his way to join Brutus when he heard of the changed situation in Rome, and he returned to assume the leadership of the anti-Caesarians. Antony left Rome for Cisalpine Gaul early in December 44, and Cicero induced the Senate to ally with Octavian against him. In his *Philippic Orations* he gave full vent to his hatred of Antony and aroused the latter's enmity.

WAR AT MUTINA: DECEMBER 44–APRIL 43 B.C. In Cisalpine Gaul Decimus Brutus, relying upon the support of the Senate, refused to yield to Antony. He was blockaded in Mutina, and the Senate made preparations for his relief. Antony was ordered to leave the province, and Hirtius and Pansa, who became consuls in January 43, took the field against him. The aid of Octavian was indispensable, and the Senate conferred on him propraetorian *imperium* with consular rank in the Senate. The combined armies defeated Antony in two battles near Mutina, forcing him to raise the siege and flee toward Transalpine Gaul. Pansa died of wounds received in the first engagement, and Hirtius fell in the course of the second. Ignoring Octavian, the Senate entrusted Brutus with pursuit of Antony. The power of the Senate seemed reestablished, for Marcus Brutus and Cassius succeeded in their design of gaining control of the East, Dolabella having perished in the conflict, and they headed a considerable military and naval force. The Senate conferred upon them supreme military authority (*maius imperium*) in the East and gave to Sextus Pompey, then at Massilia, a naval command. At last Cicero could induce the senators to declare Antony a public enemy. He no longer felt the support of Octavian a necessity and expressed the attitude of many senators toward him by saying he was to be praised, honored, and shelved. The experienced orator entirely misjudged this young man who, so far from being a tool of the Senate, had used that body for his own ends. Octavian refused to aid Decimus Brutus and demanded from the Senate his own appointment as consul, a triumph, and rewards for his troops. His demands were rejected, whereupon he marched on Rome, occupied the city and on August 19 had himself elected consul at the incredible age of nineteen with Quintus Pedius as colleague. The latter carried a bill establishing a special court to try Caesar's murderers, who were condemned and banished. The same penalty was pronounced on Sextus Pompey.

The Senate's decree against Antony was revoked and the way was open for a possible reconciliation between Octavian and Antony, whose ambitions could only be furthered by a coalition.

II. TRIUMVIRATE OF 43 B.C.

ANTONY, OCTAVIAN, AND LEPIDUS.   On his way to Transalpine Gaul Antony met Lepidus, whom the Senate summoned from Spain to assist Decimus Brutus. Lepidus was a Caesarian and, alarmed by the success of Marcus Brutus and Cassius, allowed his troops to desert to Antony. Decimus Brutus, pursuing Antony, joined forces with Plancus, governor of Narbonese Gaul. Upon news of the events in Rome, Plancus abandoned Brutus and joined Antony. Brutus in turn was deserted by his troops and killed while fleeing in Gaul. Antony and Lepidus now marched on Italy.

Octavian had been entrusted with the defense of Italy and moved north to meet them. Both sides were ready to come to terms and unite to crush their common enemies, Brutus and Cassius. At a conference of the three leaders on an island in the river Renus near Bononia, a reconciliation between Antony and Octavian was effected and plans laid for their immediate cooperation. The three decided to have themselves appointed triumvirs for the settlement of the commonwealth (*triumviri reipublicae constituendae*) for a term of five years. They had consular *imperium* with the right to appoint magistrates, and their acts were to be valid without the approval of the Senate. They divided the western provinces among themselves. Antony received those previously assigned to him; Lepidus took the Spains and Narbonese Gaul, while to Octavian fell Sardinia, Sicily, and Africa. Octavian resigned his consulship but next year was to be joint commander with Antony in a campaign against the republican armies in the East while Lepidus protected Rome. The Triumvirate was legalized by a tribunician law (the *lex Titia*) of November 27, 43, and they entered office formally the first of January following. Unlike the secret coalition of Pompey, Crassus, and Caesar, this one was a formal commission exercising almost supreme public powers.

THE TRIUMVIRS IN ITALY. The triumvirs proscribed their enemies, partly for vengeance but largely to secure money for their troops from the confiscation of property. Among the chief victims was Cicero, whose death Antony demanded. He died courageously for the republican ideal to which he was devoted, but it must be recognized that this devotion was to an oligarchy, whose crimes he refused to share, although he condoned and justified them. The exactions of the triumvirs did not end with the confiscation of the goods of the proscribed. Special taxes were laid on the propertied classes in Italy, and eighteen flourishing municipalities were marked out as sites for veterans' colonies.

In 42 Octavian dedicated a temple to Julius Caesar in the Forum, where his body had been burned. Later by a special law Caesar became a state god with the name Divus Julius. Meanwhile Octavian had difficulty in occupying his provinces. Africa was eventually conquered by one of his lieutenants, but Sextus Pompey, who controlled the sea, occupied Sardinia and Sicily. His forces were augmented by many of the proscribed and by adventurers, and Octavian could not dislodge him before setting out against Brutus and Cassius.

PHILIPPI: 42 B.C. The republican generals had raised an army of 80,000 Romans, in addition to allied contingents, and taken up a position in Thrace to await the triumvirs. In the summer of 42 the latter transported their troops across the Adriatic, despite their enemies' fleet, and the two armies met near Philippi on the borders of Macedonia and Thrace. An indecisive battle was fought. Antony defeated Cassius, who committed suicide, but the troops of Brutus routed those of Octavian, who was incapacitated by illness. Shortly afterwards Brutus was forced by his soldiers to risk another battle. This time they were completely defeated, and Brutus took his own life amidst carnage rivalling that of Cannae or Arausio.

DIVISION OF THE EMPIRE. The two victorious triumvirs now redistributed the western provinces. Lepidus, whom they suspected of intrigues with Sextus Pompey and whose hostility they could now risk, was for the time ignored. Cisalpine Gaul, because of its strategic situation, was not assigned, ceased to be a province, and was annexed to Italy, whose political boundaries at length coincided with its geographical frontiers. Transalpine Gaul was given to Antony; Octavian received the two Spains, Sardinia, and Africa on the understanding that he would turn over Africa to Lepidus if his conduct warranted it. After the meeting near Bononia Antony was chief of the coalition, and his prestige was enhanced by his success at Philippi. It was now agreed that he should settle conditions in the East and raise funds there, while Octavian should return to Italy and assign the promised lands to their troops. This decision was of momentous consequence for the future. In the summer of 41 Antony officially summoned Cleopatra to Tarsus in Cilicia to demand money of her. He had probably known her when she had been Caesar's mistress. She now became his, but there is no indication that Antony was madly in love with her. He followed her to Egypt that winter, but he left soon thereafter, and the two did not meet again for four years.

OCTAVIAN IN ITALY: 42–40 B.C. In Italy Octavian was confronted with the task of providing lands for some 50,000 veterans. The eighteen municipalities previously selected for this purpose proved insufficient, and a general confiscation of small holdings took place, rendering many persons homeless and destitute. A few, like the poet Vergil, found compensation through the influence of a powerful patron. Confiscations, following closely the proscription, only further embittered Octavian's relations with the propertied classes, especially the senatorial oligarchy, which regarded him as a pitiless and opportunistic revolutionary. His administration was also hampered by opposition from the partisans of Antony, led by the latter's wife Fulvia and his brother Lucius Antonius. Hostilities broke out in which Lucius was besieged in Perusia and starved into submission (40). Fulvia went to join Antony, while others of their faction fled to Sextus Pompey, who still held Sicily. Of great importance to Octavian was his acquisition of Gaul, which fell to him through the death of Antony's legate, Calenus. He could now safely turn over Africa with a considerable garrison to Lepidus. An indication of an approaching break between Octavian and Antony was the former's divorce of his wife Clodia, a stepdaughter of Antony, and his marriage with Scribonia, a relative of Sextus Pompey, whom he hoped to win over.

TREATY OF BRUNDISIUM: 40 B.C.   While Octavian was involved in the Perusian war, the Parthians overran Syria, and, in conjunction with them, Quintus Labienus, a follower of Brutus and Cassius, penetrated Asia Minor as far as the Aegean. Antony returned to Italy to restore his waning influence there and to gather troops to reestablish Roman authority in the East. Both he and Octavian were prepared for war, and hostilities began around Brundisium, which refused to admit Antony. At the insistence of soldiers in both armies, however, reconciliation was effected, and an agreement known as the Treaty of Brundisium was made. It provided that Octavian should have Spain, Gaul, Sardinia, Sicily, and Dalmatia, while Antony should hold the Roman possessions east of the Ionian Sea. Lepidus retained Africa, and Italy was held in common. To cement the alliance Antony, whose wife Fulvia had died, married Octavia, Octavian's sister.

TREATY OF MISENIUM: 39 B.C.   The following year Antony and Octavian came to terms with Sextus Pompey, who still held Sicily and had wrested Sardinia from Octavian. His command of these islands and of the seas about Italy enabled him to cut off the grain supply of Rome, where famine broke out. This brought about a meeting of the three at Misenum, in which it was agreed that Sextus should govern Sardinia, Sicily, and Achaea for five years, should be consul and augur, and be compensated for his father's property in Rome. In return he engaged to secure peace at sea and convoy the grain supply for the city. The terms of the treaty were never fully carried out, however, and in the next year Octavian and Sextus were again at war. The former regained possession of Sardinia but failed in an attack upon Sicily (38).

TREATY OF TARENTUM: 37 B.C.   In 39 Antony returned to the East, where Illyrians were threatening the Macedonian frontier and the Parthians still occupied Asia Minor and Syria. One of his generals won a decisive victory over the Illyrians; another drove Labienus out of Asia Minor, recovered Syria, and repelled a second Parthian inroad. In 38 Antony returned to Italy at the request of Octavian, who was alarmed at the activities of Sextus Pompey, but a meeting of the triumvirs did not take place until the next year, when they conferred at Tarentum. Octavian needed Antony's support after his defeat by Sextus and Antony wanted more Italian troops for his projected invasion of Parthia. Despite their mutual suspicions they were formally reconciled by Octavia. They agreed that Antony should supply Octavian with 120 warships for his operations against Sextus, in return for which Octavian should give him four of the legions in Africa. Antony fulfilled his share of the bargain, but not Octavian. Since the power of the triumvirs legally terminated on December 31, 38, they decided to be reappointed for another five years, until the close of 33. This appointment was perhaps carried into effect by a special law, like the first.

DEFEAT OF SEXTUS POMPEY: 36 B.C. Octavian then attacked Sicily, while Lepidus cooperated by besieging Lilybaeum. At length, in September, 36, Marcus Vipsanius Agrippa, Octavian's ablest general, destroyed Sextus' fleet in a battle off Naulochus. Pompey fled to Asia, where two years later he was captured by Antony's forces and executed. After the flight of Sextus, Lepidus challenged Octavian's claim to Sicily, but his troops deserted him for Octavian, and he was forced to ask for the latter's mercy. Stripped of power and retaining only his office of *pontifex maximus*, he lived under guard in an Italian municipality until his death in 12 B.C. His provinces were taken by Octavian. The defeat of Sextus Pompey and the deposition of Lepidus gave Octavian sole power over the western half of the Empire and inevitably tended to sharpen the rivalry and antagonism that had long existed between him and Antony. In the same year Octavian was granted tribunician sacrosanctity and the right to sit on the tribune's bench in the Senate. Of even greater significance in the long run was his assiduous building up of a political clientele, especially in the years after the Treaty of Brundisium. Not only was he patronizing equestrians and new men, he also openly sought the support of republican oligarchs by furthering their careers. The young revolutionary was clearly trying to reconcile himself to the classes that mattered and was extending his political nexus throughout Italy against the day of possible conflict with Antony.

III. VICTORY OF OCTAVIAN

ANTONY'S FAILURE AGAINST PARTHIA. After the treaty of Tarentum, Antony proceeded to Syria to prepare the invasion of Parthia which he began in 36. Avoiding the Mesopotamian desert with its fateful memories of Crassus, he took a more northerly route through Armenia into Media Atropatene, relying upon support of the Armenian king, Artavasdes. The latter proved false, however, and the Parthians destroyed the Roman train of siege engines and their reserve supplies of food. After a vain attempt to reduce the fortress of Praaspa, Antony was obliged to abandon his expedition and retreat. Although vigorously pursued by the Parthian horsemen, he managed by skillful and courageous generalship to lead most of his troops back to Armenia. His losses were heavy, however, and his reputation suffered from his failure. Without reinforcements from the West it was hopeless for him to think of further moves against Parthia. When Octavian returned those of his ships that had survived the naval battles around Sicily without the promised legions, he realized that Octavian planned to cut him off from Italy and that he must reestablish himself in the West or resign himself to an inferior position. All that he could do for the moment was to conclude an alliance with a rebellious Parthian vassal, the king of Media Atropatene, and to occupy Armenia, whose king was imprisoned in punishment for his disloyalty.

ANTONY AND CLEOPATRA. The breach between Antony and Octavian was widened by Antony's connection with Cleopatra. Antony married the Egyptian Queen in Antioch in 37, and after his Parthian defeat he refused Octavia, his legal Roman wife, permission to join him. This was equivalent to renunciation of his friendship with Octavian. Although he was emotionally involved with Cleopatra, his marriage may be attributed more to the financial support she brought him from Egypt for his Parthian war than to any blind infatuation. It is not so clear what tangible benefits Cleopatra expected from the connection. Her immediate aim seems to have been the extension of Ptolemaic influence and the revival of her empire. This was the apparent point of a pageant staged at Alexandria in 34. Antony and Cleopatra, the latter in the guise of the goddess Isis,[2] appeared seated on golden thrones. In an address to the assembled public, Antony proclaimed Cleopatra "Queen of Kings" and ruler of Egypt, Cyprus, Crete, and Coele-Syria. Joint ruler with her as "King of Kings" was her son Ptolemy Caesarion, whom Antony formally recognized as the child of Julius Caesar. The two young sons of Antony and Cleopatra also received royal titles: the elder as King of Armenia, Media, and Parthia; the younger as King of Syria, Phoenicia, and Cilicia. Their daughter Cleopatra, received Cyrene as her portion. Antony claimed no royal title for himself, but Cleopatra prompted him to make territorial arrangements that Octavian could represent as an unpatriotic partition of Rome's eastern provinces made at the behest of a foreign queen.

FINAL BREAK: 32 B.C. During the years 35 to 33 Octavian waged a series of victorious campaigns against Illyrian tribes east of the Adriatic, thus keeping his forces in fighting trim and adding to his reputation for courage if not brilliant leadership. In 33, the news of Antony's acknowledgment of Caesarion as Caesar's son provoked Octavian to protest as he had against Antony's treatment of Octavia. At the same time he gave no satisfactory answer to Antony's request for more troops from Italy and land grants for his veterans. Both principals, actively supported by their followers, indulged in a campaign of mutual vilification. The effect of this propaganda is seen in the confused and contradictory accounts of these years in later historical works. It is extremely difficult, if not impossible, for us to recover an accurate picture of many aspects of the situation. In particular it is impossible to estimate the real worth of Antony, who apparently was both able and worthy of respect, and not the indolent drunkard portrayed in Octavian's propaganda.

---

[2] As early as 38, while in Athens, Antony had taken the title of New Dionysos, anticipating that he, like Dionysos of Greek legend, would be a conqueror of Asia. He did not, however, make regular use of this title, nor did he consider that it deified him in the eyes of Romans.

The Triumvirate terminated legally at the close of 33. For the next year the consuls were Antony's nominees. To win support in Rome, Antony wrote a letter to the Senate in which he asked approval for all actions and arrangements he made in the East and offered to surrender his powers as triumvir and restore the old constitution. The consuls were unwilling to divulge the contents of the letter because they feared the effect on public opinion of the request for approval of Antony's grants of kingdoms to Cleopatra and her children. One of them attacked Octavian, however, and only by a tribune's veto was he prevented from introducing a motion that Octavian should surrender his *imperium* at once. Octavian then overawed the Senate by appearing with an armed bodyguard, with interesting results. Both consuls and perhaps a third of the Senate, including numerous and prominent statesmen of republican and Caesarian background, fled to Antony. Antony was clearly no mere adventurer if he could attract such a following, and just as clearly Octavian, in spite of his efforts, had failed to win over many members of the governing establishment. Antony's reply was to divorce Octavia publicly, which would only be interpreted as a declaration of war on her brother. Octavian then produced what he claimed to be Antony's will. There is no way of telling whether it was authentic or not. In any case, the published parts were intended to inflame public opinion against Antony and Cleopatra, in particular the ones confirming dispositions he had made in favor of the Ptolemaic dynasty. Having prepared the way through clever propaganda, Octavian was ready in 32 to take a momentous step to unite the citizenry behind him in the coming conflict and to broaden by extraconstitutional means his political clientele and to transcend all factions. He requested all Romans in Italy and the western provinces to give him a personal oath of allegiance in order to become the leader of all factions, *dux partium*. This was done in many places without coercion by his agents. It was this oath of allegiance that provided him with a basis of authority, for the powers of the Triumvirate had lapsed. Fortified by this expression of public confidence, Octavian had Antony's *imperium* abrogated and his designation as consul for 31 canceled. Not wishing to appear the instigator of civil strife, Octavian finally proclaimed a *bellum iustum* against Cleoparta.

ACTIUM AND AFTER. In the fall of 33 Antony and Cleopatra began to mobilize their forces at Ephesus. Many prominent Romans in Antony's suite objected to Cleopatra, realizing that her presence was adding grist to Octavian's propaganda mill, but she stayed. It was her money that was financing the war. The next year an army of some 90,000 men and a fleet of 500 warships were assembled and led across the Aegean to Greece. Since a landing in Italy could not yet be effected, Antony's forces wintered in the Gulf of Ambracia (32–31). In the spring of 31 Octavian and his general Agrippa crossed the Adriatic with an approximately equal force and confronted their enemies outside the Ambracian Gulf at Actium. Agrippa successfully blockaded Antony's fleet, while Octavian's army cut off Antony's supplies by occupying strategic points on the mainland. Antony's position rapidly worsened. Cleopatra's presence depressed morale, and desertions to Octavian increased. What happened next is uncertain. Antony decided either to fight at Actium or to break the blockade. A naval battle followed, a minor engagement magnified later by Augustan propaganda. For unknown reasons Cleopatra fled with her treasure ship, and Antony followed her to Egypt. Resistance on land and sea against Octavian promptly collapsed.

The victor advanced slowly eastward and in the summer of 30 invaded Egypt. Antony's attempts at defense were unavailing; his troops deserted to Octavian, who occupied Alexandria. Hearing a rumor that Cleopatra had taken her life, Antony committed suicide. Cleopatra was taken prisoner. Finding that her conqueror was inexorable and that it was impossible for her to save her kingdom for herself or for her children, she followed Antony's example rather than grace Octavian's triumph in Rome. This was probably what the latter had hoped for. He had magnified her part in the struggle in order to solidify Italian opinion behind him, but he had no wish to be held responsible for her execution. Ptolemy Caesarion, however, and Antony's elder son were executed because their lineage made them potential rivals of the victor. Egypt became a province. Its treasures reimbursed Octavian for the expenses of his late campaigns and enabled him to distribute promised bonuses to his veterans. After reestablishing the old provinces and client kingdoms in the East, but on territorial principles already established by Antony, Octavian returned to Rome in 29 and celebrated a three-day triumph over the non-Romans of Europe, Asia, and Africa, whom he or his generals had subjugated during his Triumvirate.

At the age of thirty-three Octavian had made good his claim to the political inheritance of Julius Caesar. His victory over Antony closed the century of civil strife that had begun with the tribunate of Tiberius Gracchus. War and proscriptions had exacted a heavy toll from Romans and Italians; Greece, Macedonia, and Asia had been brought to the verge of ruin; the whole Empire longed for peace. Everywhere Octavian was hailed as savior of the world. Thinking him the founder of a new golden age, men were ready to worship him as a god.

IV. SOCIETY AND INTELLECTUAL LIFE IN THE LAST CENTURY OF THE REPUBLIC

UPPER CLASSES. Perhaps the most striking socioeconomic changes during the period took place within the governing establishment, whose recruitment broadened considerably as a result of military and political exigencies that placed premiums on talent rather than noble birth. Reaching a high degree of professionalism were the military tribunes, lower military officers, and their staffs. Following their enfranchisement in the Allied War, increasing numbers of the Italian bourgeoisie having equestrian status held such posts in place of senatorial cadets. By the end of the Roman Revolution generals like Caesar made ex-centurions tribunes, which automatically gave them equestrian rank. A corresponding mobility was evident at even higher social levels as the equestrian order was politicized beginning with Gaius Gracchus. Equestrians in greater numbers competed for senatorial office and established themselves as patrons by infringing on such senatorial prerogatives as the right to be jurisprudents. The enlargements of the Senate by Sulla and Caesar also meant the promotion of many equestrians to senatorial status and signified an unprecedented infusion of new blood into the ruling oligarchy.

By the Late Republic upper-class women attained a high degree of emancipation, a characteristic that persisted for the remainder of Roman history. Marriage with *manus* by then was obsolete, which fact contributed to the frequency of divorce and the marked instability of marriage as an institution. Traditionally, divorce was easily effected simply by a declaration of either husband or wife. Normally, husbands had begun divorce actions for personal, but especially political reasons; by the Late Republic, however, some very independent women initiated divorces on their own. Perhaps the most striking and attractive feature of their emancipation was their high degree of education, which could be and was regarded as enhancing their reputation and desirability. They were frequently well read and sometimes authors themselves; they might also be adept at philosophy, oratory, mathematics, music, and the dance. Although the Romans perceived no necessary relation between the education of women and their personal liberation, the two characteristics sometimes combined to produce a new phenomenon: the literary salon presided over by women, a very important development in intellectual history. Lesbia, Catullus' courtesan,[3] held the first known salon, and the tradition was taken up by more serious and less profligate matrons patronizing poets and artists in a tradition that stretched on for several hundred years of the Roman Empire.

Roman women, of course, were always disfranchised, but especially during the Late Republic they might influence politics from behind the scenes, in one notable case overtly. In 42 B.C. a mob of noblewomen, relatives of the proscribed, publicly demonstrated in the Forum, protesting to the triumvirs the heavy taxes and penalties imposed on their own estates to support the government. They were led by Hortensia, daughter of the orator, who in a ringing speech, worthy of a modern suffragette, condemned what amounted to taxation without representation and the use of their money to promote a civil war. The demonstration was effective to the extent that the chagrined, and presumably startled, triumvirs promptly decreased by more than two thirds the number of women subject to the war tax.

Perhaps the truest test of emancipation is the fact that Late Republican noblewomen, and after them those of the Empire, had many more choices

---

[3] See p. 245.

than ever before about what to do with their lives. Many female roles were tolerated by upper-class society, and for every Lesbia there were, after all, many matrons who took pride in being discrete, virtuous *univirae* in the old tradition.

Luxury and extravagance characterized upper-class life during the period. The palaces of the wealthy in Rome were supplemented by villas in the Sabine hills, at resorts on the Campanian coast, and at other attractive points. The word *villa*, originally designating a farmhouse, now meant a country seat equipped with all the conveniences of city life. Much Italian commerce consisted in the importation of articles of luxury to adorn the town and country houses of the well-to-do. These articles included statuary, paintings, silverware, tapestries, furniture of rare woods, antiques from Greece, marble columns, and goods dyed with costly Tyrian purple, actually a shade of red.

LOWER CLASSES IN ROME.   Little is known about the life of the people thronging the rickety tenement houses and narrow, filthy streets of the capital, whose population probably numbered over 500,000 by the end of the Republic. Most people lived at or near subsistence level, the mere cost of food and lodging consuming perhaps four fifths of their income. They were typically unemployed or underemployed artisans or retailers, as Rome had never developed sufficient commerce and industry to give them a decent livelihood. The distribution of cheap grain, a fixture of life since the time of Gaius Gracchus except when temporarily suspended by Sulla, had become an outright dole by Caesar's day. He reduced the number of recipients but could not abolish totally this welfare program. Despite sometimes lavish public entertainments, living conditions were squalid, the ordinary citizen having scarcely more than a bed and chair in some badly heated and ventilated room where he very often lived, slept, and worked, a prey to fires and floods that periodically swept the city. Despite aqueducts, the water supply was inadequate and in any case was not piped into apartment houses. Under these conditions the poor were often unmarried or childless with the result that the lower-class population tended to change qualitatively, slaves, freedmen, and their descendants replacing Roman or Italian stock until they came to represent perhaps two thirds or three quarters of the population. Another element increasing the size of the city was the throngs of free aliens who had emigrated there to practice their trades.

Although the situation as described affected both sexes, the condition of lower-class women in some respects was rather special. The evidence about them is very scanty and almost exclusively urban. If they were slaves, they were typically employed in the household as weavers, spinners, nurses, general domestics, or ladies' maids. They were, of course, sexually available to their masters, sometimes also to male slaves of the household, or they might be employed as waitress–prostitutes at bars, brothels, and baths. They might informally marry slaves within their *familia*, and such relationships could be stable and enduring. If they were freed, they blended totally into the working class, and were normally employed in the same occupations they had followed as slaves. Rarely did they attain much wealth. In some respects slaves and freedwomen were more secure than city women born free; the latter, often unskilled, lacked the protection of patrons and frequently were reduced to practicing prostitution under archways on the streets. The tombstones of mostly lower-class women reveal a startling fact: their longevity was significantly less than that of men. This is perhaps accounted for by their exclusion from the dole at Rome and by the orientation of public relief programs throughout Italy toward men. It also appears that men clearly dominated the demographic sex ratio, a situation obtaining in the upper classes as well.

THE POOR THROUGHOUT ITALY. Because of the upheavals of civil war, proscriptions, and confiscations, depression was widespread in rural Italy during the last century of the Republic. Conscription for and mortality in never-ending foreign and civil wars continued to destroy the yeomanry; the wars also inhibited growth of the citizenry, which, numbering some five million at the end of the period, was probably no larger than it had been two centuries before. The Senate showed poor sense in failing to improve the wretched state of the free peasantry, because armies recruited from that class therefore felt no attachment to republican government.

It is sometimes alleged that Gracchan land reforms and successive redistributions of land in favor of the veterans of revolutionary armies redressed partially the previous buildup of *latifundia*. The Gracchan settlement proved abortive, however, as economic conditions were still working against the small farmer. Veterans' resettlement probably replaced other proprietors of middling substance, and *latifundia* were actually formed in some cases to reward leaders of dominant factions during periods of proscription. Free labor existed on Italian farms and ranches certainly, since the legislation of Julius Caesar required that one third of ranch labor be free. Some free labor was contracted for use at harvest time as a supplement to servile hands. The use of free labor as *coloni* or tenant farmers was probably more widespread than it appears in surviving sources. These tenants lived on small leaseholds into which great estates were divided. For obvious reasons they became clients of their landlords.

ROME THE CITY. The age of civil wars saw many changes and developments in the appearance of Rome. Two new aqueducts, the Tepula in 125 and the Julia in 33, served the growing population. New and superior building materials were used extensively. In place of volcanic tufa, creamy white limestone called travertine was employed from the second century in the construction of public buildings. The Romans had been developing the use of concrete since the third century; now they applied its use to ever more grandiose interpretations of Hellenistic styles. The exterior surfaces of concrete structures were regularly faced with stone, at first with small irregular fragments (*opus incertum*) and later with carefully cut square or lozenge-shaped pieces arranged to form a network pattern (*opus reticulatum*). Toward the close of the period it

VIII Four Portrait Busts. *These busts, of (top) Scipio Africanus the Elder and Pompey the Great and (bottom) Cato the Younger and Agrippina the Younger, illustrate the typical Roman interest in realistic portrayal of public personalities. (Photos: Scipio, Anderson; Pompey, Frank Brown Collection; Agrippina, German Archeological Institute, Rome.)*

was fashionable to veneer the faces of buildings with slabs of travertine or marble. Sulla, Pompey, and Julius Caesar were among those who improved the appearance of Rome by erecting new and imposing public edifices. Caesar also planned to rebuild the city extensively but did not live to carry out his projects. Sulla commenced the reconstruction of the Capitolium, temple of Jupiter Capitolinus, which was burned in 83, and Pompey erected on the Campus Martius Rome's first permanent theater (55). Another important building was the Tabularium or Public Record Office completed on the west side of the Forum by Quintus Catulus, the consul of 78. (See figure VI.) Its ruins are the most striking example of republican architecture found in Rome today. Rome suffered from great fires, of which seven are recorded for this period. Despite the addition of many fine buildings it was still rather drab and unimpressive compared to the larger cities of the Greek East.

ART. The interest of Romans in works of art, evidenced as early as the third and second centuries B.C., increased in the first. Greek influence continued paramount, as the Romans demanded copies of their masterpieces of painting and sculpture. The artists who executed such works were almost all Greek, and the mechanical copying of sculpture was facilitated by the use of pointing machines. Greek influence was no less noticeable in the minor arts like pottery, glassware, and jewelry. The period also saw an increase in the plastic decoration of tombs and especially in the continued production of realistic portrait sculpture. (See figure VIII.)

RELIGION. This period witnessed a striking decline of faith in public or official cults. This was in part due to Greek mythology, which changed the current conceptions of Roman divinities, and to Greek philosophy, with its varying doctrines on the nature and powers of the gods. The latter especially affected the upper classes, whose duty it was to maintain public cults. Throughout the period many priesthoods declined in importance; those that kept prestige did so only because they could be used for political purposes. An increase in the numbers of priestly colleges and the substitution of election for cooptation brought in many members unversed in ancient traditions, and priests in general were very ignorant of their duties, especially with regard to the state calendar. Some religious associations, like the Arval Brotherhood, ceased to exist, and knowledge of some minor deities was completely lost. Patrician priesthoods, involving serious duties and restricting the freedom of their incumbents, were avoided as much as possible. At the same time private religious rites, hereditary within family groups, decayed. While the attitude of educated circles toward the state cults was thus indifferent or skeptical, it is hard to tell about that of the common people. They probably cared little about the religious content of the state cults. It is to this period that may be attributed the first gravestone inscriptions indicating Roman belief in an afterlife. Orgiastic and emotional religions from the East appealed to all classes and took root in spite of general hostility to them by the authorities.

EDUCATION. Education from the time of the Gracchi to the age of Cicero and Caesar continued to be dominated by Greek influences, and the period marked the height of bilingualism at Rome. After receiving primary instruction at the hands of an elementary teacher (*ludi magister*), the pupil went to the school of a *grammaticus*. Here he followed a standard curriculum, which included literature, dialectic, arithmetic, geometry, astronomy, and music. These subjects were the liberal arts (*artes liberales*). Greek literature was the main curriculum and the mathematical and scientific subject matter was also Greek. Romans failed to develop the same interest in mathematics and music that was characteristic of the Greeks, being content to study the former as far as practical and preferring to leave the latter subject to professionals. Higher education was received in special schools of oratory and philosophy or was gained by private study with distinguished men. The teaching of philosophy and oratory was conducted mainly by Greek professors, and in oratory Greek was the regular language of instruction. A reaction against these Greek rhetorical schools caused the establishment of a rival Latin school by Plotius Gallus, who followed Roman models and trained his pupils in Latin. His school was suppressed for political reasons by the censors of 92, but it seems to have been later revived. In addition to pursuing these advanced studies at Rome, it was the fashion for well-to-do young Romans to complete their education in the schools of Greece itself. Cicero, whose career illustrates very well the contemporary system of higher education, was such a student. After finishing his preliminary studies, he remained in Rome, where he regularly attended the speeches of well-known orators; was introduced into law by Q. Mucius Scaevola, a leading jurisconsult; studied Greek literature and poetry, Roman history, Greek philosophy, and rhetoric with representatives of the Stoic school and the Academy; and practiced declamation, largely in Greek. Later he visited Greece, spending six months at Athens, where he studied philosophy and rhetoric. From Athens he went to Asia Minor, where he visited several cities and ended his foreign study at Rhodes. Later he was proud to acknowledge the debt owed to the teachers and schools of Greece. Cicero expressed the finest conception of education known from ancient Rome. He emphasized the need of higher cultural studies, selecting history, jurisprudence, and philosophy as those which, supplementing literature and rhetoric, comprise the fields of learning necessary for the attainment of the cultural ideal—*humanitas*.

LITERATURE. The last century of the Republic saw the completion of the fusion of Greek and Roman culture, which it was the mission of the Empire to spread among the barbarians of the West. In the midst of a collapsing political system, the upper classes enjoyed the beginning of a golden age of literature that developed new genres of poetry and the fullest expression of Latin prose. Like Hellenistic audiences, educated Romans increasingly savored a more intimate kind of poetry; to public performances in theaters, they preferred works they could hear read or read themselves in their salons.

DRAMA. In the area of drama, however, creativity ended. The last successful Roman tragedian, Accius, wrote in the period between the Gracchi and Sulla, but his work has disappeared. Comedies in Roman dress and with Italian settings, *fabulae togatae*, were in vogue for a time, and older dramatic works were revived. Of greater popularity in the long run, however, were farces and mimes. The former were derived from Oscan prototypes. With few exceptions they had no claim to being literature, since they scarcely ever rose above the level of ribaldry, as highly improvised as it was crude. The mimes, which ultimately derived from Greek prototypes well known in South Italy, were especially notorious for their vulgar language and plots. Theatrical exhibitions were produced on an increasingly lavish scale and were often given in conjunction with public games.

POETRY. The really creative movements in Roman poetry were limited to artists following the lead of Lucilius,[4] writing for an elite audience, and expressing personal emotions rather than epic themes. The best such work was done by a circle native to Cisalpine Gaul, calling themselves "modernists" (*neoteroi*) and taking their inspiration from the love poems and epigrams of Greek writers, especially Theocritus of Alexandria and Meleager of Gadara. Most of the modernists have survived as little more than names, except for the poetry of Catullus (ca. 84–54), a member of the Veronese gentry and probably the best of the school. He was known for his lampoons against Caesar, which were forgiven, but his serious poetry concerns his own life and describes in outspoken terms his tortured love affair with "Lesbia," probably Clodia, sister of Cicero's enemy, the tribune Clodius. Despite his use of Greek poetic form, structure, and meter, he was no slavish imitator but rather an outstanding innovator in love poetry—for example, his use of the first person. He invented a complicated elegaic style, used themes dramatically, and produced a poetic world that blended real and invented, novel and traditional, Greek and Roman elements.

Standing apart from the modernist movement and a different kind of poetic genius was T. Lucretius Carus (ca. 99–55), an obscure personality who was either a client or member of the aristocratic clan of Lucretii. Unlike the modernists, he believed, as did old-fashioned poets such as Ennius, that poetry's function was primarily didactic rather than entertaining, that the poet was essentially a teacher. In a strangely moving epic, *On the Nature of the Universe* (*De rerum natura*), he expounded the Epicurean doctrine that the world was mechanistic, originating and functioning without divine intervention, and that true happiness existed in withdrawal from public life, a view congenial to many propertied Italians during the First Triumvirate. His view of the world is shot through with original, imaginative vision sustained, however, by a sense of logic, which was very foreign to the modernists, who made a virtue of unexpected ideas.

---

[4] See p. 157f.

A doctrine so closely related to the science of physics might scarcely seem a subject for esthetic development in the grand manner, but Lucretius was able to transform it into an always eloquent and often majestic poem designed to liberate man from unhappiness and superstition. Reception of his work varied. In general the senatorial intelligentsia tried to ignore it, since Epicureanism was widely regarded as subversive, undermining as it did the state religion on which their political control depended in part. Some poets, however, like Vergil and Horace were deeply influenced by it.

ORATORY. It was through the study and practice of oratory, one of the most typically Roman interests, that Latin prose attained its perfection between the time of the Gracchi and Julius Caesar. Political and legal orations were weapons of party strife and were frequently polished and edited as political pamphlets. Along with such political documents appeared orations that were not written to be delivered in the Forum or Senate but were addressed solely to a reading public. Two oratorical styles competed for primacy: the Asian, showy and ornamental, and the Attic, simpler and more direct. Among the great forensic orators of the age were the two Gracchi, of whom the younger, Gaius, was reputed to be the most effective speaker that Rome ever knew. Others of note were Marcus Antonius, grandfather of the Triumvir, Lucius Licinius Crassus, and Quintus Hortensius Hortalus. But it was Cicero who brought to its perfection the Roman oration in its literary form.

Cicero (106-43) epitomized the intellectual and literary interests of the senatorial intelligentsia of the Late Republic. He was above all things an orator. Until past the age of fifty his literary productivity was almost entirely in this field, and he made significant contributions to the theoretical study of the forensic art. Steering a middle course between the Asian and Attic styles, he produced a style peculiarly his own—sonorous, rhythmical, and shot through when needed with brilliant irony and invective. In his hands Latin prose attained its highest development as a vehicle for the expression of human thought. In his later years, when the opportunity for free forensic oratory was being limited by political developments, he turned increasingly to Greek philosophy and undertook the great task of making it accessible to the Roman world. Acquainted with the leading philosophies of classical Greek and Hellenistic civilizations, he was an eclectic, a popularizer and transmitter rather than an original thinker. All of Western civilization is deeply indebted to him, however, since he embodied Rome's cultural mission in the world: the transmission of the values of classical antiquity. In a series of brilliant essays he expressed his views on political theory and ethics. Platonic inspiration is evident in his De Republica, in which he set forth the actual constitution of an ideal state. The Stoic substratum to much of his ethical thinking, stressing as it did an active life in improving mankind, is revealed in works like De Officiis and De Senectute. In addition to speeches and oratorical and philosophical treaties, Cicero left a great collection of letters, which were collected and published by his freedman secretary, Tiro. His correspondence with his friends is a mine of information for the student of society and politics in the last century of the Republic, especially because it is so candid. Cicero has been criticized occasionally for his vanity, his opportunism, and his attachment to a form of government that was not worth saving. In his defense it may be said that in many ways he was a child of his age. At crucial moments he was courageous in upholding his political beliefs, no matter how unrealistic. In any case, his possibly real personal weaknesses cannot obscure the fact that he holds a preeminent place among men of letters in Western civilization.

HISTORICAL WRITING. History, along with oratory, continued to command the attention of Rome's educated elite. Indeed, political events following the Gracchi further stimulated interest in the subject, and a flood of historical literature resulted. Two developments are noteworthy in this connection: the continued influence on Roman letters of universal history in the tradition of Polybius, whose exponents were almost all Greek, and, more importantly, the emergence of annalistic history.

The annalistic approach to history, characteristically Roman, was stimulated about 123 by publication by the *pontifex maximus* of the *Annales Maximi*, lists of magistrates and important events that had been kept for several centuries. The works of annalists of the latter second and early first centuries have not survived, but two of them writing during the Sullan period—Q. Claudius Quadrigarius and Valerius Antias—deserve mention because they were later used by Livy. The reliability of the Sullan historians was not great, since they consciously embroidered their narrative for rhetorical effect and since family and political considerations often compelled them to convert history into heroic legend.

More significant was Gaius Sallustius Crispus (86–ca. 34), whom subsequent generations ranked as the foremost Roman historian. Sallust served with Caesar in the Civil War, governed Africa, was indicted for extortion but escaped conviction, and occupied the remainder of his life with writing. His reputation rested primarily upon his *Histories*, a detailed treatment of the period 78–67, which unfortunately is almost entirely lost. His shorter works, the *War with Jugurtha* and the *War with Catiline*, have been preserved. Although not incapable of portraying fairly his political enemies and the faults of his own party, he did not attain a high level of objectivity. He owed his reputation more to his stylistic ability than to the historical significance of his writings. His spare, epigrammatic style, modeled on Thucydides, served as an inspiration to Tacitus.

The biographer Cornelius Nepos also may be classed among the historians. Only parts of one of his works survive, a collection of biographies of eminent Romans and foreigners. The lives are both uncritical and lacking in redeeming literary qualities.

Outranking Sallust for the immediacy of their themes were the works of Julius Caesar, as fascinating a man of letters as one of action. Caesar, writing

Commentaries on the Gallic and Civil Wars, contributed to a prose genre the Romans ranked only just behind history in importance. His works were intended to make it impossible to deny, underrate, or fail to reward his *dignitas*. The fact that they are propaganda is not their most striking feature, that is, the consciousness of the author's own preeminence, heightened by the air of detachment and understatement implicit in his use of the third person. The style is utterly Caesarian: spare, to the point, unornamented by rhetorical devices, yet elegant.

Of great interest to later ages were the works of the antiquarian and philologist, Marcus Terentius Varro, (116–27), the most learned Roman of his time. His great work on Roman religious and political antiquities is lost, but a part of his study *On the Latin Language* is still extant, as well as his three books *On Rural Conditions*. The latter give a good picture of farming on the plantations of the larger landholders during the period 67 to 54.

JURISPRUDENCE. Law continued its development both in substance and in theory. Contacts with foreign legal systems and philosophies proved a fruitful stimulus. In Italy the praetor for aliens (*praetor peregrinus*), and in the provinces Roman governors, administered law to foreigners. They had to face the problem of providing a law that would give substantial justice to litigants. Since the Civil Law applied only to Roman citizens, it could not serve their purpose. They solved the problem by publishing in their edicts legal rules that could be enforced between Romans and aliens, as well as between aliens of different citizenships, when these sued in courts presided over by Roman magistrates. Thus a body of law applicable to free persons, irrespective of citizenship, was formed. This law possessed advantages in its liberality, i.e., freedom from technicalities, and in its fairness (*aequitas*); thus much of it was taken over in the Civil Law by the adoption of its rules in the edict of the urban praetor, particularly after the extension of Roman citizenship to all of Italy. From the Roman point of view this new element in the law was called the *ius gentium*, or Law of Nations, which was defined as "that part of the law which we apply both to ourselves and to foreigners." Through this channel the Civil Law accepted principles and usages developed by Greeks and other foreigners, but only when they had become thoroughly assimilated and Romanized. From Greek philosophy, Roman juristic writers derived another concept of the Law of Nations as a law "common to all mankind." From the same source they also received the idea of a Law of Nature (*ius naturae* or *naturale*)—that is, a universal divine law emanating from right reason, the power that governs the universe. This Law of Nature was looked upon as the source of the Law of Nations or as being identical with it. These philosophic concepts did not contribute anything to the substance of Civil Law, but they provided Roman jurists with a philosophic justification of law and encouraged them to attempt to systematize Roman law according to fundamental legal principles.

The most influential legal writers were Quintus Mucius Scaevola, who compiled a systematic treatment of the Civil Law in eighteen books, Servius

Sulpicius Rufus, a contemporary of Cicero, and his pupil Aulus Ofilius, a friend of Caesar. Sulpicius was a productive author, whose works included *Commentaries* on the Twelve Tables and on the Praetor's Edict, as well as studies on special aspects of law. Ofilius was also a voluminous writer, notable as the first to arrange the Praetor's Edict systematically. During the last century of the Republic interpretation of the law was no longer the prerogative of a few oligarchs who had held priesthoods. The circle of *jurisprudentes* broadened considerably to include lower classes, and equestrians and even freedmen set themselves up as legal authorities. Since these latter often had only a superficial acquaintance with Roman legal tradition, and since the state exercised no control over them, their interpretations of law tended to confuse rather than to enlighten. The plans of Pompey and Caesar to codify the law were in part prompted by the desire to end this confusion.

PART
III
PRINCIPATE OR EARLY EMPIRE: 27 B.C.–A.D. 285

CHAPTER 16
ESTABLISHMENT OF
THE PRINCIPATE:[1]
27 B.C.–A.D. 14

Only a small part of the extensive Roman and Greek literature dealing with the history of the Empire from 27 B.C. to A.D. 235 has survived. Until A.D. 96, the basic works are Cassius Dio's *History*, of which the extant portion runs to A.D. 46; the *Annals* of Tacitus, which, with some gaps, covers the years A.D. 14 to 66; and the remains of his *Histories*, which deal with events of the years A.D. 69 and 70. These are supplemented chiefly by Suetonius' *Lives* of the emperors from Augustus to Domitian, the appropriate portion of Velleius Paterculus, whose history stopped with A.D. 30, and several brief historical surveys and biographical collections compiled in the fourth and fifth centuries A.D. Much historical information is also contained in the *Geography* of the Greek Strabo, written in A.D. 17–18. The inadequacies of the literary record are partially made good by thousands of Latin and Greek inscriptions from Italy and the provinces, and of papyri from Egypt, which illustrate in detail administrative, economic, and social life. An inscription that is also a notable historical document is the record of his career composed by the emperor Augustus and set up after his death in Rome and in the provinces under the title of the *Deeds of Augustus* (*Res Gestae Divi Augusti*).

---

[1] The spelling Principate (with a capital *P*) is used to distinguish the form of government prevailing between 27 B.C. and A.D. 284 from the principate as the office of the *princeps*.

I. THE PRINCEPS

SETTLEMENT OF 27 B.C. Octavian, the young revolutionary, pitiless proscriber, and clever propagandist had developed into a statesman of the highest order during the fifteen years following Caesar's death. During his sixth and seventh consulships, in the years 28 and 27, Octavian surrendered the extraordinary powers he had exercised during the war against Antony and Cleopatra and, as he later expressed it, he placed the commonwealth at the disposal of the Senate and the Roman people. This step did not imply that the old machinery of government was restored without modifications and restrictions or that Octavian intended to abdicate his position as arbiter of the Roman world. He would hardly have been justified in so doing, for such action would probably have led to a repetition of the anarchy that followed the retirement and death of Sulla. In disposing of his rivals, Octavian had assumed the obligation of stabilizing Roman imperial government. He might truly claim to have been called by consent of the Roman world to reorganize it, and public sentiment was prepared to allow him great latitude in this task. It demanded strong administration, even if this could be attained only at the expense of republican institutions.

While ambition and duty alike forbade him to relinquish his hold on the state, Octavian shrank from realizing the ideal of Julius Caesar and establishing an explicit autocracy. From this he was deterred by the fate of his adoptive father and by his own devious conservatism, which gave him such shrewd understanding of Roman temperament. His solution of the problem was to retain the constitution as far as was practicable, while securing powers to enable him to uphold and prevent a renewal of civil war. What powers and honors were necessary to this end, Octavian determined on the basis of practical experience and much experimentation between 27 and 2 B.C. His restoration of the commonwealth thus signified the end of a regime of force and paved the way for new authority legally conferred upon him.

THE IMPERIUM. Nothing contributed more directly to the failure of the Republic than the growth of the client army and the inability of the Senate to control its commanders. It was therefore absolutely necessary for the guardian of peace and the constitution to command supreme military authority. On January 13, 27 B.C.—the birthday of the new order—Octavian, by vote of Assembly and Senate, received for ten years the command and administration of the provinces of Spain, Gaul, and Syria, the chief provinces where peace was not yet firmly established and which consequently required the presence of most of the Roman armies. Egypt, which he had annexed to the Empire in 30 B.C., was also subject to his *imperium*. It is uncertain, however, whether the *imperium* granted him over those provinces in 27 was proconsular or whether it was part of his *provincia* as consul. Provinces controlled by the Senate did not come under his *imperium*, although he could guide their administration by virtue of his *auctoritas*. His solution of the military problem was an extraordinary command that found its precedents in those of Lucullus, Pompey, and Caesar but was of such scope and duration that it made him, in effect, commander in chief of the imperial army.

TITLES AUGUSTUS AND IMPERATOR. On January 16, 27 B.C. the Senate conferred upon Octavian the title of Augustus (Greek, *Sebastos*), "Reverend," by which he was henceforth known. It was a term implying no definite powers but, being an epithet equally applicable to gods or men, was well adapted to express his exalted position. It signified a person or force bringing prosperity to the state and was derived from *augere*, the Latin for "increase." A second title was that of Imperator. Following republican custom, this had been conferred upon Augustus by his army and the Senate after his victory at Mutina in 43, and in imitation of Julius Caesar he converted this temporary title of honor into a permanent one. Finally in 38, he placed it first among his personal names (as a *praenomen*). After 27 Augustus made twofold use of the term: as a permanent *praenomen*, and as a title of honor assumed upon victories won by his officers. From this time the *praenomen* Imperator was a prerogative of the Roman commander in chief. In the Greek-speaking provinces, where his power rested exclusively upon his military authority, the title Imperator was understood as the expression of his unlimited *imperium* and was translated in that sense by *autocrator*. From the *praenomen* Imperator is derived the term emperor, commonly used today to designate Augustus and his successors.

TRIBUNICIAN AUTHORITY: 23 B.C. From 27 to 23 the authority of Augustus rested upon his annual tenure of the consulship and his provincial command. In the latter year Augustus faced crises in his regime which included an important conspiracy, an almost fatal illness, and quite possibly, a temporary split in his own faction regarding the *de facto* designation of his own nephew as his successor, and he was forced to modify the powers of the Principate. He resigned the consulship, since its perpetual tenure violated republican precedent and since by holding it, he reduced the opportunity of senators to obtain nobility. In its stead he received for life, in the summer of 23, the tribunician authority (*tribunicia potestas*) from the Senate and people. As early as 36 he had been granted the personal inviolability of tribunes, and in 30 their right of giving aid (*auxilium*). To these privileges must now be added the right of intercession and of summoning the Plebeian Council (*jus agendi cum populo*). In this way Augustus incidentally acquired control over comitial and senatorial legislation and openly assumed the position of protector of the city plebs whom he cultivated as never before. He thus placed himself squarely in the tradition of popular leaders going back to the Gracchi and advertised his status as patron of the plebs. His tenure of the tribunate was intended as a constant reminder to the Senate that, if the senators subverted his regime, he would turn for support to the common people in the revolutionary tradition of the Late Republic. He was thus amply compensated for the loss of civil power, which his resignation of the consulship involved, and he also got rid of an office

which must be shared with a colleague of equal rank and the perpetual tenure of which was a violation of tradition. The tribunician authority was regarded as being held for annual periods, which Augustus reckoned from 23.

SUPPLEMENTARY POWERS AND HONORS.   His abdication of the consulship caused readjustment in his control of "imperial" provinces and their garrisons. Following the precedent perhaps established for Pompey the Great by the Gabinian Law of 67 B.C., the Senate definitely established his authority there as that of a proconsul, defining his proconsular *imperium* as "greater" (*maius*) than that of other proconsuls. He was voted the command initially for a five-year period; when it was about to lapse in 18 B.C., he had it renewed for five years and subsequently for another term of five and then three of ten years, thus preserving the continuity of his proconsular command until his death. Holding, apparently since 27 B.C., the unrestricted right of making war and peace, he was granted the right to call meetings of the Senate in 22 B.C., and he accepted censorial powers in 29, 19, and 12 B.C. on the occasion of forthcoming *lectiones senatus*.

The settlement of 23 B.C. had one basic flaw, since it left Augustus without *imperium* in Rome and Italy, where for that reason he could not formally command troops or exercise criminal jurisdiction. Partly because he had no *locus standi* there, partly to permit the new system to function without his presence, he spent the next four years abroad. The plebs were restive during his absence, because it seemed that he had abandoned them to the republican aristocrats holding normal magistracies whom they mistrusted. They unsuccessfully urged on him a dictatorship and in 19 B.C. even rioted as normal elections were being held, triggering fears in the Senate of impending social revolution. When Augustus returned, the Senate was quick to acquiesce in his being voted additional power in the capital and Italy. This was apparently a consular *imperium* without, however, his formal tenure of that office. He was accorded also the consular insignia, with twelve lictors, and the privilege of taking his seat on a curule chair between the consuls in office. His constitutional position was essentially complete in 19 B.C. with his tribunician power, consular and proconsular *imperium*. In 12 B.C. he added one more office, more decorative than useful, that of *pontifex maximus* or head of the state cult, held by the old triumvir, Lepidus, until his death in that year.

THE PRINCIPATE.   It was by the gradual acquisition of all these powers that the position of Augustus finally evolved. This may be defined as that of a magistrate whose province was a combination of various powers conferred on

IX Augustus (Syracuse Museum). Unlike most Roman portrait busts, this one of the first emperor is surely very idealized. It suggests that Augustus used the arts to project a favorable public "image" for himself and his regime. (Photo: German Archeological Institute, Rome.)

him by the Senate and people, who differed from other magistrates in the immensely wider scope of his functions and the greater length of his term. These powers were separately conferred upon him and for each he could urge constitutional precedents. His dominant position, if it rested in the last analysis on control of armed force and support of the governing establishment, was derived no less from that general *auctoritas* always wielded by senior statesmen. It cannot be said that his word was law, but it would have been inconceivable and un-Roman to question the judgment of a man whose prestige obviously outclassed that of any senator. He had no definite official title, but in receiving such wide powers he came to surpass all other Romans in authority, in the influence he was able to exercise on account of his political position, and so he came, at first informally, to be designated as *princeps*, i.e., the first of the Roman citizens (*princeps civium Romanorum*). This was good republican usage because leading statesmen, especially ex-consuls, normally were called *principes*, "princes of the state," enjoyed considerable *auctoritas*, and were habitually consulted for their advice by statesmen in office. Beginning with Augustus there was a difference, however. If previously there had been many *principes*, i.e., many senior statesmen heading factions and possessed of approximately equal prestige, henceforward there was room for only one. The *princeps* in this latter sense was the ultimate source of all patronage, and other statesmen could only bask in his reflected glory. From the word *princeps* arose the term "principate" to designate the tenure of office of *princeps*, a term which we now apply also to the system of government that Augustus established for the Empire. The culmination in the evolution of his principate and the crowning honor of his career was received by Augustus in 2 B.C., when the Senate, on the motion of one who had fought under Brutus at Philippi, conferred on him the title of "Father of His Country" (*pater patriae*), thus marking the reconciliation between the bulk of the old aristocracy and the new regime.

II. SENATE, EQUESTRIANS, AND LOWER CLASSES

THREE ORDERS.   The social classification of the Romans into the senatorial, equestrian, and lower classes was untouched, if more sharply defined by Augustus. For each class a distinct field of opportunity and public service was provided, conforming to previous traditions: for senators, the magistracies and the chief military posts; for the *equites*, a new career in the civil and military service of the *princeps*; and for the lower classes, service as privates and subaltern officers in the professional army. These orders were by no means closed castes, however, and successful men could advance from the lower to the higher grades and infuse fresh vitality into the ranks of the latter.

THE SENATE AND THE SENATORIAL ORDER.   The senatorial order was composed of members of the Senate and their families. Its distinctive emblem was the broad purple stripe on the toga. Sons of senators assumed this badge by right of birth; equestrians, by grant of the *princeps*. Of the former, however, those who failed to qualify for the Senate were reduced to the rank of equestrians. The possession of property valued at 1,000,000 sesterces was made a requirement for admission to the Senate.

The prospective senator, after completing a term of military service as tribune in a Roman legion or a prefect of a detachment of auxiliary cavalry, was obliged to fill one of the minor city magistracies known as the board of twenty (viginti-virate), and then, at the age of twenty-five, to become a candidate for the quaestorship, which admitted one to the Senate. From the quaestorship the senatorial career led through the regular magistracies, the aedileship or tribunate and the praetorship, to the consulship. As an ex-praetor and ex-consul, a senator might become a curator (superintendent) in charge of some administrative commission in Rome or Italy, or, as under the Republic, leave Rome to govern a province as a promagistrate or command a legion. Others especially close to the emperor would be appointed by him to govern a province covered by his pronconsular imperium, because Augustus normally resided in Italy and, like Pompey, used legati of senatorial rank. The post of imperial legate was more desirable to ambitious senators than the governorship of a public province as it provided an opportunity to command troops and to win status in the imperial system.

The Senate was still very important, and Augustus was sincerely interested in maintaining its prestige. Having defined senatorial status in terms of wealth, he helped with his own funds noble but impoverished families to qualify financially. More delicate was the matter of purging the Senate of undesirables, since it had grown to unmanageable size, over 1,000 men strong, following the lavish promotion of his associates during the Second Triumvirate. Not all of these men had proved either morally decorative or politically reliable. In 28 B.C. Augustus supervised a revision of the senatorial list, and 200 unworthy persons were excluded. On that occasion his name was placed at the head of the new roll as the princeps senatus. A second recension ten years later reduced membership to 600. A third in 11 B.C. conducted by Augustus, and a fourth in A.D. 4 carried out through a specially chosen committee of three, left the number unchanged. The Senate was recruited automatically by the annual admission of the twenty retiring quaestors,[2] but since tenure of the higher magistracies carried with it senatorial rank, the princeps could use recommendations to the quaestorship, praetorship, and consulship to appoint men who had not met normal requirements for enrollment. Thus many prominent equestrians became senators.

In the latter part of his principate, the prestige of the Senate was enhanced by its employment as a court of justice, sitting under the presidency of the consuls for the trial of serious charges brought against senators. Its resolutions also gained added importance because they tended to acquire the force of law

---

[2] The number of quaestors had been reduced from forty to twenty in 27 B.C.

and because the Senate thereby was gradually becoming a legislative body replacing the popular assemblies. Although the Senate lost executive functions to the *princeps*, it was essential as a forum through which the governing establishment could be informed of policy, on which, in a certain sense, it could even express opinions. In his relations with the Senate, Augustus perhaps revealed most clearly the true nature of the Principate, for he showed that, if authoritarian, he was not arbitrary. He had the first and last word in politics, but unlike Julius Caesar, who had tended to monopolize every word in between, Augustus was eager to entertain the opinions of other men. There is no means of telling how often others influenced him to change his mind on important issues in his desire to satisfy his faction and establishment.

A master political stroke designed to create good liaison with the latter was his creation, probably between 27 and 18 B.C., of a standing committee (*consilium*) composed of prominent magistrates and fifteen senators chosen by lot. This committee advised the *princeps* and, with him, prepared the agenda for plenary sessions of the Senate. This probouleutic cabinet was replaced by another advisory committee in A.D. 13, which was designed to facilitate the coming transition of power from Augustus to his successor Tiberius. Apart from these two formal councils, there were also informal advisory committees made up of political friends of the emperor, whom he would consult from time to time on various administrative and judicial matters. Augustus successfully reconciled the Senate to one-man rule. He did so by accommodating his regime to the traditional senatorial desire for attainment of *dignitas* through office-holding, which once again became respectable and safe. Now, however, political advancement was a function of imperial patronage, and in dispensing it to the senatorial order, Augustus was characteristically cautious.

EQUESTRIAN ORDER. For the conduct of public administration, the *princeps* required a great number of assistants in his personal employ. For his legates to command the legions or his provinces with delegated military authority, Augustus could draw on senators, but both custom and senatorial prestige forbade their entering his service in other capacities. Yet, freedmen and slaves, who might well be employed in a clerical position, obviously could not be made the sole civil servants of the *princeps*. Augustus therefore drew into his service equestrians, whose business interests and connection with finances seemed to make them peculiarly fitted as his agents in the financial administration of the provinces. He had been closely associated with the equestrians at the beginning of his career when he appealed primarily to the municipal equestrian gentry of Italy, and the first important connections he had, until he made his peace with the senatorial nobility, were in this class. He had good reason to use equestrians widely by encouraging their advancement and election to high office because, as his men, they would be so many extra guarantees for the loyalty of the Senate. He thus increased the degree of upward mobility into the senatorial order from the equestrian class beyond even that of Caesar's day—his most radical change within the governing classes.

The equestrian order was open to all Roman citizens who were eighteen years of age, of free birth and good character, and possessed a census rating of 400,000 sesterces. Admission to the order was controlled by the *princeps* and carried the right to wear a narrow purple stripe on the tunic and to receive a public horse, the possession of which qualified an equestrian for civil and military service. With bestowal of the public horse, Augustus revived the long-neglected annual parade and inspection of the *equites* in Rome.

Like the career of the senators, that of the equestrians included both military and civil appointments. Beginning his public career, the equestrian held several military appointments, which later came regularly to include a prefecture in an auxiliary infantry or cavalry corps, a tribunate of a cohort of troops stationed in Rome, and a regular legionary tribunate. He was then eligible for a procurator-ship, that is, a post in the civil service, usually the administration of the finances. After filling several procuratorships, he might finally attain one of the great new prefectures, as commander of the city watch, administrator of the grain supply of Rome, commander of the imperial guards, or governor of Egypt. At the end of his career he might be enrolled in the senatorial order. The equestrian class itself was continually enlarged and rejuvenated by the admission of select members of the lower classes, in special cases even freedmen.

THE ASSEMBLIES AND THE LOWER CLASSES. The assemblies, which had supposedly voiced the will of the Roman people, were not abolished, although they could no longer claim to speak for the Roman citizenry. They still functioned as elective and legislative bodies. Because the emperor had, in a sense, "nationalized" certain benefits like poor relief, mass entertainment, and public works, the offices traditionally associated with them, principally the tribunate and aedileship, tended to become sinecures. Despite the limitations by the regime on freedom, which were real though not apparent, there could be keen competition in the Centuriate Assembly for quaestorships, praetorships, and consulships, the emperor only rarely availing himself of his right to com-mend candidates as this seemed autocratic.

After the first wave of popularity for Augustus' regime had passed, genteel voters in the Centuriate Assembly returned to traditional habits and for most of his reign elected as consuls senators of the old republican nobility. Augustus was loath to permit even the possibility that these nobles might become inde-pendent. Beginning in A.D. 5 and pursuant to a *lex Valeria Cornelia*, he rigged consular elections by establishing "prerogative" voting units in the Centuriate Assembly, ostensibly in honor of his dead grandsons. These centuries, voting first, gave a strong lead in elections, virtually assuring success of their own candidates. Since the prerogative centuries were packed with equestrians, the most enthusiastic supporters of the Principate, they tended to elect as consuls "new men" from their own class, actions which Augustus foresaw and intended.

While the city mob, accustomed to receive free distributions of grain and to be entertained at costly public spectacles, was a heavy drain on the state, the vigorous third estate in the Italian municipalities supplied the lower officers of the legions. These were the centurions, mainstay of discipline and efficiency of the troops, who sometimes advanced to an equestrian career.

III. MILITARY ESTABLISHMENT

REORGANIZATION OF THE ARMY. Upon his return to Italy in 30 B.C., Augustus found himself at the head of an army of about 250,000 citizens. Of these he released more than 140,000 and settled them in colonies or in their native municipalities, sometimes on lands expropriated from Antonian partisans. Partly to meet military and strategic needs, he established a state posting service (*cursus publicus*) along the highways and rivers of the Empire to transmit dispatches, and to move troops and supplies. He then proceeded to reorganize the military establishment by gradually rationalizing the precedents of the century of civil war. Whereas before there had been many standing armies, Augustus now created one force equal to all emergencies. Voluntary enlistment supplied most of the recruits, as Augustus tried wherever possible to avoid unpopular conscription. He made an important change in the officer cadres. During the civil wars such posts had been held with increasing frequency by men of low social background who had risen from the ranks, and a professional officer class tended to develop. By restoring such posts—in particular the legionary tribunate—to equestrians and fledgling senators and by reintegrating thereby officers' military and civilian careers, he restored the prestige of the office and prevented the development of a possibly dangerous military vested interest. The army continued to comprise the two traditional categories of troops, legionaries and auxiliaries. At first the legionaries served for sixteen years, which had been the maximum legal limit for military service during the Republic.

LEGIONS AND AUXILIARIES. As during the civil wars, legionaries were recruited from Roman citizens living in Italy or the provinces or from provincials who now received Roman citizenship upon their enlistment. The legions each comprised nominally 6,000 men, of whom 120 were cavalry and the rest infantry, but often they were not maintained at full strength. By 13 B.C., apparently, there were twenty-eight legions under arms; but when three were lost in Germany in A.D. 9 they were not replaced, so that the number remained at twenty-five, giving a total of about 150,000. The auxiliaries, who took the place of contingents regularly raised from Roman allies during the Republic, were recruited from among the most warlike subject peoples of the Empire, and their numbers were approximately equal to the legionaries. Augustus began to systematize their organization into small infantry and cavalry corps (cohorts and *alae*), each 480 or 960 men strong, to enlist them under Roman direction for definite terms of service, and to give them Roman officers. It was not until much later that this regime was imposed on all auxiliary units, and many of them continued to be raised and led by native chieftains and for varying periods of service. At the expiration of their term, the auxiliaries might be granted Roman citizenship.

PRAETORIANS. A third category of troops, which, greatly inferior in number and military value to the legions and auxiliaries although very influential in the Principate, was the praetorian guard. This was the force that attended Augustus in his capacity of military commander in chief. Its organization was thoroughly precedented and corresponded to the headquarters guard of commanders of the Republic. It was influential because it was kept in Italy, at first partly and later entirely at Rome, while other troops were stationed in the provinces. Under Augustus the praetorian guard comprised nine cohorts, each 1,000 strong, the whole commanded by two praetorian prefects of equestrian rank. The praetorians were recruited exclusively from Italy and enjoyed shorter service and higher pay than the other corps. The police and fire brigade of Rome should be also reckoned among imperial armed forces, since these had a military organization and were under the command of the *princeps*. Together they numbered 10,000 men.

CONDITIONS OF SERVICE It was not until A.D. 6 that the term of enlistment and the conditions of discharge were fixed formally for the several classes of troops. From that date service in the praetorian guard was for sixteen years, in the legions, twenty, and in the *auxilia*, twenty-five. This signified a substantial lengthening of service for legionaries, an indication that Augustus was finding it difficult to pay discharge benefits. This difficulty persisted to the end of his reign, when he was forced to keep some legionaries under the colors far beyond their "normal" twenty-year term. On discharge the praetorians received a bonus of 5,000 denarii, while the legionaries were given 3,000 denarii in addition to land. Discharged legionaries were regularly settled in colonies throughout the Empire. What provision was made for veterans of the auxiliary forces is unknown. To meet this increased expense Augustus was obliged to establish a military treasury (*aerarium militare*), endowed out of his private patrimony and supported by revenue derived from two newly imposed taxes, a 5 per cent inheritance tax (*vicesima hereditatium*), which affected all Roman citizens, and a 1 per cent tax on all goods publicly sold (*centesima rerum venalium*).

NAVY. For policing the coast of Italy and the adjacent seas, Augustus created a permanent fleet with stations at Ravenna and Misenum. Conforming to the relative unimportance of the Roman navy, in contrast to its military establishment, the personnel of this fleet was recuited largely from provincials, although for some time imperial freedmen were admitted to naval service. As occasion demanded special fleets were organized to cooperate in military expeditions.

The military system emphasized the predominance of Italy and Italians over provincials. Both officers and *élite* troops were drawn almost exclusively from Italy or the Latinized parts of the western provinces. In like manner reservation of the higher grades of civil administration, the second prop of Roman rule, to Roman senators and equestrians, as well as exclusion of the provincial imperial cult from Italy, marked clearly the distinction between the conquering and the subject races. At the same time, Augustus himself pointed the way to the ultimate Romanization of the provincials by the bestowal of citizenship as a reward for military service and by the settlement of veteran colonies in the provinces.

IV. REVIVAL OF RELIGION AND MORALITY

IDEALS OF AUGUSTUS. Augustus conceived moral regeneration of the Roman people as the basis for a new era of peace and prosperity. The reawakening of morality was necessarily preceded by a revival of religious rites and ceremonies, which recently had fallen into neglect through the attraction of new cults, the growth of skepticism, and the disorder into which the administration had fallen as a result of civil strife.

REVIVAL OF PUBLIC RELIGION. One step in restoring the public state cults was the reestablishment of ancient priestly colleges devoted to the performance of particular rites or the cult of particular deities. To provide these colleges with the required number of patrician members, Augustus created new patrician families. He himself was enrolled in each of these colleges and after 12 B.C., was chief pontiff (*pontifex maximus*), head of the state religion. A second measure was the repair of ruined temples and shrines. The temple of Jupiter Capitolinus, those of Quirinus and Magna Mater, and eighty-two shrines of lesser fame were repaired or restored by him. One of his generals, Munatius Plancus, renewed the temple of Saturn in the Forum. Augustus was pious in the sense of unimaginatively and even superstitiously believing in formal religious institutions of the Roman state. Although he had briefly flirted with foreign cults, like that of Isis, at the beginning of the Triumvirate, as emperor he was concerned exclusively with the worship of old-fashioned Roman, rather than foreign, gods.

Realizing that confusion and uncertainty of the Civil Wars had stimulated the worship of such deities as Fortune, Peace, Mercury the god of wealth, and Hercules the bestower of earthly goods, Augustus fostered their cults, building new shrines in their honor and linking himself with them publicly by giving them, in such forms as Fortuna Augusta, Pax Augusta, and Mercurius Augustus, his own surname. He also sought to impress people with the religious affiliations of his Julian *gens*, and, consequently, with the divine atmosphere around him. With this in mind he erected a new temple to Mars the Avenger in his new Forum and another to the deified Julius in the old one where Caesar's body was burned. On the Palatine hill, adjacent to Augustus' residence, arose a magnificent temple of Apollo, also a protector of the Julian house, whom

Augustus honored as the giver of victory over his rivals and the savior of the state from the Civil Wars.

THE LARES AND THE GENIUS AUGUSTI. Among the divinities whose cult had been revived were the Lares, guardian deities of crossroads and protectors of household peace and prosperity, whose worship was especially practiced by lower classes. Between the years 12 and 7 B.C., each of the 265 precincts or *vici* into which the city of Rome was then divided was provided with a shrine dedicated to the Lares and the Genius of Augustus, that is, the divine spirit protecting his fortunes. Worship was conducted by a committee of masters, annually elected by the inhabitants of each precinct. In this way the city mob, while not worshipping the *princeps* himself, were yet encouraged to look upon him as their protector and guardian.

IMPERIAL CULT. Of much greater significance was the wielding of politics and religion to enhance the mystique of imperial power in the cult of Roma and Augustus, the imperial cult. Worship of the goddess Roma, the personification of the state, sprang up voluntarily in the cities of Greece and Asia after 197 B.C., when Rome began to supplant the power of Hellenistic monarchs, whose deification by their subjects was a basis of their autocracy. Such voluntary worship had also been accorded to individuals like Flamininus, Sulla, Caesar, and Mark Antony. As early as 29 B.C. the cities of Pergamon in Asia and Nicomedia in Bithynia erected temples dedicated to Roma and Augustus and established quinquennial religious festivals called *Romaia Sebasta*. Other cities followed their example, and before the death of Augustus each Eastern province had at least one altar dedicated to Roma and the *princeps*. Augustus accepted, fostered, and directed development of the cult, because he realized the political value of such an expression of reverence and devotion.

The imperial cult was also transplanted to the West. In the year 12 B.C. an altar of Roma and Augustus was established at the junction of the rivers Rhone and Sâone, opposite the town of Lugdunum (modern Lyons), the administrative center of Transalpine Gaul apart from the Narbonese province. Here the peoples of Gaul were to unite in the outward manifestation of their loyalty to Roman rule. A similar altar was erected at what is now Cologne, in the land of the Ubii, between 9 B.C. and A.D. 9, but the cult did not spread into other Western provinces until after his reign. Both in the East and West its maintenance was the duty of provincial councils, composed of upper classes in municipal or tribal units.

MUNICIPAL CULT OF AUGUSTUS IN ITALY. The imperial cult in the provinces was an expression of the absolute authority of Rome and Augustus. Augustus could not admit its development in Italy, for this would deny his claim to be a Roman magistrate, deriving his authority from the Roman people, among whom he was the chief citizen, and would stamp his government as monarchical and autocratic. In Italy there was a strong tendency, however, to see in Augustus a divine deliverer from war and strife and a guardian deity of peace and security—the inaugurator of a new world era. In 27 B.C. the poet Horace acclaimed him as Mercury incarnate, and municipalities and individuals in southern Italy spontaneously established his worship. There is no evidence that this direct cult of Augustus was encouraged or even persisted in any official form, although after 12 B.C., in many Italian municipalities there were created religious colleges of *Augustales* or priestly officers called *Seviri Augustales*, whose name indicates that they were concerned with some phase of the cult of the *princeps*. Probably they served to maintain a cult of the Genius of Augustus, either alone or in conjunction with some other divinity, such as Mercury or Hercules. As the *Augustales* were drawn largely from the class of freedmen who were no longer admitted wholesale to full Roman citizenship, Augustus both assured himself of their loyalty and gratified their pride by encouraging their municipal office. Other municipal institutions serving to reawaken an interest in religion, to maintain a martial spirit and military exercises, and to enhance the atmosphere of religious mystique surrounding the personality of Augustus were the associations or clubs of young men (*iuvenes*) that were widely revived and reorganized under his patronage. These clubs were not restricted to the municipalities but also flourished in Rome.

SOCIAL LEGISLATION. Augustus did not trust solely to the moral effects of religious exercise. He also resorted to legislative action to check the unpuritanical tendencies of his age. The Julian Laws of 19 and 18 B.C. aimed at the restoration of family life, the encouragement of marriage, and the discouragement of childlessness by placing disabilities upon unmarried and childless persons. These measures provoked great opposition, but Augustus was in earnest and supplemented his earlier laws by the Papian Poppaean Law of A.D. 9 that gave precedence to fathers among the candidates for public office. These laws failed signally to achieve their moral and demographic purposes. By example as well as by precept, Augustus sought to check the luxurious tendencies of the age, and in his own household he furnished a model of ancient Roman simplicity.

To curb the dispersion of family property in the upper classes, Augustus sponsored two laws, the Fufian Caninian of 2 B.C. and the Aelian Sentian of A.D. 4: the first limited the number of slaves a master could liberate by his will, and the second placed severe restrictions on a slaveholder's right to free slaves during his lifetime. A Junian Law, passed probably in 17 B.C., granted a new kind of Latin citizenship to the considerable number of former slaves who had been emancipated by their owners without the formalties necessary to secure citizenship for them or public recognition of their freedom. For the future, slaves thus informally liberated joined this class of Julian Latins. Such freedmen could exercise the public rights of Roman citizens if they produced at least one child a year old. This is a clear indication that Augustus was anxious that freedmen citizens should propagate no less than the Italian stock.

X Altar of Peace of Augustus. *Consecrated in 13 B.C. and dedicated in 9 B.C., the Altar of Peace was erected in the Campus Martius at Rome and decorated with majestic reliefs depicting the imperial family and their official entourage. (Photo: Fototeca Unione.)*

V. THE GOLDEN AGE OF AUGUSTUS

The epochal nature of the changes wrought by Augustus in his world were reflected in literary production, and it is no accident that his age marks the culmination in the development of Roman poetry. Through certain poetic genres and personalities, the literary history of the Augustan Age was linked to the last decades of the Republic. Some of the great talents were maturing artistically during the final phases of the civil wars. Some had even been republican in their political outlook and had suffered for it. Augustus early realized the propaganda value inherent in poetry as a means of advertising the ideals of his regime, and even during his career as a revolutionary he sought to attract the loyalty of the rising generation of artistic talent. He was acting within Roman tradition, since it had long been usual for aristocrats to display munificence and increase their fame by drawing poets and artists into their clientele. If Augustus was not the sole patron of Roman letters, even during his principate, he was by far the most important. He was aided in this role by the equestrian Maecenas, who identified and encouraged artistic endeavor at the emperor's behest. Only a brief outline of the literary creativity guided by these men can be attempted here.

The inspiration and interests of Augustan poets certainly owed much to the New Poetry of Catullus. Like the modernists, they disregarded drama and were eager to develop erotic genres. Although their love poems were undoubtedly their most popular, the most exciting new direction in Roman poetry was provided by contemporary political themes in lyric verse. The best of these poets brilliantly exploited the emotive forces in Roman institutions; their glorification of the imperial regime and its ideals rang true because they believed in it and in Augustus as the restorer of his world. Despite the efforts of Maecenas, the commitment of other writers to the new order was more qualified, but even those who refused his patronage made interesting and even brilliant contributions to literature.

VERGIL. Publius Vergilius Maro (70–19 B.C.), without a doubt the most imaginative Roman poet of any age, lost his farm near Mantua during the proscription of 42 B.C. He cannot have suffered financially, because he always had powerful connections in Rome where he had lived since adolescence, and Maecenas saw that he was properly compensated. Shy, introspective, with a haunting sensitivity for nature and human emotions, Vergil worked painstakingly and produced only a few works during a rather short lifetime. His earliest poetry, which he later tried to suppress, owed much to Catullus. About 37 B.C. he published his *Eclogues*, pastoral verses written in a Theocritan and modernist vein, blending imagination and realism, innocence and sophistication. A decade later he published the *Georgics*, written allegedly at Maecenas' behest. A kind of artistic farmer's almanac glorifying the Italian countryside, they are didactic poems inspired by Alexandrine models and, it seems, by Lucretius' *De rerum natura*. His greatest work was the *Aeneid*, whose theme was suggested to him by Octavian in 29. A mighty epic describing the transplantation of the Roman race from Troy to Italy, the *Aeneid* moves on many levels and in many ways was the artistic quintescence of all the Romans demanded from poetry, a work written in the service of a national ideal. It holds up as worthy of emulation the old-fashioned virtues of *gravitas*, *pietas*, and *fides* incarnated by Aeneas himself, who was fated to subordinate his personal feelings as the chosen instrument of the gods in establishing the destiny of Rome. Thoughtful readers were intended to see, by poetic allusion, that Augustus himself embodied such qualities. In its best passages the *Aeneid* moves with great tenderness and appreciation of human tragedy, as when Vergil described the ill-starred love affair between Aeneas and Dido, Queen of Carthage. Vergil had not finished revising the work when he died, and, perfectionist that he was, he wanted it destroyed. Augustus countermanded his request, and so it survives as one of the greatest literary monuments of civilization.

HORACE. Vergil's friend, Horace (Quintus Horatius Flaccus 65–8 B.C.), was a very different kind of man, gregarious and urbane. The son of a south Italian freedman, he fought on the losing side at Philippi and then worked for a time as a minor government clerk. He began his literary career ca. 35 B.C. by writing his first book of *Satires*, further developing the genre first invented by Lucilius, who had found no successor among the modernists. Shortly thereafter he accepted Maecenas' patronage, receiving from him the gift of a delightful farm in the Sabine hills outside Rome. Horace's early *Satires* were vulgar, even vicious attacks on obscure people, and the measure of his artistry was his ability to mellow through his increasing interest in lyric poetry, as evidenced in his *Epodes*. In his second book of *Satires* (29 B.C.) were more mature, amused, and tolerantly detached observations of human foibles. His first *Odes* (23 B.C.) lack the rebellious quality of his earliest works and combine his commentaries on contemporary politics with a philosophy of life, expressed also in his later *Epistles*, the search for comfort without ambition, passion, or greed. After Vergil's death, Horace became Augustus' poet laureate and thereby lost even more of his initial fire. His *Secular Hymn* of 17 B.C., written to celebrate the Augustan New Age, was an experiment with a Pindaric genre, and, despite a certain academic quality, effective. In the *Ars Poetica* of the same year he attempted a hexameter essay on literary questions. Expounding a new classicism, he criticized a growing belief that poetry should be not an expression of the poet's imagination, but an attempt to make an immediate impression on an audience.

ELEGAIC POETS. Undoubtedly the most popular genre of the period was the erotic elegy. In fact, the first "Augustan" poet to publish was Cornelius Gallus (70–26 B.C.), Catullus' immediate literary successor and the man who introduced Vergil to Octavian. His work has not survived. The genre is best represented by Tibullus (54–19 B.C.) and Propertius (50–15 B.C.), both of them, like Catullus, propertied gentlemen of central Italy. Little is known about Tibullus, except that he was a friend of Horace and began to write ca. 27 B.C. His elegies are notably conversational, his most original contribution to poetic composition being the subtle transitions of his thoughts. Propertius (fl. 28–16 B.C.), an equestrian from Assisi, lost his property in Octavian's proscription before being patronized by Maecenas. He began to publish ca. 29 B.C. and developed into a moving, even inspired craftsman, immortalizing the love for his Cynthia by reflecting sentimentally, if rather morbidly, on the sorrow inherent in it.

OVID. The youngest and most brilliant erotic poet was Ovid (P. Ovidius Naso, 43 B.C.–A.D. 17), who began to write ca. 13 B.C. Facile, witty, ironic, Ovid was technically the most flawless of the Augustans. Unlike Propertius, he refused to take love seriously and was its amused spectator in the frivolous *Amores*, in which he described his affairs with his mistresses, especially the fabulous Corinna. His *Art of Love* (*Ars Amatoria*), intended to be a harmless spoof on didactic poetry in general, was followed ca. 2 B.C. by *Metamorphoses*, an epic, using old myths, on love's insuperable power. He evidently desired official recognition as a serious poet and so began the *Fasti*, in which he poeticized the ceremonial observances of the religious calendar, as near as he could come to writing on a patriotic subject. The *Fasti* remained unfinished, however, since Ovid was exiled to Tomi on the Black Sea ca. A.D. 9. His love poetry had hardly endeared him to a puritanical emperor interested in reforming upper-class sexual morals, and Ovid himself may have also been implicated in a scandal involving Augustus' granddaughter, Julia. He wrote a series of poems from exile complaining to the emperor that he had been unjustly treated and requesting reinstatement, but he was never permitted to return.

LIVY. The Augustan Age also produced a prose genius, Livy of Padua (Titus Livius, 59 B.C.–A.D. 17), whose history of Rome from its foundation to 9 B.C. (*Ab urbe condita libri*) was recognized by the reading public as the canonical version of the past. Although a member of the municipal Italian gentry, his original political sympathies were republican, and he never became an enthusiastic supporter of the Augustan regime. The old-fashioned ideals he emphasized in his book were congenial to the emperor, but Livy was in no sense the official historian of the government, to which he was at best indifferent. He wrote in a Hellenistic tradition that conceived of history as a literary genre for the narration of dramatic and tragic events. He was not so interested in doing research as he was in digesting data in works of earlier historians, which he then presented in his own, extremely attractive literary style. It was more important for him to portray the psychology of his characters or make his narrative exciting than it was to get facts straight although he gave real unity to his work by infusing it with his patriotic and religious prejudices. His book is undoubtedly very important as a work of art and also, despite his frequently uncritical approach to his sources, as history, because it is the only surviving literary narrative for many periods of early Rome.

VI. PROVINCES AND FRONTIERS

IMPERIAL ADMINISTRATION. Although conferment of his great provincial command upon Augustus in 27 B.C. led to the eventual division of the Roman provinces into two classes, senatorial and imperial, this was so only formally in the sense that appointments to certain governorships were made by the Senate or emperor. Legally, the Senate, by virtue of its general provincial oversight, and the emperor, exercising his *maius imperium*, could, and on occasion did, intervene anywhere in the Empire. Legates might report to the Senate, proconsuls to the emperor, and vice versa, since the Romans conceived of imperial administration not as involving strictly defined, hierarchical chains of command but rather as an array of coordinate, yet independent officials and institutions. The emperor, of course, was from the beginning a far more powerful instrument of government than the Senate, so governors of whatever rank tended to look to him for advice and instruction. Imperial power is evident in the fact that in 7–6 B.C. Augustus issued two edicts, correcting abuses in the judicial administration of Crete and Cyrenaica, which together formed a senatorial province, and, in 4 B.C. he published in Cyrenaica a decree passed by the Senate in the recommendation of which he had concurred. This greatly simplified and reduced the cost of bringing to trial Roman officials accused of having practiced extortion in any province. It also established the Senate, instead of the former court, as the body having cognizance of such cases. In announcing the decree, Augustus wrote that it would "show to all the inhabitants of the provinces the pains taken by the Senate and himself to prevent any of their subjects being made the victim of unjust treatment or extortion." This formulated a policy at Rome of enlightened imperialism directed toward the welfare of the subjects. In conformity with this new policy provincial taxation was revised and put on a sounder basis. This was important, since the main expense of the military and civil establishment was defrayed by provincial revenues. To estimate their resources for purposes of taxation and recruitment, Augustus ordered a comprehensive census of the population and an evaluation of property in each newly organized district and provided for a systematic revision of the census in all the imperial provinces. A general chart of the Empire was compiled on the basis of an extended survey conducted under the direction of Agrippa.

SENATORIAL AND IMPERIAL PROVINCES. Although, in general, it might be said that imperial provinces were those with legionary garrisons and the senatorial those without such garrisons, this distinction did not always hold good. For varying periods the proconsuls of Macedonia, Illyricum, and Africa had legions at their disposal and surrendered them only when the frontiers passed beyond their provinces. Nor was the original allotment of the provinces permanent. In 22 B.C. Augustus gave Gallia Narbonensis back to the Senate because the rapid progress of Roman colonization there had made it "more a part of Italy than a province." Similarly, Baetica, comprising a large part of Farther Spain, and southern Greece (Achaia), previously under the control of the governors of Macedonia, were also made senatorial provinces. On the other hand, Augustus in 11 B.C. took over Illyricum, where pacification had been interrupted by the war with Antony and Cleopatra and where Rome was confronted by warlike and restless peoples in the hinterland. Somewhat later Cilicia and in A.D. 6 Sardinia became imperial provinces because of conditions necessitating military action. Finally, new provinces organized by Augustus in territories conquered by his generals remained imperial.

Outside the two classes of provinces but really within the Empire, Augustus permitted some client kingdoms to exist. They enjoyed internal autonomy and were not subject to taxation by Rome, but their foreign relations were controlled by the *princeps*, and they were bound to render military aid. Their rulers acknowledged Roman overlordship and in some cases were dependent on Roman support for their authority. Such kingdoms were Mauretania, Thrace, Judaea, Galatia, Cappadocia, Pontus, Commagene, and Lesser Armenia, of which Galatia and Judaea were transformed into provinces by Augustus.

PROVINCIAL OFFICIALS. Government in the senatorial provinces continued as it had under the Republic. Governors for senatorial provinces were selected by lot from eligible ex-consuls and ex-praetors, the former having been ten, the latter five years out of office. All were now called proconsuls, although only Asia and Africa were reserved for those actually ex-consuls. The term of office was still normally one year. Each proconsul had as his assistants a quaestor and three propraetorian legates whose appointment was approved by the *princeps*. In imperial provinces officials were deputies of the *princeps*, and this fact is reflected both in their titles and in their conditions of service. As governors of the more important provinces with legionary garrisons, Augustus appointed legates of propraetorian rank (*legati Augusti pro praetore*) from senators who had held the consulship or praetorship, without reference to the period which had elapsed since their magistracies. An exception was the governor of Egypt, who was an equestrian with the title of prefect, although he had three legions under his orders. In the imperial provinces of lesser military importance garrisoned only by auxiliary troops, the governors were not senators but equestrians, whose title was, as a rule, prefect, later procurator. Other officials in larger provinces were the legates commanding legions (*legati legionis*), in Egypt prefects, who were subordinates of the legate of Augustus, and imperial procurators who had charge of provincial finances. Being appointed directly by the *princeps*, these latter were practically independent of the governors. There was no limit on the term of service of imperial officials, who were kept at their posts at the imperial pleasure. Both imperial and senatorial officials now received regular salaries, which were intended to remove one of the earlier causes of extortion by provincial governors.

FOREIGN POLICY OF AUGUSTUS. Augustus, since he was commander-in-chief of the armies and of administration of the most important border provinces, was entrusted by the Senate with the direction of foreign relations. Although personally not an outstandng general, Augustus was as mindful of the lures of military glory as the great *principes* of the Republic. No Roman added more territory to the Empire than he. This expansion did not seem defensive to Augustan poets, who presumably were propagandizing the emperor's aims. There seems good reason to believe that Augustus was an aggressive imperialist, forced to be content with the attainment of defensive frontiers by pressing manpower problems throughout his reign and by events that occurred toward its end.

SETTLEMENT IN SPAIN. The northwestern corner of Spain was still occupied by independent peoples, the Cantabri, Astures, and the Callaeci, who harassed the pacified inhabitants of the provinces. To secure peace in this quarter, Augustus determined to subjugate these peoples. In 26 B.C. he himself, and next year his lieutenants, Antistius and Carisius, conducted campaigns in their mountain fastnesses and, overcoming their desperate resistance, settled them in the valleys and secured Roman territory by founding colonies of veterans not only there but also elsewhere, as at Emerita (Merida) and Caesaraugusta (Saragossa). A subsequent revolt in 20–19 B.C. was crushed by Agrippa. After the pacification of Spain Augustus surrendered Baetica to the Senate, while he created a new imperial province called Lusitania in the western part.

PACIFICATION OF THE ALPINE DISTRICTS: 25–8 B.C. A similar problem was presented by Alpine peoples, who not only ravaged northern Italy but also occupied passes in the west offering the most direct routes between Italy and Transalpine Gaul. In 26 B.C. near the Little St. Bernard, the Salassi, who had been subdued eight years before, revolted. In the following year they were completely subjugated, and those who escaped slaughter were sold into slavery. A highway was built across the pass guarded by a military colony at Augusta Praetoria (Aosta). In 16 B.C. the district of Noricum (modern Tyrol and Salzburg) was occupied by Publius Silius Nerva, after a raid by the Noricans into Istria. In 15 B.C. the stepson of Augustus, Nero Claudius Drusus, crossed the Brenner Pass and forced his way over the Vorarlberg range to Lake Constance, subduing the Raeti. On the shores of Lake Constance he met his elder brother, Tiberius Claudius Nero, who had marched eastward from Gaul. Together they subjugated the Vindelici. The Danube was now the Roman frontier on the north, and the way was open for the greatest military project of his reign, expansion beyond that river into Germany. A number of isolated campaigns completed subjugation of the remaining Alpine peoples by 8 B.C.

GAUL AND GERMANY. Caesar left Gallia Comata pacified but still unsettled and not fully incorporated. Augustus completed its organization, between 27 and 13 B.C. Subsequent to the transfer of Gallia Narbonensis to the Senate, Gallia Comata was divided into three districts: Aquitania, Lugdunensis, and Belgica. Under Augustus, however, these formed a unit under one governor, with subordinate legates in each district. The colony of Lugdunum was the seat of administration and the imperial cult. No attempt was made to latinize the three Gauls by founding other Roman colonies; they remained divided into sixty-four separate peoples, called *civitates*, with tribal organization under native nobility. As early as 27 B.C. Augustus took a census of Gaul and fixed its tax obligations on this basis. Gaul was important as a source of imperial revenue, as a recruiting area for the auxiliary forces, and as a western base for his projected expansion against Germany.

Such expansion was prompted only in part by a desire to keep Gaul, restive under its new burdens, from being stirred up by Germanic invasions from beyond the Rhine like those of the Sugambri in 17 and 12 B.C. For some years Augustus seems to have been preparing for a grandiose German war, a project that was to occupy him almost to the end of his reign. He aimed first at subduing the area between the Rhine and Elbe. Initially at least he may not have excluded the notion of expansion beyond the latter river. The Germans, like the Gauls at the time of the Roman conquest, were divided into a number of independent tribes usually fighting among themselves and hence incapable of allying permanently against a common foe. Individually they were powerful and courageous, but their military efficiency was impaired by their lack of unity and discipline.

Drusus, conqueror of the Raeti, was appointed commander of the Roman army. He first secured the Rhine by construction of fortresses stretching from Vindonissa (near Basle) to Castra Vetera (near Xanten). The latter and Mogontiacum (Mainz) were his chief bases. Crossing the river, he overran and subjugated the territory between the Rhine and the Elbe in four campaigns (12–9 B.C.). His operations were aided by his fleet, for whose use he constructed a canal from the Rhine to the Zuider Zee, to provide a shorter and safer route to the mouth of the Elbe. Cooperation of the fleet also facilitated the conquest of the coast peoples, among them the Batavi, who became firm Roman allies. On the return from the Elbe in 9 B.C., Drusus was fatally injured by a fall from his horse. His brother Tiberius succeeded him and strengthened the Roman hold on the transrhenane conquests.

MIDDLE AND LOWER DANUBE. To the east of the Adriatic the provinces of Illyricum and Macedonia were subject to constant incursions by the Pannonians, Getae (or Dacians), and Bastarnae, peoples settled in the middle and lower Danube valley. Marcus Licinius Crassus, governor of Macedonia, defeated the Getae and Bastarnae in 30 and 29 B.C., crossed the Balkans, carried Roman arms to the Danube, and subdued the Moesi to the south. It was some time, however, before various Thracian tribes were finally pacified, and a client kingdom under the Thracian prince Cotys interposed between Macedonia and the lower Danube. Meantime, to secure the south German front, the Pannonians were conquered in hard-fought campaigns, which were successfully concluded by Tiberius (12–9 B.C.), who made the Danube the boundary. The contemporaneous and related conquest of Pannonia and of Germany between the Rhine and the Elbe was one of the greatest feats of Roman arms and reveals the army at the height of its discipline and organization. In 13 B.C., during a lull in these frontier struggles, the Senate voted the erection of an altar to the peace of Augustus (ara pacis Augustae), in recognition of his maintenance of peace within the Empire and pacification of foreign enemies.

REVOLTS IN ILLYRICUM AND GERMANY. Following the death of Drusus no further conquests were attempted until A.D. 4, when Tiberius was again appointed to command the army of the Rhine. After assuring himself of the allegiance of the Germans by a demonstration as far as the Elbe and by establishing fortified posts, he prepared to complete the Roman conquest west of that river by attacking the kingdom of the Marcomanni, in modern Bohemia, between the Elbe and the Danube. In A.D. 6 Tiberius was about to advance northward from the Danube, in cooperation with Gaius Saturninus, who was to move eastward from the Rhine, when a revolt broke out in Illyricum, which forced abandonment of the undertaking and the conclusion of peace with Maroboduus, king of the Marcomanni. This revolt, in which both Pannonians and Dalmatians joined, was caused largely by the fact that these tribes had not been thoroughly subjugated, but also by the severity of Roman exactions, especially levies for the army. For a moment Italy was threatened with invasion. In raising new legions even freedmen were conscripted. But the arrival of reinforcements from other provinces enabled Tiberius after three years of ruthless warfare utterly to crush the rebels (A.D. 9). The organization of Pannonia and Moesia as separate provinces followed reestablishment of peace.

Until the last year of the war in Illyricum the Germanic tribes had remained quiet under Roman overlordship. In A.D. 9, provoked by the attempt of the new Roman commander, Publius Quinctilius Varus, to control them more strictly, they united to free themselves. The Cherusci and Chatti were important peoples in the coalition, and Arminius, a young chieftain of the Cherusci who had served in the Roman *auxilia* and received citizenship and equestrian rank, was its leading spirit. Varus and his army of three legions were surprised on the march in the Teutoburg Forest and completely annihilated. Rome was in panic over the news, but the Germans did not follow up their success. Tiberius was again sent to the danger point and led two successful expeditions across the Rhine. No attempt was made to recover permanently lost ground. The idea of possibly limitless expansion in central Europe was given up, and the Rhine became the frontier, with momentous consequences for the future of the Empire and of Europe. The coast peoples remained Roman allies, however, and a narrow strip of territory was held on the right bank of the Rhine. The reason for this retreat to the Rhine lay in the weakness of the Roman military organization, already strained to the utmost by the Illyrian revolt and the difficulty of finding recruits for the legions. The cry of Augustus, "Quinctilius Varus, give back the legions!" gives the clue to his abandonment of Germany.

EASTERN FRONTIER. Between the Roman provinces in Asia Minor and the upper Euphrates lay a number of client kingdoms—Galatia, Pontus, Cappadocia and Lesser Armenia, and Commagene. At the death of Amyntas, king of Galatia, (25 B.C.), his kingdom was made into a province, but the others were left under native dynasts. Across the Euphrates lay Armenia, a buffer state between Roman possessions and Parthia, and strategically important because it commanded the military routes between Asia Minor and the heart of Parthia. To establish a protectorate over Armenia was therefore one of Augustus' great ambitions. Defeat or even conquest of Parthia, cornerstone of his eastern policy during much of his reign, would reassert the glory of Roman arms, wipe out the shame of the defeats of Crassus and Antony, and guarantee Roman territory from Parthian attack. During the presence of Augustus in the

East (22–19 B.C.), Tiberius placed a Roman nominee on the Armenian throne and received by diplomatic means from the Parthian king, Phraates IV, the Roman standards and captives in Parthian hands, a success that earned Augustus the salutation as Imperator by his troops. Later Phraates sent four of his sons to Rome as hostages. The power of Parthia was therefore defused. With Armenia also dependent on Rome, it seemed only a question of time before Roman armies would cross the Euphrates and force the annexation of Parthia. But unforeseen events in Armenia diverted Augustus' attention, and the final confrontation with Parthia never took place. The Roman protectorate over Armenia was impermanent. By about 6 B.C. the national, pro-Parthian faction had gained the upper hand. Between 1 B.C. and A.D. 2 Gaius Caesar, grandson of Augustus, restored Roman influence, but none of the several Roman appointees to the Armenian throne was able to retain his position. At the death of Augustus, the kingdom, then without a ruler, escaped from Roman control. The northern flank of Asia Minor had meantime been made secure through the organization of the Bosporan kingdom as a client state by Agrippa in 14 B.C.

To the south of Syria lay the kingdom of Judaea, ruled by Herod the Great from about 37 B.C. to his death in 4 B.C. His kingdom was divided among his three sons, Philip, Herod Antipas, and Archelaus. Archelaus inherited Judaea, but proving unpopular, he was deposed at the request of both Jews and Samaritans, and exiled by the Romans in A.D. 6. Judaea then became a province, ruled by a prefect residing at Caesarea. Augustus was aware of Jewish religious sensibilities, and Roman rule was tactful.

In Arabia, Augustus sought to bring under control the spice land of Arabia Felix, the southwestern coast of the peninsula. The invasion of Arabia Felix in pursuit of revenue shows that Augustus' foreign policy was not solely defensive and aimed at attaining greater security. Success would have given the Romans control of trade between the Mediterranean and India by way of the Red Sea, for this was the point of transshipment of goods from India and Somaliland, on their way to the markets of Syria and Egypt. Relying on the support of Nabataean Arabs, who controlled the region south and east of the Dead Sea, Aelius Gallus, the Roman commander, assembled a large force in Egypt in 25 B.C. and transported it across the Red Sea to the Arabian shore. The following year he marched south through a desert where his troops suffered from lack of food and water. Shortage of necessities at length forced him to abandon the expedition and return ingloriously to Egypt. It was not a complete failure, however, since the Arabs, impressed by Rome's show of strength, accepted friendship with Rome and abandoned their monopoly of the straits at the south end of the Red Sea.

EGYPT AND NORTH AFRICA.   In 25 B.C. upper Egypt was invaded and ravaged by Ethiopians. They were defeated and driven out by the prefect Gaius Petronius. Petronius pursued them far into the Sudan and took their capital, Napata. He then secured the southern frontier of Egypt by annexing and garrisoning it south of the First Cataract. Although the attempt to occupy Arabia Felix failed, Rome came to control through Egypt a very large share of the Indian trade since, owing to the recent discovery of the monsoon winds in the Indian Ocean, many merchantmen began to make annual voyages from the Red Sea ports of Egypt directly to India and Ceylon.

Further west on the North African coast, Augustus enlarged the province of Africa by adding to it Numidia. He then appointed the former Numidian king, Juba II (whose wife was Cleopatra, the daughter of Mark Antony) to be king of Mauretania (25 B.C.), which he reestablished as a client kingdom, thus placing the tribes of Algeria and Morocco under a dependable Roman ally.

Augustus was a realist. Teutoburg and his difficulties with Armenia taught him that the Empire could not sustain the imperialistic aims he had so long pursued. At his death he left it as a maxim for his successors to abstain from future expansion, which meant that the conquests realized by him were to establish in their essential features the future boundaries of the Empire.

VII. ADMINISTRATION OF ROME

POLICE AND FIRE PROTECTION. Augustus intended that the administration of the city of Rome, like that of Italy, should be conducted by the Senate through its magistrates. Because some very important branches of city government were either neglected or mismanaged, he felt compelled, however, partly in response to popular appeals, to organize them efficiently and to assume responsibility for them. Of prime importance since the days of the Gracchi was the problem of policing Rome and the suppression of mob violence, which had threatened orderly government. The formation of the praetorian guard rather served to overawe the city mob and to prevent any revolutionary movement, even though at first only three of their cohorts were stationed in the city. To check nonpolitical disorders, suppress crime, and carry on other police functions, Augustus found it necessary to organize three urban cohorts, each originally of 1,500 men, who as soldiers ranked above legionaries but below praetorians. By the time of his death, command of these cohorts was held by the City Prefect (*praefectus urbi*), a permanent office held by senators of consular rank.

Between 12 and 7 B.C., for other administrative purposes, Augustus divided Rome into fourteen regions subdivided into 265 precincts (*vici*). Each region was placed under a tribune or aedile. Almost as important as the problem of police was fire protection, almost completely neglected under the Republic. As early as 21 B.C. Augustus tried to improve the situation by supplying the aediles responsible for this sphere of government with a force of 600 slaves. This proved ineffective, and in A.D. 6 he created a special corps of 7,000 men to serve as a fire brigade and night police. This corps was organized in seven cohorts, one for every two of the fourteen regions, and was commanded by an equestrian appointee of the *princeps* whose title was prefect of the watch (*praefectus vigilum*).

GRAIN SUPPLY. Another vital problem was maintaining an adequate grain supply. Frequently under the Republic this had presented such difficulties that extraordinary measures had been necessary to avert famine, but no permanent solution had been reached. A famine in 22 B.C. was so serious that the Senate was forced to call upon Augustus to cope with it. He assumed a temporary curatorship of the grain supply, and thereafter he may have exercised general supervision of it. Actual administration, however, seems to have remained for some time under the special aediles whose office Caesar had created. At the next crisis, in A.D. 6, they were replaced temporarily by two senatorial curators, they in turn by an equestrian prefect of the grain supply (*praefectus annonae*). His duty was to see that there was always enough grain imported into Rome to supply the market at a reasonable price. Other equestrian prefects of lower rank were in charge of the regular monthly distribution of free grain to the city mob. By 2 B.C. the number on relief had been fixed at 200,000 properly registered Romans. With the creation of the prefecture of the grain supply, Augustus assumed responsibility for the whole problem of the city's provisioning.

Other aspects of the government of Rome taken away from annual magistrates were turned over to permanent commissions composed of senatorial curators of consular or praetorian rank. Such were commissions in charge of aqueducts, temples and other public buildings, and that which was established in the year after the death of Augustus to supervise the banks and channel of the Tiber to prevent floods.

A parallel encroachment on the Senate's administrative control of Italy, also in the interests of efficiency, was made when Augustus was entrusted in 20 B.C. with the administration of Italian highways. This he also carried on through a commission of senatorial curators.

VIII. PROBLEM OF SUCCESSION

POLICY OF AUGUSTUS. Augustus was a valetudinarian and fully expected that illness would kill him prematurely, an unfounded expectation as he lived to be almost 76. The frequently precarious state of his health, however, confronted him with a dilemma as a statesman and politician. He felt that he must find a successor to consolidate and develop the Principate should he die before his work was finished, and he inevitably thought of the succession in family terms. There was nothing shocking to republican aristocrats in the idea of political dynasties and dynastic marriages, but the situation posed by the Principate was novel. One family, the emperor's own, had acquired pretensions dwarfing those of all the others. Yet the position of emperor was elective by the Senate and people rather than heritable at law, and Augustus' maneuvers to assure the election of an heir of his body to the powers he held increasingly revealed him as a monarch in disguise. This caused resentment both within his faction and the larger governing establishment because other senators, both "new men" and nobles, who claimed to be worthy of election (*capaces imperii*) by the sovereign Roman people to imperial powers. In part to silence any criticism, Augustus had as many of his relatives as possible marry into prominent senatorial families so as to implicate the latter in his dynastic plans, which then became the vested interest of these families.

MARCUS MARCELLUS AND AGRIPPA.   His immediate family, however, was small, and his designs were complicated by the ambitions of his third and last wife, Livia Drusilla, whom he married in 38 B.C., and who was interested in furthering the careers of her sons by her first marriage (to Tiberius Claudius Nero), Tiberius and Drusus. Augustus only had one child of his own, a daughter Julia by his second wife Scribonia, and Julia was obviously essential to his dynastic plans. He married her off to three likely husbands in the hope that she would produce grandsons and that if he died prematurely, their father would be their guardian until they were old enough to assume power. He chose Marcellus, his nephew, as Julia's first husband in 25 B.C., thus destroying Livia's hopes for her own sons and alienating Agrippa, who presumably expected to succeed himself. The next year, at age nineteen, Marcellus was admitted to the Senate, and in 23 B.C. as aedile he won popular favor with magnificent public shows. He died the same year, his marriage to Julia having produced no issue. Augustus then turned to Agrippa, who married Julia in 21 and in 18 B.C. received proconsular *imperium* and *tribunicia potestas* for five years, powers reconferred with those of Augustus in 13 B.C. The union of Agrippa and Julia was agreeably happy and produced a brood of five children, including two likely grandsons, Gaius and Lucius.

TIBERIUS.   But Agrippa himself died in 12 B.C., and the emperor was forced to marry Julia off once again, and to a man he found able but uncongenial, Livia's elder son, his own stepson, Tiberius, the conqueror of Noricum, whom he forced to divorce his beloved wife. Tiberius was immediately given an important Illyrian command, followed in 6 B.C. by tribunician authority for a five-year term. Proud, complex, morose, Tiberius was acutely conscious of his Claudian blood and resentful that, after all, he was merely supposed to be the eventual guardian of Agrippa's children. He also found himself utterly incompatible with the frivolous Julia. His situation became intolerable when he learned that Julia was an adulteress, and he set the stage for tragedy within the imperial house by retiring voluntarily to Rhodes in 6 B.C. Augustus subsequently heard of his daughter's escapades, whereupon he banished her to the desolate island of Pandataria off the Italian coast. Her lovers were also banished although one was executed on charges of treason (1 B.C.). Julia's like-named elder daughter herself was also later condemned and banished for adultery.

GAIUS AND LUCIUS CAESAR.   Gaius and Lucius, their ageing grandfather's pride, were showered with increasingly princely honors, assuming the garb of manhood (*toga virilis*) at the age of fifteen in 5 and 2 B.C., respectively.

On these occasions Augustus held the consulship and gave his grandsons the title of *princeps iuventutis*, thus designating them heads of the cadets of the equestrian order. They were exempted from the limitations of the *cursus honorum* so that each might become consul in his twentieth year. In A.D. 1 Gaius was sent to the East with proconsular *imperium* to pacify Armenia. There in the siege of a petty fortress he received a mortal wound and died in A.D. 4. Two years previously Lucius had fallen a victim to fever while on his way to Spain.

TIBERIUS AGAIN. The bereaved emperor then turned again to Tiberius, who was permitted to leave Rhodes at the intercession of Livia. In A.D. 4 he was adopted by Augustus and received the *tribunicia potestas* for ten years. In A.D. 13 his tribunician power was renewed, and he was made the colleague of Augustus in proconsular *imperium*. Tiberius was, in effect, coregent, lacking only Augustus' *auctoritas* and the consular *imperium* in Italy. Tiberius himself was obliged to adopt his nephew Germanicus, the son of Drusus, who married Agrippina, the younger daughter of Agrippa and Julia. Before his own death Augustus had thus set the precedent of designating the successor in the principate by association in authority, and adoption where necessary.

IX. ACHIEVEMENT OF AUGUSTUS

DEATH OF AUGUSTUS. In A.D. 14 Augustus set up in Rome an inscription recording his exploits and the sums he had expended on the state. One copy of this was found inscribed on the walls of the temple of Roma and Augustus at Ancyra (modern Ankara) (see figure p. 280) in Asia Minor. Another, less complete, has been discovered at Antioch in Pisidia. On August 19, A.D. 14 Augustus died at Nola in Campania, at the age of seventy-five.

AUGUSTUS AS POLITICIAN AND STATESMAN. Augustus was successful because he was able to extend his political faction, step by step, in the period 44–27 B.C. until it embraced the whole state. Realizing the paramount importance of patronage in Roman life, he saw to it that every important class, vested interest, and pressure group looked ultimately to him alone for rewards and advancement. A ruthless revolutionary in his early career, he nevertheless developed into a statesman of the highest order. What he established was a stable regime, a disguised kind of monarchy cleverly hidden behind a constitutional, republican facade. What followed him—a new era of peace and consolidation of Roman civilization—was the greatest justification of his work, to which both Rome and Western civilization are deeply indebted.

XI Temple of Rome and Augustus. *Erected at ancient Ancyra (modern Ankara, Turkey), one of several temples throughout the Empire honoring the first emperor, this temple is historically important because its walls were inscribed with a bilingual Greek and Latin record of Augustus' official career, the* Res Gestae. *(Photo: Fototeca Unione.)*

WEAKNESSES OF HIS SYSTEM. However successful Augustus' reforms proved to be, they were flawed from several points of view. Neither he nor immediately following emperors were able to resolve the contradictions inherent in the elective theory supporting the Principate and its dynastic practice. The result was tension between emperors and their governing establishment, the attitudes of which toward the executives were rather ambivalent. While quickly accepting the notion of a monarchic prince as a necessary evil and nurturing republican ideals of *libertas* in only a reminiscent sense, senators resented imperial absolutism, over which they had only tenuous control. Inevitably, even under Augustus, the relics of a "free" state, senatorial independence of action and the sovereignty of a people legislating and electing magistrates in popular assembly, withered away. Of even greater importance was Augustus' ultimate reliance on the control of military force as the single most important prop to imperial authority, from which followed the eventual realization by the military that it could make or unmake emperors. Furthermore, although he basically reformed the political structure of the Roman state, he did not touch its social and economic organization. Augustus' system of government rested primarily on the support of the upper classes, who as a matter of course were left to enjoy their traditional privileges. In effect, Augustus sanctioned and petrified the top-heavy class structure of the Greco-Roman world. The economic expansion that followed in the wake of the peace he created thus unequally benefited various classes of the population. The producing lower classes continued to live near subsistence level and were the first in the Empire to feel the effects of economic recession, when the Augustan system became increasingly expensive to operate.

CHAPTER 17
THE PRINCIPATE
UNDER THE
JULIO-CLAUDIANS AND
FLAVIANS: A.D. 14–96

Establishment of the Principate profoundly changed the character of Roman political history, as absolutism inherent in the imperial office became more obvious and moved toward autocracy openly exercised and buttressed by a developing bureaucracy with power depending ultimately on control of the armed forces. These trends were operative under "good" and "bad" emperors alike, historical judgment passed on them depending not on any freedom of action they permitted but on the respect (or lack of it) they showed their establishment. Although the importance of imperial personalities in determining policy and law should not be underestimated, it must be remembered that administration at all times depended as much on imperial advisers and on factions in the governing establishment supporting the emperors as it did on the emperors themselves. The government of the Empire was always evolutionary, and rulers making seemingly basic reforms often merely coordinated or rationalized *ad hoc* changes in government made by their subordinates or predecessors.

In the first century A.D. the system resulted in two short dynasties, frequently disturbed by plots directed against the emperors, who responded by purging senatorial rivals. The immediate successors to Augustus, members of the Julio-Claudian house, were related to him by blood or by adoption. Their family tree was as complicated as that of many other aristocratic clans of the Republic.[1] The emperors springing from it varied widely in ability. Like many Republican nobles, they were all very colorful, and sometimes very eccentric. The exotic historical tradition surrounding them that lends a decidedly technicolor quality to their rule must be carefully weighed, however because it derives ultimately from a senatorial class eager to damn emperors, even with the most subtle kind of slander.

I. TIBERIUS: A.D. 14–37

TIBERIUS PRINCEPS. At the death of Augustus, Tiberius Caesar assumed command of the army by right of his *imperium* and, through his tribunician authority, convoked the Senate to pay last honors to Augustus and decide on his successor. Like Julius Caesar, Augustus was deified, and a priestly college of *Augustales*, chosen from the senatorial order, was founded to maintain his worship. In accordance with a wish expressed in his will, his widow Livia was honored with the name Augusta. The title of Augustus was bequeathed to Tiberius, who now received from the Senate and Assembly other honors and powers his predecessor had made prerogatives of the *princeps*. His *imperium* was conferred for life, however, not for a limited period. The ease of his succession shows how solidly the Principate was established at the death of its founder.

CHARACTER AND POLICY. Tiberius was now fifty-five years of age. He had spent most of his life in public service and had a full appreciation of the responsibility the *princeps* must assume. He was the incarnation of the Roman sense of duty and at the same time exhibited the proud reserve of a Roman patrician. Stern in his maintenance of law and order, he made an excellent subordinate; as emperor, his greatest failing was hesitation and lack of decision. The incidents of his marriage with Julia and his retirement at Rhodes, which practically amounted to exile, rendered him bitter and suspicious, and he utterly lacked the charm and adaptability of his predecessor. Although he continued the policy of consulting groups of his political friends on matters of public policy, he did not revive Augustus' standing committee of senators, which perhaps accounts for his frequent misunderstandings with the Senate. Such an incident occurred during meetings of the Senate after the death of Augustus. Tiberius, uncertain of his popularity, sought to have the Senate press on him the appointment as successor to Augustus and appeared reluctant to accept, a course that made the senators suspect he was laying a trap for possible rivals. No *princeps*, however, tried more conscientiously to govern in the spirit of Augustus or upheld, perhaps unrealistically, the rights and dignity of the Senate. At the beginning of his principate he transferred from the Centuriate Assembly to the Senate the right of election to the magistracies,

---

[1] Note genealogical table in appendix.

thus relieving candidates from the expense and annoyance of canvassing the populace.[2]

MUTINIES IN ILLYRICUM AND ON THE RHINE. Two serious mutinies followed his accession, one in the army stationed in Illyricum, the other on the Rhine. Failure to discharge those who had completed their terms of service and the severity of service itself caused dissatisfaction. The Illyrian mutiny was quelled by Tiberius' own son Drusus, and the army of the Rhine was returned to its allegiance by his nephew Germanicus, the son of his brother, the elder Drusus, whom Tiberius had adopted at the command of Augustus in A.D. 4. Germanicus had married Agrippina, daughter of Agrippa and Julia, and was regarded as the heir of Tiberius, in preference to the latter's younger and less popular son, Drusus.

CAMPAIGNS OF GERMANICUS: A.D. 14–17. To restore discipline among his troops, relieve them from the monotony of camp life, and to emulate his father, Germanicus, without the authorization of Tiberius, led his army across the Rhine. Although the Germans were still united in the coalition formed at the time of Varus and, under their leaders Arminius and Inguiomerus, vigorously opposed the Roman invasion, Germanicus was able to ravage the territory between the Rhine and the Weser in three successive campaigns (14–16) and won several costly victories. One army narrowly escaped the fate of the legions of Varus, and twice transports of Germanicus were struck by storms in the North Sea. For these reasons Tiberius ordered an end to the war and recalled Germanicus, trusting to diplomacy rather than force of arms. On his departure each of the three Gauls (Aquitania, Belgica, and Lugdunensis) was made a province, and two new administrative districts, called Upper and Lower Germany, under consular legates, were created on the left bank of the Rhine. Financial administration of the two Germanies remained united with that of *Gallia Belgica*. Freed from the danger of a Roman invasion, the tribes led by Arminius now waged a bitter war with Maroboduus, king of the Marcomanni, which led ultimately to the latter's overthrow. Not long afterward Arminius himself fell victim to a plot by his fellow tribesmen (19). The rest of Tiberius' reign was utterly peaceful, except for a brief rising in Gaul (21) and a rather prolonged struggle with Tacfarinas, a rebellious Berber chieftain in Numidia.

EASTERN MISSION AND DEATH OF GERMANICUS: A.D. 17–19. After his return from Gaul, Germanicus was sent by Tiberius on a special mission, with an *imperium* outranking that of provincial governors, to settle affairs in the East, where Armenia was restive. Once again an Armenian king, this time the choice of his own people, received his diadem from the representative of Rome. In the East, Germanicus was as indifferent to the policy of the *princeps*

---

[2] The honorary prerogative centuries mentioned on p. 261 persisted in the Centuriate Assembly until at least A.D. 23.

as he had been in the West. He violated the rule established by Augustus that no senator should visit Egypt without special permission. During his stay there he alleviated a famine in Alexandria by distributing grain. This visit earned him a severe rebuke from Tiberius, who was alarmed by his conduct. A bitter quarrel developed in Syria between Germanicus and Piso, the legate of the province. When Germanicus fell ill and died there, many accused Piso of having poisoned him. Piso was called to Rome to be tried on that charge, as well as better founded ones of insubordination and violence. Finding that the popularity of Germanicus had biased popular opinion against him and that Tiberius refused him protection because he had attempted to assert his rights by armed force, he committed suicide. Agrippina, the ambitious wife of Germanicus, believing that Tiberius was responsible for her husband's death, openly displayed her hostility to the *princeps* and plotted with her own faction to secure the succession for her children.

PLOT OF SEJANUS. Tiberius also intended that one of his family should succeed to the Principate, but the question of succession was exacerbated by the hostility between Tiberius, Agrippina, and their respective factions, as well as by the ambitions of the praetorian prefect, Sejanus. In 23 Drusus died. Since the death of Germanicus he had been looked upon as the logical heir to the Principate. It was later alleged that Sejanus had poisoned Drusus. Grieving over the loss of his son and possibly disturbed by the conduct of Agrippina, whose elder sons Nero and Drusus were now presumptive successors, Tiberius withdrew from Rome in 26 and took up residence on the island of Capri off the Bay of Naples. This gave rise to further misunderstandings between himself and the Senate, but of much greater importance was the opportunity it furnished Sejanus to amass power that would ensure his own regency over an imperial prince upon Tiberius' eventual death. Sejanus seems to have had in mind the young and presumably pliable Gaius, Agrippina's youngest son, and he therefore played on Tiberius'suspicions to remove the other members of the house of Germanicus. On charges of treason, Nero and Agrippina were deported from Italy, the former being forced to commit suicide. Young Drusus was imprisoned in Rome. Sejanus shared the consulship with Tiberius and received from the Senate proconsular *imperium* in the provinces. He also persuaded the *princeps* to sanction his betrothal to Julia, Tiberius' granddaughter. In the end he overplayed his hand. An influential faction of senators, although tolerant of an equestrian *novus homo* in the governing oligarchy, refused absolutely to accept him as a possible regent with powers and pretensions far greater than their own. What happened next is obscure. This faction may have threatened to withdraw support from Tiberius' government if Sejanus were not dropped. Sejanus, probably aware that his position was precarious, prepared a *coup d'état*. Of this Tiberius was informed. The emperor acted secretly and energetically. In 31 Sejanus and many of his supporters were arrested and executed. Agrippina was left to die in exile, her son Drusus perishing in prison.

LAST YEARS OF TIBERIUS. The emperor became increasingly morose as the years passed, and his fears of treachery increased. The law of treason (*lex de maiestate*) was rigorously enforced, even though the concept of treason, as it applied to emperors, was ill-defined, since technically they were magistrates and not kings. Tiberius took "treason" to mean plots against his life. In some cases he discouraged frivolous charges, but he also seems to have accepted as cases of *maiestas* tales brought to him by informers (*delatores*) of trivial or imagined insults to his person. Matters were further complicated by his insistence that the Senate sit as a court of law in treason trials, which meant that senators felt that he was forcing them to do his dirty work. The emperor's estrangement from the Senate at the end was complete, and news of his death on March 16, A.D. 37, was received with undisguised relief.

The memory of his later years, represented by Tacitus and Suetonius, caused Tiberius to pass down in the traditions of the senatorial order as a ruthless tyrant. His enigmatic character certainly obscures his limited services as an effective administrator. Because of his indecision and cronyism, he left his friends for prolonged periods in high office—even if they were corrupt. While professing eagerness to relieve his subjects' tax burdens, he was also stingy with imperial funds, which restricted cash flow and even led at one point to financial panic in Italy, which, admittedly, he alleviated. Despite good intentions, he was not one of the more successful emperors.

II. GAIUS CALIGULA: A.D. 37–41

ACCESSION. Tiberius left as heirs his adoptive grandson Gaius, the sole surviving son of Germanicus—better known by his childhood nickname of Caligula ("Bootsie") acquired in the camps on the Rhine—and his grandson by birth, Tiberius Gemellus, the son of Drusus. Prompted by a powerful faction, the Senate immediately conferred the powers of the Principate upon Gaius, the elder of the two, then twenty-five years of age. Resentment of senators toward Tiberius found expression in their refusing him the posthumous honor of deification. Gaius adopted his cousin but within a year had him executed.

HIS CHARACTER. Caligula was a ruler whose personality is lost in a biased, not to say fantastic, historical tradition. Attempts have been made to rationalize both that tradition and his personality, to see behind the ancient accounts of his reign, described as being absolutely depraved, a distortion of his alleged attempts to convert the Principate into an exotic monarchy of Hellenistic type. Such rationalization is unconvincing, however, and it is simpler to assume that Caligula was at the very least perverse and unstable, but more probably quite mad. The evidence suggests that heredity and environment combined to make him a megalomaniac. It would have required an extraordinarily strong personality, which he did not have, to overcome the impressions of his boyhood, the intrigues and executions that had virtually wiped out his immediate family, and a serious illness shortly after his accession may have abetted his tendency to derangement.

The first months of his rule seemed the dawn of a new era. He won popularity by pardoning political offenders, banishing informers, reducing taxes, and spending lavishly on public entertainments and donations. Soon, however, he revealed his despotic conception of his office. He was the first emperor in Rome to insist on being a "living god," claiming deification for his sisters, allegedly building a bridge connecting the Palatine hill with the Capitoline, so that he might communicate with Jupiter, his brother god. He prescribed the sacrifices to be offered to himself and was accused of adopting the Ptolemaic custom of sister marriage. Thoroughly consistent with absolutism was his scorn of republican magistracies, his disregard of the Senate, and his attempt to have himself called *dominus* or "lord."

CONFLICT WITH THE JEWS. His demand for deification by all inhabitants of the Empire brought Gaius into conflict with the Jews, who had been exempted from this formal expression of loyalty. In Alexandria there was a large Jewish colony, hated by Greek residents for claiming citizenship in the city and enjoying exceptional privileges. During a visit of Herod Agrippa, king of a Jewish principality, the Greeks insulted the Jews by burlesquing him and his followers. Then, to avoid the consequences of this mockery of Gaius' friend, they showed their loyalty by forcing the Jews to worship images of the *princeps*. Refusal of this demand gave the mob a pretext for sacking Jewish quarters and forcibly installing statues in some synagogues. The Jews sent a delegation to plead their case before Gaius but could obtain no redress. In the meantime Gaius ordered Petronius, the legate of Syria, to set up his statue in the temple at Jerusalem, by force, if necessary. The prudent Petronius, anticipating a Jewish revolt, delayed obeying the order, and then the death of Gaius relieved him of the necessity of its execution.

TYRANNY AND ITS END. In less than a year the reckless extravagance of Gaius had exhausted the treasury surplus Tiberius had left. To secure new funds he resorted to tyrannical measures, extraordinary taxes, judicial murders, confiscations, and forced legacies. By these means money was extorted not only from Romans of all classes but from provincials as well. Ptolemy, king of Mauretania, was executed for the sake of his treasure and his kingdom claimed as a province. With the annexation of Mauretania, the Roman encirclement of the Mediterranean was completed.

Gaius contemplated invasions of Germany and of Britain, but the former ended with a military parade across the Rhine and the latter with a march to the Strait of Dover. The fear awakened by his capricious violence soon resulted in a conspiracy against his life. In January 41 he was assassinated by a tribune of the praetorian guards whom he had insulted and by others who feared that they might fall victims to his caprice. His wife and infant daughter shared his fate.

III. CLAUDIUS· A.D. 41-54

NOMINATION AND APPOINTMENT. Caligula's assassination produced the first great constitutional crisis in the Principate since 23 B.C. because he died without an heir or provision for a successor. The Senate alone legally had the power to invest emperors by its vote, or even, theoretically, to decide whether it wanted to maintain the Principate. For a few hours following Caligula's death it seemed that the Senate might have had a choice in the matter, unrestricted by dynastic considerations or other pressures. Some senators even flirted with the heady idea of restoring the Republic, although more sensible and realistic were those who wanted the free election of a new emperor with themselves as candidates. They had no choice in the matter because praetorian guardsmen ransacking the palace discovered a genuine, surviving Julio-Claudian, Germanicus' brother and Caligula's uncle Claudius, who was hiding in a closet. So great was their dynastic feeling that they acclaimed him emperor and compelled the Senate to confirm their choice. Although Claudius was not the first to buy military loyalty, his rewarding of the praetorians with a donative set a regrettable precedent for future emperors.

The new emperor was a man of fifty years, an ungainly, unheroic person who limped and slobbered, possibly the victim of a spastic condition or polio. His stepgrandfather, Augustus, who preferred to surround himself with hand-some, decorous people, had largely ignored him while admitting that he might have talent. He had not been taken seriously by the imperial family; he lived in relative obscurity during the reigns of Tiberius and Caligula although the latter allegedly enjoyed playing practical jokes on his foolish-appearing uncle. But Claudius' unprepossessing body sheltered a perceptive mind, and he may well have cultivated the impression he gave of being dull-witted in the interests of his own survival. He was also a fussy and pedantic person. Tutored by Livy as a boy, he was a historian, could read Etruscan, and published several works of Roman and Etruscan history. His least attractive quality was a certain lack of will power, which meant that he was sometimes influenced unduly by stronger personalities around him, especially his wives and freedmen.

GOVERNMENT POLICY. Claudius was conservative in his general policy. Toward the Senate he showed the greatest respect and tried unrealistically to force it to take an independent part in government. He assumed the censorship in 47 for the traditional term of eighteen months, an office Augustus had avoided because its tenure might have seemed too autocratic. In this office he followed the Republican practice and took a colleague. Claudius attempted to check abuses in application of the law of treason and to restrain professional informers. Despite such gestures of good will, many senators and equestrians conspired against him, and were executed on charges of treason. Others fell as a result of cabals concocted by his freedmen and by his last two wives, Messalina and Agrippina, all of whom sought to destroy possible enemies. In the adminis-tration of the treasury and of roads and public works in Rome and Italy, the *princeps* encroached still further on the Senate's sphere of action. Of particular importance was the building of a new harbor with docks and warehouses at Ostia, to improve the handling of the grain supply. The most significant innovation was his conversion of a number of secretaryships, held since Augustus by freedmen in the household of the emperors, into influential ministries of state. Claudius' freedmen functioning in these ministerial posts were able and ambitious men. Pallas, as *a rationibus*, was minister of finance; his rival Narcissus was minister of correspondence (*ab epistulis*). Other ministers were in charge of petitions addressed to the *princeps* (*a libellis*), of judicial investigations or trials he conducted (*a cognitionibus*), and of the imperial library (*a studiis*). Through these positions, freedmen supervised practically all branches of government directed by the *princeps* and so came to have a great influence upon his decisions and policies. Often they abused their power to amass riches by the sale of favors, some of them thus accumulating great fortunes. It was a result of their influence that many freedmen were given appointments as imperial procurators and that the latter officials in the provinces were granted judicial authority in matters affecting the claims of the financial administration.

THE PROVINCES. Following the precedent of Julius Caesar rather than that of Augustus, Claudius decided to annex Britain. In this he was motivated apparently by an exaggerated estimate of the resources of the island and the advisability of popularizing himself with the legions by a successful campaign. There was some justification for the expedition in the fact that the free Belgian tribes of Britain were a potential menace to the peace of Gaul. Conditions in Britain had changed in some ways since the days of Julius Caesar. In the southeast of the island a kingdom had been established by Cunobelinus (Cymbeline, died A.D. 40) with its capital at Camulodunum (Colchester). Although primarily agricultural, this kingdom also developed a lively commerce with the continent, and this trade was steadily improving the standard of living of the British nobility and drawing them toward the orbit of civilization. To the west were tribes composed of descendants of refugees from Caesar's invasion of Gaul. The king of one such tribe, dispossessed by Cymbeline, appealed in Rome to Claudius for reinstatement, the immediate justification for Roman invasion. In 43 the emperor's legates Aulus Plautius, Flavius Vespasianus, and Ostorius Scapula overran Britain as far as the Thames. Claudius himself was in nominal command at the crossing of the Thames and the occupation of Camulodunum, which was made a Roman colony and capital of the province of Britain, formed out of the conquered territory. With the erection of a temple to Rome and Augustus at Camulodunum, the imperial cult was set up in the new province. After the return of Claudius to Rome, Roman authority was extended steadily over wider areas. A frontier was established along the Trent and Severn Rivers, north of which Roman legions occasionally ventured on punitive missions.

In North Africa, Claudius was faced by a revolt that broke out in Mauretania as the result of Gaius' attempt to convert that kingdom into a province. After two years of hard fighting, resistance was crushed and Mauretania was divided into two imperial provinces, Mauretania Caesariensis in the east and Mauretania Tingitana (Tangier) in the west (42). Another new province was formed in 46 by the annexation of Thrace upon the death of the client king. This policy was also carried out in Judaea, which Claudius had placed in 41 under Herod Agrippa, a gesture of reconciliation toward the Jews following the excesses of Caligula and a reward to a personal friend who had been instrumental in securing Claudius' own throne. Upon the death of King Herod in 44, however, the greater part of the country reverted to provincial status and was governed by a procurator.

Throughout the provinces Claudius was active in founding colonies and in promoting the organization of towns as Roman or Latin municipalities. While censor he defended before the Senate, in a speech that has been preserved in part, his liberality in extending Roman citizenship, and apparently he enrolled some Gallic notables in the Senate. He did open the public magistracies to Roman citizens in Gaul, which meant that henceforth they were eligible, as were Romans of Italy, for admission to the senatorial order. Claudius personally paid much attention to provincial administration. Here he showed himself to be a well-meaning ruler, who tried to make his subordinates efficient and honest. His reply—recently found on a papyrus from Egypt—to the petition of the Alexandrians for permission to form a city council throws a favorable light on his statesmanship.

AGRIPPINA THE YOUNGER AND THE DEATH OF CLAUDIUS. In 48 a crisis occurred in the household of the *princeps*. His wife Messalina became infatuated with a young noble Gaius Silius, and it seemed that they were conspiring to have Silius seize the Principate. The freedmen of Claudius felt endangered and decided that Messalina must be removed. Their spokesman Narcissus induced Claudius to have her executed. Then Pallas induced the *princeps* to take as his fourth wife his own niece Agrippina, daughter of Germanicus. (See illustration, p. 242). By Messalina, Claudius had a son, Britannicus, and a daughter, Octavia. The former was regarded as the future successor of Claudius, but Agrippina determined to secure the Principate for her own son Domitius, whose father was her first husband Gnaeus Domitius Ahenobarbus. In 50 she succeeded in having Claudius adopt Domitius with the name of Nero Claudius Caesar. A year later, when he was only thirteen years old, Nero was given the title *princeps iuventutis* and granted proconsular *imperium* outside of Rome. Thus he was designated as the future emperor. In 53 he married Octavia, his sister by adoption. Narcissus still championed the cause of Britannicus, however, and Agrippina, who feared that further delay would endanger her plans, had Claudius poisoned.

XII   Amphitheater at Verona. *Birthplace of the poet Catullus, Verona was a flourishing city in imperial times, a fact attested by many surviving ruins, including this magnificent amphitheater of the first century A.D. (Photo: Fototeca Unione.)*

IV. NERO: A.D. 54–68

FIRST YEARS. The accession of Nero was expected, and his appointment to the Principate was smoothly effected as Agrippina had secured support of the praetorians by the promise of a handsome donative. Nero was only sixteen years old when he succeeded Claudius, and for five years the government was actually carried on by his most influential advisers, the praetorian prefect Afranius Burrus from Gallia Narbonensis and Lucius Annaeus Seneca, the famous philosopher from Spain, whom Agrippina had appointed as his tutor in 49. Under their direction the administration, while strongly autocratic in tone, was efficient and conducted with consideration of the best interests of the Empire. Agrippina did not mean to be excluded from the regency, however, and attempted to regain the influence she had acquired toward the end of Claudius' reign. She was opposed both by Nero and by his advisers, who catered to his baser instincts to keep him under their control. In 55 Nero had his adoptive brother Britannicus poisoned, through fear of his rivalry. Finally, influenced by his mistress, Poppaea Sabina, the wife of Marcus Salvius Otho, he had Agrippina murdered (59). Thereupon he divorced Octavia (later banished and executed) and married Poppaea.

NERO AT THE HELM.   Freed from any rival influence, Nero, now twenty-two years of age, began to run the government. After the death of Burrus in 62, Seneca lost influence over the *princeps*, who took as his chief adviser the syco-phant praetorian prefect, Tigellinus. The Senate, whose support had been courted by Burrus and Seneca, was now without any influence, and, because his wanton extravagances emptied the treasury, Nero resorted to oppressive measures to satisfy his needs. Perhaps his most genuine, and certainly most harmless, interests were whimsically artistic. The senatorial establishment viewed as scandalous his public forays into the theater, where he appeared as a singer and musician in 65. Surviving fragments of his poetry suggest that he may not have been completely without artistic talent. He professed to be a sincere and enthusiastic admirer of Greek civilization, visited Greece, lavishly exempted ancient seats of culture there from taxation, and personally per-formed in athletic and other festivals held at Delphi and Olympia in 66.

FIRE IN ROME AND ITS CONSEQUENCES: A.D. 64: The most famous single event of Nero's reign was the great fire in Rome that broke out in the summer of 64 and devastated two thirds of the city. In this instance Nero played the part of a serious ruler, acting effectively and quickly to care for the survivors and to rebuild the capital. The fire had two important consequences. It resulted in the first known confrontation between Rome and the tiny sect of Christians, who were persecuted for allegedly having started the con-flagration. The fire also permitted Nero to indulge his artistic imagination by constructing a new palace, the Golden House, in the burned-out center of the capital, under the direction of the architect Severus. Nero gave him *carte blanche* to depart radically from standard post-and-lintel building, and the Golden House initiated what was to be a revolutionary new period in Roman architecture.

ARMENIAN PROBLEM: A.D. 51–67.   In 51 an ambitious ruler, Vologases, became Parthian king. When the Roman client king of Armenia was killed by neighboring Iberians, Vologases seized the opportunity to place his brother Tiridates on the Armenian throne. After the accession of Nero, Gnaeus Domitius Corbulo was sent to Asia Minor to reassert Roman suzerainty over Armenia, but not until late in 57 was he able to mobilize his forces. In two campaigns he overran Armenia and set up a Roman puppet as king (60).

Vologases was unable to oppose Corbulo because of a serious domestic rebellion. In 61, however, he set out to reestablish his brother in his lost kingdom. Upon failure of negotiations with Rome, he invaded it, blockaded the Roman governor of Cappadocia, Caesennius Paetus, who tried to anticipate the Parthian attack, and forced him to evacuate Armenian territory (62). The situation was saved by Corbulo, then legate of Syria, who, entrusted with the sole command of operations, forced Vologases to meet Roman terms (63). Tiridates retained the Armenian throne but acknowledged Roman overlordship by coming to Rome to receive his crown from Nero. A much greater potential problem even than Armenia was a rebellion in Palestine that broke out in 66 and was still raging two years later at the time of Nero's death.

REVOLT IN BRITAIN: A.D. 60. Under Claudius the Romans extended their dominion in Britain northward to the Humber and westward to Cornwall and Wales. In 59 Suetonius Paulinus occupied the island of Mona (Anglesea), chief seat of the Druids. While he was so engaged, a serious revolt broke out among the Iceni and Trinovantes, who lived between The Wash and the Thames. It was caused by the severity of Roman administration and in parti-cular by Roman procurators' ill-treatment of Boadicea, queen of the Iceni, who headed the insurrection. The Roman towns of Camulodunum (Colchester), Verulamium (St. Alban's), and Londinium (London) were destroyed, and thousands of Romans killed. A legion was defeated, and not until Paulinus returned and united the scattered Roman forces were the insurgents defeated, Boadicea committing suicide.

CONSPIRACY OF PISO: A.D. 65. About 62 a series of treason trials began in Rome, occasioned partly by the desire to confiscate the property of the accused, partly by suspicion of the emperor. Resulting insecurity among the senatorial order naturally produced a real attempt to overthrow the *princeps*. A wide-reaching conspiracy led by the senator Gaius Calpurnius Piso and involving one of the praetorian prefects, was discovered in 65. Among those executed for complicity were the poet Lucan and his uncle Seneca. Later notable victims of Nero's vengeance were Thrasea Paetus and Barea Soranus, Stoic senators, whose guilt was their silent but unmistakable disapproval of his tyranny. No prominent man was safe; even the general Corbulo was forced to commit suicide in 67. Nero sought to strengthen his position by appointing reliable men to strategic commands, but the loyalty of these very appointees was undermined, since they could easily be persuaded that the erratic emperor might soon threaten them. Their insecurity was to be the cause of Nero's downfall.

REBELLION OF VINDEX: A.D. 68. On Nero's return from Greece, a more serious movement began in Gaul, where Gaius Julius Vindex, legate of Lugdunensis, revolted with support of the provincials, who were suffering from excessive taxation. Vindex was joined by Sulpicius Galba, governor of Hither Spain, who assumed leadership of the revolution and who quickly built up a faction among other legates. The commander of Upper Germany, Verginius

Rufus, disapproved of revolts, because he believed that only an uncoerced Senate should name a *princeps*. After a conference with Vindex, his troops got out of hand and slaughtered the Gauls in his colleague's army. Vindex committed suicide, and Verginius declined the Principate when it was offered him by his officers and troops. Nero found support among the officers of other provincial field armies, but his fate was sealed by his own cowardice and by the treachery of the prefect Nymphidius Sabinus, who bought the support of the praetorian guards for Galba. The Senate followed their lead, and Nero fled from Rome, killing himself with the help of a faithful freedman. With Nero's death the Julio-Claudian dynasty came to an end.

V. YEAR OF THE FOUR EMPERORS: A.D. 68–69

POWER OF THE ARMY. The year 68–69 witnessed the accession of four emperors, each the nominee of powerful factions in the officer cadres of their respective field armies. Up to this time the praetorian guard had already acclaimed emperors. Now, as Tacitus expressed it, the secret of the Empire was discovered, namely, that the *princeps* could be nominated elsewhere than in Rome. The crisis of the Four Emperors' Year was the most serious that the Principate had experienced, because for the first time it was afflicted with civil war. Events of the year also revealed how fragile dynastic practice was because, lacking a dynasty, provincial field marshalls felt free to exploit the loyalty of their own troops, unclaimed by an imperial house, to fulfill their ambitions.

GALBA: A.D. 68. Galba, Nero's successor, was a man of noble family but moderate attainments and soon showed himself unable to maintain his authority. That he would have been held "fit to rule, had he not ruled," was the judgment of Tacitus. He was never enthusiastically supported by the Rhine legions or the praetorians. His severity in maintaining discipline, added to his failure to pay the promised donative, completely alienated the guards. At the news that the troops in Upper and Lower Germany had declared for Aulus Vitellius, legate of the latter province (January 1, 69), Galba sought to strengthen his position by adopting as his son and destined successor, Lucius Calpurnius Piso, a young aristocrat lacking experience. In so doing, he offended Marcus Salvius Otho, the ex-husband of Nero's wife Poppaea Sabina and one of Galba's staunch adherents, who hoped to succeed. Otho now won over the disgruntled praetorian guards, who slew Galba and Piso and proclaimed Otho Imperator.

OTHO: JANUARY–APRIL, A.D. 69. The Senate acquiesced in this decision, but not the legions of Vitellius, already on the march to Italy. They crossed the Alps unopposed but were checked by Otho at Bedriacum, north of the Po. Without waiting for the arrival of reinforcements from the Danubian army, Otho ordered an attack on the Vitellians at Cremona. His army was defeated, and he took his own life.

VITELLIUS: APRIL–DECEMBER, A.D. 69. Vitellius was then recognized as *princeps* by the Senate, and his forces occupied Rome. He owed his nomination to the legates Valens and Caecina, and although well-meaning and by no means tyrannical, he lacked energy and forcefulness. His soldiers got out of control and plundered the Italian towns, and his officers enriched themselves at public expense while he devoted himself to gastronomical pleasures.

Meanwhile the army of the East, which had recognized Galba, Otho, and, at first, Vitellius, set up its own emperor, Titus Flavius Vespasianus, who, as legate of Judaea, was conducting the war against the Jews. Vespasian occupied Egypt, thus cutting off the grain supply, while his ablest lieutenant, Mucianus, set out for Italy. The Danubian legions, which had supported Otho, now declared themselves for Vespasian and, led by Antonius Primus, marched on Italy. The fleet at Ravenna espoused Vespasian's cause, and Caecina, who led the Vitellians against Primus, contemplated treachery. His troops remained loyal, but they were defeated in a bloody night battle at Cremona. Vitellius then opened negotiations and offered to abdicate, but his soldiers would not let him and suppressed a rising in Rome led by Vespasian's brother. The city was then stormed and sacked by the army of Primus, and Vitellius was slain.

VESPASIAN: DECEMBER, A.D. 69. Vespasian obtained his recognition as *princeps* from the Senate and the troops in the West and entered Rome early in 70.

VI. VESPASIAN AND TITUS: A.D. 69–81

THE NEW DYNASTY. Vespasian (Titus Flavius Vespasianus), a crusty old man of sixty when he assumed power, dated his reign from the acclamation by his army, not from the confirmation he duly received by the Senate six months afterward. He established his own dynasty, called Flavian from the name of his clan. His reign marks a new moment in the development of the imperial office. Unlike the ancient, patrician, Julio-Claudians, Vespasian's family hailed from an Italian municipality, Rieti, rather than Rome, and was of only recent senatorial status, Vespasian's own father having been an equestrian tax collector. His accession shows the rewards possible for the Italian gentry built into the Principate by Augustus. Those of upward social mobility broadened support for the imperial regime by catering to the ambitions of a talented class.

REBELLION IN GAUL AND GERMANY: A.D. 69. The new *princeps* inherited two serious wars, both national revolts against Roman rule, one in Gaul and Lower Germany, the other in Judaea. The movement in Lower Germany was headed by Julius Civilis, a Batavian chieftain, formerly a Roman officer, who won over eight Batavian cohorts attached to the Rhine army. The Batavians were disaffected because Roman authorities had recently attempted to reorganize on stricter lines[3] the auxiliary cohorts they had traditionally provided the Roman army. At first Civilis posed as a supporter of Vespasian against Vitellius and besieged the Vitellian garrison at Vetera in the lower

---

[3] The reorganization of auxiliary forces begun by Augustus was not yet complete.

Rhineland, but at the news of the former's victory he renounced his allegiance to Rome and called to his aid Germanic tribes from across the Rhine. Simultaneously the Gallic Treveri and Lingones, the former led by Julius Classicus and Julius Tutor, the latter by Julius Sabinus—both nobles who had served as Roman officers and enjoyed Roman citizenship—revolted and sought to establish a native state with its capital at Trèves (Augusta Trevororum). They were joined by the Roman legions stationed on the Rhine. The remaining Gauls, however, refused to join the revolt, preferring peace to a renewal of old intertribal struggles.

Upon the arrival of an adequate Roman force despatched by Mucianus, Vespasian's representative in Rome, the mutinous legions returned to duty, the Treveri and Lingones were subdued, and Civilis was forced to flee into Germany. The Batavi again became Roman allies (70), and the auxiliary forces they furnished the Roman army were henceforth led and organized along lines originally established for *auxilia* by Augustus.

FRICTION IN JUDAEA. From the year A.D. 6 Judaea had been a Roman province, except for its brief incorporation in the principality of Herod Agrippa I (41–44). During this time Jews had occupied a privileged position among Rome's subjects, being exempted from military service and the obligation of the imperial cult, despite Caligula's abortive efforts to the contrary. These privileges were a constant source of friction between Jews and Greco-Syrian inhabitants of Palestine, frequently necessitating intercession by Roman officials. Another cause of unrest in Judaea was the pressure of taxation, which rendered agriculture unprofitable and drove many persons from plains to the mountains where they became brigands. A more deep-seated cause of animosity to Roman rule was the Jewish notion of a religious community, for them national loyalty being identical with an uncompromising devotion to their religion. They resented the rule of foreigners, not merely because it meant loss of political freedom but because it was an offense to their religion. The situation was not helped by incompetence and tactlessness of Roman officials whose actions often needlessly wounded Jewish susceptibilities. The Jews themselves were not united. There were groups of various religious attitudes, like the Essenes, some of whose Dead Sea scrolls have survived. In addition, there was an upper class of wealthy landholders and also a lower class that included many impoverished peasants. The former were the party of the Sadducees, who monopolized higher religious offices, including that of the High Priest. Opposed to them were the Pharisees, who held most of the lower priesthoods and laid great stress on strict observance of Jewish law in all its aspects. In general, the Sadducees were inclined to cooperate with the Romans, who in turn supported them, whereas the Pharisees were strongly nationalistic and anti-Roman. It is improbable that the Pharisees actually wished to bring about a revolt, but they set in motion events they could not control and strengthened the development of a party of extremists, the Zealots, who aimed to liberate Judaea from the Romans by force, trusting in the support of Yahweh. By 66 all Judaea was in a ferment, and it required little incitement to produce a revolt.

THE JEWISH REBELLION: A.D. 66–70.   Hostilities broke out in 66 in Jerusalem, where the Roman garrison was driven out by the rebels. Simultaneously, a decision by Rome that Jews were not entitled to citizenship in Caesarea, the capital of the province, provoked a riot in which the Greek population massacred the Jews. Similar outbreaks occurred in other towns of Judaea, now one party now the other being the aggressor, and the disorders spread to Syria and Egypt. The Romans realized the situation was serious when the legate of Syria, Cestius Gallus, who had marched on Jerusalem, was forced to retreat hastily.

Late in 67 Vespasian was appointed to command an army of 50,000 assembled for the reconquest of Judaea. In this and the following year he reduced the open country and isolated fortresses and prepared to blockade Jerusalem, where most Jews had taken refuge. Upon hearing of Nero's death, he postponed his attack on the city and did not resume active operations until Vitellius' accession. Shortly afterward, however, his own elevation to the Principate caused a further suspension of hostilities for ten months, during which factional strife raged fiercely in the city.

Vespasian entrusted the conclusion of the war to his son Titus, who at once began the siege of Jerusalem (70). The city had a triple line of fortifications, and within the inner wall were two natural citadels, the temple and the old city of Mount Zion. The population, swollen by many refugees, suffered terribly from hunger but resisted furiously. Experience and numbers told; the walls were stormed, and the Romans forced their way into the temple, which was destroyed by fire. Mount Zion still held out but finally was stormed. Jerusalem was destroyed, and Judaea became a province under an imperial legate. The political community of the Jews was dissolved, and they were subjected to a yearly head tax of two denarii each, payable to the temple of Jupiter Capitolinus, in consideration of which they enjoyed their previous immunities. Titus commemorated his victory by the arch which still stands near the Forum. One of its reliefs represents the spoils from the temple, carried in the triumphal procession at Rome.

VESPASIAN'S ADMINISTRATION.   In order to establish a link between his family and the Julio-Claudian line, Vespasian followed the example of Galba, Otho, and Vitellius in assuming the name of Caesar, which was becoming a title rather than a family name. Thereafter its use became a prerogative of the imperial family. He also made regular use of Imperator at the beginning of his titles, a practice neglected under the successors of Augustus but revived in the later years of Nero.

Vespasian has sometimes been called the "second founder of the Roman Empire" by virtue of his success in pulling together the administrative and military machinery of government shaken so severely by Nero's excesses and subsequent revolution. As ruler he was thrifty and industrious, insistent on maintaining the respect due his office yet also capable of indulging a sometimes vulgar sense of humor, which betrayed his comparatively rustic origins.

To the Senate, Vespasian accorded respect and recognition of its judicial authority, but he excluded it from any effective participation in government. In 73 he assumed the censorship with Titus as his colleague and took a census, simultaneously filling the ranks of the Senate, depleted by executions and recent civil wars. He took this opportunity of introducing into the Senate many distinguished provincials, of making extensive grants of citizenship in the provinces, and of bestowing Latin status upon all non-Roman communities in Spain, as a step preliminary to Romanization. At first some senators tried to assert some control over policy, but their efforts were cut short, as was an attempt to prosecute informers who had flourished under Nero. Very soon most of the Senate was reconciled to the situation, and subsequent friction between Vespasian and certain groups was entirely caused by their intransigent attitude. One of these groups, led by Helvidius Priscus, son-in-law of the Thrasea Paetus whom Nero had executed and like him a Stoic, indulged in advocacy of republicanism in a cult of Brutus and Cato the Younger. Priscus even abused and insulted the *princeps* publicly and was therefore exiled. Subsequently he was executed, probably for conspiracy. Another group of philosophers, apparently Cynics rather than Stoics, was so violent in its attacks, not only upon the *princeps* and the Principate but upon government in general, that Vespasian banished professional astrologers and philosophers from the capital.

Vespasian set about making the nearly bankrupt state solvent again by raising new taxes, which were apparently absorbed easily by the expanding economy, and by managing revenues more efficiently. To do so he established, under imperial procurators at Rome, new treasuries to which flowed revenues from rich provinces like Asia and Egypt. He also carried out extensive building operations in Italy and the provinces. In Rome the Capitoline Temple, burned in the fighting with the Vitellians, was rebuilt, a temple of Peace was erected on the Forum, and the Colosseum arose on the site of a lake within Nero's Golden House. Vespasian also granted state subsidies to teachers of Greek and Roman oratory in Rome.

Another problem was the restoration of military discipline. It has been seen, in connection with repression of the revolt in Germany, how the dangers of national loyalties among auxiliaries were averted by tighter organization. It remained to deal with citizen soldiers. Four mutinous legions from the Rhineland garrison were disbanded and replaced by new ones. The praetorian guard, dissolved by Vitellius and replaced by detachments drawn from his legionaries, was reconstituted with cohorts of Italians as before. In order to assure himself of its loyalty, Vespasian appointed his son Titus as prefect.

PROVINCES AND FRONTIERS. The emperor's efficiency and honesty were reflected in the provincial officials he appointed and in the tone of provincial government. He deprived Greece of the tax-free status Nero had granted and made it again a senatorial province, while Sardinia and Corsica reverted to imperial control. Rhodes, Samos, and Byzantium lost their status of free and federate communities and were incorporated in adjacent provinces. A new province was formed in Lycia and Pamphylia in Asia Minor. Most changes probably were made to increase imperial revenues, but there were others that showed Vespasian's care for frontier defense. The Roman hold on Britain was strengthened by the conquest of the Brigantes north of the Humber River and the Silures in southern Wales. Roman influence was reasserted among German tribes on the right bank of the lower Rhine. In upper Germany Vespasian annexed the territory between the Rhine and the upper Danube, including the Schwarzwald and Odenwald areas, thus obliterating a dangerous salient in the frontier and shortening communications between the armies in Germany and on the Danube. The exposed boundary between Rhine and Danube was soon fortified by his successors.

Further east on the Danube two camps for legionary troops were constructed at Carnuntum and Vindobona (modern Vienna). The Euphrates frontier was strengthened by the creation of a single large province embracing Galatia, Cappadocia, and some adjacent districts, as well as by the establishment of Roman garrisons at strategic Satala and Melitene, which controlled routes across the upper Euphrates into Armenia. To the south the client kingdom of Commagene, which Caligula had restored to its native dynasty, was added to Syria. Syria was further enlarged by extension of its eastern frontier to include several minor principalities, probably including the caravan city of Palmyra. In Africa, a brief campaign sufficed to quiet the Garamantes, who had disturbed Roman territory to the south of the Gulf of Syrtis.

PRINCIPATE OF TITUS: A.D. 79–81. On the death of Vespasian, Titus was not only praetorian prefect but also his father's colleague in the *imperium* and tribunician authority. This made his succession a matter of course, and without delay he received the powers and honors of the Principate from the Senate. During his rule of little over two years, he showed himself worthy of his high office. He repressed professional informers, and, despite his generosity, kept careful watch on finances.

Two great disasters marred his otherwise uneventful principate. In 79 an eruption of Vesuvius buried the cities of Pompeii, Herculaneum, and Stabii near the Bay of Naples beneath a thick deposit of ash and lava. Thus protected, these towns have been preserved to a remarkable degree, and the excavation of Pompeii in particular has revealed with wonderful freshness an Italian municipality of the early Principate. In the following year Rome was once more devastated by fire, which raged for three days and destroyed Vespasian's new temple of Jupiter Capitolinus.

Titus died following an attack of fever in September 81. He was mourned by the Roman world, his memory treasured as that of an ideal *princeps*. Like Vespasian, he received posthumous deification from the Senate.

VII. DOMITIAN: A.D. 81–96

AUTOCRATIC IDEALS. Titus was succeeded by his younger brother, Domitian, who was saluted as Imperator by the praetorians and received from the Senate without opposition the powers and titles of the Principate on September 14, 81. Domitian had not been given any active share in government by either Vespasian or Titus. From the beginning of his principate he displayed increasingly strong autocratic tendencies. He held numerous consulships and, in addition, a perpetual censorship (*censor perpetuus*) from 85 onward. His outlook becomes clear in the title "Lord and God" (*dominus et deus*), which was used unofficially but publicly by officers of the imperial household, by contemporary writers, and even by the emperor himself. He seems also to have made an oath by the genius of the *princeps* obligatory in certain public documents. The same tendencies found expression in his establishment of the priestly college of *Flaviales*, modeled on that of the *Augustales* in Rome, to perpetuate the worship of his deified father and brother. It was abundantly clear that he intended to keep the Senate subservient and to control the government completely. Such a course inevitably provoked hostility among the nobility, which also resented his philhellenic leanings, evidenced in the establishment of a festival in honor of Capitoline Jupiter in imitation of the Olympic Games and in other Greek practices.

RETURN OF THE TERROR. In the winter of 88–89 Antonius Saturninus, the legate of Upper Germany, was hailed emperor by the two legions under his command at Mogontiacum (Mainz). He counted on the adherence of other provincial commanders and on aid from the German Chatti, who invaded Roman territory on the right bank of the Rhine. The Germans were unable to cross the river owing to the breakup of ice that had temporarily bridged it, and Saturninus was defeated and killed by the governor of Lower Germany, who remained loyal to the emperor. Alarmed at the outbreak, Domitian punished relentlessly all those suspected of complicity in the conspiracy. Fearful of other plots, he began to suspect leading senators and officers and listened to false accusations made by informers. Thus began another reign of terror for the nobility, which not only made them hate him and his works but also strongly biased the attitude of the historian Tacitus toward the Principate and its founder. Philosophers were banished again from Italy; many prominent persons were executed on charges of treason, others because of "atheism." Among the latter were some notable converts to Judaism or Christianity, whose beliefs ran counter to Domitian's leanings toward deification. His own cousin, Flavius Clemens, fell victim to this charge; and the latter's wife, Domitilla, a niece of Domitian, who, if not an active Christian, was at least a patron of Christians in Rome, was exiled.

ADMINISTRATION. Domitian cannot be dismissed as a mere tyrant. He was an energetic administrator who personally directed all branches of government and required of his subordinates high standards of public service. Of

XIII Aqua Claudia near Rome. *This aqueduct, one of the principal ones of ancient Rome, is a typical feat of Roman architectural engineering using arches and was built in A.D. 47 at the behest of the emperor Claudius. (Photo: Fototeca Unione.)*

special interest was his probable reorganization of the military supply service in which a central headquarters, the *castra peregrinorum*, was set up at Rome for couriers and supply officials going to and from the capital and legionary headquarters. These couriers, the *frumentarii*, were shortly to take on subsidiary functions as secret service agents. Domitian also used mounted units at the capital, the *equites singulares*, recruited from noncitizens of the Rhine-Danube frontier areas and serving as a personal bodyguard.

In Rome, he improved the water system, increased the facilities for storing grain and other provisions, and completed reconstruction necessitated by the great fire of 80. This gave him the opportunity to rebuild the temple of Capitoline Jupiter on a magnificent scale and to restore the damaged public libraries, in which he was particularly interested. He also completed other unfinished structures and built new ones. Among them were the temple of Vespasian and Titus and another of the Flavian Gens. At the Alban lake he built a costly villa. The urban populace was kept content with shows and distributions of money, while the pay of the soldiers was increased by one third, an increase that scarcely compensated the troops for inflation. These expenditures, added to the costs of border wars, strained the treasury. Domitian, who took over a financially sound state, was liberal in money matters and at first remitted unpaid taxes of five years' standing. He was no spendthrift, however, and insisted upon strict collection of future public revenues. His persecution of the senators has been blamed on his desire to increase his income by confiscating property of the condemned, but on the whole these judicial murders seem to have been political rather than economic.

Domitian's legislation was tinged with severe, old-fashioned morality. He restricted the performance of mimes and farces, tried to suppress vice, and made it more difficult for slaves to obtain freedom. He enforced the death penalty for Vestal Virgins convicted of adultery and in one case revived the antiquated form of punishment by burying alive. Such cruelty shocked public opinion, all the more since the *princeps* himself had a niece as his mistress. In spite of his use of informers, he punished many who brought unfounded accusations, along with the writers of defamatory or scurrilous attacks upon prominent persons. During his reign, the administration of justice was largely freed from bribery and partiality.

In the provinces Domitian pushed the work of Romanization his father had undertaken. As governors and other provincial officers, he tried to select honest men with the result that the provinces flourished under his rule. He favored small farmers by granting freehold possession to those established on odd lots of land not included in the regular surveys, but his attempt to check the spread of vineyards by forbidding the planting of new ones in Italy and the transformation of one half of those in the provinces into grain land was an unsound venture in agricultural legislation. It does not seem to have been enforced rigorously, although the newer winelands of Gaul and the Danubian provinces may have been affected by it.

DEFENSE OF THE EMPIRE. Although he did not depart radically from Augustan precepts of nonexpansion, Domitian realized the value of military success as a support for autocracy, and he carried on a vigorous frontier policy. In Africa, a revolt of the Nasamones in eastern Tripoli ended with their annihilation (85–86), and energetic action was taken against other nomads in Mauretania who resented the Roman policy of fostering argiculture at the expense of pasturage. More important was the expansion in Britain directed by the legate Julius Agricola, who commanded the province from 77 to 84.

After seizing the island of Mona (Anglesea), and completing the subjugation of northern England, Agricola led his armies deep into Scotland. In the mountainous country beyond the Clyde and the Firth of Forth, he defeated the Caledonians under their chief Calgacus (84). His fleet, skirting the coast, sailed around the north of Scotland and reaffirmed the fact, discovered centuries before by a Greek navigator, that Britain was an island. With the northern frontier of Britain secured, Agricola was recalled before he could carry out a projected invasion of Ireland.

The military situation on the Rhine frontier required concentrated effort. In 83, Domitian himself led an army across the Rhine from Mogontiacum and campaigned successfully against the Chatti, who were stirring up trouble locally. The Romans occupied Wetterau between the Lahn and Main rivers as far as the crest of the Taunus mountains and protected it by a chain of forts and watchtowers. During the revolt of Saturninus (89), the Chatti overran part of this area, but the Roman frontier was reestablished when the rebellion was put down. It was the experience with Saturninus that led Domitian to adopt the policy of not quartering more than one legion in any permanent frontier camp. At the same time he separated the financial administration of the two German provinces from that of Gallia Belgica, with which it had hitherto been united. Between the Upper Rhine and the Danube, Domitian advanced the line of forts to shorten and strengthen the frontier and communications in the angle of the two rivers.

Powerful tribes faced the Romans across the middle and lower Danube, and in dealing with them Domitian was less successful than on the Rhine. These were the Germanic Marcomanni and Quadi in Bohemia, the Sarmatian Iazyges between the Danube and Theiss, and the Dacians, who occupied the greater portion of modern Hungary and Rumania. Of all these, the Dacians were the most dangerous, for they had been welded together by an able king, Decebalus. In 85 a Dacian band crossed the Danube into Moesia, where they defeated and killed the governor. Domitian brought reinforcements and drove the invaders back across the river. In attempting to invade Dacia, however, the praetorian prefect Cornelius Fuscus suffered a disastrous defeat, in which he and most of his army perished. In 88 a new Roman general, Tattius Julianus, was more successful and won a signal victory. At this point the Marcomanni, Quadi, and Iazyges, who previously had been friendly to Rome, revolted. Domitian again took the field, invaded their territory, and met with a reverse that forced him to resort to diplomacy. He came to terms with Decebalus, who gave up his prisoners of war and formally acknowledged the overlordship of Rome but received in return an annual subsidy and the services of Roman engineers (89). This treaty enabled Domitian to enjoy the honor of a double triumph, over the Dacians and Chatti, and to concentrate his attention on the Iazyges and their German neighbors. It was not until 93 that order was reestablished along the middle Danube. For the moment, Domitian succeeded in relieving the Danubian provinces of barbarian pressure, but his settlement was to prove only temporary. In the course of the Dacian war, the province of Moesia was divided in two, Upper and Lower Moesia.

DOMITIAN'S ASSASSINATION. The closing years of Domitian's rule were occupied largely with the trials of suspected conspirators. No one, whatever his rank, seemed safe. In self-defense, some of those on his blacklist decided to anticipate their own execution by striking first. A plot was formed in which his wife Domitia and the two praetorian prefects were leaders, and on September 18, 96, he was killed by an assassin's dagger. His memory was cursed by an exultant Senate, and his name was erased from public monuments.

VIII. THE PRINCIPATE IN THEORY AND PRACTICE

At the death of Domitian the Principate had been in existence for 123 years. During this period, with the exception of parts of the years 68 and 69, it was ruled by two dynasties: the Julio-Claudian and the Flavian. This reveals clearly the strength of dynastic loyalty and the desire of emperors to found or to perpetuate a dynasty, which was voiced by Vespasian when he declared that either his sons should succeed him or no one. In the face of these tendencies it was impossible for the Senate to exercise any freedom of choice in the selection of a new appointee. Its role was virtually limited to conferring appropriate powers and honors upon a candidate chosen by forces beyond its control. Application of the dynastic principle did not prove a thoroughly satisfactory basis for the selection of emperors, since it produced such unworthy and incompetent rulers as Caligula and Nero, as well as the oppressive autocrat Domitian.

Another grave weakness was the absence of any constitutional means of removing an unsatisfactory *princeps*. His powers were conferred upon him for life, and so long as he had the support of the praetorian guard and the rest of the military, he could defy any attempt to depose him. The only recourse was conspiracy leading to assassination or open rebellion resulting in civil wars between troops stationed in different provinces. A certain standard of efficiency, justice, and personal conduct came to be regarded as essential in a *princeps*, and failure to measure up to it endangered his life, or, at least, led to withholding posthumous honors by the Senate. The judgment of senators, who voiced the opinion of the governing classes, when not overridden by the succeeding *princeps*, may be taken as evidence of the degree to which each emperor met the exacting requirements of his office as set by Augustus and confirmed by public opinion. When Augustus, Claudius, Vespasian, and Titus received deification after death, it meant that they had exercised their powers constitutionally. When, on the contrary, the Senate formally execrated the memory of Nero and Domitian,[4] it expressed the view that their actions had been unconstitutional. It did not

---

[4] Caligula was never officially condemned.

mean, however, a blanket invalidation of their acts, since this would have led to unnecessary confusion and uncertainty in law and administration. When Tiberius, Galba, Otho, and Vitellius received neither deification nor execration, the Senate was refusing to endorse but was not prepared openly to condemn them, an attitude easily understood in view of the short principates of the latter three.

It had become clear, however, that even under a constitutional principate the *princeps* himself must be the ruler and that there was no room for independent action by the Senate and magistrates. This realization was responsible at times for resentment by some senators, who engaged in a pointless criticism of the Principate as a form of government and personal attacks on certain emperors, thus provoking retaliation. The Principate could not be abolished, and more was to be gained by loyal support of a constitutional *princeps* than by hostile noncooperation. For the Empire as a whole, the new form of government had proved to be generally beneficial .

CHAPTER 18
ROMAN PEACE AND
THE MILITARIZATION
OF THE GOVERNMENT:
A.D. 96–235

The period between the death of Domitian in 96 and that of Severus Alexander in 235 falls into two parts. During the first of these, which closes with the death of Marcus Aurelius in 180, the Roman Empire reached its maximum territorial extent, population, and material prosperity. This was due to a combination of internal peace and well-intentioned government, which produced for the Mediterranean area an otherwise unexampled degree of security and well-being to the extent that this epoch has been looked upon as the golden age of Roman imperialism. In the latter part of the period, these enviable conditions were disturbed by oppression, by a renewal of civil war between the armies, and by economic difficulties, all of which produced a crisis. Unfortunately, no adequate literary narrative exists for either part of the period. Of Cassius Dio's great work, which ran to 222, all that survives are parts of the last two books, while for the rest there is only an epitome made in the eleventh century. The only even relatively contemporary history that has survived was written by another Greek, Herodian, who, shortly before 250, composed a narrative for the years 180 to 238. A series of imperial biographies, beginning with Hadrian's, is supplied by the fourth-century compilation known as the *Augustan History* (*Historia Augusta*). For the period in question the *Lives* in this collection contain much worthless material. Of considerable worth are the *Letters* of Pliny the Younger, which contain his correspondence during his governorship of Bithynia in 111–113. Finally there are late epitomes and brief biographical collections, also valuable for the earlier period of the Principate. Owing to the relative dearth of literary evidence, we must rely all the more on contemporary inscriptions, papyri, coins, and material remains in order to gain even a reasonably complete picture of the civilization of the Roman Empire at its height.

I. NERVA: A.D. 96–98

NERVA'S ACCESSION. Before assassinating Domitian, those involved in the conspiracy had selected a successor acceptable to the Senate. Their choice was Marcus Cocceius Nerva, a leading senator, distantly related on his mother's side to the Julio-Claudian line. Nerva was sixty years old and had had a distinguished public career without, however, any military experience that might have won him the support of the soldiery, among whom Domitian was very popular. Nevertheless, when the Senate appointed him *princeps*, the provincial officer cadres acquiesced in their action. The praetorians, whose prefects had taken part in Domitian's assassination, were temporarily pacified by a donative. The policy of the new *princeps* contrasted with his predecessor's. He won the confidence of the nobility by taking an oath never to execute a senator and by suspending the operation of laws against high treason. He recalled political exiles and philosophers and permitted victims of informers to prosecute them

NERVA AND ITALY. During his brief rule Nerva, because of his previous experience and because he wished to consolidate support for his regime, displayed a much greater interest in Italy than in the provinces. Immunity from the 5 per cent inheritance tax was extended more widely than heretofore, an improvement was made in the method of adjudicating controversies between the treasury and subjects, and an agrarian law provided for a distribution of lands to needy citizens. Nerva also established a relief system for poor farmers and the children of paupers. This scheme was extended by succeeding emperors.

SELECTION OF A COLLEAGUE AND SUCCESSOR. Despite its honesty and respect for constitutional practice, Nerva's government failed to win the prestige necessary to keep the praetorian guard under control. In 97 the guard mutinied and killed several of those who had taken part in Domitian's assassination. After this it was clear that the old, ailing, and childless *princeps* could save his authority and his life only by adopting as successor a man who could discipline the praetorians and receive the unanimous support of the legions, whose loyalty to Nerva was more than suspect. Nerva formally adopted as his son Marcus Ulpius Traianus, a tried legate commanding Upper Germany. From the Senate, Trajan received the title of Caesar marking him as Nerva's prospective successor, together with tribunician authority and proconsular *imperium*, which made him virtually a colleague of the *princeps*. Three months later, on January 25, 98, Nerva died peacefully in Rome, and a grateful Senate added his name to those of his deified predecessors. Nerva was well-intentioned but weak. The most important event of his reign was his adoption of Trajan. By designating such a successor, he probably prevented the outbreak of a civil war on the part of field commanders, which could have rivalled in gravity the events of 68–69.

II. TRAJAN: A.D. 98–117

A PROVINCIAL AS PRINCEPS. Upon the death of Nerva, Trajan automatically became emperor. At first he spent some two years touring the strategic northern frontiers to insure their security, to reorganize their defense, and to show himself to the troops and consolidate support among their commanders. A native of the Roman colony of Italica in Farther Spain, whose father had been a distinguished senator, he was the first *princeps* of provincial origin. His appointment indicates the declining dominance of the strictly Italian element within the Empire and the emergence of a new imperial nobility of wealthy provincials who had won recognition in imperial service. Trajan himself possessed unusual qualifications for his office. A bluff, hearty, uncomplicated man, he won rapturous praise from leading senators, like Pliny the Younger. His military training had been unusually thorough. He was a general of outstanding merit, and his main interest was military. He was also an energetic and conscientious administrator who kept himself well informed on governmental problems and displayed sound judgment in dealing with them. From the outset he was a firm ruler. The praetorian guard was brought under control, and senatorial governors who had taken advantage of Nerva's inertia to abuse their office were tried before the Senate. There was no suspicion of tyranny. Trajan repeated Nerva's oath not to condemn to death a senator and rejected all ceremonies and customs associated with deification.

BENEVOLENT PATERNALISM. In Italy, Trajan extended the system of relief to children of the poor, a step first taken by private patrons in the case of municipalities and made public policy by Nerva. The government made loans to landholders at low interest rates, and income from this source was paid to municipal authorities, who used it to support needy boys and girls. At the same time in Rome 5,000 children were granted the right to share the public distributions of grain. The primary purpose of this scheme seems to have been to check a decline in the population of Italy by encouraging parents to raise more children. The farm loans were also a stimulus to Italian agriculture, and in general the government seems to have been trying to combat a threatened economic decline in Italy.

Another example of Trajan's benevolent paternalism is to be seen in his attempt to rehabilitate municipal finances. Some Italian municipalities became heavily indebted because of mismanagement of public funds and extravagant building programs. To help them out of their difficulties, the *princeps* appointed commissioners called curators to direct or advise them. This practice was not limited to Italy but extended to provincial towns as well. In special cases imperial officials were empowered to deal with finances over wide areas, like the commissioner entrusted with the task of restoring order in the free cities of Achaea. For a time Trajan took over the administration of Bithynia from the Senate, and sent out Pliny as his legate to end confusion in the administration of municipalities there.

Trajan also showed concern for provincial welfare by improving communications through extensive repairs to existing highways and the construction of new ones. Some of the latter were designed primarily to serve military purposes, but they also proved advantageous to trade and travel. He reorganized the state postal system (*cursus publicus*) by placing at its head an equestrian *praefectus vehiculorum*. Use of the highways by officials became much more frequent during his reign. In addition to roads, the *princeps* built many other useful public works such as aqueducts, bridges, canals, and harbor facilities. Rome also was the scene of numerous and costly building operations (see illustration, p. 311), the most notable being the construction of a magnificent forum named after Trajan himself. The generosity of the *princeps* was revealed further in his liberal treatment of citizens of the capital. He rebuilt the harbor works at Ostia, where grain for the city was unloaded, and subsidized millers and bakers. His public distributions of money (*congiaria*) made on three successive occasions were lavish, and the entertainments he provided to celebrate his victories were unprecedented in duration and splendor. Those given in 107 to mark final victory over the Dacians lasted 126 days, which were taken up largely with gladiatorial combats and wild-beast hunts.

AGGRESSIVE IMPERIALISM: DACIAN WARS. In his foreign policy Trajan broke with precepts laid down by Augustus at the end of his reign, and, confident in his own leadership and the strength of imperial armies, he reverted to aggressive imperialism. His first objective was Dacia, for Domitian's agreement with Decebalus was regarded as unsatisfactory, because a strong Dacia perpetually menaced the peace of the lower Danubian provinces. The immediate cause of hostilities is unknown, but in 101 Trajan personally led an invasion of Dacia. He was opposed vigorously by King Decebalus, a valiant opponent. In his first campaign Trajan failed to obtain a decisive result, but in 102 he penetrated the heart of Dacia and forced Decebalus to make peace. The Dacian king gave up the technicians he had received from Domitian, together with his military machines, acknowledged Roman overlordship, and promised military service to the Empire. Trajan returned to Rome and

XIV Market of Trajan at Rome. *A work of public utility built into a flank of the Quirinal hill near Trajan's forum, it was very probably built by the brilliant architect and engineer Apollodorus of Damascus, a favorite of Trajan. (Photo: Fototeca Unione.)*

celebrated his victory with a triumph. At his orders a permanent stone bridge was built across the Danube below the Iron Gates to communicate with the northern bank. Decebalus was not content to remain a Roman vassal and prepared to recover his independence. In 105 he provoked resumption of war by attacking the Iazyges, who were Roman allies. This was followed by annihilation of the small Roman garrisons left in Dacia. Trajan left Rome for

the front, where he held the Dacians in check while he mobilized a force for a new offensive and won the allegiance of neighboring tribes who had joined Decebalus. The following year he invaded Dacia for the second time. His victory in 106 was complete. The Dacian capital was taken, and Decebalus committed suicide. Dacians who did not surrender or abandon their country were hunted down and exterminated. Dacia was made a province and was peopled with settlers from different parts of the Empire, particularly from Asia Minor and Syria. From the Dacian gold mines, placed under imperial control, came a steady income that helped materially to meet the increased governmental expenditure occasioned by Trajan's policies. The occupation of Dacia was significant because the Romans now had a bulwark protecting the provinces south of the Danube and a vantage point for controlling tribes both east and west of the new province. To commemorate his Dacian wars, Trajan erected a stone column over 100 feet high in his new forum. The column, still in place, is decorated with a spiral band of sculptured reliefs vividly depicting the successive campaigns.

In North Africa, Trajan continued the policy of his predecessors. He advanced the southern frontier of Numidia to the Sahara and thus opened up much new land for agricultural settlement. Desert tribes were held in check by stationing the provincial legionary garrison at Lambaesis, near where the colony of Thamugadi (Timgad) was founded.

INVASION OF PARTHIA. Even during his preoccupation with Dacia, Trajan found time to devote attention to the Eastern frontier. In 105, he ordered the governor of Syria to annex the kingdom of the Nabataean Arabs, which lay to the southeast of Syria and Palestine. This task was carried out easily, and the occupied territory was organized as the province of Arabia (106). Possession of the region gave the Romans control of caravan routes leading from the Arabian coast of the Red Sea northward to Damascus and the harbors of Syria.

Much more serious was Trajan's attempt to apply to the Armenian and Mesopotamian frontiers the methods that had proved successful on the Lower Danube. The opportunity came in about 110, when the Parthian king Osroes deposed the Armenian ruler, a Roman client, and appointed as king another member of the Parthian royal house without consulting the Roman emperor, thus breaking the arrangement that had preserved peace between Rome and Parthia since the time of Nero. Trajan, knowing that the Parthians had negotiated with Decebalus, determined to take advantage of this infringement of Rome's rights in Armenia to effect a settlement of frontier difficulties on a new basis. Leaving Rome in the autumn of 113, he proceeded to the East and invaded Armenia the following summer at the head of a large army. Little resistance was encountered, the Armenian king was removed, and his country was made an imperial province. From Armenia, Trajan led his forces into upper Mesopotamia, where the rulers of several petty states either acknowledged his overlordship or fled. After the Roman occupation of Armenia, this region for strategic reasons could not be left in Parthian hands, and it, too, became a province. Leaving garrisons in newly won territories, Trajan withdrew to winter in Antioch (115–116). After his conquest of Armenia he added the name Optimus to his official titles. The lack of opposition thus far encountered decided Trajan to complete the conquest of Mesopotamia. In the spring of 116 he opened his offensive with an attack on Adiabene, on the left bank of the Tigris whose king remained loyal to Parthia. Adiabene fell easily, and from it was formed another province, Assyria. The way was now open to the Parthian capital, Ctesiphon, which surrendered at the approach of the Emperor. During the winter of 115–116, Trajan sailed down the Tigris from here to the head of the Persian Gulf, and then returned to Babylon. There he learned that Assyria and Mesopotamia were in revolt and that Parthian armies were advancing on Assyria and Armenia. The situation was dangerous for the Romans. They had overrun rather than conquered the annexed lands because Osroes was engaged in suppressing revolts among his own people and could not spare troops to oppose them. Now he attempted recovery of his lost dominions. Trajan and his generals proved equal to the emergency. After some initial defeats, the Roman armies recovered control of both northern and southern Mesopotamia. Adiabene was lost, however, and the Parthian invasion of Armenia was checked only by the surrender of part of the country. Trajan felt that it would be too difficult to hold on to southern Mesopotamia, so he turned it over to a Parthian noble who had deserted to the Romans and who was crowned at Ctesiphon as king of Parthia. Trajan himself withdrew to Antioch.

The partial surrender of Roman conquests was largely due to a serious rebellion of Jews in the Eastern provinces. This began in Cyrenaica in 115 and spread rapidly to Cyprus, Egypt, Palestine, and Mesopotamia. The movement was caused by Messianic Jewish yearnings and was actually led by a Jewish "king." It was waged against their Hellenic or Hellenized neighbors and their gods, but developed also into a challenge to Roman authority, particularly after the Parthian successes of 116. In the course of the war, Jews and Greeks perpetrated horrible atrocities on one another. Trajan acted promptly, and the rebels were ruthlessly suppressed. Order was restored everywhere except in Egypt, where fighting continued to rage under Trajan's successor.

DEATH OF TRAJAN. In the early summer of 117 Trajan prepared for another campaign in Mesopotamia to support his appointee to the Parthian throne, who was unable to maintain his position. Worn out by his strenuous exertions of the preceding three years, however, he fell ill and left Antioch for Rome. On the way he died at Selinus in Cilicia about August 9, 117. On his deathbed he adopted as his son his younger relative and one-time ward, Publius Aelius Hadrianus, whom he had left in command in the East. Trajan's conduct and achievements in war and peace alike caught the imagination of the Romans and caused his memory to be treasured through the following centuries.

He proved to be a model emperor, Optimus Princeps, to such an extent that hundreds of years later senators were still acclaiming new rulers with the wish that they would be "more fortunate than Augustus and even better than Trajan."

III. HADRIAN: A.D. 117–138

HADRIAN'S ACCESSION. When the report of Hadrian's adoption reached the army in Syria, the soldiers immediately saluted him as Imperator. He at once assumed the power and titles of the Principate, and when the news reached Rome the Senate could only accept the accomplished fact and confirm him in his authority. Hadrian's family also came from Italica in Spain although he seems to have been born in Italy. He was a son of a cousin of Trajan's, and had married Sabina, a granddaughter of Trajan's sister Marciana.

Perhaps the most interesting of all the emperors as a person, Hadrian was a very different kind of man from his predecessor, moody, impressionable, an artist and intellectual, a first-rate poet and architect, and an even more enthusiastic and genuine admirer of Greek civilization than Nero. It seems that Trajan and Hadrian were personally incompatible, since the late emperor had not distinguished the younger man by granting him much power during his own lifetime. Rumors were even current at the time of his accession that the notice of his adoption by Trajan on his deathbed was a fiction invented by Trajan's widow, Plotina, who was Hadrian's partisan. The new *princeps* was an experienced soldier and enjoyed the loyal support and confidence of the army, so that he appears to have been the logical choice to follow his countryman in the Principate. The only opposition seems to have come from a small faction of Trajan's generals who were Hadrian's rivals and may have resented his abandonment of Trajan's policies. Four outstanding members of this group, among them the noted Moorish cavalry leader Lusius Quietus, were accused of conspiring against Hadrian in 118 and condemned to death by the Senate, even before the *princeps* returned to Italy. Hadrian made an unusually generous donation to the soldiers upon his accession. When he arrived in Rome he treated the city populace as liberally, and soon after he remitted to defaulting taxpayers in Italy and the provinces the arrears of the past fifteen years.

GOVERNMENTAL POLICY. Hadrian's accession heralded a reign whose goals were consolidation, centralization, and unification of the government. Far more than any of his predecessors, the new *princeps* took a broadly imperial conception of the Empire and the objectives of imperial policy.

Hadrian was a man of restless energy and extraordinary versatility. Taking as his motto the dictum that "the ruler exists for the state, not the state for the ruler," he exhibited unsparing devotion to duty in his endeavor to govern by this standard. There was no branch of administration in which he was not interested. To acquaint himself thoroughly with the needs of the various sections of the Empire and to take measures for their welfare, he made two extended tours through the provinces—one in 121–126, the other in 129–132—spending altogether more than half of his principate outside Italy. Like Trajan, he treated the Senate with respect and consideration. He took an oath, which he carefully observed until toward the close of his reign—not to condemn its members to death—but he did not accord it any significant share in government.

DEFENSIVE IMPERIALISM. Trajan's invasion of Parthia depleted the Roman treasury and failed to settle the eastern frontier. The Roman hold on Armenia and Mesopotamia was precarious, and the Roman nominee to the Parthian throne was deposed. Trouble had broken out also on the lower Danube, in Mauretania, and in Britain, while the Jewish revolt was not yet completely suppressed. Peace and recuperation were a necessity, and Hadrian immediately took steps to secure them. He concluded peace with the Parthians, surrendering Assyria and Mesopotamia, and reverted to the previous policy of treating Armenia as a client kingdom under a Parthian ruler who acknowledged Roman overlordship. In his frontier policy Hadrian went on the defensive. His ideal was a peaceful and prosperous state, adequately protected against attack from without, devoting its energies to development of economic and other resources. On all sides he strengthened the borders and their garrisons, particularly in Britain, where he ordered the construction of his famous Wall from the mouth of the Tyne to the Solway Firth, and along the frontier in Germany. Hadrian's defensive policy accentuated the already existing tendency for imperial armies to become garrison troops recruited locally from the border provinces where they were stationed. Under the Emperor's watchful eye the highest standards of military discipline and efficiency were maintained. The only serious war Hadrian was called upon to undertake was the suppression of a new rebellion of the Jews in Palestine. This was occasioned by their resentment at the founding of a Roman colony at Jerusalem with an altar to Jupiter on the site of the former Temple of Yahweh, and Hadrian's prohibition of circumcision, which he regarded as inhumane. Under the leadership of Simon, called Bar Kochba (Son of the Star), the Jews seized Jerusalem and defied the Roman armies. Hadrian's genocidal repression of the rebellion after a fierce, two-year struggle (132–134) stained what was an otherwise enlightened reign.

ADMINISTRATIVE REFORMS. Hadrian was both a coordinator of tendencies already operating in government and an innovator. To aid him in administering justice and framing legislation, he used jurists more frequently in his *ad hoc* councils than had his predecessors. Under his auspices Salvius Julianus, one of the most influential Roman legal writers, codified and edited the Praetor's Edict, which now embodied to a substantial degree the principles and procedures of Roman civil law. The Praetor's Edict was in effect "frozen," and an important avenue of adding to the law independent of the emperor was closed. Even before Hadrian, few magistrates would have dared to change the edict on their own initiative. In order to relieve the praetor's courts of excessively heavy dockets, Italy outside of Rome was divided into four districts,

XV Vale of Canopus at Hadrian's Villa. *In A.D. 125–134 Hadrian erected a villa, the largest and richest built by any emperor, in the foothills at Tibur (modern Tivoli), where he created replicas of famous places he had seen while travelling throughout the provinces. This illustration shows his interpretation of the Vale of Canopus leading to the temple of Serapis, which he saw near Alexandria. (Photo: Fototeca Unione.)*

each under a consular judge appointed by the emperor. This was a further step in the gradual elimination of the Senate's administrative control of Italy and in the approximation of its status to that of a province. Hadrian enhanced the importance of the equestrian class and its influence in government. He increased the number of procurators and generalized the tendency under previous emperors to appoint equestrians rather than freedmen to the great secretary-ships of the treasury, of correspondence, and so on, which had been established in the preceding century, although freedman executives did not disappear completely. Another change was creation of a class of officials called advocates of the fiscus (*advocati fisci*) as prosecutors for the treasury, whose office was regarded as an alternative to subordinate military commands in the equestrian career. An important innovation in military administration was made when Hadrian gave an official table of strength and organization to the non-commissioned officer cadres in the army and defined their use in the head-quarters clerical staffs of their commanders.

PUBLIC WORKS. Hadrian's handling of imperial finances enabled him to carry out an extensive building program. He founded many cities, among them Antinoöpolis in Egypt in honor of his favorite Antinous, who was drowned in the Nile, and Adrianople in European Turkey, which still preserves his name. He was particularly devoted to Athens, where he was archon and where he completed the temple of Olympian Zeus besides adding a new suburb. In Rome, in addition to many lesser structures, Hadrian erected a magnificent double temple to Venus and Roma and his own mausoleum, the present Castel Sant'Angelo. At Tibur (Tivoli) he built a rambling, luxurious villa.

CHOICE OF A SUCCESSOR. Hadrian had no children and no intimate and trusted friends with whom he shared his plans. His aloofness made the Senate at first suspicious, later hostile. In 136 he fell painfully and incurably ill, a warning that he must provide for a successor. His aged brother-in-law, who showed signs of aspiring to the Principate, was executed together with his youthful grandson. His choice then fell on a senator, Lucius Ceionius Commodus, whom he adopted as Lucius Aelius Caesar and who was given tribunician authority. When Aelius died early in 138, Hadrian adopted another senator, Titus Aurelius Antoninus, member of a Roman family from Narbonese Gaul. Since Antoninus was already middle aged, Hadrian made him adopt in turn the son of the deceased Commodus, Lucius Verus, and also Marcus Aurelius Antoninus, a nephew of the emperor's wife and, like her, of Spanish-Roman descent. Titus Aurelius Antoninus received both the *imperium* and tribunician authority and became Hadrian's partner in the Principate. Hadrian then died on July 10, 138.

IV. THE ANTONINES: A.D. 138–192

ANTONINUS PIUS: A.D. 138–161. The death of Hadrian made Titus Aurelius Antoninus emperor. His action in securing the deification of his adoptive father from the reluctant Senate won for him the title of Pius, as the personification of the Roman virtue of piety or sense of obligation in divine and human affairs. His filial piety was shown further in his completion of Hadrian's tomb and the erection of a temple for his worship as Divus Hadrianus. Just and mild in public and private life, Antoninus acted in perfect harmony with the Senate, at whose request he removed the four judges whom Hadrian had appointed over Italy.

The policies of Antoninus were generally a continuation of Hadrian's. Although called on to repress serious frontier troubles in Britain and Mauretania, to check vigorously Parthian encroachments in Armenia, and to put down some minor insurrections in the Eastern provinces, he adhered to a defensive frontier policy. He improved the border defenses, notably in Raetia and in Britain, where he had an earthen wall built between the Firths of Clyde and Forth well to the north of Hadrian's Wall. Unlike Hadrian, however, Antoninus refrained from visiting the provinces in person, because of the expense imperial journeys caused communities. Owing to his careful handling of finances, he was able to entertain the populace liberally, carry out numerous building projects, and yet remit delinquent taxes. Probably the greatest achievement of this principate was in the field of law. He insisted on the impartial administration of justice, and the law itself was greatly liberalized through the introduction of principles of equity and began to receive at the hands of jurisprudents its characteristically systematic form.

In 139 Antoninus conferred the title of Casear upon the elder of his adopted sons, Marcus Aurelius, to whom six years later he gave his daughter in marriage. Then in 146 he had the Senate confer on Marcus the tribunician authority and the *imperium* outside of Rome, and when Antoninus died in March 161, Marcus at once became sole *princeps*.

DUAL PRINCIPATE: MARCUS AURELIUS (161–180) AND LUCIUS VERUS (161–169). Marcus Aurelius took as his colleague his adoptive brother, Lucius Verus, and for the first time a principate was inaugurated jointly by two Augusti. Real power rested in the hands of Marcus, for Verus was weak and indolent. His chief merit was that in governmental matters, at least, he loyally deferred to his brother's judgment. Marcus Aurelius was by nature a student and philosopher and a devoted Stoic. His introspective and even mystical character is revealed in his communings with himself, his *Meditations*. Fired by no ambition and lacking any enthusiasm for his task, he nevertheless was a dutiful emperor and devoted himself unsparingly to public service. It was ironic that he, ideally fitted for peace, should have had to spend his remaining years in almost unceasing struggle to save the state from its foreign foes.

WAR WITH THE PARTHIANS: A.D. 161–165. At the very beginning of the new regime, the Parthian king, Vologases III, invaded Armenia. The Roman legate of Cappadocia, who led an opposing army, was defeated and killed. The Parthians broke into Syria, where they won a victory over the Roman garrison and ravaged the country. In view of the crisis, Marcus Aurelius sent Verus to the East, where, although he displayed neither energy nor capacity, his able generals restored the situation. In 163, Statius Priscus reestablished Roman authority over Armenia and installed a new Roman vassal. In 164–165 Avidius Cassius marched into Mesopotamia and captured both Seleucia and the Parthian capital, Ctesiphon. He was unable to follow up his victory because an outbreak of disease among his troops forced him to retreat, the army suffering serious losses from sickness and hunger. The Parthians momentarily recovered ground in Mesopotamia and even regained control of Armenia. In 166, the Romans resumed the offensive, drove the Parthians out of northern Mesopotamia and permanently occupied it as far east as the Khabur river. A few years later the Parthian governor of Armenia was removed, and it became once again a Roman client state. These gains hardly compensated for the havoc wrought by the plague, possibly smallpox, which soldiers returning from the East spread throughout the Empire and which claimed many victims.

WAR ON THE DANUBIAN FRONTIER: A.D. 167–175. Before the Eastern situation had been settled satisfactorily, a much more serious condition had developed on the Danube. There the Marcomanni, Quadi, Iazyges, and some lesser tribes united to invade the provinces. The army of the Danube, weakened by the withdrawal of detachments for service in the East, was unable to repulse them; Noricum and Pannonia were overrun, the barbarians reaching Aquileia at the head of the Adriatic. Conditions were critical, owing to lack of manpower, disorganization caused in army camps by plague, and depletion of the treasury through the expenses involved in the Parthian War. Marcus Aurelius was forced to adopt heroic measures to cope with them. He raised money by auctioning off treasures of the imperial household, drafted slaves and gladiators into the army, and even hired German and Scythian mercenaries. Marcus himself, accompanied by Verus, commanded operations against the invaders. Aquileia was relieved, and the struggle for the recovery of Noricum and Pannonia began. While this was still in progress, Lucius Verus died of apoplexy (169), leaving Marcus as sole Augustus. He continued to press the war vigorously, the barbarians being driven back across the Danube, and, despite a serious invasion of Dacia and a raid of the Costoboci that penetrated the Balkans as far as Athens, the Romans prevailed. In 172 the emperor crossed the Danube and defeated the Quadi in their own territory and then defeated the Marcomanni in the following year. Both peoples were forced to surrender their captives, together with large numbers of cattle and horses; some thousands of them were settled on waste lands in the provinces with the obligation of tilling the soil and serving in Roman armies. The Iazyges and the Costoboci of eastern Galicia also were attacked in their homelands with the aid of German allies of the Romans, while the Quadi were punished again for having broken their treaty. Marcus became convinced that the only way to obtain lasting peace was to follow Trajan's example in dealing with the Dacians, and he therefore planned to annex the lands of the Marcomanni and Sarmatians. News of the rise of a usurper in Syria compelled him to forego this project and be content with imposing the same terms on the Iazyges as he had upon the Marcomanni and Quadi (175). The victories of the campaigns of 172–175 were commemorated by a column erected in Rome by Marcus' son and successor with reliefs depicting military operations in imitation of Trajan's memorial of the Dacian Wars.

DUAL PRINCIPATE AGAIN: MARCUS AURELIUS AND COMMODUS: A.D. 177–180.   While he was combatting the barbarians of central Europe, the peace of the Empire, was further disturbed by an outbreak in Gaul, a rising of Moorish tribes in Mauretania, and a serious rebellion of herdsmen in the Nile Delta, which was put down by the general of the Parthian War, Avidius Cassius, who was legate in his native province of Syria since 167, and, since 169, was entrusted with the general supervision of the East. Upon a false report of the death of Marcus, Cassius proclaimed himself emperor and won recognition in Syria, Judaea, Cilicia, and Egypt (175). News of this usurpation forced Marcus to conclude hurriedly the war with the Iazyges so that he could proceed to the East. Upon arrival there he found that news of his approach had caused Cassius to be deserted and executed by his own followers. The episode warned Marcus that he must provide for a successor. Upon his return to Rome he had his son Lucius Aelius Aurelius Commodus, a mere youth of sixteen, proclaimed Augustus and his partner.

DANUBIAN PROBLEM ONCE MORE: A.D. 178–180.   The restless tribes on the Danubian frontier soon caused fresh troubles, which forced Marcus Aurelius again to command forces in the field, where he was joined later by Commodus. Once more he subdued the Marcomanni and the Quadi and planned for permanent Roman occupation of their territory, which included modern Bohemia and Moravia, in order to strengthen defences. For a second time he was robbed of victory, this time by his own death. Marcus Aurelius died at Vindobona (Vienna) on March 17, 180, and the Principate passed to Commodus, whom he had enjoined to conclude the war successfully.

COMMODUS SOLE PRINCEPS: A.D. 180–182.   The ignoble Commodus, is one of few Roman emperors of whom nothing good can be said. Although it may seem strange that Marcus Aurelius, who could not have ignored his weaknesses, took him as a colleague and designated him his successor, it must be remembered that, short of executing him, it was practically impossible to exclude him from the Principate. One possibility remained untried: to have given him a senior colleague who might have dominated him as Marcus himself had dominated Verus. Perhaps Marcus hoped that the responsibilities of office would sober the young man or that he would follow his father's trusted advisers.

Disregarding parental injunctions, Commodus made peace with the Marcomanni and Quadi upon the terms they previously enjoyed, and even these he subsequently relaxed. As soon as possible he returned to Rome to enjoy the delights of the capital. He pursued a sybaritic life and left government to a succession of favorites who used their power to feather their own nests. Proud of his physical strength, he sought to win plaudits by appearing in the arena as a hunter of wild beasts or as a gladiator who incurred no risks in killing his opponents. He regarded himself the living manifestation of his patron god, Hercules, whose emblems of club and lion's skin were depicted on his statues and coins.

Indifferent to any principles of government, Commodus scorned the Senate, and when a conspiracy against his life was discovered, he executed many senators. By largesse and favors, he kept the support of the praetorians, who protected him from his enemies. Despite his neglect of duty, provincial commanders maintained the integrity of the Empire. Border wars with the Moors, with the Caledonians in Britain, and with other tribes in Dacia were waged with success, but a mutiny of troops in Britain was checked only by acquiescence to their demands. More alarming were serious outbreaks within the Empire, due apparently to economic distress. Gangs of brigands roamed Italy and in Gaul formed bands large enough to capture cities and wage open war with government forces.

The extravagance of the *princeps* and his associates emptied the treasury and created a financial crisis. Informers reappeared, through whose agency judicial murders were perpetrated with widespread confiscation of property. In his infatuation with gladiatorial exploits he allegedly determined to assume the consulate on January 1, 193, in gladiator costume. On the preceding night, however, he was strangled by his wrestling companion, who had been bribed by the praetorian prefect, Quintus Aemilius Laetus, who feared for his own safety, with the collusion of the favorite mistress and the chamberlain of the neurotic ruler.

V. DYNASTY OF THE SEVERI: A.D. 193–235

SECOND WAR OF THE LEGIONS: A.D. 193. Events of the years following the death of Commodus and the extinction of the Antonine dynasty resemble those of 68–69. The praetorian guard appointed a *princeps*, only to find that commanders of the frontier armies refused to acquiesce in its action and engaged in civil war to make themselves candidates. The praetorians accepted the nominee of their prefect Laetus, Publius Helvius Pertinax, a senator of proved military and administrative capacity, who was then City Prefect. His nomination was approved by the Senate, which readily accorded him the honors and power of the Principate. Pertinax was no tool of his backers and he maintained firm discipline in the guard. This, coupled with economies necessitated by a nearly empty treasury, cost him the support of both praetorians and courtiers. After a rule of less than three months, he was murdered by a mutinous detachment of praetorians (March 28, 193), who then auctioned off the Principate to an elderly, wealthy senator, Marcus Didius Julianus, who promised them a donative of 25,000 sesterces apiece. The Senate could only confirm their choice.

News of the death of Pertinax and the succession of Julianus provoked revolts in two of the great army corps in the East and on the Danubian frontier. The speed with which they acted suggests that their commanders had already contemplated and prepared their *coups d'état*. Almost simultaneously Gaius Pescennius Niger, the legate of Syria, and Publius Septimius Severus, legate of Upper Pannonia, engineered their salutation as Imperator by the troops under their respective commands. The people and Senate in Rome seem to have supported Niger, but Severus was nearer Rome and took advantage of his position to gain recognition. Assured of the support of the four legions on the Rhine, as well as of at least eleven of the twelve stationed along the Danube, he marched rapidly on Rome, assuming the name Pertinax to indicate that he was the avenger of the murdered *princeps* and adherent of his principles. Julianus at first prepared resistance, then tried vainly to make terms with Severus. When the praetorians tried to save themselves by deserting their appointee, the Senate, forced by Julianus to proclaim Severus a public enemy, now dared to deify the dead Pertinax, to condemn Julianus himself to death, and to ratify the nomination of Severus. A soldier murdered Julianus on June 1, and a few days later Severus entered Rome at the head of his troops. He distributed the customary donation to the soldiery and populace, took the by then usual oath not to execute a senator without a trial before the Senate, and punished through its agency some of the supporters of Julianus. Besides executing those praetorians who had taken part in the murder of Pertinax, Severus disarmed and disbanded the guard, and replaced it with a new one of 15,000 veterans from the Danubian legions whom he could trust. His position was not secure, however, since Pescennius Niger obtained recognition in the Eastern provinces, was in a position to cut off the Egyptian supply of grain, and had already sent an advance guard to occupy Byzantium, which commanded the crossing of the Bosporus. Before leaving for the East, Severus guarded against a revolt by the legate in Britain, Clodius Albinus, who, like Niger, was popular in Rome and was suspected of imperial designs. He offered Albinus the position of Caesar, an indication that he was successor-designate and, when Albinus accepted, had this title conferred upon him by the Senate.

WAR WITH PESCENNIUS NIGER: A.D. 193–194. Severus then followed the troops he had already dispatched to check Niger's advance. Before he arrived on the scene, however, his generals blockaded Byzantium and landed in Asia Minor, where they won two victories over their opponents, one near Cyzicus, the other near Nicaea. When Severus brought up reinforcements, Niger withdrew into Syria south of the Taurus mountains. In the spring of 194 Severus descended into Cilicia and defeated Niger in a decisive battle at Issus. Niger tried to escape into Parthia but was overtaken and killed. Heavy penalties were meted out to individuals and communities that had supported him. Severus then invaded Mesopotamia, where the client state of Osrhoëne revolted and Roman influence was endangered. Overrunning Osrhoëne and upper Mesopotamia as far as the Tigris, he sent an army across that river into Adiabene. From these exploits he was recalled to meet a new danger in the West in December 195. In the meantime, Byzantium, which held out against its besiegers for more than two years, was starved into surrender. Its fortifications were destroyed, its officials and garrison killed, the property of its citizens confiscated, and it was reduced to the status of a village dependent upon the neighboring city of Perinthus.

DEFEAT OF CLODIUS ALBINUS: A.D. 196–197. The situation demanding the presence of Severus in the West was brought about by Albinus' claim to the Principate. He had gradually come to realize that Severus and his ambitious Syrian wife, Julia Domna, had no intention of allowing him to succeed rather than their own sons, and that unless he acted quickly he could not escape destruction. Acting in collusion with many senators in Rome, he had himself proclaimed Augustus by his soldiery and landed in Gaul, establishing his headquarters at Lugdunum (Lyons). Severus replied by having Albinus declared a public enemy by the army in Mesopotamia and later by having his eldest son, Bassianus, better known as Caracalla, proclaimed Caesar, with the name of Marcus Aurelius Antoninus.

In February 197, the armies of the rivals faced each other at Lyons. The Danubian legions won the desperate struggle, and Albinus took his own life. Lugdunum, the richest city in the western provinces, was sacked and burned and never recovered its prosperity in antiquity. Severus was now the unchallenged ruler and could take vengeance on his enemies. Supporters of Albinus in Gaul, Germany, Britain, and Spain were relentlessly hunted down, and in Rome twenty-nine senators convicted of intriguing with him were summarily executed. At the demand of Severus, the Senate confirmed the army's nomination of Caracalla as Caesar, together with his use of the Antonine name, to which they added the title of Emperor Designate (*imperator destinatus*). After a short stay in Rome, Severus was recalled to the East because of Parthian aggression.

SECOND PARTHIAN WAR: A.D. 197–199. Taking advantage of Roman preoccupation with the struggle between rival emperors, Vologases IV, king of Parthia, invaded Armenia and northern Mesopotamia, where he laid siege to the stronghold of Nisibis. At the approach of Severus in the winter of 197/198, Vologases raised the siege of Nisibis and retreated as the Romans pressed on into Parthian territory. Seleucia on the Tigris was occupied unopposed, and Ctesiphon, although vigorously defended, was taken and sacked. On his return march up the Tigris valley, Severus attempted, without success, to capture the rock fortress of Hatra, which had defied similar efforts of Trajan. A second attempt in 199 was equally unsuccessful. Northern Mesopotamia remained firmly in Roman hands, however, and was organized as a province with Nisibis as its capital. Failure of the Parthians to check the Roman invasion and prevent destruction of their capital hastened the internal decay of their empire. After spending two more years in the East visiting Egypt and other provinces, Severus and his family returned to Rome in 202 to celebrate the tenth anniversary of his salutation as Imperator.

GOVERNMENT OF SEPTIMIUS SEVERUS. Severus was a native of Leptis Magna in Tripoli, part of the province of Africa, which retained Punic linguistic and cultural traditions dating back to the days of Carthage. His influential and ambitious wife, Julia Domna, was Syrian. Establishment of their dynasty, more cosmopolitan than any preceding, symbolized the arrival at the center of power of the senatorial aristocracy from southern and eastern provinces. Political regionalism was foreign to the imperial mentality, and aside from keeping a sentimental attachment to his native city, which he lavishly patronized, Severus was completely Roman in outlook. Born to equestrian rank, he had begun his career as an advocate of the *fiscus* but was admitted to senatorial status by Marcus Aurelius. An energetic and ruthless man with first-rate administrative and military talents, he understood and appreciated the realities of imperial power, which he used to serve the state and his own ambitions. Imperial history and his own experience taught him that the rule of any emperor rested essentially on the dynastic loyalty of the troops, which he secured in several ways. In 194 he proclaimed his descent—fictitious, of course— from Marcus Aurelius, thereby making himself the descendant and heir of deified emperors since Nerva. To vindicate the honor of his family, he made the Senate annul their condemnation of Commodus and deify him, as the army had already done at his instigation. The ruling family then became a deified household (*domus divina*), to some degree basing its claim to rule on its divine ancestry. The term *dominus* came into regular use for such a *princeps* with this background, and the imperial residence was called the "sacred" city.

Although the net result of the changes he introduced was a marked acceleration of the movement of imperial power toward autocracy and militarization, Severus cannot be accused of intentionally riding roughshod over the conventions observed by the best of his predecessors. He merely read the signs of his age, and, like any able Roman, reacted to them realistically. If he excluded the Senate from any real share in government, he merely furthered a tendency operative long before him under good and bad emperors alike. Like his immediate predecessors, he tended to admit to the Senate more easterners and Africans than westerners, an indication that he acknowledged the Romanization of such areas. In general, the Senate appreciated his talents and regarded him with sincere if wary respect. After the initial reign of terror involving Albinus, it gave him grudging loyalty in return for his protection of their status and property and for his formal notification to them of matters involving public policy.

He made noncommissioned officer cadres of the army more mobile by nominating the sons of the highest legionary centurions to equestrian posts and encouraged equestrians to specialize in military careers. Since such specialists were increasingly in demand, he named acting governors of equestrian rank in place of senatorial legates, substituted equestrians for senators in other administrative positions, and placed the three legions he raised for his second Parthian War under the command of equestrian prefects.

The exceptional status of Italy, already modified by Hadrian, was further changed by Severus. The praetorian guard was henceforward recruited from the legions and thereby reflected their general provincialization. He did not exclude Italians from the guard, however, and Italians continued to serve in it until it was disbanded early in the fourth century. He did break precedent by stationing one of the newly raised legions on Italian soil near Rome. The old standing courts presided over by the praetors were abolished, and jurisdiction in the cases they had tried was transferred to the city prefect in Rome and within a circuit of one hundred miles of the city, and to the praetorian prefect beyond that limit.

As the importance of the senatorial order declined, that of the equestrians in imperial service rose correspondingly as Septimus increased the number of procuratorial posts. In particular, the praetorian prefecture gained greatly in power and prestige. Not only did the prefect judge cases arising in Italy beyond the hundredth milestone from Rome, he also, as the deputy of the *princeps*, heard appeals from provincial tribunals. The supervision of the transportation of grain to Rome was taken from the prefect of the grain supply and given to the praetorian prefecture. In the absence of the *princeps*, the praetorian prefect presided over his judicial councils, and he was the commander in chief of all the armed forces in Italy. From 193 to 205, this office was held by Gaius Fulvius Plautianus (who, like Severus, was born in Africa) at first with a colleague but alone after 200. Owing to the concentration of authority in his hands and the confidence of Severus in him, he was even more powerful than Sejanus under Tiberius. Despite his unpopularity with the empress, Julia Domna, Plautianus induced Severus to marry his daughter, Plautilla, to Caracalla, then co-Augustus with his father (202). Later Caracalla, influenced by his mother and resenting the influence of Plautianus, caused his downfall. He falsely charged his father-in-law with treason, and, when the latter denied the accusation, had him killed by a lictor in the presence of the *princeps* himself. Thereafter Severus revived the practice of having two praetorian prefects in office at the same time, and his choice of the jurist Papinianus as one of his new appointees testifies to the increased importance of the prefecture's judicial duties.

Severus was legally minded. This, added to the presence of several distinguished lawyers in his councils, accounts for the numerous and important changes in law that date from his principate. In general these follow humanitarian tendencies shown in the legislation of Hadrian, Antoninus Pius, and Marcus Aurelius, liberalizing the law by introducing principles and practices drawn from legal systems of non-Roman origin in vogue in the Hellenistic East and by developing legal concepts based on Stoicism. Characteristic also was the effort to protect weaker classes against oppression or exploitation by the stronger, and those of inferior political status (*humiliores*) against the pressure of the officials (*honestiores*).

Severus regarded the army as the prime source of imperial authority and accorded the soldiery preferential treatment. He owed his own nomination and his victory over his rivals to his legions, and the importance he attached to their role in the choice of a *princeps* is shown by his having them declare Albinus a public enemy, Caracalla a Caesar, and Commodus a *divus*, all before the Senate confirmed these actions. The recruitment of the praetorian guard from selected legionaries and especially the garrisoning of a legion at the Alban lake may be regarded as measures to eliminate opposition to the ruler in Rome and Italy. They also served to create the nucleus of a mobile field force ready to operate where needed under the emperor's command. Although Severus increased the pay of the legionaries by one third, this probably was only a cost-of-living raise. The greater prestige of the military is also shown by the widespread admission of discharged centurions to the equestrian order and to the civil service and the emergence of veterans as an important element to the governing class of provincial municipalities. Severus granted the troops permission to contract legal marriages while in service and to live with their families in settlements adjacent to army camps. This is certainly an indication of his favor to the military, although he was merely giving official sanction to common-law connections that had always existed. Severus maintained high standards of training and discipline. There can be little doubt that his policy, in general, made the army more conscious of its superiority to the civilian elements in the Empire.

Severus paid great attention to the welfare of provincials. He endeavored to protect them from outside attack as well as from internal disorders. Border defenses were repaired or improved, and much was done to stimulate municipal prosperity as well as to repair losses caused by civil wars and brigandage. Antioch, once punished for its support of Niger, recovered its autonomy, as did Byzantium, which was rebuilt on a generous scale. Syria and Britain were each divided into two provinces, and Numidia was separated from Africa, probably to weaken the influence of their governors. Governors, now generally called *praesides*, were strictly supervised in an attempt to prevent them from exploiting provincials. Great attention was paid to municipal organization, including the rights and duties of different classes. For fiscal reasons, Alexandria and native towns of Egypt were granted municipal councils, which now became responsible, as elsewhere, for the collection of local taxes and the performance of other obligations. Although associations of businessmen and craftsmen obliged to undertake public services were exempt from other duties, their own responsibilities were more clearly defined and sharply enforced. In Syria, the Danubian provinces, and particularly in Africa imperial policy brought notable prosperity. These regions also profited greatly from imperial generosity in the construction of public works.

Severus inherited an empty treasury and had to undertake two costly wars at the outset of his principate. His building program, his generosity to the city populace and the soldiers, and an increase in the military and civil services added to normal expenses. The need of more money was met in part by depreciating the silver coinage by about one third and, at least early in his reign, by many issues of it. The result was inflationary. Additional revenue was provided from the confiscation of property of the partisans of his rival, Albinus. The extent of these properties was so great that their administration necessitated creation of a separate treasury department called the *Res* or *Ratio Privata* (the Private Purse). Although, as the name indicates, the estates of the *Res Privata* were regarded as the personal property of the *princeps*, the officials in charge of this department were imperial bureaucrats, and the revenues they administered were used largely to meet costs of government.

WAR IN BRITAIN AND DEATH OF SEVERUS: A.D. 208-211. Withdrawal of the troops of Albinus from Britain in 196 so weakened its garrison that the province suffered repeated raids of Caledonians from the north. The Romans were forced to give up the land between the Walls of Hadrian and Antoninus Pius, and even Hadrian's Wall was breached. Between 204 and 207 Roman commanders gradually restored the situation and rebuilt the Wall, as well as fortifications farther south. In 208 Severus took the field, accompanied by both his sons, very probably to give them a chance to share in a victory. Caracalla, the elder, had been saluted as Augustus by the army as early as 198, while younger Geta had been made Caesar at the same time. After a successful campaign in which he penetrated far into Scotland, Severus conferred the title of Augustus on Geta also (209). Fighting was resumed in 210 and 211. In the course of preparations for a campaign in 211, Severus died at Eburacum (York) in February, at the age of sixty-five. Caracalla thereupon made peace with the Caledonians and, accompanied by Geta, returned to Rome, where they held the funeral for their father and secured him the honor of deification.

CARACALLA:[1] A.D. 211-217, AND GETA: A.D. 211-212. The enmity that had long existed between the two brothers broke into the open with the removal of their father's restraining influence. Each sought to build up a strong faction among officials and soldiers. Their mother vainly tried to reconcile them. After little more than a year of joint rule, Caracalla had Geta murdered. Alleging that he had acted in self-defense because of a conspiracy directed against him, he won over the praetorians by bribes and executed many suspected of belonging to Geta's faction. Among them was the prefect Papinian.

INTERNAL POLICY. Caracalla resembled his father in talents and personality, although in his person Severan traits were grossly brutalized. His early elevation as Augustus without the chastening influence of a career of

---

[1] So-called because of his custom of wearing a modified form of the *Caracalla*, a close-fitting Gallic coat. Note genealogical table in the appendix.

public service strengthened his natural tendency to despotism, and led him to scorn constitutional practices. The advice attributed to his father, to enrich the soldiery and neglect all else, may well be taken as the most consistent trait in his policy. He courted their good will by a general increase of their pay by one half and by frequent and lavish donations. Soon after the assassination of Geta, in 212, Caracalla issued the famous *Constitutio Antoniniana* (Antoninian Constitution), by which he conferred Roman citizenship upon all free residents of the Empire who were members of organized communities. Those affected were primarily provincials who, according to Roman law, had the status of aliens or Latins. Roman citizenship was already widespread in the Western provinces, but the change in status affected many subjects in the East, where the granting of it had been only to individuals among the upper classes, especially town councillors. Although the event appears significant as the final act of Romanization that had begun with the cities of the Latin League 550 years before, it is difficult to estimate its impact on the newly enfranchised. Roman law did not apply at once to most of them because many local magistrates and advocates did not know or practice it. The advantages of having Roman citizenship, like the eligibility to vote or to be protected from arbitrary treatment had lapsed for most of the population, granted the distinction between legally privileged *honestiores* and unprivileged *humiliores*. Enfranchisement may have seemed an added disability to new citizens because they were for the first time subject to the inheritance tax, paid only by Romans and levied even on modest estates, a tax which Caracalla doubled to 10 per cent. Enfranchisement did, eventually, introduce some unity of law and even of sentiment, but its importance should not be exaggerated. On the whole, Caracalla took little interest in internal administration, leaving it to his mother, the imperial councils, and higher officials, who carried on in the spirit of Severus.

GERMANIC AND PARTHIAN WARS. Caracalla devoted much attention to military matters and personally assumed command of his field armies. In 213 he campaigned successfully against the Alamanni, a newly formed group of Germanic peoples who threatened the province of Raetia. He then proceeded against tribes on the upper Rhine, whose attack he bought off and whom he subsidized as allies. Under his direction the frontier fortifications in Raetia and Upper Germany were strengthened.

After settling affairs on the northern frontier, Caracalla in 214 proceeded to the East, where he sought to imitate his hero, Alexander the Great, whose reincarnation he believed himself to be. Before departure, Caracalla strengthened his hand by treacherously seizing the kings of Osrhoëne and Armenia. Owing to the struggle between two brothers, Vologases V and Artabanus, for the Parthian throne, conditions seemed favorable for an attack upon Rome's eastern rival. The opening of hostilities was deferred by the desire of Vologases to avoid war and his yielding to Caracalla's demands. Caracalla then visited

Egypt, where for unknown reasons he massacred large numbers of Alexandrians. Upon his return to Syria, he demanded that Artabanus, who meantime had gotten control of Parthia, give him his daughter in marriage. When Artabanus refused, Caracalla invaded and ravaged Media unopposed (216). He prepared to renew his attack the following spring, but was assassinated near Carrhae on April 8, 217, by orders of the praetorian prefect, Marcus Opellius Macrinus.

MACRINUS AND DIADUMENIANUS: A.D. 217–218. Macrinus was saluted Imperator by Caracalla's army and was recognized without opposition by the Senate. He at once bestowed the title of Caesar on his young son Diadumenianus, whom he later proclaimed Augustus. Macrinus was a native of Mauretania and the first equestrian to attain the Principate without having entered the senatorial order. He owed his advancement to his administrative and legal talents and displayed moderation and good sense in his conduct of government. He lacked the prestige of an established dynasty and sought to win support by generous donations to the soldiery and citizens of Rome, by deference toward the Senate, and by securing the deification of Caracalla, to placate the Severan faction. Defeated by Artabanus in Mesopotamia, he purchased an expensive peace from the Parthians and also made concessions to the Armenian king. Such conduct alienated what little good will he had managed to develop among the troops.

RESTORATION OF THE SEVERAN DYNASTY; THE ROLE OF JULIA MAESA. Taking advantage of this situation, the members and followers of the house of Severus in Syria attempted to regain the Principate for their dynasty. The movement was led by Julia Maesa, sister of Julia Domna, who died soon after the murder of her son Caracalla. As claimant to imperial power, Maesa presented as Caracalla's alleged illegitimate son the fourteen-year-old Varius Avitus Bassianus, true son of her daughter Julia Soaemias and a Syrian senator. Bassianus was thus a grandnephew of Julia Domna and hence, by marriage, of Septimius Severus also. The Syrian army, won over, saluted Bassianus as Imperator under the name of Marcus Aurelianus Antoninus. The forces loyal to Macrinus were defeated (June 218), and both he and his son were subsequently captured and killed. Bassianus assumed the imperial titles and was accepted by the Senate. A few governors who opposed his claims were executed.

ELAGABALUS: A.D. 218–222. Bassianus by hereditary right was priest of the sun god worshipped under the name of Elagabal at Emesa, and hence he was himself generally known as Elagabalus. Elagabalus is represented in the historical tradition as debauched. Even if tales of his depravity are discounted, he appears to have been a worthless ruler, his most creative interest being the worship of his god, represented by a meteorite, which he brought with him to Rome. His grandmother, Julia Maesa, really directed the government. Realizing the hostility developing against Elagablus and conscious of his complete ineptitude, she prevailed upon him to adopt his cousin Alexianus, son of Julia Mamaea, his aunt, as Marcus Aurelius Alexander and to appoint him Caesar (221). Elagabalus repented of his decision and tried to rid himself of Alexander. Thereupon the praetorians, instigated probably by Maesa and Mamaea, murdered Elagabalus and his mother, along with many of his despised associates (222). The memory of the late *princeps* was condemned and the god Elagabalus sent back to Syria.

SEVERUS ALEXANDER: A.D. 222–235. The Principate passed without incident to Alexander, who took the cognomen Severus to emphasize his affiliation with the dynasty. Like his cousin, the new Augustus was a boy of fourteen at his accession, incompetent to rule alone. Amiable and weak, he was dominated by powerful personalities like Ulpianus, praetorian prefect and famous jurist, who was *de facto* regent in the early years of the reign, and by his own grandmother and mother. According to one perhaps doubtful tradition a council of senators was formed to confirm matters of policy decided on by the emperor and his ministers. At least in appearances senatorial interests were protected. When Alexander's grandmother died in 226, his mother acquired additional influence. Already enjoying the rank of Augusta, she soon acquired the grandiose title"Mother of Augustus and the camps and the Senate and the fatherland" (*mater Augusti et castrorum et senatus et patriae*), which indicated her dominant position. Her jealousy of a rival caused her to drive even her son's wife into exile. General government policy continued the traditions established by Septimius Severus. Attempts were made to strengthen finances and to improve efficiency. The spread of elementary education seems to have been encouraged, and abuses in the application of the law of treason were corrected. The prestige of the praetorian prefecture was enhanced by the admission of some prefects to senatorial rank while still in office. Control of the soldiery continued to be a crucial problem.

Mamaea's training had made her son both studious and virtuous, but as he grew up Alexander showed himself lacking in courage and self-reliance and never emancipated himself from his mother. He was utterly unfitted for military command and failed to win the respect of the armies. In 228 the praetorians mutinied and murdered their prefect, Ulpianus, in the palace without the *princeps* being able to protect him or punish those responsible. Alexander's incompetence as a general was disastrous since new and aggressive foes began to threaten the Empire. In 226 or 227 the Parthian Empire of the Arsacids was overthrown by a vassal Ardaschir (Ataxerxes), King of Persia, who founded a new Persian Empire under his own dynasty, the Sassanids. This revival of Persia was accompanied by one of the national Mazdean or Zoroastrian religion. The nationalistic character of the new state was also reflected in its foreign policy, for it claimed all the territories once a part of the old Persian Empire, including the Asiatic provinces of Rome and Egypt. After an unsuccessful attack on Armenia, Ardaschir invaded Roman Mesopotamia in 230 and 231.

He won no great successes, but the situation in the Near East had become serious for Rome, and all attempts at negotiation failing, Alexander was compelled to fight. In the spring of 232, the Romans tried to invade Persia by three separate routes. They were unsuccessful, and one division suffered severe defeat. The Persians' losses were so heavy that they could not exploit their victory, however. Although no formal peace was made, the Roman frontier was restored, and Alexander returned to Rome to celebrate an unmerited triumph (233).

Alexander's return to the West was hastened by news that Germanic tribes were threatening the Rhine and the Danube. Preparations were made to attack the Alamanni, and the *princeps*, accompanied by his mother, took command of the army with headquarters at Mainz. Influenced by Mamaea, he preferred to negotiate rather than fight and bought peace from the barbarians. This cost him the respect of his troops, who were also disgruntled at his subservience to his mother, whom they accused of parsimony. A mutiny broke out, led by Gaius Julius Verus Maximinus, a Thracian who had risen from the ranks to high command. Alexander and Mamaea were executed, and Maximinus was proclaimed Augustus (235). With this rebellion the Empire entered upon a half century of crisis and civil war.

VI. DEVELOPMENT OF THE PRINCIPATE TO SEVERUS ALEXANDER

The emperors from Nerva to Marcus Aurelius inclusive are often called the "good emperors," as if they alone had been worthy rulers. While inaccurate, the term does suggest the legal character of their reigns, contrasting with the insecurity felt under their predecessor Domitian as well as the lack of principles of their successor Commodus. It also reflects the favorable opinion of the senatorial class upon their constitutionality when compared with the autocratic tendencies of Domitian and the Severi. The capacity displayed by Trajan, Hadrian, Antoninus, and Marcus Aurelius also showed the advantages of selection by adoption over the dynastic principle, which brought Commodus, Caracalla, and Elagabalus to the Principate.

The former four emperors kept the army under strict control, so that it had not interfered with imperial nominations. With the death of Commodus first the praetorians and then the legions again assumed the right to select their Imperator. The soldiery always exhibited a strong feeling of dynastic loyalty, which accounts for the Severan restoration in the person of Elagabalus. Under the later Severi, however, even this sense of loyalty dwindled under weak rulers and as the troops realized that the fate of the Empire rested in their hands, even though action by the Senate was necessary to confer appropriate authority on the new *princeps*. With Marcus Aurelius, Verus, and Commodus, and later with Septimius Severus and his sons, the Principate was held in partnership by two or more Augusti, a situation that foreshadowed the regular practice of the later Empire. The only attempt really to share the office with a colleague was made by Marcus Aurelius with Verus. His conferment of the rank of Augustus on Commodus, like the action of Severus with Caracalla and Geta, was motivated by concern for the succession. Significant was the attempt of Septimius Severus to establish the legitimacy of his dynasty by claiming descent from Marcus Aurelius, to gain as ancestors deified emperors. His example was followed by Elagabalus and Severus Alexander, both of whom fictitiously claimed Caracalla as a parent. Notable also was the role played by the Syrian princesses of the Severan house, who followed, but with greater success, the example set by Agrippina, the mother of Nero.

This period saw the Senate gradually surrender to the *princeps* and his officers all active participation in government. The process went on under both constitutional and autocratic emperors. Extension of the functions of prefects of the watch and grain supply, and of commissions Augustus and his successors had set up to superintend construction and maintenance of public works in Rome and Italy, deprived most of the regular city magistrates of any responsibility. When, under Severus Alexander, the tribunate and aedileship ceased to be required steps in the senatorial career, these offices became sinecures. Beginning with Augustus, senatorial curators presided over public works commissions, but Claudius added equestrian procurators who took over direction of their activities. Severus dispensed with curators and placed procurators in charge. As early as Nero, control of the old treasury (*aerarium Saturni*) was virtually removed from the Senate's jurisdiction by the appointment of two prefects of praetorian rank designated by the *princeps* as its directors. The diversion of its revenues to ministers of the *princeps* caused it to diminish steadily in importance, until after Severus it gradually became a municipal treasury for the city of Rome. By the time of Nero the Senate had lost any real freedom in the elections to various magistracies, and between his principate and the death of Severus, it was also deprived of any share in legislation. The Assembly rapidly declined in importance during the first century A.D., and no trace of it as a formal organization can be found later than the time of Nerva. For a time this enhanced the legislative importance of the Senate, whose decrees acquired the validity of law, but by the time of Hadrian, if not earlier, the influence of the *princeps* seriously encroached on its freedom of action and discussion. In effect, the Senate was rapidly abdicating its roll as the chief deliberative body in the state to imperial councils. By the time of the Severans, the Senate enjoyed only the passive function of registering its approval of decrees drafted by the *princeps* and read to it by his representative. Expansion of judicial functions of the urban and praetorian prefects resulted in the abolition of the standing courts of praetors, that indirectly came under the supervision of the Senate, whose judicial competence was reduced to the trial of senators for treason. Even under Severus Alexander there was no revival of the Senate's power, although concessions were made to its prestige to conciliate its members and win their approbation. One important right remained vested in the Senate—the power to confer or withhold deification. Even here its freedom to act was occasionally hampered by the pressure of a new *princeps*. Although the Senate had lost much competence and prestige, it still remained influential, because of tradition and because of the standing of individual senators and their class. Interesting changes in the composition of the Senate are observable, reflecting basic social and economic facts of life in the Empire. Matrimonial connections of the oldest republican families with the Julio-Claudian house had been their own undoing during the various persecutions before A.D. 68, by which date they were almost eliminated. The senatorial order as a whole had never reproduced itself. From the very beginning of the Principate its membership was rejuvenated by the admission under imperial patronage of equestrian "new men" from Italy and the most Romanized provinces, and, on occasion, individual emperors strengthened their following by admitting senators from specific provinces. More important in changing recruitment of that body was the occasional difficulty emperors had in finding men in Italy with the wealth, experience, and inclination to become senators. Naturally the government looked for recruits in those provinces where the *pax Romana* had produced a wealthy and ambitious class eager for prestige. In the course of the late first and early second centuries A.D., the proportion of senators of Western provincial origin thus increased, followed in the second century by recruitment in Africa, and in the late second and early third centuries by an increase of Easterners. The Senate nevertheless was strongly Italian in tone, since senators invested in Italian estates and since many of them moved to Italy.

The extension of the powers of the Principate in administration was equaled if not surpassed in the field of law. Not only did the *princeps* legislate through controlled decrees of the Senate, but he acquired independent legislative authority, because like other magistrates, he could issue edicts valid during his term of office within the sphere of his *imperium*. He could also hand down *decreta* or judicial verdicts and issue responses to petitions of his subordinates or persons under his authority, as well as mandates or instructions to officials subject to his orders. Originally, the edicts were valid only during the principate of their author, and other pronouncements merely applied to cases or individuals to whom they were directed. Gradually, however, all these constitutions, as they came to be called, gained recognition as establishing rules of law and remained in force unless revoked by another imperial constitution. Jurisconsults advising Hadrian found a constitutional basis for the authority of the *princeps* in legislative matters. Gaius, a legal writer (ca. 150), enumerated constitutions of the emperors, along with other sources of law and went on to say: "A constitution of a *princeps* is what an emperor has authorized by decree, edict, or letter. Nor is it ever doubted that this has the force of law, since the emperor himself receives his *imperium* by a law."[2] In other words, the act which conferred *imperium* on a *princeps* transferred to him the legislative authority of

---

[2] *Institutes*, I, 5. Compare the parallel statement in Justinian, *Institutes*, I, 2, 6.

XVI Capitolium at Douggha.   *The province of Africa (roughly modern Tunisia)
was the scene of intense urbanization during the early Principate, as suggested by the
remains at Douggha (ancient Thugga) showing the Capitolium, or temple of Jupiter.
(Photo: Fototeca Unione.)*

the Roman people. By the third century, imperial constitutions were the regular form for legislation.

The *princeps* did not have jurisdiction over citizens in Rome and Italy. Strictly speaking, his right to judge senators was not recognized even under the Severans. There is no doubt, however, that the *princeps* influenced the administration of justice in the Senate and the other tribunals. Frequently, moreover, autocratic or tyrannical emperors abused their power by extending their right to hold preliminary investigations (*cognitiones*) to cover pronouncement and execution of sentences, and at times they used force to execute their orders as if these were legal judgments. Such conduct was always regarded as unconstitutional, however, and was deeply resented. The case was quite different with the judicial authority that the *princeps* derived from his *imperium*. By virtue of his authority he could judge cases arising in the military establishment, civil service, and the provinces under his command. His appointees, imperial officials, administered justice in their respective spheres only by virtue of authority he delegated to them, and appeals from their decisions might be directed to him. Under Hadrian this appellate jurisdiction of the *princeps* was extended by constitutional lawyers to include all appeals. They argued that, since the emperor derived his powers from the people and hence acted in their place, an appeal to him was the exercise of the age-old citizen's right of appeal from the action of a magistrate to the judgment of the people in assembly. With the extension of the judicial powers of the praetorian prefect, city prefect, and prefects of the watch and grain supply, and the consequent disappearance of the courts of praetors and minor city magistrates, all jurisdiction in Rome and Italy, except for the limited civil jurisdiction of local municipal courts, was exercised by appointees of the *princeps*, subject to appeals to him. Thus the *princeps* came to exercise supreme jurisdiction over the Empire.

The principate of the third century A.D., then the ultimate source of all administrative, legislative, and judicial activity, was by no means the same office as that organized by Augustus or reestablished by Vespasian. It had become far more autocratic and assumed many regal characteristics. In theory, in its titulature, its form of investiture, and other features, it still preserved magisterial traditions. A jurist like Ulpian might declare that the *princeps* was above the laws, but there were still influential circles not prepared to accept a ruler clothed with symbols expressing autocratic power.

CHAPTER 19
PUBLIC ADMINISTRATION UNDER THE PRINCIPATE

I. RISE OF IMPERIAL BUREAUCRACY

RESPONSIBILITY OF THE PRINCEPS. Emperors taking their jobs seriously, which is to say the majority, were very busy men. Quite aside from the claims made on their time by military campaigning, they were personally involved in much routine paper work. Subordinates in Rome and the provinces expected, and the emperors gave, their advice on matters which even some highly centralized modern states would leave to the judgment of local administrators. This may be seen, for example, in the correspondence between Trajan and Pliny the Younger, acting as imperial legate in Bithynia, the emperor being requested to decide even whether the citizens of rather out-of-the-way places in Asia Minor should be permitted to organize themselves into fire brigades.

As an administrator, the *princeps* depended on an imperial civil service, whose officials were nominated by him and promoted or removed at his pleasure. In this, Augustus had taken the first steps by establishing equestrian procuratorships and prefectures and creating an equestrian career. The number of these posts increased with the extension of the administrative sphere of the *princeps* at the expense of the Senate. The idea of governing through various departments manned by permanent salaried officials was foreign to the Republic, which employed such servants only as clerks of minor importance in

Rome. The chaotic conditions that obtained under the republican system demanded change, and the concentration of administration in the hands of the *princeps* encouraged development of an organized civil service. This was stimulated and influenced by the incorporation in the Empire of Egypt, which possessed a very bureaucratic system that continued to function. As control of the *princeps* over administration widened at the expense of the Senate, imperial officials took over an ever-increasing share of government, until by the end of the Severan dynasty, it was largely carried on by them.

EQUESTRIANS OR FREEDMEN. At first the imperial civil service lacked system, and there was little or no connection between administrative offices in Italy and in the provinces. Augustus and his immediate successors conducted the administration as part of their private business, contacting imperial officials through private secretaries of their households, that is to say, their freedmen, who, in another capacity, managed the private estate of the *princeps*. An important change was introduced under Claudius, when these secretaryships were changed into powerful ministries with titles that indicated the normal sphere of their duties. Establishment of these ministries in the imperial household tended to centralize the imperial administration more completely and to make it more uniform and regular. The influence of freedmen who occupied these important positions was also responsible for the admission of freedmen to many minor procuratorships. The freedmen did not maintain indefinitely their hold on the imperial service, however. Otho, Domitian, and Trajan chose equestrian secretaries, and Hadrian generalized this practice, so that only occasionally thereafter were they held by freedmen. This step transformed what were till then palace offices into civil service positions with a consequent improvement of their official status and the conduct of their holders. Hadrian was also responsible for the removal of freedmen from most of the imperial procutatorships in the provinces.

THE EXPANSION OF THE SERVICE. The first, second, and early third centuries saw a great expansion of the imperial civil service in the interest of efficiency. The number of equestrian procurators rose steadily from about 23 under Augustus to 170 under Septimius Severus. The more noteworthy increases in numbers of personnel were made by the latter emperor and by Trajan and Hadrian. Under Hadrian such officials had control of all branches of administration that were later characteristic of them. Of particular interest were his reforms of tax collection. Under him the system of farming the revenues was virtually abolished, and bureaucrats replaced private contractors who had handled this branch of public business. He also created the post of advocate of the *fiscus*, whose holders prosecuted the claims of the state against delinquent taxpayers. When Septimius Severus gave general supervision of the imperial service to the praetorian prefects, the process of centralization reached completion. A bureaucratic system of government had developed, elaborate, highly specialized, and at the same time well coordinated.

Augustus insisted upon a preliminary military career preceding appointment to administrative procuratorships, and this prerequisite was not formally abandoned under his successors. There was, however, room in the system for equestrians who had had no military service. Hadrian opened careers for such men, which were restricted mainly to holding procuratorships at the capital. Especially noteworthy was the promotion to civil and procuratorial careers by Septimius Severus of soldiers who had risen from the ranks—an indication of that emperor's favor to the military and of the Romanized state of the army.

SALARY CLASSES IN THE IMPERIAL SERVICE. The ordinary career of an official in the civil service included many procuratorships in Rome, Italy, or the provinces. Although beginning with Augustus a salary was paid to all these offices, it was not until the end of the second century at the latest that four classes of procurators were recognized in terms of pay. These four classes, known as *sexagenarii, centenarii, ducenarii,* and *trecenarii,* who received respectively an annual salary of 60,000, 100,000, 200,000, and 300,000 sesterces, remained unchanged until the close of the third century. At that time the highest class included ministers whose title was then master (*magister*). The salary of the four chief equestrian prefectures was probably higher still. Although it is surprising that relatively few such executives were required to run the Empire, payment of their salaries—not to mention their numerous subordinates and officials in other branches of government—became increasingly burdensome. The procuratorial service alone was perhaps five times as expensive to run under Septimius Severus as it had been under Augustus.

THE EQUESTRIAN ORDER. The senatorial order was, of course, recruited from the upper class of the equestrians. A good example of such advancement is seen in the case of the praetorian prefects. After the time of Trajan they frequently entered the Senate ranking as ex-consuls and in the third century were generally promoted to the senatorial office of city prefect. Vacancies in the upper ranks of equestrians caused by such promotions were filled from the lower grades of the order, which in turn were recruited from still lower classes, such as freedmen, soldiers of low commissioned rank, and municipal and provincial aristocracies. This process transformed the equestrians, like the senators, from a national Roman to an imperial cosmopolitan body. During the first century the proportion of admissions from Italy and the West declined, that from Africa and Asia Minor increased in the second century, Syria, Egypt, and Arabia showing a similar advance in the third. This increase in recruits of Eastern origin coincides with the period of the maximum number of admissions from the freedman class.

An ever-growing emphasis on official prestige, rank, and precedence, led to a hereditary title, *clarissimus* (most distinguished or noble), for the senatorial order. By the second century this title became formal and official. Following the senatorial example, equestrians also acquired honorary titles which depended upon their rank. From the time of Hadrian the title *vir eminentissimus* (most eminent) was the prerogative of the praetorian prefects. Under Marcus Aurelius two other equestrian titles appeared, *vir perfectissimus* (most perfect) and *vir egregius* (honorable). In the third century the latter was held by imperial procurators, while the former was reserved for the higher prefectures (apart from the praetorian), chief treasury officials, and imperial ministers.

ADMINISTRATION OF THE IMPERIAL FINANCES. (*a*) *Fisci*. The most important branch of the civil administration was that of public finances, which merit special consideration. Under Augustus the traditional treasury of the Republic, the *aerarium Saturni*, remained at Rome as the principal one. Revenue from all provinces flowed into it, and from it the emperor, like any republican magistrate, was voted funds for his official functions. There also existed in all the provinces, both senatorial and imperial, local branches of the *aerarium* called *fisci* (chests), where taxes were deposited and whence magistrates, like the emperor, could withdraw funds for local administrative purposes. Little cash actually flowed from the *fisci* to the central *aerarium*, except in the case of certain rich provinces, like Asia and Egypt, that tended always to produce revenue surpluses. In most cases only accounts of balances on hand were sent to the capital. The *aerarium militare*, established by Augustus to pension off veteran troops, also had the character of a public, as distinguished from an imperial, treasury and was administered by three ex-praetors Whereas senators continued to manage the *aerarium Saturni*, the accounts of the *fisci* already under Augustus were prepared by a domestic freedman called *a rationibus*. Augustus acknowledged strict accountability of such monies to the Senate, as did Tiberius and, for a time, Caligula, after which the practice lapsed. Important changes in this system were made under the Flavians, especially Vespasian, who established new *fisci* at Rome, whence flowed the surpluses from rich provinces that had formerly nourished the *aerarium Saturni*. These new *fisci* were placed under the management of imperial procurators rather than senators. This change resulted in the progressive impoverishment of the senatorial treasury. Henceforward emperors could bypass that treasury by drawing on the *fisci* at Rome for expenditures in Italy. From a popular viewpoint all *fisci* under imperial officials came to be regarded as an aggregate of fiscal organizations distinct from the *aerarium*.

(*b*) *Patrimonium*. Emperors beginning with Augustus had, of course, their own fortunes as private individuals, their patrimony, but because of their position the distinction between its administration and that of other monies expended for reasons of state was often blurred. Emperors frequently contributed sums from their immense private fortunes to the *aerarium*, and upon their deaths their estates inevitably were regarded and managed as state property. At the latest from the reign of Claudius, procurators headed the management of patrimonial estates, and treasuries into which patrimonial income flowed were known as *fisci*, like various state chests.

(c) *Res Privata or Private Purse.* This situation continued until the accession of Septimius Severus, whose enormous confiscations of property of the adherents of Niger and Albinus were incorporated into his personal estate, known as the *patrimonium privatum.* Septimius Severus then reorganized the financial administration. He consolidated the management of the old patrimonial estates inherited from preceding reigns with his own *patrimonium privatum* and placed it under a new department, the *ratio* or *res privata,* headed by a secretary called *procurator,* later *magister, rei privatae.* He also consolidated the administration of various *fisci* into a single treasury under an official called *rationalis.* Both may be regarded as departments of the imperial Fiscus, a term which, in a pregnant sense, had gradually become predominant in speaking of emperors' wealth. The *aerarium Saturni* still existed, but it was of little consequence in the third century.

Under the Republic a class of professional government clerks developed from whom the various magistrates, including provincial governors, recruited personnel. After the establishment of the Principate this practice was continued by most appointees of the Senate. Imperial officials, however, used imperial freedmen and slaves or, particularly if they exercised military authority, soldiers who were detailed from their units for such service. This latter practice, also republican in origin, became especially important by the reign of Hadrian. Under the Severans such soldiers had come to constitute an integral part of the lower echelons of the bureaucracy. So widespread was their use that the titles of the various posts in these offices were taken largely from those in the military.

II. THE ARMY AND DEFENSE OF THE FRONTIERS

CONDITIONS OF SERVICE. Service in the legions was one way in which talented men might better their social status, although it tended to be unattractive in highly developed parts of the Empire, like Italy itself, where the standard of living had attained relatively high levels. The overwhelming preponderance of legionary recruits at all times came from peasant classes, for whom military service seemed a more secure and rewarding life than the one they had been leading. Legionary careers, however, could be as arduous as those of the French Foreign Legion. Discipline was severe, marriage in service was prohibited (until Septimius), and the pay was meager, at least for private soldiers. Conditions tended to become more relaxed, however, as the legions campaigned infrequently and became sedentary, the troopers themselves making what amounted to common-law marriages with camp followers.

Augustus paid his privates 225 denarii a year, Domitian and his immediate successors, 300. This was little more than a bare subsistence, although privates might save a bit after paying for their rations and equipment, which the state did not provide. They could at least look forward to occasional windfalls coming their way in the form of booty, perhaps also eventual promotion to the noncommissioned ranks or to elite units like the praetorian guard, both of which enjoyed much more substantial remuneration. Eventually, if they survived, soldiers could expect handsome demobilization benefits at the end of their service amounting to more than ten years' pay or its equivalent in land, which would have made them men of substance. The low pay earned by privates and the harsh conditions under which they frequently served probably account for their tendency to mutiny and plunder the civilian population whenever discipline was relaxed. Such situations occurred only rarely under the early Principate, but this occasionally surfacing undercurrent of lawlessness was one of several grave defects in the Augustan military establishment pointing the way to eventual crisis.

PROVINCIALIZATION OF THE LEGIONS AND THE PRAETORIANS. Augustus restricted admission to the legions to Roman citizens and to freeborn inhabitants of provincial municipalities who received citizenship upon entering the service. The gradual provincialization of the recruitment of such professional citizen-soldiers is a significant fact in the military history of the Principate.

Augustus gradually instituted recruitment on a territorial basis, recruiting legions stationed in the West from Italy and the Romanized provinces there, the Eastern legions from the Greek East and Galatia. By the end of the Julio-Claudian dynasty, provincial citizens accounted for about half the legionary strength, and by the beginning of the second century they outnumbered Italians by almost five to one. Along with the provincialization of manpower there went a parallel and equally organic development, the recruitment of legionaries first from the provinces where they were stationed and then from the immediate vicinity of the garrisons themselves. This was perhaps inevitable, granted the defensive nature of the military establishment, which tended to transform the legions into garrisons. It was cheaper for the Empire to recruit its soldiers from the immediate hinterland of various headquarters, and recruits would be easier to find if they could serve close to home. Very often a family tradition of military service arose. By the second century the normal term of legionary enlistment had been raised to twenty-five years. Down to the Severan dynasty the Roman army remained the most powerful Romanizing catalyst in the Empire. Recruitment for the praetorian guard followed the same tendencies as those obtaining among the legionaries, except that as an elite corps its provincialization was slower. Provincial praetorians are known from the first century A.D., while Italians remained a heavy majority until the reign of Septimius Severus. Septimius reconstituted the guard by recruiting it from legionary troops, which meant that henceforth the guard was largely provincialized.

AUXILIARIES. Organization of the auxiliary corps as troops raised and officered by Romans and for a specified term of twenty-five years was begun by Augustus but was not completed until the reign of Vespasian. Generally speaking, the *auxilia*, like the legions, were recruited where they served, and the removal of the Batavi to a far distant frontier after their revolt in A.D. 69 was exceptional. At first they were not citizens until discharge, but already in the first century some of them were citizens while in service and this proportion had risen to half by Hadrian's time. The extension of Roman citizenship to practically the whole Roman world by Caracalla in 212 removed the basic juridical distinction between Romans and auxiliaries. Tactically, they had also been largely assimilated to legionary status by the second century and received the same training and weapons as legionaries.

NUMERI. As the auxiliary units increasingly approximated the legions, their place was gradually taken in the military establishment, probably beginning with Trajan, by organizations known as *numeri*. National contingents of barbarians or non-Romanized frontier peoples, they kept their own weapons and methods of warfare. They were commanded by Roman officers and used Latin as the language of commands, but the degree of Romanization they attained in service is questionable. Their functions and tactical organization corresponded to that of the original *auxilia* when the latter had been a force supporting the legions.

THE STRENGTH OF THE ARMY. At the death of Augustus the number of the legions was twenty-five, under Nero it was twenty-eight, under Trajan it was thirty, and Severus increased it to thirty-three, comprising over 180,000 men when fully staffed. A corresponding increase was made in the numbers of the auxiliaries. From about 150,000 in the time of Augustus, they had increased to about 220,000 in the second century. The total paper strength of troops in Roman service at the opening of the third century was therefore about 400,000.

SYSTEM OF FRONTIER DEFENSE. A second momentous fact in the history of the Principate was the transformation of the army from a field force into garrison troops. This was the result of the system developed for frontier defense. Augustus, his imperialistic designs having failed, finally decided that the Empire should attain only a frontier protected by natural barriers. Roughly speaking, these were the ocean on the west, the Rhine and the Danube on the north, and the desert on the east and south. At strategic points behind this frontier, Augustus stationed troops in large fortified camps, quartering both legionaries and auxiliaries. They served as bases of operations, and from them military roads were constructed to strategic points on the frontier to permit the rapid movement of troops. Such roads were called *limites* (sing. *limes*), a name which subsequently was used in the sense of frontiers. The *limites* were protected by small forts manned by auxiliary troops. Although Claudius and Vespasian discarded the maxims of Augustus in favor of an aggressive border policy, they adhered to his system for protecting new acquisitions in Britain and southern Germany. These conquests, however, and that of the Wetterau by Domitian pushed the frontier beyond natural boundaries and led to the characteristic Flavian interest in constructing an artificial barrier as a substitute. Another notable feature of Flavian military policy was the use of legionary detachments or *vexillationes* behind the fortified frontier.

GERMANIC AND RAETIAN LIMITES. By the third century the frontier in Germany was protected by a continuous system of fortifications and barriers that followed an irregular line around the area of Roman occupation from Rheinbrohl on the Rhine to Heinheim on the Danube, a distance of about 345 miles. The northwestern section of this line was called the Germanic, the eastern section the Raetian, *limes*. The dividing point was near Lorch on the borders of Germania Superior and Raetia. The final form of the *limites* was attained only after a long development in which the frontier was frequently changed and the system of defenses varied. Domitian laid the foundations of the system by constructing a continuous barrier along these frontiers in the form of a low embankment of earth, which in places gave way to wooden fences. Along this line were placed wooden watchtowers at irregular intervals, and some distance to the rear was a series of earthen forts, each garrisoned by a corps of auxiliaries and linked by roads to the barrier. While auxiliary troops were thus distributed along the frontiers in small detachments, Domitian broke up the larger legionary cantonments, so that after A.D. 89 none regularly contained more than a single legion. This had the effect of scattering the legions along the frontiers as support for the line of auxiliary forts. Trajan strengthened the fortifications of Domitian but rather stressed improving the system of communication between the border provinces by building highways from the Rhine to the Black Sea, and in Arabia and Africa. The principate of Hadrian marked a new stage in the development of the Germanic and Raetian *limites*. Along them he erected an unbroken palisade, constructed of the split trunks of oak trees set upright nine feet high in a shallow trench. To facilitate observation and signaling from the watchtowers, he shortened and straightened the line of the *limites* which now ran in rectilinear sections as far as possible without regard to topography. The adoption of the new line brought about abandonment of some of the older forts for newer ones of earth or of earth and wood placed close to the palisade. Antoninus Pius, who carried on Hadrian's policy of strengthening border defenses, converted these advance forts into stone structures; and Commodus reinforced the barrier still more by substituting in some places a stone wall for Hadrian's palisade. Finally Caracalla completed the process by providing the Raetian *limes* with a wall of stone six to nine feet high and four feet thick which ran along its whole front for about 105 miles, while he also had a wide ditch dug along the Germanic *limes* just behind the palisade. These fortifications were by no means impenetrable and were not intended to serve as a permanent barrier against large forces, but it enabled the Romans to control communications along the frontier and was a formidable obstacle to raiding parties, whose entry would be reported quickly to the nearest garrisons and who would with great difficulty escape with their booty across the *limes*.

LIMES IN BRITAIN. In the time of Domitian, Agricola built a road guarded by forts placed at irregular intervals along the 76-mile stretch from Newcastle-upon-Tyne to the Solway Firth. Along this line, under the direction of Hadrian between 122 and 127, the fortification system was constructed known as Hadrian's Wall. A stone wall about twenty feet high and eight feet thick, it linked a series of fourteen forts, each accommodating a detachment of about 1,000 auxiliaries. In front was a deep V-shaped ditch, thirty feet wide at the top. Incorporated in the wall were castles for garrisons of 100 men, situated at regular mile intervals. Between the castles were stone turrets likewise spaced at fixed intervals. In contrast to the Germanic *limes*, the wall in Britain had considerable defensive value against more than mere raiding parties. The Roman sphere of influence extended northward into Scotland, however, and, to protect this territory from highland tribes, Antoninus Pius in 143 built another wall 36 miles long from the Firth of Forth to the Clyde constructed of turf blocks laid like bricks and containing twenty forts of earth or earth and stone construction. Both the wall of Hadrian and that of Antoninus were partially destroyed by a Pictish invasion in 181. Severus later rebuilt Hadrian's Wall, but the wall in Scotland was permanently abandoned.

DANUBIAN FRONTIERS. Where the Danube marked the northern frontier, it was defended by a line of auxiliary forts and legionary encampments on the Roman side of the river. Roman advance to the north, particularly in Dacia, led to the development of frontier delimitation and defense similar to that in Germany and Raetia. Only relatively short stretches of these *limites* are traceable today. An earthen wall running west to east for about 63 miles from the Danube to the Theiss protected Moesia north of the Danube in the enclave between these two rivers. The line of another wall has been found on part of the northern frontier of Dacia, and two lines of fortifications roughly parallel to the Aluta river seem to have formed part of its eastern defenses. Of three walls that run from the Danube eastward to the Black Sea near Tomi, one, a large wall of turf, is pre-Trajanic and formed a temporary *limes* in that part of Moesia; the other two seem to be post-Roman.

LIMITES IN ASIA AND AFRICA. Neither in Asia nor in Africa was there a continuous line of frontier defenses, but the *limites* were marked by roads protected by chains of small forts and stations from which patrols operated. Behind the *limites*, often at considerable distances, were large fortified camps at strategic points. The difference in the *limes* organization of Britain and Europe from that of Asia and Africa is explained by the difference in physical features of the boundary lands, and in the character of frontier peoples and warfare on the northern, eastern, and southern borders.

THE IMPERIAL NAVY. The navy played an important if subordinate part in imperial defense. Two main fleets based at Misenum and Ravenna secured communications by sea between Italy and the provinces and served to convoy troops and supplies. Provincial squadrons were maintained in Egypt, Syria, Mauretania, in the Black Sea, on the Danube and its tributaries, the

Save and the Drave, on the Rhine, and in the English Channel. In addition to routine police duties, they suppressed piracy, checked barbarian raids, and helped the army in its operations.

CONSEQUENCES OF THE SYSTEM OF FRONTIER DEFENSE. The result of the construction of permanent frontier fortifications was the immobilization of auxiliary corps. Often stationed continuously in the same sectors from early in the second century and recruited increasingly from among the children of the camps, in the third century, they were granted frontier lands upon condition of their defending them. A semimilitary status was given to civilians in certain frontier districts by the Severi, who concentrated them in small castles and other defensible posts. Scattering of the legions along the frontiers slowed assembly of any mobile force. Fortifications, while checking predatory raids by isolated bands and in regulating intercourse across the frontiers, proved incapable of preventing invasion by larger forces. When the barbarians broke through the *limites* in the third century, they found no forces capable of checking them until they had penetrated deep into the provinces.

The chaos following the death of Severus Alexander was the result of a military policy that had left the richest and most highly civilized provinces without any self-defense and created a professional army whose rank and file placed its own vested interest before the state's and rendered the army itself incapable of fighting efficiently by often blurring the distinction between soldier and civilian.

THE ROMAN ARMY AS A CIVILIZING AGENCY. On the other hand, the army was one of the most influential agents in the spread of all aspects of Roman civilization. Highways, bridges, fortifications, and numerous other public works were constructed by soldiers. Every camp was a center for the spread of Latin and of Roman discipline, and the number of Roman citizens was augmented continuously by the stream of discharged auxiliaries. In the *canabae*, or towns of civilian camp-followers, sprang up organized communities of veterans with institutions and material advantages of municipal life. The movement of troops from one quarter to another facilitated exchange of cultural, and in particular of religious, ideas. To the ideal of a Roman Empire the army remained loyal, although this loyalty was generally interpreted in the light of its own vested interest. Not only did the army support the power of the *princeps*, it was also the mainstay of the Roman Peace, which endured with two brief interruptions from the battle of Actium to the death of Severus Alexander and was the necessary condition for the civilizing mission of Rome.

III. THE PROVINCES UNDER THE PRINCIPATE

A true appreciation of the beneficial aspects of Roman government during the Principate may be found in the state of the provinces. As Mommsen[1] said: "It is in the agricultural towns of Africa, in the homes of the vine-dressers on

---

[1] *Provinces of the Roman Empire*, I, 5, trans. Dickson, Scribner's, 1906.

the Moselle, in the flourishing townships of the Lycian mountains, and on the margin of the Syrian desert that the work of the imperial period is to be sought and found." In this sphere the chief tasks of the Principate were the maintenance of peace and the extension of Greco-Roman civilization over the barbarian provinces of the west and north. The material remains of once flourishing communities and the extent to which the civilization of Western Europe rests upon the basis of Roman culture attest its success.

THE PROVINCES. At the establishment of the Principate there were about thirteen provinces, at the death of Augustus twenty-eight, and under Hadrian, forty-five. In the course of the third century the number was considerably increased. New provinces were formed partly by the organization of newly conquered countries and partly by subdivision of larger units. This subdivision was made to relieve a governor of an excessively heavy task and to improve the administration, or to lessen the dangers of revolt by breaking up large military commands. The principle established by Augustus that garrisoned provinces should come under the *princeps* was adhered to, and consequently provinces were at times taken over by the emperor for military necessities, while others were transferred to the Senate. As a rule, new provinces were placed under imperial governors, so that these soon outnumbered the senatorial.

ADMINISTRATIVE OFFICIALS. The governors of senatorial provinces were called proconsuls, even if they were of praetorian rank. Asia and Africa, however, were reserved for ex-consuls. Following the law of Pompey, a period of five years intervened between holding a magistracy and a promagisterial appointment. Each proconsul was assisted by a quaestor and three propraetorian *legati* whose appointment was approved by the *princeps*. Imperial governors were of two classes, legates of Augustus (*legati Augusti*) and procurators. In the time of Hadrian there were eleven proconsuls, twenty-four legates of Augustus, and nine procurators, besides the prefect of Egypt. Subordinates of the legates of Augustus were legates in command of legions and fiscal procurators. Procuratorial governors, at first called prefects, were equestrians and placed in command of lesser military districts, garrisoned by auxiliaries only. An exception to this practice was Egypt, which was governed by a prefect who at first was the highest ranking equestrian but later ranked second to the praetorian prefect. He had under his orders at first three and later two legions besides auxiliary corps. In place of the usual senatorial legates, these legions were commanded by equestrian prefects. From the time of Septimius Severus equestrian procurators frequently were appointed to act as deputy governors in imperial provinces normally commanded by senatorial legates. During the second century the title *praeses* (plural *praesides*) came into general use for senatorial governors serving the *princeps*.

ENLIGHTENED IMPERIALISM. As under the Republic, governors exercised administrative, judicial, and (in imperial provinces) military authority. Augustus inaugurated a policy of enlightened imperialism with his two edicts of 7–6 B.C., which protected non-Roman provincials of Crete and Cyrene from judicial oppression by Romans residing there, and his sponsorship of the Senate's decree of 4 B.C., which provided a more direct and less expensive method for redress of wrongs suffered from provincial officials.[2] It is often assumed that higher standards of administration resulted in marked amelioration in the well-being of the provinces during the early Principate. Such a view demands serious qualification. That the provinces by ancient standards flourished in the first two centuries of imperial rule, there can be no doubt, and it is obvious that the emperors, as a whole, were sincerely interested in the welfare of their subjects. But it can be argued that the improved economic status of the Empire was due primarily to the Roman Peace following an era of civil wars and that standards of public morality, despite the best of imperial intentions, were not much higher than those of the Republic. Despite the introduction of salaries for provincial governors and other public servants, officials tended to be corrupt, and it was difficult to bring them to justice. The problem of dishonesty in administration increased as imperial bureaucracy expanded. The Empire, it seems, flourished in spite of rather than because of the conduct of many of its civil servants.

PROVINCIAL TAXATION. Under Augustus taxation was revised to correspond more closely to taxpaying capacity. These taxes were of two kinds, direct (*tributa*) and indirect (*vectigalia*). The *tributa* comprised a land tax (*tributum soli*) and a personal tax (*tributum capitis*). The land tax was assessed on all land not granted the exceptional status of Italian soil (*ius Italicum*); the personal tax was levied on all property not subject to the land tax. Poll taxes and taxes on trades and occupations were also collected in certain provinces. The chief indirect taxes were customs dues (*portoria*), the 5 per cent tax on the value of emancipated slaves, possibly the 1 per cent sales tax and the 5 (after Caracalla, 10) per cent inheritance tax, levied on Romans only. In imperial provinces the land tax was a fixed proportion of the annual yield, whereas in senatorial provinces it was a sum (*stipendium*) annually fixed for each community. Provincials were also liable to furnish supplies to troops and officials (*annona*), to provide transport animals for the post service, and to perform personal services (*munera*) for the state. Although compensation was provided for both goods and services requisitioned, such exactions proved more burdensome than regular taxation, for they often were a serious economic drain and gave many opportunities for graft and oppression.

The Principate did not break abruptly with the practice of employing associations of *publicani* to collect revenues. They had been excluded from Asia by Julius Caesar, and it is possible that Augustus dispensed with them for raising direct taxes in imperial provinces, but even under Tiberius they seem to have been active in collecting the *tributa* in some senatorial provinces. Their place in imperial provinces was taken by the procurator and his agents, in

---

[2] See p. 271.

senatorial at first by the proconsul assisted by the taxpaying communities and later by imperial officials.

Indirect taxes long continued to be raised exclusively by corporations of tax collectors everywhere. The operations of *publicani*, however, were supervised by imperial procurators. In place of the previous custom of paying a fixed sum to the state in return for a right to the total returns from the taxes in question, *publicani* now received a fixed percentage of the amount actually collected. Under Hadrian companies of *publicani* collecting customs dues began to be superseded by individual contractors (*conductores*), who, like the companies, received a percentage of the amount raised. About the time of Commodus the system of direct collection by public officials was introduced and contractors gave way to imperial procurators. The 5 per cent tax on inheritances and manumissions was also at first farmed out but later (under Hadrian in the case of inheritances) collected directly by agents of the state.

LOCAL GOVERNMENT. Each province comprised many communities (*civitates*), some of which were organized towns while others were tribes or villages. From the beginning of the Principate it was imperial policy to convert rural communities into municipalities, which undertook local administration. Under the Republic there had been three classes of provincial communities: free and federate (*liberae et foederatae*), free and immune (*liberae et immunes*), and tributary (*stipendiariae*). In addition to native communities there began to appear in the provinces Roman and Latin colonies. Toward the close of the Republic and in the early Principate most free communities lost their immunity from taxation and became tributary. Some of them exchanged the status of federate allies for that of Roman colonies. At the same time the number of colonies of both types was greatly increased by founding new settlements or planting colonists in provincial towns. Some of the latter also became municipalities. Thus a great variety of provincial communities arose, well-illustrated by conditions in Baetica (Farther Spain) under Vespasian. This province then contained 9 colonies and 8 municipalities of Roman citizens, 29 Latin towns, 6 free, 3 federate towns, and 120 tributary communities.

The rapid transformation of rural communities into organized municipalities may be gathered from the fact that in Tarraconensis (Hither Spain) the number of rural districts sank from 114 to 27 between the reign of Vespasian and that of Hadrian. A parallel movement was conversion of native towns into Roman colonies and municipalities, often through the transitional stage of Latin communities, a status existing only in the provinces. Acquirement of Roman or Latin status brought exemption from the poll tax, while the former opened the way to all civil offices. An added advantage to being a Roman colony was usually immunity from the land tax. The last step in the Romanization of provincial towns was Caracalla's edict of 212, which conferred Roman citizenship on all non-Roman municipalities.

THE THREE GAULS. Two districts were at first excluded from this municipalization: the three Gauls (Aquitania, Lugdunensis, and Belgica) and Egypt. At the time of its conquest Gaul was a rich agricultural country, with sharply defined tribal communities but little or no city development. This condition Augustus judged well adapted, under strict imperial control, to furnishing recruits, money, and produce for the army of the Rhine. He therefore continued the division of Gaul into 64 tribal units (*civitates*), each controlled by its native nobility. His policy was adhered to for about two hundred years, but during the third century the municipal system was introduced into Gaul by converting the chief town of each *civitas* into a municipality with the rest of the *civitas* as *territorium* under its control.

EGYPT. Although Augustus incorporated Egypt as a province, it occupied a peculiar status within his *imperium* and was kept more directly under his control than other provinces. This was primarily because of its wealth and importance for the grain supply of Rome. In Egypt he appeared as the heir of the Ptolemies by right of conquest and was recognized by the Egyptians as "king of upper Egypt and king of lower Egypt, lord of the two lands, *autocrator*, son of the Sun." For the Greek residents he was an absolute deified ruler of the Hellenistic type. Thus Egypt, although a part of the Empire, was looked upon at times as subject to the *princeps'* personal rule. As in the theory of government, so in political institutions, the Romans adapted to their purposes existing conditions.

Under Augustus there were three Greek towns in Egypt, Alexandria the capital, Ptolemais, and Naucratis. To these Hadrian added a fourth, Antinoöpolis. Ptolemais, Naucratis, and Antinoöpolis were municipalities, but Alexandria, because of the turbulence of its population, was ruled by imperial officials, following Ptolemaic practice. The rest of the population lived in villages throughout the Nile valley, which was divided into thirty-six districts (nomes). Most of Egypt was imperial or public domain, and most Egyptians were imperial tenants. For collection of the land tax, poll tax, professional and other taxes, for the supervision of irrigation, and for maintenance of public records of the cultivated acreage and the population (for which a census was taken every fourteen years), there had been developed a highly organized bureaucracy with central offices at Alexandria and agents in the nomes. This system was maintained by the Romans and undoubtedly influenced the organization of the imperial civil service. The chief burden laid upon Egypt was to supply one third of the grain consumed at Rome, or about 5,000,000 bushels annually. This amount was drawn partly from the land tax, paid in kind, and partly from grain purchased by the government.

The first step toward spreading municipal government throughout Egypt was taken in A.D. 200 when Septimius Severus organized a senate, or town council, in Alexandria and in the metropolis or administrative seat of each nome. His object was to create bodies that could be made responsible for administration.

THE PROVINCES AND IMPERIAL GOVERNMENT. The Principate's greatest service to the provinces was two and a half centuries of peace. This led in many areas to material development unequalled in these regions before or since. In these centuries the history of Rome becomes the history of the provinces. At the opening of the period the Italians occupied a privileged position within the Empire; at its close they and their former subjects were on the same level. The army and the senatorial and equestrian orders were increasingly provincialized, and the emperors were usually provincials. Rome was still the seat of administration, adorned with the spoils of Empire, its populace regaled with bread and public entertainments. It remained the center of Roman political traditions, but from the constitutional point of view its status differed little from that of a provincial municipality.

Obviously imperial government had no desire to create or to maintain a spirit of provincial nationalism. Consequently, it never sought to build up provincial self-government. The only institution that served to voice the opinion of a province was the council, which directed the provincial cult of Rome and Augustus. Provincial councils had not been unknown under the Republic. More of them were instituted during the Principate, but by no means everywhere. They were composed of representatives from municipalities or other local units who belonged to the upper classes of their respective communities. They could address petitions, recommendations, and complaints either to the governor or to the *princeps*. They might have been an important factor in the prosecution of governors for maladministration, but such prosecution was difficult and dangerous, and the councils often preferred to flatter outgoing governors who could no longer oppress them but who, as senators, might become their patrons at the capital. The councils themselves never exercised political functions.

It is difficult to estimate the extent to which the provincials had been "Romanized," because the meaning of "Romanization" is debatable. Apart from administrative organization, imperial government made virtually no effort to impose uniformity by supplanting local languages, religions, customs, and even laws by those of Rome. This was particularly true of the Hellenistic East, where Western cultural influences made little impression. But even in the African provinces (apart from Egypt and Cyrenaica), on the Danube, in the Rhineland, Gaul, Spain, and Britain, survivals of pre-Roman institutions, customs, and ways of life were numerous and persistent. The rapid and widespread reception of Latin culture in certain areas was due to the influences radiating from Roman colonies and Roman camps, from Roman businessmen and officials, and to the general appeal exerted by the culture of a ruling element rather than to any conscious imperial policy.

Under the Principate, as under the Republic, respect for local prejudices went far to reconcile conquered peoples to Roman rule and develop a feeling of loyalty to the Empire. Perhaps it is here that one should look for the real test of Romanization—namely, the degree to which articulate and therefore upper-class provincials took pride in being "Romans," as citizens of the Empire, and in taking an active share in its defense and its government. Development of this attitude found expression in the participation of provincials in imperial service and their incorporation in the senatorial order, which reflected the economic and cultural condition of the areas from which they came and the attitude of leading men toward the Empire.

IV. MUNICIPAL LIFE

Under the Principate the Empire became the greatest state the world had yet seen, surpassing both the old Persian Empire and that of Alexander the Great. Its area was approximately three and a half million square miles, its population possibly seventy million. To the Greek rhetorician Aelius Aristides, who in 143 delivered a speech in Rome in praise of her rule, this vast empire, coextensive with the civilized world, appeared as an aggregate of cities held together by Roman civil administration and the military establishment. This view is substantially correct, despite the existence in many provinces of large areas, especially imperial domains, without municipal organization. Most of the Empire consisted of many locally autonomous communities serving as units for taxation, jurisdiction, and conscription and in general relieving imperial administration of the burdens of local government. They were municipalities, each responsible for an area under its jurisdiction and constituting its territory (*territorium*) and were of two general types: the Hellenistic in the East and the Italian in the West.

HELLENISTIC MUNICIPALITIES. Hellenistic municipalities developed from the *poleis*, or city-states, which existed prior to the Roman conquest in Greece and the Hellenized areas of Asia and Africa. Municipal towns organized there subsequent to Roman occupation were similar. Their language was Greek. The characteristic institutions of the Hellenistic municipalities were a popular assembly, a council or *boule*, and annual magistrates. The assembly initiated legislation; the council and magistrates were elected by it or were chosen by lot. Even under the Republic these democratic institutions were modified in the interests of the wealthier classes. Timocratic constitutions were established, with property qualifications for citizenship and for the council and offices, the Principate accentuating this development. Assemblies lost their right to initiate legislation, a power that passed to the magistrates, while the council tended to become a body of ex-magistrates who held their seats for life. In spite of this approximation to the Italian type, Greek official terminology remained unchanged throughout the first three centuries A.D.

ITALIAN MUNICIPALITIES. The Latin type of municipality developed in Italy with the extension of Roman domination and was given uniformity by legislation of Julius Caesar. With the Romanization of Western Europe, it spread to Africa, Spain, Gaul, Britain, Germany, and the Danubian provinces. Despite distinctions between Roman and Latin colonies and *municipia*, all municipalities were of the same general type, as is revealed in the Julian Municipal Law (45 B.C.), the charter of the Roman *Colonia Genetiva Iulia* (44 B.C.), and those of Latin municipalities of Malaca and Salpensa (A.D. 81–84).

They were patterned after Rome, although certain titles, like those of consul and Senate, were reserved for the capital city. Like Rome, municipal towns had their officials, council (*curia, ordo*), and assembly. The chief magistrates were a pair of duovirs (or at times a college of quattuorvirs), who were assisted by two aediles and two quaestors. The duovirs were in charge of local administration of justice and conducted all public affairs of the community. Every fifth year they were called *quinquennales* and took the census. Aediles had charge of public works and market and police regulations, while quaestors were treasury officials. All were popularly elected, but a property qualification was required of each candidate. If no candidates presented themselves for a particular office, provision was made for the nomination of candidates obliged to serve if elected. At his election each magistrate paid into the treasury, or expended by order of the council, a sum of money (*summa honoraria*), which varied for each office in different communities. Often these officers did not restrict themselves to the required sum but took this opportunity for philanthropic display. As other prominent citizens followed their example, municipalities were richly provided with useful and ornamental public works. Thus municipal offices, being unsalaried, were a heavy drain upon the resources of their holders. They also offered almost the sole opportunity for gratifying political ambitions of the prosperous middle class in the provinces. In addition to civil officials, each community had its colleges of pontiffs and augurs.

Members of the *curia* were called *decuriones* and were usually one hundred in number. Their wealth, like that of the imperial senatorial order, was derived almost exclusively from land. They comprised those who had held some local magistracy, and others having enough property and enrolled directly (*adlecti*) in the council. The council supervised the magistrates and directed municipal administration. As in early Rome, so in municipalities, the people were grouped in *curiae*, which were voting units in the local assembly or *comitia*. This assembly elected the magistrates and had legislative powers like those of the Roman

XVII Theater at Leptis Magna. *This city (in modern Libya) was granted colonial Roman status by Trajan and extensively patronized by its most famous native son, Septimius Severus. The theater was begun by Augustus and embellished by subsequent emperors. (Photo: Fototeca Unione.)*

assemblies. In the second century A.D., however, these legislative powers passed into the hands of the council, whose decrees became the sole form of municipal legislation.

GUILDS AND COLLEGES. Although the lower classes of Rome and the municipalities had little opportunity for political activity, they found compensation in guilds. These were associations of persons who had some common tie, such as trade or profession, worship, or the desire to secure a decent burial. Thus arose professional, religious, and funerary colleges organized like municipalities. They had their patrons, presidents (*magistri*, or *quinquennales*), quaestors,

and treasury, sustained by initiation fees, monthly dues, fines, contributions, gifts, and legacies. The membership was called plebs or *populus*. The chief element in the life of the colleges was social, and their most important gatherings were for a common banquet. Professional colleges were unlike modern trade unions; they attempted no collective bargaining with regard to wages, prices, or working hours, although they did not altogether neglect common professional interests.

Apparently until late republican times no restrictions were placed on such associations. In 64 B.C. all of them in Rome were abolished because of the disorders occasioned by political clubs. In 58 B.C. complete freedom of association was restored, only to be revoked again by Julius Caesar, who permitted only old and reputable professional and religious colleges. Under Augustus a law regulated their character, organization, and activities. New colleges could be established in Italy or the provinces only if sanctioned by the Senate or an edict of the *princeps*, and membership in an unauthorized college was treasonable. Trajan authorized unrestricted formation of funerary colleges (*collegia tenuiorum*) in Rome, and Septimius Severus extended this privilege to Italy and the provinces. Under Marcus Aurelius colleges were recognized as juristic persons, with power to manumit slaves and receive legacies. Not only men of free birth but also freedmen and slaves, and in many cases women, were freely admitted to membership.

V. BEGINNINGS OF ECONOMIC DECLINE

In the second century A.D., under the aegis of imperial government, the ancient world reached the height of prosperity. In spite of generally favorable conditions, even in the second century there were signs that all was not well with the economy of the Empire, and before the close of the Severan dynasty these indications had become much more apparent.

BURDEN OF TAXATION. The total cost of government was clearly increasing, although it apparently did not force taxpayers to draw on their capital wealth. The maintenance of local government constituted an indirect tax upon property, whereas the superstructure of provincial and imperial government was supported by taxation collected by imperial or local agents in municipal and other administrative units. In addition, the central government could requisition upon its own terms supplies and services from its subjects, over and above normal taxes.

One increasingly expensive item was the army, whose numbers had grown considerably over those established by Augustus. The permanent fortifications constructed on the frontiers and new highways, built largely by labor of the troops, added still more to military expenditures. A second factor increasing the cost of government was the gradual expansion of the imperial civil service with its numerous departments and officials. Other significant factors were development of the imperial post; construction of public works, including roads, bridges, aqueducts, temples, theaters, amphitheaters, and public baths; the ever more elaborate system of doles, largesses, and entertainments for the populace of the capital; and expenditures on education, public health, and Italian farm relief. The fundamental causes for this expansion of public services were in most cases the search for efficiency and a corresponding growth of a sense of responsibility by the government toward its subjects. Laudable as these motives were, the result rendered the financial situation so precarious that a long war or a spendthrift emperor at times actually bankrupted the treasury. The cost of defending and governing the Empire sometimes strained to the utmost the taxpaying power of its population. One of the chief reasons for giving up the attempt to occupy the region between the Rhine and Elbe and for relinquishing to the Parthians the conquests of Trajan in Armenia and Mesopotamia was inability to afford their conquest and defense. The heavy burden of taxation played a large part in the rebellion in Judaea in A.D. 66. Both Hadrian and Marcus Aurelius were obliged to remit arrears of taxation that had accumulated over the years, and the latter received repeated requests from municipalities for financial aid or reduction of taxes. Marcus Aurelius expressed frankly the desperate condition of the public finances when he answered the petition of his victorious troops for an increase in pay with the words: "Anything you receive over and above your regular wages must be exacted from the blood of your parents and relations."[3] Financial stringency led to the debasement of coinage in order to secure a temporary profit for the treasury. Nero reduced the silver content of the denarius by 10 per cent. Under Trajan the debasement with copper increased to 15 per cent, under Marcus Aurelius to 25 per cent, and under Septimius Severus to almost 40 per cent. Caracalla issued a new silver coin, the Antoninianus, supposedly equal to two denarii, but it also contained scarcely 60 per cent silver. Not only the denarius but also the standard gold coin, the aureus, was reduced in weight. These inflationary expedients brought no permanent relief, however.

FISCAL OPPRESSION. From Egypt comes the most striking evidence of the fiscal burden. It is true that for a long time conditions in Egypt were not typical for all provinces, because the absence of municipal autonomy, the extent of public domain, and the highly developed bureaucracy there made possible fiscal exploitation that would have been difficult elsewhere. Ultimately, however, the situation in other provinces came to approximate closely that of Egypt. Even in Egypt it was not the intention of the imperial government to ruin its subjects, but rather to make them prosperous so that they might produce more revenue. The combined weight of imperial and local administration was a load greater than even this rich area could support. As early as the principate of Nero the peasantry and poorer townspeople complained of oppression to which they were subjected by local tax collectors. Since the government held

---

[3] Cassius Dio, *Epitome*, LXXI, 3.

the properties of the collectors themselves as security for the total they were supposed to collect, they used every means, legal or illegal, to force taxpayers to contribute the full amount. If anyone was unable to meet his obligations, his relatives or, in default of these, fellow townsmen and villagers were forced to make good the deficit. The demands of the tax collectors were enforced brutally, at times with the aid of police and soldiers. When harvests failed, farmers who could not pay fled, leaving their lands untilled for the next season. The result was that, by A.D. 60, a serious decline had taken place in the population of many villages even in so rich a part of Egypt as the Fayum.

Despite attempts made by some prefects and emperors to curb illegal exactions and to improve the condition of the peasants, the situation gradually grew worse, because the requirements of government increased. More and more peasants refused to lease public lands, since the burdens involved were too heavy. To prevent loss of revenue, officials assigned unleased plots to adjacent villages or to individual private landholders, who thereby became responsible for their cultivation and the payment of taxes assessed against them. This made heavier the burden on those who remained on the land, and more and more peasants simply fled. These runaways were responsible for the armed revolts of A.D. 152 and 172, as well as for the appearance of brigandage on a wide scale under Septimius Severus.

Although tenant farmers were the first to suffer, it was not long before landholders and well-to-do townspeople were also affected. At first, following the Ptolemaic custom, Roman government employed salaried officials in the lower administrative posts throughout Egypt. In the second half of the first century A.D. these were displaced by officials drafted from the propertied classes of communities in the nomes. They were unsalaried, their service constituting a property surtax. This practice was not new in the Hellenistic East, for it originated in the well-known Greek institution of the liturgy, or obligatory personal service imposed on people who possessed the property qualification. The Romans, however, applied it on a hitherto unexampled scale. As office-holders were responsible with their properties for any deficiencies in tax returns, they were more merciless than ever in exacting full payment from helpless peasants. The fear under which men lived is reflected in questions addressed to temple oracles in the second century A.D.: whether the petitioner should run away, or whether the government was going to sell his property to settle tax accounts.

DECLINE OF MUNICIPAL AUTONOMY. The prosperity of the municipalities was a gauge of that of the whole Empire and their condition was watched with anxiety by the government. By the second century A.D. many of these communities were in financial difficulties. The causes of this condition are not everywhere easy to trace. Among them were the ruin of some wealthier families by the requirements of office holding, withdrawal from municipal life of men who entered imperial service, overtaxation, bad management of local finances, and at times decline of the rural population that furnished a market for manufacturers and merchants of the towns. This situation invited imperial interference, and Trajan appointed curators and other commissioners to rehabilitate the finances of individual municipalities or those of whole provinces. They were chosen from senators and equestrians and at first were appointed for emergencies. By the time of Severus Alexander they were a fixture in many municipalities and were appointed from the local decurions. Here government paternalism, which at first sought to guide the towns through economic crises, ended in placing the operation of municipal finances under the control of the central administration. For this the apathy of the municipal governing classes was largely to blame.

Another aspect of the decline of municipal autonomy is seen in the change that took place in the character of local magistracies and the relationship of municipal councils to imperial authorities. In the second century A.D. magistracies were still looked upon as an honor, for which candidates presented themselves voluntarily, although there were signs that in some districts they were regarded as a burden. Since in default of voluntary candidates for the magistracies, eligible citizens could be forced to run, public office was an inescapable obligation for the propertied. By the third century, magistrates came to be appointees of the decurions, and membership in municipal councils likewise became obligatory for those with enough property. The principle developed that municipal councils or their representatives were responsible to the state for revenues due from municipal territories. In the Eastern provinces committees of ten, called *decaprotoi* or "first ten," were nominated by the councils and put in charge of collecting imperial taxes. These *decaprotoi* had to make good from their personal properties uncollected taxes. Because of this new function of the councils Septimius Severus organized them in the nome capitals of Egypt, where they were charged with responsibility for local financial administration and for nominating and acting as sureties for both municipal officials and local agents of the provincial administration. The municipalities had thus lost control over their own finances and also became agents of the imperial government for raising public revenues.

THE STATE AND THE PROFESSIONAL GUILDS. The loss of municipal independence was accompanied by an encroachment upon the freedom of voluntary professional colleges. From the beginning of the Principate, the government depended largely on private initiative for the performance of many necessary services in connection with provisioning the city of Rome, which became increasingly complicated when the state undertook the distribution of olive oil under Septimius Severus. Therefore guilds like those of the shipowners (*navicularii*), bakers (*pistores*), pork merchants (*suarii*), wine merchants (*vinarii*), and oil merchants (*olerarii*) received official encouragement. Their members individually assumed public contracts and were exempted from certain municipal obligations, since it was recognized that they were performing necessary services. Marcus Aurelius, Severus, and Caracalla were emperors who thus fostered the guilds. Gradually the idea developed that these services were public duties (*munera*) to which the colleges were obligated, and under Severus Alexander the initiative in organizing new ones passed to the state. He also appointed judicial representatives from each guild and placed them under the jurisdiction of certain courts. The colleges henceforward operated under governmental supervision and really formed a part of the administration, although they had not yet become compulsory and hereditary organizations.

The history of guilds in the municipalities paralleled that of the Roman guilds, although it cannot be traced so clearly in detail. The best known of the municipal colleges are those of carpenters (*fabri*), makers of rag cloths (*centonarii*), and woodcutters (*dendrophori*). The organization of these colleges was everywhere encouraged because their members were obliged to act as a local fire brigade, although in exercising their trades they were not in the service of their communities.

CHAPTER 20
SOCIAL,
INTELLECTUAL, AND
RELIGIOUS LIFE
UNDER THE
PRINCIPATE

I. SOCIAL AND ECONOMIC CONDITIONS

IMPERIAL ROME. Roman society under the Principate was generally similar to that of the last century of the Republic. Rome itself was a cosmopolitan city, where the concentration of wealth and political power attracted the ambitious, adventurous, and curious from all lands. Whole quarters were occupied by various nationalities, most prominent among whom were the Greeks, Syrians, and Jews, speaking their own languages and plying their native trades. With the freeborn population mingled thousands of slaves and freedmen of every race and tongue. During the first two centuries the population of Rome probably varied in the neighborhood of 750,000 souls. Inevitably in such a city there were the sharpest contrasts between riches and poverty, luxurious palaces of the wealthy and squalid tenements of the proletariat. Rome's appearance underwent a transformation that made her worthy to be the capital of so vast an Empire. This was largely the result of the many public buildings erected by the emperors and to the lavish employment of marble in public and private architecture from the time of Augustus. The temples, basilicas, fora, aqueducts, public baths, theaters, palaces, triumphal arches, statues, and parks combined to arouse the admiration of travelers and the pride of its inhabitants. After the great fire of A.D. 64 many improvements were made in the plan of the city, restrictions were placed on the height of buildings, and fireproof construction required for the lower stories, but the streets remained narrow and filthy, the lofty tenements flimsy and in perpetual danger of collapse, and devastating conflagrations occurred periodically.

The task of feeding and entertaining the city mob was a ruinous legacy left by the Republic to the Principate. Augustus and his successors maintained the number of recipients of free grain at 200,000. There were also frequent distributions of money (*congiaria*) by emperors, and public spectacles became ever more numerous and magnificent. Under Tiberius 87 days of the year were regularly occupied by entertainments, and by the time of Marcus Aurelius there were 135 such holidays. In addition there were extraordinary festivals, such as the 123-day carnival given by Trajan at his second Dacian triumph in A.D. 106. The spectacles were of three main types: chariot races in the circus, gladiatorial combats and animal baiting in the amphitheater, and dramatic and other performances in the theater. The expense of these celebrations fell upon senators and the *princeps*. The most important function of the consulship, praetorship, and, until its disappearance in the third century, the aedileship, came to be the celebration of regular festivals. Sums provided for such purposes by the state were inadequate, so the cost had to be met largely from the magistrates' private resources. Extraordinary spectacles were all given by the *princeps*, who also at times granted subventions to favored senators from the imperial purse. Financing of public shows placed as heavy a drain on senatorial fortunes, as did the office fees and local expenditures on those of the decurions.

A new feature of society under the Principate was the growth of the imperial court. Despite the wishes of Augustus and some of his successors to live on equal footing with the nobility, the unique position of the *princeps* inevitably gave a corresponding importance to his household. Offices developed within it not only for the conduct of public business but also to control slaves and freedmen in the domestic service. The chief household officials were his chamberlain (*a cubiculo*) and the chief usher (*ab admissione*). Because of their intimate personal association with the *princeps* their influence over him was great, and as a rule they used their position to take bribes from those seeking imperial favor. Among senators and equestrians the *princeps* had intimate associates and advisers who were called his "friends." When forming part of his cortege away from Rome, they were known as his companions (*comites Augusti*). Imperial audiences became ceremonious, with fixed forms of salutation differentiating the rank and station of those in attendance. In the society of the capital the personal tastes of the *princeps* set the fashion.

CLIENTS. A new form of clientage characterized the times, a voluntary association of master and paid retainer. Under the Republic eminent men had throngs of adherents to greet them at their morning reception and accompany them to the Forum. Custom now demanded that virtually every wealthy man maintain such a retinue, to be at his beck and call at all hours of the day and prepared to serve him. In return the patron helped to support his clients with fees, food, and clothing, and rendered them other favors. The clients were recruited partly from freedmen, partly from citizens of low birth, and partly from genteel but impoverished persons. In general, the lot of these pensioners was not very happy—even their patrons' slaves despised them—and their large numbers are attributed to the lack of industrial employment in Rome.

SLAVES AND FREEDMEN. In the early Principate slaveholding continued on as large a scale as in the late Republic. Palaces of the wealthy in Rome could count slaves by hundreds; on larger plantations they were numbered by thousands. Trained slaves were also employed in great numbers in trades and industries. Their treatment varied according to their employment and the character of their owners, but there was a steady progress toward greater humanitarianism, largely due to the influence of Stoicism. Under the Antonines this produced legislation limiting the power of the master over his slave. Gradually the number of slaves diminished, in part because of the infrequency of foreign wars after Augustus, in part because of a great increase in manumission. Not only were many set free at their owner's death as a final act of generosity, but also many found it profitable to liberate their slaves and provide them with capital to engage in business. Many slaves also had good opportunities for accumulating some money (*peculium*) with which they could purchase their freedom.

The result of these wholesale manumissions was a tremendous increase in the freedmen class. The importance of freedmen in Roman society corresponded to their numbers. From them were recruited the lower ranks of the civil service, they filled every trade and profession, the commerce of Italy was largely theirs, and they became managers of estates and of business undertakings. Pursuit of money was their common characteristic, and "freedman's wealth" was a proverbial expression for riches quickly acquired. The more successful of their class became landholders in Italy and aped the life and manners of the nobility. Their sons often attained equestrian rank, and their more remote descendants sometimes became senators. Their lack of good taste, so common to the *nouveaux riches* of all ages, afforded a good target for the jibes of satirists. A few among them attained positions of political importance and great influence through imperial favor. Despise the freedmen though they might, the Romans found them indispensable for the conduct of public and private business.

COMMERCE AND INDUSTRY. Restoration of peace, suppression of piracy, extension of highways throughout all the provinces, establishment of a single currency valid for the whole Empire, and low duties levied at provincial customs frontiers combined to produce an unprecedented development of commerce. Traders from all parts of the Empire thronged the ports of Italy, and one merchant of Hierapolis in Phrygia has left a record of his twenty-two voyages between Asia Minor and Italy. Puteoli on the Bay of Naples was Italy's chief port,

Ostia its second. The government's attitude toward the economy was one of laissez faire, but production and distribution of certain strategic commodities were regulated. Sea-borne trade was not left entirely to individual enterprise, since the imperial government supervised guilds of shipowners both of Italy and the provinces to maintain the grain supply of Rome and the transportation of supplies for the armies.

Commerce was not confined within the borders of the Empire; it also flourished abroad, particularly in the East. A brisk caravan trade through the Parthian Empire from Mesopotamia across the Iranian plateau to Turkestan and thence to China brought products of that country, especially silk and silk goods, to Syrian ports. From Egyptian harbors on the Red Sea large merchant fleets sailed for southern Arabia and thence across the Arabian Sea to India and Ceylon. Numerous finds of Roman coins in India, evidence of the presence of Greek merchants from Egypt there, and visits of ambassadors of Indian princes to Rome attest the regularity and importance of the Indian trade. Roman traders did not stop at India. They crossed the Bay of Bengal to the Malay Peninsula, passed through the Strait of Malacca, and followed the coast of Indochina until some of them finally reached the southern ports of China. Chinese sources even record the presence of a Roman embassy in China at the time of Marcus Aurelius, but this was probably not an official mission. Active trade relations were maintained with interior Russia through the cities on the north shore of the Black Sea, and Roman traders and their wares crossed Germany to the Baltic. In Africa, isolated Roman officials ventured far into the Sahara Desert and followed the Nile deep into the Sudan, but traffic with these regions remained in the hands of natives who brought their wares to the Roman frontiers.

Among all peoples of the Empire, the most active merchants were Syrians, whose presence may be traced not only in commercial centers of the East but also in ports of Italy and all the western provinces. The increased opportunities for trading stimulated the development of manufacturing, for not only could raw materials be more easily procured but towns favorably situated for the manufacture of particular goods could find wider markets for their products.

In the history of Italian industry the first two centuries of the Principate form a single epoch with the last century of the Republic. The industrial development of Italy then reached its height, largely owing to two factors: concentration of free capital in the hands of emperors and the abundant supply of slave labor at low cost. The preference for investing capital in lands, loans, and trading ventures rather than in industrial enterprises checked the growth of Italian manufacturers. Usually the wealthy tried to make their town and country establishments self-sustaining by employing slaves and tenants in making articles for farm use and by having among their slaves craftsmen trained as bakers, weavers, dyers, shoemakers, masons, smiths, carpenters, and even jewelers and glass blowers. They made themselves independent of outside production, for which poor landholders and city dwellers provided a larger and steadier market. Among important industries catering to more than local trade were bronzeworking and ironworking, manufacture of pottery, lamps, bricks, and tiles, glass blowing, and the weaving of linen and woolen textiles. These industries tended to be concentrated in special centers, determined by the presence of raw materials or a situation advantageous for distribution. Thus the centers for ironworking were Como in Cisalpine Gaul and Puteoli in Campania. Capua was the leading center for bronze work, and Arretium in Etruria for pottery. Certain industries, such as brick, tile, and pottery making, were frequently carried on in rural districts, oftentimes as an adjunct to a plantation. A peculiar feature of industrial life was the activity of the *princeps*, i.e. the State, in certain manufactures competing with private enterprise. This rivalry was limited largely to the production of materials for the construction and maintenance of public works, such as bricks, tiles, cement, lead pipes, and the like. Mass- and small-scale production flourished side by side, the latter by far more general. As a result industrial organization never attained a high degree of development. In the production of articles of bronze, silver, glass, and pottery, an approach to a true factory system developed in that successive steps in the manufacture of each article were performed by different specialists. In general, however, this was not so; a finished article was usually the product of one man's labor. The workers fell into several categories: free hired laborers, freedmen working for patrons or for others, and slaves employed by their owners or leased out to other employers. The evidence bearing upon the relative numbers in these classes is incomplete, but it seems that most workers in large and small industries alike were slaves, that freedmen were numerous, and that the proportion of freeborn persons engaged in industry was not nearly so great as in agriculture. A majority of the slaves and freedmen were Greeks and Hellenized Orientals, and their presence explains why technically and artistically Italian industry in this period could hold its own with that of the East.

The development of Italian industries was the result of export trade in the first century of the Principate. Among leading Italian exports were bronze work to transalpine countries; Arretine pottery and pottery lamps to the West, North, and East; and glass to Spain, Gaul, and the Danube. The development of Gallic pottery drove Arretine ware from the western provinces by the Flavian dynasty; by the end of the first century A.D. Gallic bronze and silver work virtually excluded Italian imports; simultaneously the glass industry of Gaul and Germany, with its final center at Cologne, monopolized the trade of the western part of the Empire. Italian glass and metal work dominated the home market, however, while its woolen manufactures at least met foreign competition.

The balance of trade ran against Italy, which demanded foodstuffs, raw materials, and manufactured articles far beyond the value of her exports. From Egypt, Italy imported glassware, linens, paper, jewelry, and ointments; from

Syria, glass, purple dyestuffs, and silk goods; from Asia Minor, woolens, iron, and steel. Greece supplied the best olive oil, figs, and marble. Africa sent oil, fruit, grain, fish and marble; Spain exported tin, lead, copper, gold, silver, cloth, wool, flax, wine, oil, and fish; Gaul contributed agricultural products, meat, wool, and woven goods; from Britain came gold, silver, iron, hides, fleeces, cattle, slaves, poultry, and oysters; and the Danubian regions furnished both raw and worked iron, hides, wild beasts for the games, and slaves. The products of the Far East reached Rome through Alexandria and Syrian ports, where raw materials were often converted into finished products. The bulk of these Eastern imports came from India, or at least through India, whence the Romans procured linens, cottons, silk, ivory, precious stones, spices, tortoiseshell, and rare wild animals. In return, the Empire sent to India copper, lead, tin, silverware, glass, wine, clothing, musical instruments, slaves, and above all specie. This steady flow of coinage eastward, noticed by the Romans, constituted a drain upon the supply of precious metals in the Empire.

Although the expansion of commerce and industry was an outstanding economic feature, agriculture still remained the basic occupation engaging the activities of the vast majority of the population and constituting the bulk of invested wealth for several reasons. Landholding enjoyed greater social prestige than other forms of business and was a safer form of investment, so that the profits of commerce and industry were largely devoted to development of land and not reinvested in industry. From the technological standpoint industry showed no advance over the Hellenistic Age. Its expansion, therefore, consisted in exploiting hitherto underdeveloped areas and the concentration of more workers at certain centers rather than in improvement of efficiency or productivity. Preference for the small shop over factories and failure to invent and apply machinery to replace manual labor and lower the cost of production reflect the static condition of industry. Owing to the extensive use of slaves and the abundance of cheap free labor, there was little incentive to develop labor-saving devices. The lack of legal recognition of patent rights removed a powerful stimulus to invention. Neglect of scientific investigations made unlikely any revolutionary discoveries that might have had industrial uses. Furthermore, Roman law, while recognizing corporations with limited liability for shareholders undertaking public contracts, forbade them in private business enterprises. In this area the only legal form of organization was a partnership, each partner responsible for all the firm's obligations and the association dissolved when one of the partners died.

A potent deterrent to industrial progress lay in the conditions that governed markets. Owing to slow transportation by land and the risks and delays attending transportation by sea, it was cheaper to produce articles locally, provided that raw materials and an adequate labor supply were available, than to import them from any distance. Thus, although underdeveloped districts absorbed surplus manufactures of developed areas, with the advance of civilization they began to provide an ever-increasing share of their own necessities, and the regions formerly supplying them had to rely more and more on local consumption. When the Empire ceased to expand, no new areas were opened up to replace self-supplying markets. Furthermore, the Empire never succeeded in creating wealth in depth or a mass class of consumers, except for the most basic necessities of life, which meant that production could never develop beyond a fairly primitive level. Industry and commerce thus stagnated and failed to create new sources of wealth to keep pace with the increasing cost of government. Economic decline set in when, as a result of overtaxation, the peasant population was impoverished, so that its ability to consume the products of towns diminished. Local production and imports shrank correspondingly.

AGRICULTURE. Like industry, agriculture made practically no technical advances over the Hellenistic period. Conditions of land tenure and farm economy varied according to the soil and climate in different parts of the Empire. New areas were opened up for farming in Gaul, Britain, Germany, the Danubian provinces, Africa, and in Arabia and Syria. There is little evidence of soil exhaustion resulting from overcropping or erosion, except in parts of Greece and Italy, where this condition existed previously and apparently did not grow much worse.

Agriculture in Italy rather flourished during the first two centuries A.D. It was carried on very skillfully, as we know from Columella, a Neronian agronomist, whose work shows good knowledge of the principles of fertilization and crop rotation. As under the late Republic, *latifundia* dominated agriculture, but peasant holdings persisted, particularly in north central Italy and the Po valley. On the *latifundia* slave labor tended to be replaced by free tenant farmers (*coloni*). This followed the drying-up of sources of the supply of slaves through suppression of piracy and cessation of foreign wars, generous manumissions, the growth of humanitarian tendencies that checked exploitation of slave labor, and the growing realization that the employment of free labor was in the long run more profitable when slaves were becoming more expensive. The breeding of domestic slaves replenished the supply somewhat, but not sufficiently to check the trend towards tenant farming. The *coloni*, many freedmen or the descendants of freedmen, were sharecroppers tilling their holdings for a fixed share of the harvest. In Italy agricultural prosperity probably reached its height about A.D. 100. Signs of weakness in agriculture then became apparent, when Domitian sought to protect cereal farming and viticulture from provincial competition.

At the beginning of the Principate in Africa cultivable land, outside municipal territories, fell into three classes: public land, private estates, and imperial domains. Under the early emperors, particularly Nero, most private estates passed by legacy or confiscation to the *princeps* and were incorporated in imperial domains. Administration of public land not absorbed into new municipal territories, rested also with the *princeps*. Domain land was divided into large districts (*tractus, regiones*) administered by imperial procurators, each district comprising estates (*saltus, fundi*). Whatever slave labor had been used in African farming was, by the early Principate, largely displaced by *coloni*, who were either Italian immigrants or tributary natives.

Procurators leased estates to tenant contractors (*conductores*), who retained part of them under their own supervision and sublet the remainder to *coloni*. The relation of *coloni* to contractors, as well as to private estate owners or their bailiffs (*vilici*), was regulated by an edict of Mancia, apparently a Flavian procurator. By this edict the *coloni* had to pay part of their crop as rental and to work a certain number of days, with their teams, on the leasor's land. The *coloni*, both landless residents on estates and small landholders from neighboring villages, were encouraged to occupy vacant land and cultivate it. Over plowland they obtained a life tenancy, but orchards became hereditary, while in both cases the occupant was required to pay rent in kind to the state. Hadrian tried to further the development of peasant landholdings by permitting *coloni* to occupy land not tilled by middlemen and giving them possession over all other types. Forced service still remained the chief grievance of the *coloni*. The government faced a dilemma; if middlemen were restrained from undue exactions often much land remained untilled, and if the *coloni* were oppressed they absconded and left holdings untenanted.

The land system in Asia Minor reflected conditions established prior to Roman occupation. Most land was incorporated in city territories. There were also many large estates, which were private property. There is little evidence for agricultural slavery, farm labor being conducted by free peasants living in villages on municipal lands or private property. At first imperial estates were not very extensive there. Their increase was gradual, and after the confiscations made by Septimius Severus at the expense of the faction supporting Pescennius Niger, they became a major factor in agriculture. Although we do not have much evidence for their management, they probably were operated along the same lines as imperial estates in Africa.

In Gaul and Britain, farming was intensified, but the land system shows a development from Celtic origins and customs. Throughout Gaul, the unit of agriculture was the farm with an isolated farmstead the home of the proprietor or tenant. On larger estates, the farmstead was a villa comprising the residence of the owner, quarters for laborers, and other buildings necessary to care for livestock and other operations. Smaller farms, whether operated by their owners or by free or servile tenants, were correspondingly modest. With the development of urbanism in the first two centuries A.D., wealthier proprietors moved to the cities to share in municipal life and government, leaving their properties to the care of bailiffs or tenants. The villa system flourished in Britain, especially among the wealthier Romanized landholders. Most farmers, however, seem to have been free peasants who lived on small farms surrounded by fields that they tilled themselves.

Agriculture in Egypt, like its administration, was exceptional, owing to the survival of Pharaonic and Ptolemaic conditions. Agricultural life depended on the Nile, with its annual floods, and the irrigation system that distributed flood water. The government regulated and maintained this system and therefore had greater control over crops and agricultural labor than elsewhere. Under the Ptolemies most of the land had been royal or state property, and much of this remained public land after Augustus. Roman government did, however, encourage the development of private property on waste or marginal land not normally inundated by the Nile but irrigated by artificial methods. In order to facilitate such development and maintain production the administration improved and extended the system of irrigation canals. As a result, there was for a time an increase in prosperity and population. Increasing taxation gradually undermined this prosperity, however, and brought about a decline in agriculture. Attempting to control tenants of public land, the Romans continued the Ptolemaic practice of compelling the inhabitants of village communities to perform corvées, such as work on canals and dykes and the cultivation of royal lands not let out on contract, within the boundaries of the community in which each was registered (his *idia*). This practice was applied with greater precision. All land registered in each village had to be cultivated by the residents of that village, either as owners or tenants. At times, the inhabitants were forced to work distant vacant lands. During sowing and harvest the presence of every villager was required in his *idia*.

II. THE INTELLECTUAL WORLD

CULTURAL DEVELOPMENTS. The historical function of cities under imperial rule, as with Hellenistic cities before them, was to diffuse classical civilization widely but thinly. As a result of urbanism, out-of-the-way and previously backward districts produced famous writers, artists, philosophers, and religious leaders along with older centers in Greece, Italy, and the already Hellenized parts of the Near East.

From a linguistic point of view, the Empire was split into two halves, based on the Greek and Latin languages. Despite its duration, Roman rule in the East had little effect on the civilization of the area. Cultural influences continued to flow rather in the other direction, the Romans always acknowledging their inferiority to, and reverence for, Hellenism. This latter feeling was not reciprocated because, although they respected Roman power, the Greeks never stopped regarding its culture as essentially inferior. They kept their own civilization rather unadulterated because they were conspicuously uninterested in Romanizing themselves and because there was never an official program of Romanization. There were very few Roman colonies and municipalities in the

East, and those that existed were gradually absorbed by their environment, so that Greek rather quickly replaced Latin as the language of the original settlers' descendants. The normal language of administration in the East was Greek, as was that of law and political assemblies. Only in the army was Latin the official language of command, but soldiers from the very beginning of the Empire tended to be recruited locally and hence to know some Greek, whatever their native language, if they came from the East.

EDUCATION. Linguistic differences aside, a characteristic feature of Greco-Roman civilization was uniformity. This derived from the rhetorical nature of an educational system in vogue since Hellenistic times, which the Romans had adopted and spread throughout the West. An educated Roman subject could travel from Scotland to Mesopotamia and find everywhere in cities other people who had read the same books and appreciated the same literature. Literacy was never more widespread in antiquity than it was in the first two centuries A.D., although knowledge of anything beyond the rudiments of reading and writing was restricted to the well-to-do who could afford tuition.

Educational theory was expounded by the Spanish Roman Quintilian, who lived, taught, and wrote at Rome during the Flavian dynasty. In his *Institutes of Oratory*, Quintilian emphasized the aim of rhetorical education: cultivation of the ability to communicate ideas gracefully and logically and cultivation of morality. Its method stressed memorization, listening to instruction, and reading. It gave first priority to appreciation and imitation of canonical literary models rather than to inventiveness. The Hellenistic curriculum remained virtually unchanged. In the West the core consisted of classical Greek authors, to which were added a choice selection of Roman writers such as Cicero, the Augustan poets, Sallust, and Livy. Consequently, cultivated Westerners were more or less bilingual in the two classical languages. The Greek East, confident of its own cultural superiority, studied seriously only its own authors.

This rhetorical orientation contributed to a certain unreality in education because students were expected to produce impressive declamations on far-fetched topics involving almost insolubly paradoxical situations, which, it was assumed, would sharpen their reasoning power and make their brains more nimble. Interest in rhetoric and oratory by the educated public also produced a cultural phenomenon known to the Hellenistic period but most typical of the Empire: the literary seance. Declamations before a select group of one's own literary works seem to have been held first toward the end of Augustus' reign by one Asinius Pollio and then quickly to have become fashionable. Even more than dilettante authors, teachers of rhetoric capitalized on the entertainment value of declamation by lecturing for fees on practically any subject. The most famous of them were Greek luminaries, who enjoyed wide popularity by virtue of their theatrical presentations on the public platform. One Polemo of

Smyrna (A.D. 88–144) is said to have earned half a million drachmas yearly in lecture fees, so popular was his florid Asian style, and Herodes Atticus, a teacher of Marcus Aurelius and benefactor of Athens, was equally famous as a public speaker.

THE SILVER AGE AND SECOND SOPHISTIC. With the passing of the Augustan authors the literary history of the Empire entered a period generally called the "Silver Age" in the field of Latin literature, the "Second Sophistic" in that of Greek. The term "Silver Age" implies a decline from the literary standards attained by the greatest writers of the first emperor's reign. The implication is justified, even though the Silver Age produced some of the most interesting and characteristic works of Latin literature. Poetry and prose in the Silver Age were affected by many factors, such as the essentially authoritarian nature of the imperial system, which demanded avoidance of politically controversial subjects, but especially by rhetoric, which only then realized its full potential in molding literary taste. Since declaimers aimed to hold the attention of audiences already conversant with all known literary devices, they felt compelled to make their compositions as showy as possible, using any stylistic techniques that could captivate their listeners. This meant that Silver Age poetry was "pointed," preoccupied with style and form, frequently at the expense of content. A second tendency was criticism by poets of the manners of a sophisticated yet frivolous upper-class society. This led to a further development of satire, which lost its original meaning as a kind of very personal, miscellaneous, verse and came to signify caustic, humorous, and colloquial poetry lampooning contemporary life with an eye to its reform.

The bulk of Silver Age poetry has not survived because it did not have an epochal appeal, most writers of poetry being gentlemen who thought that mere knowledge of rules of meter and style was a satisfactory substitute for genius. Of interest, however, is the work of Aulus Persius Flaccus (34–64? A.D.). Born of a good family and a practicing Stoic, he took Horace as his literary model and produced satires in which he derided the artificial nature of post-Augustan poetry and the poets' mania for recitation. Despite the sincerity of his Stoic ideals and the depth of his scorn for literary contemporaries, his own work reflected some of their values. His style is vivid and forceful, but it is also so allusive as to be obscure. For all his exhibitionism, he was unable to master the art of creating, like Horace, a dramatic setting for his works.

Of greater natural poetic gifts was Marcus Annaeus Lucanus (39–65). A nephew of Seneca and like his uncle a Roman from Spain, Lucan was interested in politics and was implicated with Seneca in the Pisonian conspiracy against Nero, in which he betrayed his own mother. Lucan's entire output was crammed into the last five years of his life, in which he feverishly produced occasional poems and ten books of his unfinished epic, the *Pharsalia*. Characterized by what has been called psychotic emotionalism, the *Pharsalia* mixes Stoic philosophy and history. A passionate work, it is possibly the most significant creation of rhetorical poetry. Lucan expressed in this poem his own anti-imperial sentiments by making Pompey the hero in the civil war against Julius Caesar, which results in a kind of Stoic tragedy in which the hero is foredoomed. Prolix, analytical, studded with brilliant descriptions interspersed with occasionally irrelevant interludes, the *Pharsalia* illustrates the possibilities and limitations of rhetoric as epic.

As a man of letters, Lucan's uncle, Lucius Annaeus Seneca (3 B.C.–A.D. 66) is best known today as a Stoic philosopher, although he also wrote significant verse. To his contemporaries he was above all a politician. Banished from Claudius' court in 41, he later returned to imperial favor, was Nero's tutor and regent before the emperor forced him into retirement and finally invited him to die following the Pisonian conspiracy. His lyric poems, including satires and epigrams, are conventionally rhetorical, exaggeratedly pointed, and strain after effect. Of greater interest are his nine tragedies, important because they were the versions of classical tragedy imitated by Shakespeare and his immediate predecessors in Elizabethan drama. The titles of some of his works—*Medea, Hercules, Oedipus, Thyestes,* and *Agamemnon*—suggest the Greek, chiefly Euripidean, models. Unlike the Greeks', however, Seneca's plays were intended for public recitation, not performance by actors in theaters, and so they lacked the realism imposed on works written for the stage.

Of the Flavian writers only the work of three epic poets has survived. Statius (39–100?), the son of a Neopolitan grammar school teacher, was patronized by Domitian. His *Silvae*, occasional poems to friends and patrons expressing condolence, congratulation, and thanks, are conventional in their exaggerated sentiment and learned allusions. His epic *Thebaid*, in which he interpreted the Aeschylean play *Seven Against Thebes*, is stylistically modelled after Vergil, but even more closely resembles Senecan tragedy with its abundance of horrors designed to thrill audiences and to show off the author's command of rhetoric. Self-consciously melodramatic, Statius was more interested in the reaction of his audiences than the perfection of his work. His epic was more episodic and less dramatic than his Vergilian model.

His contemporary, Valerius Flaccus (ca. 50–91) also treated epically a mythological theme in his *Argonautica*, in which he concealed rhetorical devices better than Lucan or Statius. He ran into difficulties, however, in developing his main protagonists, Jason and Medea, and was forced to abandon the poem before its completion. The work of Silius Italicus, who enjoyed a political career under Nero and Vespasian, foreshadows a reaction against rhetoric and satire. Silius wrote a *Punica*, an epic on the Hannibalic war, which was a throwback to the style of Ennius more than Vergil. His poem, however, lacks unity, is overly annalistic in structure, and is uninspired.

Poetry of the Silver Age culminates with two talented figures, Martial and Juvenal, the most interesting satirists since the Age of Augustus. Martial (ca. 40–104) came from a Spanish mining town in his early twenties to Neronian Rome just when his compatriots Seneca and Lucan held the center of literary attention. He remained there until the last five years of his life, when he returned to Spain. Writing mainly under Domitian, Martial was famous for his satirical epigrams. He was far more controlled in his emotions, despite his frequently coarse humor, than his model, Catullus. Rarely bitter, he was an attractive man because of his humane outlook on life and his devotion to his friends, including Juvenal. Perhaps not a sublimely inspired poet, he had the gift of commenting on the outrageous and ridiculous in everyday life and illuminating its trivialities.

Juvenal (ca. 60–128) of Aquinum, a different kind of man, brought to an end a literary era beginning with Lucilius in the second century B.C., one in which the personal element dominated Latin poetry. Reasonably well off, he was exposed to rhetorical training but he was repelled by the divorcement from life that rhetorically inspired poetry induced. An angry man, indignant at the vices he observed at the capital, he combined his social outrage and his poetic gifts to produce fifteen powerful satires in the period 100–128. These were vignettes in which he castigated in bitter, but vivid, imagery subjects ranging widely over imperial cabinet meetings, evil women, *nouveaux riches*, and fawning clients.

PROSE. Rhetorical influences are equally evident in the large body of surviving prose works. Since Hellenistic times the educational system encouraged dilettante scholarship characterized by the collection of exotic information in dictionaries and encyclopedias. Since research was conceived as imitative rather than creative, scholarly works were little more than the results of voluminous reading and notetaking without much discrimination or critical evaluation. The encyclopedist Varro under the first Augustus domesticated this genre at Rome, and his fame as a researcher was equalled by the senator Pliny the Elder (20?–79). Pliny took notes during almost every waking minute but he was a credulous, unimaginative compiler of all sorts of antiquarian information. He read 2,000 books as sources for his *Natural History*, and at his death he left his heir and nephew, the younger Pliny, some 160 volumes of notes. The passion for notetaking was reflected in the second century by the work of Aulus Gellius, who produced a book of miscellany and literary criticism called *Attic Nights*, by Marcus Aurelius in his *Meditations*, and by the observations of his court physician, Galen, on the human body and diseases.

The writing of history was assumed to be a branch of *belles-lettres*, in that style took precedence over factual content or objectivity. It remained very much the spare-time activity of gentlemen. The edifying, pragmatic value of history was undoubted although it was dangerous to treat current events or the immediate past because of political conditions. Almost all of the historical writing of the first century A.D. has disappeared, except for a scrappy history of Rome by the equestrian, Velleius Paterculus, that is notable for his adulation of Tiberius.

Of far greater stature and significance was Publius Cornelius Tacitus (ca. 55–123), in the opinion of many, Rome's greatest historian. Born probably in Narbonese Gaul, Tacitus came of an only recently senatorial family, his father having been an equestrian official. Although he had very mixed feelings about the regime, Tacitus pursued a political career, availed himself of the patronage of the tyrant, Domitian, whom he later excoriated, was a consul under Nerva and proconsul of Asia under Trajan. The liberal regimes of the first "good emperors" encouraged him to write, and his monographs and historical works reveal his intellectual development. Apparently under Nerva he first produced a short biography of his father-in-law, Julius Agricola, governor of Britain under Domitian, who fell from imperial favor before dying under mysterious circumstances. In describing Agricola, Tacitus also was portraying the moral and political ideals of the new imperial aristocracy. The maintenance of an empire, it seemed to Tacitus, required the habit of subordination and obedience, a rational deference to imperial authority by aristocrats.

The *Agricola* was followed, it seems, early in Trajan's reign by *Germania*, a treatise on the northern barbarians that would find an interested audience during the reign of an emperor who promised brilliant campaigns against them. The *Germania*, for all its value, is a derivative work excerpted from sources as old as Julius Caesar and Pliny the Elder. About 107 Tacitus wrote his *Dialogue on Orators*, an essay of literary criticism that is interesting because it examines the present rather than the past. Tacitus discussed in it the reasons for what seemed to be a decline in standards of forensic eloquence between Cicero's day and his own. He decided that the free interplay of politics made the old orators great, implying that even under good emperors the imperial system restricted free speech.

While working on the *Dialogue*, Tacitus was writing a history of the period 68–96, one contemporary to his own lifetime and of which he had personal knowledge. He apparently published it about 109. Only those parts of it dealing with the Year of the Four Emperors have survived, but this is enough to show that he had his characteristically annalistic form under control, and that he was capable of a sustained artistic narrative. He took as his literary models historians of Rome's civil wars, especially Sallust; this is reflected in his style which is filled with spare, Sallustian phrases that express far more than they say.

The *Histories* were followed, early in Hadrian's reign it would seem, by his masterpiece, the *Annals*, the bulk of which has survived. Covering the reigns of the Julio-Claudian dynasty, the *Annals* are a gloomy and cynical appraisal of the Principate, which seemed to Tacitus to be a form of government as necessary as it was regrettable. In this work Tacitus succeeded in transcending the facts he chose to relate (with general accuracy) by using a highly personal kind of innuendo, which places the emperors in the most unfavorable light. Whatever the undoubted limitations of his craft as a historian—particularly his disinterest in the minutiae of military campaigns and in affairs not directly

XVIII So-called Temple of Bacchus at Baalbek. *Baalbeck (in modern Lebanon), the ancient Heliopolis, was an oracular site sacred to the sun god Baal. Beginning in the first century A.D. a complex of temples arose there, including this one now thought to be dedicated to Venus rather than Bacchus. (Photo: A. H. McLeod.)*

concerning the senatorial class—his book stands as the most striking example of history conceived as a work of literary art.

Works of history written in the grand manner had a limited appeal even in educated circles, which typically preferred less austere and more entertaining books than those of Tacitus, who was read infrequently by later generations. Popular demand for essentially light reading led to the production of easily digested abridgements of historical works, notably of Livy's long history. It also stimulated a genre of history whose prototype *The Lives of the Twelve Caesars* was a work by the Hadrianic bureaucrat, Suetonius (ca. 70–140). A piquant compilation of imperial biographies, the *Lives* were widely read because they were short, superficial, and anecdotal. Since they more nearly suited popular taste than Tacitus or even Livy, they were imitated by authors throughout the rest of antiquity and even into the Middle Ages. Equally popular were other kinds of biographical works like the *Parallel Lives* of famous Greeks and Romans written by Plutarch (ca. 46–120), probably the most well-known personality of the Second Sophistic. Plutarch did not claim to be a historian, and so it seems rather unfair to fault him because he so frequently failed to weigh sources or treat them critically. Plutarch intended to edify and give moral instruction to his readers, which meant that he was concerned with developing the character of the personalities he treated.

Readers also sought entertainment in works which approximated novels, fictional narratives which did not, however, stress the psychological development of figures portrayed in them. The most famous of such works is undoubtedly the *Satyricon* of Petronius, the so-called arbiter of elegance at Nero's court. The story of the erotic and other adventures of two freedmen in South Italy, the *Satyricon* is a ribald, boisterous, and yet sophisticated work. It has sometimes been called the first picaresque romance in the Western tradition. Linguistically, it is interesting because it is largely written in everyday colloquial Latin as it was spoken in the first century, not the highly stylized literary language of more conventional books. Rather different is the work of the African Apuleius, who produced in the second century a rambling work, the *Golden Ass*, a satirical spoof of commonly held beliefs in magic and superstition. Imbedded in this book is the romance of *Cupid and Psyche*, apparently an allegory on the attainment by mankind of peace through love. Apuleius' is a first-rate work, outstanding in an age of literary insincerity for its unsentimental qualities and for its sparkling style.

THE EARLY THIRD CENTURY. Traditional literary tastes and interests continued to produce significant works under the Severan dynasty. Of interest from that period is the *Roman History* from Aeneas to A.D. 229 written by the senator Cassius Dio, a Greek from Bithynia (ca. 163–after 229). Owing much to rhetorical influence, Dio was far from being a "scientific" historian. His judgments on human nature, the instability of fortune, the need for the exercise of mercy by the powerful, and his contrast of vicious and benevolent rulers are banal. His real importance lies in his interpretation of events, frequently as an eyewitness, occurring during his own lifetime. His commentary presumably reflects what was known and felt about imperial power in senatorial circles under the Severan dynasty.

Dio veiled a comprehensive plan for coping with the threats confronting the senatorial class of the third century in a commentary treating the reign of the first Augustus. Dio believed that senatorial status should be assured, even at the expense of any claim by the Senate to dispose of imperial power. The most that senators could hope for under the imperial system, Dio felt, was to salvage their security. The Empire should assure a strictly graded society with a minimum of disorder and change, the status quo depending for defense on a disciplined, professional army. Imperial economic policy should be conciliatory to landlords, with emperors living on their own income and cash reserve and abandonment of confiscation of senatorial real estate. Dio's awareness of Severan antipathy toward the senatorial class is revealed in his suggestion that equestrians be banned from provincial government, that the broadening functions of praetorian prefects be limited to their original command of the guard, and that senators be permitted to hold more governmental posts and for longer periods.

The literate class, long trained by their education to appreciate antiquarianism mixed with a certain kind of pedantry, continued to enjoy collections of miscellany, which remained popular long after more significant classical genres ceased being either written or read. A typical anthology of trivial information was written early in the third century by one Athenaeus of Naucratis, whose *Gentlemen at Dinner* preserves a wide range of observations on food, drink, dancing girls, and games, which cultivated audiences of the day found amusing. Light reading also embraced a very old literary tradition that blended eroticism, myth, travellers' tales, and history. *Daphnis and Chloe* by the Greek sophist Longus (ca. 200), destined to have some effect on modern literature and opera, is the most famous of such romances. Transpiring in a never-never land, its plot is simple: the passion of two foundlings, reared by shepherds and separated by various adventures, only to be reunited and live happily ever after.

In addition to speciously learned anthologies and piquant love stories, the literate public continued to be entertained by biographies, sometimes highly fictionalized. One that became a best seller in the early third century was the *Life* of the philosopher Apollonius of Tyana, written by Philostratus the Athenian at the request of his patroness, Julia Domna, Septimius Severus' empress. Apollonius, who lived under the Flavians, was a very ascetic Pythagorean, famous as a prophet and miracle worker. As portrayed by Philostratus, Apollonius appeared to his readers as a mystic attaining the knowledge of divinity through self-purification. His biography points toward the most important cultural trend of the third century: an increasing religiosity and interest in otherworldly matters among all classes.

PAGAN PHILOSOPHY AND RELIGION. Traditional schools of Greek philosophy continued to flourish during the early Principate, despite the low priority given to them in the educational system. Philosophers existed to teach and, in a sense, to save souls for the Good Life by imparting dogmatic rules of living. For the introspective, philosophy rather than religion was the real sphere in which true conversions could be made in life-styles and morality. Withal, the various philosophies tended to converge and become alike, as they freely borrowed doctrines from each other. Platonic thought was rather unique, because it also showed the capacity for independent development of its own by moving toward an ever more mystical, and even quasi-religious, conception of the universe.

Philosophy produced some striking types, individuals regarded by contemporaries as ideal, the saints of pagan antiquity. Some of them were Cynics, who, especially in the period ca. 50–100, wandered about the Empire exciting the lower classes by advertising their opposition against tyranny, more accurately, against any authority. Ostentatiously they practiced a life of poverty and were at once identifiable by their long hair, beards, and dirty clothes. Such philosophers in contact with the credulous masses frequently claimed to be masters of divination, oracle givers, miracle workers, and as such frequently acquired a wide reputation. Perhaps the most famous of such men was the Neo-Pythagorean Apollonius of Tyana, whose life-style was the most ascetic of them all.

The upper classes were more receptive to Epicureanism, which was still widely practiced, especially by Roman senators, and Stoicism, which produced still more striking figures. Seneca, from his palace preaching in a series of *Moral Essays* the glories of poverty, was also affected in his thinking by Platonists and skeptics who insisted on the ultimate uncertainty of truth. Possibly more attractive as a person was the freedman Epictetus, who stood up to Domitian. Living by the Stoic motto "Bear and Forebear," Epictetus considered himself a true citizen of the world and displayed a striking warmth and humanity to his fellow men. The long line of famous ancient Stoics came to an end with Marcus Aurelius, whose *Meditations*, rather like Dag Hammerskjöld's *Jottings*, were a disorganized, random selection of his thought. His *Meditations* have seemed to some to be a kind of gospel of self-reliance, of withdrawal into one's own resources, which makes Stoicism seem unnecessarily grim. For Marcus, Stoic nature and brotherhood were impersonal, his duties as emperor a service imposed on him by the world order.

Philosophers of certain types, like the Cynics, came into contact with all classes of people and affected them by publicizing their own ideals. Nevertheless, the number of people modeling their lives on philosophical doctrines was always very small. The population at large continued to find emotional release and adjustment to the world in religion, especially Eastern cults. These latter, widely practiced in the Hellenistic East and known to Romans during the Republic, spread throughout the Empire during the early Principate. They existed side by side with the official state gods and the cult of living and dead emperors, symbolic of the state's existence and of patriotic feelings. Imperial government was concerned with the worship of foreign gods, the traditional view still obtaining that only those cults that encouraged loyalty and involved no moral impropriety might receive official sanction. The first Augustus, for example, tried to prohibit on moral grounds the practice by individuals of the cult of Isis and other orgiastic oriental rites. The private practice of Mithraism, on the other hand, at once won official approval, since it preached soldierly ideals compatible with imperial policy.

Near Eastern cults were diffused throughout virtually every province. The Roman Peace and the consequent movement of more people than ever before in commercial and other pursuits and of soldiers from one frontier to another accounted especially for the spread of new religions. Cults also acquired a widespread reputation by virtue of the great visual attraction of their temples and public ceremonies or through their propaganda publicizing oracular or miracle-working powers. Miracle working was axiomatic as the test of divinity, and hymns, votive inscriptions, and works of art publicized to the world the greatness of certain gods. The public was interested in any manifestations of divine favor or pity, but especially in obtaining supernatural information directly from a god. Belief in astrology was widespread, and the desire for liberation from a world order that was celestially preordained led to a rise in popularity of gods who became lords of the stars and thus were able to overrule fate. Although at the beginning of the Principate educated people commonly doubted survival after death, interest in cults holding out hopes of immortality increased thereafter among all classes. Even more popular were those claiming to offer protection against demons.

Granted the widely held conviction that there was a straightforward ethical explanation of the universe, people commonly wished to be initiated into as many mystery cults as possible, to get to the heart of the matter, to discover the nature of the soul and to realize happiness. Many mystery sects therefore had gnostic characteristics as they claimed to give mankind special religious insights and privileges. The personal and emotional rather than rational or logical bent taken by religious urges is illustrated by revelation through dreams, especially popular under the Antonines.

The relative strength of different cults is difficult to estimate. Syrian cults, like those of Astarte, the Baalim, and the Sun, were widely diffused. Anatolian religions like the worship of Cybele and Adonis found devotees as far away as the municipalities of Gaul and Africa. Two cults, however, of Isis and Mithra, seem to have attracted more worshippers than any of the others. Despite initial imperial disapproval, the cult of Isis spread from Egypt throughout the Empire during the first three centuries A.D. The worship of Isis was extremely flexible, and she was identified, sometimes inconsistently, with many other goddesses of the pagan pantheon. She was a goddess of life, death, and love; she could work miracles, cure the sick, and give everlasting life. Egyptian lore knew her as a wife, mother, and whore, so that she had a ready-made appeal to many kinds of women. But she also had certain qualities traditionally ascribed to male divinities as she ruled the sky and created the earth. She appealed to both sexes and all classes although women were undoubtedly her most numerous and enthusiastic devotees.

In some sense rivaling Isis and contrasting with her cult was Mithraism, whose orientation was totally masculine. In the Zoroastrian religion of ancient Persia, Mithra appears as the chief spiritual agent of the god of light Ormuzd in his struggle against Ahriman, the god of darkness. He was a beneficent force in the world and morally was the champion of righteousness against the powers of evil. Under Babylonian and Greek influences Mithra was identified with the Sun-god and appeared in Rome with the title Unconquered Sun-god Mithra (*deus invictus sol Mithra*). Mithra, the god of battles, was a patron deity of soldiers, who became his zealous missionaries in frontier camps. Unlike other Oriental cults, Mithraism was a religion for men only and lacked a professional clergy.

There was no general organization or feeling of unity among any such religions although each preached that it was the religion of mankind. From the point of view of a polytheistic population having attachments to several cults, the addition of a new one to a personal pantheon meant no more than, perhaps, the veneration by a Catholic Christian in modern times of a new saint. The essence of most of these religions was ritualistic, the guaranteeing of proper human relations with uncharted natural forces rather than demanding a special way of life from their practitioners.

III. JUDAISM AND CHRISTIANITY IN THEIR RELATION TO THE STATE

JUDAISM AND CHRISTIANITY. Two religions, Judaism and Christianity, differed from their pagan counterparts in their dogmatism: they were unique in demanding the conversion of the life-style of worshippers. Both sects came into conflict with the society of the Empire and sometimes with its government although many Romans, like Hellenistic Greeks before them, respected the teachings of Judaism. Many pagans sympathized with the doctrine of Yahweh, although the depth of their understanding of Judaism, and of their convictions, was often questionable. There were relatively few Jewish converts, in any case because even Judaising pagans were loath to give up their own gods and worship Yahweh exclusively and because they found unattractive Jewish dietary rules and abhored circumcision. Jews were concentrated in the Greek-speaking parts of the Empire but were also widely scattered in communities elsewhere, including Rome. Despite the appreciation of Judaism by some sophisticates, Jews were frequently disliked. The Empire inherited anti-Semitic feelings from the Hellenistic period, which derived from the demands by orthodoxy of aloofness from predominantly gentile communities, which made Jews seem antisocial. At most, Jews taking their religion seriously merely tolerated the existence of the Empire, even when Roman governors were especially respectful of Jewish religious sensibilities. The Romans seemed to interpose themselves between the Jews and Yahweh, and so to be delaying the realization of God's plan for them: the establishment of a terrestrial state under a Messiah who would outshine even David. This basic hostility to Roman rule combined with Messianic hopes and reactions against gentile anti-Semitism to trigger the great Jewish rebellions under Nero, Trajan, and Hadrian.

The problems faced by Christianity were at first related to its Jewish origin. Arising from the doctrine of one Joshua (Jesus), called by his followers "the anointed of God" (Christ), Christianity was an extremely reformed kind of Judaism, Christ having insisted that he was fulfilling Yahweh's Law and not destroying it. He stood in the tradition of Jewish prophets by emphasizing the spiritual side of Judaism and by championing weak and lowly people. He transcended the prophetic tradition, however, by expressing new ideas, some of which at least superficially resembled those of an Essene. He played down the importance of ritual and implied that the Kingdom of God was not necessarily a terrestrial reward for the faithful, but one for piety in eternal life beyond the grave. He either himself believed, or was held by his followers to believe, that he was indeed the Messiah and son of God. After his death his disciples added an important and novel dimension to this kind of Judaism by holding that he had fulfilled his role as Messiah by suffering vicariously for sinners, whom he redeemed through his death.

Like earlier prophets, Jesus got into difficulties with the Jewish religious establishment, which perceived him as a threat. Tried by the Pharisaic court, the Sanhedrin, for sacrilege, he was found guilty and handed over to the Roman authorities for punishment. The Roman governor, the equestrian prefect Pontius Pilate, publicly washed his hands of the affair, thus acknowleding the right of Jews to regulate internal matters, especially touchy ones involving religion, and carried out the Sanhedrin's sentence of death ca. A.D. 29.

Christianity would, perhaps, have remained a Jewish sect, like the Essenes, of only local importance and confined to Palestine, had it not been given a completely new dimension by the converted Pharisee, Paul, who was undoubtedly even more important than Peter for the spread of the sect beyond Palestine. Paul preached widely ca. 40–50, especially in the Greek East, principally in synagogues, where he intended to reach Hellenized Jews living in dispersion. Unlike wandering Cynics, he did not address random public gatherings. This established a tradition followed by Christian teachers until the end of the second century, with the result that pagans came into only casual contact with the young religion. Because of Paul, however, even that contact was effective, since he carried to its logical conclusion Christ's deemphasis on Jewish ritual and his implication that the truly Chosen People were simply those having faith. So conceived, Christianity preserved many of the features of Judaism that pagans could find attractive, while eliminating ritual hindrances to conversion. The number of pagan converts gradually increased; the ties of the sect to Palestine loosened, to be severed after the destruction of the Temple at Jerusalem in 70.

In the beginning, Christianity was inconspicuous. As a tiny sect of elect members, it only gradually acquired an interest in proselytizing outside of Jewish circles. Since early Christians were poor and uneducated, they produced few preachers with sufficient oratorical skill to attract large public audiences. Unlike other Near Eastern sectaries, they had no eye-catching outdoor ceremonies, no mystery dramas, and made no attempt to develop an appealing ritual to compete with pagan religions for converts. To outsiders, early Christian ceremonies might have appeared boring because in pagan terms they resembled the meetings of a philosophical society, so simple was their rite. Even the large and growing body of Christian literature, known historically as the New Testament, dealing with Christ's life and the teaching of Paul and other apostles, circulated mainly among the faithful. Until about A.D. 200 Christian literature was not intended to explain and develop its sometimes subtle and loosely defined doctrine for pagan benefit, and it was written in the colloquial Greek koine that educated pagans regarded as not worthy of serious perusal.

The reasons for the increasing success of Christianity are obscure. Its very dogmatism perhaps contributed to it because converts were assured that they had found the one true means to eternal happiness. Nevertheless, converts may have found it difficult to accept Christianity's startling rejection of idolatry; its demand that one acknowledge sinfulness, not purity, before approaching the Divinity; and its belief that prayer should replace astrology and magic in averting the maleficent influences of demons. Christianity seemed to unite in a peculiar way ritual sacramentalism and philosophy and, unlike pagan religions, to demand a definite, severely ascetic style of life. This asceticism tended to moderate as the sect grew from a tiny band cut off from the temptations of this world to a far-flung group in necessary contact with the sinful temptations of everyday life.

Despite its peculiarities, there was much in the Christian ethic that pagans found familiar, and this fact contributed to the ease of conversion. The idea that a certain kind of life-style was necessary for earthly happiness and salvation was a philosophical commonplace that for the first time received a religious sanction. The Christian requirement that devotees love their fellow men was rather broader than any pagan doctrine although even Platonists believed in turning the other cheek. The notion of God the Father could easily be accepted by a world accustomed to thinking of Zeus as being the father of all mankind. Even the idea of Jesus as the son of God was not repellent because ancient myths knew of gods having sons and held that the latter, too, might die without losing their immortality. Pagans were familiar with the notion of approaching divinity through divine intermediaries, in which category it seemed proper to place

Jesus whose evident humanity nevertheless encouraged resistance in the popular mind to the idea of his divine incarnation.

Finally, the organization of Christian religion was potentially advantageous for the sect because, unlike pagan cults, Christian cells kept in touch with each other and took care of their own poor and even of traveling worshippers, all of which gave them a feeling of special identity. Christian congregations were commonly headed by boards of elders or bishops, one of whom in some places frequently, when persecution threatened, led their local churches. This episcopal system only gradually developed during the first two centuries; within it certain sees attained a greater prominence than others either because they were located in important cities or because they were said to have been founded by Christ's apostles as in the case of Peter at Rome itself. Roman bishops at an early date seem to have insisted on the special right to lead other sees because of their location in the imperial capital, but such claims were generally ignored, except in Rome's immediate vicinity.

PERSECUTION OF CHRISTIANS. Despite their apparently harmless doctrines, Christians were very unpopular. Their withdrawal from the world seemed nasty and exclusive, and their beliefs in, and hopes for, the quick end to earthly kingdoms (especially the Empire), the second coming of Christ, and the establishment of his spiritual kingdom could easily be interpreted as subversive. The private nature of their worship, which few even educated pagans attempted to investigate, lent itself to stories that their ritual involved cannibalism and incest. Like the Jews the Christians also objected to the official cult of living emperors, even though they apparently ascribed to ritual ruler worship more content than it possessed. Otherwise they were reasonably loyal subjects.

As early as the reign of Nero their reputation for being antisocial was sufficiently widespread to permit them to become scapegoats punished for the burning of Rome. For several generations thereafter, however, initiative against them came rather from their local enemies, including orthodox Jews, rather than from Roman authorities. The emperor Trajan expressed what was until his reign undoubtedly the normal attitude of enlightened rulers toward the sect in answer to a request of Pliny the Younger, legate of Bithynia in 111–113, who wanted guidance in his treatment of Christians. The emperor told him never to respect anonymous accusations against alleged Christians or to indulge in witch-hunts, to execute them if they were caught red-handed in the midst of their ritual, but to pardon apostates. Official pressure and popular hatred combined thereafter to produce local persecutions by magistrates, especially under Marcus Aurelius and Septimius Severus. They called forth the one type of Christian then known to the population at large: the martyr.

CHRISTIAN APOLOGETICS. By the end of the second century the first notable works of Christian literature were produced for a pagan readership and having apologetic and philosophical aims. Some Christian thinkers by about 200 were willing to rationalize their religious beliefs by regarding secular authority, in some sense, as desirable, since it postponed the frightening final end of earthly things; it also could be interpreted as divinely instituted, since it seemed to exist as punishment for an unworthy humanity. Even so, leading theologians like the Greeks Irenaeus of Lyons and Hippolytus of Rome could still express the primitive feelings of the Church toward the State, which, by drawing allegorically on the dream of Nebuchadnezzar in the Book of Daniel, they portrayed as the ultimate expression of hideous, brute power.

Both Irenaeus and Hipppolytus, however, accepted the participation of Christians in a pagan world as inevitable. Understandably enough they were concerned with defining the position of their Church in it. This theme became predominant in the works of Tertullian and Cyprian, who wrote under the Severans in Africa, the most Christianized area in the West. Tertullian's *Apology*, an open letter to Roman magistrates, is a passionate defense of Christian values against common pagan charges that they were atheistic, immoral, and subversive. Brilliantly invective, he insisted that it was really the pagans themselves who were responsible for offenses against society and the State, that denial by Christians of the gods and any form of emperor-worship implied no immorality on their own part; on the contrary, Christians had high moral standards and were patriotic subjects. If they would not pray *to* the emperor, they would pray *for* him and the safety of his Empire, provided that it guaranteed justice and peace.

An indication of accommodation already made between Christians and the State is Tertullian's evident pride in the numbers of faithful then serving as soldiers and civil servants. There is, however, a strident undertone of confident militancy in his *Apology* expressed in the notion that Christians were soldiers of Christ, to whom they owed primary allegiance in any confrontation with the State. It was this very militancy, also emphasized by Cyprian and other theologians, that viewed martyrdom under persecution as the perfect test of the true Christian.

Christian attitudes were as profoundly influenced by Greek philosophy in the late second and early third centuries as they were by Church–State relations. By then the growing sect was under attack by pagan intellectuals like the Platonist Celsus writing under Marcus Aurelius, who accused it of being unworthy of civilized minds. At the same time Christian doctrine remained loose to the extent that it permitted various interpretations, like those of the Gnostics, who insisted that true knowledge of God came through revelation rather than rational investigation. Christian theologians were thus interested in making their religion intellectually respectable and in defining more closely orthodox belief. They naturally turned to Greek philosophy, the rich repository of ideas relating man to the world, to create for the first time a sophisticated and precise theology.

The most influential philosophical theories of the day ultimately derived from Pythagoras and Plato and emphasized the spiritual and quasi-religious aspects of the Greek intellectual tradition. As organized and refined by a series of philosophers working at Alexandria in the early third century, this body of doctrine has come to be known historically as Neoplatonism. The core of Neoplatonic belief was the idea that the terrestrial, measurable world was evil because imperfect and that a life of virtue consisted of the contemplation of divinity, which was remote from mankind, perfect, and ideal.

The Christian intelligentsia adopted much of this to enrich their theology and make it intelligible to educated pagans, although acceptance of Neoplatonic duality, and even hostility, of matter and spirit soon provoked controversy within the Church. The absorption of Neoplatonism by Christianity proceeded at several levels, from the conception of God as a supreme Intelligence, the "Word" or *logos*, to the creation of sometimes subtle theological systems. It was easiest for educated converts to accept a melding of Neoplatonism and Christianity, since they embraced their new religion with an intellectual outlook already molded in pagan schools. Typical of such people was Clement of Alexandria (ca. 200), who continued to insist after his conversion that the study of philosophy deepened understanding of the Christian *logos*. Neoplatonic influence is also evident in his belief that virtue consisted in a total, ascetic, even mystical immersion in Christianity until attainment of union with the Godhead.

IV. SCIENCE, ARCHITECTURE, AND ART

SCIENCE. The Principate inherited tendencies that had already aborted the development of Hellenistic science, so that there were few discernible advances. Almost all the noteworthy scientists were Greek. Exceptional Romans at least popularized certain discoveries made by Greeks, which they used in a few very practical fields in which they themselves excelled. The architect Vitruvius (ca. 30 B.C.), for example, understood the concept of acoustics as involving the existence of sound waves modified by particular types of building, and Frontinus (ca. A.D. 100) in a book on aqueducts, showed the mastery of a competent civil engineer over the principles of hydrostatics.

The center for medical studies remained at Alexandria, where cadavers were still being dissected, although the further development of medicine there was not helped by the quarreling of various schools. The so-called dogmatists were nearest to the early Hippocratics in their empirical approach to medicine, but they disagreed with doctors calling themselves "skeptics," who disbelieved in the study of anatomy. Surgery was known and practiced, but more common forms of treatment involved the bleeding, cupping, purging, and sweating of patients. Ancient medicine culminated in the career of Galen, court physician to Marcus Aurelius. Galen displayed true genius in his ability to digest and assimilate the classical medical tradition. His career also illustrated the limitations imposed on ancient medicine in particular, and ancient science in general, by his belief that the function of bodily organs could be discovered by divine revelation.

Something approaching the Hellenistic spirit of scientific investigation lingered in the work of Heron of Alexandria (fl. A.D. 50–100) sometimes called the "father of the turbine." Like Archimedes, however, he seems to have regarded his inventions as little more than toys; among them was a coin-vending machine he developed for dispensing holy water. Among those passing for scientists during the Second Sophistic there was general agreement on the question of the earth's sphericity but disagreement on its size and position in the universe. By the second century A.D. belief in geocentricity was established by the authority of Claudius Ptolemy of Alexandria, who, despite his monumental error, was one of the greatest scientific figures of antiquity. His *Almagest* was an important astronomical treatise, his *Geography* a popular book on the subject, which he treated mathematically.

ARCHITECTURE.   The early Principate marked the culmination of Roman architecture, one of Rome's most characteristic and original contributions to the Western tradition. A revolution took place toward the middle of the first century A.D. in building styles and engineering techniques, one that may be pinpointed to the reign of Nero. This revolution involved the more extensive use of arches and vaults known at Rome since the third century B.C. and was made possible by the use of concrete, mortar, and bricks.

There had been, of course, many vaulted structures in Rome and Italy before Nero's day, and certain public buildings created during the regime of Sulla, like the Tabularium in Rome and the Temple of Fortune at Praeneste (see illustrations, pp. 163 and 191) prefigured the new architectural imagery of the imperial period. Realization of that imagery, however, was postponed by the taste of the first Augustus, who, conservative in his approach to architecture as in other matters, preferred traditional post-and-lintel conceptions to any new trends. This official conservatism was reflected in a famous book on architectural design by Vitruvius, who described only standard building types and was not concerned with new conceptions involving vaults and curves. Later Julio-Claudians experimented with variations in barrel vaulting, especially in the construction of their palaces that spread over the Palatine. Such techniques were radically transformed only by the Neronian architect Severus, who deserves to rank as a great architectural innovator. At the behest of his emperor he created a New Architecture in the construction of the Golden House, a country villa set down in the midst of a metropolis, rambling over the Palatine and Esquiline hills and the lowlands in between in areas devastated by the great fire of A.D. 64.

Traditional Roman house architecture with atria and peristyles had been characterized by flat planes and was spatially inert. Severus built on the purely technological understanding of the use of vaulted spaces by preceding palace architects, who were striving blindly after a new idiom. He was able to infuse the use of vaults with a completely new esthetic and artistic, as opposed to a purely technological, approach. The New Architecture stressed interior effects made by curving surfaces, which produced unusual vistas. It was thus concerned with the creation of space rather than mass, a kind of space that would both embrace and direct the observer's attention. From an engineering point of view the New Architecture lacked interior supports, used centralizing axes, and, most typically, used a kind of construction in which concrete was covered with a brick face.

Some of the most famous surviving examples of the New Architecture date from the reigns of Trajan and Hadrian. Apollodorus, Trajan's favorite architect, challenged the ascendancy in public buildings of the basilica floor plan and colonnaded structures by his creation of innovative works in connection with the emperor's magnificent new forum, placed in the hollow between the Capitoline and Esquiline hills created by a remarkable feat of excavation. Perhaps the most striking building in the new style was a market, which attested to the emperor's interest in urban buildings having social utility (see illustration, p. 311). Apollodorus was on bad terms with Hadrian, Trajan's successor, who was himself a talented architect but resentful of Apollodorus' criticism, which may have earned his banishment and even execution. Apollodorus apparently did not work on a building thought by many architects to be the artistic quintescence of the Roman experience, the Pantheon, a temple to all the gods (see frontispiece). Originally built by Agrippa in the Campus Martius, it was reconstructed early in Hadrian's reign and has survived to this day virtually intact. Its great dome has suggested to some a kind of planetary rotundity, a "seeking for comprehension of things beyond knowledge." It has even been allegorically interpreted as a kind of Temple to Romanism, as expressive of an age as the Parthenon at Athens. Influence of the New Architecture is also evident in other Hadrianic buildings, especially his rambling villa at Tivoli near Rome.

The New Architecture spread throughout the provinces, the second century witnessing the construction in almost every major city of magnificent public buildings in this style. Sometimes, as at Ostia, extensive quarters were levelled for renewal on modern lines, so that a certain uniformity in appearance characterized towns far distant from one another. Architectural experience after Nero's reign was in some respects like that of twentieth-century America in its evident desire to make cities conform to a modern age, in its secular orientation, concern for novelty, and for the visual and social condition of the environment.

ART. Developments in art were less revolutionary than those in architecture. Little Roman painting has survived, except at Pompeii, where the eruption of Vesuvius in A.D. 79 preserved houses with interiors decorated in several styles derived from Hellenistic prototypes. Works of relief sculpture sponsored by emperors sometimes advertised imperial ideals, like the appropriately solemn Altar of Peace erected by Augustus. Sometimes they portrayed historical events, as in the case of bas-reliefs on the Arch of Titus that treated the triumph celebrated over the Jews, and the Column of Trajan, whose spiral decoration narrated artistically that emperor's Dacian wars. Perhaps the most interesting trend in sculpture was a certain archaism apparent in statuary of the second century and encouraged by the tastes of the emperor Hadrian. This revived interest in fifth century B.C. statuary, as distinguished from Hellenistic styles. Many such works, then copied from the originals by pointing machines, survive as the only known versions of statues by famous Hellenic artists.

Portrait sculpture under the Severans displayed both idealizing and realistic styles. Busts tended to become more "spiritual" in the sense that artists chose to emphasize and even exaggerate striking facial characteristics suggesting the psychology of the model. Developments pointing to the future then took place in historical reliefs. The arches erected by Septimius Severus in Rome and Leptis Magna reveal a departure from the rather literal rendering of similar scenes on earlier monuments. The emperor is portrayed frontally and becomes the immediate center of the observer's attention, while the rendering of other figures is flat and stiff, a departure from classical canons.

Abandonment of classical interpretations is also evident in late second and early third century mosaics, many of which have survived in villas in North Africa. There, mosaicists frequently failed to give any rational unity to their work by the use of perspective, and they even depicted farming scenes in strips where perspective was actually inverted. It is difficult to account for such striking departures from realism. The simplest and probably best explanation is that folk artists, less technically proficient than those of the imperial court and the big cities, were unable to master their medium.

Religious developments, especially those involving changing burial customs and Christianity, influenced both sculpture and painting. Pagans learned to appreciate the idea of personal immortality and so, like Christians and other sectaries anticipating an afterlife, they began to practice inhumation in sarcophagi on a large scale in the second century rather than cremation in urns to dispose of their dead. These were frequently decorated in sculptured relief, sometimes with religious scenes, sometimes with the portrayal of outstanding events in the life of the deceased in a style that was baroque and impressionistic.

Because of its Jewish origins early Christianity had a certain antipathy toward images, even those sculptured on sarcophagi. At first there was a poverty of Christian art for this reason and because Christians met in private homes, having no church buildings of their own before the third century. But even in artistic matters, Christianity came to terms with the world and gradually permitted the development of an artistic symbolism, at first primitive, but increasingly sophisticated, on sarcophagi, in underground burial places or catacombs, in houses, and eventually churches.

CHAPTER 21
DISINTEGRATION AND
RECOVERY: A.D. 235–285

During the period between 235 and 285, the Empire and ancient civilization passed through a great crisis. The causes of this crisis are ultimately attributable to basic defects in the reorganization undertaken by Augustus: reliance of emperors on military force to maintain their power against rivals; creation of a government that, in the long run, could not be supported by the resources of the Empire; and perpetuation of a class structure that failed to give the producing classes rewards equal to the taxes imposed on them. Within the Empire disorder reigned as a result of continuous military mutinies and struggles between their leaders for power. From without came waves of barbarian invaders, accompanied by repeated invasions from rulers of a revived Persia. In the wake of devastation caused by war and plundering, epidemics ravaged the population. Commerce and industry declined and the economic foundations of ancient civilized life were badly shaken. Despairing of the ability of the Empire to cope with disaster, men set up independent states, both in the East and West, to protect themselves. In order to rally the whole population in a united front against their enemies, certain emperors tried to force the Christians to conform to the state religion. Eventually, the soldiery were controlled, the Empire was cleared of foreign foes, and its political unity was reestablished. Victory was achieved at great cost. Politically, economically, and culturally the Roman world that emerged from the ordeal was far different from the Principate. Greco-Roman civilization had received a mortal blow, and the dawn of the Middle Ages was at hand.

The sources of information about this period are by no means commensurate with its importance. Herodian's history stops at 238, and for following years there is no continuous contemporary narrative. Conditions did not stimulate historical writing, and, of the little that was produced, little has survived. Biographical sketches of the emperors are given in the fourth century *Augustan History*, but these are full of falsifications. Additional information is supplied by epitomators and chroniclers of the fourth and fifth centuries and by Byzantine authors. The earliest historical works by Christian authors, the *Ecclesiastical History* of Eusebius, bishop of Caesarea, and the pamphlet *On the Death of the Persecutors* by Lactantius, both dating from the early fourth century, are new sources of information for relations of Christians and the government. The dearth of literary sources renders especially valuable contemporary inscriptions, papyri, coins, and archaeological remains. Unfortunately prevailing poverty caused a great falling-off in the number of both public and private inscriptions.

I. MUTINY OF THE SOLDIERY

SOLDIER EMPERORS. With the murder of Severus Alexander in 235 and the nomination of Maximinus the Thracian as *princeps* by the mutinous soldiery a fifty-year-long repetition began of the shorter epochs of civil war from 68 to 69 and 193 to 197. In the resulting turmoil, the Roman Peace, greatest achievement of the Principate, came to an end. Between 235 and 285 no less than twenty-six Augusti, including colleagues in imperial power, were recognized in Rome. Only one of these escaped violent death. Although five Augusti were nominated by the Senate and about the same number by emperors in office, the majority were revolutionary officers who engineered acclamation as emperors by their soldiers. In addition to those whose authority was confirmed by the Senate and so claimed legal right to *imperium*, there were many unsuccessful claimants defeated and killed by rivals. One emperor alone, Gallienus, had to suppress no fewer than eighteen of them. Soldier emperors were generally men of superior military capacities and achievements. Successful generalship was the main criterion applied by soldiers in their support of candidates for the Principate. As a rule, once in office, they conscientiously tried to restore peace and order, but all too often their efforts were nullified by the treachery of their own subordinates or the rise of more powerful rivals.

CAUSES AND CHARACTER OF THE REVOLTS. The causes of these chaotic conditions lay principally in the ambitions of the officer class, abetted by the greedy and undisciplined spirit of the professional soldiery. Such an attitude had been displayed by armies even under the Republic, and under the Empire on numerous occasions by the praetorians, and by legionaries also in the crises of 68–69 and 193, but disorder now became chronic and permeated all branches of the military. General loss of loyalty to the Empire is not easy to explain. Provincialization of the legions had led gradually to recruitment first on a territorial and then on a local basis, which meant that by the early third century most soldiers came from the immediate vicinity of frontier garrisons in what were the most rustic but by no means un-Romanized provinces. At least down to the Severan dynasty, the military establishment was generally loyal to the civilizing ideals of Rome and a not insignificant number of soldiers were sons of the municipal gentry of frontier provinces, scarcely types to form a revolutionary soldiery. A partial explanation may be the granting of citizenship to virtually all subjects in 212, which, by removing an incentive that attracted the better type of recruit, led to the enlistment of less Romanized subjects. More important, however, in the barbarization of the army was the scramble by revolutionary commanders to recruit troops in the chaos following 235. Revolutionaries willingly enlisted the roughest types from within the Empire and barbarians from outside it. At the same time, particularly because of the Severan policy of emphasizing the degree to which their authority was based on the army, the soldiers felt themselves more than ever a vested interest and lost feelings of obligation toward the state. Their appetite whetted by donations distributed by previous emperors, they determined to enrich themselves at the expense of civilians and the treasury. Jealousy between frontier armies and the praetorians and rivalries between various corps long stationed in different parts of the Empire prevented the soldiery from acting as a single unit. Different provincial armies, and at times formations brought together for campaigns, sought separately to force the recognition of their nominees to the Principate. Each hailed as Imperator the commander who led them to victory over foreign foes or other mutinous troops and forced him, often unwillingly, to march on Rome, in the expectation of receiving increases in pay and largess. Soldiers plundered impartially both peasants and townfolk through whose territories they marched and showed no indication of sharing with the former whatever spoils they wrested from the latter. Nor did they attempt to alter conditions of land ownership or land tenure in the interests of the peasantry or to alleviate heavy taxes and other burdens.

II. COLLAPSE OF THE IMPERIAL DEFENSES

NORTHERN BARBARIANS. The Roman world was simultaneously exposed to barbarian invasion. This was not caused merely, or even primarily, by the appearance of new and more aggressive barbarian nations along the frontiers. It was the direct result of the old policy of recruiting barbarians to serve in the army. Such recruitment, known even under the first emperors, increased notably in the second century and reached a flood in the third, as various pretenders sought to effect their claims with the use of barbarian contingents. The frontiers had thus long acted as a magnet for warlike bands looking for the material advantages offered them in Roman service. Now the way was open for such bands, already attracted to the frontier, to find the rewards of plunder and booty through invasion because some borders were then denuded of troops, withdrawn to meet attacks elsewhere and because armies were diverted from frontier defense to engage in civil war.

These bands placed themselves in the service of barbarian nations, some now appearing for the first time on Rome's borders, and encouraged them to engage in raids designed to plunder rather than win territory for permanent settlement. These nations included the Saxons who occupied the North Sea coast between the Rhine and Weser and whose fleets raided the shores of Britain and Gaul; the Franks, who were at home across the lower Rhine; and the Alamanni, who threatened the *limes* in Upper Germany and Raetia. Further east, the Marcomanni and Quadi still held their position on the Upper Danube, and Dacia and Lower Moesia were menaced by their old neighbors the Sarmatians and Carpi, as well as by the Vandals, who occupied part of Hungary. Potentially more dangerous, however, were the Goths, who had made their way from the Baltic to the north shore of the Black Sea, where they were joined by the Heruli. In no case do the names given these nations reflect any great degree of ethnic unity in so far as they affected the Empire. Each "nation" was the result of an amalgamation between barbarians moving to the frontiers and those already there. Once the frontier defense system was broken through, the invaders met with little opposition, for the emperors had no adequate mobile forces to deal with such attacks and required much time to organize field armies to cope with them. It is inaccurate to speak of barbarian invasions in terms of "hordes." Their effective strength was, in general, rather small, and most nations could field armies no larger than several tens of thousands of men.

GOTHIC INVASIONS. By a successful campaign against the Alamanni in 235, the emperor Maximinus secured a tranquil period on the Rhine, but under him and his successors the Danubian provinces were subjected to continual invasions by Sarmatians, Carpi, and Goths, who suffered numerous defeats but could not be subdued. It was even necessary to buy off the Goths with annual subsidies. The seriousness of the Gothic menace was first clearly realized during the principate of Decius (249–251). In 249 a Gothic host crossed the Danube into Lower Moesia and, although defeated by the emperor, moved southward into Thrace. When Decius followed them he was surprised and defeated with heavy losses (250). As the Goths withdrew with plunder and captives, Decius attacked them again. After initial success, his army was trapped and annihilated. Both Decius and his son, whom he had made co-emperor, fell in battle. Thereafter Danubian provinces were subjected to incursions of Gothic and other tribes, against whom no effective resistance could be offered.

Main Gothic activities then shifted further east. In 253 a series of raids by sea began against the Asia Minor and Aegean coasts, but the chronology is uncertain. That of 256 or 257 passed through the Bosporus and devastated the leading cities of Bithynia. Particularly disastrous was the assault on Asia Minor some years later. The Goths, descending into the Aegean by way of the Bosporus and Hellespont, ravaged coastal Ionia. Plundering, they then marched inland as far east as Galatia and Cappadocia. They finally turned north to Heraclea on the Black Sea, whence they sailed home with their booty. In 267 a large fleet manned by the Heruli and an army of Goths and associated tribes skirted the west shore of the Black Sea and descended upon Greece, which they devastated as far south as Sparta. Among other cities, Athens was seized and plundered. An imperial army then led by the emperor Gallienus (253–268) cut off their retreat and defeated them in a bloody battle at Naissus in Moesia, thousands of barbarians dying on the field. The rest sought refuge in a fortified encampment. Gallienus was forced to return to face a usurper in Italy, where he was assassinated by his own staff. His successor, Claudius (268–270), took over the command in the Balkans, winning several victories and forcing the surrender of the survivors of the former Gothic invasion and of fresh bands that crossed the Danube to aid them. The captives were partly settled in depopulated areas and partly incorporated in the Roman army. His victories brought Claudius the well-deserved surname of Gothicus. Although Gothic inroads did not cease entirely, later ones were not comparable to those of 267. The Gothic peril was averted for over a hundred years.

FRANKS AND ALAMANNI. Meantime the Western barbarians added to the general desolation and disintegration. Between 254 and 258 Gallienus was occupied in clearing Gaul and the Rhineland of Franks and Alamanni who had overrun the frontiers. At about the same time Pannonia was raided by the Marcomanni, Quadi, and Iazyges. The Marcomanni even reached Italy, advancing as far as Ravenna (254). To stop their attacks Gallienus had to grant them districts in Upper Pannonia. In 259–260 when Gallienus had to withdraw part of his forces to meet a revolt in Pannonia, the Franks again crossed the Rhine. Traversing Gaul they entered Spain and, obtaining ships in the harbors of Hispania Tarraconensis, landed in Mauretania. Meanwhile the Alamanni descended into the Rhone valley, which they occupied for three years and from which they raided other parts of Gaul. One band crossed the Alps into Italy and threatened Rome. Gallienus returned to Italy to meet the raiders, whom he defeated near Milan. As a result of these invasions the Romans lost their outposts across the middle Rhine and were also forced to give up the angle between the Rhine and Danube. Even Raetia, south of the Danube, could not be adequately protected, for the emperor Claudius had to cope with another Alamannic band that pushed through the Alps to the borders of Italy (269).

Even Africa was invaded by border tribes. A league of desert peoples called the Five Nations (*Quinquegentiani*), as well as other tribes from Mauretania, fell upon Numidia, which was, however, successfully defended by the Romans.

PERSIAN WARS. Persia under its new Sassanian dynasty claimed the eastern provinces of the Empire and initiated action that led Severus Alexander to undertake an invasion of Persia. A period of frequent conflict between the two powers ensued, but the chronology of the wars is difficult to establish because of meager sources. Although the Roman attack failed, the Persians were checked for a time, and they did not again take the offensive until 237–238. King Ardaschir invaded Roman Mesopotamia and took Nisibis and Carrhae. Ardaschir's son, Shapur I, who succeeded him about 240, at once opened a more vigorous offensive. Syria was overrun and Antioch endangered. Emperor Gordian III (238–244) took the field, and his able praetorian prefect and father-in-law Timesitheus drove the Persians out of Syria in 243 and recovered both Carrhae and Nisibis. The death of Timesitheus late that year, followed by the murder of Gordian—possibly by the new prefect, Philip the Arabian, who became emperor—prevented the Romans from exploiting their victory. Philip was content to make peace with Shapur, who accepted the former Roman boundary, but the Persian merely shifted the direction of his attack. After taking Media Atropatene, he had assassinated Chosroes, king of Armenia, a loyal Roman ally, and then set a Persian nominee on the throne (252). The way to Asia Minor was now open. Shapur raided Mesopotamia, Syria, and Cappadocia, which brought the emperor Valerian to the East. Valerian defeated the Persians in 257 and 259, but his army was weakened by disease. When he tried to relieve the siege of Edessa in 259 he was forced to negotiate with Shapur, who enticed him to a conference and took him prisoner. This was a tremendous blow to Roman prestige and a great triumph for the Persian king, who commemorated his exploit in rock reliefs still to be seen in Persia. Shapur at once marched into Syria and seized Antioch, while other Persian armies overran Cilicia and Cappadocia. When they scattered on plundering raids, the Romans began to organize resistance and to cut off isolated detachments. Shapur retreated laden with booty and captives. Before he reached his own territory, however, he was robbed of part of his spoils by the Arabs of Hatra and, in the neighborhood of Carrhae, suffered a serious defeat by Odenathus, the Roman client prince of Palmyra. This disaster ended Persian aggression for many years but could not repair the damage done to devastated provinces.

III. GAUL AND PALMYRA

ROMAN EMPIRE OF THE GAULS.   The inability of Gallienus to protect Gaul from invasion and his occupation with usurpers elsewhere, coupled with the capture of his father and senior colleague Valerian by the Persians, led to the temporary creation of an independent state in the West. In 259 troops under the orders of Marcus Cassianus Latinius Postumus, after a victory over the Franks, proclaimed him emperor and murdered the young Caesar Saloninus (Valerianus), who had been left by his father Gallienus in nominal command on the Rhine. For the moment Postumus contented himself with securing his position in Gaul and made no attempt to extend his authority. In 263 Gallienus proceeded against him, but he could not overthrow him, owing to the treachery of one of his own generals and a wound that forced him to abandon the campaign. Left to himself, Postumus won over both Spain and Britain and set up an imperial government with his capital at Trèves (*Augusta Treverorum*). There he appointed a Senate and annual consuls, issued coinage, and maintained his own praetorian guard. When Gallienus was called to the Balkans in 267 to cope with the great invasion of that year, the general Aureolus, whom he had left in guard Italy, defected to Postumus. The latter received only brief recognition in north Italy for Aureolus was besieged in Milan by Gallienus, whose successor Claudius forced him to surrender and executed him.

In Gaul, however, Postumus kept the barbarians at bay and maintained internal peace, which helped the country to recover partially from its disasters. His troops proved disloyal, however, and in 268 forced him to accept as colleague an officer, Victorinus, to fight against a rival emperor, Laelianus. Postumus defeated Laelianus at Mainz (*Mogontiacum*), but when he refused his victorious soldiers the right to sack the city they mutinied and killed him. Victorinus also fell victim to rebellion in 270. He was succeeded by Tetricus, governor of Aquitania and member of the Gallo-Roman aristocracy, who reigned until the collapse of the Gallic Empire in 274.

RISE OF PALMYRA   Palmyra, ancient Tadmor, situated in an oasis of the Syrian desert, owed its importance to its position at the junction of caravan routes between the Mediterranean ports of Syria and the Euphrates, as well as those connecting Arabia with North Syria and upper Mesopotamia. Its significance was early recognized by the Romans who gradually obtained control over it during the first century A.D. Hadrian granted it the right of Italian soil (*ius Italicum*), and under the Severi its ruling family were Roman citizens, some of senatorial rank. Detachments of Palmyrene archers served as Roman auxiliaries on the Syrian frontier. When the invasion of Shapur called Valerian to the East in 256, the prince of Palmyra was Septimius Odenathus, whose adherence to Rome was rewarded by consular rank. The capture of Valerian and the Persian march to the sea gave Odenathus an opportunity to play a more decisive and independent role. After inflicting severe losses on Shapur's army on its retreat through Mesopotamia, he turned upon and defeated the usurper Quietus, one of two emperors proclaimed in the East in 260, while the other, Macrianus, unsuccessfully attempted to secure recognition in the West. Gallienus rewarded Odenathus by entrusting him with command of Persian operations as Commander of the Romans (*dux Romanorum*). Odenathus recovered Roman Mesopotamia and carried the war to the Persian capital, Ctesiphon. When the Goths swarmed over Asia Minor in the 260s, Odenathus came to the rescue, although he was too late to prevent their withdrawal by way of Heraclea. In 267 or 268 he was murdered, along with his eldest son and chosen successor Herodian, by a relative, Maeonius, who himself soon was assassinated. By the close of his career, Odenathus was very influential in the Orient. For his victories over the Persians, Gallienus had conferred upon him the title Imperator. To this was added that of *corrector totius Orientis*, which gave him supervision of the region between Egypt and Asia Minor. After his first victory over Shapur, Odenathus took the title King of Palmyra and King of Kings, although he was still a Roman subject, in fact the highest Roman official in the Near East.

PALMYRA'S CHALLENGE TO ROME. With the death of Odenathus, power in Palmyra passed to his beautiful and gifted widow, Septimia Zenobia. Zenobia secured the crown of Palmyra for her son Vaballathus, his mother's willing tool. Conscious of the momentary weakness of Rome and the successes of Odenathus, she became convinced that Palmyra should seize the opportunity to establish independent rule over the East. She devoted her unusual energy and ability to realize this aim. The break with Rome was not immediate. Throughout the brief principate of Claudius Gothicus, Palmyra remained nominally part of the Empire, although its rulers gradually strengthened their hold upon Syria and extended it over eastern Asia Minor. When Claudius died of plague in 270, Palmyra refused to recognize the authority of his brother and successor Quintillus, and its troops occupied Egypt and western Asia Minor. When Quintillus, after about three months' reign, was succeeded by the general Aurelian, Zenobia and Vaballathus returned, nominally at least, to their allegiance, without, however, giving up control of seized territories. For the moment Aurelian was obliged to temporize and recognized Vaballathus as Imperator of the Romans but not as a colleague. In 271 Zenobia decided that the moment had come for Palmyrene independence. Vaballathus took the title Augustus, while Zenobia became Augusta. The East, like Gaul and the adjacent western provinces, had then separated from the central government, and it seemed probable that the Empire would permanently disintegrate.

IV. IMPERIAL UNITY RESTORED

AURELIAN, "RESTORER OF THE WORLD": A.D. 270–275. At this critical moment the soldiery chose Lucius Domitius Aurelianus, commander of the imperial cavalry under Claudius, who had contributed to crushing the Goths in the Balkans. By birth a humble Illyrian, Aurelian had risen from the ranks to high command by virtue of his soldierly qualities. Of great physical strength and outstanding courage, a natural leader and a skillful general, he was a stern disciplinarian, unyielding, undiplomatic, and hot-tempered. "Hand on Steel" (*manu ad ferrum*) his soldiers called him, and this epithet well expressed his character. Such was the emperor destined to reestablish political unity.

Aurelian's first task was to free the heart of the Empire from new waves of barbarians. While on his way to Rome from the middle Danube, he was forced to return to Pannonia to cope with an invasion by Vandals and Sarmatians. After a severe struggle, the invaders were defeated and allowed to return home upon condition of supplying cavalry to the Roman army. Then came word of a devastating invasion of north Italy from the upper Danube by the Juthungi, apparently Germanic peoples who had been subsidized as Roman allies. Aurelian met this enemy in the Po valley. After several battles, in which the barbarians at times gained victories, the emperor drove them north beyond the Danube. A senatorial conspiracy called Aurelian to Rome, where he suppressed a serious revolt of employees of the imperial mint, who resented attempts to check profiteering on debased coins. He also ordered the fortification of Rome as a protection against future barbarian inroads. Rome had not been in danger of attack by foreign enemies since Hannibal's invasion, and the city had outgrown its old defenses, which had fallen into decay. It was now surrounded by a brick wall twenty feet high, twelve feet wide, and twelve miles in circuit. This wall, begun in 271, was completed after Aurelian's death.

RECONQUEST OF THE EAST. Once Italy was secured by the defeats of the Juthungi and Vandals, Aurelian attempted to recover the East, where Vaballathus and Zenobia had proclaimed their independence. Marching eastward in 271, the emperor crossed the Danube and inflicted a severe defeat on a Gothic king. He then abandoned the province of Dacia because he lacked troops to defend so exposed an area. Gallienus had already given up the northern part of the province, and now Aurelian began to withdraw its garrison and civilians who wished to retreat south of the Danube. There he organized a new Dacian province at the expense of Moesia and Thrace. Resuming his march, he passed through Asia Minor and entered Syria, where the Greek population went over to him. Near Antioch he encountered the Palmyrene army, which included both the famous mounted archers and equally formidable lancers whose heavy horses, like their riders, were armored. Here, and again at Emesa, Aurelian's superior generalship won victories, and Zenobia withdrew to Palmyra. Aurelian followed and, overcoming the difficulties presented by the desert and its nomads, besieged the city. Zenobia, trying to flee to Persia, was caught, and Palmyra surrendered (272). Zenobia, Vaballathus, and other notables were taken to Rome; Palmyra itself received lenient treatment. When Aurelian campaigned against the Carpi later in the same year, the Palmyrenes rebelled and massacred their Roman garrison. Without delay Aurelian marched again to the East and retook the city (273). This time it was sacked and destroyed. Meantime a rebellion had broken out in Alexandria, which cut off the wheat supply for Rome. Aurelian easily suppressed the revolt and dismantled the fortifications of the city.

RECOVERY OF GAUL. Aurelian then directed his attention to Gaul. There the elderly Emperor Tetricus could barely ward off the barbarians and repress rebellions among his own commanders. He was unwilling and unable seriously to oppose the reunion of Gaul with the Empire, and perhaps he was already acting in collusion with Aurelian when the latter attacked (273 or 274). Aurelian crossed the Alps unhindered, and, when his troops compelled Tetricus to offer battle near Chalons, he deserted them and surrendered to his opponent. Aurelian's victory was complete. Both Gaul and Britain returned to the Empire. Reestablishment of imperial unity was achieved, and Aurelian returned to Rome to celebrate a splendid triumph graced by his captives Zenobia and Tetricus. Both received honorable treatment, the latter becoming governor of Lucania. On his coins Aurelian assumed the title "Restorer of the World" (*restitutor orbis*).

AURELIAN AND THE SOLAR CULT. In Rome Aurelian erected a temple to the Unconquered Sun God whom he established as the protective deity of the Empire. In this he was influenced by his belief that Elagabalus, the Sun God of Emesa, had aided him in his victory over Palmyra. He did not transplant to Rome the form of the cult practised at Emesa, however. In Roman fashion a college of senatorial priests supervised the ritual of the new "Lord of the Roman Empire." The Sun God of Aurelian was no mere local divinity but was looked upon as the highest god, whom all recognizing any solar divinity could unite in worshipping. The Sun God was then thought of as the source of imperial authority and in a special sense the emperor's protector.

Aurelian did not confine his attention to purely military or political matters but also interested himself in economic ones. He probably changed the status of professional guilds in the city of Rome, where he substituted a dole of baked bread for the former public distribution of grain and also issued allowances of pork, oil, and salt to the population. He attempted a rehabilitation of the silver coinage on the basis of the sestertius instead of the denarius, which was hopelessly inflated, but the reform was not sufficiently far-reaching. Like so many of his predecessors, Aurelian fell victim to military conspiracy. Early in 275, while on his way East to deal with Persia, he was murdered by a group of his officers who had been falsely informed by his secretary—himself in danger of punishment—that they were soon to be executed.

PROBUS, EMPEROR: A.D. 276–282. The Principate then was bestowed on Marcus Claudius Tacitus, an elderly senator, nominated by the Senate at the request of the army. Tacitus was killed by his troops after a war-filled rule of six months and was succeeded by his brother Florianus, who seized the *imperium*. He found a rival in Probus, the nominee of armies in Egypt and Syria. In less than three months Florianus was murdered by his troops, and Probus was recognized sole emperor. Marcus Aurelius Probus, like Aurelian, was Illyrian. An outstanding person, he devoted himself unsparingly to complete the work Aurelian had so well begun, by restoring order throughout the provinces and reestablishing military discipline. He cleared Gaul of Franks and Alamanni, who had resumed their incursions, and subdued rebellious Isaurians in the mountains of Asia Minor. Everywhere he successfully upheld imperial authority, suppressing usurpers and checking foreign enemies. Not the least of his services was the reclamation of abandoned or hitherto unexploited lands, which he accomplished in part by settlement of many conquered barbarians.

In this he was motivated largely by a desire to assure adequate provisions for the military. In many enterprises he also used the labor of soldiers, and this demand upon their services in peacetime, as well as his strict discipline, led to a mutiny which cost his life

CARUS, CARINUS, AND NUMERIANUS: A.D. 282–285. Marcus Aurelius Carus, praetorian prefect under Probus, was forced by his troops to accept their salutation of Imperator while Probus was still alive. Apparently a native of Narbonne in Gaul, he was very able and energetic. Upon his accession, he appointed his sons Carinus and Numerianus as Caesars. His chief exploit was a successful campaign against Persia, which recovered upper Mesopotamia, and the capture of Ctesiphon. In the midst of his success he died mysteriously, probably a victim of his praetorian prefect Aper (283). At his death Carinus and Numerianus were proclaimed Augusti. Carinus had been left in Rome to supervise the government of the West, where his cruelty made him detested. Numerianus had accompanied his father to the East. As the army was returning through Asia Minor, Aper had him assassinated. Instead of Aper, the army acclaimed as emperor Diocles, commander of the imperial bodyguard, who promptly executed Aper (284). Carinus at once rallied the troops under his command and met Diocles at the river Margus in Moesia. There the Western army prevailed, but Carinus was murdered by one of his officers (285). His leaderless army accepted Diocles as their Imperator, who then adopted the name Diocletian. With the consolidation of imperial power in his hands a new period of Roman history began.

V. CHRISTIANITY IN DANGER

PROBLEM OF THE CHRISTIANS. By about 250 the Christian Church was flourishing. With adherents in all classes and professions, it was nevertheless a religion that appealed mainly to the urban lower and middle classes, and it still had many more converts in the East than in the West. Its leaders were increasingly men of culture and ability, and, abandoning the attitude of the early Church, Christians were taking an increasingly active part in society. The number of the Christians was so great as to disquiet the government, as they were still traitors at law, in view of their attitude toward the cults of the state. Individual congregations, bound in a strong organization under bishops, seemed to form a state within the state. Many thoughtful pagans believed that the catastrophies besetting the Empire after 235 were due to divine wrath, that the Christians had disturbed the proper relationship between the state and the gods, that *pax deorum* that was the emperors' responsibility to maintain. Under the circumstances, it is remarkable that empirewide persecution occurred only twice during the anarchy.

Under Maximinus the Thracian, Christians experienced a brief persecution, an attack against the higher clergy as the ones responsible for propagation of Christian doctrines. He did not initiate a general persecution, and the effects of his hostility were mainly limited to Rome and Palestine. After his death (238), the policy of Trajan was resumed, and under the emperor Philip in particular the Christians enjoyed general immunity. This respite was merely a lull before the storm.

PERSECUTION OF DECIUS: A.D. 250–251. Under the emperor Decius, the successor of Philip, the first attempt was made to abolish Christianity totally. In 250 Decius issued an edict ordering all the citizens of Italy and the provinces, according to their municipalities, publicly to worship the state gods. Those who refused were liable to death. This edict threatened the destruction of all the Church communities, for it was directed against lay as well as clerical members. It also meant that Christians were to be sought out and revealed by compelling universal public registration for sacrifices. Many of the certificates of conformity granted to those who performed the sacrifices before the authorities have been found among papyri recovered in Egypt. The persecution was fairly successful from the pagan viewpoint, because many well-to-do Christians complied with the regulations to avoid punishment and death and apostatized their faith. Poor Christians apparently hoped that their obscurity would protect them if they failed to obey the law, but a few hardy souls won martyrdom for standing by their beliefs.

PERSECUTION OF VALERIAN: 257–259. The persecution of Decius was terminated by his death in 251, but his policy was renewed by Valerian in 257, whose resolution to stamp out Christianity was even firmer than Decius'. He began by prohibiting Christian meetings, then launched a campaign directed against the clergy. For all its thoroughness, this persecution seems to have had only mixed success because priests stood their ground more firmly than their parishioners. Many of the latter apostatized under the pressures of the moment, only to seek readmission to the Church once persecution stopped. There was always bitter disagreement within the Church whether the lapsed should be readmitted, but the policy in most places was liberal and forgiving. Valerian's persecution ended with his death in 259, and Gallienus, who in many respects did not sympathize with his father's policies, restored a period of toleration that lasted for over forty years.

VI. END OF THE PRINCIPATE

PRINCEPS AND SENATE. In the period between 235 and 285 the Principate came to an end. Its termination was marked by the complete elimination of the Senate as a factor in government and as the authority that legally conferred the powers of *princeps* on a new emperor. An accompanying and closely related development was the exclusion of the senatorial order from military command and to a large extent from civil administration. These changes were the logical, perhaps inevitable, outcome of trends that were manifest before the close of the Severan dynasty and were effected gradually and organically. Sometimes the Senate displayed much independence and initiative, but it did not command armed forces, and any influence it exerted was only temporary. It recognized Gordian I and his son Gordian II as emperors while Maximinus was still alive and took over the defense of Italy for them. At their death it declared them Divi and appointed as their successors Balbinus and Pupienus, but it was unable to protect them against the praetorians, who murdered them and forced the Senate to accept their own choice, the infant Gordian III (238). Later, when the army called on the Senate at the death of Aurelian to name the new *princeps*, it declined to take the responsibility and referred the decision back to the soldiers only to yield and make the appointment when they insisted. Although the Senate resented the actions of emperors like Gallienus and Aurelian, who deprived it of some of its remaining prerogatives or failed to respect its dignity, it could do nothing to protect its interests.

Until the accession of Carus (282), the Senate regularly confirmed the position of new emperors proclaimed by their armies, even though the rulers themselves need not have regarded such confirmation as essential to their power. When Carus was acclaimed emperor by the soldiers, he regarded himself as in full and legal possession of imperial authority by virtue of the action of the army alone, and he so informed the Senate. Diocletian followed his example in disregarding the Senate's traditional role in confirming an emperor, and henceforth it was admitted that the right to confer *imperium* had passed from the Senate to the army.

The Senate's loss of the right to make emperors found a counterpart in the increased emphasis laid upon divine aspects of the imperial office. This doctrine found its clearest expression under Aurelian, who called Hercules his "consort." In harmony with this was Aurelian's adoption of the diadem, long the symbol of deified autocracy in the ancient world, and his declaration to his troops that not they but God alone decided the choice of an emperor and the length of his rule. Aurelian's example was generally followed by his successors, whose coins show at times the emperor and a god side by side.

RISE OF THE EQUESTRIANS. Of great interest was the progressive exclusion of senators from military, and even civil posts, which had begun under Septimius Severus. This development is testimony to the continued tension between emperors and Senate, imperial fears of senatorial rivals, and in some sense the importance of the Senate as a corporation, despite imperial autocracy. An ancient source alleges that Gallienus excluded senators from all military commands, which he then entrusted to equestrians. This actually does not seem quite to have been the case, although he replaced all the legionary commanders with equestrian prefects and most of the senatorial legates who governed imperial provinces by equestrian officials who took the legates' title of *praesides*. He found a precedent in the practice of the early third century by which equestrians acted as temporary substitutes for senators in imperial and senatorial provinces. The successors of Gallienus continued his policy although a few imperial provinces still retained senatorial governors as late as the accession of

Diocletian. It is uncertain to what extent equestrians supplanted proconsuls in the senatorial provinces, but it seems probable that they did so very often. A sign of the new spirit was the appointment of curators to administer different parts of Italy, a prelude to its division into provinces. Symbolic also of the rise of equestrians was the continued extension of the powers of the praetorian prefect. Although the judicial development of the office ceased with Philip, prefects were given control of imposts in kind levied in support of the army (*annona*). They also acquired the right to issue general regulations, provided that they conformed to existing laws. In their military capacity they commanded all troops stationed in Italy, and when accompanying emperors in the field they were the highest general officers. It is not surprising that the praetorian prefecture became in several instances a steppingstone to the Principate. Militarization of the equestrian order, a process greatly accelerated under the Severi, became still more pronounced under Gallienus, who conferred equestrian rank at birth upon the sons of legionary centurions and subordinate officers.

MILITARY REFORMS. The failure of the system of frontier defenses, developed in the second century to check barbarian invasions, caused a regrouping of the army. This was essentially a return to the practice of the early Principate, when strong mobile forces were stationed at strategic points well back of the frontiers, ready to move rapidly against an enemy that broke through border fortifications and garrisons. Frontier units increasingly assumed the character of militiamen, particularly since, owing to increasing manpower shortage, they were reinforced by many barbarian captives and sometimes client tribes given lands along the *limites* if they promised to defend them. Other significant changes, dictated by the character of warfare in the third century, occurred in legionary equipment and training. The need for greater mobility both on the march and on the battlefield led to the abandonment of construction of fortified camps at the end of each day's march, and also to replacement of the breastplate by a leather jacket, sometimes covered with metal scales, and of the heavy shield by a small, round buckler. Since the ancient weapons of the legionary, the javelin and short straight sword, proved ineffective against cavalry of the day, they were given up in favor of lances and the long sword used by auxiliaries. Of far-reaching consequence was the gradual disappearance of Romanized officers, whose place was taken by provincials of inferior culture and education. Under these conditions knowledge of military traditions and organization among the lower officers declined as did training and discipline among the rank and file. Until about 250, however, the legions were the élite troops, and their formation determined the order of battle. Under Gallienus the Romans began to look upon cavalry as more important and developed such a force, organized independently and able to take the field without legionary support. This consisted of the already famous Moorish cavalry, cavalry formerly attached to legions, and new units recruited in Dalmatia. In equipping cavalry, Romans displayed traditional readiness to adapt to their own use their enemies' weapons. They had already used Osrhoënian and Palmyrene mounted archers armed with the powerful Asiatic laminated bow and to a lesser extent heavy-mailed lancers of the Persian type (*cataphractarii*). Many European cavalry regiments were then also organized as archers or heavy cavalry. The cavalry corps, with headquarters at Milan, was further strengthened by Aurelian, himself a great leader of horse, who increased the number of *cataphractarii*. The importance of the cavalry was shown by its enjoyment of status equal to the praetorians, and from the date of its organization its commander rivalled, if he did not eclipse, the praetorian prefect. Both Claudius Gothicus and Aurelian advanced from the command of the cavalry directly to the Principate.

An important stage in the barbarization of the army was the inclusion of German soldiers, not merely in irregular corps called *numeri* or as allies (*foederati*), but also in regular auxiliary units. Following earlier precedents Aurelian enrolled new auxiliary corps recruited among the Vandals, Alamanni, and Juthungi. In this period also the term *dux* (duke) became a formal military title, used of generals commanding special corps like the field armies and the cavalry or forces grouped in particular areas not corresponding to older provincial commands.

ECONOMIC DECLINE. It was inevitable that foreign invasions and civil strife should result in a disruption of agriculture, industry, and commerce. Apart from the destruction of property and the interruption of communication, much movable wealth was carried off as booty by Persians and barbarians. There was also an increasingly acute shortage of agricultural and military manpower, although the causes and development of what was undoubtedly an absolute decline in numbers are difficult to describe, granted the almost complete lack of reliable statistics. Certainly the barbarian invasions and revolutions, and probably the plague that began in 251, contributed to the phenomenon. Peasant classes in particular, on whom the entire economy of the Empire finally rested, did not reproduce themselves in sufficient numbers as they had little sustenance left after they had paid taxes to support such numerous unproductive classes as the soldiers, urban proletariat, bureaucrats, and estate holders with their numerous retinues.

One of the most obvious results of the anarchy was a notable currency inflation. Innocent of modern notions of public credit, government bonds, and national debts, yet faced with vastly increased expenditures to wage more frequent war, emperors saw their tax revenues shrink as the population and its productivity declined during invasions and revolutions. They reverted to the most convenient means they knew to balance their budget: debasement of silver coinage. Even during the Roman Peace and beginning with Nero, emperors had gradually, if moderately, increased the amount of base metal in their denarii as administrative expenses rose. The debasement, increasing markedly under the Severans, reached catastrophic proportions during and after Gallienus, whose coins were really only base metal with a slight silver wash. In the period 258–270 prices in terms of current silver coins rose as much as 1,000 per cent. Gresham's Law came into operation. Less debased coins of earlier reigns were driven out of circulation, hoarded, or treated as bullion.

The government and its employees were the chief sufferers in the inflation. A commentary on the primitive economic notions then obtaining is the fact that emperors did not raise fixed taxes as prices rose, so that the value of their revenue in coin fell alarmingly. At the same time they economized by not giving civil servants and soldiers cost-of-living increases, so that their salaries lost purchasing power. To avert a collapse of the system, emperors resorted to an expedient occasionally used even during the early Principate: extraordinary levies and disbursements in kind, especially wheat, to supplement fixed salaries in coin that were eroded by inflation. Even with these added emoluments, the purchasing power of officials and soldiers was much reduced below levels of the second century, which encouraged bribe-taking and plunder in their dealings with the civil population.

One important byproduct of the new fiscal policy was greater pressure by the government on the decurions charged with tax collection and on certain guilds that were made responsible for the distribution of comestibles they normally handled in the course of their retail trades. Otherwise the effects of inflation varied widely. Peasants living on a subsistence economy were scarcely affected, in so far as they were able to harvest and consume their own crops without harassment. Monetary wages of laborers tended to rise with price levels although they lagged behind inflation. Property owners, especially senators, equestrians, and decurions, kept the real value of their land, and, like the government itself, were preoccupied with the collection of rents in kind rather than coin as a hedge against monetary inflation. On the other hand, holders of long-term leases at fixed rates or of similarly pegged mortgages and institutions depending on fixed endowments were all but wiped out. The most affected in this way were provincial city governments.

CULTURAL DEVELOPMENTS.   The prolonged anarchy adversely affected cultural developments to the extent that the economic situation limited patronage of the arts by emperors and municipal governments. The third century nevertheless witnessed important developments in literature, philosophy, and art. Some of them were rooted essentially in the classical past; others derived their inspiration from outside the mainstream of Greco-Roman civilization. The most interesting cultural forces of the age were religious, Christianity in particular emerging as a peculiarly vital synthesis of both non-classical and classical outlooks.

Limited by an ossified educational system, pagan *belles-lettres* produced few important works of prose or poetry. At least worthy of mention is Herodian, a younger Greek contemporary of Dio, who just before 250 finished a superficial and highly rhetorical history covering the period from the death of Marcus Aurelius to A.D. 238. Although lacking Dio's scope, Herodian's work has some value because he, too, held official positions and was an eyewitness to important events. Dio and Herodian are the only historians whose works have survived from the third century although other authors are known by name or reputation.

Perhaps the most important cultural trend of the third century was an increasing religiosity and interest in other worldly matters among all classes that had been building up during the Principate. In different ways Christianity, pagan mystery religions, and developments in philosophy were important manifestations of this movement, and their interaction produced an important turning point in the intellectual history of Western man, what one modern observer has called the ultimate product of a certain "failure of nerve" in ancient society.

Neoplatonism, having already influenced Christian thinkers early in the century, was essential to the movement. It continued to influence the sons of well-to-do Christian families, who were exposed to pagan doctrine, because there were no Christian schools of higher learning. One such figure, a towering personality deserving to rank with Augustine because of the nature and importance of his theology, was Origen (ca. 185–254). Born of Christian parents, Origen studied as a young man at Alexandria with Ammonius Saccas, the most influential pagan Neoplatonist of his day. Origen later wrote on a wide range of subjects involving Christian doctrine. He was particularly interested in explanation or exegesis of Biblical passages, which he regarded as a philosophical exercise revealing hidden, allegorical meanings in the Testaments. His interest in exegesis also led him to anticipate Jerome in textual criticism of the Bible, by comparing variant Hebrew and Greek versions.

Origen's theology soon became controversial, since his Platonism led him to treat touchy subjects like the Trinity, the exercise of free will, and redemption. Platonic is his notion that only God the Father was *logos*, despite the divinity of Christ begotten of Him before all time, an interpretation of the Trinity that eventually earned him condemnation as a heretic in the sixth century. The influence of Ammonius Saccas is discernible in his belief that the world consists of a hierarchy of souls and spirits, more or less God-like to the extent that they refuse to be part of, and corrupted by, the physical world. Origen finally proclaimed the salvation of souls by the imitation of Christ, denial of physical life leading to a mystical union with God. Even more than Clement, Origen's theology espoused a divorcement from the temptations of this world and assured the firm penetration of Neoplatonic philosophy into both the manner of thinking and vocabulary of Christian intellectuals. Despite his eventual condemnation for heresy, his reputation made him the spiritual father of contemplative monasticism in the early Middle Ages.

The influence of Neoplatonism, of course, flowed in two directions, and if Christians like Clement and Origen were affected by it, and through them the Church, its impact on pagan intellectuals was no less marked. The pagan counterpart to Origen was his younger contemporary Plotinus (205–270), one of the most important figures in the intellectual history of Western man and the last creative representative of pagan philosophy. Born, it seems, in Upper Egypt, he too studied with Ammonius Saccas in Alexandria before accompanying the emperor Gordian on a Persian campaign in 242. He impressed the emperor Gallienus, who urged him to establish a city in southern Italy as a center for Neoplatonic studies, but the foundation was never realized.

Difficult because his notions of reality are so divorced from empirical tests of truth, the surviving works (*Enneads*) of Plotinus are the most comprehensive expression of Neoplatonic ideas on the intelligent essence of the universe, the dichotomy between material and spiritual worlds, and the ecstatic virtues of immersion in the latter. Unlike Christian Neoplatonists, however, Plotinus did not spell out the place of religion in his cosmos or identify the ideal *logos* as God. Despite his visionary thought, he had rather conventional ideas on the efficacy of astrology and ritual although he denied that praying to statues had any other than psychological benefits for worshippers. His disciples, however, especially Porphyry and Iamblichus, more clearly adapted the thought of their master to pagan religion. Thereafter, Neoplatonic sophisticates believed in a kind of basic monotheism of a perfect cosmic One, to be worshipped ascetically and intellectually, of which the old gods of the Greco-Roman pantheon were simply allegorical or poetical manifestations, important chiefly because of their sentimental links with the past.

ART. During the anarchy, artistic production declined in quantity, and in some cases quality, when patronage by individuals and cities was hard to come by. The imperial government continued to support artists and thus, on an official level, exercised great influence in determining taste. At mid-century there was a temporary reaction to a certain baroque fussiness apparent in official art produced during the Severan dynasty. The consequent reversion to a quieter, more classical style, is generally referred to as the "Gallienic Renaissance." Nevertheless, throughout the third century there was an increasingly strong movement, originating in the East, toward an art whose canons were more abstract than those of the Greco-Roman tradition.

The developing iconography of Christian art varied. Sometimes it was utterly terse and symbolic, the bare rendering of a fish, loaf of bread, or cup of wine alluding to the mysteries of the faith, but it also borrowed from pagan motifs. The Christian idea of Paradise was expressed in pastoral scenes, garlands of flowers, clusters of grapes and olive branches, and even in erotic figures, all having artistic roots going far back into the pagan Roman and even Hellenistic past. A standard type in ancient sculpture, a young man holding a ram on his shoulders, became the Christian Good Shepherd; Roman Pietas became a commonly depicted "praying" figure with arms and hands uplifted to God, and scenes of Christians reading the Holy Book were modeled after philosophers portrayed in pagan art.

PART
IV

AUTOCRACY OR
LATE EMPIRE:
A.D. 285–565

Diocletian - augusti - East
Galerias Caesar - East
Maximian - augusti - west
Constantius - caesar - west

235-285 Anarchy

285-395 United   285-305 Tetrachy

auto
cratic   {   395 - 518 divided

518 - 565 Attempts at.
              Reunification

CHAPTER 22
THE EMPIRE STANDS
UNITED: A.D. 285–395

The political history of the Empire from 285 to 565 falls into three main periods. During the first, from 285 to 395, the Empire remained united and maintained its integrity against barbarians and rebellion. During the second, from 395 to 518, the Empire split into Eastern and Western halves; the latter gradually crumbled and gave way to a number of Germanic kingdoms, while the former succeeded in surviving disintegration eventually as the Byzantine Empire. The third period, from 518 to 565, is characterized by the partially successful attempt made by the East to reestablish imperial authority in the West and so preserve the ideal of a universal Empire. Although the second and third periods will be treated in later chapters, it will be convenient to survey here our principal sources for the whole epoch.

For the fourth century the most valuable sources are the surviving books, 14 to 31, of the history of Ammianus Marcellinus, which give a detailed account of the years 353 to 378. This is paralleled and supplemented by the *New History* of Zosimus, covering the period from 270 to 410. There are also brief manuals referred to in preceding chapters: Sextus Aurelius Victor's *Caesars*, a short series of imperial lives from Augustus to 360; the so-called *Epitome of the Caesars*, which runs to 395; Eutropius' *Breviary* of Roman History to 364; and the work of Paulus Orosius entitled *Against the Pagans*, ending with 417. For most of the fifth century, however, there is no important historical literature. The events of Justinian's reign, however, are recorded in the noteworthy *History* of Procopius, whose work, ending with 554, covers the Vandal, Gothic, and Persian Wars. Procopius has left a valuable account of Justinian's building activities. A continuation of Procopius is to be found in Agathias' *On the Reign of Justinian*, in which he narrates the events of the years 552 to 558. The gaps in the narrative history are partially filled by chronicles of the fourth, fifth, sixth, and later centuries. Of these, one of the most important is the Greek chronicle of Eusebius, which ran to 325 and is partly preserved in the Latin version of St. Jerome, who brought it down to 378. This chronicle was continued by others in both Latin and Greek until nearly 600. Another similar work is the Greek *Pascal Chronicle*, a chronological record from the creation of the world to 629.

Among more specialized historical works are various Church histories by Eusebius and others and the already mentioned tract of Lactantius. Useful also are histories of the Goths, Franks, and other Germanic peoples written by Romans or others who carried on traditions of Roman culture in lands lost to the barbarians. There is also much material in contemporary nonhistorical writings of churchmen, panegyrics addressed to emperors, collections of speeches and letters, and other literature. Invaluable material is also presented in compilations of law, the *Theodosian Code* of 438; its supplement the *Novellae* or "New Constitutions" dating between 438 and 472; and the *Code* of Justinian of 534, and his *Novellae*. These collections are paralleled by others of Visigothic and Burgundian kings for their Roman subjects. An important document for the administrative organization of the Late Empire is the *Notitia Dignitatum* of the early fifth century. This is an official list of civil and military officials with their staffs and in some cases their spheres of competence. Inscriptions, although not numerous, with coins and archaeological remains, supplement literary sources. For Egypt, papyrus documents continue to throw light on all aspects of life in that province.

I. DIOCLETIAN AND THE TETRARCHY: A.D. 285–305

DIOCLETIAN'S IMPERIAL POLICY. When Diocletian became sole emperor in 285, he was about forty. By birth a Dalmatian, he had had a distinguished military career. He was dominant, courageous and strong-willed, and proceeded cautiously but with determination to effect significant reforms. Like preceding Illyrian emperors, he saw as his prime obligation the preservation of the Empire, and he sought to defend it against attack and disorder. In realizing this goal, despite a decline in manpower and economic prosperity, lies the clue to his important innovations. Foremost among them were an exaltation of imperial authority and a strengthening of military force. Autocratic tendencies that had grown ever stronger during the late Principate triumphed completely with Diocletian. Acclaimed by the army, he considered confirmation of its action by the Senate as superfluous. Even his selection by the soldiers he regarded as an expression of the will of Jupiter, and in this way claimed divine sanction. The army could not be ignored, however, and its support remained an essential base of imperial power.

AGAINST REVOLTS AND INVASIONS. In 286 Diocletian was faced by a serious rebellion in Gaul, where the peasants, impoverished by barbarian invasions and heavy taxation, had abandoned their fields. These dispossessed, known as Bagaudae, were terrorizing the countryside in formidable bands. To restore order in Gaul and rebuild Rhineland defenses, Diocletian dispatched a Pannonian officer, Valerius Maximianus, whom he raised to the rank of junior colleague, Caesar and Son of Augustus (*filius Augusti*). Maximian easily suppressed the Bagaudae. He then strengthened the Rhine frontier, which in the years 286 to 288 he successfully defended against attacks by Franks, Alamanni, and Burgundians. In 286 a more serious rebellion occurred. Carausius, an officer entrusted with the protection of the coasts of the North Sea and English Channel against pirates, occupied Britain and proclaimed himself Augustus. Diocletian then elevated Maximian from Caesar to Augustus. Having lost his fleet in a storm, Maximian failed to recover Britain and depose Carausius. This forced the two emperors to come to terms with him and recognize his authority in the area he controlled (290). Carausius claimed the status of Augustus like Diocletian and Maximian. His control of the chief channel port, Gesoriacum (Boulogne), and his alliance with barbarian tribes across the Rhine threatened Gaul, so Diocletian decided to attack again and entrusted military operations to Constantius Chlorus, an Illyrian officer whom he made a Caesar early in 293. Constantius captured Gesoriacum and then defeated the barbarian allies of Carausius, many of whom he transplanted to till vacant lands of Gaul and furnish recruits for Roman armies, and Carausius was murdered by one of his officials. In 296 Constantius landed in Britain, and the island was reunited to the Empire. This victory gave the Romans mastery of the seas off Britain and Gaul and enabled them to check Frankish pirates who had raided the coasts of Spain and North Africa. Serious disturbances in North Africa were then suppressed by Maximian (297).

The eastern parts of the Empire were threatened at the same time by barbarian tribes along the Danube, by the Persians in Asia, and by raids of the Blemmyes into upper Egypt. On the Danube, Gaius Galerius, nominated Caesar in 293, severely defeated the Iazyges and Carpi with Diocletian's support and improved the defense system. Many captured barbarians were settled on the Danube. In 296 a rebellion broke out in Egypt under a usurper named Domitianus as the result of heavy taxation and inflation. Diocletian blockaded Domitianus in Alexandria, which he took in March 297, thus ending the revolt. To check the Blemmyes, Diocletian gave up some border territory south of the First Cataract of the Nile, settling it with an allied tribe. The revolt in Egypt appeared more serious in view of the hostility of Narses, king of Persia, who attacked in 297, overrunning the Roman protectorate of Armenia and defeating the Caesar Galerius. Later in the year Galerius beat him decisively, and he was obliged to accept peace on Roman terms (298). Rome recovered Upper Mesopotamia; the Roman nominee in Armenia regained the throne; and some districts north of the Tigris became her protectorate. Along the eastern frontier new military installations were constructed.

THE TETRARCHY. Diocletian had no male heir, and the experience of his predecessors taught him the danger of entrusting serious military operations to a potential rival. For this reason, when confronted by military necessity, he appointed Maximian as his colleague, first as Caesar and then as Augustus. Military necessity again forced him to appoint two new Caesars, Constantius and Galerius, in 293. In this way a Tetrarchy, or rule of four, was created. Implicit in the Tetrarchy was the idea that ultimately the two Caesars should succeed the two Augusti as senior rulers and should in turn appoint successors. To bind them more closely to each other, Diocletian gave his daughter in marriage to Galerius, while Constantius married the daughter of Maximian. Diocletian extended the claim to divine support for his authority to his colleagues. He called himself Jovius, indicative of his being the choice of Jupiter, and he bestowed on Maximian that of Herculius, since Hercules was the mythological helper of Jupiter. When the two Caesars were appointed, Constantius became a Herculius, Galerius a Jovius. Diocletian and his associate thus claimed divine sanction and inspiration in exercising power. Any opposition to their ordinances amounted to defiance of divine will.

The Tetrarchy was held together by the dominance of Diocletian over his colleagues, based on his seniority and his strength of personality, and he formulated and directed imperial policy. Thus, there was no fourfold administrative division of the Empire, although the armed forces were divided into four commands, each under an Augustus or a Caesar. Each ruler selected as residence a city strategically placed with respect to frontiers under his particular supervision. Diocletian chose Nicomedia in Asia Minor, on the Sea of Marmora, well adapted to defend Egypt, Asia, and Thrace. Galerius, whose forces guarded the Danubian frontier, took up his quarters in Sirmium on the lower Save; Maximian established himself at Milan, in command of Raetia, Italy, North Africa, and Spain; and Constantius, to whom fell Gaul and Britain, resided at Treves (Augusta Treverorum) in northern Gaul. Rome ceased to be the imperial residence and administrative capital of the Empire, a change that reflected the decline in importance of the Senate. The Eternal City

XIX Statues of the Tetrarchs (*St. Mark's, Venice*). *These four small figures from the fourth century A.D. are commonly thought to represent Diocletian and his fellow tetrarchs embracing in fraternal concord. The style exemplifies nonclassical canons of the Late Empire. (Photo: Fototeca Unione.)*

continued to enjoy a privileged status, however, and its citizens were still fed and amused by the state.

DIOCLETIAN'S REFORMS. Diocletian's reforms profoundly affected nearly all branches of government. Many of them will be discussed in the following chapter, but it will be convenient to indicate here their scope and character. In strengthening imperial defenses, Diocletian enlarged the army, which consisted of an expanded frontier guard and the nucleus of a mobile reserve at court. He enlisted many barbarians in auxiliary units, but the bulk of his legionary recruitment came from within the Empire. Frontier provinces were divided up, largely to provide closer supervision of border garrisons and weaken the power of commanders. The provinces were grouped into new districts called *dioceses*. These changes greatly increased the number of civilian and military personnel in state service. Mistrustful of his own bureaucracy, Diocletian reorganized the imperial secret service (*frumentarii*), now called the *agentes-in-rebus*, and used it to inform on governmental operations.

The resulting increase in expenses, economic decline of the third century, and inadequacy of the old taxes, led Diocletian to establish a new and generally uniform system of taxation for the Empire. Realizing that economic instability was due in part to the great depreciation of the coinage, he attempted to introduce a new, stable gold and silver currency. His devaluation of copper coins then in circulation resulted in more inflation, accentuated by production shortages. This situation created hardships for soldiers and bureaucrats, and led Diocletian to try to control prices by law. His Edict of Prices of 301 fixed a uniform price for each commodity and every form of labor or professional service. Death was the penalty for profiteers. This law took no account of variations of supply and demand in the Empire and made no distinction between wholesale and retail trade or between good and poor workmanship. Despite the death penalty, the law was disregarded so generally that the government gave up its enforcement.

PERSECUTION OF CHRISTIANS: A.D. 303. Diocletian was responsible for the last great persecution of the Christians. They had enjoyed immunity from repressive legislation for forty years after Valerian's death. They had also increased greatly in number, including at this time perhaps as much as one sixth of the population. They were prominent in all professions, including government service. Owing to Diocletian's emphasis on the divine sanction of imperial power and on worship of the state gods, a conflict between the state and the Christians was almost inevitable. It was only after nearly twenty years of rule, however, that Diocletian decided to make Christians conform to the state religion. His reasons for doing so are unclear. He may have come to regard them as a potentially disloyal element or his pagan susceptibilities may have been offended by acts of certain Christians. Christian tradition ascribes his decision to pressure of Galerius, the most superstitious member of the Tetrarchy, but although the Caesar's attitude is clear, he was not the leader in the new policy. An indication of Diocletian's attitude toward a cult he considered a menace to religious and political unity is found in his edict of 297 against the Manicheans, followers of the third century prophet Mani. They not only rejected Roman paganism but were suspected of being Persian agents.

The first of Diocletian's three edicts against the Christians was issued early in 303. It called for destruction of Christian churches and books. The second and third edicts ordered, respectively, that clergy of all ranks be imprisoned and compelled to sacrifice to the state gods. A fourth edict in 304 prescribed that all persons make the customary sacrifices on pain of death. These edicts were not enforced everywhere with equal vigor. Constantius, in whose sphere the Christians were few, contented himself with carrying out the first edict only, whereas Maximian and Galerius were zealous persecutors. The persecution was still in progress when Diocletian's reign ended in 305.

ABDICATION OF DIOCLETIAN AND MAXIMIAN: A.D. 305. While returning to the East early in 304, Diocletian became seriously ill, perhaps suffered a stroke, and for some months was incapacitated. Recovering, he determined to abdicate on May 1, 305, and forced Maximian then to do the same. Constantius and Galerius became the new Augusti. In the appointment of new Caesars, the sons of Maximian and Constantius were passed over, and the choice fell on Severus and Maximin Daia, both favorites of Galerius. Diocletian retired to his magnificent palace near Salonae in Dalmatia, and Maximian, much against his will, to his estate in Lucania.

II. COLLAPSE OF THE TETRARCHY AND THE REIGN OF CONSTANTINE I, THE GREAT: A.D. 305–337

COLLAPSE OF THE TETRARCHY: A.D. 305–310. Diocletian's Tetrarchy did not long survive his abdication. Lacking the unifying leadership of its organizer, it was wrecked by dynastic loyalty and personal ambition. The Empire then entered a very turbulent period, one of the most complicated in Roman history, during which as many as seven men simultaneously claimed the title of Augustus. When the emperor Constantius died in Britain in 306, his army at once acclaimed his son Constantine, then twenty-six years old, as Augustus. Galerius refused to accept this, but, while he advanced Caesar Severus to the rank of Augustus, he acknowledged Constantine as Caesar to avoid civil war. Almost immediately another claimant to imperial power arose. This was Maxentius, son of Maximian, who capitalized on discontent in Rome and Italy over new taxes imposed by Severus to have himself proclaimed princeps, in the hope of being made Caesar. Galerius refused him recognition and ordered Severus to depose him. Thereupon Maximian came out of retirement to support his son and soon resumed his title Augustus. Approaching Rome Severus was deserted by his troops and surrendered to Maximian, who executed him (summer 307). Maxentius then declared himself Augustus.

Galerius prepared to intervene in the West; Maximian tried to strengthen his position by an alliance with Constantine, whom he named Augustus and to whom he gave his daughter, Fausta, in marriage (307). Constantine in return recognized him as Augustus. Galerius failed in his invasion of Italy, because his soldiers were disloyal, and called on Diocletian to return to power. This the ex-emperor refused, although he did meet Galerius and Maximian at Carnuntum (308). There Maximian was induced to abdicate again. Licinius, a protege of Galerius, was made junior Augustus, and Maxentius was treated as an outlaw. Maximin Daia and Constantine demanded from Galerius the title of Augustus but received only that of Son of Augustus (*filius Augusti*), which Constantine never accepted and Maximin soon ignored. Maximian, who had quarreled earlier with his son Maxentius and failed in an attempt to depose him, now took refuge with Constantine and appeared once more as an Augustus. Maximian soon intrigued against his son-in-law, which led to his own execution. At the close of 310 five Augusti, including Maxentius, ruled the Empire.

EDICT OF TOLERATION: A.D. 311. The persecution of the Christians initiated by Diocletian had not produced the desired result. Many leading Christians suffered martyrdom, far more suffered mutilation or were sentenced to prison or the mines; many yielded and met the formal test of pagan sacrifice; many churches were destroyed, but most Christians kept their faith. The truth was that persecution did not have the solid backing of pagans. Civilians and officials alike connived to protect their Christian neighbors from the laws. Persecution slackened or ceased, except where it was stimulated by fresh edicts, as in the sphere of Maximin Daia. Finally in 311, Galerius, then mortally ill, issued an edict as senior Augustus that gave Christians freedom to practice their religion and rebuild their churches, provided that they not offend public order.

CONSTANTINE CONQUERS MAXENTIUS: A.D. 312. With the death of Galerius rivalry sharpened among the remaining Augusti. Constantine sought possession of Italy as the next step in winning the Empire. He allied himself with Licinius, who anticipated trouble with Daia, and declared war on Maxentius, invading Italy early in 312. He defeated his rival in north Italy and pressed on to Rome. Maxentius risked a battle not far from the Milvian bridge across the Tiber. There his army was completely defeated, and he, with many troops, was drowned in the rout. Just before the battle Constantine, as the result of a vision, ordered his soldiers to mark their shields with a monogram resembling a combination of *chi* and *rho*, the first two letters of the Greek word *Christos*, meaning Christ. It was an appeal to the Christian's God, and Constantine regarded his victory as its answer. With the death of Maxentius not only Rome and Italy but also Spain and North Africa fell to Constantine, and the Senate declared him senior Augustus. In Rome, he disbanded the *equites singulares* and the praetorian guard and dismantled their barracks.

CONSTANTINE AND LICINIUS: A.D. 312–324. Early in 313 Constantine and Licinius met at Milan and agreed to grant Christians unrestricted freedom and to restore confiscated Church properties. The alliance between the two emperors was cemented by the marriage of Constantine's daughter to Licinius, but the latter got none of Maxentius' territories and was left to expand his own part of the Empire at the expense of Daia. Endangered, Daia took the offensive, crossed the Bosporus, and attacked Licinius. The latter defeated him, pursued him into Asia Minor, and when Daia died of illness, annexed all of the East (autumn 313). Letters that Licinius wrote to the governors of his newly subdued provinces explain the policy toward the Christians formulated at Milan, which does not seem to have been expressed in any general edict.

Elimination of Daia brought out the latent rivalry between Constantine and Licinius. Constantine sought to create a buffer out of territories to be ceded by each of them to a Caesar, but Licinius tried to instigate a revolt against Constantine, and this led to war. Military operations were inconclusive although Constantine had the advantage and Licinius ceded to him all his European territories except Thrace, while Constantine gave up his right as senior Augustus to legislate for all the Empire. In 317 the two emperors jointly recognized as Caesars and their future successors Crispus and Constantine, the elder sons of Constantine, and Licinianus, son of Licinius. Harmony did not prevail, and growing tension was reflected in their religious policies. While Constantine granted greater privileges and advantages to the Christians, Licinius gradually reversed his toleration and began persecution. It was obvious that Constantine aimed at being sole emperor, while Licinius sought a definite partition of the Empire. Finally in 323 Constantine, pursuing Gothic raiders, led his army into Thrace, and Licinius' resentment of this trespass led to war. In 324 Constantine routed Licinius at Adrianople, and Crispus destroyed his fleet in the Hellespont. Licinius withdrew to Asia Minor where in the same year he suffered a final defeat at Chrysopolis. He surrendered to Constantine, who shortly executed him for fresh intrigues.

FOUNDING OF CONSTANTINOPLE: A.D. 324–330. One of the early decisions of Constantine as sole emperor was to establish a new residence, Constantinople, on the site of Byzantium, the Greek city at the junction of the Bosporus and the Sea of Marmora. The choice of this site was determined by its strategic relation to the Persian and Danubian frontiers and its command of the crossing from Europe to Asia Minor and of the exit from the Black Sea to the Mediterranean. Before long the site proved equally advantageous for the growth of a world market. Construction was begun in 324, but the city plan evolved slowly, and it was not until 330 that the new imperial residence was formally dedicated. In retrospect, the foundation of Constantinople appears as the most epochal of Constantine's innovations, but he could not have foreseen the effects that the fateful and eventually permanent shift eastward of the administrative center of gravity would entail, or that his city would become the nerve center of a new world. Constantinople was a second Rome, not a new one. Upon his death he did not even designate it as the residence of his eldest son, but rather assigned it to his least important successor. Old Rome on the Tiber kept its first rank among cities, even though it was not Constantine's home. He certainly intended Constantinople to be a new Christian residence symbolizing a break with the past associated with Rome in the West. Predominantly Christian from the very beginning, it nevertheless contained pagan temples, administrators, and philosophers. It was given many of the institutions and appurtenances characteristic of an imperial city on the model of old Rome. These included a Senate, a palace, public buildings, *objets d'art* ransacked from other cities, even traditional Roman festivals and distribution of free grain to the populace.

CONSTANTINE, THE CHRISTIAN EMPEROR.   The religious influences in his life before 312 are speculative. His father was a worshipper of the sun-god, like many Illyrian soldiers of his generation. He seems also to have been not ill-disposed to monotheism; at the least his refusal to enforce strictly in his part of the Empire the anti-Christian persecution of the Tetrarchy bespeaks his toleration. A dubious tradition even claims that the women in Constantine's family were inclined toward Christianity before the Battle of the Milvian Bridge.

It would be captious to deny the reality of Constantine's Christian vision before his victory over Maxentius in 312, granted his very emotional nature or the very sincerity of his conversion to Christianity. He entrusted himself and his army to the power of the Christian God, which for him was confirmed by his stunning victory. Conversion to Christianity ideally demanded a complete break with the convert's pagan past, but in this respect Constantine's behavior was ambiguous. As emperor, he accepted the title of *pontifex maximus* and therefore headship of the pagan state cult although he did not perform the traditional sacrifices and rituals. Until 324 his coinage, always an indication of the imperial "party line," continued to show the emblem of the sun-god, clearly capable of pagan interpretation. The inscription on his arch, completed in 315 near the Colosseum in Rome, ascribed his victory over Maxentius to "inspiration of the Divinity" (*instinctu divinitatis*) but did not spell out just what god he had in mind. Although he limited pagan rites in public, he did not make Christianity the state religion in the sense of compelling his subjects to become Christians, and he did not abolish famous reminders of the old religion, like the order of the Vestal Virgins housed just off the Forum or the Altar of Victory in the Senate House.

These ambiguities need not belie the sincerity of his religious convictions. He was a child of his age and, initially at least, innocent of the sophistication of Christian doctrine. Like his contemporaries of all religious persuasions, he conceived of divinity in terms of power; he was a Christian convert because conversion in his case was effective and had made him emperor. Late antiquity was notable for its syncretism, in which the identity of many gods was interchangeable or, among the educated, all allegories of a Divine One. The association of sun and Cross in his vision, the solar heraldry of his early coins, his proclamation of Sunday as a Christian holiday, may all attest an initial tendency to identify his father's god with the Christian Divinity. His accommodation to paganism in public affairs is probably ascribable to his political astuteness, as millennial beliefs and habits of thought could not be changed overnight. Christians were only a small minority of the total population at the time of his accession; despite conversions among the governing establishment, Christianity was still predominantly a religion of the urban lower classes in the Greek East. In the West, which Constantine initially controlled, the size of the sect was minute, and the institutions and classes on which he based power—the army, senatorial aristocracy, and equestrian order—were overwhelmingly pagan.

Certainly leading Christians of his day had no doubt about his convictions and hailed enthusiastically his benefactions to the Church. It is doubtful whether Christianity ever would have triumphed as the religion of the Empire if it had not had some imperial champion such as Constantine to make it popular and powerful. It had been traditional for emperors to keep the proper relationship with the gods, and Constantine would have been un-Roman had he not striven to maintain a like relationship with his own Christian God and, by encouraging unity within the Church, to win His favor and to strengthen the Empire. This may be seen especially in the emperor's convocation of the First Ecumenical Church Council at Nicaea in 325 to decide on the orthodoxy of the Christian sect called Arian, which disputed the nature of the Trinity and was condemned as heretical.[1] Despite the intervention of the Council, Arianism remained a burning issue in the Church long after Constantine's reign.

Granted the personal religious disposition of an autocrat, the State would inevitably favor the Church and protect it against any threats. State funds subsidized bishops and built many new churches. The resources of the posting service were placed at the disposal of clergymen traveling on Church business. The tenor of imperial legislation became increasingly Christian. Disabilities on celibates were repealed, and, in certain suits, bishops were empowered to act as judges. Prelates like Hosius of Corduba frequented the imperial court and became confidants of the emperor. The new respectability of Christianity, enhanced by imperial patronage, notably encouraged conversions among the governing establishment and the army, the majority of which, however, was still pagan at the end of Constantine's reign.

CONSTANTINE'S IMPERIAL POLICY. In many respects Constantine's imperial policy followed that of Diocletian, whose ideas he developed and perfected. A convinced autocrat, he based his claim to rule on hereditary right, confirmed by divine sanction, a claim Christians and pagans could accept. As the symbol of his authority, he assumed in 325 the diadem, a narrow band around the head which had been the emblem of autocracy for both Persian and Hellenistic kings. He completed the separation of military and civil authority

---

[1] For detailed discussion of Arianism, see p. 485f.

by depriving praetorian prefects of the right of command, and by abrogating the authority of provincial governors over commanders of border garrisons. Whereas Diocletian had greatly increased the strength of the frontier forces, Constantine transferred many of their units to an enlarged mobile field army strategically stationed behind the frontiers. The place of the prefects as general officers was taken by newly created masters of horse and masters of foot. In recruiting soldiers Constantine displayed a strong partiality for barbarians and opened even the higher commands to barbarian officers. He continued the policy of transplanting tribes of barbarians into depopulated areas under obligation to furnish recruits for the army. For administrative purposes he began to place parts of his Empire under resident praetorian prefects. As they finally evolved under his successors, the prefectures were normally four in number. He also created new ministers called counts (*comes* or Companion), who formed a new council of state.

Constantine's expansion of the bureaucracy and the army, the building of Constantinople, the erection of many new and magnificent churches, and state support for the Christian clergy materially increased government expenditures and necessitated increased taxes. To help ensure their payment and to provide manpower for public services and essential economic activities, Constantine made full use of his autocratic power to develop a totalitarian regime, for which the foundations had been laid by earlier emperors. He regimented the occupations of practically all classes of the population, which were made hereditary. Constantine continued Diocletian's attempt to stabilize the coinage by issuing a standard gold coin equal to 1/72 of a pound of gold, with coins of silver and copper of smaller denominations. Metal needed to strike the new issue seems to have come from the confiscated treasures of pagan temples, but not enough coins could be issued to supply demand. Payment of salaries in kind continued, and shortages of silver and copper led the state to debase coinage, with further inflation. Constantine devoted great attention to administration of justice. By directives issued to judges he sought to secure greater protection for the poor, weak, and defenseless. Christian, Stoic, and Hellenistic Greek influences can be traced in his legislation. He forbade crucifixions and branding on the face because of resemblance of the face to heavenly beauty, humanely ordered that prisoners should be taken out of doors each day, but at the same time he prescribed excessively cruel punishments for various offenses.

CONSTANTINE AND HIS CAESARS.   Like Diocletian, Constantine realized the necessity of having partners in imperial power, but his own experience and inclination led him to choose associates from his own household. Following Crispus and Constantine the Younger, his younger sons Constantius and Constans were made Caesars in 323 and 333 respectively. A possible rival was removed by the brutal murder of young Licinianus. In 326 Constantine executed his oldest son Crispus, and in the same year his wife Fausta, the mother of his three younger sons, both allegedly for adultery. By 335 the remaining

three Caesars were entrusted with the govern̲
Empire. Constantine the Younger had Britain, (
in charge of Italy, Africa, and Pannonia; to Col
One of Constantine's nephews, Dalmatius, was ap̲
the intention that he should govern the dioceses
Another, Annibalianus, was designated as future ru
with the title of King of Kings.

CONSTANTINE'S ACHIEVEMENT. Constantine
had been an epoch-making reign. Although deficien̲
administrative training, his energy and force of ch
dominion over the Roman World. He was a great mi.
Unquestionably his greatest achievement was initiatii̲ ___ss of transforming the Roman Empire from a pagan to a Christian state. Quite properly
Christian historians honored him with the title of "the Great," and the Eastern
Orthodox Churches have made him a saint and hailed him as an "equal of the
Apostles." Actively participating in all phases of imperial government, he
completed the work of Diocletian, giving to the autocracy, bureaucracy, army,
and hereditary class system the basic forms they preserved until the collapse of
the Empire in the West and the transition to the Byzantine Empire in the East.
It cannot be denied, however, that many of his policies contributed in the long
run to disintegration, which he strove so hard and so conscientiously to arrest.

III. DYNASTY OF CONSTANTINE THE GREAT: A.D. 337-363

THREE EMPERORS, CONSTANTINE II, CONSTANTIUS II, AND CON-
STANS: A.D. 337-340. Constantine the Great's plan for succession was
thwarted by the troops at Constantinople. Allegedly instigated by Constantius
II, they refused to accept any other rulers than the sons of the deceased
emperor and put to death his other male relatives, with the exception of two
young nephews, Gallus and Julian. The three brothers then assumed the title
Augusti and divided the Empire. Constantine II, the eldest, whose seniority
was recognized by the others, retained the West, and Constantius accepted the
East with the addition of Thrace. To Constans, the youngest, were assigned the
central dioceses—Africa, Italy, and Illyricum—apparently under the supervision of Constantine II. Constans soon grew weary of being a subordinate.
He legislated independently of his brother, who then invaded Italy in 340.
Constans met and defeated him at Aquileia. Constantine II was killed in the
battle, and Constans took over the West.

RULE OF CONSTANTIUS AND CONSTANS. Constantius acquiesced in the
extension of his younger brother's sphere. He himself, from 338 onward, was
engaged in a continuous but indecisive war with Sapor II, who sought to
reestablish Persian control over Armenia and Upper Mesopotamia. Constans
energetically defended the Rhine and British frontiers against the barbarians
and restored discipline among his soldiers. A neurotic martinet, he was

e army. A conspiracy among his civil and military officials
widespread discontent among the lower classes, suffering because
tion of small change in everyday use, led to the recognition of a
n officer, Magnentius, as Augustus. Constans was executed and
nentius was recognized in the Western dioceses except Illyricum, where the
aster of foot, Vetranio, was saluted as emperor (350). A cessation of the
Persian offensive enabled Constantius to return to Europe to face the usurpers.
Vetranio, who was encouraged to assume the purple by Constantius' sister in
order to save Illyricum from Magnentius, abdicated at a meeting with the
Eastern Augustus. He was pensioned off and his army joined Constantius.
Magnentius, failing to obtain recognition, invaded Illyricum although the
forces of his opponent were twice as large as his own. After initial successes he
was soundly beaten in a battle at Mursa, which was won by the mail-clad
cavalry of Constantius (351). Magnentius escaped to northern Italy, where
Constantius followed him the next year, meanwhile using his control of the sea
to recover Africa, peninsular Italy, and Spain. Magnentius then withdrew to
Gaul and, after another defeat, committed suicide.

Constantius Sole Augustus: a.d. 353–360. In the course of his
campaign against Magnentius, Constantius appointed as Caesar his elder
cousin Gallus, who had been spared in the massacre of 337, married him to his
sister Constantia, and sent him to guard the Eastern frontier (351). Gallus
proved unworthy and cruel. His execution of officials sent by the emperor to
recall him convinced Constantius that he must be removed, and the death of
Constantia deprived him of her influential support. Gallus was induced to
return to Europe, where he was arrested, condemned to death, and beheaded
(354). Constantius himself was occupied in repelling barbarians along the
Rhine and the Danube. A brief revolt of a Frankish general, Silvanus, in Gaul
was caused by a false accusation of treason brought against him by a rival.
The death of Silvanus was followed by a disastrous invasion of the Rhineland
by Franks and Alamanni, and made the emperor realize the need of a loyal
colleague. On the advice of the empress Eudoxia, Constantius summoned to
Milan his younger and sole surviving cousin, Julian, from his studies in Athens
and appointed him Caesar. Julian was married to Helena, the daughter of
Constantius, and then dispatched to Gaul (355). He lacked military authority,
but, owing to the incompetence of the commanding general, Julian was given
the command in 357. In that year he brilliantly defeated an invading force of
Alamanni near Strassburg, pursued them across the Rhine, and recovered many
prisoners. During the next two summers he conducted successful campaigns in
barbarian territory and restored the Rhine defenses. The Salian Franks, who
earlier had settled south of the lower Rhine, were confirmed in their territory
as Roman allies.

Julian's Usurpation and Death of Constantius: a.d. 360–361.
In 359 Sapor II, having defeated tribes that disturbed his northern frontier,

invaded Roman Mesopotamia and destroyed Amida. The presence of Constantius was required, and he set out for the East early in 360. On the way he received the news that Julian had been saluted as Augustus by his army in Gaul, but he proceeded to the front where Sapor was continuing his offensive. Julian's usurpation was the result of Constantius' ordering him to dispatch many of his best troops for service in the East. For this the Persian menace was a valid excuse, but the real reason was a desire to undermine Julian's position and possibly to do away with him. From the beginning Constantius had surrounded Julian with spies and sought to hamper his activities. When he gained remarkable military success despite them, and showed himself honest and capable, popular both with the army and the civilians, Constantius decided upon more direct action. Under protest, Julian was prepared to carry out the orders of Constantius to send troops to the East, but some of his supporters persuaded the soldiers, who were reluctant to leave Gaul, to refuse to march. Julian sought to check the mutiny, but the troops saluted him as Augustus and he yielded to their acclaim (360). In 361, when he learned that Constantius refused to recognize him and was prepared to attack, Julian took the initiative and marched on Constantinople. Constantius was on his way from the East to confront him when he died at Tarsus, naming Julian as his sole successor.

POLICY OF CONSTANTIUS. Like his brothers, Constantius grew up a Christian, but he was an Arian. He zealously sought to stamp out paganism and used his authority to bring about doctrinal unity within the Church. Of only better than average military ability and unduly influenced by his palace officials and attendants, he nevertheless worked hard and conscientiously in the service of the state. He resembled Tiberius and Domitian in his approach to government. His reign was notorious for the frequent use of *agentes in rebus* and imperial secretaries as spies and informers yet toward the end of his reign he tried by legislation to correct more flagrant governmental abuses. He also defended civil authority against encroachments of the military, and profiting by the experience of Magnentius' revolution, he sought to check inflation.

JULIAN THE APOSTATE. Julian is one of the most fascinating Roman rulers because of his intellectual interests and religious orientation. Since, like Cicero, he wrote so much about himself, he stands as one of the best-known figures of antiquity. He was born in 332 and, like all the second generation of Constantine's family, raised as a Christian. For a boy of his station this still included literary training in what was, essentially, a pagan curriculum to which he was instinctively drawn. Impressionable and even puritanical, he always remembered that he had been only narrowly spared in 337 from the purge of his relatives, carried out in the name of a Christian government. During the six years of his exile, he served as a lector in a Christian church and had read both the Old and New Testaments. Indoctrination in these works, however, did not satisfy his esthetic feelings or his intellect.

Upon release from exile he studied rhetoric at Pergamon and philosophy at

XX Mosaics at Piazza Armerina. *These fourth-century A.D. mosaics are from a Sicilian villa that was, perhaps, the residence of the emperor Maximian. They illustrate hunting scenes (left) and the famous "bikini girls' performing, it seems, gymnastic exercises (right). (Photos: Fototeca Unione.)*

Athens, where he immediately found congenial the Neoplatonic doctrines of the school of Iamblichus. Julian's culturally antiquarian interests, his philosophical turn of mind, and his anti-Christian bias were satisfied by identification of the Neoplatonic One with the sun-god Helios, long a pagan favorite, and the patron deity of his own grandfather, Constantius Chlorus. He secretly renounced Christianity, embraced the cults of Zeus, Apollo, and Mithra, identical for

Neoplatonic devotees with that of Helios, and was initiated into such traditional rites as the Eleusinian mysteries. He was also a convinced believer in magic and miracle working, and even his greatest admirers criticized him for his excessive zeal in placating the gods through sacrifice.

JULIAN'S ADMINISTRATION: A.D. 361-363. A bookish ascetic might seem an unlikely candidate for power, but Julian also had first-rate administrative and military talents and commanded the loyalty of subordinates. He also had a healthy distrust of bureaucrats. He had been brilliantly successful in his five-year administration of Gaul, where, by careful economy and supervision of government, he was able to reduce taxes locally by almost three fourths and to win the respect of provincials. His short reign as emperor (361-363) was a period of abortive administrative and religious reform. For all his fine qualities, he was unrealistic in attempting to turn the clock back, and even had he lived much longer, it is unlikely that he could have arrested the decline of the Empire or reestablished a vital paganism. He effected a temporary rehabilitation of the central administration at Constantinople, dismissing the army of serving personnel at the palace, as befitted his own unostentatious living habits, and reduced the hated *agentes in rebus* and imperial secretaries to a skeleton force. He was also actively interested in reviving the finances of municipalities and of the decurion class.

Once Augustus, he revealed his paganism and pursued a program of religious reform in its favor. He reproclaimed the policy of toleration of all religions, first enunciated by Constantine and Licinius in 313, but honored in the breach by successive Christian reigns. He naturally favored pagan over Christian commanders and administrators and forbade Christians to teach rhetoric, on the rather specious grounds that their religion prevented them from properly understanding or appreciating the curriculum based on pagan classics. He did not however reinstitute persecution of the Christians, who by then had grown to be a very large minority, or in some areas even a majority, of influential classes, although he encouraged apostasy, especially by Christian soldiers, and did not intervene to prevent anti-Christian pogroms by some local administrators. He attempted to beat the Christian Church at its own game by setting up a pagan clerical hierarchy with priests and priestesses dedicated to celibacy and asceticism and providing such services as alms and poor relief. All such reforms were destined to postpone rather than prevent the ultimate demise of paganism.

For obscure reasons, Julian decided in 363 to resume the war with Persia, lately waged by Constantius II, and he may have anticipated a spectacular campaign in Mesopotamia like Trajan's 150 years before. At first he was successful, penetrating as far as Ctesiphon, which, however, he did not capture. Like other Roman generals in the desert, he was beset with supply problems and constant harassment by a mobile and elusive enemy. In a guerrilla attack, Julian was fatally wounded. With his death, the dynasty of Constantine the Great and the reign of the last legitimate pagan emperor ended.

REIGN OF JOVIAN: A.D. 363–364. The army at once asserted its right to choose a new emperor, and rival factions finally agreed on Jovian, commander of the imperial bodyguard. In order to extricate his army and return to Roman soil to secure his position, Jovian agreed to a humiliating peace with Sapor. He surrendered the districts beyond the Tigris, the eastern frontier of Mesopotamia with the great fort of Nisibis, which had defied three Persian attacks, and the protectorate over eastern Armenia. The peace was for thirty years, and Rome was to pay an annual subsidy to help Persia close the Caucasus to barbarian raiders.

Jovian was a Christian, and, once he regained Roman territory, he annulled Julian's anti-Christian legislation. He was not a persecutor and proclaimed freedom of worship. He died in Bithynia after a reign of eight months. A new dynasty began with his successor.

IV. THE HOUSE OF VALENTINIAN AND THEODOSIUS THE GREAT: A.D. 364–395

VALENTINIAN I AND VALENS: A.D. 364. After some delay following the death of Jovian, the chief military and civil officials selected as his successor Flavius Valentinianus, a veteran Pannonian officer although not of the highest rank. Yielding to demands of the army for a second emperor, Valentinian soon appointed his younger brother Valens Augustus. Valentinian chose the West as the sphere of the senior Augustus, making his capital at Milan. Dissatisfaction with the new rulers was widespread among Gallic troops loyal to Julian's memory, among former adherents of the house of Constantine I, among pagans, and in other circles. These elements gave their support to a usurper, Procopius, an official under Constantius II and a favorite of Julian, who seems to have regarded him as a possible successor. Procopius declared himself emperor at Constantinople late in 365 and occupied Thrace and Bithynia. Early in 366, however, his generals deserted him for Valens. Procopius was executed, but the rebellion was continued for a short time by a relative, Marcellinus, who was soon suppressed.

WARS OF VALENTINIAN I: A.D. 365–375. Valentinian considered his chief duty to be defense of the Empire. The situation in Gaul was particularly dangerous and required the personal presence of the emperor from 365 to 375. He and his generals defeated the Alamanni, Franks, and Saxons. Rhineland fortresses were rebuilt from Raetia to the North Sea, and strong bridgeheads established to guard the crossings. For a long time thereafter Gaul enjoyed peace. In the meantime, Valentinian's able general Theodosius cleared Britain of Picts, Scots, and other invaders and suppressed an attempted revolt by a Pannonian named Valentinus. Upon recovering from a serious illness in 367, Valentinian appointed his nine-year-old son, Gratian, as a third Augustus, in order to forestall intrigues over the succession. Valentinian also gave his attention while in Gaul to the Danubian frontier, where he strengthened the defenses of Raetia and Pannonia. After serious incursion of the Quadi in 375, he visited Pannonia. In the course of an interview with a Quadian embassy, he fell into a violent rage and suffered a fatal stroke. During his reign the African provinces suffered from invasions, misgovernment, and, ultimately, revolt. In 372 or 373 a rebellion broke out in Mauretania and Numidia, led by a Moorish chief named Firmus, who was supported by many Roman subjects. In 374 Firmus was defeated by Theodosius and committed suicide. Theodosius uncovered the intrigues of corrupt Roman officials, however, and the influence of their friends at court led to his summary execution (375 or 376), either by order of Valentinian or of Gratian, his successor in the West.

VALENS AND THE EAST: A.D. 365–378. From the beginning of his reign Valens had to cope with repeated Gothic invasions of Thrace. A Roman victory in 369 forced the barbarians to accept peace on Roman terms. In the meantime, Sapor II brought Armenia and Iberia under his control. In 371 Valens moved East and reestablished Roman influence in both countries. A Persian invasion of Mesopotamia was repelled, but no settlement had been reached by 377, when Valens was obliged to return to Europe to meet a new Gothic peril.

The new crisis in relations of the Goths to the Empire is traceable to the westward movement of the Huns, a nomadic people of Mongolian origin, whose advance from Asia into the area north of the Black Sea led to a series of great migrations among the Germanic peoples of eastern and central Europe. In 373 the Huns fell upon the kingdom of the East Goths (Ostrogoths) in the Ukraine and overwhelmed it. Then they attacked the West Goths (Visigoths) on the Dniester. Unable to resist, many of the latter retreated to the Danube and, joined by other Germanic refugees, asked to settle in Moesia or Thrace. Valens granted this, expecting to use them as army recruits, but required them to surrender their arms. Roman officials in charge of their settlement allowed them to keep their arms in return for bribes, while they issued food to the starving Goths only at high prices. The Goths then began to plunder, and, when the Romans failed to murder Gothic leaders, war broke out (377). In spite of reinforcements from the West, the generals of Valens failed to keep the Goths in check. In 378 Valens personally took command of his forces and marched to meet the enemy, whose strength had been increased by Ostrogothic and other invaders. Gratian announced that he was coming to help his uncle and asked him not to risk battle until his arrival, but Valens decided against delay and attacked the Goths, who numbered perhaps 20,000, with inferior forces near Adrianople. The battle was decided by superiority of the Goths' cavalry. The Roman army was cut to pieces, Valens was killed, and the Goths overran the Balkans.

GOVERNMENT OF VALENTINIAN AND VALENS. Unity of the imperial government was emphasized by legislation in the name of both emperors, as well as by other means. A very forceful person, Valentinian was also well educated, yet he regarded with suspicion and even hostility cultured classes. For the most part he selected as his officials and advisers cronies whose cruelty and misgovernment became notorious. Although they betrayed his confidence, he was reluctant to remove them from office. The senatorial aristocracy of Rome was treated with special severity. On charges of practicing secret magical rites, which the superstitious emperor feared and regarded as treasonable, many prominent senators were tortured, executed, or punished by exile and loss of property.

Yet, Valentinian seriously tried to lighten the burdens of the poor, both farmers and townspeople, particularly by correcting abuses in tax collection and the administration of justice. Although he reduced extravagance at his court, his need for money to defray the costs of new fortifications, to repair cities, and enlarge the army compelled him to increase taxes and accounts for his confiscation of senatorial properties. By harsh measures he restored military discipline, and he rewarded his higher officers, particularly Germans, with privileges and honors. He continued the practice of settling barbarians on depopulated lands.

Valens was much weaker than Valentinian. He lacked courage and resolution, was hot tempered, inclined to cruelty, and was badly educated. In general his policy followed his brother's; he expanded bureaucracy and strictly regulated occupation classes. Like Valentinian he sought to alleviate the burdens of the poor and tried vainly to control rapacity and corruption of officials. An incompetent commander, he nevertheless maintained discipline among his troops, to whom he added many Goths and other barbarians. Following the earthquake of 365 which devastated the eastern Mediterranean, Valens gave liberal financial aid to ruined cities. Despite the better economic condition of the Eastern as compared to the Western provinces, the high cost of wars and military and civil installations on a large scale caused a heavy drain on the treasury and prevented any lightening of tax burdens in this part of the Empire.

Valentinian was an orthodox Christian, but he followed a policy of religious toleration. He refused to be concerned with doctrine, restricting himself in his legislation affecting the Christian clergy to maintenance of public order, preservation of the fiscal interests of the state, and the administration of justice. Pagans enjoyed religious freedom except in the practice of certain rites. The right to teach and to learn was made independent of religious belief. In contrast, his brother Valens, although proclaiming freedom of religion, was very active in dogmatic strife within the Church. He was an Arian heretic. He sought to make the heresy orthodox and violently persecuted his opponents. Toward pagans he, too, was tolerant, except for his suppression of secret and magical practices.

THEODOSIUS I AND THE GOTHS: A.D. 379–382. At the death of Valentinian I government of the West passed to his son, Gratian, Augustus since 367 but only in his seventeenth year. He had received a careful education but lacked military and administrative capacity. His policy was determined by his advisers. Perhaps in order to forestall any action by the Gallic soldiery, some of the higher officials nominated Gratian's younger brother, Valentinian, at the age of four, as Augustus in Illyricum, where he received the sanction of the troops. Gratian was obliged to accept him as a colleague but allocated to him only the diocese of Illyricum, which he governed under the regency of his mother and of the Frankish general Merobaudes. Following the death of Valens, Gratian summoned from retirement in Spain Theodosius, son of the like-named general who had been executed about three years before, and appointed him first master of cavalry, then Augustus (379). The appointment of Theodosius, then some 34 years old, was given dynastic sanction by his marriage to Gratian's half-sister. For three years Theodosius fought a long but inconclusive war with the Visigoths, one costly in manpower and material resources. Unwilling to prolong the struggle indefinitely, he made peace with them on terms unprecedented in the history of Roman relations with major barbarian nations. The Visigoths were permitted, as before, to settle on the right bank of the Danube and were supposed to fight for the Empire. They were not, however, integrated with the Roman population either as farmers or soldiers. Their separate national identity was recognized in their treaty with the government, which regarded them not as subjects but as allies living under their own kings, and when mobilized for Rome fighting under their own rather than Roman commanders. This was the first instance of the admission of a large barbarian nation that would remain unassimilated, and the precedent boded ill for the future.

REVOLT OF MAXIMUS AND DEATH OF GRATIAN: A.D. 383. In the West, Gratian was a feeble administrator, more interested in hunting than ruling, leaving the government to incompetent favorites. Discontent spread among soldiers and civilians. The troops in Britain saluted their commander Magnus Maximus as emperor, and he landed in Gaul. After Gratian was deserted by his army, he took flight, was captured, and executed. The authority of Maximus was accepted in Britain, Gaul, and Spain. He demanded and received recognition from Theodosius, who did not feel strong enough to attack him. Valentinian II, however, still controlled Italy and Illyricum. The legislation of Gratian was unimportant except in the sphere of religion. A devoted Christian, he at first proclaimed religious toleration but later, influenced by orthodox advisers, he suppressed both Christian heresies and pagan practices.

OVERTHROW OF MAXIMUS: A.D. 388. The ambition of Maximus led to his downfall. He appointed his son Victor as Caesar, and in 387, when Valentinian II accepted his aid against a barbarian invasion of Pannonia, he seized the opportunity to control Italy. Valentinian fled to Thessalonica. Soon afterward Theodosius took as his second wife Valentinian's sister Galla and decided to avenge the death of her half-brother Gratian and to restore Italy to Valentinian. A treaty with Sapor II resulted in partition of Armenia between Rome and Persia, greatly to Sapor's advantage, and an Ostrogothic attempt to cross the Danube was repulsed, so that Theodosius was able to concentrate his forces against Maximus. Maximus made the Caesar Victor an Augustus and invaded Illyricum. He was forced to withdraw to Italy, however, by the fleet of Theodosius, which landed Valentinian at Ostia. Theodosius defeated the army of Maximus in two engagements in Illyricum and advanced to Aquileia at the head of the Adriatic. There Maximus was surrendered by his troops to Theodosius, who had him executed (388). Theodosius's general Arbogast recovered Gaul and put Victor to death. Maximus had governed in the tradition of emperors, but his need for money led him to persecute the wealthy and confiscate their goods. His withdrawal of troops from Britain resulted in the evacuation of Hadrian's Wall and other northern defenses, which were never reoccupied.

THEODOSIUS AND ST. AMBROSE. Theodosius took up residence at Milan, sending Valentinian II to Gaul under the protection of Arbogast. His own elder son Arcadius, whom he proclaimed Augustus in 383, remained at Constantinople. In 388 the monks of Callinicum in Mesopotamia incited a Christian mob to burn a synagogue. Theodosius ordered the bishop to restore the building. But Ambrose, the strong-willed bishop of Milan, interfered and threatened to withhold the sacrament from the emperor until he rescinded his order. Theodosius yielded but refused to accept Ambrose as his adviser, to the latter's displeasure. In 390 a riot occurred in Thessalonica in which the mob killed the general Butheric, who refused to release from prison a favorite charioteer. In a fit of anger Theodosius ordered the garrison to massacre the citizens, 3,000 of whom were killed. The emperor countermanded his order, but too late. On this occasion Ambrose notified Theodosius that he would exclude him from Church services until he did public penance for his crime. For eight months the emperor's pride prevented his yielding, but at length his guilty conscience made him publicly acknowledge his guilt. In this affair Ambrose asserted, not the supremacy of the Church over secular authority, but the right of a priest to hold even an emperor responsible for obedience to Christian moral law.

REVOLT OF ARBOGAST AND EUGENIUS: A.D. 392-394. In 391 Theodosius returned to the East, where the Goths were raiding and plundering in Thrace and there was friction among high civil officials. An end was put to the Gothic raids, partly by the skill of Roman generals, partly because of factional strife among the Goths themselves, and an all-out war was avoided. Among the favorites of Theodosius, the greatest influence was wielded by the praetorian prefect Rufinus and the half-barbarian general Stilicho, who had married a niece of the emperor. In the West, Theodosius was betrayed by one of his trusted commanders, Arbogast, who had been left to advise and protect Valentinian II. Arbogast tried to prevent the young Augustus, who was very energetic, from being independent. The conflict became so bitter that Valentinian dismissed Arbogast, who refused to vacate his post. In May 392 Valentinian was found dead, almost certainly murdered by followers of Arbogast. Ambitious though he was, Arbogast, by birth a Frank, dared not make himself emperor, but proclaimed as Augustus a prominent Roman official, the rhetorician Eugenius.

Eugenius tried to obtain recognition, but Theodosius refused. Instead, he made his younger son Honorius an Augustus in 393, and Eugenius, whose policy was dictated by Arbogast, occupied Italy. He was welcomed by the pagan senatorial faction in Rome, was acknowledged in Spain, and was supported by the commander in Africa. Finally in 394 Theodosius took the offensive. Arbogast and Eugenius awaited him with superior forces at the river Frigidus in northeastern Italy, where Theodosius won a complete victory. Eugenius was captured and beheaded, Arbogast escaped but killed himself. Once more the Empire was united, but Theodosius did not long survive his triumph. He died at Milan early in 395.

THEODOSIUS "THE GREAT." Theodosius succeeded in maintaining unity of imperial authority throughout the Empire. In many areas, however, the internal difficulties confronting the government—depopulation, impoverishment, corruption, growth of great private estates, decline of the cities—increased rather than diminished during his reign. His attempted settlement of the Gothic

question meant trouble for his successors. His desperate need of military manpower probably forced him to adopt a policy detrimental in the long run to
the state's interest. Theodosius maintained a magnificent and costly court
and enhanced the splendor of Constantinople by erecting new buildings and
monuments. His chief interest and activity were in religious spheres. A convinced orthodox Christian, he conceived it his duty to unite the Empire in
this creed, and so he took drastic steps to stamp out both paganism and Christian
heresies, although he protected the rights of the Jews. His religious policy was
the result of his own convictions, not caused by the influence of others. More
vigorously than any predecessors, he asserted the right of the emperor to
exercise authority in Church matters. To his resolute championship of
orthodoxy is due his later title "the Great."

CHAPTER 23
THE PUBLIC ADMINISTRATION UNDER THE AUTOCRACY

I. THE AUTOCRAT AND HIS COURT

THE EMPEROR. The fourth century saw the completion of the transformation of the Principate of Augustus into an undisguised autocracy that received its definitive form under Diocletian and Constantine I. All the sovereignty of the Roman people was considered to be transferred to the emperor, who based his right to rule on the grace of God revealed in his election by a human agency. An emperor could speak of the *imperium* as having been conferred on him by the heavenly majesty. The emperor was no longer the "first" Roman citizen (*primus inter pares*); all Romans were equally his subjects. He was the sole authority in all spheres of government, legislative, military, administrative, judicial. In keeping with his exalted state, the emperor's person and everything in any way belonging to him were called "sacred" or "divine," and "the imperial divinity" was a common expression.

As sole author of laws, the emperor was also their final interpreter. Because he acted under divine guidance, those who questioned his decisions and those who neglected or transgressed his ordinances were guilty of sacrilege. The emperor was held to be above the laws in the sense that he could not be held responsible for his legislative and administrative acts; and yet he was bound by the laws because he had to respect their principles and institutions and had to abide by his own edicts, for his own authority rested on obedience to them.

[431]

IMPERIAL TITLES AND REGALIA. The emperors continued to bear the titles Imperator, Caesar, and Augustus. Until Theodosius I they also counted the years of their tribunician power and styled themselves proconsuls. The new order found expression in the regular use of *Dominus* or *Dominus noster*,[1] of Victor and Triumpher, the latter two qualified as "eternal." The wearing of the "purple" (red) military cloak, formerly the right of Roman generals celebrating a triumph, became an imperial prerogative, and the robe of "purple" silk interwoven with gold, called *paragauda*, was also reserved for the emperor. The white diadem of earlier times became a purple silk band adorned with pearls. In fact, purple became a symbol of imperial power, and its manufacture and use were under government control. The privilege of "adoring the purple," i.e., of kissing the emperor's robe, was an honor reserved for favored officials. All persons entering the imperial presence had to kneel in reverence. Imperial costume and regalia, as well as prescribed salutations, were partly the result of a natural evolution in Rome since the days of Augustus, partly adoptions from the courts of Hellenistic autocrats.

SUCCESSION. There was no hereditary right to the purple. An emperor had either to be elected or appointed by another emperor. Election regularly took the form of selection by high military officers with or without participation by civilian dignitaries, followed by a presentation of the nominee to the army, which saluted him as Imperator and Augustus. He was then considered elected and was clothed in imperial robes and crowned with the diadem. In Constantinople, from the fifth century, presentation was made to the soldiers and populace assembled in the Hippodrome. Acclamation of an emperor was regarded as an expression of Divine selection. "Almighty God and your decision, most valiant fellow soldiers, have chosen me ruler," declared the emperor Leo I (457–474). At this presentation to the soldiers, an emperor first was crowned with a soldier's golden neckpiece (*torques*), afterward with the diadem. In time the torque came to be placed around the ruler's neck, and, from the time of Leo I, he was crowned with the diadem by the Patriarch of Constantinople, acting as representative of the people. An Augustus could appoint a colleague, as Caesar or as Augustus, anyone whom he wished to succeed him. In case he coopted a son, however, the latter became emperor by virtue of his father's will and not by right of birth. As history shows, the right of election might be exercised at any time. In this way usurpers arose, but a victorious usurper became a legitimate ruler. Thus the Autocracy was tempered by a legal right of revolution.

IMPERIAL PALACE. The organization of the imperial household became much more elaborate than ever before. Palace employees—ushers, chamberlains, grooms, and the like—were formed as quasi-military corps with definite regulation of uniforms, pay, terms of service, and promotion under the direction of

---

[1] From which comes the term Dominate, often used to describe the Autocracy in contrast to the Principate.

an official, the *castrensis*. The formal ceremonies were the culmination of a long development under the Principate. Their object was to emphasize the gulf separating the emperor from his subjects and to protect his person by rendering it inaccessible except to a favored few. This seclusion enhanced the influence of courtiers, in particular higher palace officials. Of these the most influential was the grand chamberlain, who supervised the attendants of the imperial bed-chamber. Before the close of the fourth century, the chamberlain, like most of his underlings often a eunuch, had become one of the great ministers with a seat in the imperial cabinet. In addition to its civilian staff the palace had an armed guard. This was formed by the scholarians, organized by Constantine I when he disbanded the praetorians in 312. The scholarians took their name from the *scholae* or palace halls to which they were assigned. Recruited from barbarians, they eventually formed five *scholae* of 500 each in the West, seven in the East.

II. MILITARY ORGANIZATION

General Characteristics. The military organization of the late Empire was the work of Diocletian and Constantine. Its chief characteristics were an initial and almost complete elimination of officers with both civil and military authority, a policy abandoned, however, whenever military emergency demanded unified command; a sharp distinction between mobile field forces and the frontier garrisons; and a large proportion of cavalry. During the fourth century the barbarian element increased both among the soldiers and also among the officers, including those of highest rank. Beginning about 400, however, this situation was reversed in the eastern half of the Empire, which found sufficient indigenous sources of military manpower, while the West fell increasingly under the control of a barbarian soldiery.

Size and Recruitment of the Army. Diocletian seems to have doubled the number of legions to 70, having a paper strength of 420,000 men, and to have increased substantially the number of auxiliary detachments. After Constantine some 200,000 men constituted the field army, about equally divided between the Eastern and Western parts of the Empire. Almost one fourth of this number were cavalry. The maintenance of armed forces at their authorized strength proved very difficult, owing to the decline of population. Recruits came from four sources. Beginning with the reign of Constantine at least, sons of veterans, if physically fit, were required to enter the army, while members of the hereditary occupation classes were forbidden to do so. There were still civilians, unencumbered by obligations of caste or occupation, who might volunteer for military service. Both these sources failed to satisfy military needs, and the imperial government instituted a draft that fell chiefly on peasants. Farmland was divided into units called *capitula*, each of which was expected to furnish a specified number of recruits. The proprietors of the *capitula* contributed money with which the recruits could be hired either by themselves or by army agents. Valens sought to modify this system by requiring the land-lords of each *capitulum* to furnish from among their own tenants recruits whose masters received monetary compensation for the loss of labor, although it still remained common to accept money instead of men from the proprietors. The scarcity of Roman recruits and their generally inferior military qualifications led the army in the fourth century to depend often on barbarian volunteers for replacements. There were three main sources for recruiting barbarians. Some joined individually as volunteers. Many more were drafted from conquered peoples already settled within the Empire (*laeti, dediticii, gentiles*). Others were raised among free tribes beyond the frontiers, which were enlisted as allies in Roman service. In return for subsidies in money and food, these allies, who came to be called *foederati*,[2] agreed to aid the Romans against other enemies. Visigoths were allied peoples of this type settled in Roman territory. Retaining political autonomy and serving under their own chiefs, they were not regarded as part of the Roman army. In the case of other threatening neighbors, the Romans purchased immunity from attack by regular payments in money which the recipients regarded as tribute.

In spite of all efforts, the army could not be maintained at full strength. Every campaign was preceded by an intensive drive for recruits, and the size of the Roman forces in critical battles was surprisingly small. Julian had only 13,000 men at Strassburg in 357, and the forces of Valens at Adrianople in 378 were not much larger. The strength of the barbarians in these engagements was not appreciably greater. Julian allegedly mustered some 65,000 for his invasion of Persia, but these included Western as well as Eastern field forces and also barbarian allies. During the invasions of the early fifth century, an appeal was made to slaves to volunteer for military service under promise of freedom.

ORGANIZATION AND COMMAND OF THE ARMY. Diocletian's policy was to provide for the defense of the Empire by strengthening the forces stationed along the frontiers. He also formed the nucleus of a mobile field army, although he dispersed the great cavalry corps built up by Gallienus and his successors. Constantine I reversed this plan. He created a large field army by detaching the more mobile units from border garrisons and grouping them at strategic points within the borders. Since these troops formed the escort (*comita-tus*) of the emperor, they received the name *comitatenses*. Certain elite units among them were further honored by being called "palace troops" (*palatini*). The frontier troops were called "borderers" (*limitanei* or *riparienses*). They were attached to the frontier defenses, and many of them received land for cultivation in the vicinity of the fortifications they manned. The borderers ranked below the field troops, their physical standards were lower, their pay was less, and

---

[2] In the fifth and sixth centuries *foederati* in the Eastern part of the Empire were no longer exclusively barbarian corps, but also included indigenous manpower.

they had to serve twenty-four years instead of the twenty of the *comitatenses*. They degenerated into militia.

Constantine I deprived the praetorian prefects of military authority. In their place he created a master of horse and a master of foot as generals of the field army. The later stationing of large corps of field troops away from the capital necessitated the appointment of other masters who, since they commanded both classes of troops, were called masters of horse and foot or masters of either service and finally masters of the soldiers, a title also given to the original masters. At the death of Theodosius I, there were in the East two masters of the soldiers stationed at Constantinople, and one each in Illyricum, Thrace, and Asia (the Orient). In the West at this time there were two masters of the soldiers (still technically called master of horse and master of foot) at the court, and a master of horse in Gaul. The frontiers were divided into military districts that corresponded to the border provinces, and the garrison in each was commanded by an officer called duke (*dux*). In certain areas several *duces* were under the orders of a higher-ranking general, a count (*comes*). Select young officers called *protectores* were assigned for training to the imperial court. There they served as a bodyguard for the emperor and received the title *domestici*.

Whereas in the East the masters of the soldiers enjoyed independent commands, by 395 there had developed in the West a concentration of supreme military power by the master of foot at the court, who outranked the master of horse. The master in Gaul and the dukes and counts in the provinces were all under his orders. This subordination was emphasized by the fact that the heads of the office staffs (*principes*) of the counts and dukes were appointed by the master of foot at court. In the East these *principes* were appointed by a civil official, the master of the offices, who was also charged with inspecting the frontier defenses and, from the opening of the fifth century, exercising judicial authority over the dukes. The latter remained subordinate to the masters of the soldiers. Thus the concentration of military power in the West in the hands of a single commander in chief prepared the way for the rise of the kingmakers of the fifth century, while the division of the higher command in the East prevented a single general from completely dominating the situation.

MILITARY EQUIPMENT, PRIVILEGES, AND DISCIPLINE. The desire to secure greater mobility, the necessity of coping with many mounted raiders and mass cavalry attacks, and the influence of barbarians enrolled in Roman service brought about changes in arms and armor. Infantry units gave up the javelin for lighter darts and lances. Longer swords came into use. The soldier's heavy pack was discarded, and, under Gratian, heavy body armor and metal helmets were generally abandoned. Among the cavalry heavily armored lancers, light horse, and archers appeared. Barbarian units recruited on a tribal basis were armed in their native fashion. Considerable use was made of artillery in the form of heavy catapults and slings, particularly during sieges.

Three fourths of the soldiers' pay was in allowances, the rest in money. In the fourth century they could defend themselves against criminal charges in the courts of their military commanders; in the fifth this right was extended to civil cases also. False muster rolls and other devices for profiting at the expense of the state indicate widespread corruption of soldiers. Requisitioning and quartering of troops among the civilian population gave rise to many abuses. With increasing barbarization, traditional discipline and methods of training tended to break down, and now the only advantages Roman armies possessed over their enemies were their strategy, fortifications, and supply services. In addition to their pay, soldiers, and in particular veterans, received advantages in the form of reduced taxation for their families and land grants. Officers enjoyed high status and became patrons of civilian landlords, defending them against the demands of tax collectors. There was a great aversion to military service among the Romans, and many prospective recruits mutilated them-selves to avoid it. Desertion and absenteeism were chronic and bands of soldiers sometimes became brigands, plundering and terrorizing defenseless peasants.

NAVAL FORCES.   The strength and organization of the navy of the Late Empire are not known. To guard against the North Sea raiders, there was a fleet based on harbors in Britain and Gaul. There were also flotillas on the Rhine and on the middle and lower Danube. No great naval force was apparently maintained in the western Mediterranean, but a large fleet was stationed near Constantinople.

III. CIVIL ADMINISTRATION

ADMINISTRATIVE FRAMEWORK.   The administration of the Autocracy was simply an elaborate outgrowth of bureaucracy developed under the Principate. All state officials were servants of the emperor, serving at his pleasure. The administration was based on the division of the Empire into prefectures, dioceses, and provinces. At the close of the fourth century there were 120 provinces, most having been created by subdivision of originally large provincial units, mainly to ensure closer supervision of administration. The provinces were grouped in fourteen dioceses, which in turn made up the four prefectures of Gaul, Italy, Illyricum, and the Orient. In the fourth century the Illyrian prefecture was at times partly or wholly merged with the Italian, but from 395 on it acquired separate status permanently and, with the prefecture of the Orient, made up the Empire in the East. The two other prefectures, those of Italy and Gaul, then constituted the Empire in the West.

GOVERNMENT OF PREFECTURES, DIOCESES, AND PROVINCES. Ruling each prefecture was a praetorian prefect, the highest civil official of the Empire. He supervised collection, storage, and distribution of taxes paid in kind and administration of justice for civilians. Subordinate to the prefect were vicars, chiefs of dioceses, and under the vicars the civil provincial governors. They had various titles—proconsul, consular, corrector, *praeses*— depending on their rank. Subordination of vicars to prefects was only superficial, for they could report directly to the emperor, and appeals from their judgments were made to him. The proconsuls of Asia, Africa, and Achaia were also under his immediate authority. Italy itself was divided into several provinces. Those north of the Apennines were united with Raetia in the diocese of Italy; those of the peninsula, with Sicily, Sardinia, and Corsica, formed the suburban region (*regio suburbicaria*), obliged to supply Rome. Rome and Constantinople were exempt from diocesan government, each being administered by an urban prefect.

CENTRAL ADMINISTRATIVE DEPARTMENTS. Branches of administration not under the control of prefects were directed by ministers resident at the Eastern and Western courts, many of whom had subordinates in the dioceses and provinces. The chief among them were the master of the offices, the quaestor, the count of the sacred largesses, and the count of the private purse. The master of the offices exercised control over the secretarial bureaus of the palace, the public post and the imperial arsenals, the imperial intelligence service (*agentes-in-rebus*), the scholarians, several branches of palace administration, and practically all personal attendants of the emperor. In the East, he also enjoyed some authority over the *duces*. The quaestor (not to be confused with republican quaestorships) was the emperor's judicial adviser, and played a large part in preparing imperial legislation. The office of count of the sacred largesses grew out of that of the *rationalis* who supervised one branch of the imperial Fiscus under the Principate. He was charged with the collection and disbursement of taxes paid in money, and his title derived from the fact that salaries of government employees paid in coin, and other objects of value distributed on various jubilee occasions, were regarded as imperial donations or largesses, just like distributions of money at the accession of an emperor or on jubilees. This minister also supervised imperial factories making silks, textiles, and purple dye. The count of the private purse was head of the department of the *res privata*, which included imperial properties as well as the ruler's private estate. These four ministers, together with the grand chamberlain, formed the council of state or consistory (*consistorium*), so called because its members had to stand in the imperial presence. They were attended there by notaries or secretaries. Under the direct orders of the emperor, these notaries were entrusted frequently with confidential missions.

Two consuls were nominated annually, one each at Rome and Constantinople. They gave their names to the year but their duties were limited to entertaining the populace. The consulship was still regarded as one of the highest honors and frequently was held by the emperor himself. Of the older city magistracies only the praetorship and quaestorship survived. They were filled by imperial appointment on recommendation of the urban prefects and their functions paralleled those of the consuls.

LESSER BUREAUCRATS. Each official directing an administrative department, civil or military, was aided by an office staff (*officium*), whose members were called *officiales*. These subordinates were freemen, generally speaking, institutionally descended from the military *officiales* of the Principate, which accounts for the quasi-military organization and nomenclature. The numbers, terms of service, promotion and discharge of these bureaucrats were regulated by imperial edicts. Since each *officium* was a permanent organization staffed by long-term civil servants, the burden of routine administration fell on them rather than on the department head whose term was short, at times annual, and for whose acts they were jointly responsible. This responsibility applied particularly to the bureau chief (*princeps*), who regularly was appointed from retiring *agentes-in-rebus* and served as a *liaison* with and at times a spy for the palace administration. Like soldiers, civil servants enjoyed exemption from ordinary courts and the privilege of defending themselves before their ministers in chief. The favorable conditions of service on the staffs of the central ministries made admission to them popular, but the situation was different in the provincial bureaus. Difficulty in recruiting employees for the latter made civil service hereditary.

CHARACTER OF THE BUREAUCRACY. The elaborate bureaucracy was cumbersome, expensive, and none too efficient, although it assured order and regularity in collecting revenues and in judicial procedures. For the civilian population the operation of the administration was oppressive. To increase their meager salaries, *officiales* demanded gratuities from those who had to deal with their offices. The emperors at first tried to prevent this sort of extortion, but they had to compromise by authorizing it within limits. *Officiales* themselves were obliged to make certain donations to other bureaucrats with each promotion in rank and, at times, upon enrollment in office. Even their superiors, governors and other administrators, frequently paid large sums for their appointments to higher officials and even to the imperial treasury.

Emperors mistrusted their officials. It was largely for this reason that they weakened many powerful offices by separating civil and military authority. They also built up a highly developed system of espionage. Despite efforts of most emperors to secure honest and efficient administration, bureaucracy nullified their efforts. An almost impassable barrier was built up between the ruler and his subjects. Their complaints seldom reached his ears, and his ordinances for their relief remained ineffective because officials cooperated with one another to conceal their misdeeds and to enrich themselves at the expense of civilians. So thoroughly had the spirit of graft and intrigue permeated all ranks of government that, to gratify personal ambition, the highest officials compromised the safety of the Empire. The increased burden imposed on taxpayers by the enlarged civil and military establishments was thus aggravated by the extortion practiced by officials.

IV. THE NOBILITY AND THE SENATE

SENATORIAL ORDER. During the third century senators were excluded from nearly all administrative offices that had been their prerogatives in the early Principate. This tendency was reversed after Diocletian, who used senators in only a few posts and relied mainly on equestrians. With the loss of all authority by the Senate as a body, there was no longer any objection to their entering imperial service, and Constantine and his successors expanded the number of senatorial positions in government and enlarged the order by promoting into it many equestrians. As a class they were virtually absorbed in the senatorial order. The senatorial aristocracy of the Late Empire had only the vaguest and most tenuous genealogical links with senatorial families of the Republic or even the Principate. Senatorial families had been small, and their vulnerability to imperial purges had often led to their early demise. Only a few late senatorial families could trace their pedigrees back beyond ca. A.D. 250, although some may have been collateral or adoptive branches of more ancient houses.

The distinguishing mark of this new senatorial order was the right to the title *clarissimus*, acquired by inheritance, by imperial grant, or by the attainment of an office conferring the clarissimate either during the term of service or upon retirement. Practically all higher officials in imperial service were *clarissimi*, and there was consequently a great increase in the number of senators during the fourth century, as many equestrian posts became senatorial.

HIGHER ORDERS OF NOBILITY. Nobility had always been dependent on membership in the senatorial order and holding higher public offices. This situation continued under the Autocracy, but development of an elaborate court ceremonial prescribed a fixed order of precedence among those admitted to imperial audiences. The great increase in the number of important civil and military officials necessitated ranking official posts, and led to the creation in the second half of the fourth century of new and more exclusive orders of nobility within the class of *clarissimi*. These were, in ascending order, the Respectables (*spectabiles*) and the Illustrious (*illustres*), also called Most Illustrious (*illustrissimi*). By 400 the praetorian prefects, masters of the soldiers, masters of the offices, quaestors, counts of the sacred largesses and private purse, and the grand chamberlains all held the rank of Illustrious. Under Justinian in the sixth century, these important officials were promoted to a still higher grade, that of the Glorious (*gloriosi*). Official positions to which these titles of rank were attached were called dignities (*dignitates*), and the great demand for admission to them, which gave their members valuable privileges, led to many honorary dignities, i.e., titles of official posts with appropriate rank but sinecures. The titles Caesar and Most Noble (*nobilissimus*) were reserved for members of the imperial household.

COUNTS AND PATRICIANS. Constantine I revived the title Count (*comes*), which had been used irregularly of the chief associates of the *princeps* in his suite during the Principate, and used it as the title of many new officials. This led to the creation of three classes of rank among counts. In time the title became permanent for certain higher civil and military officials and also one of nobility automatically attained by lesser bureaucrats in office or on retirement. Far different was "patrician," a title also revived, with a new meaning by

Constantine I. This became the highest title conferred on persons outside the imperial family. It was granted very sparingly, and in the fifth century in the West was monopolized by the senior master of the soldiers.

INEQUALITY BEFORE THE LAW. Division of subjects into two classes, *honestiores* (more honorable) and *humiliores* (more humble or "little people"), was even more distinct than under the Principate. Unlike the latter, the former class, which included imperial and municipal senators, soldiers, and veterans, was exempt from execution, except with the emperor's consent, from penal servitude, and, with some limitations, from torture in judicial investigations.

SENATE. The Senate at Rome continued to function as a municipal council and as the mouthpiece of the senatorial order. After the founding of Constantinople, a similar Senate was established there by Constantius II, probably in 340. At first all *clarissimi* had a right to participate in meetings, and their sons were expected to fill the quaestorship. After the middle of the fifth century, only those ranking as *illustres* attended sessions, which became a gathering of the highest officials and ex-officials. In addition to functions as municipal councils, the Senates made recommendations for the quaestorship and praetorship, discussed with imperial officials taxes affecting the senatorial order, and even participated sometimes in drafting imperial legislation.

The most important privilege enjoyed by senators was their exemption from the control of tax collectors of municipalities within whose territories their estates were situated. This was one of the chief reasons for the extension of their power in the provinces.

V. TOTALITARIAN STATE

NEW ECONOMIC ORDER. While the government was transformed into an autocracy, the economic policies which it pursued prescribed and limited by regulation the activities of the individual. The ultimate result was a form of totalitarian state. This did not come into being as a set plan or as the embodiment of a social theory of Diocletian or Constantine. It matured as the result of reforms initiated by them and carried to conclusion by their successors. The immediate economic problem that confronted the government was the need to raise revenues large enough to maintain the expensive military establishment, enlarged bureaucracy, and imperial court. Since income produced by the old tax system was inadequate, the emperors carried to extremes the practices of the late Principate by demanding more public service of different classes of the population and in circumscribing their freedom of activity. There was no doctrinaire attempt to eliminate freedom of initiative in industry, agriculture, or commerce, and private enterprise continued to exist in spheres in which the state was uninterested.

It would be a mistake to regard the Late Empire as a period of uninterrupted and universal economic decline. Certainly the rather primitive economic system was resilient and adapted itself, although inefficiently, to the greater demands made on it beginning with Diocletian and Constantine. There were great differences in the degrees of prosperity maintained by various provinces, so that it is very difficult to generalize regarding prevailing economic conditions. Restoration of peace and stabilization of the gold coinage did something to stimulate recovery after the chaos of the third century. Trade within or between provinces was resumed or became more active. Commerce with India and the Far East even continued, partly through Persia but mainly by the Red Sea route. Certain parts of the Empire prospered more than others. In Egypt, following the restoration of the irrigation system, which had fallen into decay, agriculture recovered partially. The commerce and industry of the Syrian cities also experienced a revival, and Antioch and its environs in particular seem to have been prosperous. Residence of the emperors at Trèves for long periods and successful defense against the Germans gave rise to a rehabilitation of agriculture and industry in Gaul and along the Rhine, as did similar conditions near Milan and Ravenna. Large landed proprietors, who were extremely prosperous, tended in some areas like Gaul and Africa to withdraw to their estates tilled by serfs, a development that prefigured the manorial social system of the early Middle Ages. Elsewhere, as in northern Italy, near Rome, and in some parts of the East, they were absentee landlords and maintained their city residences and thereby the traditional urban cultural interests that had always characterized them. Technically, agriculture was carried on less intensively and became less productive than previously, while industry resorted to more primitive practices and sometimes produced articles of inferior quality. An exception was glass-making, which enjoyed particular advantages under imperial protection. Britain was the only province that seems to have been at least as prosperous in the first half of the fourth century as before the debacle of the third because it had largely been spared devastations of civil strife and barbarian raids. In Britain as in Gaul towns declined, however, and villas became centers of economic life. The Danubian provinces in particular experienced a continuous decline in population and prosperity. Generally speaking, conditions throughout the Empire as a whole fell short of those characterizing the first and second centuries A.D. and became steadily worse, especially in the West, from the latter part of the fourth century. There can be no doubt that a manpower shortage, already manifest in the third century, became increasingly acute during the fourth and fifth. This was not only because the state demanded more from productive classes; it also reflected a decline in their numbers. The peasant classes, on whom the economy of the Empire rested, either failed to reproduce themselves or sought refuge from their burdens by fleeing to cities that had programs of social assistance, the bread and circuses that some urban governments then maintained on an expanded scale. Such cities remained reasonably populous as the result of migration, but in most cases they did not attain the demographic levels they had enjoyed under the Principate.

Except for luxury articles, industrial production beyond local needs was

XXI Late Roman Art. *Late Roman art was a varied phenomenon. The figures, above, from Constantine's Arch (A.D. 315) and, right, the head of his colossal statue (both at Rome) exemplify a style that cared little for prettiness or even technical competence. Classical canons of beauty are clearly evident, however, in the ivory consular diptych, page 444, depicting the emperor Honorius (A.D. 395–423); it is in the cathedral at Aosta. (Photos: above and right, Fototeca Unione; page 444, Alinari.)*

largely for the state, and the movement of such goods took place under its direction. The government itself became a large producer. Apart from vast imperial domains, there were imperial factories that produced arms and equipment for the troops besides articles designed for the court.

CURRENCY REFORM. Whereas Aurelian had sought to combat inflation by stabilizing the depreciated billon (copper and silver) coins of low value, Diocletian reformed the gold and silver coinage. Although the gold coins had remained pure in content, they had been made lighter and irregular in weight, and Diocletian in 286 fixed the weight of the standard gold coin (the *aureus*) at 1/60 of a pound. In 295 he issued an improved silver coin. The final reform was

made by Constantine I, however, who reduced the gold coin, now called the *solidus*, to 1/72 of a pound and issued a new silver coin called the *siliqua*, 1/24 of a *solidus*. From this time on the *solidus* retained a constant weight and purity. But owing to the shortage of both gold and silver, great use was made of billon coins of small denominations. Despite attempts at reform, this small change suffered a continuous depreciation, which was responsible for another period of serious inflation. Imperial bureaucrats whose job it was to determine the relation between this inflated billon coinage and the stable *solidus* did so at rates advantageous to themselves and the state, and the population at large, which very rarely used the gold coins, benefited little by Constantine's currency reform.

The Late Empire was based on a money economy and on the gold standard.

It inherited from the Principate, however, a system of tax collection and salary disbursements in kind; these certainly became more extensive and important than before, but the development was evolutionary. Commutation of payments in kind into payments in coin (*adaeratio*) was provided. Given the uncertain value of inflated billon coinage, different elements in the state viewed *adaeratio* in terms of their own economic advantage. The state, its functionaries, and soldiers preferred to receive taxes and wages in coin when such commutations evaluated the commodities concerned above the real or market price. The producing classes, landlords of great or moderate substance, preferred to pay in coin only when the value of their crops was set below the market price.

NEW TAX SYSTEM. Confronted by complete disorganization in public finances caused by inflation and economic decline of the third century, Diocletian revised drastically the system of taxation. The old land taxes were abolished and their place was taken by the *annona*, a tax in kind. This amounted to a regularization of the extraordinary levies that had become so important in the Late Principate. The resort to a land tax in kind rather than to an increase in monetary taxes is probably explained by a desire to protect the state against future inflation. Not only was the land tax revised but also in some provinces the method of assessment. The new land taxes in some provinces were based on a division of productive land, agricultural workers, and livestock into units of equal taxpaying liability. The system was called *capitatio* and the term *caput* (pl. *capita*) could be applied to land, personal, and animal units. A special term *iuga* (sing. *iugum*) was applied to units of land and the land tax was often called *iugatio*. Naturally the *iugum* varied in size accordingly to productivity. In Syria a *iugum* of plough land comprised twenty acres of first-class, forty of second-class, or sixty acres of third-class soil; a *iugum* of vineland, five acres; and a *iugum* in olive groves, 225 trees in lowlands, 450 in uplands. Apparently the *caput* of farm labor was one man or two women. Thus the land was taxed and also the labor to work it. A new survey and census of rural areas was required to calculate the new tax units. This was carried out apparently between 298 and 312.

INDICTION. The total land tax was announced in an annual proclamation called an indiction (*indictio*), which also specified the amount assessed against each province, and a revaluation of the tax units was made periodically. The term indiction was also used for the period between two reassessments, which occurred at first every five years and after 312 every fifteen years. Although estimates are difficult to make, it appears that from the landlords' viewpoint even though the indiction probably doubled between the reigns of Diocletian and Theodosius I, it was not prohibitively high on land of average yield, which continued to be in demand and command a high price. Marginal lands were another matter and greater taxation apparently made them unprofitable to cultivate so that they were abandoned and became waste.

MONETARY TAXES. There were other taxes payable in money. Chief of these were *chrysargyrum*, levied on all trades and professions; *aurum coronarium*, a nominally voluntary but really compulsory contribution paid by municipal councillors every five years to enable the emperor to distribute largesse to officials and troops; *aurum oblaticium*, a similar payment made by the senatorial order; and *collatio glebalis* or *follis senatoria*, a special tax imposed upon senatorial lands by Constantine I.

FORCED PUBLIC SERVICES. Besides the taxes, the government made its subjects perform public services without compensation. The most expensive such charges (*munera*) were upkeep of the public post and furnishing quarters (*hospitium*) and rendering other services in connection with movement of troops, officials, and supplies. So heavy was the burden of the post that it denuded the districts it traversed of draught animals and had to be drastically curtailed in the sixth century. In exacting these charges, collecting revenue in kind, and administering justice, imperial officials practiced extortions which weighed perhaps more heavily on taxpayers than the taxes themselves.

CURIALES. The decurions, generally called *curiales* during the Late Empire (from *curia*, senate or council), still ranked technically among the "respectable" classes. It is difficult to generalize about this class, except to say that its political functions, economic interests, and problems developed out of, and were similar to, those of the Late Principate. Beginning with Diocletian, emperors made *curiales* a legally hereditary caste, yet also, under certain circumstances, permitted them to leave their order and enter the army, civil service, or Church. Essentially, *curiales* were unpaid civil servants. When local senates became fiscal agents collecting revenues from their municipal territories for the state, *curiales*, through municipal officers or committees of the local council, had to apportion them among landholders, collect them, and be responsible for the total amount to the imperial government, their own property standing surety. They also maintained the public post and performed other services. There is no indication, at least for most of the fourth century, that *curiales* normally felt that the economic burdens they were called on to shoulder for their cities and the state were excessive.

Although membership in the curial order was a genteel and honorable estate from which the dregs of humanity like heretics, Jews, and ex-convicts were at first excluded, it was nevertheless sinking in status just when attainment of high rank for various reasons was becoming more desirable than ever before. Legally *honestiores*, they were nevertheless subject to flogging, a punishment otherwise meted out only to underprivileged lower classes, because they were less well connected than imperial senators and thus more vulnerable to the brutality of imperial agents. Many of them aspired to senatorial status that would give them prestige, protection against arbitrary treatment, and immunity from municipal responsibilities. Even under the Principate leading decurions had been motivated to enter the equestrian order, but the social and economic situation during the Late Empire greatly accelerated their upward mobility.

The government vacillated in restricting this movement, sometimes permitting *curiales* to leave the order after they held municipal offices, performed their fiscal responsibilities, willed a certain amount of land to their cities, or left an heir or substitute to take their places on town councils. Many *curiales*, however, especially the wealthier and better connected ones, connived with corrupt imperial officials entrusted with law enforcement and escaped to privileged status without complying with regulations. The government repeatedly prohibited such practices, but a commentary on the effectiveness of the law is the fact that the great offices were periodically combed for ex-*curiales*; the latter could claim immunity from service on their town councils if they proved that they had served undetected as bureaucrats for twenty or twenty-five years. The effect of massive legal and illegal defections from the order was serious. The richer, more mobile *curiales* left in their cities a dwindling number of poorer colleagues to be saddled with fiscal responsibilities that tended to increase. By the end of the fourth century many of the latter group were going bankrupt and the class as a whole was facing extinction, especially in the Western provinces.

Valentinian I attempted to aid the municipalities by making the so-called "defenders of the cities" (*defensores civitatium*), now known as "defenders of the plebs" (*d. plebis*), public officials whose duty it was to check unjust exactions and protect the people against officials and judges. These *defensores* were at first persons of influence, chosen by praetorian prefects and approved by the emperor. They were empowered to try certain cases and had the right to report directly to the emperor and to bypass the provincial governor. The *defensores* accomplished little, and in the fifth century this office became an additional obligation resting on the *curiales*.

HEREDITARY CORPORATIONS. Associations of businessmen, tradesmen, and craftsmen throughout the Empire were now called corporations (*corpora*), rather than colleges, and their members were known as *corporati*. Like *curiales*, *corporati* were required to devote much time, energy, and resources to serving the state or their municipalities. The idea that such duties constituted an obligation developed gradually during the Late Principate and was accepted as axiomatic under the Autocracy. It became more important with the introduction of the land tax in kind, for the transportation, warehousing, and distribution of such revenues necessitated the employment of many more persons than heretofore. The first step taken by the state to insure the performance of these services was to make this duty a charge that rested permanently on the property of members of the corporations, no matter into whose possession it passed. Men as well as money were needed for the performance of these charges, and to prevent a decline in numbers, the state made membership in their associations hereditary. This was really an extension of the principle that a man was bound to perform certain services in the community where he was enrolled (his *origo*). Finally, the emperors exercised the right of conscription and attached to various corporations in need of recruits persons engaged in less essential occupations.

The burden of their charges also led *corporati* to seek refuge in some other profession. They tried to enroll in the army or among the *officiales* or to become tenants of the emperor or senatorial landholders. All these havens of refuge were closed by imperial edicts. When discovered, truant *corporati* were supposedly dragged back to their associations. Such was the corruption and inefficiency of the bureaucracy enforcing these regulations that, in fact, many *corporati* remained undisturbed among privileged orders of society where they found refuge.

Although corporations probably retained their former organization and officers, their heads were now called patrons (*patroni*), who directed their public services. In Rome and Constantinople corporations were under the supervision of the city prefects; in the municipalities, under that of local magistrates and provincial governors. The professional corporations were the only ones to survive during the Late Empire. Religious and funerary associations vanished with the spread of Christianity and the impoverishment of the lower classes.

THE PEASANTRY. The vast majority of the population and economically the most important class was the peasantry, of which there were several categories. Slaves still worked on many estates but were declining in number and, except in parts of Spain and Italy, were becoming an insignificant part of the agricultural labor force. In some areas, like Syria, there were still prosperous freeholders. By far the most striking development was that of serfdom, which was encouraged by governmental decree and by social and economic conditions. The whole economic structure of the Empire rested on the peasants of whatever status, and many of them were in distress, despite the return of relatively peaceful times in the fourth century, because they paid a disproportionate share of imperial taxes. Peasant movements with revolutionary overtones, like that of the Bagaudae in Gaul, sometimes occurred. More typically, however, when driven to desperation the peasants left their land and melted into the forests, where they lived as brigands. In general, they reacted rather passively to oppression by government agents or senatorial landlords.

Abandonment of land by freeholders and tenants (*coloni*) naturally threatened government revenues in kind, and the government stepped in and attached *coloni* to estates where they had been working. It is not known when this step was taken or whether the obligation was extended to all such tenants at the same time. It seems clear, however, that the obligation had become virtually universal for tenants by 325. The status of *coloni* became hereditary, like that of *corporati*. Their condition, that of serfs, was halfway between free men and slaves. They were bound to the estate where they resided and passed with it from one owner to another, although they were not absolutely under the power of the owner and could not be disposed of by him apart from the land. They also had other rights that slaves lacked, but as time went on their condition increasingly tended to approximate servitude. "Slaves of the soil," they were called in the sixth century. As serfdom was hitherto unknown in Roman law, many edicts were issued defining the rights and duties of *coloni*.

Crushed by their obligations, the *coloni*, like the *curiales* and *corporati*, tried to change status by entering public service or another caste, but they also were legally excluded from all other occupations. Only the fugitive *colonus* who had managed to remain undetected for thirty years (in the case of women twenty years) could escape return to the land he had deserted. As in the cases of the *curiales* and *corporati*, many of these peasants, at least in the fourth century, apparently did leave the land.

GREAT LANDLORDS. The senatorial class of the Late Empire was extremely wealthy. As always its money was invested in estates widely scattered over the provinces and in palatial townhouses in the capitals. Despite purges and the confiscation of estates by emperors, from the first to the third centuries property tended to remain within the order, and its accumulation, which had been going on since the Republic, meant that by the fourth century senatorial wealth in the West was princely. The senatorial class in the East, essentially a foundation of Constantine's successors and hence more recent, was much less rich. It was recruited in the main from the municipal gentry of Eastern cities, who, if their economic interests were also agrarian, had had much less time to accumulate vast estates than Western senators. Faced by the need to maintain production for the sake of revenue, the government permitted great proprietors to take over deserted lands under various forms of heritable lease or in freehold tenure. Although the small landowner and the tenant farmer found it hard to gain a livelihood from their lands particularly in view of heavy taxation and extortionate methods of its collection, owners of big estates could operate them profitably despite low productivity.

The immunities of the senatorial order and the power of high civil and military officials tended to give an almost manorial character to the position of great landed proprietors now called *potentiores* or "more powerful." These inherited judicial powers of the procurators on imperial estates, and over their slaves and *coloni* they exercised powers of police and jurisdiction. Not subject to the municipal authorities and during the greater part of the fourth century also exempt from the jurisdiction of provincial governors, they assumed an independent position and defied municipal magistrates and even minor agents of the imperial government. Their power made their protection extremely valuable and led to a new type of patronage. Individuals and village communities, anxious to escape the exactions to which they were subject in their municipal districts, placed themselves under the patronage of a senatorial landholder, becoming his tenants. He freely protected them, albeit extralegally, against local authorities. Complaints by the latter to higher officials obtained little redress, for these officials were themselves proprietors and sided with their own class. The power of the state was thus nullified by its chief servants, and the landed aristocracy became the heirs of the Empire.

THE CASTE STATE IN PRACTICE. Late Roman emperors intended to create a rigid social structure, with each caste performing functions essential to the state. Nevertheless, there was much more social mobility than the law allowed, even more, perhaps, than during any other epoch of imperial history. The administration of edicts decreeing caste status was lax because it depended on corrupt bureaucrats for enforcement. This is indicated by the frequent re-issuance of such edicts and by the apparent freedom of movement and even choice of profession in many classes. The Principate had been a period of stability, in which most of the population did not change their ancestral status or profession. The period ca. 250–350, however, was one of flux unique in antiquity, when many more people than ever before changed jobs, professions, or status. Diocletian's probable doubling and Constantine's subsequent increase of the army meant a changeover of tens of thousands of men from civil to military status. The expansion of the bureaucracy and the senatorial order meant the similar transfer of more thousands from one walk of life to another, as did the growth of the secular church hierarchy and, in some areas, of monasticism. The traditional picture of the Late Empire is one of languishing private industry, declining commerce, and untilled fields. Such an interpretation is well grounded in fact, but striking local economic differences existed. In particular there were subtle forces at work differentiating the Western and Eastern halves of the Empire. As yet too little is known about these forces, but it would appear that the East was better able to maintain a reasonably prosperous urban tradition and that it was better able to resist the manorializing tendencies of the landlord class, which in the West increasingly escaped from the control of the central government.

CHAPTER 24
GERMANIC OCCUPATION OF ITALY AND THE WESTERN PROVINCES: A.D. 395–493

I. GENERAL CHARACTERISTICS OF THE PERIOD

PARTITION OF THE EMPIRE. With the death of Theodosius the Great the Empire passed to his sons, Arcadius a youth of eighteen, whom he had left in Constantinople, and Honorius a boy of eleven, whom he had designated as Augustus for the West. However, in the East the government was really in the hands of Rufinus, the praetorian prefect of Illyricum, while an even greater influence was exercised in the West by Stilicho, the Vandal master of the soldiers, whom Theodosius had selected as regent for young Honorius. The rivalry of these two men and the attempt by Stilicho to secure for Honorius restoration of eastern Illyricum, which had been seized by the Eastern administration for Arcadius, were the immediate causes of a real, if informal division of the Empire into Eastern and Western halves, a condition which was foreshadowed by the division of imperial power throughout most of the fourth century.

The fiction of imperial unity was preserved by the nomination of one consul each in Rome and in Constantinople, by the joint display of the statues of both Augusti everywhere, and by the issuance of imperial enactments under their joint names. There was in fact, however, a complete separation of administration. Before A.D. 395 edicts issued by one emperor required the sanction of the other before attaining validity within his own territory. After that date, the two parts of the Empire increasingly tended to separate legislatively, because edicts issued in one half were frequently not republished in the other. Furthermore, upon the death of one Augustus, the actual government of the whole Empire did not pass into his survivor's hands. The Empire had really split into two independent states, even though contemporaries did not recognize any formal division.

GERMANIC INVASIONS. The period between 395 and 493 is also marked by the complete breakdown of Roman resistance to barbarian invasion and the penetration and occupation of the Western provinces and Italy by Germanic peoples, power passing from Roman officials to Germanic kings. A barbarian soldier finally took the throne of the Western emperor, when a Germanic kingdom was established in Italy.

MILITARY DICTATORS. During this period of disintegration, real power in the Western Empire was wielded by military dictators who, with the office of senior master of the soldiers, became commanders in chief of the armies with the title patrician. The emperors exercised only nominal authority. As these dictators were either barbarians or depended on barbarian troops for their support, they were continually intrigued against and opposed by the Roman or civilian element, headed by civil officers of the court. The fall of one "kingmaker" was always followed by the rise of another, for by their aid alone could the Romans resist the flood of barbarian invasion.

THE EMPIRE MAINTAINED IN THE EAST. But while the Western Empire was thus absorbed by Germanic invaders, the East survived the crisis of the fifth century with its institutions and frontiers intact. This is in part accounted for by the ability of the central government in the East better to resist the decentralizing tendencies of the great landholders and of barbarian armies and their generals. The strength of the Eastern Empire caused the West to look to it for support, and Western emperors upon several occasions were nominated, and at other times given the sanction of legitimacy, by those in the East.

II. VISIGOTHIC MIGRATIONS

REVOLT OF ALARIC: A.D. 395. Seizing the opportunity created by the death of Theodosius and the absence of the army of the East, which he had drawn into Italy, Alaric, a prince of the Visigothic *foederati*, began to ravage Thrace and Macedonia with his own people and other tribes from across the Danube. He was opposed by Stilicho, who was leading back the troops of the Eastern emperor and intended to occupy eastern Illyricum. Stilicho was ordered by Arcadius to send the army of the East back to Constantinople, and he complied. This gave Alaric access to southern Greece, which he systematically plundered. Stilicho intervened again, transporting an army by sea to the Peloponnesus. He maneuvered Alaric into a precarious situation but came to

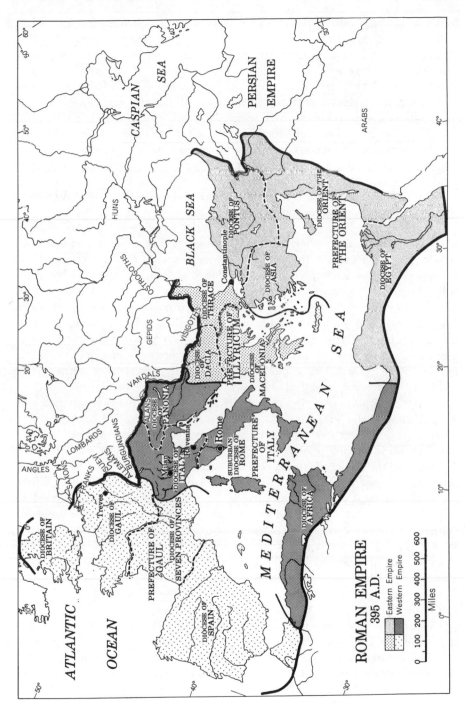

ROMAN EMPIRE
395 A.D.

Eastern Empire
Western Empire

0   100 200 300 400 500 600
Miles

terms with him, possibly because of a revolt that had broken out in Africa. Stilicho was declared an enemy by Arcadius, while Alaric, after devastating Epirus, settled there with his Goths and extorted the title of *magister militum* from the Eastern court.

DEATH OF STILICHO: A.D. 408. In 401, when Stilicho faced an inroad of Vandals and Alans into Raetia, Alaric invaded Italy. Stilicho forced him to withdraw and foiled a second attempt at invasion in 403. Alaric then held the title of master of the soldiers from Honorius and agreed to help Stilicho occupy Illyricum. When the Western Empire was embarrassed by new invasions and the appearance of a usurper in Gaul, however, he made his way into Noricum, and demanded an indemnity and employment for his troops. On Stilicho's advice Alaric was to be paid 4,000 pounds of gold. Shortly afterward, Stilicho fell victim to a plot hatched by jealous court officials (408).

VISIGOTHS IN ITALY. The death of Stilicho removed the only capable defender of Italy, and, when Honorius refused to honor the agreement with Alaric, the latter crossed the Alps. Honorius retreated to Ravenna, and the Goths marched on Rome, which was ransomed at a heavy price. As Honorius still refused to give him lands and supplies, Alaric returned to Rome and set up a new emperor, Attalus. Honorius, supported by troops from the Eastern Empire, remained obdurate, and a disagreement between Alaric and Attalus led to the latter's deposition. Rome was then occupied by the Goths, who plundered it for three days (410). Alaric next marched to South Italy intending to cross to Sicily and Africa, but his flotilla was destroyed by a storm. While retreating northward he fell ill and died.

GOTHS IN GAUL AND SPAIN. Alaric's successor was his brother-in-law, Ataulf, who led the Visigoths into Gaul (412), where he allied himself with a usurper, Jovinus, but soon deserted him to serve the Romans. When Honorius failed to subsidize him, he seized Narbonne and other towns in southern Gaul and married the emperor's sister, Galla Placidia, whom the Goths had captured in Rome. He again attempted to come to terms with the Romans but failed, and Constantius, the Roman master of the soldiers, who had succeeded to Stilicho's position and influence, forced him to abandon Gaul. Ataulf and his Goths crossed the Pyrenees into Spain, where he died in 415. His successor Wallia, facing famine and failing to invade Africa, made peace with the Romans. He surrendered Placidia and in the name of the emperor attacked Vandals and Alans who had occupied parts of Spain. Alarmed by his success, Constantius recalled the Goths to Gaul, where they settled in southern Aquitania (418).

VISIGOTHIC KINGDOM IN GAUL. The status of the Goths in Gaul was that of *foederati*, bound to render military aid to Rome but governed by their own kings. The latter, however, had no authority over the Roman population among whom the Goths settled. This condition was unsatisfactory to the Gothic rulers, who sought to establish an independent Gothic kingdom. Theodoric I, the successor of Wallia, forced the Romans to acknowledge his complete sovereignty over Aquitania but failed in his attempt to conquer Narbonese Gaul. Subsequently he joined forces with the Romans against Attila the Hun and was largely responsible for checking the latter at the battle of the Mauriac plain near Troyes (451) in which he was killed. For a time the Goths remained on friendly terms with the Empire. Under Euric, who became king in 466, the anti-Roman faction was in the ascendant, and they embarked upon expansion. In 475 Euric, after a protracted struggle, occupied the district of Auvergne, and the Roman emperor acknowledged his sovereignty over the country between the Atlantic and the Rhone, the Loire, and the Pyrenees, besides some territory in Spain. Two years later the district between the Rhone and the Alps, south of the Durance, was added to the Visigothic kingdom.

III. VANDALS

INVASIONS OF A.D. 406. In 405 a band of Vandals and Alans descended on Italy, and were utterly defeated by Stilicho. In the following year fresh swarms, united with the Suevi, crossed the Rhine near Mainz and plundered Gaul as far as the Pyrenees. For a time they were checked by the usurper Constantine, who held Gaul and Spain. Later, when he was involved in a struggle with a rival, Gerontius, they found an opportunity to enter Spain (409).

OCCUPATION OF SPAIN. They quickly occupied the whole peninsula. Despite their successes against Roman troops, lack of supplies forced them to terms. In 411 they became *foederati* and were granted lands for settlement. Under this agreement the Asdingian Vandals and the Suevi occupied the northwest part of Spain, the Alans, the center, and the Silingian Vandals, the south. Roman government made peace with the Vandals and their allies only under pressure and seized the first opportunity to be rid of them. In 416 Constantius authorized the Visigoths under Wallia to attack them. Wallia was so successful that he utterly annihilated the Silingian Vandals and so weakened the Alans that they united with the Asdingian Vandals, who escaped destruction only through the recall of the Visigoths to Gaul. The Vandals quickly recovered from their defeats, were victorious over the Suevi, who had reached an agreement with the Romans, and occupied the whole of southern Spain.

VANDAL KINGDOM IN AFRICA. In 429 under their king Gaiseric the Vandals landed in Africa, attracted by its richness and its importance as a granary of the Roman world. Their invasion was facilitated by war between Count Bonifacius, the governor of Africa, and the Western emperor. The number of the invaders was estimated at 80,000, of whom probably 15,000 or 20,000 were fighting men.

Despite a reconciliation between Bonifacius and the imperial government and their united opposition, Gaiseric overran the open country although he failed to capture the chief cities. In 435 peace was concluded, the Vandals settling in Numidia, once more as *foederati*. In 439, Gaiseric broke the peace and seized

Carthage. This was followed by the organization of a fleet, which harried the coasts of Sicily. In 442 the Western emperor acknowledged the independence of the Vandal kingdom. Peace continued until 455, when the assassination of the emperor Valentinian III gave Gaiseric the pretext to attack Italy and seize Rome, which was systematically plundered, although its buildings and monuments were not wantonly destroyed. Among the captives was Eudoxia, widow of the late emperor, and her daughters, who were valuable as hostages.

Lack of cooperation between the Eastern and Western Empires enabled the Vandals to extend their power. Their fleets controlled the Mediterranean and ravaged its western and its eastern coasts. A powerful expedition fitted out by the Eastern emperor Leo I in 468 for the invasion of Africa ended in utter failure, and in 476 his successor Zeno was compelled to acknowledge Vandal authority over the territory they controlled. At the death of Gaiseric in 477, the Vandal kingdom included all Roman Africa, the Balearic Islands, Corsica, Sardinia, and the fortress of Lilybaeum in Sicily.

IV. BURGUNDIANS, FRANKS, AND SAXONS

BURGUNDIAN INVASION OF GAUL.   The invasion of Gaul by the Vandals and Alans in 406 was followed by an inroad of Burgundians, Ripuarian Franks, and Alamanni. The latter two peoples established themselves on the left bank of the Rhine, and the Burgundians penetrated farther south. In 433 the Burgundians, at war with the Empire, were defeated by Aetius, the Roman master of the soldiers in Gaul. Subsequently they were settled in Savoy. From there, about 457, they began to occupy the valley of the Rhone as far south as the Durance.

On the whole they remained loyal *foederati*. They fought under Aetius against Attila in 451, their kings bearing the title *magister militum* until the reign of Gundobad (473–516), who was made patrician by the emperor Olybrius.

SALIAN FRANKS.   The Salian Franks—as those who had once dwelt on the shores of the North Sea were called in contrast to the Ripuarians, whose home was along the Rhine—crossed the lower Rhine before 350 and occupied Toxandria, the region between the Meuse and the Scheldt. They were defeated by Julian, who left them in this district as *foederati*. The disturbances of the early fifth century enabled them to assert their independence and expand as far south as the Somme. They fought as Roman allies against the Huns in 451, and their king Childeric, who began to rule shortly afterward, remained a faithful *foederatus* until his death in 481. In 486 Clovis, the successor of Childeric, overthrew the Gallo-Roman state south of the Somme and extended his kingdom to meet the Visigoths on the Loire. Thus the whole of Gaul passed under the rule of Germanic peoples.

SAXONS IN BRITAIN.   After the decisive defeat of the Picts and Scots by Theodosius, father of Theodosius the Great, in 368 and 369, the Romans successfully defended Britain until the close of the fourth century. In 402, however, Stilicho was obliged to recall part of the garrison to protect Italy, and in 406 Constantine, who claimed the imperial crown in Britain, took with him the remaining Roman troops to obtain recognition on the continent. The ensuing struggles with the barbarians in Gaul prevented the Romans from sending officials or troops across the channel immediately, and the Britons had to fend for themselves.

The Roman garrison was eventually restored under the command of a *comes Britanniarum*, but it was unequal to stemming the tide of Saxons, Angles, and Jutes, who made permanent settlements beginning in 428. Toward 442 the Roman garrison evacuated the island forever. Four years later the inhabitants directed one last appeal to the Roman government for help, but in vain. Because Roman civilization in Britain was a relatively thin veneer, the subsequent struggle for possession of the island resulted in the obliteration of the Latin language and of what material civilization had developed under Roman rule.

RESUMÉ. The immediate causes for such spectacular barbarian success in areas which had not experienced widespread invasion for about 150 years are difficult to establish. Like their predecessors during the third century, migrating tribes of the fifth were rather loose and disunited, waxing strong in moments of success but losing many followers to other tribes and nations under weak leaders or when defeated. They were not more numerous than earlier tribes, and it seems that normally, like the Vandals, they could not field armies much larger than 20,000 men. Although the order of battle of Roman armies during the crucial period of Stilicho's leadership is unknown, it appears that the *comitatenses* in Gaul and Italy numbered about 40,000 men each and enjoyed no great numerical superiority, if any, over several barbarian nations coalescing under successful leaders, like Alaric.

Western armies apparently suffered severe losses in the invasions of the period 395–425. During that time the *comitatenses* lost almost half their effective strength, with the attrition rate almost two thirds in Gaul. The already depopulated West was hard put to make up these losses, and the government was forced to transfer *limitanei* from the frontiers to form new units of the *comitatus*, even though the former were often second-rate units. Military disasters thus produced a cycle of further dislocation and recruitment of inferior armies, from which the West never recovered.

V. FALL OF THE WESTERN EMPIRE

HONORIUS: A.D. 395–423. After the murder of Stilicho in 408, Honorius was faced with the problem of restoring his authority in Gaul, where for a time he was forced to acknowledge the rule of the rival emperor Constantine, who had donned the purple in Britain in 406. Constantius, a Roman noble who succeeded Stilicho as master of the soldiers, was dispatched to Gaul in 411 and soon overthrew the usurper. Two years later another rival, Jovinus, was crushed with the help of the Visigoths.

Constantius, leader of the antibarbarian faction at court, was now Honorius' mainstay and used his influence to further his own ambitions. After the Visigoths returned the princess Placidia, he induced the emperor to make her his wife (417). In 421 Honorius appointed him coemperor, but he was not recognized as an Augustus at Constantinople. His death the same year was followed by a quarrel between the emperor and his sister, as a result of which Placidia and her son took refuge with the Eastern emperor, Theodosius II.

VALENTINIAN III: A.D. 423–455. Honorius died childless in 423, and Castinus, the new commander in chief, secured the nomination of John, a high court officer, as his successor. Theodosius refused him recognition, however, and his authority was defied by Bonifacius, a commander in Africa. Valentinian, the five-year-old son of Placidia and Constantius, was escorted to Italy by forces of the Eastern Empire, and John was deposed. His chief supporter Aetius, who brought an army of Huns to his aid, was induced to dismiss his troops and accept a command in Gaul with the rank of count. Placidia, who had returned to Italy with Valentinian, became regent with the title of Augusta.

AETIUS. During the reign of Valentinian III interest centered about the career of Aetius. In 429, after eliminating his enemy Felix, who had succeeded to the position of Castinus, Aetius himself became master of the soldiers, the real ruler in the West. Fearing his influence, Augusta Placidia tried to engineer his downfall by an appeal to Bonifacius, who, after his revolt of 427, fought with the Empire against the Vandals. In 432 Bonifacius returned to Italy and was appointed master of the soldiers in place of Aetius. The latter took up arms, was defeated near Ariminum, and forced to flee to his friends the Huns. Bonifacius died not long after his victory; Aetius, with Hunnish backing, forced the emperor to reappoint him to his command as patrician in 433. From then until his death in 454 he directed imperial policy in the West. He received foreign embassies, and the latter made treaties with him and not with the emperor.

ATTILA'S INVASION OF GAUL: A.D. 451. The chief efforts of Aetius were directed toward preserving central and southeastern Gaul for the Empire. He was successful, checking Franks on the north, Burgundians on the east, and Goths in the southwest. Gaul was saved, but Africa was lost to the Vandals, Britain to the Saxons, and the greater part of Spain to the Suevi. The success of Aetius in Gaul was principally because of his ability to draw on large numbers of Hunnish troops, through the influence he had with leaders of that people while their hostage. The Huns then occupied the region of modern Hungary, Rumania, and South Russia. They comprised many separate tribes, which united in 444 under the strong hand of King Attila, who extended his sway over neighboring Germans and Scythians.

At first Attila remained a friend of Aetius, but his ambitions and his interference in Gaul led to friction and to his demand for the hand of Honoria, sister of Valentinian III, with half the Western Empire as her dowry. When the emperor refused, Attila led an army across the Rhine into Gaul and besieged

Orleans. Their common danger united the Romans and the Germans of Gaul, and Aetius faced the Huns with an army strengthened by the kings of the Visigoths and the Franks. Repulsed at Orleans, Attila withdrew to the Mauriac plain, where, near Troyes, a memorable battle was fought between the Huns and the forces of Aetius. Although the result was indecisive, Attila did not risk another engagement and recrossed the Rhine. The next year he invaded Italy, but famine and disease among his own forces and the arrival of troops from the Eastern Empire induced him to listen to a Roman embassy led by the Roman bishop Leo and to withdraw without occupying Rome. Upon his death in 453 his empire fell to pieces.

MAXIMUS AND AVITUS: A.D. 455–456. The death of Attila was soon followed by that of Aetius, who was murdered by Valentinian at the instigation of his chamberlain Heraclius (454), and the next year Valentinian himself fell victim to Aetius' faction. With him the dynasty of Theodosius in the West ended. The new emperor, a senator named Petronius Maximus, compelled Valentinian's widow, Eudoxia, to marry him, but when the Vandal Gaiseric appeared in Italy in answer to her appeal, Maximus offered no resistance and died in flight. He was succeeded by Avitus, a Gallic follower of Aetius, whom he had made master of the soldiers. After ruling about a year, Avitus was deposed by his own master of the soldiers, Ricimer (456).

RICIMER. Ricimer, a German of Suevic and Gothic ancestry, succeeded to the power of Aetius and was the virtual ruler of the Western Empire from 456 until his death in 472. Backed by his mercenaries, he made and unmade emperors and never permitted his nominees to be more than puppets. Majorian, who was appointed emperor in 457, was overthrown by Ricimer in 461 and followed by Severus. After the death of Severus in 465 no emperor was appointed in the West for two years. Imperial power was nominally exercised by the Eastern emperor, Leo, while Ricimer actually controlled the government in Italy. In 467 Leo sent to Rome as emperor Anthemius, a dignitary of the Eastern court, whose daughter was married to Ricimer, to secure the latter's cooperation in a joint attack of the two empires on the Vandal kingdom. In 472 Ricimer broke with Anthemius, who had endeavored with the support of the Roman Senate to free himself from the barbarian. Anthemius was besieged in Rome and executed following its capture. Ricimer then raised to the purple Olybrius, a son-in-law of Valentinian III. Both the new emperor and his patron died the same year (472).

LAST YEARS OF THE WESTERN EMPIRE. In 473 Gundobad, the nephew of Ricimer, had Glycerius proclaimed emperor. But his appointment was not recognized by Leo, who nominated Julius Nepos. The next year Nepos invaded Italy and overthrew his rival, only to die at the hands of Orestes, his master of the soldiers (475). Orestes did not become emperor, but nominated his son Romulus Augustulus. Orestes held power only shortly. Germanic mercenaries in Italy—Heruli, Sciri, and others—led by Odovacar demanded lands there such as others had been granted as *foederati* in the provinces. When they were refused, they mutinied and killed Orestes. Romulus abdicated, and Odovacar assumed the title of king (476). His soldiers settled in Italy, and barbarians acquired full control of the Western Empire.

RULE OF ODOVACAR: A.D. 476–493. With the deposition of Romulus Augustulus, imperial authority was united again, nominally through the Eastern emperor, who without recognizing Odovacar as king, gave qualified sanction to his rule by granting him the title of patrician, which had been held already by Aetius, Ricimer, and Orestes. Odovacar obtained authority only in Italy. The last remnants of Roman authority vanished in Gaul and Spain, while Raetia and Noricum were abandoned to the Alamanni, Thuringi, and Rugii.

OSTROGOTHIC CONQUEST OF ITALY: A.D. 488–493. In 488 the position of Odovacar was challenged by Theodoric the Amal, king of the Ostrogoths. This people, after having long been subject to the Huns, recovered their freedom at Attila's death and settled in Pannonia as *foederati* of the eastern Empire. Theodoric, who became sole ruler of the Ostrogoths in 481, proved himself a troublesome ally of the emperor Zeno, who mistrusted him. When Theodoric demanded an imperial commission to attack Odovacar in Italy, Zeno readily granted him authority, together with the office of patrician in the special Western sense, to remove him far from Constantinople. In 488 Theodoric invaded Italy. Odovacar was defeated in two battles and in 490 blockaded in Ravenna. After a long siege he surrendered, upon condition that he and Theodoric should rule jointly. Shortly afterward he and most of his followers were assassinated by the Ostrogoths (493). Theodoric was proclaimed king by his army, although, like Odovacar he was never recognized legally as imperial vice-regent by the Eastern court.

VI. SURVIVAL OF THE EMPIRE IN THE EAST

ARCADIUS: A.D. 395–408. The year Theodosius the Great died the Asiatic provinces of the Empire were overrun by Huns, who ravaged Syria and Asia Minor as Visigoths under Alaric devastated the Balkan peninsula. The presence of Eastern troops in Italy prevented the government from offering any effective opposition. When Stilicho came to the rescue from Italy and was holding the Visigoths in check, his rival, the praetorian prefect Rufinus, regent to the young Arcadius, induced the emperor to order Stilicho to withdraw and send the troops of the East to Constantinople. This order resulted in the death of Rufinus, who was killed by the returning soldiery at the orders of their commander, the Goth Gainas.

The influential position of Rufinus at court devolved upon the grand chamberlain Eutropius, who had been an enemy of his predecessor. He induced Arcadius to marry Eudoxia, a daughter of a Frankish chief, instead of the daughter of Rufinus, as the latter had desired. The fall of Eutropius in turn was brought about by Gainas, now a master of the soldiers, who sought to play the role of Stilicho in the East, and by the empress Eudoxia, who chafed under the domination of the chamberlain. In 399, when Gothic troops in Phrygia revolted, Gainas held aloof, and the failure of a nominee of Eutropius to crush the movement gave Gainas the opportunity to recommend the latter's dismissal. The plots of Eudoxia against the eunuch finally brought about his fall from power and eventually his death.

Gainas' aspirations to become an Eastern Stilicho were not realized. He and his troops were unpopular at Constantinople because of their Arianism, and upon the removal of Eutropius preponderant influence at court fell to an antibarbarian faction supported by the empress and led by the praetorian prefect, Aurelian. A massacre of thousands of Gothic soldiers in Constantinople followed, and with the aid of a loyal Goth, Fravitta, Gainas was driven north of the Danube, where he was killed by the Huns (400). Units composed of indigenous troops were soon raised by Arcadius to replace the barbarians. This was the first step taken by the Eastern court to combat the barbarization of the army and to rely on a predominantly "national" military establishment.

Eudoxia, of course, was more influential than ever following the fall of Eutropius. But she herself found a critic in the eloquent bishop of Constantinople, John Chrysostom, who inveighed against the extravagance and dissipation of the court and censured the empress in particular. Ultimately, in 404, Eudoxia had him deposed from his see. Four years later Arcadius died, leaving the Empire to his eight-year-old son Theodosius II.

THEODOSIUS II: A.D. 408–450. At the beginning of the reign of Theodosius II, the government was in the hands of the praetorian prefect Anthemius, an able administrator during the last years of Arcadius. In 414, the emperor's elder sister, Pulcheria, was made regent with the title of Augusta. She was strong-willed and for many years dominated the emperor, who lacked character and energy. In 421 Pulcheria selected as a wife for Theodosius, Athenais, the daughter of an Athenian sophist, who took the name Eudocia upon accepting Christianity. After some years, differences arose between the empress and her sister-in-law, which led to the latter's withdrawal from court (after 431). About 440 Eudocia lost her influence over the emperor, and she was compelled to retire from Constantinople and reside in Jerusalem, where she lived until her death in 460. Power then passed to the grand chamberlain Chrysaphius, whose corrupt administration rivalled that of Eutropius.

During the reign of Theodosius II peace was broken by war with Persia and by inroads of the Huns. The Persian war, which began in 421 as a result of persecutions of the Christians in Persia, was concluded victoriously the next year. A second war, following a Persian invasion in 441, ended with Persian defeat in 442. With the Huns the Romans were not so fortunate. In 424 King Rua, the ruler of the Huns in Hungary, had extorted from the Empire payment of an annual tribute. At the accession of Attila and his brother in 433, this tribute was raised to 700 pounds of gold, and Romans were forbidden to shelter Hunnish defectors. Payment of tribute failed to win a permanent respite, for Attila was bent on draining the wealth of the Empire and making it helpless. In 441–443 the Huns swarmed over the Balkans and defeated imperial armies. An indemnity of 6,000 pounds of gold was exacted and the annual payment increased to 2,100 pounds. Another disastrous raid occurred in 447. The Empire could offer no resistance, and Attila even claimed to regard himself as the overlord of Theodosius. Chrysaphius plotted the assassination of Attila, but the plot was detected.

The reign of Theodosius II was important for several events. It witnessed the emergence of a new heresy, involving a dispute over the nature of Christ, called Monophysitic. The Monophysites were destined to be at the center of bitter religious disputes that plagued the East for many generations.[1] The erection of a new city wall in 413 under the administration of Anthemius was also noteworthy. The wall stretched from the Sea of Marmora to the Golden Horn, and its circuit was much greater than that the old wall of Constantine, which the city had outgrown. Theodosius' wall made Constantinople virtually impregnable, and its ruins remain to this day one of the landmarks of the city. Possibly influenced by the philosopher-empress Eudocia, Theodosius refounded the school of higher learning in the capital. Originally an establishment of Constantine's, now, after 425, it was endowed with ten chairs of Greek and ten of Latin grammar, five of Greek and three of Latin rhetoric, two of law, and one of philosophy. Of great importance for the development of law was the publication in 438 of the Theodosian Code, which was supposed to contain for purposes of ready reference all the still valid imperial ordinances, beginning with the reign of Constantine.

MARCIAN: A.D. 450–457.   Choice of a new emperor was left to Augusta Pulcheria. She selected Marcian, a tried officer, whom she married. Marcian was able and conscientious. He refused to continue the indemnity to Attila and adhered to this policy as the latter invaded the West and subsequently died. He also permitted the Ostrogoths to settle as *foederati* in Pannonia (454).

LEO I: A.D. 457–474.   At the death of Marcian in 457, imperial authority was conferred upon Leo, an officer of Dacian origin, who was appointed because of the support of the Alan Aspar, one of the masters of the soldiers. Aspar's power rivalled that of Ricimer in the West. Since the breakup of the Hunnish Empire, the number of Gothic barbarians in East Roman armies had increased, a tendency the would-be barbarian kingmaker furthered. Leo was alive to the danger of becoming the puppet of a powerful general, who was unpopular and even suspected of treason when he failed to support properly the unsuccessful expedition against the Vandals. As a counterpoise to Gothic mercenaries and *foederati*, the mainstay of Aspar's power, Leo enlisted Isaurians, warlike mountaineers of southern Anatolia, who, if they were little better than

---

[1] For fuller discussion of Monophysitism, see p. 486.

barbarians themselves, were good soldiers and imperial subjects. The emperor's eldest daughter married Zeno, an Isaurian, who was made master of the soldiers in the East. In 470 Aspar was still strong enough to force Leo to marry his second daughter to his son Leontius and to appoint the latter Caesar, but the next year when Zeno returned to Constantinople, Aspar and his eldest son were assassinated in the palace. The second notable attempt by barbarians to take over the army of the East thus failed; thereafter indigenous elements tended to predominate among the officer cadres and rank and file of East Roman armies.

LEO II: A.D. 473–474. In 473 Leo took as his colleague and destined successor his grandson, also called Leo, the son of Zeno. The elder Leo died early in 474, and the younger soon crowned his father Zeno coemperor. When Leo II died before the year ended, Zeno became sole ruler.

ZENO: A.D. 474–491. The reign of Zeno was an almost uninterrupted struggle against usurpers and Gothic *foederati*. In 474 the latter revolted under their king Theodoric, called Strabo or "the Squinter," who ruled over the Goths settled in Thrace as master of the soldiers. Before this revolt was put down, unpopularity of the Isaurians induced Basiliscus, brother-in-law of Leo I, to plot a *coup d'état*. He was supported by his sister, the ex-empress Verina, and Illus, chief Isaurian officer in Zeno's service. The conspirators seized Constantinople and proclaimed Basiliscus emperor in 475. His heretical religious views aroused opposition, however, and he was deserted by both Verina and Illus. Zeno reentered the capital, and Basiliscus was executed.

During the revolt Zeno was supported by Theodoric the Amal, a Gothic prince who was a rival of Theodoric Strabo. The emperor tried to crush the latter with the former's help, whom he made a master of the soldiers with patrician rank, but the two Theodorics came to an agreement and acted in concert against Zeno in 478. In 479 peace was made with Strabo, but hostilities continued with the Amal. At this time a brief insurrection broke out in Constantinople, under the leadership of Marcian, a son-in-law of Leo I, against the predominance of Isaurians, Illus in particular.

Theodoric Strabo, was killed in 481, and in 483 Zeno made peace with Theodoric the Amal, restoring his office of master of the soldiers and granting him lands in Dacia and lower Moesia. These concessions were made because of a falling-out between the emperor and his all-powerful minister Illus. This ill feeling culminated in 484, when Illus, master of the soldiers in the East, induced the dowager empress Verina to crown a general, Leontius, as emperor. Outside of Isauria the movement found little support. After a long siege in an Isaurian fortress, the leaders of the revolt were taken and put to death (488). In the meantime Theodoric the Amal had asked and received permission to attack Italy. With the departure of the Goths the Eastern Empire was delivered from the danger of Germanic invasion. Zeno died in April 491.

ANASTASIUS: A.D. 491–518. Choice of a successor was left to the empress Ariadne, who selected as emperor and husband an experienced courtier, Anastasius. Anastasius removed the Isaurian officials and troops from

Constantinople. This led to an Isaurian rebellion in southern Asia Minor, which was not stamped out until 498. The power of the Isaurians was broken, their strongholds were captured, part of their population was transported to Thrace, and they ceased to menace the peace.

In place of the Goths, new enemies appeared on the Danube—Slavic Getae and Bulgars—who overran the depopulated provinces of the northern Balkans. Their ravages were widespread. So utterly did the imperial troops fail to hold them in check that Anastasius was obliged to repair a protective wall built some years before outside the city across the peninsula upon which Constantinople stood. Anastasius also coped with a serious Persian war, which began with an invasion of Roman Armenia and Mesopotamia by King Kawad in 502. After four years of warfare in which the Persians gained initial success but were ultimately defeated by the master of the offices Celer, peace was reestablished on the basis of the *status quo*.

Anastasius' reign is noteworthy for the abolition of the tax called *chrysargyrum* (498) and for his relief of *curiales* from responsibility for the collection of municipal taxes. The former step was taken because the impoverishment and decline of tradesmen and workers had made *chrysargyrum* both a crushing burden and unprofitable, and the latter because the virtual disappearance of municipal landholders had rendered their councils useless as tax-collecting agencies. A land tax paid in money replaced the tax on the urban populace. A testimony of the increasing influences of Christian morality was the abolition of certain pagan festivals and of combats between gladiators and wild beasts.

Despite the justice and efficiency of his administration, the reign of Anastasius was marked by several popular uprisings in Constantinople and in other cities of the Empire. The cause lay in his sympathy for the Monophysite doctrine, which was vigorously opposed by orthodox Christians. In 512 the appointment of a Monophysite bishop at Constantinople provoked a serious rebellion that almost cost Anastasius his throne.

Although the emperor was able to quiet the city, the prevailing religious discord encouraged Vitalian, the commander of Bulgarian *foederati* in the Thracian army, to revolt in 513. He defeated all forces sent against him and endangered the capital, but he was induced to withdraw by a ransom of 5,000 pounds of gold and the office of master of the soldiers in Thrace. The truce was only temporary, and in 515 he again advanced on Constantinople. This time his forces were crushed on land and sea, and the rebellion ended. Three years later Anastasius died, leaving an immense treasury surplus, which was to be the economic basis for the program of expansion soon to be undertaken by Justinian.

CHAPTER 25
AGE OF JUSTINIAN:
A.D. 518–565

I. GERMANIC KINGDOMS IN THE WEST TO A.D. 533

GERMANS AND ROMANS. The passing of Italy and the Western provinces under Germanic kings was the result of the settlement of many barbarians in the conquered territories. This necessitated a division of land and a definition of the status of Romans and invaders, who were everywhere less numerous than the natives. These questions were settled in different ways.

UNDER THE VISIGOTHS. In the Visigothic kingdom in Gaul, Goths and Romans lived side by side as separate peoples, each enjoying its own laws, and the Romans were not regarded as subjects without rights, although inter-marriage between the two races was forbidden. The law that applied to the Romans was published by King Alaric II in 506 as the *Lex Romana Visigothorum*, or the Breviary of Alaric. His predecessor Euric sponsored the compilation of a code of Gothic customary law, in imitation of the Theodosian Code.

The settlement of Goths on the land took the form of *hospitium* or quartering. By this arrangement Roman landholders yielded two thirds of their property both land and cattle, *coloni*, and slaves. What the Goths received was not taxable.

For purposes of administration the Roman provincial and municipal divisions were retained (*provinciae* and *civitates*), the former being placed under dukes and the latter under counts of the cities (*comites civitatium*). The Goths settled within these districts formed their own national associations of tens, hundreds, and thousands, under Gothic officers. Adoption of settled life deeply affected Gothic institutions. Their national assembly could no longer be easily assembled and came to exist in the army alone. In the division of land, the more influential warriors and friends of the king received larger shares, and this stimulated the rise of a landed nobility. The government was established at Toulouse, where central ministries were set up, modeled on those of the Roman court. This led to a considerable strengthening of royal power. The language of government remained Gothic for the Goths, Latin for the Romans, but the leading Goths appear to have been bilingual.

UNDER THE VANDALS. In Vandal Africa the Romans were treated as conquered subjects. As under the Goths, intermarriage between them and the conquering race was prohibited. In the province of Zeugitana (old Africa), site of the main Vandal settlement, Roman landowners were completely dispossessed and their estates turned over to the new proprietors. *Coloni* and other tenants remained on the soil, and the Vandal landlords entrusted the management of their properties to Roman stewards. Elsewhere the Romans were undisturbed.

Roman divisions were retained, but regions settled by Vandals were special enclaves. Here the Vandals preserved tribal divisions of hundreds and thousands. Their own officials administered justice for the Vandals according to their customary laws; for the Romans it remained with their previous authorities, administered according to Roman law but under the supervision of the Vandal king.

The Vandal kingdom was strongly centralized. This led to the development of a service nobility. The African climate and sudden wealth enabling them to enjoy all the extravagances of Roman life in the upper classes soon weakened them. Although they lacked political rights, the Roman agricultural population of Africa found Vandal rule less oppressive than Roman bureaucracy. The Arianism of the Vandals prevented their winning the loyalty of Roman subjects, however.

THE OSTROGOTHS. In Italy, Odovacar had maintained the Roman administrative system, and Theodoric continued his policy. He assumed the *de facto* powers of a master of the soldiers and could even be styled unofficially *princeps* or Augustus by his subjects, but essentially he ruled as a king. He retained the Roman administrative organization, and all his civil officials were Romans. He published an edict that constituted a code of laws applicable to Goths and Romans alike. So thoroughly Roman was Theodoric's administration that even the army was open to Romans, who appear among his prominent generals.

The Ostrogoths were assigned land in Italy, but it seems that there was no confiscation of private property, one third of the state lands being allotted for his purpose. Ravenna was the royal residence and capital, but the Roman

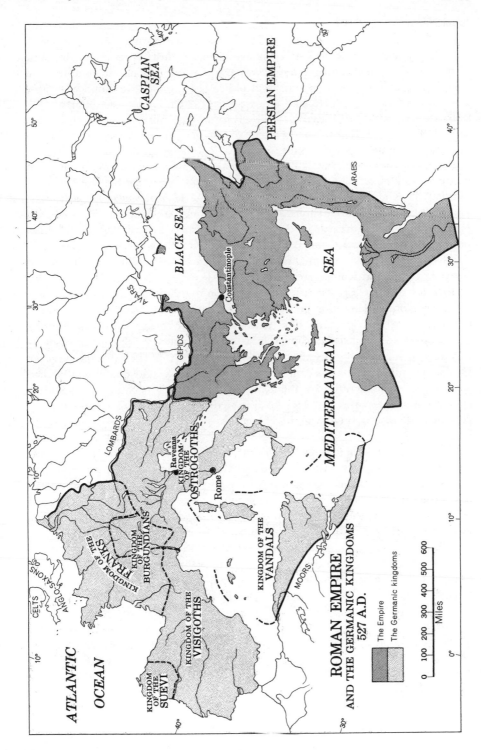

ROMAN EMPIRE
AND THE GERMANIC KINGDOMS
527 A.D.

The Empire
The Germanic kingdoms

0   100   200   300   400   500   600
Miles

Senate exercised much influence and until the later years of his reign, cordially supported the authority of Theodoric. Until the very end the reign of Theodoric was enlightened, since it stressed the peaceful coexistence of Goths and Romans. It must have seemed a golden age, compared with the economic conditions in Italy resulting from the wars and fiscal policies of the East Roman administration during Justinian's reign that followed.

BURGUNDIANS AND FRANKS.   The Burgundians in the Rhone valley were settled, like the Visigoths, according to *hospitium*. Their relations with the Roman population were peaceful, intermarriage between the two peoples was sanctioned, and Burgundian kings showed themselves appreciative of Roman culture. Gundobad, who reigned from 473 to 516, issued both a code of Burgundian laws and the Burgundian Roman Law (*Lex Romana Burgundionum*), which applied to Roman subjects and to Burgundians in their disputes with Romans. In their advance to the Seine the Franks annihilated the Roman population of northern Gaul. Between the Seine and the Loire, however, they left Romans in possession of their property, the kings making no distinction between Frank and Roman subjects.

THE RELIGIOUS QUESTION.   In addition to ethnic differences, there was also a religious demarcation between Goths, Vandals, and Burgundians on the one hand, and the Romans. The Goths and neighboring Germanic peoples were converted to Christianity in the latter half of the fourth century, largely through the missionary activities of Ulfila, who translated the Bible into Gothic. Under his influence they became Arian not orthodox, and consequently they were regarded as heretics by the Romans, who never became reconciled to rulers of another confession. This hostility led frequently to government intervention and persecution, but in this respect the policy of the Germanic kingdoms varied.

In general the Visigoths were tolerant, leaving the orthodox clergy undisturbed except when the latter were disloyal. At the time of their settlement in Zeugitana the Vandals confiscated property of the orthodox Church and turned it over to their own Arian clergy. Elsewhere in Africa Catholics remained unmolested during the reign of Gaiseric but were persecuted by his successors. Generally speaking, Vandal occupation dealt a mortal blow to orthodoxy in Africa. In the Ostrogothic kingdom in Italy Theodoric, although an Arian, gave complete freedom to the orthodox Church throughout most of his reign, but his policy changed in 523 when the emperor Justin began to persecute Arians in the East. The ban against Arianism was supported by Romans in

XXII   Mosaics from S. Apollinare in Classe. *Mosaics from this church, consecrated at Ravenna in A.D. 549, illustrate the Transfiguration of Christ, who is represented by a Latin cross. This and other mosaics of the city are generally considered masterpieces of the early Byzantine mosaicists. (Photo: Alinari.)*

Italy, particularly by the orthodox clergy and senators. This led Theodoric to suspect that the emperor's action had been stimulated by a faction in the Roman Senate. Realizing the effect that imperial proscription of Arianism would have on relations between his Roman and Gothic subjects, Theodoric sent a delegation to Constantinople, headed by the bishop of Rome, to have the anti-Arian decree annulled. Although Justin apparently agreed to this, Theodoric was angered by the favor shown the pope by the emperor, which emphasized the solidarity of Eastern and Western orthodoxy. Theodoric died in 526 before religious peace was restored in Italy.

The Burgundians were also Arians, which prevented their winning the loyal support of the orthodox clergy, who recognized the authority of the Burgundian kings. Although Sigismund, son of Gundobad, who came to the throne in 516, was converted to orthodoxy, it was too late to heal the religious breach before the fall of Burgundian power.

Unlike their neighbors, the Visigoths and Burgundians, the Franks were pagans when they settled in Roman territory and remained so until the end of the fifth century. In 496 the Frankish king Clovis was converted to orthodox Christianity, a fact of great importance in his conquests in Gaul.

EXPANSION OF THE FRANKS. The foreign policy of Theodoric was directed toward strengthening his position in Italy by establishing friendly relations with western Germanic kingdoms and maintaining peace and a balance of power among them. To this end he contracted a series of family alliances with the rulers of these states. In 492 he married a sister of Clovis the Frank and gave his own sister in marriage to the Vandal king Thrasamund. One of his daughters became the wife of Sigismund, king of the Burgundians; and another was married to Alaric II, who succeeded Euric as Visigothic king.

Theodoric's scheme was disturbed by the ambitions of Clovis. In 496 Clovis conquered the Alamanni. He next forced the Burgundians to acknowledge him as overlord, and with these allies he attacked the Visigoths in 507. The conquests of Euric in Gaul and Spain overtaxed Visigothic strength and weakened their hold on the territory they occupied, and their Roman subjects aided the orthodox Clovis. In a battle near Poitiers the Visigoths were defeated and their king, Alaric II, was killed. Theodoric was prevented at first from intervening personally by the emperor Anastasius, who sanctioned the action of Clovis and sent him consular insignia. In 508, however, the Ostrogothic king came to the aid of the Visigoths. He repulsed the Franks and Burgundians before Arles and recovered Narbonese Gaul. Most of Aquitania remained under the Franks. Theodoric established his grandson Amalaric as Visigothic king and became his regent (510). Clovis died in 511, and expansion of the Franks ceased for a time, but the death of Theodoric in 526 led to fresh disturbances. The Visigothic king Amalaric at once asserted his independence in southern Gaul and Spain. Not long afterward, in 531, he fell in battle against the Franks, who seized remaining Visigothic possessions in Gaul except Septimania—the coast between the Pyrenees and Rhone. Three years later the Franks overthrew the Burgundians and so brought under their sway the whole of Gaul outside of Septimania and Provence.

In 533 the situation in the West was as follows. Gaul was mainly in the hands of the Franks, Spain was under the Visigoths, the Vandals were still established in Africa, and the Ostrogoths in Italy. Both of the latter kingdoms, however, were showing signs of internal weakness. In addition to hostility between Germanic conquerors and the subject Roman population, strife had broken out over the succession to the throne. Evidence of the declining power of the Vandals was the success of Moorish tribes in winning independence. By 525 both Mauretania and Numidia were lost to them, and the tribes of Tripolis had shaken off the Vandal yoke. In 530 the Moors of southern Byzacene inflicted a severe defeat on the Vandals, which led to deposition of the king. The weakness of these states seemed to offer a favorable opportunity for the reestablishment of imperial authority in the West.

II. RESTORATION OF IMPERIAL POWER IN THE WEST: A.D. 533–554

JUSTIN I: A.D. 518–527.   Anastasius died in 518 and was succeeded by Justin, a lowly Illyrian who had risen to the post of commander of the imperial bodyguard (*comes excubitorum*). Unlike his predecessor, Justin was orthodox, and at the beginning of his reign an influential position was held by the general Vitalian, the champion of orthodoxy against Anastasius. He became master of the soldiers at Constantinople and in 520 was honored with a consulship. His power and ambitions constituted a real menace to the emperor, and the latter arranged his murder. Justin reigned for nine years. He was an experienced soldier but personally unequal to imperial government. The guiding spirit of his administration was his nephew Justinian, who was responsible for Vitalian's removal. In fact the reign of Justin was a brief introduction to that of Justinian himself, whom his uncle crowned colleague in 527 and who became sole emperor at the latter's death the same year.

JUSTINIAN'S IMPERIAL POLICY.   Justinian was by birth a Latin peasant, probably from near Scupi (modern Uskub) in Upper Moesia, but through his uncle he had been able to enjoy all the educational advantages of Constantinople. Justinian insisted on his own West Roman orientation, which colored many of his policies as emperor. Latin was once again to be the language of administration; religious orthodoxy as understood in the West was to be enforced; and the Western provinces were to be reconquered and imperial rule reestablished throughout the Mediterranean basin. Roman law was to be codified and used as a consolidating force. Justinian's ambitions outran his resources. He was methodical rather than brilliant, and many of his aims were unrealistic and his achievements temporary. Some of them, however, were destined to affect the future development of Western civilization, and even his ephemeral conquests reminded the West that Roman power, living on in the Byzantine Empire, still had ecumenical claims.

THEODORA AND BELISARIUS. Justinian's name is commonly linked with that of his imperial consort, the empress Theodora, one of the most fascinating women of any period, and that of his faithful general, Belisarius, who effected the most important imperial conquests. Theodora was low-born, the daughter of a member of the "green" circus faction who entertained the populace with a trained bear during the intermissions between horse races at the hippodrome. She became an actress when this was synonymous with prostitution, acquired a notorious reputation, and after abandoning lovers on three continents, reformed her life and settled down in the capital where she earned her living as a seamstress. Justinian first knew of her in this situation during Justin's reign and fell in love. A law on the statute books prohibiting marriage between prostitutes and senators was conveniently repealed, and the couple was married.

Despite her unpromising early career and the scandalous rumors concerning her behavior even after her marriage circulated by her enemies, she seems to have been a faithful wife. She was even interested, as empress, in rehabilitating girls of the street like herself by establishing lodging for them in an abandoned palace, where, it is alleged, they were so bored they sought escape by throwing themselves out of the windows. Proud, willful, imperious, she is sometimes depicted as the real power behind Justinian's throne. She disagreed with him on a number of issues and meddled in politics and intrigued to get her way. Nevertheless, until her premature death of cancer in 548, she rarely swayed the emperor in matters of state.

More important to Justinian as a public figure was Belisarius, a brilliant commander and self-effacing subordinate. Belisarius deserved well of the government by virtue of his victories against foreign enemies. The emperor's support of his wars was not consistent, however, and Belisarius' campaigns sometimes failed of complete success because he lacked the proper resources. At crucial periods the emperor's confidence in his chief general wavered; he interpreted military checks or failure as caused by the lack of proper effort, and his suspicions were encouraged by Theodora, who was jealous of Belisarius' influence with the emperor. Belisarius was occasionally recalled from the front and replaced by other generals; at the very end of the reign he seems to have fallen into disgrace, only to be asked to defend Constantinople itself from barbarian attack.

INTERNAL PROBLEMS. Justinian sought to protect his subjects against the rapacity of bureaucrats and soldiers and to curb the patronage over peasants exercised by magnates. Attempting to centralize and streamline his government, he sometimes departed from the principle of separate civil and military jurisdiction in the provinces. Although undertaken on a piecemeal basis and hesitantly, this concentration of provincial authority in the hands of generals pointed the way to the gradual militarization of administration characteristic of the medieval Byzantine Empire. Despite his interest in improving the government, like most other late Roman emperors his intentions were better than their realization, and the men on whom he relied were frequently corrupt even if they efficiently collected the high taxes he needed to attain his goals.

Popular feeling exploded early in his reign (532) in a revolution originating among the circus factions, called the "Nika" revolt from their watchword, "Victory." Justinian and his entourage were surrounded in the palace as the mob controlled the capital, and the emperor himself seems to have considered fleeing into exile until he was galvanized into action by Theodora's determination to stay. Belisarius subdued the revolutionaries by using the imperial bodyguard, and concessions were made to the popular mood by dismissing certain administrators. This was the only internal challenge to his reign, and later hated but efficient bureaucrats like John the Cappadocian and Peter the Scissors reappeared to fleece his subjects.

A more serious problem was the Monophysite heresy. Both Justin and Justinian reversed the pro-Monophysitic position taken by previous emperors, and this reflected their own essentially Latin, or Western, orientation. Justinian in particular felt it his duty to demand religious conformity of his subjects; he himself was a learned theologian and laboriously investigated varying shades of religious opinion. In attempting to impose some kind of orthodox position on his subjects, he ran into insurmountable difficulties at the imperial court and in the provinces. Theodora herself was a passionate Monophysite and until her death continually intrigued to have the emperor influenced by churchmen of her persuasion.

Justinian tried to discover religious formulas on which both sides could agree to as orthodox. His efforts culminated in the fifth Ecumenical Council convened at Constantinople in 553, in which Pope Vigilius, summoned for the occasion, was forced to agree to condemnation of the so-called Three Chapters, anti-Monophysitic tracts, which could also be interpreted by orthodox theologians as heretical. The Council satisfied neither side, and toward the end of his reign the emperor was about to advocate as orthodox a doctrine close to the Monophysite—that the body of Christ was incorruptible—but he died before he could get it promulgated. The Monophysite problem was settled only when those provinces where the heresy was most strongly entrenched were occupied by the Moslems in the seventh century, and even thereafter echoes of it were heard in the famous iconoclastic controversy of the eighth and ninth. Justinian was implacable, of course, in his eradication of all traces of lingering paganism. Thus, he brought to an end an era in Western intellectual history when in 529 he closed the Neoplatonic Academy in Athens, founded some 900 years before by Plato. Its professors, for a time, took refuge at the court of the Persian king.

JUSTINIAN'S BUILDINGS. Justinian conceived of himself as a builder on a grandiose scale, and he filled his provinces with forts, public buildings, and churches. The destruction of large parts of Constantinople during the Nika revolt provided him with a unique opportunity to embellish his capital, and on the site of the burned-out Church of the Holy Wisdom (Hagia Sophia) he erected a magnificent sepulchre, which he expected would outdo the splendor of Solomon's Biblical Temple (see illustration, p. 483). This hope was realized, and the new Hagia Sophia remains to this day as a culminating achievement of imperial architecture. Designed by two architects of Asia Minor, Anthemius of Miletus and Isidore of Tralles, it was especially famous for its great dome, still one of the largest in the world, which was, however, shaken down in an earthquake in 558 and rebuilt on a slightly smaller scale.

THE LAW CODE.   Of much greater significance was Justinian's compilation of Roman law. He was also interested in centralizing and thereby controlling the teaching and interpretation of law by jurisprudents and suppressed all law schools except those officially recognized at Beirut, Rome, and Constantinople. Roman imperial government had always been inefficient in collecting the many edicts and mandates of emperors and senateconsults, as well as their commentary by either professional or private jurisprudents. The body of law was as tremendous as the commentaries and consisted of regulations still valid as well as legislation subsequently repealed. All of this information, some inconsistent with current legal practice or out of date, was scattered in archives of the central and provincial administration as well as in the libraries of law schools and jurisconsults. Under these conditions it was sometimes difficult to discover just what the current state of the law was, and even central administrators and emperors had only a very imperfect knowledge of precedents stretching back over hundreds of years of legal development. As early as the third century A.D. private compilations of the law were in circulation, but these were unofficial and incomplete. The first imperial codification of the law had been undertaken by Theodosius II in 438, but the Theodosian Code was restricted to edicts issued by emperors beginning with Constantine in 312, ignored the important commentaries of jurists as well as all edicts issued before that date, and in some cases did not even include all of the latter in the period 312–438.

Because the earlier code was very imperfect, Justinian set himself the enormous task of replacing it. He assigned a committee headed by his quaestor, the brilliant but corrupt Tribonian, the task of reading thousands of law books and millions of lines of legal texts with several goals: (1) the creation of a standard textbook or syllabus for the use of students; (2) the collection of commentary of jurisconsults on the law; and (3) the collection and editing with a view to their currency of all legislation still valid. The commission worked with great speed and produced the first edition of Justinian's Code in 529. Its work, hasty and inaccurate, required a revised edition, which appeared in 534 and incorporated Justinian's own legislation postdating 529.

The Code consisted of three parts, corresponding to Justinian's aims: (1) the Institutes, or legal textbook; (2) the Digest, or commentary of jurists on the civil law beginning with the second century A.D., but stressing those of the "classical" period of jurisprudence, especially Paul, Ulpian, and Papinian of the Severan age; and (3) imperial legislation still in force, beginning with the "freezing" of the Praetor's Edict under Hadrian and continuing down to Justinian's own day. This third volume, the *Corpus Iuris Civilis*, was divided into twelve books like Rome's original law. In abridging or editing edicts, the committee sometimes garbled the original meaning and intention of imperial legislation, which nevertheless reveals their understanding of it as of the sixth century. Because law was a living institution, it could not be frozen forever in a code, emperors in the future having to legislate for new situations. Justinian himself felt this need and even after 534 issued new laws (*Novellae* or Novels), which were appended to the *Corpus Iuris Civilis*.

Whatever its limitations, the Code was a useful compendium and significant summation of the most important Roman experience. It remained a basic document for the further evolution of law within the Byzantine Empire although knowledge of it in the West soon died out, as it was too sophisticated for barbarian successor states. It was reintroduced, however, into continental Europe in the eleventh and twelfth centuries, when its authoritarian tenor was found congenial for buttressing the claims to centralized power by emerging dynastic monarchies. The *Code Napoleon* guaranteed that it would remain the foundation of civil law in continental Europe; of European countries only England, with its Common Law, has generally escaped its influence.

THE WARS. Justinian's reign was noteworthy for his wars, by which he changed for a time the balance of power in the Mediterranean and reestablished his Empire's ecumenical claims. Had he been a different kind of ruler, he would perhaps have devoted greater attention to those frontiers most strategic to its survival along the lower Danube, but especially in the East where he was confronted by Chosroes, an unusually energetic Persian king. Belisarius' first assignment, in fact, was a Persian campaign in 527, but Justinian was soon hypnotized by vistas of Western conquest, and weakened the Eastern frontier to wage wars in Africa and Italy. Chosroes capitalized on his advantage, ravaged the Eastern provinces, and even took the Empire's third city, Antioch, in 540. Thereafter, Justinian tried to keep peace by paying the Persians a large subsidy, but even then outbreaks of fighting were frequent until a fifty-years' peace was concluded in 561. An indirect result of the Persian wars was domestication within the Empire of the silkworm and consequent development of a flourishing domestic industry of silk weaving. Raw silk had traditionally been imported from central Asia with Persians acting as middlemen. Persia was circumvented when monks smuggled into the Empire silkworms hidden in their hollow canes.

The situation in the West seemed to invite Justinian's interference. In Africa the Romanized population languished under the harsh rule of their Arian Vandalic overlords, and a revolution bringing to the throne Gelimer, who was anti-Roman, was the formal occasion to intervene. In Italy the death of Theodoric in 526 brought a succession of weaklings to the throne, and Byzantine intrigues appealed to the Catholic population and won support of the Papacy and Senate. Against the advice of his councillors, Justinian mounted an expedition under Belisarius against the Vandals in 533. A landing in Africa was effected, and the Vandals were defeated and Gelimer was captured the next year. In 535 Belisarius next attacked Italy. The campaign there was long and trying. The Ostrogoths found capable leadership under their kings Vitigis and Totila, and Belisarius did not receive reenforcements and supplies. The wars meant the ruin of many sections of Italy. The city of Rome was ravaged after changing hands several times. With aqueducts cut and walls breached, it entered the medieval period of its existence as a miserable place scarcely larger than a village; for one six-week period during the wars it was totally abandoned. The capture of Ravenna seemed to conclude the war in 540, but the Ostrogoths soon revolted, and not until 554 was Italy, for a time, once again pacified. In the same year Justinian's ambitions took him to the far western Mediterranean, where, in Spain, he intervened in a struggle between Visigothic princes, his armies subsequently occupying the southeastern coast. Although the Empire had increased in territory substantially by the end of his reign, vast areas, particularly Gaul, still remained unrecoverable.

The reoccupation by Byzantine forces of Africa, Italy, and Spain brought mixed blessings to the inhabitants. Some areas, like Africa, which suffered from continued incursions by Moors from the desert, were never really pacified, and the initial acceptance of imperial rule by the Catholic Roman population soon was tempered by the misgivings prompted by the expensive bureaucracy set up in the wake of East Roman armies. In Italy the tranquility of the Ostrogothic regime was replaced by a government that, even if Roman, was oppressive.

Justinian is frequently criticized for having unduly drained the Empire of its resources to fight his Western wars. Had his ambitions been modest, he might have strengthened the Empire against its threatening enemies in the east and north, but there is no indication that the Western wars were not well within imperial means, at least initially. A commentary on the strength of the Vandalic and Ostrogothic kingdoms is the size of Belisarius' armies, which numbered no more than a few thousand. However, it is undeniable that once conquered the reclaimed provinces did not pay their own way, and the continued military efforts there were a steady drain on imperial finances and manpower. So tenuous was Byzantine control over Italy that only three years after Justinian's death in 568 renewed attacks from the north by the Lombards soon reduced imperial authority to a few strong points, and in the next century Moslem onslaughts swept away the last traces of Byzantine rule in Africa and Spain.

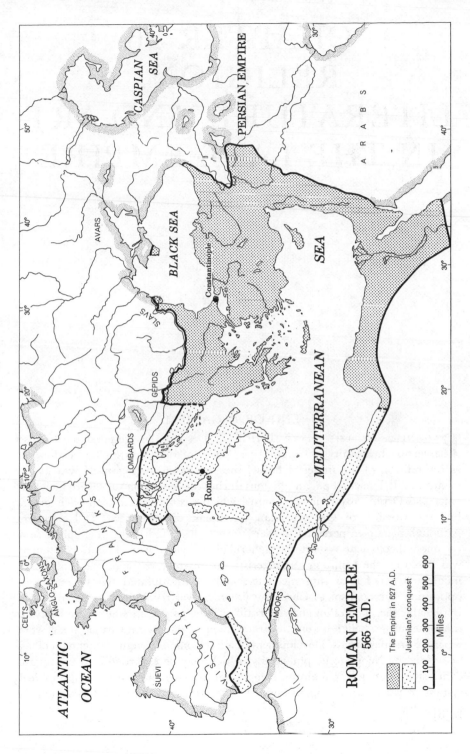

ATLANTIC
OCEAN

CELTS

ANGLO-SAXONS

SUEVI

F R A N K S

L O M B A R D S

MOORS

ROMAN EMPIRE
565 A.D.

The Empire in 527 A.D.

Justinian's conquest

0   100 200 300 400 500 600
Miles

Rome

LOMBARDS

GEPIDS

SLAVS

MEDITERRANEAN   SEA

Constantinople

BLACK SEA

AVARS

CASPIAN
SEA

PERSIAN EMPIRE

A R A B S

CHAPTER 26
RELIGION,
LITERATURE, AND ART
IN THE LATE EMPIRE

I. END OF PAGANISM

PAGANISM OF THE LATE EMPIRE. Despite the tremendous impulse given to Christianity by Constantine's policy of toleration and by its adoption as the religion of the imperial house, the extinction of paganism was by no means rapid. The chief pagan religions during the fourth century were Oriental cults and Orphic mysteries of Eleusis, which strongly resembled each other, but the worship of Greco-Roman Olympian divinities was still popular. Although paganism persisted in many forms, these had found their place in a common theological system through religious syncretism. This development was based on the common characteristics of mystery religions, each of which inculcated belief in a supreme deity, and was stimulated by the conscious opposition of paganism to Christianity, which was recognized as its common, implacable foe. The chief characteristic of later paganism was its tendency to monotheism—a belief in one abstract divinity of whom various gods were separate manifestations. Development of a harmonious system of pagan theology was aided by Neoplatonic philosophy, which may be regarded as the ultimate expression of ancient paganism. Neoplatonism was more than a philosophical system; it was then a religion and, like Oriental cults, preached salvation. It

[478]

was essentially a pantheism, in which all life was regarded as emanations of the divine mind.

CAUSES OF THE PERSISTENCE OF PAGANISM. Oriental and Orphic cults exercised a powerful hold over their votaries and their appeal resembled that of Christianity. Stoicism, with its high ideal of conduct, remained a strong tradition among the upper classes; Neoplatonism had a special attraction for men of intelligence and culture. Municipal patriotism where it still existed also fostered at least nominal worship of traditional city gods, especially among the curial class. Roman patriotism encouraged loyalty to gods who had made Rome great, and until about 400 pagan influences in the Roman Senate made it an indefatigable champion of the ancient faith. More potent was the fact that Greco-Roman literature was utterly pagan. This was the only material available for instruction in the schools and formed the basis of rhetorical and philosophical studies. Generally speaking, in the East articulate opposition to Christianity was intellectual and came from the schools of higher learning and from professors rather than from the governing establishment, because the Senate of Constantinople had been predominantly Christian since its foundation.

PERSECUTION OF PAGANISM. Constantine I sought to convert all his subjects to Christianity and to make it eventually the official religion of the Empire, although for political reasons he did not severely restrict paganism. Not until the reign of Theodosius I (379–395) did Christianity in fact become the state religion. In converting the classes that mattered, Constantine and his successors were aided by the heterogeneous nature of the new imperial service-nobility which, in contrast to the paganism of urban West Roman senators, was not a firmly entrenched aristocracy hostile to religious changes. The new ruling classes of the Late Empire were dependent upon imperial patronage for their advancement, and they tended to be subservient to the court in religious matters. Christianity soon became fashionable and respectable in the East through imperial support. The gradual conversion of the urban senatorial aristocracy in West Rome was not smooth; often relations between it and the court were embittered because of religious antagonism.

Constantine's sons, Constantius and Constans, initiated Christian persecution of paganism. They prohibited public sacrifices, forbade the adoration of statues of the gods, removed them from temples, closed many of the latter and turned them over to the Christian clergy. Nevertheless, they continued to appoint pagans to high administrative offices. Under Julian antipagan laws were abrogated, restrictions were placed upon Christians, and a vain attempt made to create a pagan state church. This pagan reaction ended with Julian's death and his successors, Jovian, Valentinian I, and Valens, restored Christianity to its former status, but adhered to a policy of toleration of paganism much like Constantine I.

With Gratian and Theodosius I official persecution of paganism was renewed. Theodosius was the first emperor to refuse the title of *pontifex maximus* at his accession, and he influenced his colleague Gratian to do the same. In 382 Gratian withdrew all official recognition of pagan worship, deprived the Roman priesthoods of public support, confiscated temple properties, and abolished the privilege of pagan priests. He also removed from the Senate house in Rome the altar and statue of Victory, which Julian had replaced after its removal by Constantius. For many senators this altar was the symbol of the state, and their spokesman Symmachus made an eloquent plea for its restoration.. Under the influence of his Christian advisers, Gratian remained obdurate. Later appeals to Valentinian II and Theodosius were equally vain. Although the brief reign of Eugenius produced a revival of pagan influence in Rome, the cause of paganism was already lost there. After his victory over Arbogast and Eugenius, Theodosius pardoned their supporters in the Roman Senate on condition that they accepted Christianity. By the fifth century the Senate was thoroughly Christian. As early as 380 Theodosius had ordered all his subjects to accept the Christian creed formulated at the Council of Nicaea in 325. In 391 he ordered the destruction of the image and temple of Sarapis in Alexandria, a step portending the end of paganism in the Eastern part of the Empire. The following year he unconditionally forbade pagan worship under the penalties for treason and sacrilege, and in 393 he ended the Olympic Games and their traditional pagan associations. Theodosius II continued vigorous persecution of pagans. Adherence to pagan beliefs was declared criminal, and in the Theodosian Code laws against pagans were included among those regulating civic life.

Many prominent persons continued to be secret devotees of paganism, and pagan philosophy was taught in the schools of Athens until they were closed by Justinian. Acceptance of Christianity was more rapid and complete in the cities than in the country. This gave rise to the use of the term pagan (*paganus*, "rural" in the sense of "barbarian") to designate a non-Christian, a usage that became official by 370.

The long association between pagans and Christians and the rapid incorporation of new converts into the Church exercised a profound influence upon Christian beliefs and practices. Pagan belief in magic contributed largely to Christian belief in miracles, and the development of the cult of saints was stimulated by pagan concepts of inferior divinities, demigods and demons. Finally, many pagan festivals were Christianized.

II. THE CHURCH IN THE CHRISTIAN EMPIRE

THE CHURCH AND THE EMPEROR. The right of emperors to legislate for the religious welfare of their subjects was inherent in imperial power and was accepted by Christians, clergy and laity alike. Constantine established the procedure regularly followed by emperors in dealing with problems that arose within the Church. He was willing to accept the decision of the clergy in determining the correct or orthodox position in dogma and discipline, but he took the responsibility of enforcing such decisions. His view was that, because he had been selected by divine will to rule Rome, it was his duty to God to prevent the spread of errors and strife within the Church.

To obtain the judgment of clergy on disputed matters, Constantine adopted the Christian practice of calling synods or councils. These councils had already been organized on a provincial basis; Constantine simply made them representative of larger areas, even of the whole Empire. His first council was the Synod of Arles called in 314 to settle the Donatist controversy in Africa. Bishop Donatus and his followers took the position that clergymen who yielded to the edicts of Diocletian's persecution and handed over Christian religious works should not be readmitted to their offices. Their opponents, headed by the bishop Cecilian, advocated pardon and restitution in office for those who repented. Strife between the two groups became so widespread that two sets of clergy appeared in almost all the towns of Africa and Numidia, and public order was endangered. When Constantine obtained control of Africa in 312, he recognized the Cecilianists as orthodox and reserved to them the benefits granted to the Christian clergy and congregations. The Donatists appealed to the emperor. After a small council of bishops, acting by imperial authority, decided against them, they made a second appeal. Constantine then convoked the Synod of Arles, a council of Western bishops, to settle the controversy. This synod condemned the Donatists anew and defined the orthodox position. The Donatists refused the Synod's verdict and for more than a century violently opposed Church and state alike, but the Synod of Arles set a precedent for future Church councils. The first Ecumenical or Empire-wide Council was summoned by Constantine in 325 to deal with the Arian heresy.

Procedure in the councils was modeled on that of the Roman Senate; the emperor or his deputy presided; all attending bishops had the right to speak and to vote; decisions were accepted and approved by the emperor, who transmitted them to the appropriate parties with his sanction that made them legal.

Constantine's successors followed his example of summoning Church councils to settle sectarian controversies, although, many like Constantius sought to influence decisions of the councils in favor of doctrines they supported. Since the general councils seemed to accentuate rather than allay strife, the emperor Zeno substituted a referendum of bishops by provinces, but his example was not followed by his successors. Justinian most effectively asserted his authority over the Church. He issued edicts on purely theological questions and matters of Church discipline without reference to councils, and he received from the populace of Constantinople the salutation "High Priest and King."[1] The Council of 553, influenced by Justinian, seemed to favor the heretical sect of the Monophysites, and provoked an attack upon the sacerdotal power of the

---

[1] *Archiereus basileus*. The title Basileus (King) was in common use in the Eastern part of the Empire from the fourth century, but it was not assumed officially by the emperors until 629.

emperor by Facundus, bishop of Hermiania in Africa, who declared that priests and not the emperor should rule the Church. This opposition, however, had no immediate effect, and Justinian remained the successful embodiment of "Caesaro-papism." The attitude of the Church toward the emperor's right to intervene in religion was generally consistent: that the clergy acknowledged the emperor's sole right to call ecumenical councils, but that in these councils the bishops alone had the right to speak and vote, that the emperor had the right and duty to enforce their decisions and the right to legislate in religious matters on his own initiative, provided that such legislation conformed to orthodoxy established by councils.

RISE OF THE PAPACY.   The Late Empire witnessed a rapid extension of the authority of the bishopric of Rome, which even previously laid claim to primacy among the episcopal sees. In the West the title "pope" (from the Greek *pappas*, "father") became the prerogative of the bishop of Rome after the fourth century. The papacy was the only Western patriarchate or bishopric with jurisdiction over metropolitan and provincial bishops, and it was the sole representative of the Western Church in dealings with Eastern bishops. At ecumenical councils the seniority of the Roman see over other bishoprics was recognized. The ideal of the papacy was to organize the Church on the model of the Empire, with the pope as its religious head. Despite appeals by Eastern bishops to the pope on questions of orthodoxy, the Eastern Church never fully admitted papal authority.

The claim of the papacy was pushed with particular vigor by Innocent I (402–417) and Leo I (440–461). Leo laid particular stress upon the primacy of Peter among the Apostles and taught that this had descended to his successors in the Roman see. On this ground he induced the emperor Valentinian III in 455 to order the whole Western Church to obey the bishops of Rome. Pope Gelasius (492–496) wrote to Anastasius that the power of priests was superior to imperial authority, but the establishment of the Ostrogothic kingdom in Italy and its reconquest by Justinian weakened papal independence. Justinian forced the popes to submit to his authority in religious controversies.

PATRIARCHATE OF CONSTANTINOPLE.   A papal rival developed in the patriarchate of Constantinople, which at the Council of Constantinople in 381 was recognized as taking precedence over other Eastern bishoprics and ranking next to that of Rome. This council also established the authority of

XXIII Interior of Hagia Sophia at Istanbul. *The Church of the Holy Wisdom, built after its predecessor was destroyed during the Nika revolt of A.D. 532, shows Justinian's taste and munificence. Its conception was original, combining as it did a circular core with what was essentially a basilica floor plan. Its present appearance reflects several centuries of use of the building as a mosque after the fall of Constantinople to the Turks in 1453. (Photo: Fototeca Unione.)*

other Eastern patriarchates, Alexandria, Antioch, Ephesus, Caesarea of
Cappadocia, and Heraclea in Thrace, and their dioceses. The primacy of
Constantinople was not readily accepted by Alexandria, Antioch, and Ephesus
—all apostolic foundations—whereas the claims of Constantinople to that honor
were more than dubious. Between 381 and 451 the patriarchs of Alexandria
successfully challenged the doctrinal authority of Constantinople, but its
primacy was reasserted in the latter year at the Council of Chalcedon. This
Council also recognized the bishopric of Jerusalem as a patriarchate. The
patriarch of Constantinople was made equal to the pope, a decision against
which Pope Leo I protested in vain. But the patriarchs of Constantinople
never acquired papal power and independence. However, situated as they
were in the emperor's shadow, they owed their ecclesiastic authority as well
as their appointments to secular authority. They rarely offered strong opposition
to the emperors. The position of the patriarch under Justinian has been described
as that of a "minister of state in the department of religion."

TEMPORAL POWER OF THE CLERGY. When Christianity became the
favored and then the state religion, it was inevitable that the clergy should
occupy a privileged position. Constantine the Great exempted them from
personal services (*munera*) in 313 and from taxation in 319. Clerics were expected
to abandon all worldly pursuits, and an imperial edict of 452 excluded them
from all employment. In addition to their authority in dogma and church
discipline, bishops also acquired considerable power in secular affairs. During
persecution Christians had regularly submitted legal differences among themselves to the arbitration of their bishops, rather than resort to tribunals of state.
Constantine the Great gave legal sanction to episcopal arbitration in civil
cases; Arcadius restricted its use to cases in which litigants voluntarily submitted
to the bishops' judgment. Bishops enjoyed no direct criminal jurisdiction,
although the right of sanctuary was accorded to churches, and they were
frequently able to intercede for refugees in them. To enforce moral and humanitarian legislation, the state called for episcopal cooperation.

The influence of bishops as religious heads of towns led to their being given a
place in the municipal administration. In protecting impoverished taxpayers
against imperial officers, they were more effective than the *defensores plebis*.
During barbarian invasions, when representatives of imperial authority were
driven from the provinces, bishops became leaders of the Roman population in
dealings with the barbarians.

Clearly, the growth of the Church contributed materially to the decline of
the Empire and to its extinction in the West. The Church hierarchy was a
magnet that attracted ambitious and able men who might otherwise have
served the state in civil capacities. The Church also attracted funds that might
otherwise have contributed to shoring up ancient institutions. Monasticism
provided an important alternative to city life and helped to undermine the
military and political structure of the state. The Church in the West contributed

to the feelings of defeatism that aided imperial collapse. Western Church fathers, by searchingly criticizing imperial institutions, seemed to imply that the Empire was not worth saving. They collaborated with the barbarians when the latter displaced Roman imperial leadership. In the East, however, the Church seems to have recognized the greater vitality of imperial institutions, to have thought of them as worth saving, and to have stood by New Rome in its struggle with its enemies.

III. SECTARIAN STRIFE

SECTARIANISM. The history of the Church from Constantine to Justinian is largely that of sectarian strife, which had its origin in doctrinal controversies. While the Western Church generally abstained from bitter theological discussions, adhered strictly to the orthodox or established creed, and devoted its energies to the development of church organization, the Eastern Church, imbued with the Greek philosophic spirit, tried to solve the mysteries of the faith and was a fruitful source of heterodoxy. Strife between the adherents of various sects was waged bitterly and frequently culminated in riots and bloodshed. Toleration was unknown, and heretics, like pagans, were classed as criminals and excluded from orthodox communion. Of many sects that arose in the fourth and fifth centuries, two were of outstanding importance: the Arians and Monophysites.

ARIANISM. Arianism was an attempt to express precisely the relation of the three members of the Holy Trinity: God the Father, the Son, and the Spirit. About 318 Arius, a presbyter of Alexandria, taught that God was eternal but that the Son and the Spirit were his creations. A controversy arose over the teaching of Arius that threatened the unity of the Church. Constantine intervened and summoned the Ecumenical Council of Nicaea in 325 to decide on the orthodoxy of Arianism. The Council accepted the formula that the Son was of the same substance (*homo-ousion*) as the Father, begotten but not created, which was the doctrine of the West. Arius was exiled.

The struggle was by no means over, for the Nicene creed was opposed by many Eastern bishops who regarded it as a radical innovation to doctrine. The leader of this party was Eusebius of Nicomedia. In 335 they brought about the deposition of Athanasius, chief opponent of Arius, who had been bishop of Alexandria since 328. After the death of Constantine, Athanasius returned to his see, only to be expelled again in 339 by Constantius, who was influenced by Eusebius. He took refuge in the West, where Pope Julius gave him his support. At a council of the Church held at Serdica (Sofia) in 343, there was a sharp division of opinion, but the supporters of Athanasius were in the majority, and he and other orthodox Eastern bishops were reinstated in their sees (345).

When Constantius became sole emperor (353), the enemies of Athanasius once more prevailed. The emperor forced a general council, convoked at Milan in 353, to condemn and depose Athanasius, while Pope Liberius, who supported him, was exiled to Macedonia. A new council, held at Sirmium in 357, tried to secure religious peace by forbidding the use of the word "substance" in defining the relation of the Father and the Son and sanctioned only the term *homoios* (like). Although adherents of this creed were not Arians, their solution was rejected by conservatives everywhere. In 359 a double council was held, the Western bishops meeting at Ariminum, the Eastern at Seleucia. The result was the acceptance of the Sirmian creed, although the Western council almost had to be starved into yielding. Under Julian and Jovian Arians enjoyed full toleration; Valentinian I pursued a similar policy, while Valens went further and supported Arianism.

Meantime three great Cappadocians—Basil of Caesarea, Gregory of Nazianzus, and Gregory of Nyssa—did much to reconcile Eastern bishops to the Nicean confession, and with the accession of Theodosius I the fate of Arianism was sealed. An Ecumenical Council met at Constantinople in 381 and accepted the Nicene creed, adding a definition of the nature of the Holy Spirit as one of the Trinity. Arian bishops were deposed and assemblies of heretics forbidden by imperial edicts. Arianism died out among the subjects of the Empire, although it existed for a century and a half as the faith of several Germanic peoples.

MONOPHYSITE CONTROVERSY. While dogmatic controversies of the fourth century concerned the relation of God to the Son and Holy Spirit, the burning question of the fifth and sixth centuries was the nature of Christ. Like the former, the latter dispute arose in the East, originating in divergent views of theological schools at Antioch and Alexandria. The former stressed the two natures in Christ—the divine and the human; the latter emphasized his divinity to the exclusion of his humanity, and hence its adherents were called Monophysites. The Diophysite Antiochene position was the orthodox view held universally in the West, where the duality of Christ was accepted without any attempt to define the relationship of his divine and human qualities. Beneath doctrinal controversy lay rivalry between the patriarchates of Alexandria and Constantinople and awakening national antagonism of native Egyptians and Syrians toward Greeks.

The conflict began in 429 with an attack of Cyril, patriarch of Alexandria, on the teachings of Nestorius, patriarch of Constantinople. Cyril, believing that the nature of Christ was human made fully divine, justified the use of the word *Theotokos* (Mother of God), which was popularly applied to the Virgin Mary. Nestorius criticized its use and argued in favor of the term Mother of Christ. Cyril won the support of the bishop of Rome, who desired to weaken the authority of the see of Constantinople, and Nestorius was condemned at the Ecumenical Council of Ephesus in 431.

The next phase of the struggle opened in 448, when Dioscorus, Patriarch of Alexandria, assailed Flavian, the patriarch of the capital, for having deposed Eutyches, a Monophysite abbot of Constantinople. At the so-called "Robber Council" of Ephesus in 449, Dioscorus succeeded in having Flavian deposed, and

Pope Leo I pronounced in favor of the duality of Christ, In 451 the new emperor Marcian called an Ecumenical Council at Chalcedon, which reasserted the primacy of the see of Constantinople in the East, approved the use of *Theotokos*, and declared that Christ was of two natures. The attempt to enforce the decisions of this Council provoked disturbances in Egypt, Palestine, and Eastern countries. In Palestine armed force was required to suppress a usurping Monophysite bishop. In Egypt, enforcement led to a split between the orthodox Greek and the Monophysitic Coptic Churches.

As opposition to the decree of Chalcedon still disturbed the Church, the emperor Zeno in 482, instigated by patriarchs Acacius of Constantinople and Peter of Alexandria, tried to settle the dispute by exercise of imperial authority. He issued a letter to the Church of Egypt called the *Henoticon*, which, while acknowledging the Councils of Nicaea and of Constantinople, condemned that of Chalcedon and declared that "Christ is one and not two." This doctrine was at once condemned by Pope Silvanus. The rupture with Rome lasted until 519, when a reconciliation was effected at the price of complete submission by the East and rehabilitation of the Council of Chalcedon. This in turn antagonized the Monophysites of Syria and Egypt and led Justinian to embark on his hopeless task of reestablishing complete religious unity by holding the Western and winning back the Eastern Church.

Justinian hoped to reconcile the Monophysites by an interpretation of the discussions at the Council of Chalcedon acceptable to them. This led him (544) to condemn the so-called Three Chapters, anti-Monophysitic doctrines. Although this step implied a condemnation of the Council of Chalcedon and was consequently opposed in the West, he forced the fifth Ecumenical Council of Constantinople in 553 to sanction it. Neither this concession nor still greater ones at the very end of his reign availed to win back the extreme Monophysites of Egypt and Syria.

IV. MONASTICISM

ORIGIN OF MONASTICISM. Monasticism (from the Greek *monos*, "alone,"), so marked a feature of religious life in the Middle Ages, originated in the ascetic tendencies of early Christianity, which harmonized with Eastern religious and philosophical ideals of a purely contemplative life. It also gave expression to feelings of despair over social and economic conditions. The chief characteristics of early Christian monasticism were celibacy, fasting, prayer, surrender of worldly goods, and the adoption of a hermit's life.

MONASTICISM IN EGYPT. Monastic life first developed in Egypt in the late third and early fourth centuries, when many men and women renounced a worldly life and began living on the edge of the desert or in oases. A leading figure in this movement was St. Anthony whose monastic career began in 285. His life, written by Athanasius, had a great influence on the expansion of monasticism. The reputation for sanctity acquired by Anthony and others attracted numerous monks. In this way the earliest monastic communities arose—gatherings of monks living in separate cells entirely independent of their neighbors.

From these unregulated colonies gradually evolved monastic communities whose members lived a common life within a walled enclosure under the direction of a single head, the abbot, who enforced rules governing their religious life and daily labor. The first such cenobitic monastery was established in upper Egypt about 325 by Pachomius, whose "rule" of monastic life was widely adopted.

SPREAD OF THE MONASTIC MOVEMENT. During the fourth century monasticism spread throughout the East, partly under Egyptian influence, partly as the result of parallel developments elsewhere. A peculiar feature of Syrian monasticism were the Stylites, who passed many years on the tops of high columns. Eastern monks were noted for their fanaticism, and they eagerly participated in religious disorders. Everywhere the abuses of unregulated monastic life led to the formulation of cenobitic rules and attempts to subject those monks who were not regular clergy to episcopal authority. The most influential organizer of monasticism in Asia Minor was St. Basil, who founded a monastery at Neocaesarea in 360. His rule, which discouraged excessive asceticism and stressed study and useful labor, became very popular.

WESTERN MONASTICISM. Athanasius brought monks with him from Egypt when he took refuge in Rome in 341. Monasticism then found a foothold in Italy, whence it spread to Gaul and elsewhere. The great organizer of Western monasticism was Benedict, founder of the monastery at Monte Cassino about 520. The Benedictine rule for cenobitic life required monks to read as well as to work and to worship. This stimulated the collection of libraries in the monasteries and made the monks the guardians of classical and biblical literature through the Middle Ages. As yet no distinct monastic orders had developed, each monastery being autonomous under its abbot.

MONASTICISM AND THE STATE. The spread of monasticism created a situation disquieting to the government. For one thing, adoption of celibacy by many thousands of men and women helped to accelerate depopulation—a trend already well established. For another, withdrawal of such numbers of able-bodied persons from the ranks of agricultural workers, craftsmen, and other occupations lessened productivity and accentuated the manpower shortage felt in both public and private services.

V. THE WORLD OF LETTERS AND ART

EDUCATION. The civilization of the Late Empire was a new cultural synthesis based on classical traditions inherited from pagan antiquity but combined with certain important new elements introduced by the troubles of the third century and by the rise of Christianity. In many respects the orientation of imperial culture had changed but little, and a cultivated gentleman of the second century A.D., such as Tacitus, would have found much that was familiar in the fourth and fifth centuries.

The Empire was still divided rather sharply into two cultural areas, one Latin-speaking, the other, Greek, both superimposed on various native cultures whose languages were unwritten peasant patois. Punic was still the language of the countryside near Carthage well into the fifth century, as was Celtic in parts of Gaul and Asia Minor. Because the survival of the two classical languages depended on the existence of the establishment that spoke and wrote them and supported a government that made their use official, in many parts of the Mediterranean world Greek and Latin did not long outlive the break-up of the Empire.

Another characteristic was the increasing linguistic divorcement between the educated classes of East and West. Latin, of course, was the official language of administration and law in both parts of the Empire, but it never made much headway in the East, even in official circles. The use of Latin in the East was gradually restricted to certain judicial *formulae*, a few commands and technical military terms current in the army, and the drafting of imperial edicts—even in the central offices of the imperial court at Constantinople. It was increasingly difficult to find either executives or clerks who were bilingual; anything more than a rudimentary knowledge of Latin was exceptional. Those few Greeks who learned their Latin well, such as authors writing for a Western audience or lawyers ambitious for a brilliant career, did so for such special reasons. Among educated classes in the West, Greek was still studied, but, it appears, rarely beyond an elementary level. Educated Latin speakers preferred to read their Greek classics in translations, and even in large cities it was difficult to find suitably trained professors of Greek. The increasing linguistic separation within the Late Empire was symptomatic of a basic cultural and even political division that had been latent from the beginning.

The educational system showed little change from the practices of the Principate. As earlier, the orientation of the curriculum was literary and consisted primarily of the study of grammar and rhetoric, although "liberal" studies normally included a smattering of other subjects. The literary works of men trained in the system tended to be drearily antiquarian, bombastic, and vapid. The state and municipalities did in many places pay salaries more frequently than before to professors of rhetoric because the government was interested in the training of literate administrators. The professors, however, regarded such endowments, which were frequently very handsome, as being only part of their legitimate income. They continued to charge substantial fees, thus excluding poor boys from their tuition.

Much is known about the teaching profession at the most advanced level from the many surviving orations and letters of the most famous teacher of late antiquity, Libanius of Antioch (314–ca. 393), who attracted to his school hundreds of the sons of the great and near-great during a career spanning most of the fourth century. Competition among professors of rhetoric was keen, and they frequently attempted to steal one another's students or blacken rival reputations. Other cities tried to entice prominent teachers from home base by holding out the prospect of better working conditions or higher salaries. Libanius himself was called to teach at Constantinople, but declined the blandishments of a post at the imperial capital and remained loyal to his native Antioch. He stands out as an attractive figure, genuinely interested in his students and in his city, the last representative of education in the classical Greek sense.

The normal rhetorical curriculum occasionally faced competition from other fields of study that were also of interest to the government, and some emperors preferred to staff their bureaucracy with technically rather than rhetorically trained personnel, much to the disgust of such professors as Libanius of the traditional educational establishment. Constantius II was notorious for promoting to confidential posts low-born men trained in shorthand, and Theodosius I seems to have preferred people educated in law.

The Christian Church did not develop schools of its own to replace those in which the subject matter was totally pagan, except in a few cases for the training of monks. Upper-class Christian boys were still steeped in a literature filled with references to pagan gods regarded by their faith as demonic and corrupting. Roman education was very conservative, and the impact of Christianity on the Late Empire did not immediately bring about a cultural revolution. For most people the fundamental literary monuments of the Christian faith, the Testaments and hagiographical writings, could still not compete stylistically with the pagan classics and were not worthy of a cultivated society steeped in classical literary conventions. Symptomatic of this situation was the attempt made by certain Christian clerics to convert Biblical stories into esthetically attractive poems by using the meters of pagan literature. This occured when Julian the Apostate forbade Christians to teach rhetoric, but the effort was solitary, feeble, and abortive.

SECULAR LITERATURE. The ascetic wing of the Church always insisted that the reading of pagan works should be totally prohibited. Such opinions were increasingly influential, but fortunately for the Church and for Western civilization more reasonable attitudes prevailed among educated churchmen although the clash between the esthetic claims of their own education and the fundamentalist demands of their religious conscience was often acute. St. Jerome emotionally consigned to the flames his editions of Cicero after an angel informed him in a dream that he was a Ciceronian rather than a Christian, but he could not deny the typically classical interest in literary craftsmanship that always colored his work. The influence of Cicero on St. Augustine was absolutely basic for his development as a Christian. His reading of one of Cicero's now-lost tracts, the *Hortensius*, led the cleric to embrace a life of religious speculation and influenced his notions on the immortality of the soul.

In many ways typical of the age was the Christian Ausonius of Burdigala

(Bordeaux) (d. ca. 395), son of a doctor and himself professor of rhetoric at that city, tutor to the young emperor Gratian, a man who parlayed his literary talents into high civil office for himself and his relatives. His verse is urbane, scholarly, and facile, and as a product of pagan literary culture closer to the Muses, Apollo, and Jove than to Christ. It is also unreal, placid, and contented, divorced from the serious problems that were wracking the Empire during his lifetime. Occasionally his poems are personal and even moving, as when he describes the beauty of one of his German slave girls or the Moselle valley filled with prosperous villas and fishermen.

A different type was Claudius Claudianus (d. ca. 404), a Greek from Egypt, who attained the status of poet laureate at the Western court towards the end of the fourth century. Claudian was at his best in epic verse in which he glorified the accomplishments of the emperor and his courtiers, and stylistically his better pieces are worthy of Vergil. Claudian resembled Ausonius in his fondness for classical pagan allusions and in his divorcement from the reality of the contemporary political situation. For him the Empire was still powerful, united, and flourishing, as if the government were not tottering under the impact of barbarian invasion.

It was the exception for Latin prose to produce work of lasting interest. History was still a subject that attracted the leisure time of Roman senators, but their works were curious, anecdotal, and antiquarian. One such work, the so-called *Augustan History*, was a series of imperial lives beginning with Hadrian and ending with Diocletian's accession. It allegedly was written by a group of senators during the reigns of Diocletian and Constantine although more probably it was composed anonymously late in the fourth century. The *Augustan History* is a peculiar combination of accurate and fanciful information, depending on the value of the sources its author(s) followed; it is nonetheless important because it is the only continuous literary narrative that has survived for crucial periods of the second and third centuries A.D.

An exceptional figure in what is otherwise a dreary period of secular Latin literature was Ammianus Marcellinus (ca. 330–395), who deserves to rank with Livy and Tacitus as one of the most important historians writing in Latin. Like Claudian, he was a Greek, born of a decurion of Antioch, and like Claudian he chose to write in Latin because he intended to reach an influential Western audience. Initially he pursued a military career, served among the *protectores domestici*, and in the course of his service saw many parts of the Empire and was in a position to know more than the average subject about events at the centers of power. Toward the end of his life he settled in Rome to write his history, in which he apparently conceived of himself as the literary successor to Tacitus. Beginning in A.D. 96 where Tacitus had ended his *Histories*, he traced imperial developments down to the Battle of Adrianople in 378. Only those portions of his work covering the years 353–378 have survived, but these were the most important as they represented the bulk of his book and the parts in which he could bring to bear his firsthand observations. Ammianus surpassed Tacitus in his objectivity and breadth of vision. Although a pagan, he could admire Christians who practiced what they preached; he attempted detached estimations of the good and bad qualities of contemporary emperors and did not refrain, for example, from criticizing even Julian the Apostate, otherwise his hero. Unlike Tacitus, he was interested in the impact of imperial rule on the provinces, and his pages are filled with penetrating indictments of the corruption and repression he saw around him. Ammianus is difficult reading because his style is so rhetorical and bombastic. A few parts are vividly realistic, however, as when he describes the frivolity of the upper and lower classes at the old capital in that part of his work known as the "Roman Satire."

The cultural interests of late pagan intelligentsia are perhaps best seen in the circle affiliated with the senator Symmachus, which flourished in the final decades of the fourth century. Symmachus, prefect of Rome in 384 and later consul, was famous among contemporaries as an orator and letter-writer. He was on friendly terms with Ambrose, bishop of Milan, with whom he competed unsuccessfully for the emperor's ear in his attempt to have the Altar of Victory reinstated in the senate house. His surviving orations are remarkable for verbosity without substance, as are most of his letters, mainly to recommend men seeking political preferment to his wide circle of friends. Epistolography, of course, was an accepted branch of literature since the days of Cicero, and prominent men wrote letters with an eye to their eventual editing for publication. Symmachus' letters, unfortunately, are documents filled with polite trivialities; of greater historical interest are his surviving reports to the imperial court in his capacity as city-prefect, but even these are turgid. He also figures in a series of possibly idealized literary seances described by the fifth-century author, Macrobius (ca. 430), in which Symmachus and his friends discussed pagan lore, dear to the hearts of the senatorial aristocracy. This circle was said to have produced studies of Vergil and Cicero remarkable for the variety and miscellany of their urbane observations. Sentimental literary antiquarianism among such classes produced the collation and editing of Latin classics, a tradition maintained for several generations in prominent senatorial families of the West, that preserved standard versions of literary works that otherwise would have been lost.

Literature of the fifth and sixth centuries continued trends noted in the fourth, except that the pagan element became increasingly insignificant. The only pagan poet of note is Rutilius Namatianus, whose work describing his return home to Gaul from Rome in 415 is mainly of historical rather than esthetic interest. A reader of Rutilius would scarcely imagine that the old capital had been occupied by Alaric only a few years before and that Gaul itself was overrun with barbarian tribes.

Interesting for other reasons is the work of the Gallo-Roman nobleman Sidonius Apollinaris (ca. 430–479) who, after holding posts in the civil administration, ended his life as bishop of Clermont-Ferrand. Sidonius wrote poetry, but his correspondence is more interesting because it reveals the state of the Gallo-Roman nobility as their province was slipping under barbarian rule and suggests their attitudes toward the new rulers. Sidonius' world resembles that of Symmachus, and his letters reveal a pleasant round of house parties at country villas with scarcely any reference to barbarian incursion and the collapse of imperial power.

The period of Ostrogothic rule in Italy produced two distinguished writers. Boethius, a Roman senator and civil servant under Theodoric until he fell from favor and was executed, conceived of preserving Plato and Aristotle from oblivion in a West that no longer knew its Greek by translating both authors into Latin and commenting on them. He got only as far as the *Logic* of Aristotle, but even this modest accomplishment was important because it was the only version of Aristotle known in the West until the Renaissance. While in prison awaiting execution, Boethius also composed a poignant account of the importance of philosophy in his own life, *On the Consolation of Philosophy*. Another Latin writer, a far lesser stylist, was Cassiodorus (ca. 490–583), who also served Theodoric and his successors. As head of the chancery, he composed administrative directives for his barbarian masters, but these are verbose, bombastic, and vapid. He also wrote a history of the Gothic nation, which has been preserved in a later epitome.

Greek letters were rather more flourishing in the fifth and sixth centuries. There was even a revival of historical interest, although this did not generally rise above the writing of chronicles. Worthy of mention is the pagan Zosimus, whose work, while bitterly prejudiced against Christian emperors, is nevertheless scholarly. The most important secular writer in Greek was the historian Procopius (b. ca. 500), thanks to whom we know so much about the reign of Justinian. Procopius was the private secretary to Belisarius, whom he accompanied to the Persian, African, and Italian fronts. He was thus an eyewitness to important events, which he reported capably. His histories of Belisarius' wars are precious documents, but he also wrote other works. As a panegyric to Justinian he produced a fulsome account of imperial buildings, yet all the while he was apparently nursing a grudge against both the emperor and empress. The reasons are obscure; perhaps he was resentful of their shabby treatment of his idol, Belisarius, or their failure to patronize his own career. In any case, he anonymously wrote a scandalous book called the *Anekdota* or *Secret History*, in which he portrayed Justinian and Theodora as fiends incarnate, capable of any depravity. The *Secret History* is not a sober work and belongs in the category of sensational literature.

CLERICAL CIVILIZATION. In contrast to such secular *literati* were the great Church fathers, whose work ushered in a Golden Age of patrology in both Latin and Greek. Clerics wrote on a wide range of subjects including history, saints' lives, sermons, and doctrinal tracts explaining or justifying their own viewpoints or instructing the faithful. The attitude of Christian historians was especially interesting. Once Christianity had become legal, then the preferred, and finally the state religion, they could afford to abandon *apologiae* of their faith and devote their attention to the history of its development. The first important figure in this respect was Lactantius (ca. 240–320), tutor to Constantine's sons, who wrote a bitter tract, *On the Deaths of the Persecutors*, in which he rather gleefully and vengefully recounted what seemed to him to be the bitter end of rulers like Diocletian and Galerius. More significant was the work of Bishop Eusebius of Caesarea, (ca. 260–340), especially his first-rate *Ecclesiastical History*. Eusebius revealed what was to become a typical Christian preoccupation: the writing of history on eschatalogical lines, not unlike those familiar to Judaism, in which all of history was seen as the unfolding of God's divine plan for His Chosen (now Christian) People. The ecclesiastical histories of Socrates and Sozomen in the fifth century illustrate clerical interest in such eschatological history although they also wove into their narratives accounts of secular happenings. Christian writers were generally not interested in writing the histories of secular figures, that they left to pagans. Exception was made for Constantine, of course, and Eusebius himself wrote a tendentious biography of the first Christian emperor.

Among the ecclesiastical writers of the fourth and early fifth centuries two stand out as literary giants: Jerome and Augustine. Both of them, like many other clerics, were converted from secular lives to religious introspection by crucial moments of spiritual truth. Jerome (348–420), a native of Dalmatia, was a student of law before becoming a cleric. He was early attracted to monasticism, spent time as a solitary in Syria, and, after a short sojourn in Rome as secretary to Pope Damasus, returned to a cell in Bethlehem where he remained until his death. Jerome had some very human failings. High-strung and sensitive, he was also irascible and capable of petulant criticism of spiritual and secular colleagues that frequently made him disagreeable. He was important to Church literature as a translator and exegete. An accomplished linguist, he mastered Greek and Hebrew, the latter as an ascetic exercise, in addition to his native Latin. To his great life's work, the translation of the Old Testament into Latin, he applied his philological instincts as he wanted to establish the standard text from variant Greek and Hebrew versions. Jerome's Vulgate Old Testament only attained widespread use later in the Middle Ages. His Biblical exegesis was characterized by deep scholarship based on knowledge gained from his first-hand acquaintance with Palestine, tempered by occasional flights of allegory.

A personality more attractive and certainly more subtle was Augustine (354–430), who has exercised a profound effect on the thought of Western civilization. Son of a *curialis* of the province of Africa, Augustine led an extremely worldly life as a student there and as a professor of rhetoric in Rome and Milan before his final conversion to Christian asceticism in 388. Developments leading him in that direction were tortuous and are revealed in his autobiography, the *Confessions*, a frank and even moving account of the conflict between his fleshly and spiritual inclinations and of the many influences on his life. These included his pagan education, in which Cicero and Vergil colored his philosophical and esthetic viewpoints, Manicheism, whose duality of Good and Evil he found attractive as a young man, and finally Neoplatonism, which led him back to orthodox Christian monotheism because it suggested that evil had no existence separate from good but merely indicated its absence.

During his middle and old age Augustine was bishop of Hippo in North Africa, and it was in this capacity that he crowned his career by writing one of the mightiest works of philosophy produced by Western civilization. Criticism of the Christian Church by pagans who alleged that abandonment of the old pagan gods had caused the disaster of A.D. 410, evoked examination of imperial institutions by clerics. The most important work in this genre was Augustine's *The City of God*, which developed an allegorical interpretation of the Christian view that history unfolded according to a divine plan consisting of interaction between God and His Chosen People. According to Augustine, the world was divided between the Divine City, composed of those essentially spiritual Christians who would earn salvation, and the Terrestrial City of the damned, whose interests were carnal. Augustine did not identify this terrestrial city with any particular state, but a thoughtful reader of his book could easily conclude that it was the Roman Empire. Augustine seemed to imply that Rome, although great, was nevertheless wicked because it was of this earth. The fact that the Empire had become Christian did not guarantee its eternal triumph over enemies; the Empire was irrelevant to the Divine scheme of things, since the allegiance of true Christians was to the Spiritual Kingdom, through which they would attain their salvation. *The City of God* opens a new era in the intellectual history of Western man with its emphasis on other-worldly values; its effect was defeatist for a civilization traditionally oriented to this world, and its audience could conclude that the Empire was not worth saving. More explicit expressions of this viewpoint are apparent in the works of the churchmen Orosius and Salvian, who bitterly condemned Western imperial rule and contrasted the evils of secular society with alleged barbarian virtue.

ART. Like *belles-lettres*, late imperial art and architecture were the products of both old and new developments. Classical traditions of painting and sculpture had been almost destroyed by the anarchy of the third century. When stabilized again in the fourth, several kinds of artistic styles were evident. Classical canons of expression in which the sculptor interpreted his subjects both rationally and idealistically were by no means dead and constantly appeared on sarcophagi, mosaics, consular diptychs (see illustration, p. 444), and other rather small objects made for emperors, their court, and the upper classes.

This classicism sometimes was mixed with and sometimes stood in direct contrast to less highly proficient folk art reflecting esthetic trends already observable in the third century A.D. Portrait busts of third-century emperors, for example, had been sculptured in a style that tended to represent not individual personalities but psychological, even transcendental types. This tendency was abetted by the emphasis on the charismatic nature of imperial power by Diocletian and Constantine. The result was work like a colossal statue of Constantine, the surviving head of which forcefully depicts power rather than a particular man (see illustration, p. 443). It seems obvious that for whatever reasons artists emphasized those parts of the body that were effective, especially the eyes, which are frequently depicted as large and staring into the distance. The remainder of the body tended to receive scant attention, and the portrayal of folds and drapery in clothing became flat and unrealistic.

Bas-reliefs perhaps show best the increasing influence of folk art. Early pieces were vigorous, lively, and rather naive; frequently they depicted genre scenes of the workaday world, but they clearly owed their inspiration to forces outside the classical Greco-Roman canon. Artists working in this tradition emphasized frontality, made their figures short and stubby rather than idealized and pretty, and were generally incapable of expressing perspective or foreshortening. The clash between such styles and classical ones is vividly apparent on the Arch of Constantine, which incorporates contemporary work by folk artists along with decorations ransacked from earlier Roman monuments done in the classical tradition. The contemporary reliefs make the emperor larger than his entourage because he is more important, and the soldiers and populace surrounding him are reduced to lines of dwarf-like and even misshapen figures (see illustration, p. 442).

Both technically and artistically the most interesting medium was now that of mosaic, especially those that covered the walls of Christian churches for the edification of the faithful. Late Romans, and after them the Byzantines, were extremely proficient mosaicists, and their creations mark one of the most brilliant phases in Western art history (see illustrations, pp. 469 and 483). Here, too, classicizing canons and those whose effect was more transcendental were in a constant state of interplay. Frontality, lack of perspective, and emphasis on those parts of the body that inspired awe and respect existed side by side with a more idealized iconography whose subject matter was occasionally lifted from the realm of pagan art.

Public building revived from the chaos of the third century and, like the plastic and pictorial arts, architecture reflected the mixture of sometimes slovenly and primitive technique along with new and inventive changes. Buildings were constructed and ruins repaired frequently by the simple expedient of cannibalizing material from other structures. After the closing of pagan temples, these especially seemed fair game as quarries, even though the imperial government, regarding them worthy of preservation at least as monuments or museums, attempted to protect them. Brickwork, formerly the pride of imperial builders, became unesthetic and sloppy, and elements of many buildings,

especially columns taken from other structures, presented a confusing jumble
of styles. Notable public works in the city of Rome, like the immense baths
built by Diocletian and the famous basilica begun by Maxentius but dedicated
by Constantine, brought to a grandiose conclusion the classic use of arches
and vaults to enclose space, and Diocletian's palace at Salonae was an interesting adaptation of the architecture of military camps to a luxurious private
residence. Much public building was undertaken, of course, at Constantinople,
but otherwise the financial exigencies of municipalities and the curial class
drastically reduced the amount of new construction.

The most significant new trend was in the building of churches, which
boomed with the legalization of the faith and the subsequent development of
many congregations. Although they expropriated and used many temples as
churches, these did not suffice by far and the need for places of worship was
pressing and immediate. The Church turned to the basilica as its most common
form. While perhaps uninventive from an architectural point of view, this
type of structure at least had the advantage of being simple, easily constructed,
and adaptable to the use of large congregations. As it ultimately evolved, it
was a rectangular structure with a nave and two side-aisles, lighted by a clere-
story and roofed with wood. As befitted a house of God, the basilica was lavishly
decorated with stories of the Bible and saints where they could be viewed by
the congregation both in the interior, typically with mosaics, and at the doors,
which were often sculptured pictorially in wood.

EPILOGUE

LOMBARD AND SLAVIC INVASIONS. In 568 the Lombards descended on Italy from Pannonia and occupied the Po valley and part of central Italy. The Romans were confined to Ravenna, Rome, and the southern part of the peninsula. Toward the close of the sixth century (after 581) Bulgars and Slavs migrated across the Danube, resulting in the Slavic occupation of Illyricum and the interposition of a barbarous, heathen people between the Eastern Empire and Western Europe. Early in the seventh century Roman possessions in Spain were lost to the Goths.

THE PAPACY AND THE HOLY ROMAN EMPIRE. The weakness of imperial authority in the West led to the strengthening of the papacy and its acquisition of political power in Italy. It was the papacy that kept alive in Western Europe the ideal of a universal imperial Church, for Western Christendom came to acknowledge the supremacy of the Roman see. Nor was the concept of a reestablished Western Empire lost to view; it was destined to be realized in the Holy Roman Empire of Charlemagne and his successors. Of great future importance for the development of European civilization was the fact that the Western part of the Roman world passed to peoples either already Christianized or soon to become so and that the Church, chiefly through the monasteries, was thus able to become the guardian of the remnants of ancient culture.

[498]

THE BYZANTINE EMPIRE. The loss of the Western provinces and Illyricum transferred the center of gravity in the Empire from the Latin to the Greek element and accelerated the transformation of the Eastern Roman Empire into an essentially Greek state—the Byzantine Empire. The Byzantine Empire inherited from the Roman its organization and the name Romaioi (Romans) for its citizens, but before 600 Greek had supplanted Latin as the language of government. This transformation further accentuated the religious differences between East and West, which led ultimately to the separation of the Greek Orthodox and Roman Catholic Churches.

THE MOSLEM INVASION. Before 650 Egypt and Syria were occupied by the Moslems, whose conquest was facilitated by the animosity of Monophysite natives toward the rule of an orthodox emperor. The loss of these territories gave fresh solidarity to the Empire in the East by restricting its authority to the religiously and linguistically homogeneous and thoroughly loyal population of Asia Minor and the eastern Balkans. This solidarity enabled the Byzantine Empire to fulfill its historic mission of forming the eastern bulwark of Christian Europe against the Moslems throughout the Middle Ages.

THE PROBLEM OF ROME'S FALL. For the student of Roman history, the major problem is to find the causes of the political, economic, and cultural changes that overtook the Roman World by the third Christian century and led ultimately to the collapse of the Roman Empire and classical culture in the West. An allied problem is to understand why it simultaneously survived in the East and later revived. Although all parts of the Empire were to some extent subject to identical stress, diverse pressures did not have the same effects everywhere, in part because they were stronger in the West, in part because the East could better withstand them. A truism sometimes forgotten is the fact that barbarian invasion was the immediate cause of the disappearance of West Roman political control. Why the West Roman response to this challenge was feeble is another matter.

Strategic considerations help to explain the West's failure to cope with the situation. The Rhine-Danube frontier was the principal area of penetration. Most of it was under the jurisdiction of West Roman emperors, and because of its length this frontier was the hardest to defend. The Eastern Empire had a strategic advantage because the lower Danube valley, although subject to frequent invasion, was not essential to its survival. Tribes entering the Balkans generally struck glancing but not mortal blows and then tended to move west into Italy. The East also had the luck not to be forced into fighting simultaneous wars on two fronts when it had its troubles in the Balkans, because the Persian frontier was exceptionally peaceful during the fifth century. Other considerations played their part. Constantinople was virtually impregnable and was destined to remain the nerve center and unassailable symbol of the Eastern Empire, whose heartland, Asia Minor, also escaped invasion. There was no such administrative focus in the West. Rome, twice taken and sacked in the fifth century, was never really replaced in the imagination of its subjects by cities like Milan and Ravenna, the usual residences of the imperial court.

The concentration of power in the hands of a series of generalissimos suggested that there was an alternative to imperial power in the West and that the imperial system was politically redundant. This feeling was abetted by the Western Church, which not only criticized local conditions but tended to cooperate with the barbarians whom it regarded as objects of conversion to orthodoxy rather than as enemies. This viewpoint contrasted sharply with that of the Greek Church, which already displayed an identification with secular rule that was characteristically Byzantine. Eastern churchmen at crucial junctures rallied the population against barbarian takeovers or otherwise in support of the government, implying that East Rome was worth saving. In the East, even though many fifth-century emperors were weaklings or undistinguished, the dispersion of military power in a college of equal-ranking field marshals provided no alternative to imperial rule, and even though the emperors were dominated by their courtiers, these latter were at least civilian personalities.

Perhaps most important were the resources of the East, which made it better able to withstand corruption from within and military pressures from without. The West was relatively underdeveloped, less populous and provided with cities, and less well endowed with the means to produce the kind of wealth on which antiquity lived. Certainly both halves of the Empire then suffered from depopulation, but the East had started with an initially higher population base and could better provide the manpower to support the economy and staff essential services than could the West. This may be seen in the problem of military recruitment. The West was forced to rely on the recruitment of barbarian mercenaries and federate allies *en bloc* because its supply of indigenous troops was inadequate. The East, on the other hand, could always rely on a nucleus of native cadres as it had excellent recruiting areas within or near its own borders in the Balkans, Asia Minor, and Armenia.

Important also was the development in the West of the senatorial aristocracy as a powerful vested interest that thwarted centralization and thus encouraged the collapse of imperial authority. The senatorial class in the East, however, as it was a more recent aristocracy, had not yet built up landholdings as vast as those of their western colleagues. Consequently, there were many more independent peasants in the East, and these latter, because they were relatively defenseless, could be made to pay their taxes or be drafted. Furthermore, although the descendants of relatively lowly men ennobled as senators in the East soon acquired aristocratic airs and occupied the highest offices, they did not exercise such a stranglehold over the government as did Western senators. In the East there were always many more executives who had risen in the bureaucratic hierarchy by virtue of imperial patronage. They owed their status to the imperial system as such, not to the connivance of senatorial vested interest, and even if they were frequently corrupt, they at least had greater allegiance to the central government and more reason to want it to work effectively.

APPENDIX

CHRONOLOGICAL
TABLE

B.C.	To ca. 9000	Palaeolithic Age. Cro-Magnon Culture.
	ca. 9000–3500	Mesolithic Age.
	ca. 3500–2500	Opening of the Neolithic Age and Introduction of Agriculture.
	ca. 2000	Earliest Palafitte lake villages.
	ca. 2000–1800	Copper-Stone Age.
	ca. 1800–1300	Beginning of the Bronze Age.
	ca. 1700	Terremare villages.
	ca. 1000–800	Transition to the Iron Age.
	Early or Middle VIII Cent. ?	Iron Age settlement on Palatine Hill.
	Late VIII Cent.	Greek colonization of Sicily and south Italy begins.
	ca. 725–700	Foundation of Carthage.
	VII–VI Cent.	Etruscan expansion in Latium, Campania, and the Po Valley.
	VII Cent.	Rome of the Four Regions.
	ca. 509	Overthrow of Etruscan supremacy at Rome. End of the early monarchy. The first consuls appointed. Dedication of the Capitoline temple.

ca. 493 (486)	?	Alliance of Rome and the Latins.
ca. 450	?	Foundation of plebeian Tribunate.
ca. 451–449 (444–442)		The Decemvirate. Codification of the Law.
ca. 445 (437)		Lex Canuleia.
ca. 435		Censorship established.
ca. 426 (417)	?	Office of military tribune with consular powers established.
ca. 400		Celtic migration into Po Valley.
ca. 392		Capture of Veii.
390 (387)		Battle of the Allia. Sack of Rome by the Gauls.
367 (363)		Sextio-Licinian Laws.
366 (362)		Praetorship established.
343–341		First Samnite War.
340 (338)– 338 (336)		The Latin War.
340	?	Alliance of Rome and the Campanians.
339		Lex Publilia.
326 (324)–304		Second Samnite War.
321 (319)		The Caudine Forks.
309–308		War with the Etruscans.
312 (310)		Appius Claudius Censor.
300		Lex Ogulnia.
298–290		War with Samnites, Etruscans, and Gauls.
295		Battle of Sentinum.
290		Subjugation of Samnium.
287		Secession of the Plebs. Lex Hortensia.
285		Occupation of the Ager Gallicus. Defeat of Gauls and Etruscans at Lake Vadimo.
281–272		War with Tarentum and Pyrrhus.
280		Battle of Heraclea.
279		Battle of Asculum. Alliance of Rome and Carthage.
278		Pyrrhus invades Sicily.
275		Battle of Beneventum.
264–241		First Punic War.
263		Alliance of Rome and Syracuse.
260		Naval Victory at Mylae.
256–255		Roman invasion of Africa.
250		Roman naval disaster at Drepana.
242		Battle of the Aegates Is. Office of *praetor peregrinus* established.
241		Silicy ceded to Rome.
241/40		Reform of the Centuriate Assembly.

241–238	Revolt of Carthaginian mercenaries. Sardinia and Corsica ceded to Rome.
237	Hamilcar in Spain.
232	Colonization of Ager Gallicus.
229–228	First Illyrian War.
229	Hasdrubal succeeds Hamilcar in Spain.
227	Provinces of Sicily, and Sardinia and Corsica organized.
226	Roman treaty with Hasdrubal.
225	Gauls defeated at Telamon.
224–222	Conquest of Boii and Insubres.
221	Hannibal Carthaginian commander in Spain.
220–219	Second Illyrian War.
219	Siege of Saguntum.
218–201	Second Punic War.
218	Hannibal's passage of the Pyrenees and Alps. Roman invasion of Spain.
217	Battle of Trasimene Lake. Q. Fabius dictator.
216	Cannae. Revolt of Capua.
215	Alliance of Hannibal and Philip V of Macedon. First Macedonian War.
214	Revolt of Syracuse.
214	Syracuse and Capua recovered. Roman Alliance with the Aetolians. Roman disasters in Spain.
210	P. Cornelius Scipio Roman commander in Spain.
207	Battle of the Metaurus.
205	Peace between Philip of Macedon and Rome.
204	Scipio invades Africa.
202	Zama.
201	Annexation of Carthaginian Spain.
200–196	Second Macedonian War.
197	Battle of Cynoscephalae. Provinces of Hither and Farther Spain organized.
196	Flamininus proclaims the "freedom of the Hellenes."
192–189	War with Antiochus the Great and Aetolians.
191	Antiochus defeated at Thermopylae.
190	Battle of Magnesia.
186	Dissolution of the Bacchanalian societies.
184	Cato the Elder censor.
180	*Lex Villia annalis.*
171–167	Third Macedonian War.
168	Battle of Pydna.
167	Achaean political prisoners held in Italy.

149–146	Third Punic War.
149	Calpurnian Law.
149–148	Fourth Macedonian War.
148	Macedonia a Roman province.
147–139	War with Viriathus in Spain.
146	Revolt of the Achaeans. Sack of Corinth. Dissolution of the Achaean Confederacy. Destruction of Carthage. Africa a Roman province.
143–133	Numantine War.
136–132	Slave War in Sicily.
133	Kingdom of Pergamon willed to Rome. Tribunate of Tiberius Gracchus.
129	Province of Asia organized.
123–122	C. Gracchus tribune.
113	Siege of Cirta.
111–105	Jugurthine War.
105	Romans defeated by Cimbri and Teutones at Arausio.
104–100	Successive consulships of Marius. Slave war in Sicily.
104	Domitian Law.
102	Teutones defeated at Aquae Sextiae.
101	Cimbri defeated at Vercellae. Province of Gallia Narbonenis organized.
100	Affair of Saturninus and Glaucia.
91	Tribunate of Livius Drusus.
90–88	Italian or Marsic War.
90	Julian Law.
89	Plautian Papirian Law. Pompeian Law.
89–95	First Mithridatic War.
88	Massacre of Italians in Asia. Mithridates invades Greece.
87	Marian revolt at Rome.
87–86	Siege of Athens and Piraeus.
86	Seventh consulship of Marius. Chaeronea and Orchomenus.
83	Sulla's return to Italy.
82–81	Sulla dictator.
77–71	Pompey's command in Spain.
75	Bithynia a Roman province.
74–63	Third Mithridatic War.
74–66	Command of Lucullus in the East.
73–71	Revolt of the gladiators.
70	First consulate of Pompey and Crassus. Trial of Verres.
67	Gabinian Law.

66	Manilian Law.
63	Cicero consul. Conspiracy of Catiline. Annexation of Syria. Death of Mithridates.
60	Coalition of Pompey, Caesar, and Crassus (First Triumvirate).
59	Caesar consul. Vatinian Law.
58	Cicero exiled.
58–56	Subjugation of Gaul.
57	Cicero recalled. Pompey Curator of the Grain Supply.
56	Conference at Luca.
55	Second consulate of Pompey and Crassus.
55–54	Caesar's invasions of Britain.
53	Death of Crassus at Carrhae.
52–51	Revolt of Vercingetorix.
52	Pompey sole consul.
49–46	War between Caesar and his opponents.
48	Pharsalus. Death of Pompey.
48–47	Alexandrine War.
47	War with Pharnaces.
46	Thapsus.
45	Munda. Julian Municipal Law.
44	Assassination of Julius Caesar (March 15).
44–43	War at Mutina.
43	Octavian consul. Coalition of Antony, Lepidus, and Octavian (Second Triumvirate).
42	Battles of Philippi.
41	War at Perusia.
40	Treaty of Brundisium.
39	Treaty of Misenum.
37	Treaty of Tarentum. Second term of the Triumvirate begins.
36	Defeat of Sextus Pompey. Lepidus deposed. Parthian War.
31	Battle of Actium.
30	Death of Antony and Cleopatra. Annexation of Egypt.
27	Octavian Princeps and Augustus.
27 B.C.–A.D. 14	AUGUSTUS.
25	Annexation of Galatia.
23	Second Imperial Act of Settlement by Augustus.
20	Agreement with Parthia.
18	Julian Law on Marriage.
16	Conquest of Noricum.
15	Subjugation of the Raeti and Vindelici.

	14–9	Conquest of Pannonia.
	12	Augustus Pontifex Maximus. Altar of Rome and Augustus at Lugdunum. Invasion of Germany. Death of M. Agrippa.
	9	Death of Drusus.
	6	Subjugation of the Alpine peoples completed.
A.D.	6–9	Revolt of Pannonia.
	9	Revolt of Arminius. Papian Poppaean Law.
	14–37	TIBERIUS.
	14–17	Campaigns of Germanicus.
	19	Death of Germanicus.
	26	Tiberius retires to Capri.
	31	Fall of Sejanus.
	37–41	GAIUS CALIGULA.
	40	Annexation of Mauretania.
	41–54	CLAUDIUS.
	43	Invasion and annexation of southern Britain.
	48	Aedui receive admission to magistracies and the Senate.
	54–68	NERO.
	58–63	Parthian War.
	59–60	Rebellion of Boudicca.
	64	Great Fire in Rome.
	65	Conspiracy of Piso. Death of Seneca.
	66–67	Nero in Greece.
	66	Rebellion of the Jews.
	68	Rebellion of Vindex.
	68 (June)–69 (January)	GALBA.
	69 January–March.	OTHO.
	69 April–December.	VITELLIUS.
	69 (December)–79	VESPASIANUS.
	69	Revolt of Civilis and the Batavi.
	70	Destruction of Jerusalem. End of the Jewish Rebellion.
	79–81	TITUS.
	79	Eruption of Vesuvius. Destruction of Pompeii and Herculaneum.
	81–96	DOMITIANUS.
	83	Battle of Mons Graupius. War with the Chatti.
	84	Domitian perpetual censor.
	85–89	Dacian Wars.
	88–89	Revolt of Saturninus.
	96–98	NERVA.
	98–117	TRAIANUS.

101–102	First Dacian War.
105–106	Second Dacian War. Annexation of Dacia.
106	Annexation of Arabia Petrea.
114–117	Parthian War.
114	Occupation of Armenia and Upper Mesopotamia.
115	Jewish Rebellion in Cyrene.
116	Annexation of Assyria and Lower Mesopotamia. Revolt in Mesopotamia.
117–138	HADRIANUS.
117	Abandonment of Assyria and Mesopotamia. Armenia a client kingdom.
121–126	Hadrian's first tour of the provinces.
129–134	Second tour of the provinces.
132–134	Revolt of Jews in the East.
138–161	ANTONINUS PIUS.
161–180	MARCUS AURELIUS.
161–169	LUCIUS VERUS.
161–166	Parthian War.
166	Plague spreads throughout the Empire.
167–175	War with Marcomanni, Quadi, and Iazyges.
175	Revolt of Avidius Cassius.
177–192	COMMODUS.
177–180	War with Quadi and Marcomanni.
180	Death of Marcus Aurelius, Commodus sole emperor.
193 January–March.	PERTINAX.
193 March–June.	DIDIUS JULIANUS.
193	Revolts of Septimius Severus, Pescennius Niger, Clodius Albinus.
193–211	SEPTIMIUS SEVERUS.
194	Defeat of Pescennius Niger.
195–196	Invasion of Parthia.
197	Defeat of Albinus at Lugdunum.
197–199	Parthian War renewed. Conquest of Upper Mesopotamia.
208	Caledonians invade Britain.
211–217	CARACALLA and
211–212	GETA.
212	Antoninian Constitution.
214	Parthian War.
217–218	MACRINUS.
218–222	ELAGABALUS.
222–235	SEVERUS ALEXANDER.
227	Establishment of Persian Sassanid Kingdom.

230–233   War with Persia.
234   War on Rhine frontier.
235–238   MAXIMINUS.
238   GORDIANUS I and GORDIANUS II. BALBINUS and
          PUPIENUS.
238–244   GORDIANUS III.
243–249   PHILIPPUS ARABUS.
247–249   PHILIPPUS JUNIOR.
249–251   DECIUS.
249   Persecution of the Christians.
251–253   GALLUS and VOLUSIANUS.
253   AEMILIANUS.
253–260   VALERIANUS and
253–268   GALLIENUS.
257   Persecution of the Christians renewed.
258   Postumus establishes Roman Empire in Gaul.
259   Valerian defeated and captured by the Persians.
          Gallienus sole emperor.
267   Sack of Athens by the Goths.
268–270   CLAUDIUS GOTHICUS.
270   QUINTILLUS.
270–275   AURELIANUS.
271   Revolt of Palmyra.
272   Reconquest of Palmyra and the East.
274   Recovery of Gaul and Britain.
275–276   TACITUS.
276   FLORIANUS.
276–282   PROBUS.
282–283   CARUS.
283–285   CARINUS.
284–305   DIOCLETIANUS and
286–305   MAXIMIANUS.
286   Revolt of Carausius in Britain.
293   Galerius and Constantius Caesars.
296   Recovery of Britain.
297   Persian invasion.
301   Edict of Prices.
303–304   Edicts against the Christians.
305   Abdication of Diocletian and Maximian. GALERIUS
          and CONSTANTIUS. Severus and Daia Caesars.
306   GALERIUS and SEVERUS. Constantinus Caesar. Revolt
          of Maxentius.

307	GALERIUS, LICINIUS, CONSTANTINUS, DAIA, and MAXENTIUS.
311	Edict of Toleration.
312	Battle of Milvian Bridge.
313	Fall of Daia.
324	Battle of Chrysopolis.
324–337	CONSTANTINUS sole Augustus.
325	Council of Nicaea.
330	Constantinople the imperial residence.
337–340	CONSTANTINUS II.
337–350	CONSTANS.
337–361	CONSTANTIUS.
343	Council of Serdica.
350	Revolt of Magnentius.
351	Gallus Caesar. Battle of Mursa.
354	Death of Gallus.
355	Julian Caesar.
357	Julian's victory over the Alamanni at Strassburg.
359	War with Persia.
360–363	JULIANUS.
363	Invasion of Persia. Death of Julian.
363–364	JOVIANUS.
364–375	VALENTINIANUS I.
364–378	VALENS.
367–383	GRATIANUS.
375–392	VALENTINIANUS II.
376	Visigoths cross the Danube.
378	Battle of Adrianople.
379–395	THEODOSIUS I.
380–382	Settlement of Visigoths as allies (*foederati*) in Moesia.
381	Council of Constantinople.
382	Altar of Victory removed from the Senate.
383	Revolt of Maximus in Britain. Death of Gratian.
383–408	ARCADIUS.
388	Maximus defeated and killed.
390	Massacre at Thessalonica.
391	Edicts against Paganism. Destruction of the Serapaeum.
392	Revolt of Arbogast. Murder of Valentinian II. Eugenius proclaimed Augustus.
393–423	HONORIUS.
394	Battle of Frigidus. Death of Arbogast and Eugenius.

395	Death of Theodosius I. Division of the Empire. ARCADIUS emperor in the East, HONORIUS in the West. Revolt of Alaric and the Visigoths.
396	Alaric defeated by Stilicho in Greece.
406	Barbarian invasion of Gaul. Roman garrison leaves Britain.
408	Murder of Stilicho. Alaric invades Italy.
408–450	THEODOSIUS II eastern emperor.
409	Vandals, Alans, and Sueves invade Spain.
410	Visigoths capture Rome. Death of Alaric.
412	Visigoths enter Gaul.
415	Visigoths cross into Spain.
418	Visigoths settled in Aquitania.
423–455	VALENTINIANUS III western emperor.
427	Aetius Master of the Soldiers.
429	Vandal invasion of Africa.
438	The Theodosian Code.
439	Vandals seize Carthage.
450	MARCIANUS eastern emperor.
451	Battle of the Mauriac Plains. Council of Chalcedon.
453	Death of Attila.
454	Aetius assassinated. Ostrogoths settled in Pannonia.
455	MAXIMUS western emperor. Vandals sack Rome.
455–456	AVITUS western emperor. Ricimer Master of the Soldiers.
457–474	LEO I eastern emperor.
457–461	MAJORIANUS western emperor.
461–465	SEVERUS western emperor.
465–467	No emperor in the West.
467–472	ANTHEMIUS western emperor.
472	OLYBRIUS western emperor. Death of Ricimer.
473–474	GLYCERIUS western emperor. LEO II eastern emperor.
474–475	(480) NEPOS western emperor.
474–491	ZENO eastern emperor.
475–476	ROMULUS AUGUSTULUS western emperor.
476	Odovacar king in Italy.
477	Death of Gaiseric.
486	Clovis conquers Syagrius and the Romans in Gaul.
488	Theodoric and the Ostrogoths invade Italy.
491–518	ANASTASIUS eastern emperor.
493	Defeat and death of Odovacar.
506	Roman Law of the Visigoths.
507	Clovis defeats the Visigoths.

518–527   JUSTINUS I eastern emperor.
526   Death of Theodoric.
527–565   JUSTINIANUS eastern emperor.
532   The "Nika" riot.
533–534   Reconquest of Africa.
534   Franks overthrow the Burgundian kingdom.
529–534   Publication of the *Corpus Iuris Civilis*.
535–554   Wars for recovery of Italy.
554   Reoccupation of the coast of Spain.
565   Death of Justinian.

GENEALOGICAL
TABLES

TABLE I. THE JULIO-CLAUDIAN LINE

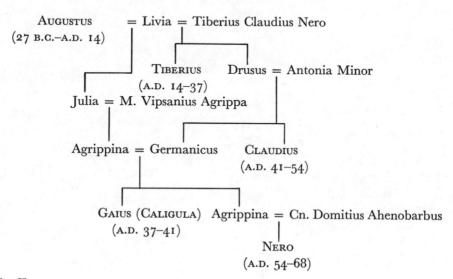

TABLE II. THE DYNASTY OF THE SEVERI

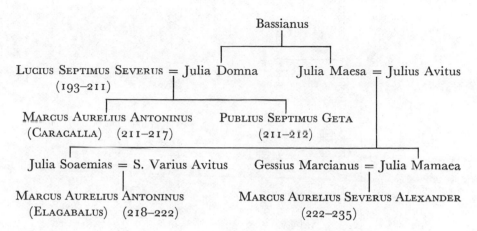

Bassianus

LUCIUS SEPTIMUS SEVERUS = Julia Domna   Julia Maesa = Julius Avitus
       (193–211)

   MARCUS AURELIUS ANTONINUS   PUBLIUS SEPTIMUS GETA
   (CARACALLA) (211–217)   (211–212)

   Julia Soaemias = S. Varius Avitus   Gessius Marcianus = Julia Mamaea

MARCUS AURELIUS ANTONINUS   MARCUS AURELIUS SEVERUS ALEXANDER
   (ELAGABALUS) (218–222)   (222–235)

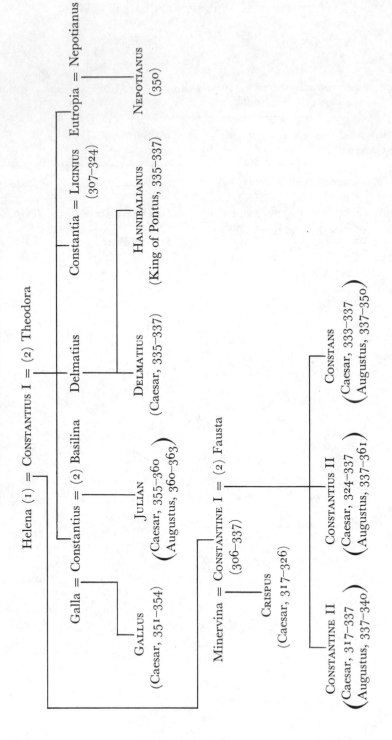

TABLE III. THE HOUSE OF CONSTANTIUS

TABLE IV. THE DYNASTY OF VALENTINIAN AND THEODOSIUS

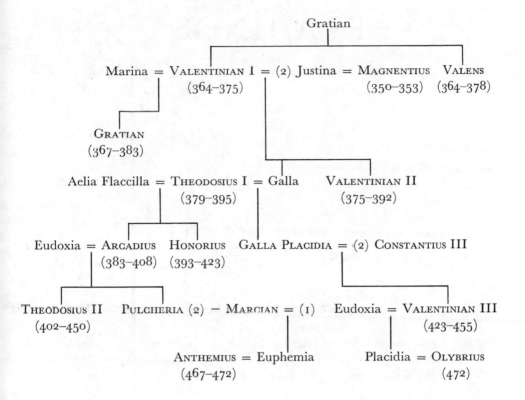

SUPPLEMENTARY READINGS

This list of supplementary readings is not meant to be a comprehensive bibliography of Roman 'history. Rather, it is conceived as a guide for students who wish to find basic and up-to-date discussions of problems and periods in the field.

BIBLIOGRAPHY AND SOURCES

Detailed bibliographies of the sources and modern literature pertaining to Roman History are given in the pertinent volumes of the *Cambridge Ancient History* (12 Vols., 1924–1939; currently being rewritten). Roman historical writing is also treated in H. Bengtson, *Grundriss der römischen Geschichte mit Quellenkunde* (1967); J. T. Shotwell, *The History of History*, Vol. I, 1939, Part iv; M. L. W. Laistner, *The Greater Roman Historians*, 1947; A. H. McDonald, "Historiography, Roman," *Oxford Classical Dictionary*, 2nd ed., 1970; H. Bengtson, *Introduction to Ancient History* (1970); and T. A. Dorey ed., *The Latin Historians* (1966). Recent trends in the literature of the field are surveyed in two important articles in Vol. 50 (1960) of the *Journal of Roman Studies*: A. H. McDonald, "Fifty Years of Republican History," and C. G. Starr, "The History of the Roman Empire, 1911–60." Chap. 12. The most important current bibliography of research on all phases of classical antiquity, including Roman History and Civilization, published yearly, is J. Marouzeau and Juliette Ernst (eds.), *L'année philologique* (1924–present). The most important encyclopedia of classical antiquity, now essentially complete, is Pauly-Wissowa-Kroll et al., *Realencyclopädie der klassischen Altertumswissenschaft* (1894–present). A recent, first-rate atlas is A. A. M. van der Heyden and H. H. Scullard, *Atlas of the Classical World* (1959). Their *Shorter Atlas of the Classical World* (1967) and M. Grant, *Ancient History Atlas* (1971) may also be consulted.

EARLY ITALY AND THE FOUNDATION OF ROME

Alföldi, A., *Early Rome and the Latins* (1964).
Altheim, F., *Der Ursprung der Etrusker* (1950).
Bloch, R., *The Origins of Rome* (1960).
Boëthius, A., et al., *Etruscan Culture, Land and People* (1962).
Cary, M., *The Geographic Background of Greek and Roman History* (1949).
Dunbabin, T. J., *The Western Greeks* (1948).
Etruscan number of *Historia*, Vol. 6 (1957).
Fraccaro, P., *La storia romana arcaica* in *Opuscula*, Vol. 1 (1956), 1ff.
Gjerstad, E., *Early Rome* (1953–1960).
Gjerstad, E., et al., *Les origines de la république romaine* (1967).
Holland, L. A., *Janus and the Bridge* (1961).
"Italy: Topography," *Encyclopaedia Britannica* (14th ed.).
Momigliano, A., "An Interim Report on the Origins of Rome," *Journal of Roman Studies*, Vol. 53 (1963), 95ff.
Mueller-Karpe, H. *Vom Anfang Roms* (1959).
———, *Zur Stadtwerdung Roms* (1962).
Pallottino, M., *The Etruscans* (6th ed., 1974).
Pulgram, E., *The Tongues of Italy: Prehistory and History* (1958).
Richardson, E., *The Etruscans. Their Art and Civilization* (1964).
Ryberg, I. Scott, *An Archaeological Record of Rome from the Seventh to the Second Century B.C.* (1940).
Schachermeyr, F., *Etruskische Fruehgeschichte* (1929).
Siegfried, A., *The Mediterranean* (1948).
Strong, D., *The Early Etruscans* (1968).
Thompson, J. O., *History of Ancient Geography* (1948).
Werner, R., *Der Beginn der rœmischen Republik* (1963).
Whatmough, J., *The Foundations of Roman Italy* (1937).
Woodhead, A. G., *The Greeks in the West* (1962).

THE REPUBLIC

Astin, A. E., *Scipio Aemilianus* (1967).
Badian, E., *Foreign Clientelae 264–70 B.C.* (1958).
———, *Publicans and Sinners* (1972).
———, *Roman Imperialism in the Late Republic* (2nd ed., 1968).
———, *Studies in Greek and Roman History* (1964).

Bleicken, J., *Das Volkstribunat der klassischen Republik* (1955).

Boren, H. C., *The Gracchi* (1968).

Broughton, T. R. S., *Magistrates of the Roman Republic* (2 vols. with supplements, 1951/2–1960).

Brunt, P. A., *Italian Manpower 225 B.C.–A.D. 14* (1971).

Carney, T. F., *A Biography of C. Marius* (1962).

Cassola, F., *I gruppi politici romani nel 3. secolo a. C.* (1962).

Dickinson, J., *Death of the Republic: Politics and Political Thought at Rome, 59–44 B.C.* (1963).

Dorey, T. A., ed., *Cicero* (1965).

Frank, T., *Roman Imperialism* (1914).

Gabba, E., *Appiano e la storia delle guerre civili* (1956).

Gelzer, M., *Caesar: Politician and Statesman* (6th ed., 1968).

——, *The Roman Nobility* (1969).

——, *Cicero und Caesar* (1968).

——, *Pompeius* (2nd ed., 1959).

Graff, J., *Ciceros Selbstauffassung* (1963).

Grimal, P., *Hellenism and the Rise of Rome* (1968).

Gruen, E. S., *The Last Generation of the Roman Republic* (1974).

Hadas, M., *Sextus Pompey* (1930).

Hardy, E. G., *The Catilinarian Conspiracy* (1924).

Holmes, T. R., *Caesar's Conquest of Gaul* (1911).

Kienast, D., *Cato der Zensor* (1954).

Lintott, A. W., *Violence in Republican Rome* (1968).

Marsh, F. B., *A History of the Roman World from 146 to 30 B.C.* (3rd ed., 1964).

Meier, Ch., *Res Publica Amissa* (1966).

Meyer, E., *Caesars Monarchie und das Principat des Pompeijus* (3rd ed., 1922).

Mommsen, T., *The History of Rome* (5 vols., 1894).

Muenzer, F., *Roemische Adelsparteien und Adelsfamilien* (1920).

Nicolet, C., *L'ordre équestre à l'époque republicaine (312–43 av. J.-C.)* (1966).

Ooteghem, P. van, *Pompée le Grand* (1954).

Palmer, R. E. A., *The Archaic Community of the Romans* (1970).

Proctor, D., *Hannibal's March in History* (1971).

Salmon, E. T., *Roman Colonization* (1971).

——, *Samnium and the Samnites* (1968).

Scullard, H. H., *The Etruscan Cities and Rome* (1967).

——, *From the Gracchi to Nero* (2nd ed., 1963).

——, *History of the Roman World 753–146 B.C.* (3rd ed., 1969).

——, *Roman Politics 220–150 B.C.* (2nd ed., 1973).

——, *Scipio Africanus: Soldier and Politician* (1970).

Seel, O., *Cicero* (1953).

Sihler, E. G., *Cicero of Arpinum* (1914).

Stockton, D., *Cicero: A Political Biography* (1971).
Suolahti, J., *The Roman Censors* (1963).
Taylor, L. R., *Party Politics in the Age of Caesar* (1949).
Volkmann, H., *Kleopatra* (1953).
———, *Sullas Marsch auf Rom* (1958).
Warmington, B. H., *Carthage* (1960).

PRINCIPATE

Balsdon, J. P. V. D., *The Emperor Gaius* (1934).
Birley, A., *Marcus Aurelius* (1966).
———, *Septimius Severus* (1971).
Bowersock, G. W., *Augustus and the Greek World* (1966).
Charlesworth, M. P., *Five Men: Character Studies from the Roman Empire* (1936).
Colledge, M. A. R., *The Parthians* (1967).
Dudley, D. R., and Webster, G., *The Rebellion of Boudicca* (1962).
Earl, D., *The Age of Augustus* (1968).
Farquharson, A. S. L., *Marcus Aurelius* (1951).
Grant, M., *The Climax of Rome* (1968).
Hammond, M., *The Augustan Principate in Theory and Practice* (1968).
Henderson, B. W., *Civil War and Rebellion in the Roman Empire A.D. 68–70* (1908).
———, *Five Roman Emperors* (1927).
———, *Life and Principate of the Emperor Hadrian A.D. 76–138* (1923).
———, *Life and Principate of the Emperor Nero* (1903).
Holmes, T. R., *The Architect of the Roman Empire* (1928–31).
———, *The Roman Republic and the Founder of the Empire* (1923).
Homo, L., *Vespasien, L'empereur du bon sense* (1949).
Huettl, W., *Antoninus Pius* (2 vols., 1933–36).
Jardé, A., *Etudes critiques sur la vie et la règne de Sévère Alexandre* (1925).
Jones, A. H. M., *Augustus* (1970).
Lepper, F. A., *Trajan's Parthian War* (1948).
Levi, M. A., *Nerone e i suoi tempi* (1949).
Marsh, F. B., *The Founding of the Roman Empire* (2nd ed., 1927).
———, *The Reign of Tiberius* (1931).
Mattingly, H., *Roman Imperial Civilisation* (1957).
Millar, F., *The Roman Empire and Its Neighbours* (1967).
Momigliano, A., *Claudius* (repr. 1961).
Orgeval, B. d'., *L'empereur Hadrien* (1950).
Paribeni, R., *Optimus Princeps* (2 vols. 1926–27).
Parker, H. M. D., *A History of the Roman World from A.D. 138 to A.D. 337* (2nd ed., 1958).
Premerstein, A. von, *Vom Werden und Wesen des Prinzipats* (1937).

Reinhold, M., *Marcus Agrippa* (1933).

Rogers, R. S., *Criminal Trials and Criminal Legislation under Tiberius* (1935).

————, *Studies in the Reign of Tiberius* (1943).

Salmon, E. T., *A History of the Roman World from 30 B.C. to A.D. 138*, (6th ed., 1968).

Scramuzza, V. M., *The Emperor Claudius* (1940).

Scullard, H. H., *From the Gracchi to Nero* (2nd ed., 1963).

Seager, R., *Tiberius* (1972).

Sedgwick, H. D., *Marcus Aurelius, A Biography* (1921).

Syme, R., *The Roman Revolution* (repr. 1951).

————, *Tacitus* (2 vols., 1958).

Timpe, D., *Untersuchungen zur Kontinuität des frühen Prinzipats* (1962).

Vittinghoff, F., *Kaiser Augustus* (1959).

————, *Römische Kolonisation und Bürgerrechtspolitik unter Caesar und Augustus* (1952).

Vitucci, G., *L'imperatore Probo* (1952).

Walser, G., and Pekáry, T., *Die Krise des römischen Reiches* (1962).

Wells, C. M., *The German Policy of Augustus* (1972).

Wright, F. A., *Marcus Agrippa* (1937).

Yavetz, Z., *Plebs and Princeps* (1969).

LATE EMPIRE

Alföldi, A., *A Conflict of Ideas in the Late Roman Empire* (1952).

————, *The Conversion of Constantine and Pagan Rome* (1948).

Arnheim, M. T. W., *The Senatorial Aristocracy in the Late Roman Empire* (1972).

Baynes, N. H., and Moss, H. S. L. B., *Byzantium. An Introduction to East Roman Civilization* (1948).

Bidez, J., *La vie de l'empereur Julien* (1930).

Boak, A. E. R., *Manpower Shortage and the Fall of the Roman Empire in the West* (1955).

————, *The Master of the Offices in the Later Roman and Byzantine Empires* (1924).

Brown, P., *The World of Late Antiquity* (1971).

Browning, R., *Justinian and Theodora* (1971).

Burckhardt, J., *The Age of Constantine the Great* (1956 ed.).

Bury, J. B., *History of the Later Roman Empire from the Death of Theodosius I to the Death of Justinian* (2 vols., 1923).

Charanis, P., *Church and State in the Later Roman Empire* (1939).

Chastagnol, A., *La préfecture urbaine à Rome sous les Bas-Empire* (1960).

Dill, S., *Roman Society in the Last Century of the Western Empire* (1899).

Doerries, H., *Konstantin der Grosse* (1958).

Downey, G., *Antioch in the Age of Theodosius The Great* (1962).

Ensslin, W., *Theoderich der Grosse* (1947).

————, *Zur Geschichtsschreibung und Weltanschauung des Ammianus Marcellinus* (1923).

Gibbon, E., *Decline and Fall of the Roman Empire* (7 vols., 1896–1900, ed. J. B. Bury).

Harmand, L., *Libanius, Discours sur les patronages* (1955).

Holmes, W., *The Age of Justinian and Theodora* (2nd ed., 1912).

Jones, A. H. M., *The Decline of the Ancient World* (1966).

———, *The Latter Roman Empire 284–602* (3 Vols., 1964).

Laistner, M. L. W., *Christianity and Pagan Culture* (1951).

———, *Thought and Letters in Western Europe*, A.D. 500–900 (1957 ed.).

Liebeschuetz, J. H. W. G., *Antioch: City and Imperial Administration in the Later Roman Empire* (1972).

MacMullen, R., *Constantine* (1970).

Martin, E., *The Emperor Julian* (1919).

Mazzarino, S., *Aspetti Sociali del quarto secolo* (1951).

Meer, F. van der, *Augustine the Bishop: The Life and Work of a Father of the Church* (1961).

Momigliano, A. (ed.), *The Conflict Between Paganism and Christianity in the Fourth Century* (1963).

Oost, S. I., *Galla Placidia Augusta* (1968).

Ostrogorsky, G., *History of the Byzantine State* (English ed. 1957).

Petit, P., *Libanius et la vie municipale à Antioche au IVe siècle après J. C.* (1955).

———, *Les étudiants de Libanius* (1957).

Piganiol, A., *L'empereur Constantin* (1932).

———, *L'empire chrétien* (1947).

Quasten, J., *Patrology*, Vol. 3: *The Golden Age of Greek Patristic Literature From the Council of Nicaea to the Council of Chalcedon* (1960).

Ruggini, L., *Ebrei e Orientali nell'Italia settentrionale fra il IV e il VI secolo D.Chr.*, in *Studia et Documenta Historiae et Iuris* (1959), 186ff.

———, *Economia e società nell'Italia Annonaria* (1961).

Seeck, O., *Geschichte des Untergangs der antiken Welt* (6 vols., 1901–20).

Seston, W., *Dioclétien et la Tétrarchie* (Paris, 1947).

Sirago, A., *Galla Placidia e la trasformazione dell'Occidente* (1961).

Stein, E., *Histoire du bas-empire* (2 vols., 1949–59).

Stroheker, K., *Der senatorische Adel im spätantiken Gallien* (1948).

Ure, P. N., *Justinian and His Age* (1951).

Vasiliev, *History of the Byzantine Empire* (1952).

———, *Justin the First* (1950).

Vogt, J., *Constantin der Grosse und sein Jahrhundert* (2nd ed., 1960).

———, *The Decline of Rome* (1967).

POLITICS AND GOVERNMENT

Abbott, F. F., *A History and Description of Roman Political Institutions* (3rd ed., repr. 1963).

Adocock, F. E., *Roman Political Ideas and Practice* (1959).

Boissier, G., *L'opposition sous les Césars* (4th ed., 1900).

Botsford, G. W., *The Roman Assemblies* (1909).

Crook, J., *Consilium Principis* (1955).

——, *Tiberius Gracchus: A Study in Politics* (1963).

Earl, D. C., *The Moral and Political Tradition of Rome* (1967).

Grant, M., *From Imperium to Auctoritas* (1946).

Greenridge, A. H. J., *Roman Public Life* (1901).

Gruen, E. S., *Roman Politics and the Criminal Courts* (1968).

Hammond, M., *The Antonine Monarchy* (1959).

Homo, L., *Roman Political Institutions from City to State* (repr. 1962).

Jones, A. H. M., *Studies in Roman Government and Law* (1960).

Kornemann, E., *Doppelprinzipat und Reichsteilung im Imperium Romanum* (1930).

Lacey, W. K., "Nomination and the Elections under Tiberius," *Historia*, Vol. 12 (1963), 167ff.

Laet, S. J. de, *Portorium* (1949).

Lambrechts, P., *La composition du sénat romain de l'accession d'Hadrien à la mort de Commode* (1936).

——, *La composition du sénat romain de Septime Sévère à Dioclétien* (193–284) (1937).

Larsen, J. A. O., *Representative Government in Greek and Roman History* (1955).

Magdelain, A., *Auctoritas principis* (1947).

Oliver, J. H., *The Ruling Power. A Study of the Roman Empire in the Second Century after Christ Through the Roman Oration of Aelius Aristides* (Transactions of the American Philosophical Society, Vol. 43, Part 4, 1953).

Pflaum, H. G., *Les carrieres procuratoriennes équestres sous le haut empire romain* (4 vols., 1960–61).

——, *Les procurateurs équestres sous le haut-empire romain* (1950).

Sherwin-White, A. N., *The Roman Citizenship* (1939).

Stavely, E. S., *Greek and Roman Voting and Elections* (1972).

Taylor, L. R., *Roman Voting Assemblies* (1966).

——, *Voting Districts of the Roman Republic* (1960).

Wirszubski, C., *Libertas as a Political Idea at Rome* (1950).

REGIONAL STUDIES AND MUNICIPALITIES

Abott, F. F., and Johnson, A. C., *Municipal Administration in the Roman Empire* (1926).

Arnold, W. T., *The Roman System of Provincial Administration* (3rd ed., 1914).

Bouchier, E. S., *Life and Letters in Roman Africa* (1913).

——, *Sardinia in Ancient Times* (1917).

——, *Spain Under the Roman Empire* (1914).

——, *Syria as a Roman Province* (1916).

Broughton, T. R. S., *The Romanization of Africa Proconsularis* (1929).

Chilver, G. E. F., *Cisalpine Gaul* (1941).

Collingwood, R., *Roman Britain* (1923).
———, *Roman Britain and the English Settlements* (2nd ed., 1937; *Oxford History of England*, Vol. 1).
Debevoise, N. C., *A Political History of Parthia* (1938).
Grenier, A., *Les Gaulois* (1945).
Gwatkin, W., *Cappadocia as a Roman Procuratorial Province* (1930).
Haverfield, F., *The Romanization of Roman Britain* (rev. ed., 1924).
Jones, A. H. M., *Cities of the Eastern Roman Provinces* (1937).
———, *The Herods of Judaea* (1938).
Jullian, C., *Histoire de la Gaule* Vol. 2 (4th ed., 1921).
Magie, D., *The Roman Rule in Asia Minor* (1950).
Milne, J., *A History of Egypt under Roman Rule* (3rd ed., 1924).
Mommsen, Th., *The Provinces of the Roman Empire* (1909).
Parvan, V., *Dacia* (1928).
Powell, T. G. E., *The Celts* (1958).
Reid, J. S., *The Municipalities of the Roman Empire* (1913).
Richmond, I. A., *Roman Britain* (1960).
Romanelli, P., *Storia delle provincie romane dell'Africa* (1959).
Stevenson, G., *Roman Provincial Administration* (1939).
Sutherland, C. H. V., *The Romans in Spain* (1939).
Welch, G. P., *Britannia; The Roman Conquest and Occupation of Britain* (1963).
Wheeler, M., *Rome Beyond the Imperial Frontiers* (1954).
Witt, N. J. de, *Urbanization and the Franchise in Roman Gaul* (1940).

LAW

Crook, J. A., *Law and Life of Rome* (1967).
Cramer, F., *Astrology in Roman Law and Politics* (1954).
Daube, D., *Roman Law: Linguistic, Social and Philosophical Aspects* (1969).
Garnsey, P., *Social Status and Legal Privilege in the Roman Empire* (1970).
Jolowicz, H. F., *Historical Introduction to the Study of Roman Law* (2nd ed. 1952).
———, *Roman Foundations of Modern Law* (1957).
Kunkel, W., *Herkunft und soziale Stellung der römischen Juristen* (1952).
———, *Römische Rechtsgeschichte* (2nd ed., 1948).
Martino, F. de, *Storia della costituzione romana* (1951).
Nicholas, B., *An Introduction to Roman Law* (1962).
Schulz, F., *Classical Roman Law* (1951).
———, *History of Roman Legal Science* (2nd ed., 1953).
———, *Principles of Roman Law* (1936).
Sherwin-White, A. N., *Roman Society and Roman Law in the New Testament* (1963).

SOCIETY

Abbott, F. F., *Society and Politics in Ancient Rome* (repr. 1963).
André, J., *L'alimentation et la cuisine à Rome* (1961).

Balsdon, J. P. V. D., *Roman Women: Their History and Habits* (1962).
———, *Life and Leisure in Ancient Rome* (1969).
Barrow, R. H., *Slavery in the Roman Empire* (1928).
Brunt, P. A., *Social Conflict in the Roman Republic* (1971).
Carcopino, J., *Daily Life in Ancient Rome* (1940).
Corte, M. della, *Case ed abitanti a Pompeii* (2nd ed., 1954).
Cowell, F. R., *Cicero and the Roman Republic* (1948).
———, *Everyday Life in Ancient Rome* (2nd ed., 1962).
Dill, S., *Roman Society from Nero to Marcus Aurelius* (1905).
Duff, A. M., *Freedmen in the Early Roman Empire* (1928).
Finley, M. I., ed., *Slavery in Classical Antiquity* (1968).
Fowler, W., *Social Life in Rome in the Days of Cicero* (1909).
Friedlaender, L., *Roman Life and Manners under the Early Empire* (1908).
Hands, A. R., *Charities and Social Aid in Greece and Rome* (1968).
Hill, H., *The Roman Middle Class in the Republican Period* (1952).
MacMullen, R., *Enemies of the Roman Order* (1966).
———, *Roman Social Relations (50 B.C.–A.D. 284)* (1973).
Pomeroy, S. B., *Goddesses, Whores, Wives and Slaves. Women in Classical Antiquity* (1975).
Rowell, H. T., *Rome in the Augustan Age* (1962).
Syme, R., *Colonial Elites* (1958).
Treggiari, S., *Roman Freedmen During the Late Republic* (1969).
Weaver, P. R. C., *Familia Caesaris: A Social Study of the Emperor's Freedmen and Slaves* (1969).
Wiseman, T. P., *New Men in the Roman Senate* (1971).

ECONOMY

Adams, L., *A Study in the Commerce of Latium from the Early Iron Age through the Sixth Century B.C.* (1921).
Bolin, S., *State and Currency in the Roman Empire to 300 A.D.* (1958).
Burford, A., *Craftsmen in Greek and Roman Society* (1972).
Cary, M., and Warmington, E. H., *The Ancient Explorers* (1929).
Casson, L., *The Ancient Mariners: Seafarers and Sea Fighters of the Mediterranean in Ancient Times* (1959).
Charlesworth, M. P., *Trade Routes and Commerce of the Roman Empire* (2nd ed., 1926).
Duncan-Jones, R., *The Economy of the Roman Empire* (1974).
Finley, M. I., *The Ancient Economy* (1973).
Frank, T., *Economic History of Rome* (2nd ed., 1927).
———, *Economic Survey of Ancient Rome* (5 vols., 1933–40).
Grant, M., *Roman History from Coins* (1958).
Hatzfeld, J., *Les trafiquants italiens dans l'orient hellénique* (1919).
Heichelheim, F., *An Economic History of the Ancient World* (2 Vols., 1958–1964).

Heitland, W. E., *Agricola, A Study of Agriculture and Rustic Life in the Greco-Roman World from the Standpoint of Labour* (1931).

Klausing, R., *The Roman Colonate* (1925).

Loane, H. J., *Industry and Commerce of the City of Rome (50 B.C.–200 A.D.)* (1938).

Louis, P., *Ancient Rome at Work* (1927).

Mattingly, H., *Roman Coins* (2nd ed., 1960).

Maxey, M., *Occupations of the Lower Classes in Roman Society* (1928).

Meiggs, R., *Roman Ostia* (1960).

Milne, J. G., *The Development of Roman Coinage* (1937).

Rickman, G. E., *Roman Granaries and Store Buildings* (1971).

Robertis, F. M. de, *Il diritto associativo romano dai collegi della repubblica alle corporazioni del basso impero* (1938).

Rostovtzeff, M., *Caravan Cities* (1932).

———, *Social and Economic History of the Roman Empire* (2nd ed., 1957).

———, *Studien zur Geschichte des römischen Kolonats* (1910).

Sutherland, C. H. V., *Coinage in Roman Imperial Policy, 31 B.C.–A.D. 68* (1951).

Sydenham, E. A., *The Coinage of the Roman Republic* (1952).

Thomsen, R., *Early Roman Coinage* (3 vols., 1957–61).

Waltzing, J. P., *Etude historique sur les corporations professionelles chez les Romains* (4 vols. 1895–1900).

Warmington, E. H., *The Commerce Between the Roman Empire and India* (1928).

White, K. D., *Roman Farming* (1970).

ROMAN CIVILIZATION

Adcock, F. E., *Caesar as a Man of Letters* (1956).

Allbutt, T., *Greek Medicine in Rome* (1921).

Bailey, C., *Lucretius* (3 vols., 1947).

Baynes, N. H., *The Historia Augusta, Its Date and Purpose* (1926).

Beare, W., *The Roman Stage* (1950).

Bieber, M., *The History of the Greek and Roman Theater* (2nd ed., 1961).

Boissier, G., *Cicero and His Friends* (1929 ed.).

Bowersock, G. W., *Greek Sophists in the Roman Empire* (1969).

Cameron, A., *Claudian* (1970).

Clarke, M. L., *The Roman Mind* (1956).

Dorey, T. A., ed., *Latin Biography* (1971).

———, *The Latin Historians* (1966).

Dorey, T. A., and Dudley, D. P., eds., *Roman Drama* (1965).

Duff, J. W., *A Literary History of Rome from the Origins to the Close of the Golden Age* (repr., 1953).

———, *A Literary History of Rome in the Silver Age* (rev. ed., 1959).

———, *Roman Satire* (1937).

Earl, D. C., *The Political Thought of Sallust* (1961).

Edelstein, L., *The Meaning of Stoicism* (1966).

Evans, G. A. S., *Procopius* (1972).

Fraenkel, E., *Horace* (1957).

Frank, T., *Life and Literature in the Roman Republic* (1930).

Fuchs, H., *Der geistige Widerstand gegen Rom in der antiken Welt* (1938).

Glover, T., *Life and Letters in the Fourth Century* (1901).

Grant, M., *The World of Rome* (1959).

Haarhoff, T. J., *The Schools of Gaul* (1920).

Hadas, M., *History of Latin Literature* (1952).

————, *Stoic Philosophy of Seneca* (1958).

Havelock, E. A., *The Lyric Genius of Catullus* (1939).

Heitland, W., *The Roman Fate* (1922).

Highet, G., *Poets in a Landscape* (1957).

Hunt, H. A. K., *The Humanism of Cicero* (1954).

Jones, T., *The Silver Plated Age* (1962).

Kennedy, G., *The Art of Rhetoric in the Roman World* (1972).

Klingner, F., *Römische Geisteswelt* (4th ed., 1961).

Kroll, W., *Die Kultur der ciceronischen Zeit* (1933).

Laistner, M. L. W., *The Greater Roman Historians* (1947).

Marrou, H. L., *A History of Education in Antiquity* (1956).

Mendell, C. W., *Latin Poetry. The Age of Rhetoric and Satire* (1967).

Millar, F., *A Study of Cassius Dio* (1964).

Otis, B., *Vergil. A Study of Civilized Poetry* (1963).

Rose, H. J., *A Handbook of Latin Literature* (2nd ed., 1949).

Seel, O., *Cicero* (1953).

Sihler, E. G., *Cicero of Arpinum* (1914).

Sikes, E. E., *Lucretius, Poet and Philosopher* (1936).

Sinclair, T. A., and Wright, F. A., *A History of the Later Latin Literature* (1931).

Stahl, W., *Roman Science* (1962).

Starr, C., *Civilization and the Caesars: the Intellectual Revolution in the Roman Empire* (1954).

Syme, R., *Emperors and Biography: Studies in the Historia Augusta* (1971).

————, *Ammianus and the Historia Augusta* (1968).

————, *Sallust* (1964).

————, *Tacitus* (2 vols., 1958).

Walbank, F., *Polybius* (1972).

Walsh, P. G., *Livy: His Historical Aims and Methods* (1961).

Wilkinson, *Horace and his Lyric Poetry* (2nd ed., 1951).

————, *Ovid Recalled* (1955).

Williams, G., *Tradition and Originality in Roman Poetry* (1968).

ART AND ARCHITECTURE

Boëthius, A., *The Golden House of Nero* (1960).

————, *Roman and Greek Town Architecture* (1948).

Brown, F. E., *Roman Architecture* (1961).

Encyclopaedia of World Art (1959–   ); Articles: "Etrusco-Italian" (M. Pallottino), "Hellenistic-Roman," (O. Vessberg), "Italo-Roman Folk Art" (G. Mansuelli).

L'Orange, H. P., *Art Forms and Civic Life in the Late Roman Empire* (1965).

Macdonald, W., *The Architecture of the Roman Empire* (1969).

Maiuri, A., *Roman Painting* (1953).

Morey, C. R., *Early Christian Art* (1942).

Nash, E., *Pictorial Dictionary of Ancient Rome* (2 vols., 1961–62).

Richter, G. M. A., *Ancient Italy* (1955).

Robertson, D. S., *Greek and Roman Architecture* (2nd ed., 1943).

Strong, E., *Art in Ancient Rome* (2 vols., 2nd ed., 1930).

———, *Roman Sculpture from Augustus to Constantine* (1907).

Toynbee, J. M. C., *The Hadrianic School: A Chapter in the History of Greek Art* (1934).

Walters, H. B., *Art in Ancient Rome* (2nd ed., 1930).

RELIGION

Altheim, F., *History of Roman Religion* (1938).

Bailey, C., *Phases in the Religion of Ancient Rome* (1932).

Bell, H. I., *Cults and Creeds in Greco-Roman Egypt* (1953).

Cumont, F., *Oriental Religions in Roman Paganism* (repr. 1956).

Ferguson, J., *The Religions of the Roman Empire* (1970).

Fowler, W. W., *Religious Experience of the Roman People* (1911).

Glover, T. R., *The Conflict of Religions in the Early Roman Empire* (2nd ed., 1909).

Latte, K., *Römische Religionsgeschichte* (1960).

Ogilvie, R. H., *The Romans and their Gods in the Age of Augustus* (1969).

Rose, H. J., *Ancient Roman Religion* (1948).

———, "Roman Religion, 1911–1960," *Journal of Roman Studies*, Vol. 50 (1960), 161ff.

Scott, K., *The Imperial Cult under the Flavians* (1936).

Taylor, L. R., *The Divinity of the Roman Emperor* (1931).

JUDAISM AND CHRISTIANITY

Baynes, N. H., *The Early Church and Social Life* (1927).

Burrows, M., *More Light on the Dead Sea Scrolls* (1958).

Dodds, E. R., *Pagan and Christian in an Age of Anxiety* (1965).

Farmer, W. R., *Maccabees, Zealots, and Josephus: An Inquiry into Jewish Nationalism in the Greco-Roman Period* (1956).

Frend, W., *Martyrdom and Persecution in the Early Church* (1967).

✓Grant, M., *The Jews in the Roman World* (1973).

Grant, R. M., *Gnosticism and Early Christianity* (1959).

Halliday, W. R., *The Pagan Background of Early Christianity* (1925).

Harnack, A., *Mission und Ausbreitung des Christentums in den ersten drei Jahrhunderten* (2 vols., 4th ed., 1924).

Hexter, J. A., *The Judaeo Christian Tradition* (1966).

Jaeger, W., *Early Christianity and Greek Paideia* (1961).

Kidd, B. J., *History of the Church to 461 A.D.* (1922).

Leon, H. J., *The Jews of Ancient Rome* (1960).

Lietzman, H. A., *A History of the Early Church* (2 vols., 1953).

Moore, G. F., *Judaism in the first Centuries of the Christian Era* (2 vols., 1930–32).

Mowry, L., *The Dead Sea Scrolls and the Early Church* (1962).

Nock, A. D., *Conversion: the Old and New in Religion from Alexander the Great to Augustine of Hippo* (1933).

——, *Early Gentile Christianity and Its Hellenistic Background*, in *Essays on the Trinity and the Incarnation* (1928) (ed. A. Rawlinson).

Oesterly, W. O. E., *A History of Israel*, Vol. 2, (1932).

ARMY AND NAVY

Adcock, F. E., *The Roman Art of War Under the Republic* (1940).

Baillie-Reynolds, P. K., *The Vigiles of Imperial Rome* (1926).

Berchem, D. van, *L'armée de Dioclétien et la réforme Constantinienne* (1952).

Birley, E., *Roman Britain and the Roman Army* (1953).

Cheesman, G. L., *The Auxilia of the Roman Imperial Army* (1914).

Durry, M., *Les cohortes prétoriennes* (1938).

Forni, G., *Il reclutamento delle legioni da Augusto a Diocleziano* (1953).

Grosse, R. *Römische Militärgeschichte von Gallienus bis zum Beginn der byzantinischen Themenverfassung* (1930).

Karayannopulos, J., *Die Entstehung der byzantinischen Themenordnung* (1959).

Kraft, K., *Zur Rekrutierung der Alen und Kohorten an Rhein und Donau* (1951).

MacMullen, R., *Soldier and Civilian in the Later Roman Empire* (1963).

Parker, H. M. D., *The Roman Legions* (2nd ed., 1958).

Pinsent, John, *Military Tribunes and Plebeian Consuls: The Fasti from 444 V to 342 V* (1974).

Smith, R. E., *Service in the Post-Marian Roman Army* (1958).

Starr, C. G., *The Roman Imperial Navy* (2nd ed., 1959).

Suolahti, J., *The Junior Officers of the Roman Army in the Republican Period* (1955).

Thiel, J. H. *A History of Roman Sea-Power Before the Second Punic War* (1954).

——, *Studies in the History of Roman Sea-Power in Republican Times* (1946).

Wallinga, H , *The Boarding Bridge of the Romans: Its Function in the Naval Tactics of the First Punic War* (1956).

Watson, G. R., *The Roman Soldier* (1969).

Webster, G., *The Roman Imperial Army* (1969).

INDEX

NOTE: All Romans, except emperors and men of letters, are to be found under their *gens* name: e.g. for Cato see Porcius. All others are indexed under the name most commonly used in English: e.g. Trajan, Horace, Alaric.

GROWTH OF THE
ROMAN EMPIRE
44 B.C. - 300 A.D.

Scale of Miles

0   100   200   300   400   500

The Empire in 44 B.C. ....
Additions under Augustus, 31 B.C.-14 A.D. ....
Later Annexations ....
Temporary Occupation (Screened Borders)
Losses in the Third Century ....

IRELAND

NORTH SEA

BALTIC SEA

Wall of Antoninus

82 A.D.
Hadrian's Wall

BRITAIN
(43 A.D.)

Londinium

9 B.C.

9 B.C.   9 A.D.

Cologne

GERMANI

LOWER GERMANY

Belgica

ATLANTIC

OCEAN

Lugdunensis

GAUL

UPPER GERMANY

78
155 A.D.

RAETIA
15 B.C.

Danube

NORICUM
15 B.C.

UPPER PANNONIA
9 B.C.

LOWER

12 B.C.

R

ILLYRICUM

U

MO

Lugdunum

Aquitania

Narbonensis

8 B.C.

Milan

19 B.C.

SPAIN

Tarraconensis

Lusitania

Baetica

Gades

New Carthage

BALEARIC IS.

CORSICA

SARDINIA

ADRIATIC SEA

DALMATIA

ITALY

Rome
Ostia
Naples

MAC

MEDITERRANEAN

SICILY

MALTA

Carthage

MAURETANIA
40 A.D.

AFRICA

NUMIDIA

S   A   H   A   R   A

CY

AC

EPIR

0°   10°   Longitude East of Greenwich   20°

10°   0°   10°   20

50°

40°

30°